Justice by Insurance

Justice by Insurance

The General Indian Court
of Colonial Mexico and
the Legal Aides of the Half-Real

WOODROW BORAH

University of California Press
Berkeley Los Angeles London

University of California Press
Berkeley and Los Angeles, California

University of California Press, Ltd.
London, England

© 1983 by
The Regents of the University of California

Printed in the United States of America

1 2 3 4 5 6 7 8 9

Library of Congress Cataloging in Publication Data

Borah, Woodrow Wilson, 1912–
   Justice by insurance.

   Bibliography: p.
   Includes index.
   1. New Spain.   Juzgado General de Indios.
2. Indians of Mexico—Courts.   3. Indians of
Mexico—Legal status, laws, etc.   I. Title.
LAW   347.72′01′08997   82-20177
ISBN 0-520-04845-8   347.20718997

To Lesley Byrd Simpson,
exacting teacher and warm friend,
who first planned a study
on this topic

Contents

Tables

Preface

THIS study has had a prolonged gestation. It was first conceived in 1931 by Lesley Byrd Simpson during sabbatical study and a Guggenheim fellowship in Mexico and Guatemala. During a second period as a Guggenheim fellow in 1939–40, he continued to collect materials in the form of photographs and summaries of cases, but the United States' entry into the Second World War suspended all work. Meantime, in 1938–39, while examining records at the Archivo General de la Nación in Mexico City for a study of the silk industry in colonial Mexico, I saw almost daily the delegations of Mexican village peasants waiting in the presidential patio for an audience with President Lázaro Cárdenas, and realized that I was witnessing the Juzgado General de Indios still functioning in the form it had had under the first Spanish viceroy, Antonio de Mendoza. In the early 1950s, when I mentioned my interest in the General Indian Court, Dr. Simpson generously proposed that we work jointly on the study. Our collaboration consisted of discussions as he read his materials already collected and I began the examination of widely scattered materials outside the archival sections of his searches. My own research was furthered by two periods as a Guggenheim fellow and sabbatical scholar, one in Mexico and one in Spain.

Toward the end of the 1950s, when Dr. Simpson already had retired from teaching, he withdrew from the project and urged me to make free use of his materials. I obviously have done so, and wish to record his warm, open-hearted support. Further work on the study has proceeded in spurts when possible during a long collaboration with the late Sherburne F. Cook on other topics. The first chapters of this book were drafted in 1955, rewritten several times, and reached final version only in 1979–80. Chapter IV, begun and suspended in the summer of 1955, was completed in November–December 1979; later chapters were drafted after that.

In the course of a study for which the research has been carried on over so many years, Lesley Byrd Simpson and I have received much help, which we both want to record. Both of us have benefited from periods as John Simon Guggenheim, Jr., Memorial Foundation Fellows. I have had the advantage additionally of a year in 1965–66 as a fellow of the Social Science Research Council, which financed archival research in Mexico and Peru (so that I might learn more of the parallel Peruvian institution). The University of California, Berkeley, has given much assistance through its programs of sabbatical and faculty-research fellowships and through its Associates in Tropical Bio-Geography, Center for Latin American Studies, and Committee on Research.

As I have probed the maze of an administrative system now vanished and a law now largely abolished, I have had to call upon many colleagues for help and advice. I have met everywhere with interest and assistance. Lesley Byrd Simpson, after surrendering his share in the projected study, has continued to show interest and give cogent advice. The late Jacobus tenBroek of the Department of Political Science at Berkeley, a pioneer in studying the history of social welfare, the repression of vagabondage, and the regulation of mendicity in Anglo-American society, opened my eyes to unsuspected aspects; his premature death has rendered this study far poorer than it might otherwise have been. I especially want to acknowledge the contributions of Stephan Kuttner and Thomas Izbicki at the Institute of Canon Law, School of Law, and colleagues in other departments on the Berkeley campus: Luis Monguió, Arthur L. Askins, John K. Walsh, and José Durand in the Department of Spanish and Portuguese; and Gunther Barth, Richard Herr, and Thomas Barnes in the Department of History. At the Universidad Nacional Autónoma de México in Mexico City, I have received much help and needed materials from María del Refugio González, José Luis Soberanes Fernández, and Guillermo Floris Margadant, all associated with the Instituto de Investigaciones Jurídicas or the Facultad de Derecho. Andrés Lira González of El Colegio de México, who has written on the aftermath of the abolition of the General Indian Court, has always been ready with insight and advice. A major and unexpected pleasure has been making the acquaintance of Hans W. Baade of the School of Law, University of Texas, Austin, who holds the only chair in the United States for the study of the history of civil law within its boundaries.

Finally, without much and generous assistance from the personnel of archives and libraries, this study would have been impossible. The Bancroft Library of the University of California, Berkeley, under the long administration of Dr. George Hammond, has been particularly helpful in filming materials, as has Mrs. Vivian Fisher, head of film, in making the materials available. The Archivo General de la Nación in Mexico City, under directors from 1931 to the present, has shown customary generosity in facilitating access to materials and filming them, as has its paleographer for so many years, Luis Ceballos, in helping me to read them. Antonio Pompa y Pompa, long-time director of the library of the Museo Nacional de Antropología, kindly guided my steps outside Mexico City, through his remarkable knowledge of provincial holdings. At the Archivo General de Indias, Sevilla, under two directors, José María de la Paña y Cámara and Rosario Parra—and the latter also as *subdirectora* under her predecessor—I have met equal generosity in access to materials and in eventual filming. I thank also the owner of the archive of Tulancingo and other materials, who kindly permitted me to consult and cite them. It would require much paper to record my further debt to libraries and archives in the United States, Mexico, Spain, Peru, France, Great Britain, and other countries. Let me thank them one and all collectively.

Author's Notes

Money

During the colonial period, the Spanish in Mexico kept accounts both in money of account and in money of actual circulation. The more important kinds of money of account were pesos of fine gold (*pesos de oro de minas*), worth 450 maravedís, and ducats (*ducados*), worth 375 maravedís. Each peso was divided into 8 *tomines*. After the earliest years, money in actual circulation consisted of silver pesos, sometimes called pesos of common gold, worth 272 maravedís. Each peso was divided into 8 *reales* and each real into 12 *granos*. The common denominator for the various kinds of money was the value in *maravedís*, an obsolete Spanish silver coin. Regardless of the money that records were kept in, payments were in silver pesos and reales. In this book, silver pesos and their fractions are written in an adaptation of the English system, the peso always being noted—e.g., 7/1/1 or 0/1 or 0/0/6.

Citations in Footnotes

To reduce the length of footnotes, this book uses the following system: If a cited work is the only one by that author (or anyone of the same surname) in the Bibliography, only the surname (or source) is given. If more than one work by an author (or source) is listed in the Bibliography, a short title is used. The Bibliography gives the full reference.

Since most abbreviations are to manuscript citations, the designation "ms." has been omitted. For further economy and clarity, volume number, series, and internal divisions are given in arabic numerals. For Spanish compilations of laws, the newer method of citations, which omits *libro*, *título*, and *ley* in favor of numerals separated by periods, is used here, but further modified by employing arabic numerals.

Abbreviations

AGI	Archivo General de Indias, Sevilla, Spain:
AGI-C	Contaduría
AGI-G	Audiencia de Guadalajara
AGI-IG	Indiferente General
AGI-J	Justicia
AGI-M	Audiencia de Méjico
AGI-P	Patronato
AGN	Archivo General de la Nación, Mexico City:
AGN-Civ	Civil
AGN-Crim	Criminal
AGN-GP	General de Parte
AGN-I	Indios
AGN-J	Archivo del Hospital de Jesús
AGN-Jus	Justicia
AGN-M	Mercedes
AGN-O	Ordenanzas
AGN-RC	Reales Cédulas
AGN-RCD	Reales Cédulas, Duplicados
AGN-Ti	Tierras
AGN-Tr	Tributos
AGN-V	Vínculos
AJT	Teposcolula (Oaxaca, Mexico) Archivo Judicial:
AJT-Civ	Civil
AJT-Crim	Criminal

AT   Tulancingo (Hidalgo, Mexico) Archivo

BLT   Bancroft Library (University of California, Berkeley) transcript

DCLI   Spain: Laws, Statutes, etc., *Disposiciones complementarias a las leyes de Indias*

DIE   *Colección de documentos inéditos para la historia de España*

DIHA   *Colección de documentos inéditos para la historia de Hispano-América*

DII   *Colección de documentos inéditos, relativos al descubrimiento, conquista y organización de las antiguas posesiones españolas de América y Oceanía, . . . y muy especialmente del Indias*

DIU   *Colección de documentos inéditos, relativos al descubrimiento, conquista y organización de las antiguas posesiones españolas de Ultramar*

GP   Peru (Viceroyalty), *Gobernantes del Perú: cartas y papeles, siglo XVI; documentos del Archivo de Indias*

HM   Lewis Hanke, ed., *Los virreyes españoles en América durante el gobierno de la casa de Austria: México*

HP   Lewis Hanke, ed., *Los virreyes españoles en América durante el gobierno de la casa de Austria: Perú*

LBSD   Documents Relating to the Juzgado de Indios, 1580–1826, selected by Lesley Bird Simpson from the AGN, 1939–40 [Film enlargements of documents in the AGN-Civ, -Crim, and Historia]

LBSF   Lesley Bird Simpson, Field and Archive Notebooks, 1931–1940

RLI   Spain: Laws, Statutes, etc., *Recopilación de leyes de los reynos de las Indias*, 4th ed.

VC   Correspondencia de Don Luis de Velasco con Felipe II y Felipe III, acerca de la administración de los virreinatos de Nueva España y del Perú, durante los años 1590 a 1601

Map of Provinces Within the Audiencia of Mexico, Including Yucatan, in 1786 (on following two pages)

Key to numbers on map:

1. Acapulco
2. Acatlán and Piaxtla
3. Actopan
4. Amula
5. Antequera (Spanish city, now Oaxaca)
6. Apa and Tepeapulco
7. Atlatlahuca
8. Atlixco
9. Autlán
10. Cadereita
11. Celaya
12. Zempoala
13. Zimapán
14. Zimatlán and Chichicapan
15. Sinagua and La Huacana
16. Coatepec
17. Colima
18. Córdoba
19. Cosamaloapan
20. Cuatro Villas (Oaxaca, Etla, Cuilapán, and Tlapacoya)
21. Cuautla Amilpas
22. Cuernavaca
23. Cuitzeo de la Laguna
24. Coyoacán
25. Chalco
26. Charo
27. Chiautla
28. Chietla
29. Chilapa
30. Cholula
31. Huauchinango
32. Guanajuato
33. Huatulco and Huamelula

34. Cuautitlán
35. Huajuapan
36. Huayacocotla
37. Huaymeo and Zirándaro
38. Coatzacoalcos
39. Huejotzingo
40. Huejolotitlán (Huitzo)
41. Huejutla
42. Iguala
43. Igualapa
44. Ixcateopan
45. Ixmiquilpan
46. Etzatlán
47. Ixtepeji
48. Izúcar
49. Juxtlahuaca
50. León
51. Lerma
52. Malinalco
53. Maravatío
54. Metepec
55. Mexicaltzingo
56. Mexico City
57. Metztitlán
58. Miahuatlán
59. Mitla and Tlacolula
60. Motines
61. Nejapa
62. Nochixtlán
63. Nombre de Dios
64. Orizaba
65. Otumba
66. Pachuca
67. Pánuco
68. Papantla
69. Puebla
70. Querétaro
71. San Cristóbal Ecatepec

72. San Juan de los Llanos
73. San Luis de la Paz
74. San Luis Potosí
75. San Miguel el Grande
76. Sayula
77. Xochicoatlán
78. Xochimilco
79. Tacuba
80. Tancítaro
81. Taxco
82. Tecali
83. Teziutlán and Atempan
84. Teococuilco
85. Tehuacán
86. Tehuantepec
87. Temascaltepec and Sultepec
88. Tenango del Valle
89. Teotihuacán
90. Teozacoalco
91. Tepeaca
92. Tepeji de la Seda
93. Teposcolula
94. Tetela del Río
95. Tetela del Volcán
96. Tetepango and Hueypoxtla
97. Teutila
98. Teotitlán del Camino
99. Teotlalco
100. Texcoco
101. Tingüindín
102. Tixtla
103. Tlalpujahua
104. Tlapa
105. Tlaxcala
106. Tlazazalca
107. Tochimilco

108. Toluca
109. Tula
110. Tulancingo
111. Tuxpan
112. Tuxtla and Cotaxtla
113. Valladolid (Morelia)
114. Valles
115. Venado and la Hedionda
116. Veracruz
117. Veracruz Vieja
118. Villa Alta
119. Jalapa
120. Jalapa del Marqués
121. Jicayán
122. Jilotepec
123. Jiquilpan
124. Jonotla and Tetela
125. Zacatlán
126. Zacatula
127. Zacualpán
128. Zamora and Jacona
129. Zumpango
130. Tabasco
131. Laguna de Términos
132. Bacalar
133. Beneficios Altos
134. Beneficios Bajos
135. Bolonchencauich
136. Camino Real Alto
137. Camino Real Bajo
138. Campeche
139. Costa
140. Mérida
141. Sahcabchén
142. Sierra
143. Tizimín
144. Valladolid

Sources: Adapted from Gerhard, *A Guide to the Historical Geography of New Spain*, 16 et passim, and *The Southeast Frontier of New Spain*, 19 et passim.

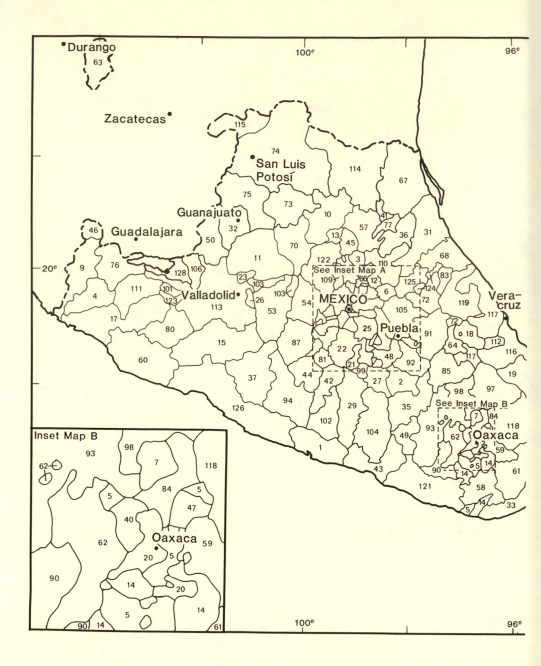

Durango
63

100°

96°

Zacatecas

115

74

San Luis
Potosí

114

67

75

73

10

41
77

36

31

Guanajuato

32

57

50

13
45

70

122   3   110

68

11

See Inset Map A

109

66   12

125

83

20°

46

Guadalajara

9

76

23

103

MEXICO

6

124

72

119

Vera-
cruz

128   106

101

103

26

54

105

117

4

111

123

Valladolid

113

53

25

Puebla

72

17

80

87

22

91

64

117

112

116

60

15

81

48

92

85

19

37

44

21   99

27   2

98

97

126

94

102

42

29

35

93

See Inset Map B

7   84

118

62

Oaxaca

1

104

49

90

14

5   14

61

43

121

58

14   33

5

Inset Map B

98

93

62

7

118

5

84

5

47

40

62

Oaxaca

59

20

5

90

14

20

5

14

90   14

61

100°

96°

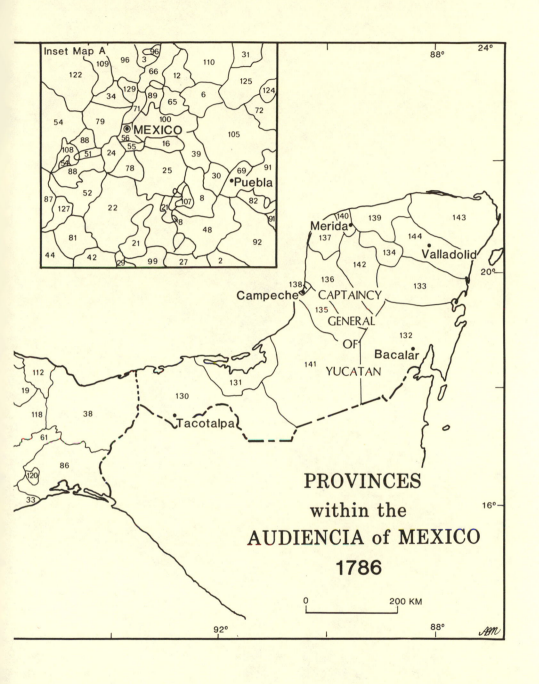

Inset Map A

96
96 3
109
122
66
12
110
31
129
89
65
6
125
124
34
71
72
54
79
100
88
MEXICO
105
108
56
16
54
51
24
55
39
88
78
25
69
91
52
30
Puebla
127
22
107
8
82
81
21
8
91
44
42
29
99
48
92
2

Merida
140
139
143
137
144
Valladolid
134
142
Campeche
138
136
133
CAPTAINCY
135
132
GENERAL
Bacalar
OF
141
YUCATAN
131
130
Tacotalpa
112
19
118
61
86
120
33

PROVINCES
within the
AUDIENCIA of MEXICO
1786

0   200 KM

88°   24°

92°   88°

20°

16°

AM

CHAPTER I

Introduction

THE problems which the Spanish government tried to solve in colonial Mexico by establishing a system of legal insurance, the General Indian Court, and the legal aides of the half-real, undoubtedly had local variations peculiar to the viceroyalty, but in their basic outlines they were present throughout the Spanish empire in America. Indeed, they are basic to the experience of mankind wherever and whenever two peoples have come into contact for more than very short periods. The closer the contact and the longer the period, the greater will be the need for accommodation and adjustment between differing ideas and provisions of law, equity, and morality. The need for adjustment becomes even more acute when one people as the possessor of superior force imposes its rule upon the other. At the time of initial contact, the problems are likely to arise from different cultures in intimate meeting and the conflicts of varying customs and laws. If the relationship continues for a relatively long span of time, during which conquerors and conquered mix their cultures and genetic stocks and come to a common language, a single religion, and a unified social structure, the relationship is likely increasingly to become one of class, with the advantages and disadvantages that attach to differential power within a culture that is progressively becoming unified.

In the Mediterranean basin, the Ius Gentium developed out of the series of decisions and arrangements forced upon the Romans by their need, on the one hand, to decide cases among foreigners resident within their gates, as well as between Romans and foreigners; and on the other hand, to decide what law to apply in their subject territories, very often among varied peoples living in the same city or province.[1] Presumably the Ius Gentium embodied what was common to all peoples and all cultures, but that concept became less valid as the Roman world succumbed to attacks by peoples of differing laws and ultimately, in the east, of a powerful new faith.

In medieval Europe, the crumbling of Roman law and the entrance into the general Latin Christian culture of large areas that had lain beyond Roman rule resulted in a patchwork of local bodies of custom and law, some written, some reaching determination only when a case came for judgment, like the English common law. The inherent shocks and lack of comparable treatment may be seen in the imposition of Norman, then English, rule on Ireland. In Irish custom, homicide, for example, was a civil matter, to be settled by payment of compensation, wergeld. So a native Irishman could be killed by an Englishman, and the finding that the deceased was Irish meant the acquittal of criminal penalty—that is, hanging—although civil liability remained. On the other hand, if an Irishman killed an Englishman, he could be tried for felony, and if found guilty, hanged. The contrast in treatment was such that Irish guilt was sometimes handled by fine or ransom. In the Tanistry case (1608), an English judge declared the entire Irish system of inheritance invalid as " 'ecounter to the Commonwealth'," and imposed the alien English one.[2] On the Slavic and Moslem frontiers of medieval Europe, where differences were in general much greater, the problems of adjustment were equally so. A Slav or Moslem who converted to Christianity abandoned not merely his own people but also their law, to assume the burdens and privileges of the Christians.[3]

Since the Renaissance, problems of adjusting differing laws and customs have become prominent in European experience in a form far beyond that of the Romans, who after all governed lands of fundamentally similar cultures; and well beyond the experience of medieval Europe, varied though that was. For as Europe made itself master of the greater part of the globe, it exercised rule over millions of people whose beliefs, folkways, and legal and administrative systems were so different that European administrators, even when they did not regard

---

1. García Gallo, "El derecho común"; Sánchez Gallego, 41–51.

2. Hand, 201–205 et passim; Elias, 104–105.

3. Wittram, 27; Kirchner, 7–11; Vryonis, 351–402; Dozy, 1:283–284, and in general vols. 1 and 2 passim; *Las Siete Partidas* (Spain: Laws, Statutes, etc.), partida 7, tits. 24–26, dealing with Jews, Moslems, and heretics, but also with converts to Christianity and apostates. The *Fuero Real* (4.2.1) set death by fire for apostasy: Pérez y López, 4:23 et seq.

the ways of their subjects as abominations to be rooted out mercilessly, had difficulty in understanding them and were apt to substitute their own laws and customs as more reasonable—that is to say, something they could understand. In the substitution the European administrators often remade the native society and not only inflicted sweeping change, or vast injustice—a result which probably did not bother most of them—but also found that enforcement could be obtained only with such difficulty that the attempt was of questionable value. For what to the European is crime may be immemorial and proper custom to the native: for example, servants' use of their masters' goods; killing aged and ailing members of the tribe; avenging the death of a relative without recourse to the courts, and exacting such vengeance even when the killing was a clear case of self-defense against felonious assault.

A classic example was India under British colonial rule. British administrators and judges, trained in English law and political structure but very often completely ignorant of Hindu custom or practice, made rules on the basis of English experience, often completely misread or misunderstood local law and custom, and imposed English common law or their own idea of what was proper and constituted justice. They substituted British ideas of litigation for the Indian one of accommodation and slow jockeying to settlement. But what the British did has remained and is the basis of the legal system and administration in India today.[4]

Whenever or wherever Europeans have settled in substantial numbers among native populations, the questions of law and custom present even more serious difficulties of adjustment, let alone justice. The difficulties that arise in our own presumably enlightened century from this mingling of two very different groups of people may be illustrated from Julius Lewin's study of the Union of South Africa, where European (i.e., Dutch–Roman) law applies to Europeans, Hindus, and Coloured, but Natives in their relations among themselves are governed by Native law and custom, and in their relations with non-Natives are subject to European law.

Just what is Native law is in itself no simple matter. In the first place, South Africa is inhabited by Negro tribes of widely varying customs. In the second place, the Courts of Native Commissioners may enforce what they consider custom only to the extent that it has not been forbidden or modified. Furthermore, they may enforce a custom not forbidden or modified only to the extent that it is not "'opposed to the principles of public policy or natural justice'"; but, whatever their

4. Derrett.

feelings on the matter, they may not declare the marriage customs of the Natives repugnant to such principles. It is obvious that the Courts of Native Commissioners and the Native Appeal Court of the Union have been developing in their decisions a body of Native law that contains a remarkable number of surprises for the Natives.[5]

Even where the decision does conform to what undoubtedly has been Native custom, the existence of two separate bodies of law leads to curious discrepancies of treatment. As between Natives, one man has no recourse when another man's cow kills the first man's horse, for that is Native custom recognized by the Union courts for Natives. But should the same cow kill the horse of a Hindu, European, or Coloured person, the injured party could recover damages, for such is the Dutch–Roman law.[6] Of course, the Native theoretically has the same recourse should his horse be killed by a European's cow—but the poorer, more ignorant, and more timid Natives are likely to assume that their own custom governs, or be unwilling to enter an alien arena. With the passage of time, more Natives undoubtedly will become aware of the remedies available to them. However, the Native who chooses to sue in such a case must do so in the ordinary Union courts and under ordinary procedures, which are alien to him and place him at a considerable disadvantage. Further, as the body of Natives divorced from their tribal backgrounds becomes numerous, a situation arises which is even more complex, for European law increasingly becomes more comprehensible to them than much of their tribal custom, and may be the most obvious body of rules for application in industrial settlements of diverse tribal origins.

In countries which have won their independence from European administration, problems of adjustment continue, for the administrative and legal systems have taken root and been set upon courses that are not easily changed. In general, the Europeanized systems are much better adapted to the new forms of a modernizing society. So, as already mentioned, English common law remains the basis of the legal system and administration in India today. In the former English possessions of West Africa, English common law continues to be applied, except that native custom is accepted by the local courts in family law, inheritance, marriage, and prescription, unless native custom embodies barbarous practice. The exception allows broad latitude for judicially imposed change. Where the succession state is a European construct, uniting territories of disparate tribal heritage (and sometimes splitting tribes between itself and neighboring states), the imposition

---

5. Section 11 (i) of the Union of South Africa Native Administration Act, no. 38 of 1927, cited in Lewin, 57. See also the discussion in Lewin, 57–94.

6. Ibid., 64 and 86.

of European law and custom often becomes a necessity, since it is the only common denominator. In Africa and Asia there does exist at least one competitor of equally overriding character, namely Islam; but the advance of Islamic law brings with it equal or even greater suppression of native law and the greater problems inherent in a comprehensive system that is less well adapted to present-day practice and needs than the European.[7]

So the retreat of European rule does not end the difficulties of adjustment and adaptation. They may appear, in addition, in another form, as the revived native or Islamic law is imposed on Europeans when colonial status or extraterritorial privileges end. Whatever their theoretical approval of this revival and the accompanying end of European domination, people of the European world may yet wince at the imposition of penalties, such as those of Islamic law, that they regard as barbarous and take pride that they themselves have abandoned.

Where European law and legal procedures have penetrated the native society deeply, too deeply to be removed, the problems of adjustment may take on other forms. Such especially is the case if there has been substantial or massive European settlement. The problems tend increasingly to become ones of class or of previously subject ethnic minorities or majorities—to use the current phrase—that exhibit characteristics of class difference within a common social and political structure, but with residues of cultural differences retained from a differing past. There thus results a spectrum at one end of which there remains the need for helping people of different law not conversant with the dominant system, but that shades toward the other end into the need for adjusting judicial protection and legal recourse so that they become available in easier and more accessible forms to poor, ignorant, and wretched folk—the *miserabiles* of Roman and medieval European jurisprudential thinking. Society has become sufficiently unified that ethnic and racial residues have far less meaning, and class differences considerably more.

In short, the General Indian Court of New Spain may no longer exist as a formal legal entity, and the agents of the half-real may have passed into history, but the problems they were established to solve are present in the world today in vitually the same or analogous forms. The system of legal insurance that supported the court and its officials remains today a remarkable innovation that has been proposed in more timid voluntary programs, but hardly on a compulsory, country-wide scale.

7. Daniels, passim; Elias, 104–120 et passim; Ollennu; Roberts-Wray.

CHAPTER II
Castilian Antecedents and Experience to 1521

CASTILE, as it entered upon the Age of the Great Discoveries and the conquest of America, had available to it the experience of Latin Christian Europe, rooted in classical and biblical antiquity. It had, further, experience that much of western Europe, except on the Slavic frontier, did not have, of close and continuing contact with non-Christians, not merely Jews but also Moslems.

General Christian theory, derived from Roman theory and augmented by numerous glossators and theologians, held that there was a natural law binding upon all people and peoples wherever they might be. That law was inherent in the universe and in man: for example, all human beings are born, all must ingest and eliminate, all die. The exact boundaries were much debated, and in the thinking of some included what others considered belonged more properly to a second body of law, the Ius Gentium, a common body of law and custom that might be found in the practices of all peoples. Beyond these two basic bodies of law binding upon all peoples lay a variety of human observance, all of it permissible so long as it did not conflict with the previous two. Christian law and custom were binding upon Christians, but not necessarily upon non-Christians.[1] Upon individual conversion, the convert was bound to observe Christian rules, forsaking the non-

---

1. Ayala, "El descubrimiento"; García Gallo, "Las bulas de Alejandro VI," 613–680, and "El derecho común," 133–139; Höffner, 3–84; Pérez de Tudela Bueso, "Ideas jurídicas y realizaciones políticas," 140–151; Rumeu de Armas, "Los problemas"; Sánchez Gallego, 41–51; Muldoon, passim.

Christian law he had observed previously.[2] When, as in the mass conversions of the Germanic nations, whole peoples became Christian, they might continue with their native law insofar as it was not contrary to what was regarded as natural law, Ius Gentium, and Christian requirements.[3] Polygyny, for example, is contrary neither to natural law nor the Ius Gentium, but is offensive to Christian precept.

Castilian experience and that of all other parts of the Iberian Peninsula, in the nearly eight centuries of an independent Moslem presence there, incorporated various degrees of accommodation to non-Christian peoples and their law. In the most galling instances for Christians, they lived under Moslem rule. In consequence, although they were allowed to apply Christian law (usually some modification of Roman and Visigothic law) among themselves, cases involving disputes with Moslems went before a Moslem judge, and all cases of serious criminal offenses fell within Moslem jurisdiction.[4] As the Christians reconquered the Peninsula, they reversed the tables. Moslems were allowed to live under their own law and custom and to resort to their own courts for matters concerning themselves. Mixed cases involving Christians as well as Moslems, and serious criminal offenses, went before a Christian judge, increasingly with the passage of time a royal one. The same general system was applied to Jews by both Moslems and Christians as each group won the upper hand. To use the term *system*, however, is to imply a uniformity that did not exist, for very often the *aljama* and the *judería* lived under terms of a specific contract with the Christian conquerors, with the purchase of modifications possible as financial needs drove the Iberian monarchs to sell concessions.[5]

Even if Christian law was imposed, there was a great deal of flexibility and accommodation inherent in it and its practice in the Penin-

2. The convert became part of a new community. The point is most graphically illustrated in discussions of the history of the European Slavic frontier: Wittram, 27; Kirchner, 7–11. The rule held as well for converts to Islam; apostasy from the dominant religion was punished by death: Dozy, 1:283–284; section "Apóstatas" in Pérez y López, 4:23 et seq., quoting clauses from canon law, the *Fuero Real* (4.1.1–2, ordering death by fire for apostates and heretics), *Las Siete Partidas*, and subsequent legislation entering the *Nueva Recopilación de Castilla*. For the ceremonies and public pomp of conversion to Islam, see Vryonis, 357–358.

3. The early codes of the Germanic peoples are obviously the result of just such adaptation.

4. Circourt, 1:25–27; Lévi-Provençal, 3:218–220.

5. Baer, vols. 1 and 2, passim; Neuman, 1:xxv–xxxi, 3–32, and 112–160; Serrano y Sanz, xi–xxix; Van Kleffens, 94 and 130–131; Fernández y González, 117–118 and 286–287; and *Ordenanzas reales de Castilla (de Montalvo)*, 8.3.16 and 25, and *Las Siete Partidas*, 7.24.5, both in Spain: Laws, Statutes, etc., *Los códigos españoles*, 6:511–512 and 514–515 and 4:430 respectively.

sula, as indeed throughout Europe, for it was essentially a patchwork of customs and law, on the one hand, and of judicial jurisdictions, on the other. Essentially, each person lived under a *fuero*, or body of customary law and privilege, written and unwritten, that inhered in him and descended to his children. It might be territorial, as in the fuero of a city and its territory; it might be personal, as in the fuero of the clergy. It might be mixed, as in the law binding upon Jews and Moslems, which both inhered in their persons and had a territorial element through the differing privileges of the two communities. The elasticity and complexity of the patchwork were much enhanced because judicial jurisdiction was also greatly divided, and in many instances exercised under seigneurial privilege or municipal right.

Conflict was eased further, and accommodation secured, by a number of rules and features. First, most of the Christian custom in the Peninsula arose from Roman law with relatively minor modifications, so that the fueros and other local bodies of custom tended to embody a reasonably common body of ideas and rules. Even Jewish and Moslem law, originating within or near the Mediterranean basin and having been much influenced by Roman theory, did not differ so markedly that there were many genuinely wide conflicts. Second, the basic principle applied almost universally was *actor sequitur forum rei*—that is, the plaintiff must sue in the court and under the law of the defendant. A person from a truly foreign jurisdiction could be held to account within the fuero of the territory in which he found himself, however; and in the instance of Moslems and Jews, the principle was modified to the benefit of Christians, as the Moslems had modified it to their benefit in their years of dominance. In regard to Jews, the crown, because of its special fiscal relation to them and need of revenue from them, sometimes modified the principle in their favor in cases involving the collection of debts due them.

Eventually the rising royal power began to assert control through the institution of royal courts of appeal, which in the end applied royal law, and through insistence that all cases involving the royal treasury, whether as plaintiff or defendant, must be tried within the royal jurisdiction. Such imposition and acceptance of an overriding law came late. Custom, when it came into conflict with royal enactment, was held at first to be paramount; and from the tenth century until at least the middle of the fourteenth, judges in Castile had considerable latitude to apply their own conception of what was right and reasonable, with binding force for all similar cases in the future. It was not until the Ordenamiento de Alcalá in 1348 that Alfonso XI set the order of precedence for categories of Castilian law. They were to be: (1) the Ordenamiento itself; (2) the fueros, especially the Fuero Real (which safeguarded the privileges of the nobility); and (3) the Siete Partidas, as amended by the Ordenamiento and without prejudice to special legislation for the nobility. True supremacy of the royal law did not come until 1505 with the Leyes de Toro, which declared that royal laws superseded all fueros and customs, even if contrary to them. Henceforth, the order of precedence was to be: (1) royal laws, past and future; (2) fueros and municipal laws, if not superseded; and (3) the Siete Partidas, even if and wherever not hitherto enforced or regarded as having binding force.[6]

Clearly, in a patchwork of this kind, with marked differences in what the judges in each territory and at each level of instance would apply, there was possible a great deal of flexibility and accommodation. Equally, of course, there lay in the future the very real possibility—and we know now, a certainty—of the imposition of uniform law through the operation of the appellate courts that would tend to obliterate local laws and customs, especially alien ones.

From the middle of the thirteenth century, when the Christians established clear dominance of the Peninsula, until 1492, when the last Moslem state fell to Christian siege, and all Jews who refused baptism were expelled, Castilian law and practice became increasingly illiberal and asserted the privileges of Christians and their law relative to non-Christians. The Siete Partidas of Alfonso the Learned of Castile, prepared in the middle of the thirteenth century, by inference allowed autonomy to Moslems and Jews, but expressly declared that in disputes between Jews and Christians, regardless who was plaintiff or defendant, the case must go before the royal judges and not the learned men of the Jews.[7] This provision meant, of course, the application of Christian custom or law and the use of Christian procedure.

The tendency of succeeding Castilian monarchs, despite local variation and occasional retreat, was to restrict the area within which their non-Christian subjects might apply their own laws and use their own judges. Jews probably were more the target than Moslems. The most drastic limitations were imposed during the minority of Juan II in the early years of the fifteenth century. One decree, issued at Soria, ordered that Jews might not be tried before their own judges on any criminal charge and, although they might continue to decide civil suits among themselves under their own law, they must associate with the Jewish judges a Christian one, whom they might select themselves from among those of the jurisdiction. Criminal cases of Jews were to

6. Van Kleffens, 130–131, 196–198, 226–228, et passim; García Gallo, "El derecho común," 133–135; Teicher, 91–94; Gibert y Sánchez de la Vega; Leyes de Toro, ley 1, in Los códigos españoles, 6:571–572; Richard Kagan, 22–32.

7. Partida 7.24.5. Título 24 deals with Jews, título 25 with Moslems.

be tried in first instance before the ordinary courts of the jurisdiction, whether seigneurial or royal, appeals from such tribunals to go before the King in his capacity as high judge of appeal.[8]

This drastic limitation of judicial autonomy was made much more severe in 1412, when a clause in further legislation aimed at all resident non-Christians forbade Jews and Moslems alike to have their own judges. Thenceforth their cases, civil and criminal, were to be tried before the ordinary judges of the districts where they lived. Criminal cases were to be decided according to Christian custom; but in purely civil cases affecting no member of another religion, the judges were enjoined to observe the customs of the non-Christian community concerned, to the extent that the judges regarded such customs as authentic and approved of them.[9] In effect, the Christian alcaldes could do as they wished.

The legislation of 1412 was too drastic not to meet with a great deal of passive resistance from the non-Christian communities. Our clearest evidence comes from the Jewish ones. Well organized as they were in the face of aggressive Christians, they were able to continue to exercise very considerable judicial powers over their own members in both civil and criminal matters; but such exercise of judicial jurisdiction remained always subject to the danger of intervention by royal or seigneurial officials, should a member of the community choose to complain and the community be unable, through purchase or bribe, to obtain official blindness.[10] In 1476 the Catholic Monarchs relaxed the most rigorous provisions of the legislation of 1412 with a decree which seemed to make concessions but actually represented a further restriction of the substantial *de facto* concessions which had been obtained since 1412. The decree of 1476 returned to the rule of Soria; that is, it recognized as legal the existence of such non-Christian courts as still functioned for civil cases within the community, provided a Christian judge was associated with the non-Christian ones. However, it added a new provision that any Moslem or Jew might bring a suit against a co-religionist before a Christian judge, notwithstanding any previous grant of privilege to a community, and that any decision by Jewish or Moslem judges might be appealed to the newly established royal court of appeal.[11] The aim was to achieve the destruc-

8. *Ordenanzas reales de Castilla*, 8.3.35, in *Los códigos españoles*, 6:514–515.

9. Ibid., ley 16, pp. 511–512. The text of the legislation of 1412 is also published in Fernández y González, 400–405.

10. Neuman, 1:112–160, demonstrates that the Jewish community courts continued to deal with both criminal and civil cases. In 1432 the Jews were able to obtain a privilege which recognized the legal existence of their community courts and gave them very extensive powers.

11. *Ordenanzas reales de Castilla*, 8.3.35, in *Los códigos españoles*, 6:514–515.

tion of non-Christian community courts envisaged in the legislation of 1412, but to encourage divisions within the communities, to abet the process, rather than to drive the non-Christian communities into unified resistance. The special status of Jews ended in 1492; that of Moslems early in the sixteenth century, through forced conversion.

Jews who were baptized became subject automatically to the Christian law of the jurisdiction.[12] For a century, the status of Moslems who were baptized remained different and perhaps most resembled that of the Indians in Spanish America. The numbers and density of settlement of the Moriscos, as they were called, made impossible immediate and complete replacement of their customs and law. In some districts like the Alpujarras, they formed almost the entire population. Accordingly, they were permitted a limited retention of previous custom and law, to the extent that such were not clearly repugnant to Christian religion and morality. In practice, the Morisco communities—in part through their own cohesion; in part with the tolerance of Christian landlords and feudal lords, who were more interested in revenue than in relentless Christianization; and in part through the fact that the local justices of first instance might themselves be *conversos*—were able to continue under much of their former law and custom, even to portions that might be held to be contrary to Christian religion and morality. On appeal to the royal courts, tolerance fell away rapidly, for the royal judges were much more likely to declare Morisco law and custom offensive to Christianity or no longer applicable. All of that came to an end through a series of rebellions and suppressions, and early in the seventeenth century the Moriscos were expelled from Spanish territory as incorrigibly unassimilable.[13]

Thus far we have dealt with differences in law, custom, and procedure arising from ethnic and religious diversity. In the later Middle Ages, Europe further was actively developing kinds of judicial accommodation aimed at easing the impact of law upon people of the same culture and custom who, because of class differences and other circumstances, found themselves at a disadvantage in demanding justice. (These kinds of accommodation were not thought of as possibilities in easing the Indians' entrance into European law and administrative systems for perhaps the first half-century of Spanish–Indian relations, but later were given much emphasis.) First was the obligation of the sovereign and all his delegates to provide special protection to widows

12. They moved, of course, out of the Jewish community to the Christian one. That move did not give them full equality, for they remained *conversos*, or New Christians, increasingly ineligible for many offices and honors and unable to demonstrate proper *limpieza de sangre*.

13. Circourt, vol. 2, passim; Lea, passim.

and orphans, the aged, crippled, and seriously ill, the poor, and in general the wretched of the earth. The theory of this obligation, as it came down to the fifteenth and sixteenth centuries, had twin origins: in the injunctions of the Old and New Testaments to be merciful, charitable, and give alms, and the special protection accorded widows, orphans, slaves, and the poor in general; and in similar injunctions in Greek thought to assist the needy. These ideas, picked up readily by Christian thinkers, were given wide extension and development in over a millennium of discussion.[14] The formal legal embodiment of the idea that widows, orphans, and the wretched in general should have special legal protection entered Roman law through an enactment of Constantine, ordering that they might not be cited out of their province and that they might cite others to the imperial tribunal.[15] Further development in western Europe enlarged this privilege into a formal obligation of protection binding upon bishops and the Merovingian and Carolingian counts. It was assumed by Charlemagne, especially once he became emperor, and was formally incorporated in a number of capitularies.[16]

Thereafter the application and nature of the protection were extended considerably, both through attempts of the Church to assert jurisdiction, especially when justice was denied widows, orphans, and other weak and needy people, and through redefinition and increase in the categories defined as weak and wretched. The additions included pilgrims, poor and ignorant countryfolk, minors, captives, the Church, clergy, persons serving them, the city, prostitutes, students, public penitents, exposed infants, the aged, the blind, those in jails, soldiers, prodigals, and people married in name only.[17] Protection to these groups came to be considered part of the proper exercise of justice[18] and was enjoined either through implication or specific statement in,

14. Lallemand, 1:1–28 and 2:3–9, 12–38, 61–89, 101–106, 149, and 163–164; Tierney, 5–20.

15. Castañeda Delgado, 259–262; Álvarez de Velasco, 2:20 (quaest. III.1) gives the text and indicates the subsequent Spanish laws based upon it. See also the commentaries on partida 3.23.20, 3.3.5, and 3.18.41, in two editions of the Siete Partidas: in Los códigos españoles, 3:316–317, 33–34, and 206; and Las Siete Partidas del sabio rey d. Alonso el IX (Spain: Laws, Statutes, etc.), 2:70–72 and 387–388.

16. Lallemand, 2:149 and 163–164; Capitulare Saxonicum, Aachen, October 28, 797, Capitulare Langobardicum, 802 and 808, and Capitulare Aquisgranense, 805, 810, and 813, in Monumenta Germaniae historica: Legum, 1:75–76, 103–105, 130, 153, and 163–164, and 2:550–554.

17. Gratianus, Corpus iuris canonici, part 1: distincts. 84 and 85, chs. 1–9; part 2: quaest. 5, ch. 23; Innocentius IV, bk. 1, tit. 29, ch. 38; Álvarez de Velasco, proem. 4 (II.3). I thank Dr. Thomas Izbicki for help on this material.

18. Kuttner; I thank Dr. Kuttner for bringing his article to my attention and lending me a copy of it.

for example, the numerous *specula principum*, which became a favorite and widely circulated form of writing in the later Middle Ages and the Renaissance.[19]

Castile participated fully in this general Christian development. The obligation of the sovereign to extend special protection to the needy and wretched was clearly stated in the thirteenth-century *Leyes del Estilo*[20] and in the *Siete Partidas*. Both declared the legal causes of widows, orphans, and *miserables* to be *casos de corte*, and so immediately within the royal jurisdiction in first instance:[21]

> And this is because, although the King is bound to defend all people of his land, he should have special concern for these [the miserable ones], for they are as people abandoned and with less counsel than the others. . . . Thus for such as these, when they appeal to him, compassion should move him, either to render justice to them himself or to appoint a judge who will do so at once.[22]

The royal legislation undoubtedly merely codified what was already common practice and widely accepted in the religious and ethical thought of the period. From the *Siete Partidas*, the clauses were incorporated in the *Nueva Recopilación de Castilla*, prepared in the time of Philip II, and remained in the various later and enlarged editions, including the *Novísima Recopilación de las leyes de España* prepared under Charles IV. It was only in 1835 that *casos de corte* were abolished in Spain.[23]

A second form of judicial accommodation for easing the impact of law upon the poor, needy, and otherwise disadvantaged came through the spread of the idea that their cases should not be heard by the long-drawn-out and expensive forms of ordinary suits and proceedings at law but should be handled by summary hearing and rapid decision. The origin of the idea as it spread through medieval and Renaissance Europe lay in Roman law, in the development of the *cognitio summaria*, which began as the use of administrative power by the praetor or consul to stop injury or order restitution. Further, a judge

---

19. Born, 471–475; Walsh, 42–46 and 91–92; this last, cap. 16, "Quel rey o principe o regidor deve ser piadoso a los buenos e omildes e a los pobres que non han esfuerço." It is notable that in the translation of Aegidius Romanus by Juan García Castrojeriz in the first half of the fourteenth century, the translator added material on the obligation to defend the poor, widows, and the defenseless from the Policratus of John of Salisbury: Aegidius Romanus, *De regimine principum*, vol. 3, and *Glosa castellana*, 3.3.11. Professor John K. Walsh has very kindly helped me with this material.

20. Ley 91, in *Los códigos españoles*, 1:323.

21. Partida 3.3.5, 3.14.6, 3.18.41, and 3.23.20, in *Los códigos españoles*, 3: 33–34, 145–146, 206, and 316–317, respectively.

22. Partida 3.23.20.

23. See the glosses to the laws cited in notes 21 and 22.

might accept summary process in a portion of a case, namely, the part dealing with proof, but written rules provided no special procedure. In slow, intricate steps from Diocletian to Justinian, abridgement of full legal process and rapid determination of cases entered Roman practice through the development of rules for less rigid handling of cases involving smaller sums, quick and summary handling of suits of the imperial treasury, limitation of the right of appeal, and a distinction between greater and lesser judges. The adoption of Christianity as the official religion of the empire added the idea that disputes over Church contracts should be handled by summary process. What in the reign of Theodosius I was exceptional, by the reign of Justinian became more usual, although hedged by the limitation that any judgment rendered by summary hearing must be provisional.[24]

The next developments, as far as they have been traced, came in papal legislation, perhaps through the renewed study of Roman law, in the twelfth and thirteenth centuries. The new papal legislation enjoined summary hearing for some cases, without written complaint, answer, and the lengthy proceedings of normal suit. In decretals of Clement V of 1306 and 1311, the *cognitio summaria* was finally sharply defined and its limits set. By then the concept was entering the enactments of civil rulers, notably Frederick II in 1231, for restitution of unjust exactions by minor officials. It was applied rapidly to the cases of those regarded as entitled to special protection: strangers, widows, orphans, poor people, those in jails, clerics, soldiers, scholars, and cases of the state treasury and pious endowments. It was abused by extending the procedure to cases of *laesa maiestatis*, or disrespect of the sovereign.[25]

From canon law and that of the Holy Roman Empire, the concept of summary process for cases of the poor and defenseless moved into local and municipal law.[26] It has been traced in Roussillon,[27] but not as yet in medieval Castile. Entrance of the concept of summary or abridged process into royal legislation in Castile came in 1534 when Charles V, at the petition of the Cortes, ordered that in civil suits and suits over debt of 1,000 maravedís and under, judgment was to be by summary procedure, "ni tela de juicio ni solemnidad alguna; salvo . . . sabida la verdad sumariamente."[28] Clearly, royal legislation, in lesser cases, was moving toward radically abridging the ponderous, ex-

---

24. Biondi.
25. Salvioli, 773–775.   26. Ibid.
27. Cots i Gorchs, 78; Lalinde Abadía, 404.
28. *Novísima recopilación* (Spain: Laws, Statutes, etc.), 11.3.8; Castillo de Bovadilla, 3.16.27–28. Castillo de Bovadilla, writing in 1593, stated that the amount had just been raised to 4,000 maravedís.

pensive, tourney-like qualities of normal litigation.[29] Extension of this benefit to the cases of the poor and unprotected, judged worthy of special royal protection, was a logical next step.[30]

A third form of legal accommodation for meeting the needs of the poor and defenseless, one which like the abridgement of ordinary judicial process also would serve to reduce or eliminate legal costs, lay in developing the concept that all lawyers and legal officials were obligated to serve them at reduced fees or no fees at all.[31] The final form of this idea in the fifteenth and sixteenth centuries was the provision of an *abogado de pobres*, a municipal or state official charged with providing free legal representation to *miserables*. A specific day each week, usually Saturday, was set aside for the trial of cases of such people.[32]

We may reduce this discussion of complex material to a few simple statements: On the one hand, in the years of first Spanish penetration into America, European experience and most of all Spanish experience included the complete incorporation of heathen into Christian law and institutions, especially in instances of individual conversion or seizure as slaves. That incorporation might be mitigated through special measures of protection already in existence for the needy, the poor, and the defenseless. On the other hand, Spanish experience also included the acceptance of non-Christian law and custom for non-Christians living under Christian rule, but in strict subordination to Christian jurisdiction in serious criminal cases, important civil ones, and appeals. Complete incorporation, of course, was likely to run into difficulties if large numbers of heathen, whether converted or seized as slaves, were left *in situ*.

On the eve of the first Hispanic incursions into America, European theory on the proper way to deal with non-Christians outside of Christian Europe also was much divided. One school held that heathen had forfeited all rights relative to Christians; another held that heathen were endowed with full human rights which Christians were bound to respect. In practice, Europeans followed an ad hoc rule of power (as have most other peoples through time). Heathen organized

29. Castilian law allowed 30 witnesses to each party for proof; but if the questions for proof were diverse, 30 for each question: *Novísima recopilación*, 11.11.2. On the complicated procedures, delays, and costs of Spanish judicial process, see the entire libro 11.

30. Ibid., 5.1.30, 5.19.7, 11.3.7, and 11.12.8. The laws are of the sixteenth century.

31. In addition to the citations in note 30, see ibid., 5.22.8 and 14; Castillo de Bovadilla, 3.14.18 and 3.15.63–64; and Lalinde Abadía, 405.

32. *Novísima recopilación*, 5.1.29 and 5.5.10.

in powerful agglomerations, easily able to retaliate, were treated with consideration, although captives taken in war could be enslaved. Heathen without significant capability to withstand the Christians, or encountered in small numbers, might be seized as slaves for transportation to Europe or elsewhere, or might be conquered.[33] Administration was thought of in terms of division of loot and the profits of rule.

Let us turn now to the early years of Spanish experience in America. The two Spanish stations on the way to the American continents were the Canaries and the West Indies. Both brought problems that differed from those of the *Reconquista* in that they involved the administration of subject peoples of technologically much more primitive cultures. In contrast to the Jews and Moslems of the Peninsula, who were the equals of their conquerors in cultural terms and shared many elements of what might be held to be a common European and Mediterranean culture, the new subjects were stone-age peoples of such different customs that accommodation was bound to present considerably greater difficulty. Equally, the Spaniards in both conquests moved rapidly to mass conversion.

The Canaries, although known earlier, were conquered and settled in the fifteenth and sixteenth centuries, the earliest occupations taking place under grants of feudal jurisdiction, the later ones under direct royal rule. Such evidence as we have indicates that the Spaniards proceeded in the conquest of the Canaries as though they were continuing the reconquest of the Peninsula, their far greater superiority in arms being most evident in their insistence upon extirpating the island religions and Christianizing their new subjects. Many were seized as slaves and shipped to the Peninsula for sale. Most undoubtedly remained in their islands as subjects of the new rulers. Practice varied from island to island, and indeed from district to district within each island. Some of the native chieftains were even permitted to continue to rule part of their lands, the remainder being reserved for distribution among the conquerors and new settlers from Europe.

In general, the islanders not shipped off as slaves were guaranteed the liberties of Spanish vassals—that is, essentially, freedom from enslavement and recourse to the royal courts. But although Christianization implied immediate assimilation, as had been the practice in the Peninsula, the islanders who remained under the rule of their own chieftains would continue to observe their former customs in civil and criminal cases affecting only themselves. Presumably, further, the European feudal lords did not interfere in local arrangements until a case

33. See note 1 of this chapter.

came before them, and then were likely to enforce Guanche (local) usage so long as it was not in direct conflict with Christian directives. The flexibility inherent in feudal devolution of judicial authority operated here in favor of the Guanches. However, when a criminal case originated in the infraction of royal legislation or a Spanish local ordinance, or involved a Spaniard in dispute or conflict with an islander, the case would go before a seigneurial or royal Spanish judge, who with some discretion presumably would judge the case under Castilian law, especially if one of the parties was a Spaniard. In any appeal, the case would move to a Spanish judge, usually a royal one, who was likely to apply Castilian law. Any Guanche as a free Spanish vassal could force a suit or case to which he was a party before a Spanish judge, removing it partially or wholly from island procedures and custom. In addition, Guanches resident in Spanish settlements lived under Spanish judges who probably applied Castilian law without much hesitation.[34]

The policy was basically that of medieval Castile in dealing with Jews and Moslems, as modified by the law of 1476. On the whole it appears to have been successful, probably because the relations between Spaniards and islanders were eased by similarity of race and because Guanche culture, although stone-age, arose out of the general European—Mediterranean matrix. The Guanches, who numbered only a few thousand, accepted Spanish culture and Christianity so rapidly that they ceased to be a separate cultural group by the end of the sixteenth century. They were not killed off; they became Spanish.[35] Complete assimilation quickly removed any problems in accommodation, and meant the unchallenged operation of full Christian law.

In the West Indies, the Spanish encountered peoples of different race, of far more different culture, and in considerably greater numbers than the Canary Islanders. They lived in a tropical environment in which both they and it turned out to be much less resistant to the impact of the European entrance. The problems of adjustment of procedures and law which inevitably arose were distinctly more complex than had been met in Spanish experience until then. Nevertheless, Spanish exploitation of the West Indies proceeded with, if anything, less attention to organizing an orderly native administration than had been evident in the Canaries and in the Peninsula. Taino inability to withstand European weapons, and distance from the seat of the royal

34. Millares Torres, 236–237, 267–269, 279, et passim; Torres Campos, 29–52 et passim; Viera y Clavijo, 2:85–86, 134–135, 178–214, 251–256, and 323–474; Zavala, "Las conquistas de Canarias y América," in his *Estudios indianos*, 32–33.

35. Introduction by Wölfel to Torriani, 1–2 and 8. Torres Campos, passim, argues for rapid assimilation.

authority in Spain, are a considerable part of the explanation. We are here concerned primarily with Hispaniola—the first large island to be occupied, the one with the largest native population, and the seat of Spanish government and then of royal authority in the form of an audiencia. Perhaps the very numbers of the Indians relative to Europeans at the outset of Spanish occupation made it impossible to think of substituting a new administrative system or of making substantial adjustments in native practice. Certainly the inability of Columbus' administration and subsequent royal ones to control the European settlers meant that attempts at orderly administration came late and remained largely paper projects.

In the earliest years, during the administrations of Christopher Columbus and Francisco de Bobadilla, the few Spaniards on Hispaniola harnessed the Indian population to yield. Most of the subjugated Indians were allotted to Spaniards, resident and in Spain, for labor in mines, fields, and houses. The men who received such grants, the encomenderos, were obviously like feudal lords in a position to exercise authority over their Indians, and often did so to avoid interference with the supply of labor. Furthermore, whenever conflict did occur between Spanish and Indian outside the encomendero relationship, the early settlers took it for granted that the interests of the Spaniard should prevail. They arrogated to themselves an illegal but thoroughly effective power of justice in dealing with the Indians; for such purposes, each Spaniard became his own judge and executioner.

In these circumstances, the only hope of protection or of fair dealing for the natives under European conceptions, let alone attention to native custom, lay in the possibility that the encomendero might object to any harm to his source of revenue. In accordance with medieval Spanish practice, the Indians at first were allowed fairly complete freedom in relations among themselves, so long as continued observance of their customs did not adversely affect the delivery of labor and tribute to the Spanish and was not held to be abhorrent to Christian morality. This concession of limited autonomy was implicit in the acceptance of caciques as *señores naturales*, native lords, who as the counterpart of European feudal seigneurs were to continue governing and judging the natives. This concession was substantially modified in practice, of course, by the crushing weight of labor service and the virtually unrestrained interference of white settlers in native affairs. Equally, redress against Spaniards probably did not exist, for until 1516 testimony of an Indian against an Old Christian (any settler from Europe) could not be accepted by a Spanish judge. Isabella's decision freeing the first Indians enslaved by Columbus, and the clause in her testament repeating that they were free vassals of the crown to be

treated well, barred wholesale slaving among the Indians of Hispaniola (but not in the Bahamas or the Lesser Antilles). Obviously, it
merely conferred a theoretical juridical status that could not protect
the luckless Indians from brutal exploitation.[36]

Formal disturbance of the body of Indian society at royal order
began with the administration of Nicolás de Ovando. The initial idea
that European settlement could be superimposed upon native society
with relatively little adjustment was implicit in his instructions of
1501. It being the royal will that the natives be well treated, Europeans
were to be restrained from mistreating them, and caciques and other
Indian nobles were to be acquainted with the royal pleasure so that
they would govern their Indians benevolently. Ovando's reports home
soon dispelled any illusion that the needs of the natives could be met
thus easily. The instruction of 1503, which represented an attempt to
remedy the truly frightful conditions on Hispaniola, created a curious
dual regime. The Indians were to be settled in towns under the care of
a trustworthy, honorable Spaniard in each town, who was to administer justice and see that the natives were not mistreated or cheated by
Spanish settlers. The Indians were also to continue under the rule of
their caciques, who were equally to be prevented from mistreating
or oppressing their followers. In effect, the native chiefs were to continue to administer justice according to native procedure and customs
not explicitly outlawed, but they were to be subject to the check of a
Spanish judge in each town, to whom their subjects could transfer
complaints and cases at will. For disputes and complaints involving
Spaniards, the Indians had to turn directly to the trustworthy and
honorable Spaniard.[37]

Just what law the honorable Spaniard applied was not specified,
and thus lay entirely in his discretion. In practice, he probably hon-
ored whatever native custom was not manifestly inconvenient or ex-
cessively foreign to his ideas; for the rest, he would turn to Castilian
rules. It is significant that the royal counselors assumed that there was
no need for royal guidance on this point. The instruction contem-

36. These paragraphs are based on Simpson, *The Encomienda in New Spain:
Forced Native Labor in the Spanish Colonies, 1492–1550*, 1–79, and *The Encomienda
in New Spain: The Beginnings of Spanish Mexico*, 1–55; Pérez de Tudela Bueso, *Las
armadas*, 159–177 and 213–217; Las Casas, *Historia de las Indias*, passim, in *Obras
escogidas*, vols. 1 and 2; Sauer, passim; Cook and Borah, *Essays*, 1:376–410; the
highly opposed theories of population density in Rosenblat, *La población indígena y el
mestizaje en América*, 1:105–120 and 293–303, and *La población de América en
1492*, 7–23; and McNeill, 199–234 et passim. The clause of the testament of Isabella is
in RLI as 6.10.1.

37. Royal instructions, Granada, September 16, 1501, and Alcalá de Henares
and Zaragoza, both March 20, 1503, in Konetzke, 1:4–6 and 9–13; Pérez de Tudela
Bueso, *Las armadas*, 177–198. The instructions also are published in DII, 31:13–25
and 156–174.

plated for the Indians of Hispaniola the complex mingling of functions and undefined jurisdictions of royal courts and local and seigneurial justice which obtained in Castile at that time. In any event, since the instruction really provided a pious cover for allotting Indians, the trustworthy Spaniard proving to be none other than the encomendero or his agent, it meant little more than formal royal approval for the encomendero's meddling in the affairs of his charges with whatever wisdom and tolerance he might muster.

In the next years, a long debate took place among Spaniards in the islands and in the Peninsula against a backdrop of ruthless exploitation of the Indians and their steady disappearance, which made all questions of institutions and choice of law illusory. The essential positions that the Indians were incapable of governing themselves and providing revenue without strict Spanish supervision, or that they should be settled in towns under the minimum of Christian supervision necessary for life as Christian vassals of the crown, involved the economic interests of the Spaniards in the islands and in Spain and the revenues of the crown. Within the debate lay also, on the one hand, delivery of the natives to a semi-feudal jurisdiction that in the circumstances of Hispaniola would have obliterated native society and usage; and on the other, some preservation, although under Spanish tutelage.[38] Later instructions to governors in the island, during the few years that the natives still constituted a substantial factor in the population, either repeated the basic idea of the instruction of 1503 for accommodating native procedures and custom to Spanish law, or accepted it without discussion. Whatever changes there were lay in details. The royal instruction of 1509 to Diego, son of Christopher Columbus, upon his recovering the family right to govern the Caribbean islands, combined the formulas of 1501 and 1503.[39] It can have had effect only to the slight extent that a few Indians were settled in new towns.

The famous reforming Laws of Burgos of 1512, despite numerous clauses calling for good treatment of the Indians, went little beyond previous instructions. Injunctions to settle Indians in new towns were repeated more insistently. In each Spanish town, the royal governor of the island was to appoint two honorable and trustworthy Spaniards as inspectors (*visitadores*), each to visit the surrounding Indian

---

38. Simpson, *The Encomienda: Forced Native Labor*, 1–79, and *The Laws of Burgos in 1512–1513: Royal Ordinances*, passim; Giménez Fernández, "La jurisdicción jeronimíta," 234–235; Pérez de Tudela Bueso's Introduction to Las Casas, *Obras escogidas*, 1:xxx–xxxii, and his "Ideas jurídicas y realizaciones," 151–154; Meza Villalobos, 11–116; Giménez Fernández, *Bartolomé de las Casas*, passim.

39. Cádiz, May 5, 1509, in Konetzke, 1:18–20, and in DII, 3:156–174.

towns separately at least twice a year in order to see that the Indians were well treated. The purpose of ordering separate inspections was to make collusion between the inspectors and Spanish settlers more difficult. The inspectors were also to enforce native compliance with Christian rules of marriage and were to act as judges for serious offenses by natives and for any complaints against natives by Spaniards who were not their encomenderos. One of the more famous clauses limited the powers of punishment of the encomenderos as well as other Spaniards:

> Also, we order and command that no person or persons shall dare to beat any Indian with sticks, or whip him, or call him dog, or address him by any name other than his proper name alone; and if an Indian should deserve to be punished for something he has done, the said person having him in charge shall bring him to the visitor for punishment. . . .

Other clauses aimed at compulsory baptism, Christian indoctrination, and the beginning of what amounted to a rationing of Indian labor.[40]

A later plan, drawn up by Las Casas and embodied in the instructions of the regent, Cisneros, to the Jeronymite friars sent to govern the West Indies in a final curious effort to save what was left of the native population, represented essentially elaboration upon the basic proposal of the Laws of Burgos and previous instructions that the Indians be permitted limited judicial autonomy and retention of their customs. According to this instruction of 1516, the Indians were to be settled in towns of 300 families. If the Indians of one cacique did not reach that number, those of nearby caciques were to be combined, each retaining authority over his original Indians, but the whole town to be under the charge of the principal cacique. Marriages between Spaniards and female heirs to the *cacicazgo* were to be encouraged, so that Spaniards might succeed to the title and the great expense of dual rule be avoided. Supervision over the Indian towns was to be exercised by the priest resident in each and by responsible and honorable Span-

40. Burgos, December 27, 1512, and Valladolid, January 23, 1513. The laws have been published a number of times, with variations that reflect either differences in the copies used or disagreements over paleography. Among the most recent are Simpson, *Studies in the Administration of the Indians in New Spain: I. The Laws of Burgos of 1512*, 4–26, publishing a copy dated at Valladolid, January 23, 1513; Konetzke, 1: 37–67, publishing a transcription for application to Puerto Rico; Muro Orejón, "Ordenanzas reales sobre los indios (las leyes de 1512–13)," publishing photographs and transcriptions of the Laws of 1512 and the amendments to them, Valladolid, July 28, 1513. An excellent English translation both of the Laws of Burgos and of the amendments of 1513 is Simpson, *The Laws of Burgos of 1512–1513: Royal Ordinances for the Good Government and Treatment of the Indians*. The quotation above, the first part of clause 24 of the Laws as issued in 1512, is from this translation, p. 32.

iards, the latter to be appointed as administrators and judges of one, two, or three Indian towns, according to the population. Each town was to have the normal complement of officials, appointed by the principal cacique, the priest, and the Spanish administrator; in case of dispute, the two Europeans were to make the appointments. The towns were to have a limited administrative and judicial autonomy:

> Also each town is to have jurisdiction within its boundaries, and the said caciques are to have jurisdiction to punish the Indians who transgress in the town where they are superior, not only as regards their own people, but also as regards those of the inferior caciques who live in the town. This is to comprehend those who deserve punishment up to whipping and no more. And upon these they are not to execute punishment on their own order alone, but at least with the supervisory advice and consent of the friar or priest who is there. The rest is to be in the hands of our ordinary justice. If the caciques should do what they ought not, they are to be punished by our ordinary justice. If also they do wrong to their inferiors, they are to make fitting reparation.

This somewhat complicated system of tutelage clearly left intact little of previous native custom except the system of caciques and such native practices as the resident priests and Spanish judges deemed compatible with Christianity and Spanish conceptions. In the provision for town officials lay the seed of an alternative government that, if given time to develop, was likely to destroy the rule of the caciques. The instruction of 1516 contained another clause which sheds much light on the status of Indians in Spanish courts: In order that Old Christians who wronged Indians might be punished, the judge at his discretion might accept the Indians as witnesses and give weight to their testimony in the case.[41] This clause indicates that until then no Indians could appear before a Spanish judge in a case involving a Spaniard, even though they must be recognized as competent witnesses in purely Indian cases that might come before Spanish judges.

It is notable that civil suits were not mentioned in the instruction of 1516. To the extent that there were any among Indians, the inten-

---

41. Madrid, September 13, 1516, in Konetzke, 1:63–67; and DIU, 9:53–74. Simpson publishes an English translation in *The Encomienda: Forced Native Labor*, 191–205, from which the clause quoted is taken (p. 195), with slight modification.

The instruction of 1516 repeated the essence of a clause in the amendments to the Laws of Burgos that Indians showing capacity for civilized, Christian life were to be allowed to live in their own settlements, subject only to payment of tribute to the crown. A similar instruction was issued in 1518: Konetzke, 1:68–70; DIU, 9:92–93; DCLI, 1:128–129; and Encinas, 2:184–185. The arrangement, if implemented, meant freedom from labor service but not from the supervision of priest and district judge. In the conditions on Hispaniola in 1518, it is doubtful that the instruction had much practical effect.

tion must have been that those of small value be judged by the caciques, with the advice and concurrence of the priest. If the suit involved more substantial value, it must have gone to a Spanish judge. Suits involving Indians of different towns, or Indians and Spaniards, would have gone before the ordinary judges for Spaniards or before the Audiencia of Santo Domingo, which was established as a royal court of appeal for the islands in 1512.[42] In the general situation of exploitation and rapidly diminishing numbers that prevailed among the Indians of Hispaniola, there may well have been no civil suits beyond purely local ones, quickly settled. A royal order of 1514 that entered later Spanish digests as referring to Indian suits turns out, on inspection of its text, to refer to disputes among Spaniards over grants of Indians.[43]

The first quarter-century of Spanish empire in America, then, did little more for Indian administration than establish on paper the practice of medieval Castile, especially as it had been formulated in the law of 1476 and as it was being formulated in the treatment of the Moriscos. Within the limits imposed by Christianization, the natives might keep their own procedures and customs for deciding relations

42. The instructions to the new audiencia, signed at Burgos, October 9, 1511, are published in DII, 11:546–555. There is no mention in them of Indian cases, but there is provision for a *procurador de pobres*, presumably for the Spanish.

43. Gobernación espiritual y temporal de las Indias, in DIU, 23:87. The order itself, dated at Valbuena, October 19, 1514, is recorded in AGI–IG, leg. 419, lib. 5, fol. 81r–v: "Para que cosa de yndios no vaya por vía de letrados y procuradores, syno solamente la verdad sabida. El rey. Don Diego Colón, etc., e nuestros jueçes de apelación del abdiencia e juzgado que resyde en la dicha ysla Española: A my es fecha relación que algunas personas en la dicha ysla han yntentado e yntentan algunos pleitos e deferençias sobre los yndios que les están encomendados e sobre otras cosas que tocan a los dichos yndios, lo qual diz que se a fecho y haze por vía hordinaria e con letrados e procuradores, como se haze en los pleitos çeviles, lo qual es cabsa que los dichos yndios se escandalizen y alteren y no sirvan con la voluntad que convernía, de que Dios, Nuestro Señor, es deservido, e porque mi voluntad es de lo mandar proveer e remediar como convenga, por ende, yo vos mando que agora e de aquí adelante no consintáys ni deys lugar que ningund pleito ni diferençia que oviere en esa dicha ysla sobre qualquier cosa que toque a los dichos yndios vaya por vía de letrados e procuradores, ni se guarde en ello los términos del derecho, salvo solamente sabida la verdad, se concluye e determine brevemente, syn tela de juizio e no de otra manera, lo qual asy hazed e cunplid, siendo primeramente tomada la razón deste my carta en la casa de la contrataçión de las Yndias que reside en la çibdad de Sevilla por los nuestros ofiçiales della. Fecha en Valbuena, a diez e nueve días de otubre de quinientos é catorze años. Yo el rey. . . . The phrase "que ningund pleito ni diferençia . . . que toque a los dichos yndios vaya por via de letrados e procuradores," etc., is sufficiently broad that it might later have been applied to suits among and by Indians, although that was not the reason for the cédula. In this other meaning it entered the *Copulata*, and from there the RLI, 5.10.10. One suspects a secretarial confusion through too brief a marginal notation of content. I thank Enrique Otte for a copy of this cédula.

among themselves, so long as no substantial sum or grave offense were involved. But the operation of their justice was to be under close Spanish supervision. Graver cases, and those involving Spaniards as well, were to go before Spanish royal judges. Presumably any native, if he dared and could afford the expense, could demand that his cause be heard by a Spanish judge, and appeals could be carried from the decisions of caciques and district judges to the new Audiencia of Santo Domingo. Alongside the native system of caciques, there was also to come into being a Spanish type of town government and set of officials that provided the possibility, perhaps certainty, of supplanting the older native arrangements. In the circumstances of Hispaniola in 1516, the intention was there, the possibility of success illusory.

That the provisions of the instruction of 1516 were implemented to any great extent, we may doubt. In the years of Jeronymite rule on Hispaniola, despite whatever measures the new administrators tried to carry out, the native population continued to die out. The Indians of the other islands of the Greater Antilles vanished with equal rapidity. By 1525 there were so few natives on Hispaniola—and most of these slaves brought from the smaller islands or the mainland—that fundamentally there was no problem of native administration. The Indians of the other large islands disappeared with equal rapidity.[44] It was only on the mainland, in areas so heavily populated that, despite heavy losses in conquest and early contact with whites, substantial native populations survived and intermingled with their conquerors in prolonged and intimate contact, that there was time to experiment, revise, and eventually arrive at an ordered system for fitting the natives and their customs within an adjusted Spanish judicial system.

44. See the references to movement of population in note 36. In 1525–28 the royal government proposed placing some of the remaining Indians of Cuba in encomiendas that fell vacant in towns under the supervision of Franciscan and Dominican friars, but the proposal quickly ran into determined opposition on the part of the Spanish settlers: Gómez Canedo, *Evangelización y conquista*, 102–107.

CHAPTER III

The Experience of New Spain, 1519–1585

In the Antilles, the problems of accommodating Spanish laws and judicial procedures to subject Indians ended with the extermination of the natives. In one sense, they were solved. But the extermination—which resulted in part from anarchic and destructive exploitation, and in greater measure from the introduction of Old World diseases into populations without acquired resistance—meant that most of the Spanish settlers were forced to seek their livelihood elsewhere. The holocaust in the West Indies was sufficiently shocking and unprofitable to the Spaniards themselves that they tried to develop more orderly and moderate systems of exploitation on the American mainland. Involved in this experimentation was the mutual adjustment of the New Christians and their conquerors' laws and procedures, judicial and executive. This adjustment took place slowly, because the very nature of the problems became clear only after the first major political and social changes due to conquest were already well under way. On the mainland, unlike the West Indies, there was time for experimentation. Despite the very serious losses which the Indians sustained in the decades after conquest, substantial nuclei of population survived in most regions, especially the uplands, so that the problems did not disappear through the extinction of the conquered, but remained long enough for the conquerors to become aware of them and, by a process of trial and reexamination, attempt solutions.

We are concerned here only with New Spain in its narrowest definition: that is, the lands of the Triple Alliance and of neighboring cities and tribes that became the territory of the Audiencia of Mexico and the core of the viceroyalty of New Spain. Destruction of Indian life within this area was very great. Most of the coastal regions, heavily populated before the coming of the white man, became virtually uninhabited, disease-ridden wastes, where nearly feral livestock replaced human beings. The most detailed of recent studies chart the trend in central Mexico—the region north and west of the Isthmus of Tehuantepec, including all of the Audiencia of Mexico (except for Yucatan) and portions of the Audiencia of Guadalajara or Nueva Galicia:

Year	Native Population
1518	25.2 million
1532	16.8
1548	6.3
1568	2.65
1585	1.9
1595	1.375
1605	1.075
1622	.75

These estimates indicate clearly the trend of Indian population in the century after the coming of the Spaniards. Despite sharp contraction, substantial numbers of that population survived during the sixteenth century. In the first half of the seventeenth century, there began a recovery that brought Indian numbers to steadily higher levels. There was thus continuing need for accommodation of laws and procedures and the time to work out the accommodation.[1]

During the same years, and indeed throughout the colonial period, Spanish settlement and interbreeding with the natives created a community of whites and mixed-bloods of Spanish culture. Another

1. Borah and Cook, *The Aboriginal Population of Central Mexico on the Eve of the Spanish Conquest*, 72–88, *The Population of Central Mexico in 1548*, 109–115 and correction, and "Conquest and Population"; Cook and Borah, *The Indian Population of Central Mexico, 1531–1610*, 33–56, *The Population of the Mixteca Alta*, 17–59, esp. 57, and *Essays in Population History*, 1:300–375 and 3:95–102; and Simpson, *Exploitation of Land in Central Mexico*, passim. The reexamination of aboriginal numbers began in Cook and Simpson, *The Population of Central Mexico in the Sixteenth Century*, passim, and has been refined and revised in the works cited above. For opposing views, see Rosenblat, *La población indígena y el mestizaje en América*, 1:59–82, 88, 102, 215–218, 240–246, and 281–293, and *La población de América en 1492*, 23–81; and Sanders. Rosenblat would admit only a small decline in Indian numbers, made up by replacement through intermixture, whereas Sanders would admit substantial decline. For the explanation in terms of epidemiology and immunology, see McNeill, 199–234.

study[2] arrives at the following estimates of so-called Spaniards (really Europeans of all kinds, and many mixed-bloods of Hispanic culture):

Year	Population
1570	57,000
1646	114,000
1742	465,000
1772	486,000
1793	780,000

There were thus two substantial communities living within the same territory, and the need to adjust their relations became more rather than less pressing as the Hispanized population increased.

During the sixteenth century, a long series of discussions and experiments attempted to settle the relations of the dominant and the subjugated communities. From perhaps 1511 on, some members of the royal bureaucracy, sincerely disturbed by the destruction of the Indian population in the Antilles and on the mainland, initiated discussions aimed at finding less murderous systems of exploitation. These discussions continued throughout the century, reaching a sharper focus in specific controversies and meetings of juntas, subsiding in other years. Debate was made very much longer by the dilatory methods of the royal bureaucracy and the difficulties of communication in the sixteenth century, so that the gathering of reports and opinions, discussion of them by juntas and councils, reaching decisions to initiate new measures, and reconsideration of the decisions upon protest by affected groups made the adoption and implementation of any measure a matter of decades rather than years.

Bound up in the discussion was the debate over the nature of the Indians. That they were human beings was hardly in question, whatever the rhetoric advanced, since no participant urged that Spaniards having sexual intercourse with Indians be punished for the then-monstrous sin of bestiality. That Indians had souls and were competent to become Christians also was not really in question, although the papal bull *Sublimis Deus* of June 2, 1537, settled whatever doubt lay in that matter. What the debate really concerned was the nature of the regime the Indians were to be subjected to. If they were of diminished capacity and understanding, they ought either to be turned over to feudal jurisdictions, which would have left them to more flexible administration, or placed under some form of Spanish tutelage. If they were of full capacity and understanding, the alternatives were that they ought to be placed in full Christian policy forthwith, with imme-

2. Borah, *New Spain's Century of Depression*, 5–18 et passim.

diate imposition of Spanish forms and substantial discarding of native custom, or that they should be left in full enjoyment of their own customs and usages, with minimum change.[3]

This search for less destructive systems of exploitation was not merely the concern of royal officials. Many of the clergy, especially the friars, were active in demanding the remedy of abuses and in proposing measures. Bartolomé de las Casas gained prominence as an agitator for reform.[4] Also active, and perhaps more effective in the long run, were such men as Francisco de Vitoria[5] and Jerónimo de Mendieta.[6] There was also among the conquerors and settlers a substantial group which, understanding the need for a durable, long-term relationship, urged measures to ease the burden on the Indian community.[7]

The discussions were characterized by almost innumerable variations of opinion and proposal, but in general three schools of thought emerged. One, led eloquently by Francisco de Vitoria, held that the Indians, having developed their own society, were entitled to their own institutions and law. Should they come under the rule of a foreign sovereign (like the Spanish king), he was bound to uphold and defend native institutions and laws and the rights of existing nobles and chiefs, since he served as the native prince. The most that might be conceded as imposed change was the minimum necessary for extirpating idolatry and introducing Christianity.[8] Such views, which required undoing a profitable occupation imposed by conquest, met a frigid reception from crown and settlers.[9]

Diametrically opposed to the Vitoria school, other men ad-

3. See the comments by Friede, 30–31. On the papal bulls of 1537, see Hera. For the controversy in general, these articles plus O'Gorman, "Sobre la naturaleza bestial," and his Introduction to Las Casas, Apologética historia sumaria, 1:xxxviii–lxxix; Gallegos Rocafull, 15–213; Biermann, 8–9, 39, 40–44, and 55–58; Gómez Canedo, "La cuestión de la racionalidad de los indios" and Evangelización y conquista, 63–68; Hanke, The Spanish Struggle for Justice, 39–41 et passim; and Góngora, 201–211. See also the two letters of Sebastián Ramírez de Fuenleal to the empress, Mexico City, November 3, 1532, and May 15, 1533, in DII, 13:259–260, and Paso y Troncoso, 15:162–165, respectively.

4. Paso y Troncoso, passim. The major proponent of the fame of Las Casas is Lewis Hanke, in The Spanish Struggle for Justice and Bartolomé de las Casas. There are numerous other expositions by Hanke and others.

5. Miranda, Vitoria y los intereses de la conquista; Vitoria, Relectio de Indis, 2–134 (parts 1 and 2) and Introductions, xiii–clviii.

6. Phelan, The Millennial Kingdom of the Franciscans, 41–91 et passim; Maravall, "La utopía político-religiosa"; and Ricard, La "conquête spirituelle," 66–68.

7. See the quotation from Luis de León Romano in this chapter, and the whole of his letter in Ricard, ed., "Un document inédit." Also see the later discussion in this chapter.

8. Vitoria, Relectio de Indis, 2–134.

9. Vitoria, Relecciones del estado, xix–xxiv.

vanced the idea of one society. That meant sweeping assimilation of the Indians to Castilian institutions, laws, and procedures. Castilian law was to be applied to the Indians in full rigor. Their customs and institutions were to be assimilated to Christian and European ones without restriction or special accommodation. Although the adherents of this view never developed the eloquence in exposition or defense of their position that flowed from the pens and teaching of the upholders of the other schools of thought, their position had very real strength, for it accorded best with the interests of the crown and the settlers. Most crown jurists held this view. Men trained in law (*letrados*), they were developing a unitary legal system which would replace feudal diversity with a uniform royal administration. In deciding questions affecting the Indians, they tended to apply Castilian procedure and law. Agreement by the colonists may be seen in such decisions as that of the municipal council of Mexico City that Indians might slaughter pigs freely and sell the meat in the city, ". . . since the Indians are free vassals of His Majesty and all the republic is one." [10] That there were difficulties in this position very quickly became apparent in such a matter, for example, as the early, episcopal inquisition—for if the Indians upon baptism were to be subject to its operation, Spanish judges would have found it necessary to burn a substantial proportion of them at the stake for continuing to hold heathen beliefs and practice idolatrous rites. [11]

The third school of thought might be called one of two republics. Recognizing that the Spanish were in America to stay, it urged that the Indians and Spaniards be organized into two separate commonwealths, each with its own laws, customs, and system of government. This was the position of Alonso de Zorita, judge of the Audiencia of Mexico, although he was exceptional among his colleagues in holding these views. [12] Jerónimo de Mendieta, one of the foremost proponents of this position, held that the Spaniards were so corrupt and given to vice that the Indians should be kept as isolated as possible. Their institutions and law should be modified to conform to Christianity and to ensure proper governance, but the Indians should retain as much as possible of the old or be moved to a new that would be different from the world of the Spaniards. He went so far as to urge that the Indian commonwealth be so completely separate that it would be linked with the Spanish only by being subject to the same viceroy. In general, the

10. Session of December 16, 1552, in Mexico City, *Actas de cabildo*, 6 : 79. See the discussion in Góngora, 198–221, esp. 210–211 and 215–216.

11. Cuevas, *Historia de la iglesia*, 1 : 417–431; Medina, *La primitiva inquisición*, 1 : 140–186 and 508–509; Greenleaf, *Zumárraga*, 68–75.

12. Zorita, *Breve y sumaria relación*, 39–54.

missionaries held to some form of these views and attempted to keep the two communities apart, even to the extent of further propagating the use of Nahuatl as a lingua franca among the various Indian linguistic groups, rather than favoring Spanish.[13]

Interestingly enough, the proponents of the two-republics position proceeded from contradictory views of the nature of the Indians. Most of the missionaries, including Mendieta, held that the natives were childlike in their understanding and, although industrious, were weak-willed, easily led astray whenever error was presented to them. They lacked the will power and physical force to resist anyone, especially Spaniards who wished to abuse them, seize their goods and women, or force them into harmful or sinful behavior. Only through rigid separation from the Europeans could the Indians be saved from corruption in their ways and physical extinction.[14] Others, such as Vasco de Quiroga and Las Casas, took the opposite view that the Indians were able, civilized people, who had governed themselves well except in matters of religion and were fully able to understand the way of civilized polity. The Indians should be kept separate from the Spaniards because under proper guidance there lay in them the possibility of a better society than the European.[15]

There were, of course, many variations and combinations of these views, some combining elements of different schools. One of the most strikingly phrased opinions was put forth in a letter to Charles V by Luis de León Romano, a Roman noble who held a number of administrative posts in the colony under the first two viceroys:

> The commonwealths of these natives appear to me to be without order and governance whatever, as much in what relates to their conversion as in what is needful for their conservation and increase. As far as I can discover, this has come about because the system of government has been turned so much to the opposite of what it once was. For the sort of people they are, their former system of government was the best that ever nation had, except for the salvation of their souls. For lack of care . . . and because of the mistake of trying to rule under one law two nations as different as men from children, the proper order of society among Indians and Spanish alike has been reversed. . . .

13. Phelan, *The Millennial Kingdom*, 41—91; Ricard, *La "conquête spirituelle,"* 61—70; Maravall, "La utopía político-religiosa"; Mörner, 17—51 et passim.

14. See note 13; further, Góngora, 204, 208—209; and Mendieta to Fray Francisco de Bustamante, Toluca, January 1, 1562, and to Philip II, Toluca, October 8, 1565, both in García Icazbalceta, *Nueva colección*, 1:1—29 and 31—45 respectively.

15. Giménez Fernández, "La jurisdicción jeronimita," 234—235; I have combined his four categories into two for the purposes of this discussion. See also Zavala, *La "utopía,"* 3—29; Hanke, *Bartolomé de las Casas*, 69—101; Las Casas, *Apologética historia sumaria*, vols. 1—2 passim and Introduction by O'Gorman.

To avoid the damages and inconveniences that I describe, this nation should be ruled by a good and wise man who will give law suited to nation and circumstance, and who will deal with such affairs and crimes as arise not by delay and recourse to written inquiry but by such rigorous and summary punishments as are suitable for subjects and were once the custom here. If this nation by force of arms were to conquer our realms and force us to accept its laws, ordinances, and customs, in what way would our commonwealth prosper? I am sure that we should rather come to grief and be made desolate. If their laws are harmful for us, ours have not been and cannot be profitable for them, since this is a people of little judgment and less substance. If Montezuma, king of these natives, preserved these realms with their laws, and, although he was more irrational than man of reason, governed them with great increase, order, and plenty, a Christian ruler should keep them in even greater prosperity, governing them in accordance with their laws and ours. . . .

In addition to all that I have said, this people should be reestablished in its customs and given a few necessary ones of ours. It should be placed under the yoke of its own centurions, as once it was. . . .[16]

Official royal policy steered an ambiguous course among all schools. It wavered between the theory of the two republics and that of one society, but occasionally showed some slight adherence to that led by Vitoria. To a considerable extent, the difficulty of detecting clear lines in royal policy arises because there were few explicit formulations of it. The crown proceeded by decisions on specific cases and problems as they arose, the decisions setting a precedent for the future and for other regions of America.[17] In part, further, the difficulty of finding clarity arises because royal policy itself changed, for the crown found itself bound by theological and legal formulations it was loath to transgress directly, yet caught in issues not easily handled unless they were transgressed or evaded. Moreover, it was beset by pressures to which it had to pay attention. When in the matter of the New Laws the crown chose to flout the interests of the colonists too directly and grievously, it learned a lesson that inhibited further drastic experiment for over two centuries.

Theoretically it might have been possible, had the crown been in full command of the situation at the outset and had it so wanted, to organize central Mexico on the basis of two entirely or nearly entirely separate racial communities. In the course of the sixteenth century, al-

16. Luis de León Romano to Charles V, Mexico City, April 20, 1553, in Ricard, "Un document inédit."

17. As is evident in the compilations of instructions and decrees. See the statement in García Gallo, *Manual*, 1:103, clause 214.

though a thorough-going decision was never reached, the crown issued a number of rules which tended to keep the two racial communities separate. Encomenderos were forbidden to settle in their Indian towns.[18] Indeed, any Spaniards, Negroes, and mixed-bloods were forbidden to settle in such towns.[19] The ordinances were so stringent that Spanish bachelors and merchants, both of whom were regarded as especially prone to teach the natives bad habits or to abuse them, were permitted to tarry only three days in an Indian town, even if they were there on proper business.[20] Furthermore, the royal government tried to keep Indians and Spaniards in separate settlements even when the needs of the Spanish required that Indians live near them in order to be available for service. Accordingly, the Indians of Mexico City were organized into four separate barrios, each with its own government.[21] When in the middle and later decades of the sixteenth century the royal government moved to concentrate the Indian population in more compact and larger settlements, Spaniards and other non-Indians were supposed to be rigidly excluded from the new towns.[22]

In practice, of course, the policy of separation proved unworkable, since the needs of the Spanish for tribute and labor meant very substantial, continuing contact between them and the Indians—so that, even if the two groups remained in separate settlements, there could be no real isolation. Actually there was very considerable intermingling, since numbers of Spaniards took up residence in Indian towns in order to establish businesses and care for properties, at the same time that large numbers of Indians were drawn into Spanish households as permanent or semi-permanent workers.[23]

18. Mörner, 85–94; royal cédula of June 23, 1571, to the Viceroy and Audiencia of Mexico, AGN-RCD, 47:fol. 541r–v. The cédula is a rebuke for not enforcing an established policy strictly.

19. Ordinances of Charles V for the good treatment of the Indians of New Spain, Toledo, December 4, 1528; royal cédula to the Viceroy of New Spain, Madrid, May 2, 1563, repeating the clause in the instruction to Luis de Velasco I, April 16, 1550, in Encinas, 4:261 and 340–341 respectively; and royal cédula to the Viceroy of New Spain, Madrid, November 25, 1568, in AGN-RCD, 6:exp. 277; royal cédula, Barcelona, January 31, 1586, citing an order of May 1573 and the instruction to Luis de Velasco I of April 16, 1550, in AGN-O, 1:fols. 94r–95v; ordinance of Luis de Velasco II, Mexico City, October 15, 1591, in AGN-RCD, 3:exp. 157; DIU, 23:108–109, summarizing royal legislation; Mörner, 94–122.

20. Ordinance of Luis de Velasco II, Mexico City, August 31, 1592, in AGN-RCD, 3:exp. 149; and the reenactment of this ordinance in broader terms, Mexico City, September 7, 1607, in Montemayor y Córdova de Cuenca, part 3:fol. 60r.

21. See the discussion by José Miranda in Caso et al., 38–39; and Gibson, *The Aztecs*, 173, and "Rotation of Alcaldes," 212–213.

22. Mörner, 42–58; ordinance of Velasco II of October 15, 1591, in AGN-RCD, 3:exp. 157. See also the summary of legislation in DIU, 21:315–321.

23. Mörner, 141–310. The parochial archives of Tlaxiaco and Teposcolula

In the minds of most advocates of the two republics, the idea of physical separation of the Indian and Spanish commonwealths was coupled with the plea for a separate and different legal and political organization for the Indians. Indeed, the former often was urged as a means of insuring the success of the latter. The conception had in its favor European respect for custom, in an age when the activity of princes and estates as lawgivers was regarded as the determination of existing custom or law—or in new situations, of whatever was least repugnant to them—rather than the enactment of innovative statutes. In medieval European thought, as it was accepted in Spanish legal thinking and had been stressed by Vitoria and his followers, each people had its own proper rulers (natural lords) and its own customs, both of which it was the duty of a conqueror to respect. Under this conception, the Indians should have been allowed to retain all of their pre-Conquest organizations and usages which were not repugnant to natural or moral law.

This conception ran counter to the thinking of the bulk of the Spanish conquerors and settlers, who, having come to America to make their fortunes, were hardly likely to respect any usages and organization that got in the way. In addition, neither the missionaries nor the members of the royal bureaucracy really wished to preserve the pre-Conquest organization of Indian society, of which a religion which both missionaries and lay Spaniards regarded themselves bound to extirpate was an integral element. The substitution of Christianity meant not merely the destruction of idols, an end to human sacrifices, and the building of churches, but rather a wholesale re-working of Indian culture and society. In the eyes of the missionaries, only construction of a new order could remove all reminders of past error and provide inducement for a Christian life. Not merely were the Indians' prayers to be Christian, but also their work, their play, their family lives, and all community activities and organization.[24] Fundamentally the crown agreed, even when it objected to the cost and the excessive extension of missionary influence.[25] Furthermore, both royal bureaucracy and the missionaries were in accord that the Indians must live in

show the existence in each town of Spanish communities sufficiently substantial that separate sets of registers were kept for them during the seventeenth and eighteenth centuries. That situation obtained over a large part of central Mexico.

24. Ricard, La "conquête spirituelle," 163–212 and 337–340.

25. Ibid., 181–185 and 202–204. The crown objected especially to the exercise of judicial power by the missionaries. See also Dr. Luis de Anguis to Philip II, Mexico City, February 1561, in Cuevas, Documentos, 252–253; royal cédula of the prince to the provincials in New Spain, Monzón, December 18, 1552, in Puga, fol. 212v; and royal cédula to the Audiencia of New Spain, Toledo, September 4, 1560, in ibid., fol. 201v, and Encinas, 4:337; see also Pazos.

proper polity; that is, that their political organization must be re-modeled to fit European conceptions. The model of proper polity naturally was the Spanish town. This royal policy was apparent from the first in the instructions of 1518 to Diego Velázquez, reissued on June 26, 1523, to Cortés, that the Indians be settled in proper polity and be placed under the sway of good customs and a proper manner of life.[26] These instructions echoed the policies of the Laws of Burgos and both earlier and later enactments for the West Indies.[27]

In consequence, the royal program for organizing Indian society in northern Mesoamerica, as it developed during the course of the sixteenth century, contained contradictory elements. On the one hand, the crown officially accepted the idea of preserving Indian organization and custom. The first comprehensive regulations for the guidance of provincial governors in New Spain, issued in 1530, expressly stated:

> Furthermore, we command that [our governors] examine the order and way of life that the Indians have for the supply and polity of towns that may be under their administration, and send a report to the president and *oidores* of the Audiencia, so that the latter may examine it and forward it to the Council of the Indies together with their opinion on what ought to be provided. In the meantime, the good usages and customs of the Indians shall be observed insofar as they are not contrary to our Christian religion.[28]

The injunction was confirmed in the New Laws of 1542.[29] In 1555, the royal cédula for the government of the Indians of the Verapaz enjoined Spanish administrators and justices to enforce the good laws and customs of the natives, without the suggestion that enforcement was to be an interim measure.[30] The following year a royal order empowering the viceregal government to appoint an Indian justice in Cortés' Marquesado del Valle explicitly enjoined respect for Indian custom.[31] There can be no doubt that through these instructions and other measures Indian custom was given formal royal recognition as proper law, and that the crown was pledged, at least to some extent, to respect the former organization of Indian society.

Within the regulations of 1530 for provincial governors in New Spain lay another clause aiming at reducing the impact of Castilian law and procedure upon the natives:

> Whereas we have commanded that an order be issued for adjudicating suits between private Indian persons, [namely,] that such

26. Encinas, 4:247–252; DII, 23:353–368.
27. See Chapter II above.   28. Puga, fol. 54f.
29. Clause 25, in DII, 14:385–386.
30. Encinas, 4:355–356.   31. August 1556, in DIU, 21:323.

suits be decided orally without recourse to documents or judicial procedure, we command that this order be observed and enforced without change. But if the suit is between town councils, justice shall be done by ordinary process with the brevity that the quality of the matter requires. For it is our intention that the Indians shall be relieved for the present from fees and costs.[32]

The reference to an earlier order is to the royal cédula of 1514 and its somewhat ambiguous wording. Clearly the intention was to invoke on behalf of the Indians the *cognitio summaria*, a civil hearing dispensing with written pleas and formalities, even with lawyers, relying instead upon the judge's investigative diligence and shrewdness to discover the facts, and ending in a summary judgment.

On the other hand, whatever the theory or rhetorical justification, and despite all palliative measures, the imposition of Spanish rule meant sweeping change for the natives, for the Castilian crown and its European subjects responded to a series of imperatives inherent in the imposition of alien sovereignty and an alien religion as well as the insertion of an alien upper class. In some instances, Spanish officials mistakenly considered that they were continuing the custom of the time of Montezuma; in other instances, they held that the Indians were being brought to proper rational and Christian practice. At all times the crown had to keep what its subjects had conquered. If it was unthinkable that the Spanish permit continued practice of idolatry and human sacrifice or continued existence of the heathen religious hierarchies, it was equally unthinkable that the Castilian crown and its officials not replace the old native political superstructures and their administrative hierarchies. In any case, religious and political functions were so deeply intertwined that extirpating the one meant a wrenching effect upon the other. So there disappeared the imperial political structures of Tenochtitlán and its allies in the Triple Alliance, of the Zapotec kingdoms, and of the Tarascan state, even though the crown and its officials accepted the policy of preserving the status of pre-Conquest chieftains. The chieftains were forbidden to use the title lord or natural lord, which would have implied a challenge to the legitimacy of Spanish rule. Instead, they were given the title caciques and the status of nobles. Lesser members of the Indian upper classes became *principales*, with the status of lesser nobles.

The perquisites of both groups were much reduced by viceregal insistence that payments to them by the Indian communities must be regulated by a formal schedule, which had to be approved by the viceroy. Their political power within their communities was substantially

32. Puga, fols. 55v–56v.

reduced or largely done away with by relocation and reorganization of the Indian towns, since the functions of government were entrusted to a new group of elected officials. The older rulers were able to retain some power by taking on the new posts; i.e., the cacique had himself elected governor and, despite the rule against re-election, held on to the office. Lesser nobles within the towns took on the other administrative posts. But the acts of all as town officials were subject to review and change by Spanish administrators and judges.[33]

Reorganization of Indian communities was inherent in the royal instructions to Diego Velázquez and Hernán Cortés that the Indians be settled in proper polity. In practice, proper polity turned out to be a European-style town, laid out in checkerboard fashion, in accordance with the best European ideas of planning, with streets meeting at right angles, and church and administrative buildings grouped around a central square.[34] The town officials were a governor, council, and lesser officials, again largely in European style that rendered the old native administrative hierarchies obsolete. The priest and his superiors were, of course, European, but a subordinate group of servants, musicians, catechists, etc., were Indian and paid from community funds.[35]

The first instances of such towns may well have been the new settlements of Indian allies close to Spanish settlements, like San Martín Mexicapan and Santo Tomás Xochimilco, both near Huaxyacac (Antequera/Oaxaca), for Mexican and Tlaxcaltecan Indians. These two towns had a Spanish-style government but may not have had the checkerboard layout.[36] As far as we now know, the full model appeared in 1526 when the Franciscans founded the Indian town of San Francisco Acámbaro in Michoacán. The audiencia confirmed the elections of officials and conferred the staves of office. In 1530 the

33. Gibson, *The Aztecs*, 9–57 and 154–181; cédula of the empress to the Audiencia of New Spain, February 26, 1538, forbidding native rulers to term themselves *señores naturales*, in Encinas, 4:291; further prohibition in royal cédula, Madrid, July 17, 1572, in Montemayor y Córdova de Cuenca, part 1: fol. 210r; Mendieta to Philip II, Toluca, October 8, 1565, in García Icazbalceta, *Nueva colección*, 1:48–49; letter of Fray Nicolás de Witte, Metztitlán, August 21, 1554, in Cuevas, *Documentos*, 221–228; Miranda, in Caso et al., 59–61; and Zorita, *Breve y sumaria relación*, 39–54. Gerhard, *A Guide*, passim, gives information on such readjustments town by town; AGN-I, vol. 1, has a series of assessments for caciques, etc. The process may be observed further in Gibson, *Tlaxcala*, 89–123 et passim, and in Spores, passim.

34. Borah, "European Cultural Influence"; Foster, 34–49; Kubler, 1:68–102; Ricard, *La "conquête spirituelle,"* 164–172.

35. Miranda, in Caso et al., 79–82; Ricard, *La "conquête spirituelle,"* 163–186; Chevalier, "Les municipalités indiennes"; Gibson, *The Aztecs*, 98–135, 154–193, and 211–219. For a case study, see Borah and Cook, "La transición" or "A Case History: Santiago Tejupan."

36. Chance, 32.

crown instructed the audiencia to appoint Indian *regidores* (council members) in Mexico City as well as Indian towns, and to use Indians as *alguaciles* (bailiffs) for investigations. The intent was clear; and so, despite some difficulties in implementation, between 1530 and 1564 local Indian settlement and government in New Spain were remade in a Spanish image, town by town. At first the Indians tried to combine the old native hierarchy and the new Spanish one, but by the middle of the century the new Spanish forms prevailed.[37] Their victory was greatly aided by a sweeping policy of relocating the Indian populations— mostly living until then in dispersed rancherías or on hilltops, for defense—into compact settlements in the valleys, laid out in the new manner. This reorganization was largely carried out during the administrations of the first two viceroys, Antonio de Mendoza and Luis de Velasco I.[38]

The Spanish program for the reorganization of Indian society thus meant very considerable change even in the terms in which royal officials conceived of it: a relatively moderate series of measures designed to implant Christianity, harness the Indians to the service of the Spanish, and cement Spanish rule beyond possibility of reversing the Conquest. But the changes, once initiated, touched off an upheaval in native society that went far beyond what the royal bureaucracy and the clergy contemplated. By the middle decades of the sixteenth century, many of the more thoughtful officials and clergy were appalled at what had been unleashed. We can see now that the Spanish Conquest called into question the relationships of power and status within aboriginal society, all of which were essentially a distillation of previous centuries and even millennia of imposition. Maintained by the preexisting array of force, they could now be challenged in the new balances of power. The occupation of land by one town rather than a neighbor, the dependence of village upon town and of town upon town with attendant payments of service and tribute, could be brought into question and perhaps undone by appeal to the Spanish.

The reorganization of native society led to a bitter fight within it to retain or obtain the most favored position possible, for the new or-

37. Chevalier, "Les municipalités indienne"; Gibson, *The Aztecs*, 166–219, and "The Transformation"; Miranda, in Caso et al., 79–82; Cristóbal de Benevente to the king, Mexico City, June 1, 1544, in Paso y Troncoso, 4:94–102; the empress to the Audiencia of New Spain, July 12, 1530, and March 20, 1532, in DIU, 10:53–54 and 117, and Encinas, 4:335–336; royal cédulas to Mendoza and to the Audiencia of New Spain, both Valladolid, October 9, 1549, in Konetzke, 1:186–187 and 260–261 respectively; and royal cédula to the Audiencia of New Spain, December 1555, in DIU, 21:321.

38. Gerhard, "Congregaciones de indios" and *A Guide*, passim; Miranda, "La pax hispanica."

ganization meant that there were far fewer posts of honor and profit available, at the same time that the shrinkage of Indian population made the Indian community less able to support the old upper stratum. Moreover, the general disorder and shuffling after the Conquest meant that natives who had not had previous noble status, but who had more rapidly learned Spanish customs and gained Spanish favor, could use their knowledge to secure higher economic and political position for themselves.[39] As we shall see, the major means for carrying on quarrels between towns and within towns was furnished almost unwittingly by the Spanish. Further, the Spanish—probably without malice, but also without genuine understanding—imposed a number of their own conceptions in important aspects of Indian life. They were strongly influenced by sixteenth-century European beliefs in natural law and in a universal substratum of civilized custom to which all peoples might properly be held. Among these conceptions were proper polity, the nature of ownership and use of land, the nature of slavery, and proper administration and relief within it.

Proper polity and the far-reaching changes brought by imposing it have been sketched already. Differences in conceptions of ownership and use of land also brought substantial change. For the Indians, land was essentially a means of production, held by the community or clan and allocated to support certain offices or functions. Tenure was fundamentally conditional and subject always to the requirement of use. Indian conceptions of the nature of land-holding most closely approximated those of the feudal linkage of land tenure to service or office. It is unlikely that aboriginal Indian society had any conception of the owning of land in the sense of Roman law, that a man could be the master of land which was his to allow to remain idle, destroy, or till as he chose, subject only to the right of the sovereign to tax or take for public use on due compensation.

The Spanish, on the other hand, not only were moving to the conception of land-ownership embodied in the Roman or Civil Law, but further declared that all land not actually occupied by Indians or used by them was vacant and thus royal domain available for grant or purchase. For the Spanish, land was not merely a means of production; ownership of far larger stretches of it than the owner could make use of directly or through tenants was a visible sign of prestige in the community and one of the few safe forms of investment. The results

39. Borah, "Population Decline"; Borah and Cook, *The Population of Central Mexico in 1548*, 54–74; Miranda, in Caso et al., 59–61; Zorita, *Breve y sumaria relación*, passim; Cook and Borah, "Quelle fut la stratification sociale"; Mendieta to Philip II, Toluca, October 8, 1565, in García Icazbalceta, *Nueva colección*, 1:48–49; and letter of Fray Nicolás de Witte, Metztitlán, August 21, 1554, in Cuevas, *Documentos*, 221–228.

were a vast series of conflicts between Spanish and natives, and far-reaching readjustments within the Indian towns as their more powerful and more alert members strove to assert and extend ownership in Spanish fashion, usually at the expense of the peasantry and other members of the pre-Conquest upper class.[40]

Slavery is another illustration of the way in which almost unwitting imposition of a Spanish conception brought sweeping change, so that a fairly benign native institution became a harsh and destructive form of exploitation. Slavery was widely known among the pre-Conquest Indians of northern Mesoamerica. It seems, in general, to have been a mild affair which entitled the owner of the slave to service for life, but left the slave very substantial rights. The latter, for example, could hold property and himself own slaves. Families might agree to provide a slave, but shift the role among members. The only truly harsh aspect of aboriginal slavery was the selection of some slaves, upon repeated resale, for fattening and eventual sacrifice and eating; but this affected only a very small percentage of the total. Under Spanish law, on the other hand, slaves had far fewer rights. They were civilly dead, chattels who might be worked like domestic animals and transported and sold like any other form of merchandise.

The initial Spanish equation of slavery under Indian custom with slavery under Castilian and Civil Law meant that Indian slaves could be subjected to merciless exploitation. Enterprising Spaniards acquired Indian slaves by purchase, levy on tributary villages, or straight kidnapping, and worked them to death in mines or shipped them for sale to new and very different lands and climates, where they soon died. Short-sighted though such practices were, they were profitable enough to bring about the destruction of the Indian population in, for example, the Pánuco region. There was for a time serious danger that the experience of the Antilles would be repeated on the mainland, through the slave trade, until the danger was averted by royal legislation. Finally put into effect in the 1550s, it abolished Indian slavery save for captives taken on the northern frontier.[41]

A third Spanish conception, which had especially far-reaching

40. Caso, "La tenencia de la tierra"; Miranda, in Caso et al., 69–72; Parry, *The Audiencia of New Galicia*, 59; Chevalier, *La formation*, 176–194; and Esquivel Obregón, 1:369–374 and 431 and 3:173–218. See the long analysis of the Huejotzingo area in Prem, 50–234.

41. Bosch García, 11–109; Vasco de Quiroga to the Council of the Indies, July 24, 1535, in DII, 10:370–372 and 390–456; Zavala, *Los esclavos indios*, 1–179; Chipman, 87–91, 157–158, 197–218, 223–229, 236–237, and 299–302; Simpson, *Studies: IV. The Emancipation of the Indian Slaves*, 3–14. For European and Castilian law, see Pérez y López, 12:117–156, esp. 122; and Spain: Laws, Statutes, etc., *Las Siete Partidas* (1843–1844), 4.21.1–8 and 4.22.1–11, esp. 8 (2:1105–1120), with the glosses.

consequences, was that of appeal against the acts or decisions of judicial and administrative officials; indeed, that any person, however high his status, including the monarch himself through his agents, could be brought into court. It is unlikely that pre-Conquest Indian society had this concept except in highly restricted and attenuated form. For the Spanish, on the other hand, the idea of appeal and accountability was part of the very fabric of the state. Castilian law and procedure made elaborate provision for appeals in judicial cases, for delaying the actions of executive officials until they could be reviewed either by a superior or by a court, and for formal accounting for an official's acts after his term of office. Today some may object that the result often was long delay and even near-paralysis, with a consequence of substantial injustice, but there can be no doubt that behind the conception lay a concern for orderly and just administration. It was unthinkable to the crown bureaucracy that a civilized and Christian state should deny the right of appeal to any subject. Furthermore, keeping open the channels for appeals greatly increased the chance that the royal government could examine the acts of its officials and implant a centralized, uniform administration.[42]

So the Indians of New Spain, after enduring the shocking losses and disruption of the first years of conquest, found that once a relatively orderly royal administration began under the Second Audiencia in 1531, they could haul any official into court and challenge his decisions; that any grant of land could be disputed; that boundaries and political arrangements could be challenged; and that any private person or corporate entity could be held to redress for damage done or be forestalled through petition for an order of *amparo*. They found very quickly, furthermore, that any decision once rendered could be appealed up the long line of reviews provided by Castilian law. The conquerors thus placed a potent weapon at the disposal of the conquered, one that might be used against them as well as the subjected. Fear of direct, extra-legal reprisal, and the reluctance of Spanish judges and officials to rule against fellow Spaniards, undoubtedly limited its use against Europeans, especially those of superior status, but the Indians made very great use of their right.

Within the Indian community, litigation before Spanish courts and petitions for administrative review and protection became the principal means of carrying on the long series of disputes unleashed by the Conquest over land, status, and virtually all other relationships. The conquerors were amazed that subjects so meek showed such ferocity and tenacity in litigation. Alonso de Zorita, who was judge of the

---

42. Esquivel Obregón, 1:430–431; Villapalos Salas, *Los recursos contra los actos: Su evolución*, passim, and "Los recursos: Notas."

audiencia in the middle years of the sixteenth century, has left a long description of *el pleitismo indígena*:

> . . . as those who have risen against their lords understand that they will be listened to, provided that they bring with them something to give those who take part in the airing of their affairs, they have arranged to rob in order to overturn their natural lords. Thus have begun the suits of Indians against Indians within towns, of subjects against lords in all New Spain, of towns against towns, and dependencies against their head towns. The result has been enormous costs and a great multitude of dead on the highroads as the Indians have gone and come on their suits, without knowing what is genuinely to their advantage, nor what they ask, nor want, nor seek, nor what they are suing about, nor why they go to the audiencia. Thus they merely use up their money and their lives, at the urging of men who devour their wealth, for that is the true reason [behind these suits].
>
> Lords and nobles have died, and many of the common people, men, women, and children, for the Indians always take with them people to carry the food they need. Many lords, nobles, and peasants have been sentenced to the mines and public works and have died there or have been left there abandoned and forgotten by their wives and children.
>
> The suits have brought about great upheavals in the provinces and towns and very great confusion everywhere. Both lords and commoners have been impoverished, brought to ruin, and their substance wasted. They have all suffered great loss, as much spiritual as material. In all New Spain there is no agreement on a single matter between the classes, because the commoners have lost their respect for their lords and nobles and have risen against them and no longer give them the obedience they once did. Yet such obedience to superiors is very necessary for good government among the Indians. . . . For the common people are like children who, when they lose fear or sense of shame, lose all the good that has been taught them. They want to be subject to those they can fear and hold in respect in order to do what they ought and are bound to do. To this end the lords and nobles were and are needed, for they understand the Indians and others do not. . . .
>
> If we had not allowed the Indians to carry on so many and such confused suits as they do, they would not have brought ruin on each other, nor would so many people have died. The desolation that now exists would have been avoided. We should have been far wiser to have turned Indian suits over to the caciques and lords who know and understand the truth of what each Indian claims, rather than listen to troublemakers given rein to cause mischief. We should have avoided much offense to Our Lord, false oaths, hates, enmities, the ruin of Indian towns and provinces, the many and grave misdeeds of those who incite and persuade the Indians in order to rob them, and finally the chaos that now exists among the Indians, which has become so bad that it seems impossible to end. All that I have described, furthermore, would have

ceased if we had observed what Your Majesty provided in one of the New Laws, that in suits among Indians or with them there should not be the usual procedures or protracted hearings, but that the cases should be decided summarily in accordance with their usages and customs, so long as these are not clearly unjust; nor should procuradores, letrados, nor solicitors aid them or carry on their suits, since all deal with matters which can be ascertained easily, so long as letrados and the rest of that tribe do not confuse and snarl the case. . . .

Many of the Indian lords, seeing what trouble-makers could do and the favor they have found, have joined them to avoid ruin, and have taken sides with part of their own people; in other matters, they have let the trouble-makers do whatever they wished. Both have robbed and have come to ask for appointments as alcaldes, governors, and councillors in order to rob more. The lords conform to the whim of the commoners and the unruly and those who persuade and incite. All rob and live on the sweat of the poor peasants. Since everything is in confusion, with a little intrigue, they get whatever they want. Thus there is now no light in the land, nor that majesty which the provinces used to have with their lords and good government. . . .[43]

By the time that Zorita wrote, the process of destruction of the old native society had gone too far to be reversed, even if the crown and the Spanish community had wished to do so. There did develop, in part of the royal bureaucracy and among the missionaries, concern over the extent of the convulsion that was taking place. Nevertheless, insofar as the older rulers and nobility retained a favored position, they did so by adapting to the new governmental structure and ways. The natural lord survived, if at all, as native boss, and the more enterprising among his former subjects could aspire to replace him. Costs in the form of expenses of the delegations, fees, gifts, and bribes were borne by the towns, usually through special assessments on the tributaries. Among the Spaniards, virtually the entire legal and notarial pro-

43. Zorita, *Breve y sumaria relación*, 42–46. See also Archbishop Montúfar to the Council of the Indies, Mexico City, May 15, 1556, in Paso y Troncoso, 8:85–87; petition of the bishops of New Spain to the Audiencia of Mexico, Mexico City, 1565, in DII, 13:288–289; Mendieta to Bustamante, Toluca, January 1, 1562, and to Philip II, Toluca, October 8, 1565, in García Icazbalceta, *Nueva colección*, 1:15–29 and 43–50 respectively; the Second Audiencia to the king, Mexico City, August 14, 1531, in DII, 41:42; and to the empress, Mexico City, February 9, 1533, in Paso y Troncoso, 3: 27–32; Alonso de la Vera Cruz, "Los avisos que se dieron al señor Marqués de Falcés," 1566, Memoria para el señor contador Hortuño de Ybarra, de las cosas que a de tractar con Su Magestad y Real Consejo de Yndias, y en Roma con Su Sanctidad, ca. March 7, 1560, and letter of Frs. Bustamante, Pedro de la Peña, and Vera Cruz to the king, Mexico City, July 26, 1561, all in Vera Cruz, 5:27–29, 167–169, and 177–181 and 187 respectively; "A relation of the commodities of Nova Hispania, and the maners of the inhabitants, written by Henry Hawks merchant . . . , 1572," in Hakluyt, 9:394.

fessions, which derived their living from honoraria and fees, showed little objection to the rain of silver.[44]

The flood of native litigation brought about substantial replacement of native usages, despite formal recognition by the crown of their validity to the extent that they did not conflict with natural law, reason, or Christian doctrine. At the lowest levels of native litigation and justice—even though few records have been found so far, and most proceedings may never have been committed to written record—it seems likely that local custom would continue to be important, for the Indian alcaldes would be better versed in it than in Spanish law and would rely upon what they knew.[45] Moreover, the community itself would insist upon its own custom.

But at any point at which the dispute involved other communities or was carried before higher authority, especially when it came before a Spanish provincial justice or before the audiencia or viceroy or the Council of the Indies, the situation changed—and the higher the level, the more fully was it reversed. Despite all prohibitions and limitations, the Indians resorted to letrados, solicitors, and other agents versed in Castilian procedures. They had to present the types of petition and testimony that Castilian law prescribed and that the royal authorities could understand. They had to pay fees and make gifts. Inevitably, the losing party appealed and one party or the other based his claim upon Castilian practice and law. Equally inevitably in the long series of claims and counterclaims, the royal authorities found themselves relying upon Castilian procedure and law rather than a strange native custom that could not be clearly ascertained because of widely conflicting testimony. In the end, the native usage was likely to be held contrary to reason or Christian doctrine. Equally, the royal injunctions to apply summary process in Indian cases ran up against the insistence of one or the other of the parties upon the full formalities of Castilian hearings. The judges of the audiencia, especially, tended to insist upon the application of Castilian procedure and law.[46] Their disposition was strengthened by the codification of Castilian law, promulgated in 1567, which provided a uniform code supposed to apply

44. See citations in note 43 and the discussion of fees and costs later in this chapter.

45. Gibson has found records of early Indian cases heard by Indian judges: Tlaxcala, 115–117. As far as the records go, the judges followed Castilian rules. Appeals went to the corregidor.

46. Gibson, Tlaxcala, 64–72 and 115–117, and The Aztecs, 91–92 and 147–149; clause 14 of the ordinances for the Council of the Indies, El Pardo, September 24, 1571, in DII, 14:415. See the comments of García Gallo, "La ley como fuente," 613–618; see also the later discussion in this chapter.

to the Indies as well as Castile except when it conflicted with specific royal enactments for the Indies.

Indian cases which poured into the Spanish courts and the audience chambers of administrators fell into two primary categories: Church and royal. Church cases might involve civil litigation or criminal offenses under ecclesiastical law, or dispensations and permissions under that law. Included were such matters as tithes, marriage, and orthodoxy of belief and religious practice. All fell within the jurisdiction of Church tribunals and administrators, who functioned under Church rules of procedure and canon and diocesan law in a gradation of levels of jurisdiction beginning with the parish and extending through the diocese, with a theoretical but rarely used right of appeal to the Rota in Rome. Judges, lawyers, notaries, and secretaries qualified under canon law and held Church appointment. Recourse to the royal jurisdiction was possible when the Church authorities appealed for the support of the *brazo secular* to enforce or execute its decisions, or when a party objected to Church jurisdiction through *recurso de fuerza*, a plea before the audiencia that rights guaranteed by royal law were being abridged. We shall not examine the category of Indian cases falling within Church jurisdiction for two reasons: (1) Much less is known about them than of civil ones, since the scholarship of the past century has devoted almost no attention to them, and (2) as far as one may judge from the little work done on such cases and the pertinent documents published, the basic problems of adaptation turned out to be much the same as for those in royal jurisdiction. In the end, considerable adjustment had to be made to Indian needs and circumstances.[47]

Royal cases fell within three basic groups: civil, criminal, and administrative, each with different laws and procedures. Involved in civil cases were the relations of people with each other and questions of personal status, essentially disputes in which the state acted as arbiter between or among subjects. I have indicated already two of the major kinds of civil disputes which developed, brought by Indians against other Indians. They were the differences of towns with each other over lands, water, and woods (in other words, boundary disputes) and the fight of dependent towns to free themselves from their *cabeceras*, or head towns. Boundary disputes became matters of community prestige

47. García Gallo, *Manual*, 1:85–86 (pars. 175–178) and 101 (par. 209); Maldonado, 281 et seq.; Greenleaf, "The Inquisition"; Llaguno, 34; Archbishop Montúfar to the Council of the Indies, Mexico City, September 18, 1555, in Paso y Troncoso, 8:42–45; royal cédula to the Viceroy and Audiencia of New Spain on its insistence on use of the *brazo secular*, with all accompanying fees, Aranjuez, May 7, 1571, in Encinas, 2:31.

and were carried on at heavy cost, which in many, perhaps most, instances far exceeded the total value of the land or water at issue.[48] The relations of *sujeto* and cabecera also involved matters of prestige and further substantial financial and social advantages, for the cabecera collected tributes, administered justice, and forced the natives of its dependencies to contribute in money, goods, and labor for community enterprises, which were centered in the head town and benefited its inhabitants far more than those of the dependencies.[49]

These two kinds of disputes were rife long before the coming of the Spaniards, but the reshuffling of relationships after the Conquest afforded a chance to demand a more favorable settlement. When the Second Audiencia attempted to insure that all of the conquered had their day in court, it opened the floodgates. The audiencia probably had little choice, since the disputes, if left unsettled or not given more peaceful outlet in litigation, frequently threatened to lead to riot and civil war. Shortly after the arrival of the Second Audiencia, for example, it was forced to intervene in a boundary dispute between Totolapan and the towns of the province of Chalco which had erupted into a riot serious enough to require a special investigation. The one unusual feature about this dispute was that Totolapan, reversing the usual practice, claimed to be a dependency of Yecapixtla in order to place itself under the government of Cortés' marquisate.[50] Need to preserve order thus forced the royal authorities to hear the complaints, even though the resulting upheaval was such that Mendieta in 1562 urged that a royal commission settle all town boundaries once and for all and that, as soon as the audiencia ratified the decisions, no suits on boundaries might be heard.[51] His proposal was not adopted, nor could it have solved the problem. Suits between towns over boundaries and on relationships within the political structure of towns became one of the most characteristic features of Mexican litigation and have remained so to the present day.

Another major subcategory of civil suit among Indians involved inheritance, especially inheritance of the property and rights of caciques. While the number of such cases was far less than those involving

48. *Relación de mando* of Martín Enríquez for his successor, the Conde de Coruña, September 25, 1580, in HM, 1:204–205.

49. *Relación de mando* of Antonio de Mendoza for Luis de Velasco I, n.d. but 1550–51, ibid., 49–50; Gibson, *The Aztecs*, 44–57 and 221–222; Taylor, *Landlord and Peasant*, 29; and Cook and Borah, *The Population of the Mixteca Alta*, 11–13 and 49.

50. Cédula of the empress to the Audiencia of Mexico, Barcelona, April 20, 1533, in Puga, fol. 85r.

51. Mendieta to Bustamante, Toluca, January 1, 1562, in García Icazbalceta, *Nueva colección*, 1:19–20.

towns, all such suits, like those of towns, had to be brought before the Spanish courts, both because of the assimilation of the caciques to Spanish noble status and the value of the lands and privileges in dispute. Aboriginal custom in succession varied from region to region and even within regions, but was seldom strictly patrilineal. In the Valley of Mexico, inheritance more frequently moved through brothers before entering the next generation, with an element of election among a group of potential heirs. In the Mixteca Alta (Oaxaca), eligibility for inheritance required descent from a ruler on both sides. Some towns, in default of a properly qualified person, returned to the original line of Tilantongo from which so many ruling houses sprang.

Although these customs did differ from Spanish law, there is nothing in them contrary to natural law or Christian doctrine. Nevertheless, as disputes over succession were brought to Spanish judges for decision, the judges began to apply Spanish ideas of rights in inheritance, holding that the cacicazgo must go to the oldest son or, in default of a son, to the nearest heir by Castilian rules. Indian custom was refused validity as contrary to reason. One of the more interesting cases concerned the failure of qualified heirs within the direct line of the ruling house of Teposcolula. When one claimant advanced the plea that the right of succession reverted to the parent house of Tilantongo in accordance with Mixtec custom, a claim that would seem to accord with Mixtec tradition, the Spanish judges dismissed it as contrary to reason. Inevitably, the proper heirs under Spanish ideas always could secure validity of their claims by recourse to a Spanish court. Indian custom, where contrary, gave way by the later sixteenth century to succession in cacicazgos through primogeniture on the Spanish model, with possessions moving *en bloc* in a form of entail.[52]

Many of the civil suits were between Indians and Spaniards—for suits were one of the few means by which Indian towns and caciques could defend their possessions and commoners from the European population settling among them. Under the prevailing rule, suits of Indians against Spaniards had to be brought in Spanish courts; the legal quality of towns and caciques equally brought cases by Spaniards against them into Spanish courts. A substantial proportion of the suits arose over land, which the Spanish acquired in one or more of three ways. (1) They might receive title to vacant land by royal grant. Such

52. Minutes of Church junta of 1532, Mexico City, May 1, 1532, in Llaguno, 152–153; Gibson, "The Transformation," 587, and *The Aztecs*, passim; Taylor "Cacicazgos coloniales," 14–15; Spores, 131–154; Caso, *Reyes y reinos*, 1:152–153; Munch, 27–28; Casas, *Apologética historia sumaria*, 2:406–409 (cap. 217); Zorita, *Breve y sumaria relación*, 42–49; suit over succession to the cacicazgo of Teposcolula, 1566–69, AGN-Tr, 24: exp. 6 (55 fols.).

grants were always subject to revocation or modification if they prejudiced the interests of a third party.[53] Initially the proceedings took
place under administrative law; but the grant, if made despite protest,
could be challenged before the Spanish courts. (2) In many instances,
the Spanish simply took lands they wanted. When they dared, the Indians sued for restitution or payment. Thus, upon the death of Hernán
Cortés, many of the Indian towns within his marquisate instituted suit
for such seizures and recovered judgment.[54] (3) A third method by
which Spaniards might acquire Indian lands was purchase or rental,
usually an amicable arrangement without suit. But this method too
meant a great deal of business before the Spanish justices, since the
crown very early insisted that any such purchases or rentals must be
made under judicial supervision. In 1536, a royal order required that
any license issued for such purchase contain a clause stipulating that
the sale must be before a judge of the audiencia.[55] The order was repeated in 1540, with the additional proviso that the Spanish might
rent the land to Indians or farm it with them on shares, but that such
contracts also must be made under the supervision of a justice.[56] The
requirement became standard. Subsequent regulations made the procedures of judicial supervision much more complicated.[57]

In addition to disputes over ownership of land, Spanish agriculture led to a long series of disputes over the extent to which Spanish-
owned livestock might graze upon Indian land. Under Castilian custom, once the crop was harvested the stubble became common pasture
which might be grazed by any livestock, however much towns and individual proprietors objected. Most of the livestock wandered loose
with insufficient guard the year around, being rounded up in an annual drive for branding and slaughter. Inevitably, many Spaniards let
their livestock invade the Indian villages before crops were harvested.
Without proper guard, it would have been difficult to prevent the

53. Such grants are to be found in the early volumes of AGN-M. Simpson, *Exploitation of Land*, passim, analyzes and tabulates such grants to 1620. See also Gibson,
The Aztecs, 257–277.

54. Resumen de los autos del pleito seguido por los indios de Coyoacán, and the
accompanying *probanza*, ca. 1561, in Mexico: AGN, *Documentos inéditos relativos a
Hernán Cortés y su familia*, 343–390; codices of the suit of the Indians of Cuernavaca
against the Marqués del Valle, in AGN-J, leg. 276; and accounts of Simón Pasca, majordomo of the Marquesado del Valle in Mexico City, 1550–1554, which show substantial
payments to Indian towns by order of the audiencia, ibid., leg. 98, exp. 6.

55. DIU, 21:336. Gibson, *Tlaxcala*, 84–88, describes the development of su-
pervisory systems and attempts at prohibition in Tlaxcala.

56. Royal provisión, Madrid, February 11, 1540, in Encinas, 4:354.

57. Royal cédulas, Madrid, July 23, 1571, and May 18, 1572, ibid., 354–
355; and ordinance of Villamanrique, Mexico City, January 15, 1588, in AGN-RCD,
3:exp. 44.

nearly feral animals from making for the Indians' corn and other crops, since these were the best grazing available. The complaints of the Indians and their demands for payment for damages by livestock became one of the most common forms of petition before Spanish justices.[58]

Yet another major category of civil dispute between Indians and Spaniards arose from the demand of the Spanish community for labor: Indian labor. In the first decades of the sixteenth century, many of the suits concerned demands by Indians held as slaves that they be recognized as free. After the virtual abolition of Indian slavery, the mass of business before the courts involved the attempts of the European community to bind its Indian laborers through the use of debt. The Indians were advanced money, to be repaid by service, the practice being that the Indians were always kept in debt and hence remained bound for service. Petitions by Spaniards demanding that Indians be turned over to them for working off debt, and the counterbalancing petitions of Indians that they be freed, on the grounds that they either did not owe money or long ago had worked off the debt, became a standard part of the business before Spanish colonial justices. A long series of royal and viceregal regulations attempted to limit the extent to which Indians might be lent money, although the crown never tried to forbid the practice. All efforts at regulation ran up against the need of the Spanish for labor. Local justices, in cooperation with Spanish owners of farms, households, mines, and workshops of all kinds, delivered Indians to their creditors for labor and returned them if they tried to flee.[59]

A second major group of Indian cases within the royal jurisdiction dealt with criminal offenses. From the first the crown planned to take jurisdiction, for its long-term policy in Spain as in America was to bring to royal judges all decisions of death or mutilation. Judgment or review in such cases was expressly reserved to the audiencia.[60] Royal

---

58. Chevalier, *La formation des grands domaines*, 102–114; Gibson, *The Aztecs*, 279–282; clause 50, ordinances of the Mesta, January 25, 1574, in Montemayor y Córdova de Cuenca, part 3: fols. 17v–40r. The custom of open grazing was much older. See RLI, 4.17.5–7, which indicates a policy dating at least from 1533 and probably from the earliest settlement in America. Complaints of invasion by Spanish livestock and petitions for redress and payment for damages may be found in AGN-I and in the provincial archives.

59. Borah, *New Spain's Century of Depression*, 38–39; Borah and Cook, *Price Trends*, 38–46; Gibson, *The Aztecs*, 242–256; Zavala and Castelo, 4:xii–xvi, 6:ix–x and xxiv–xxvi, 7:x–xii, and 8:vii–x; ordinance of Velasco I forbidding advances of money to Indians, Mexico City, August 1, 1560, in AGN-M, 5:fol. 75r–v; royal cédula to the Audiencia of Mexico, Madrid, June 20, 1567, in Encinas, 2:67–69.

60. Memoria breve de los artículos que parece al consejo, November 18, 1533, in Konetzke, 1:150–153; Tello de Sandoval to the prince, Mexico City, September 9,

judges thus found themselves forced to deal with a large number of Indian offenses against native custom. They had to decide whether to honor the custom or disallow it as contrary to reason or Christian precept. More importantly, infractions of custom and statute by Indians in and around Spanish settlements, which were regarded as the special preserve of Spanish judges, whether local or royal, gave rise to a vast number of criminal charges. Many offenses occurred as infractions of laws and ordinances which were new to the natives, or covered actions that under their custom were not improper. Many others occurred in the general weakening of Indian custom after the Conquest, with the appearance of the usual patterns of behavior of subject races. However virtuous and well-behaved the Indians may have been in their relations with each other and the state power before the Conquest, they astonished their conquerors by their proneness to theft, assault, homicide, rape, riot, drunkenness, and a host of other transgressions, most of which called for infliction of the more gory penalties of Castilian law.[61]

The attempts of the crown and its officials to deal with the problem took a number of forms. One was to declare that verbal insults and blows delivered by hand without any weapon should be matters for reprimand rather than trial and punishment.[62] Another was to commute the severer penalties such as death and mutilation. In 1531, Vasco de Quiroga urged that crimes such as rebellion, homicide, worship of idols, human sacrifice, robbery, and all those which in Spain were dealt with by service in the galleys, mutilation, or death, should be punished by service in the mines. After completing their terms and learning Christian ways, the Indians should be returned to their homes. The crown would thus both demonstrate mercy and supply the labor its Spanish subjects needed.[63] Quiroga's argument was cogent and had in its favor the further fact that the sale of the Indians' labor would enrich the royal treasury, whereas the infliction of other penalties merely cost it money. With royal consent, the audiencia during the 1530s adopted a policy of branding and selling as slaves Indians convicted of crimes that otherwise would have been punished by torture, mutilation, service in the galleys, or death.

1545, in Paso y Troncoso, 4:214; qu. 300 of Mendoza's probanza in his defense in the Tello de Sandoval visita, January 8, 1547, in García Icazbalceta, *Colección*, 2:138–140; and royal cédula to Mendoza, Valladolid, February 22, 1549, in DCLI, 1:95.

61. Cédula of the princess to the Audiencia of Mexico, in reply to a report of the audiencia of April 14, 1553, Valladolid, June 3, 1553, in Puga, fols. 155v–156r. Further see below.

62. Capítulos de gobernadores y regidores, Madrid, July 12, 1530, ibid., fol. 56r.

63. Quiroga to the Council of the Indies, Mexico City, August 14, 1531, in DII, 13:425–526.

This solution became impossible in the 1540s when the New Laws abolished Indian slavery. The audiencia again laid the problem before the crown, pointing out that the full rigor of the laws could not be enforced against the Indians, who were weak people and committed many crimes. Castilian alternatives, such as flogging or imprisonment, had very little effect, since the Indians regarded such punishments as of little consequence. Another possibility, sale of service without branding, was inadequate, because the Indians could escape easily, both evading punishment and leaving their purchasers defrauded of the money paid the royal treasury. Although the audiencia's inquiry was pointedly phrased to suggest a royal answer that slavery in punishment for crime was permissible, the crown answered unequivocally that the laws must be enforced in full rigor, with such modification as the quality of persons suggested and the laws permitted. Again in 1553 the audiencia demurred, objecting that were the crimes of Indians to be so punished, the butchery of men in Mexico City would be greater than the slaughter of animals for food. In 1555 the crown gave way, although it did pay respect to the New Laws by stipulating that no Indian might be condemned to service for life.[64]

Thereafter sale of service became standard throughout the colony as punishment for serious offenses by Indians. The practice rapidly became a profitable source of labor for the Spanish community, so that justices soon began to sell Indians for offenses which should not have been punished so severely, or even delivered them over without formality of trial as a substitute for imprisonment pending hearing. Once turned over to a Spaniard for whatever reason, an Indian rarely regained his freedom. In 1567, Philip II issued a series of stringent safeguards to insure that delivery of Indians for service as punishment or in payment for debt be confined to proper instances.[65] Whatever the attempts at reform,[66] the abuses helped meet the Spanish community's demands for labor far too well for successful inter-

64. Prince Philip to Mendoza, Castellón de Ampurias, October 28, 1548, in Konetzke, 1:248–249; and royal cédula to the Audiencia of Mexico, Valladolid, February 14, 1549, and cédula of the princess to the Audiencia of Mexico, Valladolid, June 3, 1555, both in Puga, fols. 121r and 155v–156r respectively.

65. Royal cédula to the Audiencia of Mexico, Madrid, June 20, 1567, in Encinas, 2:67–69; Borah and Cook, *Price Trends*, 38–46 and 88; and Gibson, *The Aztecs*, 243–245. Records of auctions of convict labor in Mexico City for 1569–70 may be found in the accounts of the royal treasury, Mexico City, in AGN-Tr, leg. 225, exp. 1. The same procedure was followed in the provinces.

66. For example, injunctions that penalties assessed against Indians be corporal and not pecuniary since fines usually had to be worked off by service to Spaniards: Ordinance of Montesclaros, Mexico City, February 19, 1605, in AGN-O, 2:fol. 167r–v. This is a reenactment of an older rule. The policy is most clearly apparent in the injunctions to ecclesiastical courts: Cédula of the empress to the Bishop of Mexico, Madrid,

ference. The crown and its officials were thus left with the problems of providing the Indians with an administration of Castilian criminal law which first would take into account their lack of knowledge of that law and obvious difficulties at fitting into Spanish conceptions, and second would avoid the operation of criminal trial as a device for supplying the Spanish community with labor without regard for justice.

A third major group of Indian cases within royal jurisdiction was those calling for administrative decision and remedy.[67] Very often they involved a series of proceedings that at viceregal level were not easily distinguishable from judicial process, except that the final order issued as an administrative decree rather than as a judicial writ. The number of Indian cases advanced for administrative determination may well have exceeded all other kinds of Indian suits and petitions, for most of the new relationships arising from the Conquest called for executive determination, which the crown and its agents could not forego without surrendering control of the new territories.

Because of the bewildering variety, only the more important kinds can be indicated. I have mentioned already that grants of land by the crown automatically meant validating proceedings to insure that the interests of third parties were not adversely affected. Institution of the encomienda and royal tribute meant a long series of administrative hearings and petitions for virtually each town; for, whether held in encomienda or by the crown, its tribute was assessed at fairly frequent intervals, very often with a good deal of dispute and appeal. Furthermore, all exactions by encomenderos or corregidores in excess of the schedule set and all other kinds of abuse, if the Indians dared object, meant petitions for redress to the executive. Similarly, the reduction of Indian government and the caciques to a fairly uniform pattern characterized by annual elections and written schedules of payments meant executive inspection to arrive at the proper assessment, continuing supervision to prevent abuse and extortion, demands for reassessment either by the peasants or by the officials and caciques, and annual confirmation of elections. One of the abuses most frequently brought to the attention of provincial administrators and the viceroy

---

June 26, 1536, requesting that he not fine Indians for adultery and sexual intercourse outside of marriage, in Puga, fols. 110v–111v, and royal cédula to the bishops of New Spain, Madrid, February 7, 1560, both in Encinas, 4:336–337.

67. The Spanish organization of government during the colonial period differed considerably from our conceptions. Royal government was divided into four branches: administrative, judicial, treasury, and military. Since the viceroy was supervisor of the royal treasury, appeals and petitions over tribute went to him and were handled by administrative process. The treasury officials and the fiscal of the audiencia had to be informed of the matter and had the right to be present at the hearing on behalf of the crown.

arose from the Indian practice of levying ad hoc assessments (*derramas*) for special expenses such as the costs of lawsuits or community enterprises and celebrations. The practice permitted easy misuse and the enrichment of a favored group of Indian nobles, since more could be levied than was needed for legitimate expenses. Often the entire levy was for improper purpose.

In general, all complaints of maladministration meant petitions for redress and, if investigation upheld the complaints, administrative orders for remedy. The imposition of Spanish forms of government gave rise to many. Spanish governors of towns and provinces had liberal opportunities for exploiting their charges, which almost all used extensively. To the extent that the natives objected to extra payments of tribute, forced purchases of goods, forced deliveries of other goods, unpaid or underpaid contributions of service and food, and direct brutality, they petitioned the superior of their governor for redress.[68]

The forms of Spanish government gave peculiar prominence to certain forms of inspection and intervention that were designed to secure orderly, just administration. The two most important were the *visita* and the *residencia*. The visita was the practice of sending an official at irregular intervals through a part of the colony to examine the functioning of local government, the extent to which the burdens upon the peasantry in the form of tributes and community assessments were within their ability to bear, and the extent to which they were being subjected to mistreatment and extortion. The *residencia* was an accounting that each Spanish official had to undergo at the end of his term of service. For a stated period, an official appointed for that purpose gathered all complaints of misconduct, investigated the basis for the complaints, and finally submitted his findings to superior authority for determination by a court. If there was justified basis for complaint, it was enumerated in a series of charges with suggested penalties assessed for each. In theory, at least, the two institutions should have been effective in preventing and correcting abuses; but in practice, collusion among the authorities, and the fear of the Indians that any person making complaint would be subject to reprisal, deprived both institutions of much of their effectiveness.[69] As a result, most complaints by Indians were taken *por la vía administrativa*

68. The first volumes of AGN-M and AGN-O have many orders based on complaints of these kinds and contain further moderating assessments of payments to caciques and allowances for town assessments.

69. Mendoza to the king, Mexico City, December 10, 1537, in DII, 2:183–185; Lebrón de Quiñones to the king, Taximaroa, September 10, 1554, in Paso y Troncoso, 7:223–250; royal cédulas to the Audiencia of Mexico, El Escorial, June 28, 1568, and Madrid, December 29, 1593, in AGN-RCD, 47:fols. 62v–63r and 103:fol. 42r–v respectively.

rather than to the courts, and so went to governors and viceroys. Since the Indians quickly learned that the higher they went in the administrative hierarchy the surer they were of a sympathetic hearing and an effective order for redress—if such were possible at all—most of the petitions wound up in the viceregal palace.

Two forms of administrative intervention became especially important in Indian affairs and proved of considerable effect. One, the colonial version of the present-day writ of amparo, was an order to the appropriate officials that the petitioner be protected in the possession of land or the exercise of some function which he feared might be unjustly disputed or forbidden. The writ was especially effective in quieting title to lands held by Indians. The second form of intervention was a writ to an official to carry out his duty. For example, an Indian who could not get his complaint or suit heard by the local official would petition the viceroy for an order compelling a hearing. In the marginal summaries of the seventeenth-century secretaries, the description of this writ became a play upon words, "To the justice of _____, that he do it." Petitions for both forms of writs brought much business to the viceroy and his staff.[70]

Finally, a great many Indian petitions concerned release from Spanish restrictive legislation. To insure control of the native population, the viceroys and audiencia imposed a number of prohibitions. For example, Indians might not own firearms, swords, or daggers; they might not ride horses, nor might they wear European dress.[71] Within a few years, caciques, governors of towns, and many principales were permitted exemption from these restrictions if they petitioned for special license. Within a few decades, as European customs, agriculture, and industry spread among the Indians, there was sound reason for granting many more licenses to Indian nobles, merchants, and commoners, since explicit or unwritten restrictions which impeded their living and working in the new ways threatened to curtail a production of goods and services which the Spanish community itself needed. The raising of livestock by natives, for example, usually was authorized by special license, as was engaging in European crafts. In these instances, the licenses avoided possible difficulties with local offi-

70. Lira González, *El amparo*, passim, on the colonial amparo. The volumes of AGN-M, -I, and -GP have many orders of amparo and orders for justices to hold a hearing. For summaries of some, see below.

71. Royal provisión on arms, Granada, September 17, 1501; instructions to the Audiencia of Mexico, 1528 and 1530, on arms and horses; royal cédulas to the Audiencia of Mexico on arms, Palencia, September 28, 1534, and on horses, Madrid, June 19, 1568, all in Encinas, 4:345–348. The prohibition on wearing Spanish dress is apparent from the viceregal licenses to caciques in AGN-M, vols. 1–8. See also DIU, 21: 346–347.

cials rather than exempted from specific prohibitions. Petitions for special licenses thus became another substantial category of Indian business before the viceroy.

The total amount of business represented by Indian cases under civil and criminal law and petitions for administrative relief or remedy was clearly enormous and left untouched few of the more important aspects of Indian life. As already indicated, it was one of the principal instruments of the upheaval that took place within native society after the Conquest. Further, the mass of Indian litigation and petitions served to nullify the recognition of native custom by the crown in the regulations for provincial governors of 1530 and in the New Laws. Despite continuing royal injunctions validating Indian usage, Castilian procedure and law became the basis for handling Indian suits and complaints in royal courts and administration. Inevitably the European ways moved downward into native society, displacing the older aboriginal ones. Equally, judicial and administrative machinery became even more clogged through the intricate and innumerable delays possible.

Crown validation of native custom, abortive as it proved, embodied a sincere desire to lessen the burden of the Conquest upon the Indians and to ease their transition to Christianity and European polity. The same desire gave rise to a long series of proposals for handling Indian litigation and petitions, which, although coupled in the beginning with injunctions to preserve native custom, in the end worked more effectively for adjustment within the new. Basically the proposals were of three kinds: simplification of procedures, reduction or avoidance of costs, and provision of special legal assistance. These three headings are hardly mutually exclusive, but they do point to the main directions.

Spanish legal proceedings were complicated and represented a reduction to nonviolent dispute of the pageantry of a tourney. In the presentation of testimony in law-suits, for example, each side was entitled to as many as 30 witnesses, and in addition there might be witnesses summoned by the judge. If the questions in the proof were held to be diverse, the allowance of witnesses rose to 30 per question for each side. Presentation of complaint and answer, the gathering of testimony and counter-testimony, arguments and counter-arguments by counsel, and finally decision, took months and years. After the hearing in first instance, the case could be appealed if the money value of the property or act in dispute was sufficiently high. If higher still, the case might be appealed a second time.[72] Appellate hearings invariably took

---

72. Spain: Laws, Statutes, etc., *Novísima recopilación*, 11.11.2, 4, and 5. All of libro 11 is devoted to regulating procedures, time limits, delays, and costs. See also Tomás y Valiente, *El derecho*, 153–200.

years, especially if the case was carried to the Council of the Indies and the proceedings were slowed yet further by the need to communicate by annual sailings of fleets.

The proposals of royal officials for simplifying procedures were not entirely altruistic, for they found that the mass of Indian cases so clogged royal courts and administrative offices that reform of some kind became necessary if the government was to function. The difficulty may be illustrated by the matter of appeals in criminal cases at the time of the Second Audiencia. Under Castilian law as extended to America, appeals from sentences by the audiencia of death, torture, or mutilation might be made to the Council of the Indies in Spain. Once intention of appeal was given, execution of the sentenced was suspended until the appeal could be made and an order rejecting it be received from the council. The Indians very quickly discovered this feature of Castilian law, so that those sentenced to torture, mutilation, or death by the audiencia, which had exclusive jurisdiction in such offenses by Indians, promptly announced intention to appeal. They were then content to let the case rest and to remain in prison, sound in body and prepared to take advantage of any opportunity for escape. Legally there could be no denial of the right to appeal because of failure to carry it forward, since virtually all Indians affected were paupers. Nor was the crown in those years prepared to pay the costs of transmission to Spain and counsel for a hearing before the Council of the Indies.

The audiencia, which held the prevailing view that public executions reinforced respect for law, was scandalized at the number of people in jail under suspended sentence. Its concern was strengthened by the fact that in civil suits the same device of appeal was used to delay execution of judgment for years. In 1533 it asked the Crown for a decision.[73] The following year, a royal order abrogated the right of appeal to the Council of the Indies by Indians in criminal cases. Instead, the audiencia was to hear appeals from sentences of torture, mutilation, or death.[74] Such reviews were usually carried before the entire body of the court—or in later years, when the number of judges increased, before a panel of three. The pressure of Indian business upon Spanish tribunals is further illustrated by the fact that in 1551 the Audiencia of Mexico was ordered to devote approximately half its time to Indian civil suits—two days a week and as much of Saturdays as was not needed for the suits of the poor.[75] Any measure that shortened the time of hearing, or by simplifying procedure made it possible for

73. Audiencia of Mexico to the empress, Mexico City, February 9, 1533, in Paso y Troncoso, 3:27–28.
74. Royal cédula to the Audiencia of Mexico, Madrid, October 27, 1534, in Puga, fols. 93v–94r.
75. Royal cédula of March 7, 1551, in DIHA, 8:13.

the royal tribunals to handle more business, both avoided the need for additional judges and saved the crown money.[76]

Perhaps the basic elements in most measures for simplifying legal procedures were increasing the discretionary power of the judge and dispensing with requirements for written documents. For minor criminal offenses, which were legion among the Indians, the Audiencia of Mexico early adopted the policy of having one judge, instead of the two required by Castilian law, make the weekly visit of each of the two Indian jails in the vicinity of the capital, those at Santiago Tlatelolco and San Juan Moyotlan. The one judge heard such testimony as there was and entered judgment. Very often the only written document in the trial was the record of judgment. Such summary procedure had the additional advantage of avoiding assessment of the Indians for costs. The procedure won formal royal approval in 1570[77] and presumably furnished a model for provincial courts.[78]

For civil suits, the earliest order for simplification of procedure may have antedated the Spanish entrance into Mesoamerica. As already mentioned, the somewhat ambiguous phrasing of the royal order of October 19, 1514, may have been intended to apply to suits among Indians as well as suits among Spaniards over grants of Indians. There can be no doubt that in preparing the regulations for provincial governors of 1530 the royal secretaries so read it or merely read a brief, erroneous marginal notation. Whatever the reason, the regulations of 1530 ordered that civil suits among Indians be decided orally without recourse to documents or judicial procedure, suits between towns being excepted.

The earliest substantial evidence of the use of abbreviated procedure for civil suits, although more often between Indian and Spaniard than between Indian and Indian, occurred in the 1530s in hearings on petitions for freedom of Indians held as slaves. Vasco de Quiroga sat as delegate of the audiencia for all such cases. Rather than attempt to impose the formalities of Spanish procedure where they were man-

76. Enríquez complained that the audiencia could not handle all business before it nor perform all duties assigned it. He suggested more judges and division into two chambers: Enríquez to the king, Mexico City, March 20, 1580, in AGI-M, leg. 20 (BLT).

77. Paragraph of a letter from the king to the Audiencia of Mexico, July 4, 1570, in Encinas, 2:67.

78. An injunction for summary process in Indian hearings, undoubtedly based on the instructions for provincial governors of 1530, was customary in the standard viceregal instruction: Instructions to the alcaldes mayores of Acapulco, Teposcolula, Colima, Zacatula, and Tierras Calientes of Michoacán, Mexico City, n.d. but probably November 8, 1544, in AGN-M, 4:fols. 83r–84v. An even more detailed injunction was incorporated in the standard instruction for alcaldes mayores and corregidores, adopted in 1571: Cuevas, Documentos, 246–250, esp. clause 4, pp. 246–247. (The date 1561 heading the document is an error, as may be seen by the date at the end and that of July 12, 1569, in clause 4.)

ifestly unsuitable, he summoned four of the highest of the old native judges to explain native custom in each case, heard the case as informally as possible, and accepted, rejected, or modified the suggestions of the native judges according to his own ideas. In effect, he used native judges as assessors.[79] His practice was not followed by the other judges of the audiencia, although it must have been applied to some extent by royal provincial and town governors in their capacity as justices. Unfortunately, such local justices relied for this kind of advice too much upon their interpreters, who were apt to use their position for furthering their own fortunes.[80]

The injunction to use summary procedures in Indian civil suits was repeated in the New Laws[81] and in a series of subsequent orders and enactments.[82] The audiencia dutifully passed on the royal injunctions to subordinate royal justices, and incorporated them in its standard instruction for town and provincial governors, prepared in 1571. The intention was to do away entirely with judicial process, with its complicated and expensive procedures, substituting for it an informal hearing with as little use of witnesses and documents as possible. By the middle of the sixteenth century, a further incentive for such reform was the knowledge that the Indians were committing perjury on a grand scale and that subornation of witnesses was so invariable that it could not be punished.[83]

All proposals proved difficult, if not impossible, to implement. The bulk of Indian civil suits concerned towns and nobles, who were entitled to and insisted upon full judicial process. Further, ascertaining the facts of any dispute was very difficult and, if the Indians came from any distance, virtually impossible without formal and costly investigation by special agents.[84] Under continued pressure from the crown, the audiencia did attempt in 1570–72 to reduce the complexities of ju-

79. Quiroga to the Council of the Indies, July 24, 1535, in DII, 10:349–350.
80. Gibson, *The Aztecs*, 147–149; royal cédula to the Audiencia of Mexico, Valladolid, September 12, 1537, in Encinas, 4:359. See also the royal cédula to the Audiencia of Mexico, Toledo, August 24, 1529, complaining of the exactions of interpreters, in DCLI, 2:455, and DIU, 9:430–431.
81. Clause 24, in DII, 14:385–386. The new enactment extended the scope of Indian custom to suits between Spaniards and Indians.
82. In 1550, 1559, 1561, 1563, 1569, and 1571: Royal cédula to the audiencias of the Indies, Valladolid, March 11, 1550, and ordenanza of the audiencias, 1563, in Encinas, 2:166–167; DIU, 23:87–88; royal cédulas to the Audiencia of Mexico, n.d. but 1569, and Madrid, July 6, 1571, in AGN-RCD, 47:fols. 54v–55r and 205r.
83. Petition of the bishops of New Spain to the Audiencia of Mexico, 1565, in DII, 13:288–289; Fray Pedro Xuárez de Escobar, O.S.A., to the king, n.d., n.p., ibid., 11:199; Mendieta to Bustamante, Toluca, January 1, 1562, in García Icazbalceta, *Nueva colección*, 1:17–23; *relación de mando* of Mendoza, ca. 1550–51, quoted below.
84. The sending of special agents to take testimony (*receptores*) gave rise to

dicial process for Indians. The number of witnesses permitted each party and those *de oficio* were reduced to five. Only one submission of *probanzas*—testimony in proof—was to be permitted in any suit, and none on appeal, which was limited to a single review. Moreover, the audiencia forbade use of such pleas as nullity and restitution that created subsuits within suits.[85] These provisions represented a very substantial curtailment of procedure. It is unlikely, however, that they were successful in speeding up hearings over the opposition of notaries, lawyers, judges, and other professional men who had a direct interest in prolonged litigation. The Indians themselves resisted reform, since, upon any decision that one side or the other was unwilling to accept, they raised the issues again in new suits.[86]

Costs[87] were central in the problem of Indian suits and administrative petitions. Paying them placed a heavy burden upon the population of the Indian towns. In general, the nobles were able to shift the load to the commoners. Many were able to enrich themselves through skillful incitement to suit and manipulation of the assessments for costs. According to missionaries and royal officials, another major factor in incitement and delay was the greed for fees of Spanish and mestizo agents at law and in fact, a greed shared by many of the judicial and administrative officials.[88] Yet the crown could not deal easily with the problem, for the Spanish social and political structure was far more dependent than ours on fees. The notaries, solicitors, procuradores, abogados, secretaries, and other professional men associated with judicial and administrative process, who made all or a major part

complaints that it was done to provide employment for favorites. A royal cédula to the Audiencia of Guatemala, Madrid, November 30, 1561, forbade that such agents be sent in small cases: Encinas, 2:367.

85. Autos of the Audiencia of Mexico, June 20, 1570, and May 19, 1572, in AGN-RCD, 47:fols. 457v and 382v–383r respectively. The audiencia pledged itself to hear suits between towns over lands and between Indian principales over succession to lands and cacicazgo in *acuerdo*—that is, meeting as an executive body.

86. Relación de mando of Mendoza, quoted below.

87. For a careful historical discussion of the theory and kinds of costs in Castilian and Spanish judicial proceedings and litigation, see Lalinde Abadía. The narrower topic of reimbursement for costs to the winning party, as the ideas had developed in various strands of European legal systems, may be found in Chiovenda, passim. In general, the elements covered are the fees and expenses of (1) judicial organs, (2) bureaucratic elements registering and documenting declarations, (3) executors of justice, and (4) representatives of the parties. There were additionally the costs of the parties to the suit for appearing in the appropriate places, and gifts and bribes to appropriate officials and people of influence.

88. Xuárez de Escobar to the king, n.d., n.p., in DII, 11:199; Mendieta to Bustamante, Toluca, January 1, 1562, and to Velasco II, Tlaxcala, February 20, 1591, in García Icazbalceta, *Nueva colección*, 1:1–18, and 5:109–111; Lic. Altamirano to the king, Mexico City, March 12, 1553, in DIHA, 1:214; relación de mando of Enríquez for his successor, the Conde de Coruña, September 25, 1580, in HM, 1:204–205.

of their living from fees and costs, formed a large and important proportion of the Spanish community in New Spain, and their influence was correspondingly great. Government itself was organized to a great extent on the theory that services should be paid for at the time they were given. Accordingly, there were very few officials with adequate salaries in our terms, and many with none at all. Instead, they charged fees for each exercise of duty and for each document prepared. The keepers of the jails received their compensation from charges they were entitled to levy upon the prisoners, and no prisoner might go free, even upon acquittal, until he paid. In the second half of the sixteenth century, when purchase became the common method for appointment to many offices, the price set usually involved an estimate of the probable receipts from fees.[89] Any royal attempts to curtail fees and other perquisites were certain to meet virtually united opposition, except from the friars, who were not associated directly with the Church counterpart of the royal system.

The crown and the viceregal government, aside from discouraging suits and simplifying procedures, tried to reduce the burden of fees and other costs in two ways. First, they tried to restrict levy upon the commoners of the Indian towns by requiring viceregal permission, a series of measures which seems to have met with indifferent success.[90] Second, they moved to impose moderation in the thorny matter of payments to Spanish professional men and officials. The fees charged Spaniards, they regarded as too high for the Indians; on the other hand, the functioning of their own administrations required that the Indians pay something. Accordingly, they tried a middle path of lower schedules for Indians than for Spaniards and release of the poorest from any fees at all. In 1530 the schedule of fees for officials and professional men attached to the Audiencia of Mexico was set at three times the rates charged in Valladolid and Granada, triple fees being regarded as a fair adjustment for the much higher price level of the colony.[91] In 1532 the triple schedule was extended to Indians by a royal order that the lieutenant of the judicial notary of the audiencia might collect fees from Indians unless they had made formal declaration that they were paupers, and thus under Castilian law entitled to exemption.[92]

Over the opposition of the Second Audiencia,[93] this order opened

89. See the discussion in Parry, *The Sale of Public Office*, 1–5.

90. The complaints, rebukes, and schedules may be found in AGN-M and AGN-I, initial volumes.

91. Royal provisión, Madrid, July 12, 1530, in Encinas, 2:315–318.

92. DIU, 23:224–225.

93. Audiencia of Mexico to the empress, Mexico City, February 9, 1533, in Paso y Troncoso, 3:32.

the gates wide for fee-collecting officials, who for the next twenty years made full use of the permission. In 1551 the crown finally was stirred into action. It ordered the audiencia to report on the advisability of setting a lower schedule for Indians than for Spaniards. Pending decision, Indians were to be charged the rates of Spain without multiplication. Furthermore, any Indian with assets of less than 6,000 maravedís was to be considered a pauper. No fees not customary until then might be levied.[94]

Upon the arrival of this order, the secretary of *gobernación* at once appealed for exemption on the ground that it applied only to the other notaries. Aside from asking for clarification of the royal intent, the audiencia does not seem to have enforced the order. The mere fact that there was an order may have had some effect in moderating exactions by officials.[95] When in 1559 the crown ordered strict enforcement of its order of 1551,[96] the new injunction was interpreted by the audiencia to mean that Indians were to be charged fees at triple Spanish rates, unless they had taken oath as paupers. The major question which concerned the audiencia was whether the maximum value of assets an Indian seeking to qualify as a pauper might have was to be set at 6,000 maravedís or triple. At length, it decided to set the maximum at 30 silver pesos, alleging that this was the nearest round sum to the 6,000. (Actually 30 silver pesos came to 8,160 maravedís, and 6,000 maravedís in silver coin to 22/0/6. One may wonder why 25 should be held not so round a sum as 30.) This decision was proclaimed throughout the audiencia district and a report sent to Spain.[97]

This problem of fees also extended to securing administrative papers, and ran into the same kinds of obstacles. To increase profits, for example, viceregal secretaries issued each confirmation of an annual appointment of an Indian town official as a separate document payable with a separate fee. The order of the Second Audiencia that no fees be charged at all was equally disregarded by the administrative

94. Royal cédula to the Audiencia of Mexico, Madrid, December 9, 1551, in DCLI, 2:182–183, and Puga, fols. 128v–129r. The sum in the later silver pesos was 22/0/6.

95. Zorita to the king, Mexico City, January 10, 1558, in Zorita, *Historia*, 404–405; Valderrama to the king, n.d., n.p., but Mexico City, February–March 1564, in Scholes and Adams, 7:54–55; Testimonio de unos autos hechos en la Audiencia de México en virtud de una real executoria presentada por el escribano mayor de aquella gobernación Antonio de Turcios sobre llevar derechos a los indios, Mexico City, February 21, 1564, covering orders and proceedings, December 9, 1551–February 21, 1564, and Turcios' petition of March 4, 1564, in AGI-P, leg. 231, núm. 4, ramo 12.

96. Royal cédula to the Audiencia of Mexico, Valladolid, June 6, 1559, in Encinas, 4:275–276, and Puga, fols. 209v–210r.

97. Velasco I and the Audiencia of Mexico to the king, Mexico City, February 26, 1564, in Spain: Ministerio de Fomento, *Cartas de Indias*, 277–278.

corps.[98] Crown reform took the form in 1550 of an order that all appointments of annual officials be issued in a single document to be covered by a single fee, that fee to be paid by the town. The order, repeated in 1561,[99] became part of the general ordinances for audiencias in 1563,[100] and in 1583[101] was specifically extended to the neighboring Audiencia of Nueva Galicia. One suspects that this reform was equally ineffectual, since it ran counter to the interests of the powerful fraternity of notaries and secretaries.

All attempts at limiting fees charged Indians disclosed that the major difficulty lay in enforcing any schedule at all. Most officials levied in terms of what the traffic would bear.[102] Towns and nobles were especially fair game, since they were better able to pay high fees. Provisions for exempting Indians who filed pauper's declarations were an interesting device for dealing with some Indian needs within European tradition, but they ran into the difficulty that few professional men were willing to work without pay. A poor Indian's affair was dispatched late, if at all, especially if it involved private petition or suit. Only in official business, where delay was more noticeable, were royal orders for exemption from fees given attention.[103] In the later sixteenth century, as we shall see, the burden of fees worsened considerably when disputes between the judicial and administrative hierarchies forced the Indians to take out double sets of documents for assurance, and so pay double fees. Men of the pen and the robe formed a rapacious and formidable vested interest.

Failures in relief from fees, added to increasing imposition of Castilian law and steady opposition to simplification of Castilian procedures, all pointed to the need for another kind of remedy if the natives were to live within Castilian law and yet be protected from exploitation by the European community beyond the generous measure that the crown and clergy regarded as proper. The remedy lay in special legal assistance, and perhaps a special jurisdiction for their legal business. During the sixteenth century, the crown and colonial governments tried a series of experiments toward this end. Some were of

98. Fray Pedro de Gante to the emperor, Mexico City, February 15, 1532, ibid., 97–98; Extracto de los capítulos que Fray Francisco de Mena . . . presentó al rey, n.d., in DII, 11:189.

99. Royal cédula to the Audiencia of Mexico, Valladolid, July 18, 1550, in Encinas, 4:274–275, which quotes it in the sobrecédula issued at Madrid, June 28, 1561.

100. Ibid. and 2:341.

101. Royal cédula to the Audiencia of Guadalajara, Madrid, April 19, 1583, ibid., 4:274–275.

102. See the account of Fray Francisco de Mena cited above in note 98.

103. In 1553–54, for example, a judgment on the assessment of tribute to be paid by Huejotzingo was issued with a certification that no costs or fees had been collected: AGI-IG, leg. 1092 (BLT).

lesser, some of greater promise; many led to clashes with threatened jurisdictions; nearly all raised questions of cost to a royal treasury, perennially in deficit.

A neglected possibility of legal assistance for Indians in their encounters with Spanish administration and Castilian law lay in the *abogado de pobres*, a salaried attorney for the poor, serving without fee. It was an office that became customary at higher levels of jurisdiction and in larger Spanish cities by the sixteenth century.[104] When the Audiencia of Santo Domingo was established in 1511,[105] its ordinances provided for one, as did the ordinances of other colonial audiencias.[106] Spanish cities of any size in New Spain made similar provision.[107] These abogados might have taken on the function of representing Indians—although their number in New Spain hardly would have been equal to the need—but they confined their assistance to non-Indians.

Recognition by the crown and its officials that there was need for providing legal assistance for Indians came relatively slowly, perhaps in part because they were slow to perceive the extent to which the Indians were being moved into the sphere of Castilian law and administration. The first move, in 1537, took the form of a royal order that any Indian ignorant of the Spanish language who was summoned before a Spanish justice might bring a Christian friend to make sure that translation and reporting were accurate. The order was issued in response to complaints of extortion and abuse by interpreters.[108] Any benefit must have been slender, except in the rare instances in which the Christian friend was both versed in law and prepared to serve without pay.

A more effective measure came in 1550, when at crown order the Audiencia of Mexico appointed a *procurador general de indios* as at-

104. Spain: Laws, Statutes, etc., *Novísima recopilación*, 5.1.29, 5.5.10, and 5.22.14; Castillo de Bovadilla, 3.14.18 and 3.15.63–64 (2:291–292 and 333–335); Spain: Laws, Statutes, etc.: Valladolid, *Recopilación*, fols. 73v and 77v; and Lalinde Abadía, 405–407.

105. Ordenanzas para los Jueces de Apelación de Indias, Burgos, October 5, 1511, ms. in Real Academia de la Historia, Madrid, Colección Muñoz, 39:fols. 259–262.

106. Encinas, 2:284; see also Montemayor y Córdova de Cuenca, part 2: fol. 45f.

107. See, for example, the practice of Puebla, in its Archivo de la Secretaría Municipal, Libros de cabildo, 17:fol. 41f–v (resolution of the town council, October 30, 1646, on appointment of an *abogado de pobres*).

108. Royal cédula to the Audiencia of Mexico, Valladolid, September 12, 1537, in Encinas, 4:359. See also the royal cédula to the Audiencia of Mexico, Toledo, August 24, 1529, complaining of the exactions of interpreters: DCLI, 2:455, and DIU, 10: 430–431.

torney before it for all Indian claims to freedom from slavery. His appointment was to be proclaimed over the realm, so that the natives would know of his office and make use of it. By this measure, the Indians for the first time were provided with special counsel, salaried and serving their interests without fee. Unfortunately, the appointment was a temporary one limited to the specific purpose of freeing Indian slaves.[109] It lapsed as soon as that purpose was accomplished.

In the general reforming impulse of the years after the New Laws, the crown asked the audiencia, in 1551, to report on the advisability of appointing a general salaried defender who would bring and defend Indian suits before the audiencia. Until a royal decision, the audiencia was to take such measures as it deemed desirable.[110] In 1554, after three years of discussion, the function was approved but entrusted to the audiencia's *fiscal*, or crown attorney. He was to act only for Indians qualifying as paupers in cases before the audiencia. If the suit involved the royal treasury, so that the fiscal in discharge of another of his functions had to represent the crown, the audiencia was to appoint a special attorney for the Indian.[111] This order of 1554 embodied a general policy for the Indies adopted for Peru in 1550[112] and incorporated in the general ordinances for audiencias in 1563, which made the fiscal of each audiencia protector of the Indians in his district, but with no more power than the early ecclesiastical protectors had had.[113] Unfortunately, all such proposals had serious defects in that the fiscal was already a busy official and there was no provision that counsel be provided Indians before other tribunals nor in administrative proceedings, which were perhaps more important than civil suits. One defect was remedied in 1575 by a general royal order for all of America that the fiscales of all audiencias act as attorneys for Indians in criminal as well as civil cases.[114] But this provision threw an additional burden upon officials whose careers depended upon their discharge of other functions.

Much of the effect of this inadequate provision of free legal counsel, moreover, was counteracted by a royal order of 1573 which conferred upon the ordinary judges of Spanish towns jurisdiction in

109. Paragraph of a royal letter to the Audiencia of Mexico, 1550, and royal instructions to the *procurador general de los indios*, Valladolid, July 7, 1550, in Encinas, 4:375–377.

110. Royal cédula to the Audiencia of Mexico, Valladolid, July 7, 1551, in Puga, fol. 125r–v.

111. Royal cédula to the Audiencia of Mexico, Valladolid, February 13, 1554, in ibid., fols. 150v–151r, and DCLI, 1:146.

112. DIU, 23:22.

113. Encinas, 2:269.

114. Royal cédula, Madrid, February 8, 1575, in ibid.

first instance in the smaller civil suits of Indians against Spaniards.[115] Indians who attempted to secure redress by civil suit from most Spaniards, nearly all of whom were residents of Spanish towns, were forced to appear before judges elected annually from among the Spanish residents. Such judges were sure to know their neighbors and have a solidarity of interest with them. Accordingly, the need for special legal assistance became greater, despite the fact that on appeal the Indians might be able to secure the services of the fiscal.

The greatest possibility of an adequate solution lay in the creation of a special jurisdiction for Indian legal business, whether civil, criminal, or administrative, with greatly simplified procedures and its own salaried staff forbidden to charge fees. Development of as much of this solution as was eventually adopted took almost exactly six decades from the coming of the Second Audiencia and seven from the fall of Tenochtitlán.

In the first year a possibility of this kind of development lay in the office of *protector de indios*. It was brought into being because of the disasters in the Antilles. Adequate discharge of this function demanded prompt, inexpensive settling of Indian disputes and dealing with complaints against Spaniards.[116] In Nicaragua, the first bishop, interpreting his appointment as protector to confer a grant of jurisdiction over such cases, heard disputes between Indians and those of Indians with Spaniards, and assessed criminal penalties. He even assumed jurisdiction in disputes of Spaniards over encomiendas, and so invaded one of the most jealously guarded royal preserves.[117] In New Spain, Zumárraga, similarly appointed protector, urged upon the crown an even more sweeping extension of power. In 1529 he proposed that the protector appoint a subordinate staff of trustworthy, conscientious people to be judges of the Indians in all civil and criminal cases, suggesting further that the only men suitable for such duties were friars, and that the crown even relinquish administration of visitas to them. Under his proposal, Indian society would have passed under the control of the bishops and missionaries in something very close to a separate centralized administration.[118] As the governor of Nicaragua commented on his episcopal protector, "If the office of protector is to be carried out in this manner, Your Majesty has no need of a governor."[119]

115. Royal cédula of November 20, 1573, summarized in Fonseca and Urrutia, 1:536–537.

116. Bayle, "El protector de indios," 59–64.

117. Ibid., 60–63; Molina Argüello, 141–142.

118. Bayle, "El protector," 72–73; García Icazbalceta, *Don Fray Juan de Zumárraga*, 1:50–65; Zumárraga to the king, Mexico City, August 27, 1529, in DII, 13:169–170.

119. Bayle, "El protector," 61–62.

The crown was as unwilling to surrender so substantial a part of its dominion to the clergy as it was to permit the creation of a new feudalism by the encomenderos. In 1530, in effect by return mail, Zumárraga's powers as protector were rigidly restricted to assessing small penalties against private Spanish persons guilty of abusing Indians and to reporting more serious offenses and all abuses by officials to the audiencia. He was specifically forbidden to judge criminal cases among Indians, such jurisdiction being reserved to the audiencia and ordinary justices. By implication, he was also forbidden to interfere in civil disputes among Indians, or even between Spanish and Indians if there was no clear abuse.[120] The regulations for provincial governors, issued in the same year, further underscored the royal intent that the ordinary judicial and administrative hierarchy govern without competition from new jurisdictions.[121]

The most noteworthy attempt to set up a special jurisdiction for Indian matters, but one within the normal organization of office and firmly under royal control, took place during the administrations of the first two viceroys (1535–1564). Its creation was the work of Antonio de Mendoza (1535–1550). He was in an especially advantageous position, since as viceroy he was head of the royal administration and as president of the audiencia, one of his functions, he settled the order of business for that body. Thus, even though he could not vote in judicial hearings,[122] he decided whether a matter was judicial or administrative; that is, whether it went before himself as head of the executive or before the audiencia or some inferior court. As trustee for the reserve powers of the crown, moreover, he could deal with any matter that did not fit within existing laws or institutions. Mendoza evolved a remarkably efficient arrangement for handling Indian civil disputes and administrative petitions. Criminal cases of Indians, he left to the ordinary tribunals unless there was a clear abuse of justice or failure to act. The core of the arrangement was the merging of the hearing of all Indian disputes, complaints, and petitions in a single jurisdiction exercised by the viceroy personally, so that private interests and procedural complexities could not hinder a speedy decision. Indians were encouraged to bring all complaints and disputes to the viceroy, who ordered a summary investigation, decided where remedy lay, and saw that a decision was reached quickly. If the matter was one for judicial determination, Mendoza sent it to an oidor, if it had to go to the audiencia, with instructions to hold an informal hearing in cham-

120. Cédula of the empress to Zumárraga, Madrid, August 2, 1530, in Puga, fols. 64f–65f.

121. Ibid., fols. 53f–56v.

122. Instruction, Barcelona, April 17, 1535, in HM, 1:22. Mendoza was barred from such participation as a soldier without legal training; see Schäfer, 2:10–14.

bers and report to a meeting of the audiencia in executive council, at which the viceroy was present. In other instances, Mendoza sent cases for decision to inferior judges. So, except for suits of towns and nobles, which by law could not be exempted from full procedure, the handling of all Indian business became a matter of administrative determination, since the viceroy not only decided in what jurisdiction cases fell and directed the manner in which decision was to be reached, but also required that the decision be reported to him.

An important part of Mendoza's system was the use of special investigators and judges on an ad hoc viceregal commission. For these purposes he resorted to Spanish governors of provinces and towns and to a group of trustworthy Spaniards and Indians sent out to the provinces under his personal instructions. His most interesting innovation was the formation of a panel of trustworthy Indians whom he employed as agents and even gave powers as judges on commission. The only distinction between the races was that the Spaniards on investigative or judicial commission were paid one peso a day by the parties to the case, whereas the Indians received only one-fourth as much. All these investigators and judges on commission reported back to the viceroy—who, if he accepted their reports, issued their findings and decisions in a formal order. Only in relatively rare instances, usually involving infliction of a penalty other than restitution or removal from office, did the viceroy refer reports of his agents' finding guilt in Spaniards or Indians to a justice for hearing and sentence.

Mendoza's system was so important in the later solution of the problem of Indian judicial and administrative affairs and the larger question of easing the entrance of Indians into Spanish ways that it requires examination at some length. We are fortunate to have in his *relación de mando*, his report to his successor, his own description:

> The Indians of this land are of such nature that many times they come to complain of very slight wrongs done them, which they exaggerate into genuine abuses; yet others suffer grave wrongs and keep quiet. Your Lordship must be warned that it is needful to understand and investigate the words of the Indians no matter how trivial they seem, for from the small one learns about the great. Your Lordship must be on guard not to believe the opposite, however much he is urged to do so, for he will discover that the case is as I say.
>
> I have maintained the custom always of listening to the Indians; and although very often they lie to me, I do not get angry, for I do not believe them nor issue any order until I have found out the truth. To some people it has seemed that I encourage the Indians to lie more, since I do not punish them. I judge that it would be more harmful to cast such

fear that they would cease coming to me with their troubles than that I should suffer loss of time through their children's tricks. Your Lordship should listen to them. The arrangement that I have had for this is that Monday and Thursday mornings the interpreters of the audiencia bring me all the Indians who have come with business. I listen to all of them. For those cases which I can settle at once, I issue orders. Those that are matter for judicial determination or of considerable weight, I send to one of the judges of the audiencia for hearing and investigation in chambers, with instructions that report of what has been done be brought to the audiencia in executive meeting. Matters of lesser moment, I send to provincial governors and to religious and lay persons according to the type of matter and the persons available in the regions where the Indians live, in order not to keep the latter away from their towns. At other times I appoint Indian judges, named with the consent of the parties, to investigate disputes. Through this arrangement my other days remain more nearly free for other matters. Yet not even then do I fail to hear all the other Indians who come to me at any time and hour and in any place save only the judicial and executive sessions of the audiencia.

The Indians have the custom, if any of the matters that they bring to the Spanish authorities are not settled as they want them, to wait until the matters have been forgotten and then raise them again on some pretext. Since most of their affairs are settled summarily on the basis of their pictographic accounts, there is no record except the memory of the official who handled the matter. Thus there has been great confusion. As a remedy I provided that the [viceregal] secretary keep a book for recording all settlements, and when any Indians come with a petition, the book is searched to see whether or not there has already been a provision on the matter. If no record of a previous order is found and a special judge is commissioned, a clause is put in his instructions that he have power unless another judge already has issued a decision. In addition, since the Indians are especially prone when any judge is available to raise once more all matters brought up in the past, they will do this far more with Your Lordship, since you are new come from Spain. You must be warned of this.

His Majesty has ordered that among the Indians there be no ordinary judicial process, and this order has been kept; but at times, because of the insistence of the attorneys and carelessness, the order has not been observed as fully as it should be. Your Lordship should be careful not to permit this, for it causes serious damage to the Indians.

Some will tell Your Lordship that the Indians are simple and humble people without malice, pride, or covetousness. Others will insist upon the opposite, and claim that they are very rich and lazy and do not wish to cultivate their lands. Do not believe one group or the other. Rather deal with the Indians as with any other people, without making special rules, and with caution for the devices of third parties, for there are few in this land who have no personal interest, whether it is earthly or spiritual wealth, passion or ambition, or vice. . . .

It happens usually that Indian nobles and peasants of any town come on matters of community welfare and government, for all wish to have news of what is decided. It may be that Your Lordship will be urged, because of the number who come and the stench and heat that they give off, to order that no more than one or two of the nobles enter. The others will be greatly hurt. Furthermore, there is the danger that, as has happened, the nobles will give a false account of what has been ordered. These Indians have the custom in matters of community welfare and government that all who come may enter. The interpreter should proclaim clearly and loudly whatever is provided so that all may hear. This will content the Indians, and moreover, is fitting.[123]

This unified viceregal jurisdiction was complemented by a series of special appointments of judges for Indian affairs in the provinces and Spanish cities, with jurisdiction not only over disputes among Indians but also over those between Spaniards and Indians. The Spanish cities objected and in 1573 were able to secure jurisdiction in first instance for their own alcaldes.[124]

We are further fortunate in having many of the books of the viceregal secretaries recording the handling of Indian affairs by Mendoza and by Luis de Velasco I, who continued the same arrangements. The following summaries will give an idea of the variety of matters that the two viceroys handled in personal audience and the working of their system (the initial dates are those of the final viceregal order):

1. May 20, 1542, Mexico City. The Indians of Ocuila (state of Mexico) appeal to the viceroy for determination of their dispute with the Indians of Jalatlaco over boundaries and woodlands and their further dispute with the Indians of Malinalco over the setting of boundary markers between the two towns. Mendoza issues a commission to Lorenzo de Luna, Indian noble of Texcoco, investing him with the powers of a judge for investigation and arbitration. To the end that the Indians cease civil suits, he is to hear all parties and try to reach a

123. N.d. but 1550–51, in HM, 1:41–42, 47, and 51. Further material on the operation of the system may be found in Velasco I to the king, Mexico City, February 7, 1554, in Cuevas, *Documentos*, 211–213; Sarabia Viejo, 25–26; Warren, 105–106. The description preceding the quotation from the relación de mando represents a reading also of the records in AGN-M, vols. 1–3.

124. Instruction of Puebla for its procurador in Spain, Puebla, June 25, 1544, in Paso y Troncoso, 4:126; petition of Indian officials of Tlaxiaco and Teozacoalco before Tristán de Luna y Arellano, corregidor of Guaxolotitlán and "juez en cosas tocantes a indios en la cibdad de Guaxaca y en toda su probincia por el yllmo. señor don Antonio de Mendoza visorrey e governador en esta nueva españa," Etlatongo, May 13, 1545, in AJT-Crim, leg. 2; Fonseca and Urrutia, 1:536–537.

peaceful settlement acceptable to all. The settlement is to be recorded in writing and pictographs, and boundary markers are to be set so that there may be no future doubt. If no settlement is possible, he is to take testimony and other evidence in judicial manner and report to the viceroy, who will provide what is proper. On Luna's return to Mexico City, the viceroy will issue an order for the payment of his services.[125] [This is the standard form of such orders.]

2. October 23, 1543, Mexico City. The Indians of Tixtla (Guerrero) appeal to the viceroy for settlement of land disputes between them and the people of the town's dependent villages. The viceroy commissions Agustín, Indian of Xochimilco, as judge to investigate and compose the differences. The text of the instruction is essentially the same as that of the order above and is marked on the margin, "usual commission."[126]

3. January 29, 1544, Mexico City. Don Julián, Indian noble of Tepeapulco (Hidalgo), protests to the viceroy against a settlement of land disputes between the nobles and commoners of Tepeapulco because he was not given due prior notice of the first settlement by Hernando Arias de Saavedra, corregidor of the town, who supervised it. The viceroy issues an order to the Indian governor and other officials of the city and province of Tlaxcala, directing that they meet the governor and nobles of Tepeapulco by the middle of February in order to reach a new settlement composing the differences between Don Julián and the other Indians of Tepeapulco. From 15 to 20 Indians are to attend the new negotiations, under penalty of 50 pesos' fine. The new agreement is to be brought to the viceroy for confirmation within ten days after it is made.[127]

4. October 13, 1542, Mexico City. The town officials of Huejotzingo (Puebla) petition the viceroy for protection against the Indians of Tlaxcala, who, they claim, are cutting and carrying away much timber from the lands of Huejotzingo. The viceroy issues an order of amparo to the corregidor of Tlaxcala and his lieutenant that the Indians of Huejotzingo are to be protected against invasion of their timber lands. If the Indians of Tlaxcala have any claim, they are to bring it to the viceroy.[128]

5. October 25, 1543, Mexico City. Pedro, Indian of Amatlán, a dependency of Chiautla (Puebla), petitions the viceroy for protection in his possession and operation of two mines he has discovered. Some Spaniards have tried to seize the mines on the ground that he is an

125. AGN-M, 1:fols. 40v–41f.   126. Ibid., 2:fol. 198r–v.
127. Ibid., fol. 253r–v.   128. Ibid., 1:fol. 175v.

Indian. The viceroy issues an order for amparo to the alcalde mayor of the mines of Chiautla.[129]

6. September 2, 1550, Mexico City. The Indians of Jaltepec (Oaxaca) petition the viceroy for an order of amparo to insure their quiet possession of Atleistaca, lands settled by their peasants but now claimed by the town of Tlalnavaca. They assert that Tlalnavaca has not had possession of the lands for 35 years. In the hearing before the viceroy, the representatives of Tlalnavaca admit Jaltepec has been in possession for 30 years. The viceroy issues the order of amparo.[130]

7. September 19, 1550, Mexico City. Tomás, an Indian noble of Achiutla (Oaxaca), appears before the viceroy, stating that he has lent money at interest to Indians of neighboring towns and that he has bought some Indians as slaves, since he did not know that these practices were wrong. He did not use the Indians as slaves and returned them at once. He petitions the viceroy for return of the money lent without interest and refund of the payments for the slaves. The viceroy orders the corregidor of Tejúpam to summon the parties and do justice by summary hearing and decision.[131]

8. July 29, 1550, Mexico City. Pedro Elías, an Indian noble of Taximaroa (Michoacán), complains that the Indians of the villages left to him directly by his father and indirectly through his sister, who died without other heir, suddenly refuse to pay him the tributes due. He asks that the alguaciles and other Indians not interfere and that his rights be enforced. The viceroy orders the corregidor of the nearby towns of Ucareo and Zinapécuaro to summon the parties and do justice.[132]

9. December 6, 1550, Mexico City. The Indians of Coyoacán (Distrito Federal) complain that the inhabitants of their sujeto, Tacubaya, wish to attend divine service in Mexico City instead of coming to the monastery in Coyoacán as they have done in the past. The viceroy orders that the Indians of Tacubaya go to church in Coyoacán.[133]

10. October 16, 1543, Mexico City. Rafael de Trejo, Spaniard, petitions the viceroy for confirmation of his purchase of vacant lands in an arroyo of Zacatepec (Oaxaca), sujeto of Ixtlahuaca. He has bought the lands from the Indians of Zacatepec for 60 pesos of common gold and proposes to raise cacao. The viceroy orders that the corregidor either of Jicayán or of Teposcolula investigate the transaction.

129. Ibid., 2:fol. 203v.   130. Ibid., 3:fol. 168r.
131. Ibid., fol. 191r.   132. Ibid., fol. 139v.
133. Ibid., fol. 239v.

He is to make sure that the sale is voluntary and the price fair. If the transaction is just, he is to give his approval.[134]

11. October 9, 1542, Mexico City. Ambrosio, Indian of Temoac (Morelos), petitions the viceroy for his freedom and pay for services rendered while he was held in bondage. He has been held a slave by Francisco de Solís, Spanish resident of Mexico City, who claims that he received Ambrosio as a gift from the Indians. The case is heard before the viceroy, who after examining the evidence pronounces Ambrosio free and issues a formal order to that effect.[135]

12. March 30, 1542, Mexico City. Francisco de Santa Cruz and Gutierre de Badajoz, Spanish encomenderos, inform the viceroy that many Spaniards pass through their towns and abuse the Indians. The viceroy issues an order empowering Bernabé de Albornoz, *calpisque* (encomendero's agent) of Nexpa, Tlacolula, and Tecamama (Oaxaca and Guerrero), to carry the special staff of a judge, arrest travelers molesting Indians, and send them with a report of the offense to the audiencia or the nearest Spanish justice.[136]

13. November 24, 1542, Mexico City. Juan Cermeño, encomendero of Coatlán (Guerrero), petitions that Juan Marco, his calpisque, be empowered to arrest non-Indian travelers molesting his Indians. He reports that there has been such abuse. The viceroy empowers Juan Marco to carry the special staff of a judge, make arrests, and send the culprits with a report of the offense to the alcalde mayor of Tasco for trial.[137]

14. September 20, 1542, Mexico City. The Indians of Nochixtlán (Oaxaca) complain that Pedro de Maya, their encomendero, mistreats them and levies excessive tributes. He further prevents them from coming to Mexico City to complain to the viceroy and audiencia. The viceroy orders that the Indians of Nochixtlán are not to be hindered in any way from coming to Mexico City to complain about their encomendero. Any person hindering them is to be fined 500 pesos. If Maya does so, he is to be subject to the fine and the natives are to be freed from tribute for one year.[138]

15. April 21—22, 1543, Puebla. The viceroy commissions Jerónimo Ruiz de la Mota, encomendero of Mitlantongo (Oaxaca), who is planning to visit his town, inspector and judge in all towns for 8 leagues around Mitlantongo, with the special staff of a judge, and a

134. Ibid., 2:fol. 193r.   135. Ibid., 1:fol. 166r.
136. Ibid., fol. 232r-v.   137. Ibid., fol. 200r-v.
138. Ibid., fol. 150r.

bailiff. His powers include settling suits and disputes among the Indians; punishing abuse of the natives, and excesses by governors, nobles, and others; and sentencing Spaniards living with women they have not married to 100 lashes and 50 pesos' fine. The commission is issued because the viceroy is informed that the area is so remote from Mexico City that Indians cannot come to Mexico City for remedy.[139]

16. July 18, 1542, Mexico City. The Indians of Tamazola (Oaxaca) ask permission to cut timber on the land of Tlaxiaco for building a church, since they have no timber on their own land. The viceroy grants the permission. The Indians of Tamazola are to summon those of Tlaxiaco so that the latter may make sure that as little timber as possible is cut. Should they not obey the summons, the Indians of Tamazola may proceed without them. Should the inhabitants of Tlaxiaco try to interfere, they are to be subject to a fine of 50 pesos.[140]

17. October 4, 1550, Mexico City. The Indians of Yanhuitlán (Oaxaca) complain that, when they went to make lime on their own lands for building their church, the Indians of Teposcolula set upon them, beat them with clubs, and seized the hatchets they had brought for cutting firewood. The viceroy orders the corregidor of Nochixtlán [not Teposcolula, which had a corregidor] to hear the case and arrest and punish any found guilty, so that there is no further occasion for complaint.[141]

18. March 10, 1543, Mexico City. Juan Guerrero, encomendero of Tucupan (Guerrero?), informs the viceroy that the governor and nobles of the town levy more tribute than is needed to meet assessments, force the peasants to cultivate extra land for their benefit, and commit other extortions. The viceroy commissions Alonso Temoque, Indian of the *parte de México*, as judge to go to Tucupan and its sujeto for taking a residencia of the governor and nobles. Those he finds guilty of misconduct, he is to order before the viceroy and is himself to file a report recommending penalties for the guilty parties. On his return, the viceroy will assign appropriate pay for his work.[142]

19. [May 2, 1551, Mexico City.] The Indians of Ixcuintepec, Elotepec, and other towns of the Peñoles (Oaxaca) complain that, although they have given food and domestic service to their corregidores, some make excessive demands and even force them to send food to the city of Antequera [Oaxaca today]. They petition for an

---

139. Ibid., 2:fols. 66r–v and 69r–70r. The version of April 21 has an additional section on *tamemes* and contains authorization to appoint a bailiff.

140. Ibid., 1:fol. 104r.   141. Ibid., 3:fol. 201v.

142. Ibid., 2:fol. 56r.

order that they need provide only what is in the formal assessment. The viceroy issues an order of amparo that the Indians are to provide their corregidor only such food and services as are in the formal assessment—a chicken a day for 20 days when the corregidor is in the towns of the Peñoles.[143]

20. October 12, 1543, Mexico City. The viceroy orders the governor and officials of Tlaxcala to keep a book in their town hall in which they are to record all determinations of fact and all decisions in disputes over land and inheritance that are made by the audiencia, corregidores, and other justices. There have been complaints that, notwithstanding decisions that have been issued, the Indians start new suits and demand new hearings for old cases and disputes.[144]

Handling the bulk of Indian complaints that might reach the higher Spanish authorities in Mexico City in a unified jurisdiction under the personal supervision of the highest royal official in the colony clearly provided substantial protection. The very large number of orders in the surviving records is evidence of the extent to which the Indians became aware of the possibility of remedy and brought complaint. The unified viceregal jurisdiction provided substantial relief from the burdens of litigation although it by no means eliminated them. It reduced costs markedly, especially judicial ones, although executive fees still had to be paid, but in reduced measure. It solved the costs and problems of legal counsel by avoiding to a considerable extent the need for such counsel. It avoided judicial process by converting most of the hearings into executive proceedings handled by the viceroy or his agents on direct instruction. The amount of business that Mendoza and Velasco found to be clearly judicial was small, as may be seen from the cases summarized above. The viceregal decision in favor of Tlalnavaca in its dispute with Jaltepec (no. 6), the instruction for investigation of Spanish purchase of land (no. 10), and the award of freedom to an Indian held as slave (no. 11) represented decisions in matters that normally should have been left to a tribunal. Other orders arranging for the settlement of disputes by arbitration rather than suit, or appointing special judges, were somewhat less clearly invasions of the judicial sphere, but easily could be interpreted as such. The audiencia was certain to protest this extension of administrative competence at its expense.

Mendoza's unified jurisdiction encountered two major difficulties, which became especially serious under his successor. In the

143. Ibid., 3:fol. 1v.
144. Ibid., 2:fol. 189r–v.

first place, Indians losing decisions or dissatisfied with settlements only partially in their favor attempted to carry the quarrel or complaint farther by appeal to the audiencia, alleging that the matter was one for judicial determination.[145] Towns as corporate entities and nobles, both caciques and principales, had the right of unrestricted access to Spanish courts and to ordinary legal counsel. That they were making very wide use of their rights by the end of Mendoza's administration is clear from the royal orders expressing concern at the extent and costs of Indian litigation.[146]

In the second place, the audiencia objected with increasing vehemence to the very substantial enlargement of the administrative sphere at its expense. The viceroys could claim partial royal sanction in an order of February 1537 granting them power to commission special ad hoc judges for Indian matters.[147] Furthermore, the royal legislation directed that Indian disputes be settled by summary decision without judicial process, but that injunction did not mean removing determination from the judicial to the administrative sphere. In counterclaim, the audiencia demanded that it, rather than the viceroy, appoint any special judges and issue orders for investigation and justice that might be sent to corregidores and alcaldes mayores. Early in the administration of Luis de Velasco I, the audiencia tried to declare void all proceedings that it objected to on the ground that, being determinations of judicial matters by administrative officials, they bore no legal force. In February 1554, Velasco reported these difficulties to the crown and urged the retention of Mendoza's system, since resort to judicial process would mean endless delays and the use of procedures which the Indians would never understand.[148] The royal decision in July 1555 was that the viceroy consult the audiencia when appointing Indian judges to regular posts in the Indian towns, but that he continue to

145. Mendieta to Bustamante, Toluca, January 1, 1562, in García Icazbalceta, *Nueva colección*, 1:15–23.

146. Royal cédulas of the prince to the Audiencia of Mexico, Madrid, December 9, 1551, in DCLI, 2:182–183, Puga, fols. 128v–129f (misdated 1552), and Encinas, 4:275–276, and sobrecédula repeating it, of the princess to the Audiencia of Nueva Galicia, ordering a report on desirability of a more moderate schedule of fees for Indians than for Spaniards, Valladolid, July 5, 1555, ibid., 357; to the Audiencia of Mexico,. n.p., n.d. but ca. January–February 1569, in AGN-RCD, 47:fols. 54v–55f; to the Viceroy and Audiencia of Mexico, ordering careful observance of previous orders to avoid costs and expense, Madrid, July 6, 1571, ibid., fol. 205f. Later orders are listed in RLI, 2.15.83 and 5.9.25, but one cannot be certain that they were directed to New Spain and not to other regions.

147. DIU, 23:209.

148. Velasco I to the king, Mexico City, February 7, 1554, in Cuevas, *Documentos*, 211–213.

appoint special agents and judges on commission without consultation. Such, declared the order, was the custom of Mendoza.[149]

This substantial victory for the viceroy by no means ended the objections of the audiencia. It continued to insist that disputes and complaints be brought before it and that both viceregal appointments of judges on commission and any decisions by them were void. Its views on the limits between *cosas de gobernación* and *cosas de jurisdicción* tended to place all matters within judicial determination. Obstruction by the audiencia was able to hamper viceregal activity very greatly.[150] In 1566, eleven years after the royal decision and two and a half after Velasco's sudden death, the Crown was forced to ask for a new report because there were so many disputes over jurisdiction.[151] By then the balance was tilting clearly in favor of the audiencia, for it governed the colony in the absence of a replacement for most of the time from July 1564, when Velasco died, until November 1568, when Martín Enríquez entered Mexico City, the exception being the year 1566–67 when the Marqués de Falcés was in office. Once in control of both the administrative and judicial spheres of government, the audiencia asserted its views of the proper division between them and allocated Indian matters accordingly. The administrative records for Indian affairs of the period cease to have orders for settling disputes over lands and other matters that could properly be held to be judicial.[152]

The dispute over jurisdiction involved far more than a fight for power between the highest authorities of the colony. Each authority had its own secretariat, levying fees and costs besides receiving gifts, and a group of professional men practicing before it and bound to it, who also lived on fees and perquisites. Under Mendoza's system, the *secretario de gobernación*, his staff, and the other professional men attached to or practicing before the administrative hierarchy reaped a rich harvest from the dispatch of Indian business. They constituted a strong vested interest which did not accept lightly any loss of revenue and disputed all attempts to change the older order. Success by the audiencia in asserting jurisdiction over a very much larger proportion of Indian disputes and complaints meant that the *secretario de cámara*, his officials, and the other professional men licensed to practice before the audiencia profited hugely, far more than the loss of fees and per-

149. DIU, 23:209.

150. Mendieta to Bustamante, Toluca, January 1, 1562, in García Icazbalceta, *Nueva colección*, 1:15–23.

151. Madrid, December 10, 1566, AGN-RCD, 47:fol. 328 (BLT).

152. AGN-M, vol. 8, passim.

quisites to *gobernación*, for the fees, costs, and perquisites of ad-judicature were many more and very much higher.

What lay at issue in the dispute between the two hierarchies may be gauged from a royal order of June 28, 1568, which listed the categories of Indian matters in which both claimed the right to prepare papers and dispatch business: (1) orders for the release of Indians held in jail by local justices for slight offenses; (2) orders to local justices to speed cases they were delaying through favoritism or malice; (3) complaints and suits against caciques and principales for exacting illegal derramas and personal services; (4) appeals from settlements arranged by corregidores in disputes of towns over boundaries and water; (5) complaints and suits against collectors of royal tributes for levy beyond assessments; and (6) challenges to grants of land for farming or grazing on ground of prejudice to a third party. These categories cover the bulk of Indian matters which had been dispatched by the viceroy under Mendoza's unified jurisdiction. To be sure, the royal order of 1568 enjoined the audiencia to settle the dispute and see that harmonious working relations were established between the two hierarchies;[153] but the audiencia, itself the champion of its own officials and professional men and a jealous guardian of its own prerogatives, was hardly likely to do so.

The vested interest of the administrative hierarchy, and resistance to loss of fees and perquisites by the under-officials and professional men of gobernación, explain why the audiencia was not completely successful in imposing its views. On the other hand, it was able to assert its claims to jurisdiction and the rights of its own officials with sufficient success so that Martín Enríquez, viceroy from 1568 to 1580, never was able to make the handling of Indian affairs a prerogative of the viceroy and the secretario de gobernación to any extent approaching what it had been under Mendoza and the first Velasco. The conflict continued unresolved throughout the 1570s and 1580s. Moved by criticism of its procedures, the audiencia attempted to strengthen its case by adopting a number of measures for simplifying legal forms and hearings.[154] Perhaps the worst damage of the dispute

153. AGN-RCD, 47:fols. 63r–64v and 391r–392r (the latter available as a BLT). For a further listing of the categories of Indian matters and others in dispute, see the Memorial of the Marqués de Falcés, March 23, 1567, in HM, 1:182–185. For more general accounts of disputes over jurisdiction between viceroys and audiencias, see García Gallo, "Los principios rectores," 341–345; Muro Romero, 126–136; and Villapalos Salas, "Los recursos: Notas," 10–48.

154. Autos of the Audiencia of Mexico, Mexico City, June 20, 1570, and May 19, 1572, AGN-RCD, 47:fols. 457v and 382v–r respectively; and chapter of a royal letter approving the custom of having only one judge visit each Indian jail, July 4, 1570, in Encinas, 2:67.

was that Indians coming to Mexico City with a dispute or complaint could not be certain where to take the matter. With an understandable desire for certainty, they took their business to both hierarchies, attempting to have any order or writ granted them prepared by the two secretariats. Vast confusion resulted, fees and costs multiplied, and the Indians had to resort to legal counsel, for without them it was obviously impossible to deal with the complicated and duplicated machinery.[155]

Confusion became even worse under Enríquez. In 1568 the crown established a *sala de crimen*, a panel of three lesser judges for handling civil and criminal cases brought before the audiencia in first instance within the five-league radius in which it had such jurisdiction.[156] The audiencia and the sala promptly disputed exactly what was the division of competence, the audiencia claiming jurisdiction over suits between Indians and Spaniards and the sala claiming all jurisdiction in first instance that the audiencia exercised in Indian matters, without regard to the five-league radius. The judges of the sala soon became embroiled as well with the viceroy, since he demanded that their deliberations be conducted before him and interfered with their handling of cases. All these quarrels forced the crown to define spheres of competence: The sala was to have jurisdiction in cases arising in first instance between Spaniards and Indians within the five-league radius. On the other hand, it was not to interfere in the appellate function of the audiencia nor attempt to deal with Indian matters arising outside the five-league radius.[157] The viceroy might not interfere in the sala's deliberations, but might require a report on its decisions.[158] Despite such royal clarification, the existence of another tribunal with competing claims added to the confusion of the Indians in deciding where to take their complaints and suits.

A further source of confusion and levy upon the Indians, one that took on particular vigor during the administration of Enríquez but continued until the end of the colonial period, was the multiplication of fee-levying officials as the royal government—starting with Philip II, impelled by an empty treasury—raised revenue by selling office, and created office in order to have more to sell.[159] In 1573, a second secretario de gobernación was appointed, over the protests of Enríquez. Within a few months the viceroy reported serious disputes over

155. Velasco II to the king, October 8, 1590, VC, fols. 22v–23r.

156. Schäfer, 2:112–114; royal cédula to the Audiencia of Mexico, Madrid, June 19, 1568, in Encinas, 2:73–74.

157. Royal cédulas, El Escorial, July 4, 1570, and Madrid, June 23 and July 6, 1571, in Encinas, 2:75–76, 79–80, and 82.

158. Royal cédula, Madrid, May 23, 1573, ibid., p. 92.

159. Parry, *The Sale of Public Office*, 6–47; Schäfer, 2:183–191; Tomás y Valiente, *La venta*, 51–138.

the division of business between the two secretaries, and a further, un-anticipated difficulty that there was no way of knowing who was keep-ing the records on any matter. Enríquez urged a division on the basis of bishoprics, which would not be perfect but at least an improvement. In answer, the crown, which was interested primarily in the price it had collected for the new appointment, instructed him to apply any territorial division he wished, "so long as it gave equality." [160]

Conflicts over jurisdiction thus nullified the effectiveness of Mendoza's attempt to create a special unified jurisdiction for Indian affairs. At the same time, attempts at reform within the ordinary Span-ish jurisprudence and administration clearly failed to meet the prob-lem. In the 1570s and 1580s, efforts to spare the Indians from legal costs and fees were clearly a failure. Indeed, the increase in number of notaries and other professional men as a result of royal multiplication and sales of office meant that a larger number of Spaniards tried to recover the prices of their appointments and earn a livelihood from the handling of Indian legal affairs and petitions. Schemes for providing free legal counsel for some of the Indians were grossly inadequate, and the simplification of Spanish judicial procedures of doubtful benefit. Meanwhile, the numbers of Indians visibly melted away while the His-panized population with its need for them increased. Simultaneously, the decay of Indian institutions and custom and the imposition of Spanish ways and Castilian law upon the Indians moved as an inex-orable tide.

160. Paragraph of a letter from the king to Enríquez, June 22, 1573, in Encinas, 2:340–341.

CHAPTER IV

Establishment of the General Indian Court, 1585–1607

By the 1580s, the efforts of the crown and its administrators in New Spain to ease introduction of the Indians into Spanish law and legal procedures clearly had failed. The Indians still lacked access to relatively simple, inexpensive, quick, and effective legal remedies. Awareness of this failure by the clergy and many of the higher officials in the royal bureaucracy in both the colony and the Peninsula led in the last years of the sixteenth century to renewed efforts at an effective solution. During these years the investigations and concern of the imperial government bore fruit in a number of reforms for easing the burden on the Indians in New Spain and the rest of Spanish America, notably in the great labor measures embodied in the *reales cédulas* of 1601 and 1609.[1] In the Audiencia of Mexico, they also resulted in establishment of the General Indian Court and the special Indian agents of the half-real.

The nadir of failure came with the viceregal administration of Villamanrique (1585–1590). Although the audiencia and many influential Spaniards agreed that the steadily diminishing number of Indians had reached a point at which they could not support the multitude of posts of justice and inspection for special purposes which formerly had helped to maintain worthy descendants of the conquerors—and which therefore in recent years had been left unfilled—Villamanrique insisted upon filling all, and instituted even more in connection with

1. Schäfer, 2:309–332; and Zavala and Castelo, 5:v–xxix and 6:xiii–xxiv. The text of the royal cédulas, dated Valladolid, November 24, 1601, and Aranjuez, May 26, 1609, is in Konetzke, 2:71–85 and 154–168.

the new slaughterhouses permitted in the large Indian towns. Worse, he filled these posts with members of his own entourage or made the appointments dependent upon payment to them or to himself. The audiencia, for its part, despite its show of virtue in objecting to these appointments, fought tenaciously with the viceroy to maintain its jurisdiction and the claims of the officials dependent upon it.[2] Meantime, the Indians of New Spain, steadily diminishing in number,[3] seemed doomed to disappear as completely as those of the Greater Antilles, as Fray Domingo de Betanzos had predicted in 1545, setting a term of forty years. Toward the end of the century a later generation of writers and preachers of his order recalled that prophecy and thought it taking place under their own eyes, even though in somewhat more than forty years. In the face of the onslaught of the Spaniards, wrote Mendieta, the Indians were like sardines before great whales. As Fray Domingo de Betanzos also had observed, all measures planned for the Indians' good worked to their harm.[4]

Nevertheless, despite a growing pessimism, many among the clergy and royal administrators continued their efforts to ameliorate the lot of the natives. Since the problem extended far beyond Mexico to all of the Spanish possessions in America where there were Indians, and even to the Philippines, the discussions took place throughout the Spanish world. One of the basic elements of a more effective approach to the adjustment of European law and judicial systems to the Indians developed within that general discussion. A second, elaborated in the Viceroyalty of Peru, had possibilities of application to Mexico.

The approach that developed in what one might call general discussion envisaged application of the millennial doctrine of the obligation of prince and Church to give special protection to widows, orphans, and the wretched of the earth. The Indians were to be assimilated en masse to the juridical condition of *miserabiles*. Accordingly, they were to be entitled to have their complaints and cases taken under special royal and Church protection and to have special legal assistance, special conditions of hearing, abbreviated legal process, summary judgment, and either reduced costs or free access to legal facilities.

The pioneers in urging this view were Francisco de Vitoria and Bartolomé de las Casas, an oddly contrasting pair in temperament and

2. Relación de mando of Villamanrique, Texcoco, February 14, 1590, clauses 17, 18, 26, 27, 28, and Cargos contra el Marqués de Villamanrique, April 18, 1592, passim, both in HM, 1:266–283 and 2:9–68 respectively. See also the discussion below.

3. Cook and Borah, *Essays*, 1:73–118 and 3:1–102, esp. 1 and 101–102.

4. Betanzos to provincials and procuradores going to Spain, Tepetlaoztoc, September 11, 1545, in García Icazbalceta, *Colección*, 2:199–200; Dávila Padilla, 99–103 (cap. 33); Mendieta, 365–366 (lib. 4, cap. 1).

method of action. Vitoria in his lectures at Salamanca in January 1539 tentatively raised the proposition that the Indians might be regarded as in need of special legal protection, since they were unable fully to govern themselves.[5] The jump to full declaration that the Indians should be regarded as *miserabiles* in the legal meaning of the term came from Las Casas in his customary mixture of prophetic perception and counterproductive impetuous assault on vested interests. In the early 1540s, while awaiting transportation from Spain to his new diocese of Chiapa, Las Casas called attention to the plight of Indian slaves in Sevilla, but his use of the word *miserable* was a rhetorical and descriptive one, as yet without juridical content. Once he was in the New World, appearing before the Audiencia de los Confines with his fellow bishops of Nicaragua and Guatemala, his thinking moved to give the term juridical content. In October 1545, in a written representation to the audiencia, he and the other bishops declared the Indians *miserables* in the full juridical meaning of the term, but also declared that as such they fell within Church jurisdiction, citing Gratian and the papal bull *In Coena Domini*. Las Casas repeated the demand in a letter to the audiencia outlining his needs as Bishop of Chiapa. This demand, with its assertion of an overriding Church jurisdiction, was one that the audiencia as guardian of the royal jurisdiction had to reject.[6] From that first formulation by Las Casas, however, the more moderate idea of declaring the Indians *miserables*, without asserting special Church jurisdiction, found favor in Church discussions in New Spain.[7]

Acceptance by royal jurists came much more slowly, perhaps because of the dangers of conceding Church jurisdiction. In 1563 Philip

5. The proposition occurs as an additional one after the seventh in Vitoria, *Relectio de Indis*, part 1, sec. 3:97–98, and begins: "Aliud titulus posset non quidem asseri, sed revocari in disputationem et videri aliquibus legitimus, de quo ego nihil affirmare audeo, sed nec omnino condemnare, et est talis"; also see Castañeda Delgado, 291–294.

6. Cantù, "Esigenze di giustizia," 155–163, prints the text of the representation of the bishops. For the text of the *requerimiento en derecho* of Las Casas to the audiencia, October 22, 1545, see Las Casas, *Obras*, 5:218–221, which also prints the audiencia's answer on October 26, 1545. The president of the audiencia was moved to write to Prince Philip on December 31, 1545: "'No sería malo que diese cuenta personalmente en el Real Consejo de Indias de cómo los indios son de la jurisdicción eclesiástica.'" Pérez de Tudela Bueso comments: "Las Casas se excedía al reclamar una jurisdicción que ni le competía ni la Audiencia podía delegarle": ibid., 1 (*Estudio preliminar*): clx–clxi. Las Casas, nevertheless, was asserting medieval Church theory still widely held (see Cantù, "Per un rinnovamento," 69–75), but at a most unpropitious time and to highly unwelcoming ears.

7. Castañeda Delgado, 285–291; Oliveros, 118–120; Llaguno, 1–3, 117–121, 137, and 277.

II declared heathen Indians *miserables*, to be redeemed by conversion to Christianity under Spanish tutelage; but use of the term was rhetorical rather than juridical. In 1571, in the ordinances for the Council of the Indies, the crown attorney (*fiscal*) was enjoined to give particular attention to the affairs of the Indians, "whose protection and defense, like that of poor and miserable people, is to be of pressing concern." Here the meaning was clearly moving toward acceptance of the concept, but had not yet reached full assimilation. In 1580, 1583, and 1593, the term appeared in other royal injunctions for Peru and New Granada, but with juridical meaning unclear. The meaning was more likely rhetorical.[8] By 1580 the term was clearly evident in administrative thinking in Mexico in the *relación de mando* of Viceroy Enríquez for his successor, with its recommendation that the viceroy act as father to the Indians, "and this has to be without costs or expense to them, for most of them do not have the means to find a *real* unless they sell themselves. . . ."[9] The term is equally evident in the thinking of Luis de Velasco II at the start of his viceregal administration in Mexico in 1590: ". . . these natives, because of their poverty and misery. . . ."[10] Fuller development came only in the middle years of the seventeenth century in the writings of Solórzano Pereira, the great jurist of the Audiencia of Lima, who declared that the Indians were to be regarded as *miserables* in juridical meaning, and as such were to get many but not all of the rights and privileges of minors, the poor, rustics, widows, and the wretched of the earth.[11] In this sense, the concept found place in the *Recopilación de leyes de los reynos de las Indias* of 1680.[12]

8. Oliveros, 118–119; Castañeda Delgado, 264–266. The text of the declaration of Philip II in the *Ordenanza de Audiencias* of 1563 is quoted by Altolaguirre y Duvale in a footnote to his publication of the Copulata, 3.3.31 (DIU, 21:202–203): "'. . . uno de los mayores cuidados que siempre hemos tenido es procurar por todos medios que los indios sean bien tratados y reconozcan los beneficios de Dios nuestro Señor, en sacarlos del miserable estado de su gentilidad, trayéndolos a nuestra Santa Fe Católica y vasallaje nuestro.'" The royal statement of 1571 in clause 51 of the *Ordenanzas del Consejo de Indias* enjoins the fiscal of the Council to exercise special care for the protection and needs of the Indians, ". . . de cuya proteccion y amparo, como de personas miserables y pobres, se tenga por muy encargado": Encinas, 1:16. The text of the royal cédulas is printed in Konetzke: to the governor of the province of Chucuito, Badajoz, September 23, 1580 (1:528–529); to the Audiencia of New Granada, San Lorenzo, November 1, 1583 (1:551–552); and to the Audiencia of Lima, Madrid, December 29, 1593 (2:12–13).

9. September 25, 1580, in HM, 1:204.

10. Análisis del memorial del Marqués de Villamanrique, Mexico City, February 8, 1590, in HM, 2:93.

11. Solórzano Pereira, 1:417–429 (lib. 2, cap. 28).

12. For example, RLI, 6.10.21. Lic. Francisco Ramiro de Valenzuela, the eighteenth-century commentator on Solórzano Pereira in the edition cited above, indicates other provisions in the RLI.

In at least one aspect, the entire discussion might be regarded as dealing with a null question, for no one whose opinions have come down to us held that the Indians should be dealt with in full detail and rigor of Spanish law. All regarded the Indians as a group to be given different and special treatment. After Las Casas' abortive effort in 1545 to declare an overriding Church jurisdiction, even he abandoned that idea. Later discussion among the clergy was directed toward ensuring that Church jurisdiction, to the extent that the crown allowed it, operated with as little burdening of the Indians as possible, and to urging upon the crown the same approach in the royal jurisdiction.[13] Discussion among royal jurists and administrators always centered upon the exact nature of the measures needed to ease the entrance of the Indians into life with the Spaniards.

As the sixteenth century wore on, these ideas were considerably enriched by discussion of the legal doctrine of *miserabiles*, and the nature of the measures needed became progressively clearer: reduction or elimination of legal costs and, equally, of the intervention of the normal Spanish network of fee officials, attorneys, and notaries; much more direct access to judicial and administrative relief; drastic simplification of legal process to summary hearing and decision, without the normal Spanish legal possibilities of prolonged litigation; means of persuading the Indians to remain in their villages rather than pursue litigation often at great distances; and special agencies for hearing complaints of merit. At no time were the royal jurists willing to make the leap to full application of the legal concept of *miserabiles*, for that would have made all Indian suits *casos de corte* and overridden the protection accorded the Spaniards under the prevailing doctrine that the plaintiff must sue in the court and under the law of the defendant. With that exception, the willingness of the imperial bureaucracy to adopt ameliorative measures became greater in the later sixteenth century, as the misery and diminution of the Indian populations became clearer. One very important aspect of the measures listed above should be noted: all moved basically from dealing with the Indians as a widely separate cultural group to treating them as a separate estate within what was rapidly becoming one society, despite the formal designation of two republics.[14] In other words, Spanish thinking moved steadily from debating terms of preservation of culture to the kind of protection that prevailing legal and social theory already prescribed for the European poor and wretched.

The problems of making place for the Indians within the Spanish

13. Castañeda Delgado, 273–291.

14. Lira González, in "La extinción," 299–300 and 309–311, discusses the abolition of the General Indian Court at the beginning of the nineteenth century as part of the move to end the organization of society in estates.

legal system were common to all areas of America (and the Philippines) with masses of sedentary natives. Within the Viceroyalty of Peru, the Andean regions presented problems that paralleled those found in Mexico, and the solutions attempted had as difficult and intricate a history. Despite the same basic elements, whatever regional and cultural differences, the Viceroyalty of Peru experimented with somewhat different measures which were brought into a coherent system in the 1570s through the genius and determination of Francisco de Toledo, a viceroy of a long administration, with deep experience, and one able in the end to impose measures over the opposition of the imperial bureaucracy in Madrid. At least one of the important ingredients of the plan adopted in Mexico in the 1590s came from Peruvian experience.

The Peruvian system was far more ambitious than anything attempted in Mexico. It involved a network of judges for native cases, criminal and civil; protectors, defenders, solicitors, and notaries at both provincial and audiencia or viceregal level. The network operated in both judicial and administrative spheres. Complaint or petition were as short as possible, hearings equally abbreviated, and judgment quick and summary. The number of Indians who might leave their district to press a case elsewhere was limited to two—a notable measure for restricting costly travel. The entire network operated on salary without charge to the Indians, or with minimal charge at most. Salaries came from a special fund derived by including a small additional levy in the reformed assessments for tribute, also the work of Toledo.[15]

The renewed impetus to solution in New Spain for problems of Indian legal needs, one that was to result in a far more effective and efficient system, came with Luis de Velasco II, viceroy from 1590 to 1595. As the son of Luis de Velasco I and a resident for many years in Mexico City, he knew the colony with unusual thoroughness. He was not a man with the force and improvising genius of Antonio de Mendoza or even of his father, but rather the careful, deliberate, prudent

15. Relación de mando of Francisco de Toledo, n.p., ca. 1581–82, in HP, 1: 140–142; instruction for Luis de Velasco II as Viceroy of Peru, San Lorenzo, July 22, 1595, ibid., 2:25–26. The system of taxation may be found in Peru (Viceroyalty), *Tasa de la visita general de Francisco de Toledo*, passim, which summarizes the inspections and reassessment of each district in the Audiencia of Lima and Charcas, with a statement of the amount earmarked for the salaries of the defenders and attorneys for the Indians. One beginning of the system may be seen in the appointment of a judge for Indian cases by the Conde de Nieva as viceroy, Lima, April 17, 1563 (the printed transcription reads 1573, but that is obviously a mistake): Peru (Viceroyalty), *Relaciones*, 1:364–366.

Beyond the statement in his relación de mando and the evidence in the *Tasa de la visita general*, Toledo's work may be traced in his ordinances governing the *Defensor de los Naturales*, the Interpreter-General, and the manner of handling Indian cases: Arequipa, September 10, 1575, and La Plata, December 22, 1574, ibid., 236–266. The spe-

administrator who came to the fore in the later years of Philip II, conscientious in carrying out his master's will and sufficiently trusted to have influence in forming that will. Velasco's reports to the crown during his administration give a comprehensive review of the plight of the Indians, their relations with the Spanish settlers and the royal government, the desperate need to help them, and the genuine difficulties in the way of change.[16]

The most serious social and economic problem of the colony lay in the growing disproportion between the increasing number of Spaniards and the decreasing number of Indians. As an upper class, the Spaniards drew their livelihood from the Indians, either through economic enterprises using Indian labor or through government office or official appointment drawing fees and payments or, indirectly, salary from them. By the time Velasco wrote, there were not enough posts and appointments to support the number of Spaniards who lacked other income, and the financial exigencies of the crown, which forced the abolition of many posts and appointments such as special inspectorships, lessened the number available. In addition, the sale of public offices, which became especially prominent in the 1590s, further decreased the appointments available for distribution among the more needy Europeans. At the same time, the decline in the Indian population not only cut the yield of posts dependent on fees, fines, and payments, but also heavily reduced the labor supply available for Spanish enterprises such as mining and farming. In 1591 Velasco estimated that the number of Indian laborers available for distribution through the *repartimiento* was half what it had been when the first repartimientos were instituted in the 1550s. Any efforts by the crown to lessen the burden on the Indian population were certain to incur the opposition of the Spanish, upon whose loyalty in the last analysis rested the maintenance and continuation of royal dominion.[17]

cial set of ordinances of Cuzco also contains regulations on a judge for the natives: Checacupí, October 18, 1572, ibid., 66–71. The general ones for the viceroyalty also define the jurisdiction of judges for the natives: Arequipa, November 6, 1575, ibid., 161–169. The ordinances are also published in GP, vol. 8. See also the discussion in Borah, "Juzgado General de Indios del Peru," 131–134. The number of officials and the scope of the Toledan system may be gauged by the minimum lists in Vázquez de Espinosa, 722–723 and 729–730 (pars. 2048 and 2059). Although the quota for the native legal aides cannot be ascertained from the Toledo *Tasa*, and may have varied from region to region, a royal cédula of October 23, 1638, indicates a general annual levy of 1 *tomín ensayado*, equal to 56¼ maravedís, as against the later Mexican levy of 17 maravedís a year per whole tributary: RLI, 8.27.8.

16. The reports of Velasco II to the crown were regarded as so exemplary by his contemporaries that they were copied into a special compilation, Correspondencia de Don Luis de Velasco con Felipe II y Felipe III acerca de la administración de los Virreinatos de Nueva España y del Perú durante los años 1590 a 1601 (cited as VC).

17. Velasco II to Philip II, June 5, 1590; March 4 and 9, May 5, and November

Velasco found the provincial and district governors—the *alcaldes mayores* and *corregidores*—an oppressive weight upon the Indians.[18] They had the melancholy distinction of rivaling the Indian nobles in fleecing the natives. The governors were paid grossly inadequate annual salaries, which were substantially reduced by the fact that they served sixteen months for the salary of a calendar year, the extra salary being retained in the royal treasury as *quitas y vacantes*. If there was delay in sending out a successor at the end of a governor's term, the salary for that period too escheated to the treasury. The total sum derived from retention and escheat was used to pay royal concessions of pensions and special expenses like those for carrying out *congregaciones*. As permitted by law and custom, the alcaldes mayores and corregidores supplemented their salaries by receipts of fees and their shares of fines and legal costs.

In practice, the sixteen months' administration became a business for squeezing the Indians. The luckless natives were compelled to provide food and fodder, work up materials into finished merchandise for sale by the Spanish governor, purchase merchandise brought into the district by the governor, with collection enforced by him as judge— and, in short, to contribute to the governor's fortune in as many ways as he could arrange. In the process, the collection of fines, fees, and legal costs was enormously expanded. Accounts of town treasuries were audited not once but repeatedly; those of each sujeto were audited separately, and fees charged accordingly. Licenses and certifications were required of the Indians at every opportunity, all of them at exorbitant fees, or the Indians were fined heavily for not having them. Upon the entrance of each new Spanish governor into his district, the natives were encouraged, and often forced, to revive old legal proceedings and institute new ones. From these the governor and a group of officials and professional men, including a series of special agents appointed for the intricate series of investigations and reports of Spanish legal procedure, reaped a harvest of fees and costs that was not noticeably diminished by the injunctions of the crown.

To increase the volume of legal business, the Spanish governors invaded the jurisdiction of the Indian judges in the towns and insisted upon observance of Spanish legal forms, with their richer yield. At Yanhuitlán, one of the great towns of the Mixteca, the alcalde mayor was rebuked by the viceroy in 1590 for usurping the jurisdiction of the

---

1, 1591; May 24, 1592; and April 6, 1595, all in VC. The letter of May 24, 1592, is published in Cuevas, *Documentos*, 440–441.

18. The description which follows is based upon cases in the viceregal archive, especially AGN-I, vols. 3 and 4, and upon Velasco II to Philip II, December 2, 1590, March 30, 1592, and February 25 and October 4, 1593, all in VC.

Indian alcaldes in cases of small moment, multiplying costs, and thus enriching himself and his notary.[19] In 1591 the Spanish officials and professional men in the same town were rebuked for seizing jurisdiction in the making and administration of Indian wills. The Spanish notaries and officials not only insisted that all wills be made before them, rather than the appropriate Indian authorities, but also, upon the death of the testators, inventoried the estates, auctioned off the personal effects of the testators, and administered the properties without regard to the provisions of the wills and without consulting the Indian executors.[20]

In a few instances of extreme proven abuse, Velasco adopted the extraordinary measure of forbidding the Spanish justices to reside in the towns they administered. They were to enter a town only for judging a case of sufficient importance to justify their asserting jurisdiction, and to leave as soon as the case was decided.[21] In less extreme instances, the viceroy was powerless to apply remedy without special royal grant of power. The punishment of governors was a judicial function, entrusted to the audiencia, and could be initiated only through formal preferment of charges or complaint during the residencia. The governors were always able to intimidate the Indians or persuade them to accept a private settlement. The only measure that the viceroy had within his armory, other than orders to reform, was removal from office—but, as he explained to the king, he was reluctant to take such extreme action lest he commit injustice.[22] A more practical consideration was probably the reflection that any extensive use of this power would have brought the Spanish settlers about his ears and have led the audiencia to cancel the removal as executive infliction of a judicial penalty without proper trial. Velasco's suggestions for reform were twofold: (1) that most of the posts of corregidor be abolished, so that Spanish royal supervision of the Indians would be by provincial governors, who could be paid higher salaries from the money saved and

19. Mexico City, August 30, 1592, in AGN-I, 4:exp. 95.

20. Mexico City, November 16, 1591, in AGN-I, 6, part 2:exp. 176. The difficulties of the Indians were made worse by disputes between the alcaldes mayores and corregidores over jurisdiction, the alcaldes mayores insisting that as provincial governors they had the right to administer justice, and the corregidores resisting with the claim that their powers as justices were equal to those of the provincial governors. On December 9, 1589, Villamanrique attempted to settle the dispute by ordering that the alcaldes mayores not attempt to administer justice within the districts of corregidores, even though these lay within their provinces. The order of Velasco II, Mexico City, August 5, 1591, repeats the ruling, with specific application to Mecatepec: AGN-I, 3:exp. 866.

21. Order to the corregidores of Zimatlán, Teutila, Nochistlán, and Huajuapan, Mexico City, October 25, 1591, in AGN-I, 5:exp. 975.

22. Velasco II to Philip II, December 2, 1590, in VC.

thus be persuaded to fleece the Indians less; and (2) that the viceroy be empowered to appoint ad hoc commissioners for secret investigations from which he could determine whether or not to replace the justice or, further, to prefer charges before the audiencia. Other suggestions for reform lay in Velasco's plans for providing more adequate legal protection for the Indians.[23]

Velasco's reports and the case records of his administration furnish a disheartening estimate of the ineffectualness of royal attempts to ease absorption of the Indians into Spanish laws and procedures.[24] By the early 1590s the possibility of preserving Indian custom to any substantial extent was gone. Velasco did not even discuss it in his reports, and the records made it abundantly clear that Indian civil litigation, criminal trials, and pleas for administrative relief were being dealt with under Spanish law and procedures. The invasions of the jurisdiction of Indian town justices by the alcaldes mayores and corregidores must have done much to hasten this process. El pleitismo indígena, Velasco found, continued unabated. The suits and administrative proceedings were paid for by levies upon the Indian peasantry, through whom mestizo solicitors, Spanish professional men, and Indian principales enriched themselves; the Indians' small funds were used up, and the communities were threatened with bankruptcy. A large proportion of legal proceedings concerned Indian communities or principales and caciques, and so were exempt from existing limitations. Furthermore, the function of providing free legal protection entrusted to the fiscal of the audiencia was not being discharged, and could not be by this already overburdened official. Necessarily the Indians turned to ordinary professional men, who evaded all efforts by crown and audiencia to limit their charges. Most startling of all, many cases were initiated without knowledge of the Indian plaintiff by self-appointed representatives, who thereby assured themselves a profitable course as agents.

Neither were attempts at simplification of judicial process successful. From Velasco's comments, it is clear that further efforts made under his predecessor, Villamanrique, to have Indian cases before the audiencia handled quickly and inexpensively, probably by decree rather than formal sentence under royal seal (provisión real),[25] had had little or no success. The reform was nullified, as were all attempts at sim-

23. Ibid. and letter of November 1, 1591, in VC.

24. The paragraphs following are based upon Velasco II to Philip II, Mexico City, June 5 and October 8, 1590, and October 29, 1591, in VC.

25. Royal cédula to the Audiencia of Mexico, San Lorenzo, May 11, 1588, in AGN-RCD, 2:exp. 330.

plification, by the grave difficulties resulting from the competition for jurisdiction between viceroy and audiencia, which reached its most acute phase in the insistence of the *escribano mayor de gobernación* and the *escribano mayor de cámara* that each prepare papers and orders. Indians seeking relief were forced to appear before both the audiencia and the viceroy, undertaking two separate proceedings, presenting two separate series of documents, and securing both a viceregal order and a judicial provisión so that there could be no challenge to the validity of the decision. Notaries, scribes, and other professional men seized the opportunity to multiply costs in the already costly duplication. All of these difficulties were made much worse by the fact that the audiencia, although claiming a jurisdiction virtually coterminous with that exercised by the viceroy in judicial affairs, was so burdened with business that for effective operation it needed at least two more judges and reorganization into two chambers.

Velasco's reports may have painted a somewhat gloomier picture than the situation warranted, for the case records of his early administration indicate that, despite protests from the audiencia, he continued to exercise jurisdiction through administrative decision in Indian disputes and complaints that clearly called for judicial decision. The following extracts of cases, all from the Mixteca in the present state of Oaxaca, are typical:

1. August 17, 1590, Mexico City. Don Felipe de Austria, cacique of Teposcolula, complains to the viceroy that he rented some houses he owns in the town of Achiutla to a mestizo, Juan Bautista, for 2 pesos a month. Bautista has not paid rent and, in addition, keeps pigs and horses, which are doing much damage to the houses. All efforts to secure redress have been unavailing, because Juan Bautista is protected by the alcalde mayor. Luis de Velasco II issues an order to the alcalde mayor of Teposcolula that the houses be vacated at once and all back rent be paid.[26]

2. January 19, 1591, Mexico City. Doña Ana de la Cueva, cacica, widow of Don Francisco de Arellano, cacique of Tecomastlahuaca, and mother of Don Hernando de la Cueva, her legitimate son, appears before the viceroy and complains that her husband left large properties in jewels, silver, horses, mules, sheep, cacao, cotton, houses, lands, and grain; but that the executors of the estate refuse an accounting. She petitions for such an accounting. Velasco issues an order to Miguel García Rengino, corregidor of Teozacoalco and *juez de resi-*

26. AGN-I, 4:exp. 933.

dencia of Alonso de Camas, former corregidor of Izpatepec, that he go to Tecomastlahuaca, examine the will, make whatever other investigation is necessary, and require the accounting petitioned for.[27]

3. October 29, 1591, Mexico City. Don Domingo Junda and Don Diego Xirdi, principales of the estancia of San Miguel Tulancingo, a sujeto of Tamazulapan, complain to the viceroy that a Spaniard, Martín Duarte, with the support of the local friars, has seized lands, built houses and corrals, and pastures many *ganado menor* (sheep, goats, or pigs). He and his servants force the Indians to work for them; the livestock ruins crops; and other damage is done to the Indians. Velasco orders the corregidor of Nochistlán to go with staff of justice to the sujeto and force Duarte within a short period of time to exhibit his titles to the land. If he has none, he and his livestock and servants are to be expelled from the sujeto; his corrals and buildings are to be torn down; and he is to be forbidden to return, under heavy penalties to be set by the corregidor. A marginal notation, dated November 28, 1591, states that the order was reissued, directed to Juan de Valverde, corregidor of Texupan, which is much nearer to Tamazulapan.[28]

4. November 9, 1591, Mexico City. The Indians of the estancia of San Cristóbal, sujeto of Coixtlahuaca, petition the viceroy, stating that Archbishop Moya de Contreras, as viceroy, granted them an *estancia de ganado menor*, where they now pasture 460 sheep, the profits being used to support their friars and poor and to meet other community expenses. But the Indians of the barrio of Octla, claiming a share in the land and sheep, want to sell them, causing suits and quarrels. The Indians of San Cristóbal ask the viceroy for an order forbidding the sale. Velasco orders the corregidor of Coixtlahuaca to investigate and report to the viceroy, including in his report a recommendation on what the decision should be.[29]

5. November 13, 1591, Mexico City. Don José de Mendoza, a principal of Sayula in the province of Yanhuitlán, states that when his father, Don Gonzalo de Mendoza, died, he willed 400 pesos to his younger son, Esteban, and the rest of his property to Don José as an entailed estate. Now evil persons are trying to challenge the will for their own profit. He petitions the viceroy for an order of amparo to avoid costly litigation. Velasco orders the alcalde mayor of Yanhuitlán to investigate and, if the circumstances are as alleged, to protect Don José, but without prejudice to the interests of a third party.[30]

27. Ibid., 5:exp. 125.
29. Ibid., 5:exp. 1030.

28. Ibid., 6, part 2:exp. 111.
30. Ibid., 6, part 2:exp. 158.

Velasco, like his predecessors in the viceregal palace, was exercising the unified and special executive Indian jurisdiction begun by Antonio de Mendoza. That he had substantial success is evident from the number and variety of cases that the Indians brought before him. In asserting its own claims, the audiencia was resisting what might with good reason have been regarded as executive invasion of the judicial sphere. All of these cases summarized above, had they been between Spaniards alone, would have had to be resolved by judicial process. Whatever the respective merits of the dispute over jurisdiction, nevertheless, the conflict between the two highest authorities in the colony nullified a substantial measure of the benefit that the Indians should have derived from the special executive jurisdiction. It opened the way for duplication of legal process, extortion by lawyers and other professional men, weakening of the checks upon provincial governors, and failure to observe the reforms officially adopted in judicial procedures.

The situation clearly needed remedy, and had for decades. Velasco proposed his solution in two letters.[31] Writing on June 5, 1590, he urged that the legal assistance supposed to be furnished the Indians by the fiscal be provided through appointment of a special *defensor de los indios*, who should be sole attorney for the natives in all cases, regardless of the monetary values involved. No petition or complaint of an Indian should be received unless it was prepared and presented by this official. The defender should be charged to try to reach settlements by negotiation rather than by suit wherever possible, thus substantially reducing the inconvenience and cost to the natives, even if they suffered some injustice without full remedy. Furthermore, the defender should be paid a salary to be raised through a small per-capita tax on the Indians. A similar system already existed in other areas of the Indies, notably Peru, which had Indian defenders in each of the Spanish towns and provincial capitals who were paid from the proceeds of a special tax and furnished legal advice and assistance to the Indians without additional charges.[32] Establishing a similar office of defender of the Indians in New Spain, although Velasco urged it only for Mexico City, would solve the two problems of providing adequate legal assistance and ending the exactions of solicitors and other professional men.

In a second letter of October 8, 1590, Velasco completed his proposals for ending the conflict over jurisdiction in Indian cases, duplication of process, and costly, prolonged litigation. It need hardly surprise anyone, and probably did not at the time, that his further pro-

31. VC.
32. On this point, see also Velasco II to Philip II, El Callao, May 2, 1599, in GP, 14:153–154.

posal urged that the crown confirm the special, unified, executive jurisdiction of the viceroy in such terms that there could be no further challenge to it. The viceroy, he urged, should be given jurisdiction in first instance in all civil cases affecting Indians, whether they concerned the relations of Indians with each other or the relations between Indians and Spaniards. The viceroy could handle the cases by administrative procedure with far fewer investigations, far less need for formal presentation of evidence and replies, and far fewer postponements and delays than resulted from judicial procedure. Accustomed as they already were to viceregal decisions embodied in brief orders, the Indians would accept an administrative order as a proper solution. Appeals from the viceroy's decisions could be taken to the audiencia, which could hear them and render decision by summary process. A similar type of procedure, already in use in the special court for the property of people dying intestate or with heirs in the Peninsula (*juzgado de bienes de difuntos*) was working very well. Velasco urged on behalf of his proposal that it would go far to end the burden of costs upon the Indians and would furnish quick, simple legal remedy.

These proposals, if adopted, meant that the special Indian jurisdiction of the viceroy would have a wider sphere than it had had under Mendoza. The only area of Spanish law affecting the Indians that Velasco did not propose to place within viceregal jurisdiction was the judgment of criminal cases. (The ecclesiastical jurisdiction, of course, always remained apart, governed by canon law and administered by the episcopate and special Church tribunals.) Vested with unified jurisdiction, the viceroy could hear all complaints against subordinate government officials and thus prevent or correct abuse by Spanish provincial and town governors without interference from the audiencia. On Indian petition, he could take cognizance of provincial cases, removing them from the court of the provincial or town governor whenever he agreed that there was undue delay or refusal of justice. Velasco's request for unhampered power of secret investigation of alcaldes mayores and corregidores, mentioned above, was made in a letter of December 12, 1590, soon after his second letter on Indian suits, and represented a further development of his ideas for strengthening the viceregal jurisdiction as the means for more adequate legal remedies for the Indians.

Customarily under Spanish procedures, the consideration of Velasco's proposals by the Council of the Indies and Philip II should have taken a number of years, since they embodied changes that adversely affected very substantial vested interests in the colony. But the imperial government had had decades of complaint and debate about the worsening plight of the Indians in New Spain and Peru, decades during which it had groped to provide adequate legal remedies. Its thinking may be inferred from a royal order of June 4, 1586, embodied later in the Laws of the Indies, that Indian suits and petitions of small moment be handled by both viceroys and audiencias by decree and not by formal sentences, to avoid expense to the natives.[33] It was further evident in a stiff royal order of December 29, 1593, complaining to the Audiencia of Mexico that offenses of Spaniards against Indians were punished lightly, if at all, compared to the punishments meted out to Spaniards for offenses against fellow Spaniards, and ordering that in the future offenses against the Indians by Spaniards be dealt with more harshly than those against Spaniards.[34] The thinking of king and council was evident also in the fact that the formal documents embodying the royal reply were dated April 9, 1591, only a few weeks after Velasco's second and third letters reached Madrid.

On the whole, the imperial government was prepared to grant more rather than less of what Velasco proposed. His suggestion for a salaried defender of the Indians was accepted, but expanded to include a salaried *letrado* and attorney. They were to be the sole legal agents to intervene in Indian cases. Indians were to be freed from payment of all fees whatever, without need to prove poverty; the only exceptions were to be Indian towns and caciques, who might be charged half the fees provided in the schedule for Spaniards. The only point on which the imperial government gave less was the request that all suits in first instance between Indians and Spaniards be placed under the viceroy's jurisdiction, for such a measure meant that the Europeans in the colony would be deprived of the protection of ordinary legal process and would be made subject to demands for redress under summary procedure. It would have been a major breach of the still-prevailing medieval rule that the plaintiff must sue in the court and under the law of the defendant. The proposal was too drastic and dangerous for a government whose rule in the colony depended upon the upper class of Europeans and whose major defense against riot, uprising, and invasion lay in the service of the Europeans as militia. Accordingly, the royal answer embodied a compromise: that suits of Spaniards against Indians come before the viceroy, but that the Indians continue to sue Spaniards in the ordinary tribunals. Both king and council must have been aware that a very large proportion, perhaps the majority, of Indian cases consisted of complaints against Spaniards, and further that the extent to which the ordinary tribunals would pay attention to injunctions for judging such Indian cases by summary process was prob-

33. RLI, 2.4.85. The order probably was directed to Peru.

34. Montemayor y Córdova de Cuenca, 1:fol. 215r, sum. 38; AGN-RCD, 103:fol. 42r–v. The formal act of obedience is dated Mexico City, October 10, 1594.

lematical at best. One may detect, too, a willingness to concede elements already embodied in the reforms of Francisco de Toledo in Peru, their existence and functioning in the other viceroyalty constituting a defense against charges of innovation.

The decisions of the crown were embodied in a royal order and a royal letter, both dated April 9, 1591, and both addressed to Luis de Velasco II.[35] These constitute the formal legal basis for the General Indian Court of New Spain, preserved as such in the registers of the secretariats of viceroy and audiencia, and consulted whenever question arose later. The order, after reciting the difficulties caused by the competition over jurisdiction, formally vested the viceroy with judicial power over Indian suits:

> I command that henceforth he who is or may be my viceroy of the said New Spain may take cognizance in first instance of any manner of suits that may arise among the said Indians, suits of Indians with other Indians, and also suits between Spaniards and Indians in which the said Indians are defendants; for when the Indians are plaintiffs, it is my will that they sue before the ordinary justices or before my royal audiencia as is done at present. Whatever my said viceroy may provide or decide in the said suits may be appealed to the said audiencia, which shall take cognizance of the suits in second instance, the hearing by the said viceroy counting as judgment in first instance.

The accompanying letter gave a much fuller statement of the royal intent. After repeating the content of the royal order, it authorized the appointment of salaried legal counselors for Indians, gave explicit instructions on fees, and ordered a further abridgment in executive process:[36]

> And since, furthermore, I understand that the welfare of the said Indians requires that they have a protector-defender, a letrado, and an attorney to present and further their causes, you shall search for and appoint qualified persons worthy of being entrusted with a duty of such importance. You shall set for them ample and proper salaries to be paid from fines [penas de estrados] or through levy on the Indian community treasuries as you deem better. You shall order that [the new officials] may in no wise charge fees, under heavy penalties that you shall set, and you shall instruct them in writing of their duties.

35. The text of the royal cédula and excerpts from the royal letter may be found in AGN-RCD, 103: fols. 160v–161v; this is a transcription made in 1637. The text of this cédula and the instructions on Indian cases were incorporated into a royal cédula of December 12, 1619, Madrid, extending the Juzgado de Indios system to the Philippines. The text of the 1619 cédula is printed in Viñas Mey, 325–328.

36. The translation has been paragraphed in order to make clear the topics treated.

Since, moreover, in securing documents and sentences for administrative matters, and even for judicial ones, the Indians suffer long delays which cause them expense and other hardships, you shall order that Indian affairs be settled by decree alone, signed by you personally and countersigned by the notary. Such decrees shall have legal force and be executed as though they were formal sentences under royal seal.

No notary of the administrative or judicial sphere, nor any other, may charge nor shall charge fees of the said Indians, nor shall relatores or attorneys; save only that caciques, principales, and Indian towns may be held to pay fees at one-half the rates charged Spaniards as the rates are established in the schedules.

You shall order also that when suits between Indians are heard by the audiencia, the fiscal shall serve as advocate for one party and the protector, letrado, and attorney shall serve the other.

You shall see to it also that the corregidores and alcaldes mayores, without permitting the said Indians to leave their lands, forward the papers and documents of suits and disputes to the said protector or to my fiscal of the said audiencia for appropriate hearing. When the cases have been heard, the decisions shall be sent to the said corregidores and alcaldes mayores.

You shall take very special care to report to me what is done to carry out these commands.[37]

The letter further gave Velasco his sought-for authorization to carry out investigations of subordinate officials without interference from the audiencia. He might carry out investigations publicly or secretly. He might collect information in any other way on abuses by corregidores, justices, and other officials and legal agents, most especially on abuses against Indians. For these purposes, he might appoint special judges or investigators. If the investigation disclosed any probabilities of guilt, the audiencia was to try the case; but the viceroy, notwithstanding, was to apply any appropriate administrative remedies at his discretion.[38] Again, the royal grant of power was more ample than Velasco had requested. With the power to investigate and appoint special judges without reference to the audiencia, the viceregal jurisdiction had a powerful weapon for curbing abuses by provincial officials and the notarial and legal professions. Only the judges of the audiencia were exempt from the new authorization.

37. The importance of these instructions is shown by the fact that, in addition to the accompaying royal cédula, the section on handling Indian cases by decree, amplified in 1619 to apply to all Spanish America and the Philippines, was incorporated in the RLI: the royal cédula of 1591 is in 3.3.65, the quoted section of the letter in 5.10.12.

38. Montemayor y Córdova de Cuenca, 1:fol. 157v, sum. 6. I infer that this summary of a paragraph of a letter to the Viceroy of New Spain, Madrid, April 9, 1591, is another part of the letter containing instructions on the Juzgado General de Indios.

The royal order and letter arrived in Mexico City in the late spring or early summer of 1591. On July 17, 1591, the audiencia, in the first measure of compliance with the royal will, adopted a drastic revision of the fees that might be charged Indians by its doormen.[39] On September 28, 1591, Velasco acknowledged receipt in a letter which expressed his very great pleasure at the royal decision and his hope for substantial benefit to the Indians. Nevertheless, he wrote, he felt forced to advise the king that the limitation of his new judicial power in cases involving Spaniards to those in which Indians were defendants would seriously reduce the benefit, for Indians seldom were defendants. They usually were the victims of invasions and seizures of their houses and lands by Spaniards and others, so that they were the ones who had to seek redress by petition or suit. Therefore, the viceroy should be given complete jurisdiction in first instance for all suits to which Indians were parties, whether as defendants or plaintiffs. The viceroy further detected a flaw that must have been an oversight of king and council or the secretaries who drafted the orders: the fiscal was to represent one side in Indian disputes before the audiencia, but the instructions neglected to charge him with the same function for the hearings in first instance before the viceroy. While waiting for the royal reply on his request for revision, Velasco continued, he would, in consultation with the audiencia, appoint the new Indian agents, assign salaries, and prepare rules for the dispatch of Indian affairs.[40] In another letter dated a few days later, November 1, 1591, the viceroy expressed his pleasure at his new investigative powers, which would serve as an effective restraint upon abuses by subordinate officials and legal agents.[41]

Velasco proceeded rapidly with organization of the new court. Consultations and investigations must have occupied a good deal of his time for the next three months. He decided initially to appoint two agents for Indian affairs: an attorney-general for Indians (*procurador general de indios*) who would serve as advocate and defender, and an assessor who would serve as adviser in judicial hearings. Both appointments were to be additional ones: that is, they went to people already holding posts, who agreed to discharge the added functions for an additional salary. Of the two appointments, that of assessor was by far the more important, since without advice from a *letrado* the

39. Ibid., 2:fol. 35r, auto 95. Indian commoners were not to pay the doormen anything; caciques and principales appearing on their personal cases were to pay 1 real for each presentation, new petition, or appearance; Indian towns were to pay 3 reales in similar circumstances, half what had been charged previously.

40. VC, fols. 100v–101v.

41. Ibid., fol. 105r.

viceroys, who were normally *gente de capa y espada* rather than *gente de toga*, could not function as judges. In practice, the assessor was the judge, the viceroy signing findings and decisions prepared for him.

The General Indian Court came into existence as a functioning court with the appointment of the assessor. Velasco chose as assessor Dr. Luis de Villanueva Zapata, a judge of the audiencia who had held appointment since 1560. Although he had been under suspension twice for conduct unbecoming a judge, he enjoyed royal favor even in his disgrace and had served without serious complaint since 1582. Holding the degree of doctor of law as well as *licenciado*, he was well trained in law; equally, through long residence and service in Mexico,[42] he was well acquainted with Indian problems. His salary for the additional function of assessor was set at 1,000 *pesos de minas* (coins of fine gold, but in New Spain essentially money of account). In the silver pesos of circulation, the salary came to 1,654/3/4. As attorney-general for the Indians, Velasco chose Pedro Díaz de Agüero, who was probably an abogado practicing before the audiencia. He was assigned 700 silver pesos a year. Both of the new officials were stringently forbidden to ask for or accept fees or gifts from the Indians. Their formal appointments were dated February 4, 1592.[43]

That same day, Velasco signed an ordinance making public the royal instructions; announcing the appointment of Indian legal agents; prohibiting charging Indians legal fees except for caciques, principales, and communities, who were to pay at half the official schedule; and requiring the use of simple decrees instead of sentences in Indian affairs. Justices, notaries, relatores, and secretaries in Mexico City and the provinces, including the viceregal secretaries of administration, were to be bound by the new order. The prohibition against charging fees even extended to the notaries and court officers under Church jurisdiction. That last prohibition, although certainly in the spirit of the royal instructions, might have been stretching the precise wording. The ordinance was proclaimed in Mexico City by town

42. Schäfer, 2:452. Villanueva Zapata was a canon of the cathedral chapter of Mexico City, during one of his suspensions, until marriage disqualified him for the post: Archbishop Moya de Contreras to the king, Mexico City, November 6, 1576, in Paso y Troncoso, 12:21. On the problems of corruption in the Spanish audiencias and the mildness of punishment, see Phelan, *The Kingdom of Quito*, 147–214. The first suspension by Valderrama, the visitador-general sent out from Spain, probably had a political basis, since when Villanueva Zapata and Vasco de Puga were both suspended and shipped to Spain, they were sent back promptly to Mexico with a peremptory royal command that the next visitador-general, Múñoz, return at once: Torquemada, 1:636–637 (lib. 5, cap. 20).

43. AGN-RCD, vol. 3. Díaz de Agüero's is exp. 156 and Villanueva Zapata's is exp. 159.

crier on March 2, 1592. To make sure that it was brought to the attention of Indians and officials throughout the realm, Velasco had it printed in broadside and distributed to corregidores, alcaldes mayores, and other Spanish justices. It was to be proclaimed in the Indian towns in the native tongues.[44]

This first ordinance was supplemented by additional ones signed in the last days of February, proclaimed also on March 2, 1592, and, as appropriate, also sent to the provinces. One reinforced the prohibition against charging Indians fees by forbidding any person, trained lawyer or not, to act as advocate, agent, or solicitor in royal or Church courts, whether civil or criminal, in disputes and offenses of Indians against Indians or of Indians and Spaniards. All cases in process were to be halted for future handling by the new royal officials. In the future, suits between Indians were to be dealt with through representation of one side by the new officials and on the other by the fiscal of the audiencia. Penalties for violation were stiff: suspension from office, fine of 500 pesos, and fourfold return of fees paid by the Indians.[45]

A second order, directed to all provincial justices, corregidores, and the municipal judges of the city of Mexico, forbade them to hear any Indian cases whatever, even if Spaniards, mulattos, and other non-Indians were also involved as plaintiffs. All suits pending were to be halted. Civil ones were to go to the viceroy for hearing; criminal ones to the *sala del crimen* of the audiencia. No fees of any kind were to be charged except for caciques, principales, and communities, who were to be charged at half the schedule for Spaniards. Provincial justices and those of Mexico City might continue to hear cases in which Indians were plaintiffs against Spaniards, but no attorney or agent in the audiencia or the provinces might intervene in the case on behalf of the Indians. That function was to be discharged by the royal agents. The justices were equally bound to the new rules on fees from Indians, and notified further that they were not to accept gifts, food, or service.[46]

A third ordinance dealt with the role of interpreters and further defined the prohibition against acting as solicitor. It ordered the interpreters of the audiencia to serve monthly turns in Indian cases without fees from ordinary Indians and only fees at half the Spanish schedule in the permitted categories. They might not accept gifts of any kind from anyone. They were to interpret exactly without influencing the

44. AGN-O, 2:305r–306r. The text is published in Zavala, *Ordenanzas*, 273–275.
45. Mexico City, February 28, 1592, in AGI-M, leg. 22; calendared in HM, 2:122, as no. 72-B.
46. Mexico City, February 29, 1592, in AGI-M, leg. 22; calendared in HM, 2:122, as no. 72-C.

Indians, nor might they give help in preparing papers or the pictorial manuscripts of Indian usage. In no way might they act as solicitors. Penalties for violation of the terms of the ordinance were set at loss of office, exile from the city and its territory to a distance of 10 leagues, and forfeit for the royal treasury of fourfold the money or value of other gifts or payments. The network of prohibition was reinforced by inclusion of a clause forbidding anyone to act as solicitor in Indian cases. Again, penalties for violation were stiff: ten years' exile from the colony for Spaniards; for mestizos, mulattos, and Indians, 100 lashes and five years' exile from the district.[47]

A fourth ordinance, dated May 12, 1592, and distributed as a broadside to the provinces, dealt with yet another major abuse. It ordered corregidores, alcaldes mayores, and all Spanish justices not to permit Indian town governments to levy derramas on their commoners for costs of suits or any other improper purpose.[48]

An absolute embargo on airing Indian cases at provincial level would have meant that the viceroy would be flooded with more petitions and complaints than he and his staff could handle. Some means of selection limiting the flow was imperative. Another ordinance issued in March 1592, directed to the justices of New Spain, laid down the terms. The purpose was to prevent unnecessary suits and to allow suits of small value to be heard in local courts and so avoid need for Indians to come to Mexico City. Each alcalde mayor, corregidor, or other Spanish justice was to buy a book, at the expense of the Indian communities, for his notary to record all civil Indian suits to a value of 10 silver pesos, even if concerning land. He was to hear such suits by summary executive process, recording his judgment on the margin. The procedures and rules were to apply to cases among Indians, of Indian against Spaniard, or Spaniard against Indian, so long as the value was 10 pesos or less. If the suit of a Spaniard against an Indian involved a value over 10 pesos, it was to be sent to the viceroy for decision. Suits among Indians, or of Spaniards against Indians, to the value of 100 silver pesos were to be decided locally by judicial process, but no more than five witnesses were to be allowed to each side and all proceedings were to be expeditious. Suits of a value over 100 pesos, and those concerning boundaries, agricultural land, wasteland, and the dependence of one community on another (i.e., between cabecera and sujeto over relationship), were to be heard by normal judicial process, but the Indians were to be represented by the new royal agents for Indians without intervention on their behalf of other advocates or

47. Ibid. The ordinance is probably that calendared under February 20, 1592, in HM, 2:122, as no. 72-A.

48. Medina, *La imprenta*, 1:290–291.

agents. If the local court was at too great a distance from Mexico City for the new agents to appear, the local justice was to appoint an intelligent, trustworthy person to serve in the specific case.

If the case was of a cacique, principal, or community, the court-appointed attorney might charge fees in accordance with the new rules; otherwise, his fees were to come from the receipts of justice (i.e., fines and court-retained costs). The justices were not to permit lengthy hearings, new petitions, new suit once decision was reached and recorded, derramas, nor the intervention of unauthorized persons. Caciques, principales, and communities might be charged fees at the rate of half the Spanish schedule, but no more, and anyone charging more was liable to return it fourfold. No solicitors, attorneys, or other agents were to be allowed among the Indians, nor might any outsider draw up petitions or prepare pictorial manuscripts of complaint or testimony. If any did, they were to be prosecuted by the justices.[49] This ordinance thus both regulated the exercise of jurisdiction by local justices in cases involving Indians which were assigned to them by the royal instructions, and returned part of the jurisdiction newly vested in the viceroy. Even with the proposed limitation and sifting of cases and petitions going to the viceroy, the volume was certain to be considerable, and the burden on him and his staff accordingly heavy.

The extent to which the new set of regulations applied to hearings before ecclesiastical courts is another aspect worth noticing. To inhibit such courts from hearing cases clearly within their jurisdiction would have been beyond the competence of the viceroy and, if attempted with the royal consent, might have unleashed a dispute that ultimately would have reached the papacy. It is unlikely that the regulations contemplated any such invasion. The most likely interpretation is that the viceroy forbade charging of fees by the apostolic notaries—for the Church licensed its own—and in any hearings by Church courts. Presumably Indians appearing before Church courts would be represented by the new royal officials without fee. That in turn raised the question of the ability of the small new staff to represent clients in dioceses away from Mexico City.

Sometime in February 1592 the General Indian Court held its first sessions. Within a few weeks, Velasco was able to organize regular operation. The customary times of viceregal audience for Indian affairs—Monday and Wednesday mornings and Friday afternoons—were allocated to the court. The sessions were attended by the assessor, attorney-general for Indians, secretaries for judicial and administrative affairs, and notaries of the two branches. Indian petitions for

49. AGN-M, leg. 22; calendared in HM, 2:122, as no. 72-D.

executive redress and complaints in suits within the royal limits were brought to the viceroy either by Indians in person or by the appointed officials, and were handled by summary hearing. They terminated either in an order for relief or one to an appropriate official for investigation and report so that the viceroy might issue the proper order. Written transactions and records were minimal, since the viceregal order was written on the same folio as the petition or complaint.[50] The one defect, according to Velasco's successor, was that the folio was turned over to the Indian petitioner for his use or for presentation to the Spanish official, if an order to investigate, without being copied into a central register.[51]

In his letter of June 15, 1592, Velasco reported to Philip II that the benefit of the new system was already evident, for the Indians were spared the exactions of interpreters, solicitors, attorneys, notaries, and others who had battened on them. They were also being spared the scourge of derramas. The new arrangement, he commented, was one of the best things that the king had done for the realm, adding slyly that the benefit would be even greater when the king granted the viceroy jurisdiction over cases in which Indians as plaintiffs sued non-Indians.

Velasco did not conceal the fact that there was considerable difficulty in getting the court to function. Trouble came with the first days of the court, for, since it was both judicial and administrative, the secretaries for judicial and executive affairs both had to be present. Their rivalry and disputes, which included their respective officials and notaries, over which group should dispatch what business forced the viceroy to appoint a special notary until at least temporary agreement could be reached.[52] Within a few weeks he arranged an uneasy peace through his suggestion that each group dispatch business clearly within its jurisdiction and that matters claimed by both be handled in alternation; but Velasco himself saw that the dispute might erupt anew at any moment. Behind it lay claims to fees or to compensation in lieu of them, but perhaps also the normal element of bureaucratic rivalry.[53]

As Velasco's reports for the remaining years of his first administration reveal at some length, there was substantial opposition to the

50. Velasco II to Philip II, Mexico City, March 6 and June 15, 1592, in VC, fols. 111v–112v and 130r–131v respectively. The March 6 letter is printed in Cuevas, *Documentos*, 435–438, with the marginal notations of the Council of the Indies and Philip II; that of June 15 is in ibid., 445–448, under the date of June 2, 1592.

51. Clause 6, report of Monterrey to Philip II on the General Indian Court, Mexico City, April 15, 1598, in AGI-M, leg. 24.

52. Letter of March 6, 1592, in VC and in Cuevas, *Documentos*, pp. 435–438.

53. Letter of June 15, 1592, in VC.

new system, both in Mexico City and in the provinces. The root of the opposition lay in the interdiction on levying fees and costs. A very large part, in many instances the bulk, of the income of officials, notaries, scribes, and lawyers came from fees and costs, which were either abolished or sharply curtailed by the reforms. The complaints had a very large measure of justice in that most of the officials, agents, and notaries had bought their offices from the crown at prices calculated in part upon the revenues which were now forbidden. If holding official commission, moreover, they were now ordered to serve without fee and without compensation of any kind.

Protests began as soon as the royal instructions were known. They came from virtually all groups of fee officials and professional men: the secretaries of administrative affairs; those of the judicial secretariats, both civil and criminal; the officials charged with placing the royal seal on documents; those charged with registering them; the letrados, relatores, and other attorneys admitted to practice before the audiencia; the notaries in Mexico City, the provincial capitals, and the Indian towns. All pointed out that the new regulations invaded vested interests confirmed by payment to the crown. Even the interpreters complained that their livelihood, equally secured by custom and payment to the crown, was being tampered with. Velasco duly relayed the complaints to Madrid; probably they were sent privately as well. They found no welcome on the part of the Council of the Indies and Philip II, who were adamant that the regulations be enforced. Velasco, who was not protected from the clamor by an ocean, was inclined to restore the levy of fees by public notaries in Indian towns, since the value of their offices was seriously impaired. In urging that view on the crown, he made the interesting but not impressive additional argument that such fees need not be paid by the Indians, since they had available the easy remedy of a viceregal hearing rather than attempting litigation in their own towns. But the imperial government insisted that the notaries in Indian towns, too, must abide by the new instructions, and that furthermore there was to be no compensation for the very real loss suffered.[54]

The remedy decided upon eventually was to let the posts lapse as they fell vacant.[55] That decision included all posts as chief constable in Indian towns, even though they were readily salable to Spaniards.[56]

---

54. Ibid. and letter of March 6, 1592, in VC; Cuevas, *Documentos*, pp. 435–438. See also below.

55. Velasco II to Philip II, Mexico City, October 4, 1593, in VC, fols. 145v–146v; also in AGI-M, leg. 22 (BLT), with the marginal notations of the Council of the Indies and Philip II.

56. Velasco II to Philip II, Mexico City, May 20, 1592, in VC, fol. 123v.

The resolution represented a considerable sacrifice for a government which was then facing the third bankruptcy of the reign.

Attorneys in the provinces had less legal ground for complaint, since they were barred from handling Indian suits in the provincial courts,[57] although they would have less legal business in future. Accordingly, whatever protests they made were ignored. Attorneys attached to the audiencia, on the other hand, since they did handle Indian suits, had a just complaint that they were being deprived of value they had paid for. On their petition, the audiencia ordered that the viceroy refund to each attorney 400 silver pesos of the price paid for his office. Rather than comply, the viceroy offered to buy back the offices at the original price paid. When the posts of the first two attorneys to complain brought in a new auction as much as the original price, despite the claimed loss of fees, the other attorneys dropped their demands for compensation.[58]

The major difficulty, and one not so easily settled, lay in the claims of the secretaries of gobernación and cámara that they were suffering serious losses of revenue and were being held to a very large amount of work without compensation. The rivalry between the two branches arose essentially because of competition for fees, and continued after the abolition of fees in Indian matters because of the hope that there would be either restoration of fees, legally or illegally, or substantial compensation. Without the cooperation of the secretaries, the new system could not function. This consideration probably moved the viceroy as much as the justice of the claims. In consultation with the audiencia, Velasco decided to assign 1,000 silver pesos a year to each of the two secretaries of gobernación and 650 each to the two secretaries of cámara. As part of the compromise, he imposed the condition that all fees from Indians be waived, including those the royal instructions permitted levying on caciques, principales, and towns, on the ground that permission to levy any fee opened a loophole for extortion. This condition represented a violation of explicit instructions from the crown, although he undoubtedly was right about the probability of extortion. The compromise was made somewhat more palatable to the hard-pressed imperial government by the statement that the grant was for the life of the incumbents. For its part, the crown, while insisting that its instructions on fees must be enforced without modification one way or the other, reluctantly accepted the principle of compensation for the secretaries.[59] The arrangement added four more officials to the roster of the new Indian agents. They and their

57. Velasco's letter of June 15, 1592.
58. Velasco II to Philip II, Mexico City, February 25, 1593, in VC, fol. 143v.
59. Velasco letters of June 15, 1592, and October 4, 1593, as cited above; Mon-

successors remained there for the rest of the colonial regime; for compensation, once granted, could not be withdrawn without serious impairment of service.

By June 1592 there were at least six Indian agents for whose salaries some kind of revenue had to be found. Their number steadily rose in the next months, as other officials demanded and received compensation. They included at least two subordinate attorneys (*procuradores*) for Indians at 400 silver pesos each a year, a relator at 200, a receptor or treasurer (a new fiscal officer) at 300; a solicitor at 300, an interpreter at 300, a special notary at 400 pesos, and a bailiff (*alguacil*) at 250. In addition, the complaints of the audiencia officials in charge of seal and registry were assuaged by assigning 135 pesos a year to the one and 120 to the other. The sum of salaries was far beyond what the treasury fund from fines and the royal share of court costs could possibly meet.[60] For that matter, royal grants on it already far exceeded receipts. In the royal instructions, the alternative source indicated was an assessment on the community treasuries of the Indian towns, which were in better position to bear such expenses. Even in regard to them there were difficulties, since at this time the imperial government had ordered a special additional levy of tribute at the rate of half a silver peso annually from each adult male, and the Indian community treasuries were being tapped for the expenses of the program of congregación,[61] then entering a massive phase that was to culminate in resettlement of a substantial portion of the Indian population within a decade and a half. Nevertheless, the Indian community treasuries were the best source of funds within Velasco's reach.

Each Indian tributary, defined as a married adult male, paid a silver peso and a fanega of maize a year, plus a newly added half-peso of additional *servicio* for the crown in its financial difficulties, or equivalent amounts in commodities. Further, each whole tributary paid as a general rule 2 reales a year for community expenses. Half-tributaries—i.e., widows, widowers, and single adults—paid at half these rates. Velasco proposed that the royal treasury appropriate a half-real of the community contribution of each whole tributary, and half of that for half-tributaries, to cover the costs of the system of Indian agents. The first levy of the half-real for Indian agents (*medio real*

temayor y Córdova de Cuenca, 1 : fol. 181v, sum. 2, repeating the instructions on fees in two royal cédulas of 1605 and 1608.

60. Velasco II to Philip II, Mexico City, April 6, 1595, in VC, fols. 189v–190f; Díez de la Calle, 116–117, 122, and 126–127. The receptor or treasurer at 300/ appears only in Díez de la Calle.

61. Velasco II to Philip II, Mexico City, March 20 and 25 and May 20, 1592, in VC, fols. 116r–117r, 117v–118r, and 120r–v.

de ministros) was made in 1592,[62] and clearly was tied to the appointment of a treasurer. On April 13, 1595, the levy was confirmed in a
general order to Spanish provincial and town governors that they
make sure that the half-real was collected and forwarded to Mexico
City. They were strictly charged to see that no extra sums were collected and that, again, no fees were charged Indians for legal papers
and actions, since the half-real was to defray all such costs and pay for
rapid legal remedy.[63] In another circular of the same date, Velasco
asked the prelates of New Spain (since it would have been improper to
command the members of the First Estate) to charge their clergy to
keep watch over enforcement of the order. They were to see to it especially that the Indians paid only the taxes strictly due, that local justices charged them no fees, and that the justices complied with injunctions that the Indians use the services of the new Indian agents.[64] The
medio real de ministros was thenceforth a fund within the royal treasury, collected regularly each year. Contrary to Velasco's intention and
express injunction, it usually became an additional levy beyond the
contribution for community expenses.[65]

Thus far we have examined the development of the Juzgado
General de Indios as a court within the terms of the royal instruction
of 1591. Questions of fees and disputes over jurisdiction were to en-
large its powers very substantially. The royal order and instruction
gave the viceroy partial jurisdiction in civil suits, but in its express denial of jurisdiction over civil suits in which Indians sued non-Indians
ignored the fact that the limitation easily could be evaded by re-
classification, and had been almost from the beginning of Spanish rule
in Mexico. Ever since the time of Mendoza, the viceroys of New Spain
had handled as administrative matters a wide range of Indian complaints that, if they had been brought by Spaniards against other Spaniards, would have been held to be civil suits.[66] In the new General Indian Court, Velasco continued to issue executive orders requiring
restitution to Indians for extortion by Spaniards, official and private;

62. Velasco's letter of March 6, 1592, as cited above.
63. AGN-I, 6, part 1: exp. 993.
64. Ibid., exp. 994.
65. See discussion later in this chapter.
66. The point was made very clear in the appeal of the *secretario de gobernación*
attached to the governor of Yucatan, who exercised far wider powers than most provincial governors. The secretario, claiming that the prohibition against fees applied only to
judicial matters, appealed to the Audiencia of Mexico, pointing out that there was no
official schedule in Yucatan applicable to administrative proceedings and, further, that
Spaniards did not apply for executive orders of the types sought by Indians: Velasco II
to Philip II, Mexico City, September 28, 1591, in VC, fols. 100v–101v.

expelling Spaniards from lands seized from Indians; and exacting compensation forthwith for damages to Indian crops by Spanish-owned livestock.

Perhaps the most hotly contested exercise of executive determination was in Indian cases involving so-called voluntary agreements to serve Spaniards in textile workshops (*obrages*), farms, mines, and households—cases arising from the debt peonage which by then was the main reliance of the Europeans for securing labor. Velasco ordered that disputes involving such agreements come before him. His order met immediate protest from the corregidor of Mexico City, who claimed that he had been vested by express royal order with jurisdiction over such cases within the municipal territory. His claim must have been made to the viceroy a few weeks after formal inauguration of the General Indian Court. Notwithstanding the royal order, Velasco continued to hear demands of Indians for release from debt service. In his report to the king, he explained that the corregidor's hearings were not carried out with zeal for the interests of the Indians; that the Indians were easily persuaded to confess that they owed the money claimed, and were willing to work off the debt without careful investigation by the corregidor to determine the facts. Furthermore, the corregidor and his subordinates collected heavy fees from both the Spanish and Indians. (These were understatements, for the corregidor undoubtedly worked hand-in-glove with the Spanish residents.) Cases over debt peonage, concluded Velasco, were so important to the well-being of the Indians that he wished to deal with them himself, despite the royal grant of jurisdiction to the corregidor.[67] His report was couched in terms which were certain to incite the sympathy of king and council. That the crown confirmed his exercise of executive jurisdiction in such matters may be inferred from the facts that not only did Velasco continue to hear cases of debt peonage, but also that they were one of the major forms of Indian business brought before the viceroys throughout the colonial period.

A much stiffer battle arose over the viceroy's invasion of the sphere of the *alcaldes del crimen*, who despite their name exercised civil as well as criminal jurisdiction in first instance for the audiencia. These alcaldes also protested the viceroy's exercise of jurisdiction in cases of debt service on the ground that they were civil disputes and, if the Indians complained, clearly suits in which the Indians were plain-

---

67. Letter of June 15, 1592, as cited above. The claim of the corregidor may have been based upon the royal grant of jurisdiction by the empress regent, acting for Charles V, Madrid, October 3, 1539, preserved in the RLI, 4.8.3. Although Indian cases were expressly reserved to the viceroy and audiencia, suits by Indians against Spaniards would have fallen within Spanish municipal jurisdiction.

tiffs and non-Indians defendants. They also protested all other forms of executive decision by which the viceroy handled complaints by Indians against Spaniards. All of these, the alcaldes held—and with good legal basis—were civil disputes to be settled by civil suit and judicial determination in the ordinary courts. Further, the viceroy was invading their criminal jurisdiction, for like his predecessors he continued to punish by executive order mistreatment and exactions by principales, caciques, and officials of Indian towns. The alcaldes del crimen were so infuriated that they took the extraordinary measure of complaining to Philip II without submitting the letter to the viceroy for signature in his capacity as president of the audiencia, and without informing him that a letter was being sent.[68]

Velasco's dispute with the alcaldes del crimen was complicated by the fact that the royal instruction on Indian fees applied equally to those in criminal cases. The secretaries for criminal justice and other officials serving under the alcaldes del crimen thus found themselves threatened with the same loss of revenue that had aroused other fee officials. They protested vigorously, making their protest public by not attending hearings of Indian criminal cases. Admitting that their complaints were justified, and recognizing that their refusal to serve would seriously hamper or even halt the administration of criminal justice, Velasco in October 1593 urged the crown to allow a low schedule of fees in criminal cases. His recommendation met flat rejection from king and council, who reiterated their determination that all fees be abolished as directed, but indicated that they would agree to some measure of compensation as had already been arranged for the secretaries and other officials for civil justice.[69] The complaints of the alcaldes del crimen were given short shrift by royal decision that the viceroy should exercise, in addition to the measure of jurisdiction already granted in civil cases, jurisdiction in first instance in Indian criminal cases. Although not expressly stated, the decision implicitly upheld the viceroy's stand on classification as well.[70]

Heartened by the royal confidence and sweeping enlargement of his judicial competence, Velasco enthusiastically proceeded to reorganize the handling of Indian criminal cases. The problem of compensation was urgent. That he settled in consultation with the audiencia—which was forced to assist, however unhappily, at these invasions of the sphere of judges and judicial-fee officials. The secretaries for crimi-

68. Complaint by Velasco II to Philip II, Mexico City, April 6, 1594, in VC, fols. 170r–171v.

69. Letters of March 6, 1592, and October 4, 1593, as cited above.

70. Montemayor y Córdova de Cuenca, 1: fol. 157r, sum. 8, summarizing a paragraph of a royal cédula, Madrid, May 30, 1594.

nal justice were awarded 1100 silver pesos a year each for Indian work. Since the attorney-general for the Indians and the letrado of the General Indian Court were already fully burdened by the flood of Indian civil litigation and administrative business, adding to their duties would imperil the quick dispatch commanded by the crown. The plan adopted was to have the attorney for the poor assume the additional function of Indian criminal defense for 100 silver pesos a year, and the letrado for cases of the poor act in Indian criminal cases for an additional 200 pesos annually. The notary already appointed for Indian civil matters was to handle criminal ones for additional payment of 100 pesos yearly, while a solicitor and a bailiff already appointed for Indian civil affairs also were to serve for criminal matters. The total of new salaries came to 2,600 pesos a year, to be met from proceeds of the half-real. The one provision not made was to compensate the assessor of the General Indian Court for a substantial addition to his load. Velasco urged an annual grant in aid, but left the determination of form and amount to the crown.[71]

As part of what must have been a package settlement, judicial procedures in Indian criminal cases were also overhauled in the same months of late 1594 or early 1595. Information of complaint was reduced to a summary report, and both testimony for the defense and investigation equally curtailed.[72] The changes must have concerned more serious offenses, since less serious ones had been handled for decades by summary oral procedure at the jails. With the changes, the viceroy was prepared to have his staff exercise the criminal jurisdiction vested in him.

The General Indian Court thus emerged from the first four years of negotiation, organization, and dispute immensely strengthened. It had an adequate source of revenue in the half-real, and a paid staff of officials who were to handle Indian petitions and cases without fee. The imperial government not only had upheld the exercise of executive jurisdiction in the major categories of cases at issue with the audiencia since the time of Mendoza, and thereby nullified many of its own limitations on civil jurisdiction, but also had granted broad competence to the viceroy in criminal cases. In effect, the disputes of more than half a century over the special unified jurisdiction in Indian affairs that Antonio de Mendoza had organized were settled resoundingly in favor of the viceroy, who emerged with even wider powers. The price offered for an end to substantial opposition within the audiencia and its staffs lay in the system of salaries and additional pay-

71. Velasco II to Philip II, Mexico City, April 6, 1595, in VC, fols. 189v–190v.
72. Ibid.

ments financed by the half-real. There was no attempt to assuage the anger of other fee officials. Opposition by both groups continued, in the hope that Velasco's successors and the imperial government could be persuaded to undo the new system.[73] For the next decade, the General Indian Court and its system of Indian agents of the half-real could not be regarded as definitively established until the crown was fully satisfied that they provided substantial relief for the Indians of New Spain, and accordingly was prepared to ignore all objection.

In November 1595 Velasco relinquished office to his successor, the Conde de Monterrey. Before taking ship for Peru, where he was to be viceroy, he wrote the customary memoir for his successor, discussing the most important features of government in Mexico and problems that were likely to arise. The General Indian Court, his handiwork, he found on the whole good, although he was aware that difficulties still existed:

> The good effects are many. Each day more than I can mention appear, without our being fully aware of them. The handling of Indian matters is quicker, more continuous, and less complicated. Those who complain should remember how much longer delays were before, and how insignificant in the press of business is the holding over of a few matters for a period that never is longer than two, three, or four days for hearings. But the existence of the General Indian Court is attended by two very serious difficulties: the burden in time and work to the viceroy, and the opposition of all manner of [Spanish] people.
>
> The first difficulty is of some importance, but is being remedied as experience makes it possible to expedite work and save time. If the assessor has the capacity, education, experience, and reliability that a function of such importance requires, he can carry much of the burden. I am not sure that the second difficulty is truly important, but I am sure that the very extent of the opposition does demonstrate the need for and effectiveness of the court. One quickly becomes aware that the opposition arises from selfish interest—for the letrados, relatores, attorneys, solicitors, and interpreters all object because of the losses they have sustained through the abolition of fees. The corregidores and justices also object for selfish motives, since they were able to earn the good will of their friends and professional men by steering to them so much profitable business. For the Indians now can present their complaints with great ease and speed and denounce abuses as they could not do easily before, because the justices steered them to friends among the letrados and attorneys. The owners of textile workshops, artisans, and all manner of people complain because the Indians now easily can get hearing and remedy for their wrongs. . . .
>
> In the payment of the Indian agents, there may be the difficulty

73. See discussion below.

that attends all affairs in the Indies: that is, slackness in execution. If the half-real is taken from the two which every tributary pays to his community, clearly no one suffers damage, expense, or distress. If instances of damage do arise, they should be dealt with rigorously, as I have done whenever I have had any brought to my attention. . . . What I have been most anxious to do carefully has been to choose agents with the zeal and ability that the function demands. Otherwise, the entire structure will fall. I have made my appointments with great care and scrutiny. I suspect that no better men could be found in this realm, nor would men brought from elsewhere be as good.[74]

The testing period of the General Indian Court and the new Indian agents largely coincided with the administration of the Conde de Monterrey, viceroy from November 1595 to October 1603. Monterrey lacked the winning personality of his predecessor, and began his administration without the detailed personal knowledge of the colony, derived from long previous residence, that so greatly helped Luis de Velasco II. Furthermore, he was in delicate health and either too ill or confined to his chambers a good deal of the time. A man of probity, patience, and intelligent, careful judgment, he made these difficulties a source of strength, for he reached decisions only after long investigation and looked to arrangements that would both solve problems and ease the load on himself.[75] His instructions, which came to him when he was already in Mexico, directed him to give special care to the needs of the Indians and see to their good treatment and preservation.[76] Although essentially clauses by then standard in viceregal instructions, they had special weight since the Council of the Indies during all of Monterrey's administration devoted much time and energy to problems concerning the treatment of American Indians, and after years of investigation drafted the great reform cédulas of 1601 and 1609.[77]

Upon his arrival, Monterrey found great opposition to the new judicial system for Indians. Members of the audiencia, influential friars, and other notables urged abolition. He answered that he could act only with royal consent and must wait for a year to gain knowledge before reporting to the king.[78] That year lengthened to two and a half as he probed and considered. In that period he moved to put the

74. N.d. but 1596, sect. 7, in HM, 2:102-104.
75. Torquemada, 1:725-727 (lib. 5, caps. 59-60); see also Monterrey's own comments, discussed below.
76. Aranjuez, March 20, 1596, in HM, 2:133-134 and 143, clauses 17, 18, and 52.
77. Schäfer, 2:318-332.
78. Report on the Juzgado General de Indios, Mexico City, April 15, 1598, in AGN-M, leg. 24, sect. 1; further report, sailing to Peru, April 30, 1604, ibid., leg. 26.

operations of the court and the handling of Indian business by the viceroy in greater order. A major problem was the mass of business that came to him for hearing. A substantial part arose from Indian petitions for exemptions from restrictive legislation on their riding horses or mules, owning livestock, pasturing livestock, wearing Spanish dress, bearing arms, dealing in European merchandise, and engaging in European-style trades.[79] On January 15, 1597, Monterrey issued an ordinance releasing Indians from the need for many forms of permission. They might ride mules with saddles, spurs, and reins, and each might own and use up to six pack animals. They might engage in any mechanical trades except those forbidden to them in the mines. They might buy and sell all manner of merchandise except knives, other arms, and silks from Spain. Each might pasture up to 300 sheep or 250 sheep and 50 goats without cutting tails or ears, own 6 yokes of oxen, and have 4 milch cows. They might wear Spanish dress, so long as it was locally made. Despite the royal prohibition on Indians' riding horses or bearing arms, caciques and governors during their term of office, and no others, might ride horses with saddles and reins, but none might bear arms. Indians might have Indian drums (*teponastles*) or other musical instruments and might dance their native dances (*mitotes*) by daylight without penalty or hindrance, but they might not do so by night, nor have a *volador*. Those held to personal service were to have off Holy Week and a week each at Christmas, Easter, and Pentecost. All orders, decrees, licenses, confirmations, and other rulings given to Indians by previous viceroys, if not expressly revoked or voided by new ordinances, were to continue uninterrupted, without need for confirmation by any new viceroy. Finally, from the first viceregal hearing after Easter 1597 no petitions for exemptions or changes were to be brought to the viceroy. The new Indian officials and the secretaries were not to present them, nor would the viceroy hear them. The new ordinance was sent to the provinces in printed broadsides in Spanish and Nahuatl, to be announced to the Indians of each town on a feast day when they were assembled in church.[80] If obeyed, this order closed one of the major avenues by which Spanish justices molested the Indians, and at one stroke removed from the viceregal hearings a substantial proportion of business—nearly a third, the viceroy estimated.[81]

79. Ibid., sect. 2.

80. Ibid.; AGN-I, 6, part 2: exp. 1092. An earlier version, held back for revision, is exp. 1088. A copy of the broadside is attached to the viceroy's report in AGI-M, leg. 24. It has some differences from the version in AGN-I, which must represent further revision.

81. Further report of Monterrey on the Juzgado, sailing to Peru, April 30, 1604, in AGI-M, leg. 26.

Toward the end of 1597 there arrived in Mexico City what was really one of the last royal responses to Velasco's initiatives. The alcaldes del crimen were ordered not to hear appeals in Indian cases decided in first instance by the viceroy unless the viceroy was present at the hearing or formally notified them that he was unable to attend.[82] That order was hardly likely to calm opposition, but again gave indication of the royal temper.

By the spring of 1598, Monterrey's patient probing and reflection brought him to decision, embodied in a long report dated April 15, 1598.[83] By then he was firmly convinced of the need for and utility of the new system. All that previously had been reported to the crown by his predecessors about the oppression of the Indians was accurate, and yet, grim as it was, understated the truth. The Indians were fleeced by their own caciques, principales, and community officials. They had been the prey of Spanish justices, who filled out inadequate salaries through fees and levies, however illegal. The salary of a corregidor, commented Monterrey, barely paid for the papers of his appointment and his expense in reaching his district, nor would combining corregimientos into the larger alcaldías mayores, as Velasco proposed, do any good since lieutenants would have to be appointed, with about the same results. The only remedy with hope of success was to raise salaries very substantially. Other wolves included the *doctrineros* (an interesting choice of term, for it referred to the friars); private Spaniards, who used Indians for labor and secured land grants to the detriment of the Indians, and whose livestock invaded Indian sowings and ate the crop; and the army of fee officials who had battened upon the Indians. These last made up a network of friends and interested parties that reached from the capital to the provinces. Indians were encouraged or forced to embark upon suits, and often suits were started in their names without their knowledge. Suits were deliberately mishandled, often by the representatives paid by the Indians, so that they would have to be restarted and drag on interminably, with a rich yield in fees. Spanish petitions for grants of land would be dropped if they encountered opposition, or the papers would vanish, to resurface or be started anew at a more favorable opportunity. The attorneys and other fee officials attached to the audiencia were essentially corrupt and in alliance with friends and allies in the provinces and capital, as were at times the very secretaries of the viceroy, who hid papers or misrepresented the content in their reading to the viceroy in chambers. They could be held in check only by report in public audience with the Indi-

82. Royal cédula, San Lorenzo, July 18, 1597, in AGN-RCD, 103: fol. 56v; RLI, 2.17.30.

83. The pages that follow are a summary of Monterrey's long report, attached to his letter of April 15, 1598, in AGI-M, leg. 24.

ans present. The very nature of Spain's dominion in Mexico made it impossible to remedy these abuses completely, since there had to be parish priests and Spanish justices. Equally, ". . . the avarice of the Spanish and the weakness of the Indians make it impossible that we do more than bring matters to the best state possible, or less bad, or at the least do not allow abuse so dangerous that it threatens the existence of the Indians. . . ."

The Indian Court and the new system of salaried legal aides were clearly needed and had served to spare the Indians the burden of fees in suits and petitions and to secure them much more rapid relief. Basic elements of these reforms had been ending the collection of fees and restricting Indian access to the audiencia in favor of concentrating decision as far as possible in summary hearings before the viceroy. "The variety of opinions that always exists in different heads," commented Monterrey, "upsets everything." The General Indian Court and the staff of salaried Indian agents, then, must be continued. On the other hand, their operations were attended by genuine problems that needed reform. Monterrey sorted these into five categories: (1) the increase in the number of complaints and petitions coming to Mexico City; (2) the burden on the viceroy, who had many other matters to deal with, since he was in the colony charged with *despacho universal*; (3) diminution of the dignity that should surround the viceroy, because of the tumultuous public hearings; (4) need for a central register of all orders and decisions; and (5) financing of the system through the half-real.

In discussing his first category, the increase in Indian complaints and petitions coming before the viceroy, Monterrey really complained of preexisting volume as well as increase. Even before the General Indian Court, Indians had had to apply for exemptions from restrictive legislation and for confirmation of annual elections of town officials. Many might have been handled by the local Spanish justices; but since they could no longer charge fees, except under the table, they sent all such matters to the viceroy. Similarly, the local justices, who under the general ordinance of Velasco II on jurisdiction were supposed to handle all cases of small amount without fees, deliberately sent all to the viceroy and the new Indian agents. Further, petitions on behalf of Indian communities arising from factional quarrels within the community, or Spaniards' fishing in what they hoped might be troubled waters, continued to come in substantial number to the viceroy. Monterrey reported that he had resorted to three measures as a remedy. One was the ordinance of January 15, 1597, releasing Indians from the need for many forms of viceregal permission and declaring that it was useless to petition for others. That, one would judge, was certain of substantial success.

A second, with possible likelihood of success, was to introduce the use of official seals among the Indian towns, so that papers purporting to come from them would be clearly identified in such matters as confirmation of elections and petitions for audits of town accounts. Use of such seals was spreading slowly, he reported; accordingly, any success was likely to come equally slowly. A third measure was to reissue Velasco's ordinance on division of jurisdiction, ordering that cases of small moment be dealt with locally and not referred to Mexico City. The chance of success on this was slim, since the prohibition against fees remained, and the justices and their notaries were again ordered to work without compensation.

Monterrey's discussion of his second category of problems, the burden on the viceroy, really goes beyond that to give insight into his problems of getting his own secretariat to function honestly and well. Much executive business was settled by having the secretaries read or summarize the papers in private to the viceroy, who then gave his decision. A dishonest secretary could misrepresent the matter in order to gain a decision he had been bribed to get. In addition, all secretaries had a tendency to move Spanish business, for which they got fees, and postpone Indian matters, for which they were on salary. Accordingly, such matters had to be handled in public hearings with the Indians present. At the end of each day of hearing, the viceroy had to call his officials together and see that they had carried out instructions given at the previous audience.

Lessening the burden on the viceroy was accomplished by two sets of measures. For judicial matters, since the viceroy could function only on the advice of his assessor, he left examination and reading to the assessor, who prepared recommended orders, which he signed with a rubric, and brought to the viceroy for confirmation. The viceroy intervened only in those cases that the assessor thought required discussion. For executive matters, the viceroy appeared at public hearings, but the assessor also put his rubric on the orders issued. Procedures and the functions of each official had been carefully defined and standardized through a set of regulations for the functioning of the court dated May 6, 1598. A copy was attached to the report.[84] With these changes, Monterrey considered the burden upon the viceroy little more than it had been before institution of the new system.

Monterrey's third category of problems, on lessening the dignity surrounding the viceroy through tumultuous public hearings, embraced in his view the viceroy's acting in public as an ordinary judge with dispute and objection and having his officials prove quick dispatch in public. His solution was to hold hearings in a chamber of his private apartment, one with a private outside entrance, to which Indi-

84. This is further discussed in chapters VI and VII.

ans might come without meeting Spaniards. A porter admitted Indians but excluded all Spaniards except for the Indian agents who had to be present. Monterrey's views and discussion contrast markedly with Mendoza's policy of letting all Indians come to the hearings, so that they would be satisfied that they had been heard fully and fairly. They contrast also with the medieval idea of having the royal representative demonstrate the king's function as fountainhead of justice and quick dispatch in public hearing. Accepted theories might have been changing, but it is more likely that Monterrey's delicate health led him to shun large, tumultuous hearings.

His fourth category of problems, the need for a central register of all orders and decisions, arose from the custom of returning the petition to the Indian plaintiff, with the order for investigation or redress written on the same folio. For administrative matters, the secretaries had kept a central register of orders issued since the time of Mendoza, one that in the time of Enríquez had been placed in a separate series for Indian affairs. For judicial decisions, no such recording of decisions seems to have been started, and so the only record was the original delivered to the Indian. It was impossible to make sure that a matter had not already been decided and might be being restarted to gain a different decision. Monterrey's solution was to direct that as the secretaries of administration and justice drew up orders and resolutions, another notary enter them in a central register. (Many of these volumes survive in the *ramo de indios* in the Mexican national archives, AGN). The viceroy found similar chaos in the issuance of land grants, since the original papers were given to the petitioners without being copied into a central ledger. Again, he ordered that all be copied into a central government register.

The fifth set of problems around the new system concerned the half-real. Since all Indians benefitted from the abolition of fees and the operations of the new system, the unfairness of collecting equally from all Indian tributaries, whether engaged in suits or not, could be excused. On the other hand, the half-real should not be collected from the individual tributaries, but should be paid from the community treasuries, i.e., by reducing the amount retained for community expenses; but in this, confessed the viceroy, there was much disorder. He hoped to introduce remedy. One wonders what it could be, for the caciques and principales were certain to collect from their commoners and resist any diminution of the revenues available to them through the community. Neither would the crown permit any diminution of its share of the tribute. Monterrey's discussion in this section contrasts oddly with his clear vision of the colony elsewhere in the report.

Regardless of the date of April 15, 1598, Monterrey's long report must have been in preparation for some time thereafter, for one of the attachments, the new regulations for the General Indian Court, bears the date of May 6, 1598. The docket probably arrived in Spain in the summer of 1598. It seems to have satisfied the Council of the Indies and the king for the rest of Monterrey's administration, that is, until 1603. In those remaining years, Monterrey was deeply engaged in the second major congregación, bringing dispersed and depleted Indian settlements together into new, compact, large ones. The litigation that ensued forced him to declare matters relating to congregación to be administrative ones, to be settled by summary executive process and removed from the judicial function of the General Indian Court. That measure automatically curtailed appeals to the audiencia for further review. As an additional measure, to reduce burdens on the Indians and in part on himself, Monterrey limited to two the number of people in any Indian delegation coming to him with petition or complaint about congregación, and established a hospice in Mexico City for furnishing lodging and food for them, which also ministered to Indians coming on business of the General Indian Court.[85]

In 1603 Monterrey was promoted to be viceroy of Peru, and the Marqués de Montesclaros was sent out as his successor in Mexico. Monterrey's last services in Mexico, particularly as they related to the General Indian Court, should have been to advise his successor both orally and in a written *relación de mando*, but the actual events were more complex. Opponents of the court sent so many and such convincing complaints to the Council of the Indies that, despite Monterrey's long report of 1598, the imperial government decided to reopen the matter. Three royal cédulas were prepared, dated at Valladolid July 1, 1603: one was directed to Montesclaros, then still in Spain; another to the Audiencia of Mexico; and a third to Monterrey, all of essentially the same content. The cédulas summarized the complaints against the court and the Indian agents as reported by the fiscal of the Council of the Indies: Indians were forced to travel long distances to Mexico City for a hearing, incurring many expenses in doing so and neglecting their own crops and enterprises. Their affairs suffered long delays because all business had to be funneled through one letrado, and while waiting in Mexico City many sickened and died. The system of summary process and abridged orders was so unclear that Indians were forced to return to Mexico City for clarifying orders, thereby again incurring all the ill effects enumerated. Fee officials would not handle Indian matters, since they could charge no fee, despite their

85. Monterrey to Philip III, Mexico City, May 20, 1601, in AGI-M, leg. 24 (BLT). Monterrey already had royal approval through a royal cédula of Madrid, October 20, 1598, ordering that appeals in matters of congregación go to the Council of the Indies and that orders were to be executed despite appeals: AGI-G, leg. 68 (BLT). Also see Montesclaros to Philip III, Mexico City, May 10, 1604, in AGI-M, leg. 26.

having bought their offices, nor did they receive salaries from the half-real. Salaries paid officials from the half-real were excessive, and the half-real itself unfair, since it was collected from all regardless of whether or not Indians resorted to suits. Finally, the collection was attended by extortion and fraud and yielded a sum far in excess of what was needed. Upon recommendation of the fiscal, the crown commanded that the two viceroys and the audiencia investigate with care and return their recommendations on whether or not to end the jurisdiction in first instance of the viceroy and the levy of the half-real. Montesclaros arrived in Mexico with the cédulas.[86]

Both Montesclaros and the Audiencia of Mexico prepared their reports and sent them to Spain.[87] Unfortunately, they are not in the papers found in the Archivo General de Indias. What is there is a careful answer from Monterrey, who in any case was far better informed than Montesclaros and did not take ship for Peru for half a year. After concluding his discussions with his successor, he made a leisurely progress to Acapulco, accompanied as he left Mexico City by delegations of Indians bewailing his departure, "something that they had never done for anyone else."[88] In Acapulco he composed his *relación de mando*, dated March 28, 1604; but section 3, supposed to deal with the General Indian Court, is blank, with a marginal note that the sections were drafted on separate sheets in looseleaf fashion and the one on the General Indian Court was thrown overboard by mistake. It had contained no more than a reference to the report being drafted at the same time in obedience to the royal command.[89]

Monterrey's report is dated April 30, 1604, "written at sea, bound for Peru." It is essentially a shorter version of the lengthy report of 1598, making the same points: the very great need for the General Indian Court, to give the Indians access to relief from mistreatment and oppression; the almost universal Spanish preying upon the Indians; the bad faith of the very lawyers the Indians hired to serve them, in deliberately mismanaging cases in order to prolong and restart

86. The royal cédulas to Montesclaros and the Audiencia of Mexico are in AGN-RCD, 4:exps. 28 and 41. I infer the issuance of one to Monterrey, since his further report was written in obedience to express royal order.

87. Philip III to the Audiencia of Mexico, Valladolid, June 9, 1604, in AGN-RCD, 4:exp. 47; Montesclaros to Philip III, Mexico City, October 25, 1605, in AGI-M, leg. 26.

88. Torquemada, 1:727 (lib. 5, cap. 59). Statements that the Indians grieved for the departure of Montesclaros in the same way (HM, 2:126, citing Cline, "Civil Congregations," 356, in turn citing Espinosa, cap. 21 [p. 430 in ed. of 1899; pp. 358–362 in ed. of 1945]) may stem from a misreading of Espinosa, who describes the viceroy's accompanying nuns for the founding of the royal convent of Santa Clara in Querétaro. The emotion on this journey was more probably rejoicing for the coming of the nuns.

89. HM, 2:194.

them; the need for speedy dispatch by a single agency instead of the audiencia's loose procedures, in which each item at any stage went to a different official or judge; the need to watch even the viceregal secretaries in handling petitions in chambers, and, in fact, to deal with executive matters in public audience with the Indians or their representatives present. The emphases are somewhat different from those in the report of 1598, for Monterrey apparently felt freer to discuss the shortcomings of the audiencia and his former staff.

In the new report he returned to his discussion of the two problems of burden on the viceroy and the financing through the half-real. His measures for reducing petitions and complaints coming to the viceroy and for shifting much of the work to his assessor had brought the drain on the viceroy's time to little more than it had been before institution of the General Court. On the medio real, he agreed with complaints of irregularities in its collection since, instead of turning over the half-real from the community share of tributes, many towns collected an additional half-real per tributary. Some towns even collected a whole real, because half-real coins were not easily available. Monterrey had ordered strict compliance with the original intent, and hoped that with the concentration of Indians in larger settlements remedy would be easier, at least in those settlements. He was under no illusion that the abuse could be remedied quickly since "it had deep roots." For the rest, he thought that his successor, being of robust health, should be able to handle Indian affairs with less trouble. The charges listed in the royal cédula of 1603 were either ignored or handled by oblique reference.[90]

Since Monterrey wrote his report on the high seas, it must have been forwarded to Spain from Lima and could not have arrived in Spain until late 1604 or early 1605. The report from Montesclaros, written in April 1604, undoubtedly agreed with that of Monterrey and equally enthusiastically backed the new system.[91] We have no clue to the contents of the audiencia's answer save that it was long in preparation. If negative, it could not have been convincing, for the Council of the Indies found the new round of answers decisive. On its advice, Philip III signed a royal cédula on April 19, 1605, ordering that the Juzgado General de los Indios in Mexico be continued as it existed. Its expenses were to be paid from the levy of a half-real a year from each Indian tributary, with the proviso that any surplus funds be applied to reduce the levy in the succeeding year or be used for the good of the

90. Monterrey to Philip III, April 30, 1604, in AGI-M, leg. 26; printed in HM, 2:237–242.

91. I infer the support of Montesclaros from his reply on receipt of the royal cédula ordering continuation of the General Indian Court: letter of October 25, 1605.

Indian communities. The royal order was repeated in a new cédula issued in San Lorenzo, October 5, 1606. The first order was acknowledged in a letter of Montesclaros of October 25, 1605, to the king, reporting that his command would be carried out scrupulously. As to any surplus in the funds raised by the half-real, commented Montesclaros, returning money to the Indian communities merely meant that it would be wasted by the town officials or used by the local friars at their pleasure. A better form of benefit for the Indians would come from applying any surplus to reducing arrears of tributes or making sure current ones were paid in full, a suggestion that brought a delighted marginal comment of approval.[92]

For the remainder of his administration, Montesclaros reported to Spain a number of times that the General Indian Court was functioning well.[93] Beyond that there was little to need mention. When, upon giving up office to his successor in July 1607, he prepared the obligatory *relación de mando*, he did not include reference to it.[94] By then its operations were so firmly routine, and the Indian agents so well organized, that his successor did not need special notice.

With the royal cédulas of 1605 and 1606, the long dispute between audiencia and viceroy over jurisdiction, and the almost equally long debate over the special Mexican definitions of administration in Indian affairs, came to final royal resolution; at the same time, the parallel debate over fees and summary disposition of Indian petition and complaint found solution in the royal confirmation of a unified viceregal jurisdiction, relying upon salaried officials and essentially administrative procedures, whatever the classification of the matter. The financing of the new organization through annual levy of a half-real per tributary created, in effect, a system of legal insurance, less expensive and more uniform than that of Toledo in Peru, one that represented the culmination of nearly a century of discussion and experiment in Mexico and perhaps a millennium of thinking in western Europe.

92. Ibid.; AGN-RCD, 180:cuad. 3, exp. 21 bis; RLI, 6.1.47.
93. Montesclaros to Philip III, Mexico City, November 6, 1606, and May 26, 1607, in AGI-M, legs. 26 and 27 respectively.
94. HM, 2:276–284; pp. 282–284 deal with Indian matters and lands, without mention of the General Indian Court.

CHAPTER V

The Court:
Jurisdiction and Nature of
Business—A Sampler of Cases

A. The Questions

THE General Indian Court, an integral unit of the Spanish colonial government in central Mexico from 1592 until its abolition in 1820, functioned for more than two centuries. This and the next two chapters examine its jurisdiction, the nature of business and kinds of cases it handled, procedures, the place of the court and its agents in the administrative and judicial hierarchies, the Indian approach to them, and the functions and discipline of the salaried agents of the *medio real* within the court and in other tribunals. Chapters VIII and IX will analyze the fund of the medio real, from which the agents were paid, and the existence of exempt regions within Mexico—that is, administrative areas that had parallel but separate or even different arrangements for handling Indian complaints.

The entire span of time, longer than the existence of Mexico or the United States as independent political entities, is dealt with here as a single period, for although the mix of cases varied with changes in density of population, advance of Hispanization, and the steady development of a more interpenetrated society and economy, and although the procedures and functioning of the court varied with the personality and energy of individual viceroys, there occurred no change so marked as to justify division into subperiods. The most noticeable development during the period was the slow shift from the laconic decrees of the late sixteenth and early seventeenth centuries to the much fuller recording of pleas and intermediate steps in the later colonial period. These, however, were more evidence of increasing literacy and a burgeoning bureaucracy than of any difference in nature and functioning.

Let us first consider definition or jurisdiction: What was the General Indian Court? Under the royal cédulas that established the court and defined its competence, it had alternate but not exclusive jurisdiction in first instance in suits of Indians with each other and in those of Spaniards against Indians. Suits of Indians against Spaniards, the major avenue of complaint seeking relief, were specifically removed from the competence of the court; but under colonial Mexican practice since the time of Viceroy Mendoza, they could be heard by the viceroy as petitions for administrative remedy. The court further had alternate but not exclusive jurisdiction in criminal cases against Indians. A reasonable assumption would be that the General Indian Court should be defined in these terms—terms, moreover, that were underscored by the division of labor in the viceregal audiences through distribution of the preparation and recording of documents between the *secretarios de cámara* (judicial secretaries) and the *secretarios de gobernación* (administrative secretaries). The fierce rivalry between these two groups of secretaries, backed by their staffs, for the remnants of fees and costs that were still allowable, quickly would define those matters which were clearly judicial and those clearly administrative, leaving a third category of doubtful matters to be allocated by mutual bickering and eventual viceregal decision.

Presumably only the operation of the judicial secretaries and their staffs constituted the business of the General Indian Court. That presumption would be much strengthened by a viceregal decree of August 12, 1622, that the General Indian Court issue no order in matters of grace, grant, or administration (*gracia, merced, y de gobierno*) and that attorneys present no petitions for decisions of such nature to the court.[1] Further evidence may be found in the standard royal instructions of the eighteenth century for viceroys, which essentially enjoin observance of the original royal cédulas establishing the court.[2]

If this assumption is correct, simple inspection of the range of viceregal decrees containing in their text the statement that they were issued as judgments of the General Indian Court should uphold the distinction. It does not. On the contrary, the decrees demonstrate that the preparation of documents and recording by the administrative sec-

1. AGN-I, 9: exp. 379.
2. E.g., general instruction for the Marqués de las Amarillas, Aranjuez, May 17, 1755, section 10: Mexico (Viceroyalty), *Instrucciones*, 1:423–425.

retaries, although scrupulously upholding their rights to function in administrative business, frequently were considered part of the functioning of the court and steadily issued with the statement that the matter had been examined "in our General Indian Court." Even petitions for licenses or exemptions—surely matters of grace—and for grants, administrative decisions, and administrative relief were heard in the court, and the viceregal decrees issued as court decisions. In some instances, petitions involving the administrative dependency of one Indian community upon another—to use the terms of the time, of a sujeto upon its cabecera—which by ideas held both then and now were very much an administrative matter, might be returned to the petitioners by the viceroy with the notation that they apply through the General Indian Court ("déseme cuenta por el Juzgado de Naturales").[3]

A further test—considerably more effective, since it replaces our judgments as to categories of petitions and decrees with those of the viceregal staff—lies in the sworn declarations made by the two salaried solicitors for Indian affairs in late August and early September of 1784, listing all cases and papers they were handling at the time.[4] (These declarations are presented in tabular form in the appendix.) Their statements covered business before various tribunals and administrative entities, all in Mexico City. If we ignore a slight amount of repetition, i.e., decisions listed as made in the General Indian Court but also on appeal to the audiencia, the overwhelming bulk of the business handled by the two solicitors lay in the General Indian Court (about 82%, varying from 79% for one to just under 90% for the other). The nature of the cases before the court is clearly a remarkable mingling of suits of Indian against Indian; complaints of ill-treatment brought by Indians against Spaniards; petitions to account for debts and salary; and complaints against local Spanish officials, clergy, and officials of Indian town government. Many involved petitions for viceregal *incitativas*, orders for a provincial justice to carry out some function such as rendering a report or sending on papers of an investigation so that the court could decide a complaint. The listing makes it clear beyond debate that the General Indian Court heard suits and complaints against Spaniards, whether officials or private persons, and that the formal royal restrictions on its jurisdiction were ignored even to the extent that the classification as administrative matters of

3. See the summaries of cases later in this chapter. See also the comment of Viceroy Marquina in his *relación de mando* to Iturrigaray, Tacubaya, January 1, 1803, "Advertirá V. E. que el despacho del juzgado general de naturales se hace de una manera poco compatible con un sistema de claridad e instrucción . . .": ibid., 2:644–645.

4. AGI-M, leg. 1286, fols. 47v–72v.

complaints of Indians against Spaniards—a classification accepted by the crown—did not estop the viceroy from hearing such matters in the court. Handling the papers and recording of the decision by an administrative secretary were considered part of the functioning of the tribunal.

It is proper, then, to hold the entire unified viceregal jurisdiction in Indian matters as virtually synonymous with the sphere of the General Indian Court. On the plea of an overriding, though concurrent, competence to protect and defend Indians,[5] the viceroys could and did merge judicial and administrative categories (but always, one suspects and the evidence indicates, with careful attention to the sensibilities of the respective groups of secretaries). The viceroys could and did ignore royal refusal to grant them competence in mixed cases in which Spaniards were defendants. On the same plea of overriding obligation to protect and defend the Indians, they could successfully invade other jurisdictions. The plea became a major viceregal weapon for reducing the rights of feudal jurisdiction vested in the Marquesado del Valle de Oaxaca, the immense seigneurial grant given to Hernán Cortés and his heirs as reward for the conquest of Mexico.[6]

The intermingling of judicial and administrative functions went considerably farther than is evident from the listing of cases and papers by the salaried Indian solicitors in 1784. In general, they did not intervene in criminal cases of Indians which arose within the five-league jurisdiction of the audiencia, since such cases were brought to the General Indian Court by another set of officials. They did, on the other hand, prepare papers in criminal cases of Indians brought from greater distances—that is, those which involved supersession of the jurisdiction of provincial tribunals. All criminal cases clearly were judicial in nature and within the competence of the General Indian Court by specific royal cédulas. Neither did the salaried solicitors, in general, have a role in the reporting of accounts and auditing of collections and expenditures by the Indian barrios of the Mexico City area, grouped in the two *parcialidades* of Santiago Tlatelolco and San Juan Tenochtitlán. Supervision of these two entities and their constituent barrios, essentially an administrative function, became lodged in the General Indian Court.[7] One suspects convenience rather than strict

---

5. The plea had a basis in secret royal instructions to the viceroys; e.g., the secret instruction to the Marqués de las Amarillas, sects. 3–4, Aranjuez, June 30, 1755, in *Instrucciones*, 1:521–522. This instruction was a standard one that varied little from viceroy to viceroy.

6. See, for example, García Martínez, 96. Also see the discussion later in this book, in Chapter IX.

7. Mexico: AGN, *La secretaría de cámara del virreinato*, chart 3; Estrada, 325.

logic; it was simpler for the viceroys, harried as they were with varied and complicated affairs, to turn over an essentially routine function to the legal assessor of the court rather than to discharge it themselves or appoint yet another official, with further charge upon the treasury.

Such intermingling of both judicial and administrative functions was comprehensible and justifiable in the thinking of the sixteenth and seventeenth centuries. In the eighteenth century it became progressively less acceptable, and by the end of the century obnoxious in more advanced political thinking. To the extent that opposition appeared in colonial Mexico before the wars of independence, however, it came from quarrels over jurisdiction. In his *relación de mando* to his successor, Marquina, Viceroy Azanza commented:

> . . . this court exercises jurisdiction indiscriminately in all civil and criminal cases involving Indians, even when they are plaintiffs [and Spaniard defendants]. Many are the instances in which the court has accepted and given sentence in cases against alcaldes mayores, corregidores, and subdelegados. The royal audiencia has protested this abuse in my time. . . .[8]

Marquina, in turn, took up the question in his *relación de mando* prepared for the succeeding viceroy, Iturrigaray. Marquina urged returning to the letter of the original royal cédula of creation—that is, limiting the competence of the court to suits between Indians and those in which Indians were defendants. He would have removed from its jurisdiction all suits against Spaniards, including those against local Spanish officials and clergy and those affecting clerical or military privileges (*fueros*).[9] In effect, he proposed wiping out the fiction of administrative jurisdiction over wrongs against Indians which effectively evaded the original royal restrictions. Such a change would have made the court considerably less effective as protection to the Indians. It also would have met many objections by Spaniards, but still have fallen far short of ending that mingling of the operations of two distinct branches of government which ran counter to the political thinking, gaining currency in the later eighteenth century, that there are three branches of properly constituted government and that their functions should be kept separate. Marquina's suggestion was followed a few years later by the much more drastic action of the Cortes of Cádiz.[10]

8. San Cristóbal Ecatepec, April 29, 1800, sect. 15, in Azanza, 45–46. By a royal order of June 13, 1798, the viceroys were given special jurisdiction to hear charges of repartimientos de mercancías: ibid., 47.

9. Marquina to Iturrigaray, Tacubaya, January 1, 1803, sects. 50–53, in *Instrucciones*, 2:644–646.

10. Lira González, "La extinción," 306–315.

Thus far we have considered the jurisdiction of the General Indian Court in terms of the royal cédulas establishing it, the successful allegation of administrative competence in order to circumvent limitations in those cédulas, and the mixture of administrative and judicial jurisdiction. Let us turn now to the nature or mix of business that came before the viceroy sitting in audience as the General Indian Court: in short, what kinds of cases and in what proportions? Any attempt to answer these questions is subject to certain difficulties that must be underscored. In the first place, the records of the court are scattered and incomplete. The most substantial mass is in the section, Indios, in the Mexican national archive (AGN), containing a very large residue of the administrative decrees and considerably fewer of the judicial ones. More papers are scattered through other sections of this archive, and probably give a good sample of the judicial decrees. Papers in the national archive may be supplemented by the signed original decrees that finally lodged in provincial archives, where they have sustained the ravages of neglect, plunder, sale (if fortunate, to foreigners; if unfortunate, to factories for pulping and firecrackers), and destruction in popular tumult.[11] Nevertheless, surprisingly abundant records still remain in provincial deposits. For this study I rely upon the archives of Teposcolula and Yanhuitlán, in the Mixteca Alta (Oaxaca), and those of Tulancingo (Hidalgo), now in private possession. Another scholar has plumbed the records of Tlaxcala.[12]

Enormous as is the mass of the records that do survive and have been consulted, it is but a fraction of the original mass. Moreover, the known surviving records relate to the operations of the viceregal audience; they do not cover the operations of the General Indian Court as a criminal tribunal for the Indian parcialidades around Mexico City. Those records, if they yet exist, have not been found. Furthermore, many other records, such as those arising from the audit of accounts and supervision of the parcialidades, appear only in the last volumes of Indios. They relate to years after the abolition of the court and to the plunder of the Indian entities once the protection of the court was removed.[13] While they are a most useful clue to what the court did before it was extinguished, they are not records of the years in which it did conduct audits and carry on supervision.

In the second place, the mix of business must have varied over

---

11. In Mexican popular tumults in the smaller cities and villages, archives seem to be a favorite target, perhaps on the theory that they contain records of land titles and criminal judgments; on the other hand, they simply may make good bonfires.

12. Riley.

13. Lira González, "La ciudad de México y las comunidades indígenas"; AGN-I, vol. 100, passim.

time, changing with circumstances of government ordinance, Spanish economic need and wish, and the Indian demographic nadir and then steady increase after the early seventeenth century. In the third place, our sources for determining proportions of various kinds of cases and complaints are of disparate types. On the one hand, we have the judgments of scholars who have examined substantial masses of the records, most notably the ramo of Indios. On the other hand, we have the comments of people living at the time the court was in operation, most notably viceroys and critics. Perhaps most reliable of all, we have the declarations in 1784 of the two solicitors of the court, which give us a detailed account of the court's business they were involved in during some months. If we keep firmly in mind the degree of completeness and coverage of extant records, and the fact that the mix almost certainly varied in proportion over time, there is no need for us to enter into the interesting but not informative debate that opposes present-day scholarship to the observations of people of the past, for all of the testimony and judgment is remarkably congruent.

One of the few scholars of our time who have interested themselves in the General Indian Court, Lesley Byrd Simpson, has tried to summarize his impressions upon examining the ramo of Indios:

> As I go on in the Ramo de Indios I find the cases are almost all of types: complaints of pueblos against Spaniards who are encroaching on their communal lands—the Indians are invariably given an amparo; cases of Indians being used for personal services illegally—on haciendas, in shops, etc.; many complaints against priests for extortion, interference in elections, cruelty, forced service; complaints against alcaldes mayores and other officials for using the Indians in their private enterprises; many cases of disputed elections, mostly for governors; complaints against the residence in Indian towns of Spaniards, mestizos, Negroes and mulattos. . . . Some cases of disputes between villages over conflicting boundaries and water rights. All cases are now handled by the Juzgado de Indios and the fiscal. The viceroy always decrees according to the opinion of the fiscal. In fact, the Indian problems and their settlement have been reduced almost completely to routine cases.[14]

All observers alive in the years the court existed were agreed that the largest proportion of cases and complaints concerned land, in the form of disputes over ownership, questions of grants, petitions for amparo (writs granting formal government protection in possession), sale and rental, or division among heirs. One of the most acerbic critics of the court, Hipólito Villarroel, commented that on all the globe there

14. LBSF, 10: fols. 68–70; see also the comment on fol. 137.

was no other place with so many suits over land, and yet the New World had immense stretches of fertile land unsettled and untilled.[15]

The next-largest category might be complaints against local Spanish officials, to which might be added those against priests. Other categories of relative importance were relations with Spaniards other than in disputes over land (questions of debt, service, and treatment as workers), and conflicts arising over relations within Indian towns, i.e., disputes over elections, government, mistreatment and extortion by officials, or refusal of respect or obedience by commoners. Relatively minor proportions of the cases and complaints would concern disputes among Indians not involving the town or corporate entities and a group of miscellaneous cases. The second-largest category listed, complaints against local Spanish officials and priests, is particularly revealing of affairs in the Indian towns and villages. According to Viceroy Croix, writing at the end of his administration:

> ... it is certain that the Indians are customarily oppressed by the priests and alcaldes mayores with demands for services and taxes. When the two representatives in a district are united is when they most afflict the Indians. If they fall out, there is a stinking gush of complaints, for the parish priest vents his anger against the alcalde mayor by getting his Indian parishioners to initiate complaints against the latter in Mexico City. . . .[16]

Much clearer proportions are possible for the first months of 1784 through the sworn declarations of the solicitors. It should be kept in mind that their testimony deals only with the papers they handled in the viceregal audience and elsewhere, and does not include the criminal cases of prisoners in the local Indian jails nor audit and supervision of the parcialidades. The summary in Table 5.1 gives proportions only for matters before the General Indian Court. The categories are not firmly separate, but they do indicate general proportions. Suits over money might be added to the category of other property or to that of private Indian suits not over land. Petitions for extension of time for payment of debts is a less surprising category if one remembers that the Indian economy always had commercial aspects. As declared by the solicitors, the cases and petitions listed in this category do not seem to refer to debts involving peonage, but rather standard commercial obligations.

15. Villarroel, 52–53. The situation continued with little change from the sixteenth century; see clause 3 of the relación de mando of Viceroy Enríquez, September 25, 1580, in HM, 1:204–205.

16. Croix, 56–57, clause 17. See also the comments of Viceroy Revillagigedo I in his relación de mando for the Marqués de las Amarillas, Mexico City, November 28, 1754, in Instrucciones, 1:303.

TABLE 5.1   Kinds of Cases Before the General Indian
Court Declarations of August–September 1784

Land and easements on land	32%
Other property	6
Inheritance	3
Licenses affecting land	2
Subtotal	43%
Complaints against local Spanish officials	26%
Complaints against priests	1
Labor: Indians vs. Spaniards	12
Complaints arising from town government	5
Private Indian suits (not over land)	5
Money (not peonage)	1
Extension of time on debts	2
Family quarrels and offenses	1
Miscellaneous	3
Not stated	2
Total (due to rounding)	101%

Source: Sworn affidavits of solicitadores, in AGI-M, leg. 1286.
See Appendix.

B. A Selection of Case Abstracts

Once general categories have been established for the kinds
of petitions and cases that came before the viceroy sitting as judge of
the General Indian Court, further examination is best secured by making available summaries of typical petitions, suits, and decisions. Some
records cover the full course of the case to what was intended to be the
final decision; many others give the complaint and testimony up to a
procedural decision which obviously did not settle the case nor apply
remedy to the complaint. The final papers may be elsewhere or may
have been lost. A third possibility lies in the category of suspenso—
that is, halted or dropped—for many of the complaints and cases
came to settlement by private arrangement, so that the formal proceeding before the General Indian Court was not picked up. The presentation here is organized as far as possible by the larger categories
developed in Table 5.1, but subdivisions within those categories are
more elaborate and reflect the greater detail that becomes possible on
selection from more than two centuries of records. There is much
overlap, since one case may fit in several categories. In general, the
dates or cities given refer to the viceregal decisions, but may include
provincial proceedings when they are in the docket as it comes to us.

1. Land and Property Rights

Complaints and disputes over land and property rights were at all times the largest category. Indian villages would fight each other or hacendados for decades and even centuries over boundaries, frequently spending in the suits far more than the value of the land in dispute. Contrary to a widely held current opinion, Indian villages fought more with each other in these suits than with Spaniards.[17]

a. Disputes in General

1. March 15, 1617, Mexico City. Tuxtla, province of Huajuapan, and Tamazulapan, province of Teposcolula, sue each other over land. The viceroy orders the alcalde mayor of Teposcolula and the corregidor of Huajuapan to examine the evidence and recommend a verdict. The two Spanish officials examine Indian pictorial records, question witnesses, and inspect the disputed lands from the *huerta* of the cacique of Tamazulapan. Their report, dated December 14, 1616, Tamazulapan, recommends dividing the land along a natural watershed, two-thirds to Tamazulapan and one-third to Tuxtla, placing boundary stones, and imposing perpetual silence on the parties. On February 1–2, 1617, the two letrados of the court, each acting for one of the parties, approve. The viceroy then embodies the recommendation in a formal order to the alcalde mayor of Teposcolula. Behind the report of the two Spanish officials is almost certainly a compromise negotiated in discussion with the officials of the two towns and agreed to by them.[18]

2. March 6, 1634, Mexico City. Ixtlán, province of Antequera, vs. Calpulalpan and two of its sujetos, a long suit over land and status. Ixtlán claims that the two villages are tenants on its land and exhibits the latest version of the agreement of rental, dated September 11, 1629. The two villages, declaring themselves sujetos of Calpulalpan, province of Ixtepeji, claim that the agreement is fraudulent, entered into in order to obtain water. Each side sues in different courts, Ixtlán in the General Indian Court. The viceroy orders the alcalde mayor of Antequera to investigate with personal inspection of the lands and of Indian pictographic records. On May 15, 1631, the alcalde mayor hears the case, with inspection of the agreement transcribed and translated from Zapotec in a sworn version. He reports that the lands are Ixtlán's. On August 2, 1632, the viceroy decides in favor of Ixtlán, the

---

17. See the discussion in Taylor, *Landlord and Peasant*, 83–89, 108–109, et passim.

18. AGN-I, 10: exp. 30.

other side being allowed thirty days to comply or appeal. This decision is to be enforced even if contrary judgment has been rendered elsewhere.

Calpulalpan and its two sujetos manage to get the case reopened; the alcalde mayor of the Antequera is instructed to hold new hearings and to suspend criminal proceedings for failure to comply with the previous decision. In the new hearing, Ixtlán presents two viceregal decrees of August 1632 in its favor. Again the alcalde mayor recommends judgment for Ixtlán, but with the proviso that Indians of the cabecera of Calpulalpan may enter the lands without wand of justice for collection of tribute. He negotiates a new agreement of rental, one clause of which sets a fine of 500/ for reviving the suit, half for the other party and half for the crown, plus payment of all costs. In his report to the viceroy, May 20, 1633, he includes all papers, and comments that suits are being brought in a number of courts besides the General Indian Court and both sides are incurring heavy expense. (The rent asked by Ixtlán was 6/ a year.)

Calpulalpan again asks that the case be reopened, on the ground that the agreement has been signed by people not authorized to act for the town and the two sujetos and that the alcalde mayor is prejudiced. The viceroy appoints the corregidor of Tecocuilco as special judge to investigate. All parties then give testimony before him, Calpulalpan and its two sujetos repeating their plea that the agreement of May 1633 is void and the alcalde mayor prejudiced. On January 5, 1634, the corregidor renders his opinion that the lands are clearly Ixtlán's. On February 16 the assessor of the General Indian Court recommends a decision in favor of Ixtlán on the basis of the corregidor's report, and on March 6, 1634, the viceroy signs the formal judgment as recommended. All judges and justices elsewhere are enjoined to observe the final sentence. The two sujetos are to pay 6/ a year rent, to help maintain the church of Ixtlán, and to show up with flowers and festive arches for the feast of St. Thomas, patron saint of Ixtlán.[19]

This case is an excellent example of the tenacity of Indian litigation, especially in land disputes in Oaxaca. The suits were carried on simultaneously in various jurisdictions, repeatedly renewed, and piled up costs far in excess of the value of whatever was in dispute. In this case, legal costs and the expense of sending delegations to Mexico City, Antequera, and other towns must have run to hundreds, perhaps thousands of pesos, as against a rental of 6/ a year and minimal acts of dependence.

3. November 4, 1638, Mexico City. The town of Nuestra Señora Asunción Tlaxcalilla vs. San Miguel Mezquitepec, both in the prov-

19. Ibid., 12, part 1: exp. 101 (LBSF, 8: fol. 111).

ince of San Luis Potosí, over wasteland which the latter has leased out. On the advice of the assessor of the court, the viceroy orders the Captain Protector of the Frontier to hear testimony and send it to the viceroy for decision.[20]

4. March 21, 1640. San Miguel Mezquitepec, province of San Luis Potosí, vs. the Society of Jesus. José de Celi, solicitor of the court, on behalf of the Tlaxcaltecans and Chichimecas of San Miguel Mezquitepec complains that, in violation of the town's privileges, people under the protection of the justice of the province invade the three leagues expressly reserved to the town for grazing and timber in order to secure charcoal for the mines of San Luis Potosí. The lands are held under old privilege confirmed by viceroys and the audiencia. In addition, the town disputed title to land with Gabriel Ortiz, a Spaniard. When he died, the town discovered that his widow had sold the land in dispute to the Society of Jesus. The Indians now petition, in order to avoid litigation, that their land be surveyed and boundary stones set. The viceroy so orders.[21]

Later a receptor surveys the Indian land over the protests of the Jesuits, restores the boundaries in accordance with the town's petition, and places boundary stones.[22] On January 31, 1641, in Mexico City, the town of San Miguel Mezquitepec agrees to lease the land in perpetuity to the Jesuits of San Luis for an annual rental of 75l. The viceroy approves.[23]

5. April 29, 1640, Mexico City. The Indians of Churubusco, province of Mexicaltzingo, had claimed a house held by their encomendero, Bernardo Vázquez de Tapia, and it was awarded to them. The encomendero appeals the decision, shows prior possession, and the house is awarded to him. This is one of the rare instances in which a formal decision gained by Indians in the General Indian Court was reversed in favor of the Spaniard.[24]

6. October 22, 1685, Mexico City. Santa María Ocotepec, a sujeto of Teposcolula, vs. Santiago Nuyóo, all in the province of Teposcolula. Santa María Ocotepec complains that it rented land from Chalcatongo, which it planted to bananas at a cost of 40l. On the night of August 27, 1685, the natives of Santiago came with axes, ma-

20. Ibid., 11:exp. 53. The document gives the name of one town as San Miguel Mezquitepec, and I have so copied it here. Gerhard, A Guide, 234–237, gives the name as Mezquitic, present-day spelling Mexquitic in the Mexican census of 1950. He is confirmed by the Diccionario Porrúa, 2:1339.

21. AGN-I, 12, part 2:exp. 47 (LBSF, 8:fols. 131–134).

22. Ibid., 13:fols. 7–19 (LBSF, idem.).

23. Ibid., fols. 133–145 (LBSF, 9:fol. 3).

24. Ibid., 12, part 2:exp. 82 (LBSF, 8:fol. 137).

chetes, spades, etc., and destroyed the planting, claiming the land is theirs. The complainant asks for amparo and payment of damages. The viceroy orders the local alcalde mayor to protect Santa María Ocotepec in its use of the land and to force payment for damage done.[25]

7. August 1, 1686, Mexico City. The town officials of Tlaxiaco, province of Teposcolula—"all caciques"—complain that Mateo Vázquez, who forces himself upon the town, and a nephew have built three mills on the town's river, where Tlaxiaco has its community-owned mill. The new mills take away business and consequent revenue, which went to pay church expenses. They ask that the viceroy order verification of license, and if there is none, the mills be forbidden to operate. The viceroy orders the alcalde mayor of Teposcolula to have Mateo Vázquez exhibit the documents which empower him to have the three mills built and to show title to the lands involved. He is also to report on the damage to the town, all within fifteen days.[26]

8. August 8, 1696, Mexico City. Nuestra Señora de la Limpia Concepción, sujeto of Coixtlahuaca, province of Teposcolula, complains that the town of San Antonio Abad has seized land, partly the patrimony of the cacique and the rest owned by the community, and has built a church and flimsy houses on the land, pretending to move the town there. By orders of 1589, 1605, and 1667, Nuestra Señora de la Limpia Concepción is supposed to be protected in its lands, but the lieutenant of the alcalde mayor of Teposcolula and Yanhuitlán forced the sujeto to sign an agreement dropping the suit. The sujeto asks for justice and the return of its lands. The viceroy orders the alcalde mayor of Teposcolula and Yanhuitlán to show the complaint to the town authorities of San Antonio Abad and send all papers to Mexico City for decision.[27]

A later order of September 22, 1698, Mexico City, instructs the nearest royal justice to take testimony and carry out a personal inspection of the lands in dispute since the alcalde mayor of Teposcolula and Yanhuitlán has been recused as prejudiced.[28]

9. April 16, 1741, Mexico City. The town of Teposcolula complains that a past alcalde mayor, Francisco de Alarcón, in order to remain in the province, bought a ranch of one caballería of irrigated land and one of pasture, just outside the town, through a compadre, Tomás de Azcárraga. The lands were community-owned. Notaries and town officials had been allowed to use them, and one, now dead, sold it. Alarcón as alcalde mayor and judge allowed and arranged the sale,

25. Ibid., 22 : exp. 95.
26. Ibid., 28 : exp. 276.
27. Ibid., 33 : fols. 69f–70f.
28. Ibid., 20 : fols. 257f–259f.

intimidating the Indians. He now has houses and businesses there. The viceroy already has issued a dispatch, in 1739, but to the lieutenant of Alarcón. Then Alarcón secured a writ of prohibition against Pedro Valdenebro y Robles, the new alcalde mayor. Since the latter has died, the writ is vacated. The viceroy orders the present alcalde mayor of Teposcolula to investigate the complaint and send the documents to Mexico City within one month under penalty of a fine of 500/ for failure to comply.[29]

A later order of June 7, 1742, Mexico City, cites Alarcón, "resident of Teposcolula," to the court for a hearing in the suit. The town asks for restitution of the land and all earnings from it for the time Alarcón held it.[30]

10. November 14, 1774, Mexico City. A viceregal order to the alcalde mayor of Nochixtlán to carry out promptly judicial requests of the alcalde mayor of Teposcolula in the suit of Santiago Amatlán, province of Teposcolula, against La Concepción, province of Nochixtlán, over lands. The town is to pay fees and costs, but in moderation. Both alcaldes mayores are to maintain proper and harmonious working relations on threat of a fine of 200/. Apparently each justice has been backing the town in his province. The alcalde mayor of Teposcolula has the principal documents in the case and is to hear the suit.[31]

11. September 22, 1787 – August 27, 1788, Mexico City and San Cristóbal Ecatepec. The town of Xonacahuacán, province of San Cristóbal Ecatepec, vs. Don Antonio Palazuelos, hacendado, for mistreatment and seizure of water, a long, complicated dispute with a previous history. The Indians file a long complaint with the General Indian Court, objecting to assignment of workers, general fines levied by the hacendado for late delivery of barley, and seizure of the town's water supply for irrigation. The court sends the complaint to the alcalde mayor of San Cristóbal Ecatepec for investigation, with six days to report back. In the hearings before the alcalde mayor, the Indians produce witnesses who uphold their complaints, and Palazuelos produces witnesses who testify to his good behavior. He also exhibits a viceregal decree of May 21, 1781, issued on the opinion of the viceregal assessor, that if the allegation of alternating use of water by the town and the hacienda is correct, the alcalde mayor of San Cristóbal Ecatepec is to force the town to continue the usage, penalty for violation by the town to be two months in jail for its officials. The case continues with new complaints filed on behalf of the Indians by the Indian agents and a petition on behalf of Palazuelos. All papers are sent for an opinion to

29. Ibid., 55:exp. 40.
30. Ibid., exp. 100.
31. Ibid., 63:fols. 394v–395f.

the fiscal protector, at this time the fiscal of the royal treasury acting as general protector of the Indians. His opinion points out that under a viceregal proclamation of June 3, 1784, and a royal cédula of June 4, 1787, the Indians are entitled to freedom of movement, and so there is basis for decision on one complaint. As for a dispute over water rights, the dam providing it is on town land, without evidence of permission for it to be built. The viceregal decree of 1781 is therefore void. For the rest, let the two parties prove their rights. The court accepts his opinion and so orders.

In the following round, the registry of the viceregal order of 1781 is found, but no evidence that it was preceded by any investigation. The lieutenant of the subdelegado (who replaced the alcalde mayor under the Ordinance of Intendants) testifies that the dam is in use. Palazuelos submits further testimony by witnesses, all included by the justice for the province with his report. The justice upholds the position of Palazuelos, but admits that the complaints against him are true. He does pay the Indians who work for him under order, and the water is necessary for the existence of the hacienda, which in turn is necessary for the commonweal. The viceroy orders all papers sent to the fiscal protector, a post still filled *ad interim* by the fiscal of the royal treasury. The fiscal's recommendation is that the Indians be allowed to see the papers for six days and then return them to him. Affidavits certify that this has been done. At this point the record of the case ends.[32]

A persistent element in this file is the clear partiality of the Spanish provincial governors and their lieutenants for the hacendado, which the Indians try to overcome through appeal to the General Indian Court. An interesting element is the resort to the court in 1781 by the hacendado.

12. January 4, 1794, Mexico City. The town of Acayucan vs. bounding hacendados over damages and persecution. The town petitions the court, which sends the petition to the fiscal protector. The latter recommends sending the petition to the subdelegado of Pachuca for administration of justice. The viceroy agrees, and the Indian attorney, Ignacio Covarrubias, is given the papers of the docket plus the decree, for delivery to the subdelegado of Pachuca.[33]

13. September 9, 1794, Mexico City. The Indians of Tlacintla and Los Remedios, province of Ixmiquilpan, vs. the Hacienda de Debode. The early records in the case are not here. The two villages object to quieting of title in the hacienda through a composición in 1715,

32. AGN-Crim, 12:exp. 17 (LBSD, vol. 2).
33. Ibid., 22:exp. 19 (LBSD, vol. 22).

which ignored their objections. They prove their title to the land and show that their objections to the composición were not heard. The court decree returns official title to the two villages, but stipulates that the Indians are to give up their rancherías and move to a compact settlement, with governor, alcaldes and other officials, a church, etc. Since existing maps do not permit exact demarcation of the town land, the local administrator of the sales tax, in company with one representative of each party and a third chosen by mutual agreement, is to set boundaries and place boundary stones in order to avoid future dispute.[34]

14. August 6, 1796–April 8, 1801, Mexico City and Cuautitlán. Pedro José of San Mateo Xoloque, province of Cuautitlán, vs. Don Sebastián Pérez, lessor of the Ranch of Xuchimangas, for changing the customary charges for pasturing livestock. The complaint alleges that the customary charge for pasturing livestock is 0/4 a head for horses and cattle and 0/0/6 a head for pigs, sheep, and goats. (Probably only cattle and sheep are involved here.) Pérez, a new lessor, tries to double the charge, despite an order by the subdelegado of the province in 1796 that there be no change. Upon Pérez' filing an answer, the Indian is ordered to come to Mexico City so that his attorney may prepare a counter-answer. In his opinion, the fiscal protector suggests investigation to ascertain the custom and also to discover why the town does not have enough land of its own. The court so orders. The report from the province indicates that the town has enough land and that 1/ for pasturing horses and cattle and 0/1 for other livestock are standard annual charges in the area. Thereupon the fiscal protector recommends awarding judgment to the Spaniard. All papers are sent to the *relator* (for ordering and summary). The formal final judgment is not in the docket.[35]

15. October 17, 1808–March 2, 1809, Mexico City, Temascaltepec, etc. Final papers in a suit of the town of Tlatlaya and others, province of Temascaltepec, vs. the towns of Acapetlahuaya, province of Zacualpan, and San Simón Oztuma, province of Ixcateopan, for invasion of lands and destruction of boundary markers. The plaintiffs established their case and were awarded damages and costs, which rise to 1,308/, to be paid by Acapetlahuaya, and 1,000/ by San Simón Oztuma. Commissioners sent by the viceroy seize horses and cattle of Acapetlahuaya over the protests of the town priest, who claims that they belong to pious foundations and not to the town. At auction the livestock brings in 1,053/, despite a claim on the part of Acapetla-

34. AGN-I, 70:fol. 28 (LBSF, 13:fols. 8–10).
35. AGN-Civ, vol. 2154:exp. 38 (LBSD, vol. 5).

huaya that it is worth 2,000*l*. The latter town again approaches the court with a charge of violence and excess. Despite that, the commissioners pay off the plaintiffs and report to the viceroy on January 31, 1809. The costs for the action of the commissioners and the auction come to 564/2/6 additional. In the docket there is nothing on collection of the damages and costs assessed against San Simón Oztuma. There is a sad letter to the commissioners from the town priest of Acapetlahuaya, dated November 25, 1808, asking them to locate his personal mule, which was seized in the general sequestration, and return it at his expense. He reports that the town has been in tumult all night and day, and he and the governor have been trying to bring reason without success. Some wish to pay; others refuse "*y así está todo de los demonios.*"[36]

b. *Fundo Legal*

In the second half of the colonial period, the crown established the concept of *fundo legal*, or minimum endowment of land for an Indian town or village. The germ of the idea lay in an ordinance of the viceroy, the Marqués de Falcés, of May 25, 1567, that there be 500 varas between any hacienda and Indian lands, and that Spanish ranches raising livestock must be 1,100 varas distant.[37] A royal cédula of June 4, 1687, formally defined a minimum endowment for each Indian town of 600 varas, measured from the outermost houses in the four directions, but attempts to enforce this led to complaints by Spanish landholders that the Indians were building huts and shacks in the fields to extend the *casco* of the town and establish rights to hacienda lands. So a new royal cédula of July 12, 1695, although confirming the concept of fundo legal, ordered that the 600 varas of Indian town lands be measured from the church in the center of town and not from the outermost houses. Equally, the 1,100 varas distance required between any Spanish livestock ranch and an Indian town was to be measured in the same way.[38] Royal policy for ensuring each Indian town an adequate endowment of land, water, and waste was formally restated in a royal cédula of October 15, 1713, which set the proper limits for an ejido (at that time meaning pasture and waste) at 1 league.[39] In 1786 the Ordinance of Intendants of New Spain repeated

36. Ibid., vol. 2161:exp. 15 (LBSD, vol. 3).

37. Beleña, 1, part 1:67–68, no. 102. Oddly enough, the regulation, although a viceregal ordinance, is summarized under the autos acordados of the audiencia.

38. Beleña, 1, part 5:207, no. 382. The text of the royal cédula of June 12, 1695, is printed in DCLI, 1:89–90.

39. Beleña, 1, part 5:208, no. 384; see also the preceding summary (no. 383) of a royal cédula of May 7, 1785, that suits between Spanish farmers and Indians are to be decided quickly in terms of the royal legislation on fundo legal.

the injunction to see that Indians were suitably provided with land, although in more general and less exact terms.[40] The royal cédulas of 1687 and 1695 provided the Indians with a powerful weapon in quarrels with each other and with non-Indians, since each town could thereafter plead an overriding right to its legal endowment, even at the expense of the property rights of others.

16. November 27, 1769, Mexico City. San Miguel Tixáa, province of Teposcolula, vs. Doña Juana Pérez Bontilla, over lands within the 600-vara limit. The town approaches the General Indian Court, complaining that it cannot get justice from the local Spanish officials, who are in love with Doña Juana and imprisoned the town officials until they signed documents in her favor. On the day set for the required investigation, the Spanish officials appeared with 60 men and yokes of oxen to plow the disputed land as the Indians came out from hearing mass. The alcalde mayor turned soldiers loose on women and children, one of each being killed. The wounded were dragged at horsetail to the jail of Teposcolula, three men and four women being put in chains. They ask that all be investigated. The viceroy orders the justice nearest the province of Teposcolula to go to the scene, investigate, and administer justice on pain of a fine of 200/. The justice is to have a doctor examine the wounded and slain and is to collect all evidence.[41]

17. April 4, 1794, Mexico City. The Indians of Coloxtitlán, province of Zacualpan, vs. the town of Xocotitlán and the local governing board of the miners, over assigning ejidos. The docket opens in mid-suit with a further plea by the solicitor for Indians on behalf of Coloxtitlán. The town has a right to 600 varas in the four directions, since it has all the legal requisites for possessing a fundo legal. Xocotitlán has more land than it needs, and furthermore its allegations are absurd in that they confound a parcel of land in dispute with the fundo legal claimed by Coloxtitlán. Xocotitlán further claims that Coloxtitlán is not a true town but a barrio or settlement of Tesicapan; but such a circumstance does not impair its right to land. On the advice of the fiscal, the viceroy orders all parties to the suit to appear before him within twelve days.[42]

18. February 28, 1800, Mexico City. Xocotipac, province of Teposcolula, vs. Don Manuel Dionisio Güenduláin, vecino of Oaxaca, and the town of Teotitlán. Xocotipac has petitioned for endowment of pasture, water, and land, and investigation has shown its need is truly

40. Art. 61, in Beleña, 2:appendix, xxi–xxii.
41. AGN-I, 61:fols. 325v–327v.
42. Ibid., 70:fols. 7v–8v.

stated; but a neighbor, Don Manuel Dionisio Güenduláin, opposes granting the petition on the ground that it will affect a ranch he holds as part of an entailed estate. It should therefore, he claims, go to the audiencia since the petition affects rights in entail. The town of Teotitlán also opposes. In his opinion, the fiscal protector holds sharply that Indians too have privileges, and so the case is properly before the General Indian Court. Further, the pleadings by Teotitlán are tainted by much fraud. The viceroy then signs an order to the subdelegados of Teposcolula and Teotitlán jointly to award and fix boundaries for a fundo legal for Xocotipac. The papers in the case are sent to Xocotipac for execution.[43]

c. Licenses for Sale or Rental of Indian Lands

The legal framework for supervising sales or rentals of Indian lands, either to other Indians or to Spaniards, came into existence during the first century of Spanish rule and brought many of the transactions of larger amount to the General Indian Court, once that was established. The important regulations for most of the colonial period were decreed in 1571 and 1572 by Philip II. They required judicial authorization, public announcement for thirty days, public auction for lands worth over 30/ (nine days for other property), and simple judicial license for lands worth less.[44] A viceregal ordinance of December 17, 1603, added the requirements that before the beginning of the thirty days of public proclamation, investigation establish that the lands truly belonged to the would-be seller and that he retained enough to support himself; further, all papers were to come to the viceroy after the period of public proclamation, but before the sale.[45] A few months later, on November 17, 1604, another viceregal ordinance required the justices carrying out the investigations to give the parties a properly signed and sealed copy of the papers, but to deposit the originals with the viceregal secretaries of gobernación. Until then, the originals were turned over to the parties, who were supposed to deposit them with the secretaries but often did not. In consequence, whenever question arose concerning title, new judicial investigations had to be carried out, frequently by special commissioners sent out for the purpose, with much duplication of expense and considerable confusion.[46] After 1603, all sales over 30/ had to have viceregal approval. Although such license was an administrative matter, handled by the secretaries of gobernación, it usually came within the operations of the General Indian Court.

43. Ibid., fols. 175f–176v.
44. RLI, 6.1.27.
45. Beleña, 1, part 2: 113–114, no. 135.
46. AGN-O, 2: fols. 160v–161f (BLT).

Despite all legal safeguards, alienation of Indian lands continued at an alarming rate. In 1781 Viceroy Mayorga, on the advice of the assessor of the General Indian Court, issued a new ordinance forbidding local justices to allow sales, rentals, or any other kind of disposal of Indian lands, even among Indians themselves, without express license of the viceroy, the General Indian Court, or the audiencia. Notaries were forbidden to prepare deeds or papers except after such licenses had been obtained, on penalty of a fine of 500/ and loss of office; the documents thus illegally prepared were to be void. However, on review in the Council of the Indies, the measure was disapproved as too sweeping and in violation of the *Recopilación de . . . Indias*, i.e., the decrees of Philip II of 1571 and 1572. So the next viceroy was ordered to reconsider the matter, consult the fiscal for civil affairs and the audiencia, and prepare new regulations for submission to the crown.[47] The ordinance thus was revoked, but no new one was issued. The net result was greater care and much more detailed proceedings for obtaining viceregal licenses.

19. September 3, 1616, Mexico City. José de Celi, Indian solicitor, on behalf of three Indians of Santa María Azompa, sujeto of Cuilapa, province of Cuatro Villas in the Marquesado, who bought land from a principal. The deed was executed before the justice of Cuilapan, and is now presented to the viceroy for confirmation and amparo. On the advice of the assessor of the court, the viceroy approves the sale since it is among Indians.[48]

20. November 7, 1631, Mexico City. Melchor López de Haro, Indian solicitor, on behalf of the governor, alcaldes, councilors, and community of Tenancingo, province of Malinalco, petitions for confirmation of the sale of two parcels of land by the town to Manuel Duarte, a Spaniard. All formalities and investigations required by royal cédula have been carried out. Duarte was highest bidder at the public auction. On the opinion of his assessor, the viceroy confirms the sale, with the reservation that his confirmation is not to invalidate any rights of the crown or any third party.[49]

21. June 20, 1738, Mexico City. The town of Teposcolula complains that lands of the town and its barrios, which legally cannot be alienated, have been sold to private people. The lands were used for crops which enabled the Indians to pay the royal tributes. The viceroy orders the alcalde mayor of Teposcolula, on penalty of a 200/ fine for noncompliance, to summon the purchasers of such lands, require

47. Konetzke, 3:541–543 (no. 275).
48. AGN-I, 7:exp. 104.
49. Ibid., 10, cuad. 2:exp. 125.

them to present their titles, have these copied, and send them to Mexico City for examination.[50]

22. February 20–July 9, 1805, Mexico City and Tulancingo, a full docket on one sale. On February 20, 1805, Joaquín Pérez Gavilán, Indian solicitor, presents to the General Indian Court a petition on behalf of Mariano Cristóbal, Indian widower and tributary of Tulancingo, for permission to rent out a house and a half-fanegada of land. The viceroy orders an investigation by the local justice and granting of a license if the house is a second one and under 30/ value. On March 5 the subdelegado of Tulancingo orders an investigation, and on March 8 there is written into the record an evaluation by a mason and a carpenter that the house is worth 152/5/9. In a document without date, Cristóbal petitions the subdelegado for a license to sell the house since he does not need it. On March 9 the subdelegado reports to the viceroy that the house is indeed a second one, but well over 30/ value. The viceroy sends all papers to the fiscal protector for an opinion. On April 30 the fiscal recommends granting a license for sale at public auction; May 4 the viceroy issues a decree to that effect; and on May 10 at Tulancingo the subdelegado orders that the proceedings for sale be carried out. From May 13 to June 19 the thirty days of public proclamation occur. On June 20, in Tulancingo, Juan Vicente Ordóñez offers the formal evaluation, the only bid in the public auction; July 1 the subdelegado accepts the bid. On July 5 Cristóbal, in the presence of the subdelegado, formally acknowledges receipt of the price in cash, and on July 9, 1805, in Tulancingo, certified and sealed copies of the proceedings are given as required.[51]

d. Opposition to Land Grants

All vacant land in central Mexico legally was crown property and could be granted to subjects by the viceroy. The viceregal order for the grant was supposed to be followed by an investigation to establish that the land really was not in use nor claimed by someone else, and to set boundaries. Neighbors and people with possible claims were supposed to be given full notice of the proceedings so that they might make any protests they wished at that time. The formal document of grant always specified that it was issued without prejudice to the right of any third party; and the plea that proper proceedings had not been carried out in full might be used to challenge any grant years after the event. In the seventeenth and eighteenth centuries, a series of *composiciones generales*, general inspections of land titles district by district,

50. Ibid., 54:fols. 224v–225f.
51. AT, in 14 fols.

gave royal titles to lands for payment—the purpose of the investigations—quieting title in instances of irregularity or simple usurpation of vacant land. Such titles still did not invalidate the rights of third parties.[52] In 1667, Indian towns were exempted from such composiciones generales on the ground of undue financial burden.[53]

23. June 7, 1594, Mexico City. The viceroy had made a provisional grant of an *estancia de ganado menor* in the area of Tlaxiaco, province of Teposcolula, to Juan Pérez Román. Since the investigation showed that such a ranch would be harmful to the Indians, the Spaniard has twice been required to yield the document but has not done so. Now, at the request of the Procurador General de los Indios, the viceroy issues a specific decree of cancellation.[54]

24. April 24, 1616, Mexico City. The town of San Francisco Astacameca, province of Otumba, petitions for grant of an estancia de ganado menor plus 2 caballerías of land. In the investigation, Juan Téllez Baraona presents papers in contradiction, pleading prior right. The viceroy's assessor advises sending the case for proof by both parties within fifteen days, with the full formality of notice, citation of parties, and reaching a final sentence. The viceroy issues an order to the corregidor of Otumba to hold hearings as advised by his assessor.[55]

25. June 17, 1616, Mexico City. Dr. Juan de Contreras, holder of the first chair in medicine at the University of Mexico, vs. the town of San Pedro Cangua, province of Acámbaro. Contreras is represented by Diego López de Haro, normally a salaried Indian solicitor, and San Pedro Cangua by José de Celi, Indian solicitor. The suit concerns measurement and bounding of an estancia de ganado mayor in the Valley of Puruagua. The Indians have twice appealed the formal sentence of the viceroy in the matter, on the ground that it does not reserve land around their houses of about a half-caballería, which they use for crops. They are willing to drop the suit if the land is reserved for them. Despite the sentence closing the case, the papers are sent to the Protector of the Indians and, in turn, to Dr. Luis de Cifuentes, abogado of the audiencia, acting as assessor. In view of their opinions, the viceroy orders that the ranch lands be surveyed and measured, but without innovation, and that Indian houses populated at the time of the first survey, the church, and lands the Indians cultivate for crops are not to be disturbed. The local justices are to enforce the decree and its clauses.[56]

52. Chevalier, *La formation*, 59–68, 176–181, 242–301, 348–363, et passim; Simpson, *Exploitation of Land*, passim. See also the summaries in this section.

53. Viñas Mey, 292–293 (doc. 12).

54. AGN-I, 6, part 1:exp. 800.

55. Ibid., 7:exp. 40.   56. Ibid., exp. 70.

26. March 29, 1629, Mexico City. Don Miguel, principal of Maravatío, on behalf of the town, relates that in 1610 Viceroy Luis de Velasco II granted Don Gerónimo de Padilla Barahona lands for 2 estancias de ganado mayor plus 4 caballerías. Investigation by the alcalde mayor of the mines of Tlalpujahua found no impediment and assessed the grant as worth payment to the crown of 150/. Now Don Gerónimo has given deed to his rights to the town for support of the town hospital. The town petitions for confirmation of the grant and transfer, presenting all papers. On the opinion of his assessor that new proceedings are necessary, since the old ones took place nineteen years ago, the viceroy orders the alcalde mayor of Maravatío to carry them out, with five official witnesses and five presented by the town, to be Spanish and Indian, and citing further all possible parties. He is to send his report and the papers to the office of the viceregal administrative secretaries.[57]

27. November 27, 1706, Mexico City. On October 20, 1706, Nicolás Manzano obtained a provisional viceregal grant of rough land 3 leagues from the town of Sosola, province of Antequera. In the proceedings, Sosola objected that the land was the town's, held by Nicolás Manzano on rental for pasturing livestock. The latter had paid the town 4/ a year the first two years, but had continued to use the lands without payment for another two years. The viceroy orders the local alcalde mayor to refer the Indians of Sosola to the General Indian Court and report on their complaint so that the court may hear the case.[58]

e. Cacicazgo and Inheritance

28. June 12, 1656, Mexico City. Don Gabriel de Guzmán, an Indian, complains that his older brother, Juan Manuel, has seized all property left by his father, Don Francisco de Guzmán, cacique of Yanhuitlán, who apparently died without leaving a will. The older brother refuses to divide the inheritance. The viceroy orders the local alcalde mayor of Yanhuitlán to see that justice is done. The viceregal order is really an *incitativa*, an order to a lower official or court to carry out its functions, since the alcalde mayor as justice of the province was fully competent to hear the case and was not being challenged as prejudiced. Such orders became common practice in the eighteenth century.[59]

29. March 8, 1657, Mexico City. Don Benito de Zúñiga, cacique of Coixtlahuaca, province of Teposcolula, relates to the General In-

---

57. Ibid., 10, cuad. 1 : exp. 77.
58. Ibid., 36 : fols. 348f–349f.   59. Ibid., 20 : exp. 137.

dian Court that his sister, Juana de los Angeles, married Don Juan de Gregorio. Both died, leaving a son, Melchor de los Angeles, who also died in 1646, leaving Zúñiga sole heir to the cacicazgo of the barrio of Utziniyucutepan, and all its lands and buildings in the town of Tezoatlán, province of Huajuapan. His inheritance is disputed by Don Francisco de Mendoza, who has introduced himself into the town of Tezoatlán as cacique. To avoid suits and much trouble, Zúñiga agreed to a settlement arranged before the Spanish justice of the town. He now petitions for a viceregal order to the alcalde mayor of Yanhuitlán to enforce the terms of the settlement. The viceroy orders the alcalde mayor of Yanhuitlán to extend amparo to Zúñiga, provided that his account is true and that such protection does not injure a third party.[60]

30. March 13, 1799, Mexico City. José Antonio Gómez, cacique of Tepeji del Río, province of Tula, vs. Manuel Resendes, over three ranches, a house, and other land, claimed as property of the cacicazgo. Gómez petitions the viceroy to take jurisdiction, complaining of failure of the justice of the district of Tula to reach any decision and of his fear that the justice will sell off the property in dispute. On October 2, 1798, the viceroy orders the justice to report to the General Indian Court. On October 11 the subdelegado of Tula formally acknowledges receipt of the viceregal order, and on October 13 signs a report declaring the petition mendacious and denying any attempt or intent to sell the properties. The final decree here orders that the papers are to be turned over to the petitioner's lawyers for presentation to the subdelegado of Tula.[61]

f. Grants and Special Privileges

The category here is complex, covering lands, right to bear arms, amparo against invasion by neighbors, etc. It illustrates grants and confirmations of special property rights. Grants of licenses will be found below under section 4d.

31. January 11, 1712, Mexico City. Basilio de Rivera, on behalf of Don Cristóbal Vásquez, governor of Santa María del Río, province of San Luis Potosí, a Tlaxcaltecan town on the Guachichil frontier, asks for confirmation of privileges granted by former viceroys as verified by the oidor, Tristán Manuel de Rivadeneyra, who was sent as special judge by the viceroy to investigate. The privileges specify that the nobles and principales may bear defensive and offensive arms; use drum and trumpet when appropriate, "since the town is on the frontier"; and that no Indian of the town is to be put to involuntary service

60. Ibid., 21:exp. 78.
61. AGN-V, 273:exp. 4 (BLT).

by the alcaldes mayores or their lieutenants. If the Indians do work, they are to be paid. Furthermore, no Spaniard may molest the Indians by pasturing livestock on their land, except with their consent and proper payment. The governor also complains that some younger people create disturbances when cabildos and meetings are held. The viceroy reconfirms all privileges, extends amparo against abuses, and sets a fine of 200/ for using Indian land as pasture without consent. Unruly and tumultuous Indians upsetting orderly functioning of the town are to be sentenced to forced labor in workshops at the pleasure of the court.[62]

g. Amparo

Since the Constitution of 1857, Mexicans have pointed with pride, as a great advance in the assurance of human rights, to the writ of amparo: the granting of protection in some right that is likely to be threatened, or the guarantee of existing dimensions of that right. Actually, as one Mexican legal scholar has proved, the issuance of writs and orders of amparo was common colonial practice.[63] Orders of amparo, valid within the Audiencia of Mexico, fell within the administrative prerogative of the viceroy, and their issuance began with the first viceroy. Petitions for many of them were heard in the General Indian Court, once that was established. Most orders concerned land and water, but any other right under threat of infringement might be protected.

32. March 24, 1616, Mexico City. José de Celi, Indian solicitor, on behalf of the Indians of San Nicolás Cuitlatetelco, sujeto of Mezquique (Mixquic, province of Chalco?), explains to the court that for many years the town has held its market behind its church in order and peace every Saturday, but that now certain Spaniards and some Indians from outside wish to move the market for their own purposes. He petitions for protection and that no one occupy the site. On the advice of his assessor, the viceroy issues an order to the justice of the province that the town market fair is not to be interfered with, nor are the Indians to be forced to abandon it or allow anyone to occupy it for other purposes.[64]

33. April 28, 1616, Mexico City. Alonso Jiménez de Castilla, Indian solicitor, appears before the court on behalf of Don Gabriel Miguel, native and principal of Otumba. A copy of information on 3 caballerías Don Gabriel inherited from his father near the towns of

62. AGN-I, 38:exp. 2 (LBSF, 10:fols. 153–155).
63. Lira González, *El amparo colonial*, passim.
64. AGN-I, 7:exp. 36.

San Francisco Istacameca and Santa Cruz Tlamapa was sent to a Spaniard, Pedro González Perlín, for investigation. He reported that Domingo de Lizardi was the only person who might object to assertion of ownership. Lizardi has not answered formal notification. The solicitor asks for an order of amparo, and that it and the other papers serve as title to the land. On the advice of his assessor, the viceroy orders the appropriate judges to protect Don Gabriel in possession of the land. If any Spaniard who received notification has any reason to object, he is to do so before the General Indian Court, which will do justice.[65]

34. June 7, 1616, Mexico City. The town of Chiautla presents evidence that Lic. Diego Landeras y Velasco as visitador-general of New Spain ordered that it be protected in its use of water from the arroyo of Salepango, and set penalties for Cristóbal Osorio and other persons who tried to seize the water; but the owners of the haciendas involved transferred their claim for water to others, who refuse to allow the Indians any use, even to irrigate the kitchen garden of the convent. The town asks for protection in its use of the water and that an inspector be sent to set boundaries to their lands in accordance with the Indians' titles and grants. On the advice of the assessor, the viceroy orders the justice of Texcoco to force all people to observe the decision on water rights issued by Lic. Landeras y Velasco. The town is to be protected in peaceful use, and if there is any complaint, it is to come before the viceroy in the General Indian Court. If no judge has yet been named to set boundaries to the Indians' lands, Alonso Sánchez Redondo is hereby commissioned to do so under the ordinances and with due regard to titles. All neighbors, residents, and interested parties are to be cited to the proceedings. If a judge already has been named or a suit is being heard on the matter, it is to be brought to conclusion promptly, with due opportunity for the Indians to present their claims.[66]

35. April 7, 1618, Mexico City. Fray Hernando del Villamisor, O.S.A., prior of the convent of Tlanchinolticpac, province of Pánuco, exhibits a viceregal order that tithes due from Indians not be collected by tithe collectors in person, but only by a bailiff, and that tithes be required from Indians only to the extent and on the three crops allowed by law. On the opinion of his assessor, the viceroy issues an order of amparo.[67]

36. August 3, 1628, Mexico City. Lic. Alfonso de Castro Guzmán, chaplain-major of the Hospital Real de Indios in Mexico City, asks the court for an order of amparo. The many Indians who die in

65. Ibid., exp. 41.
66. Ibid., exp. 62.
67. Ibid., exp. 275.

the hospital are buried with great expense for Indian singers from the convents of San Francisco, Santa María, and San Pablo. To reduce costs, he has brought in outsiders, master singers who constitute a formal chapel choir, but he fears that the friars will interfere and the justices molest his singers. The assessor advises that there will be no infringement of any right if the Indians sing at the hospital's festivals and burials without charge to the Indians, and if they do not appear at festivals and burials outside of the hospital's jurisdiction. The viceroy issues an order of amparo.[68]

37. October 19, 1628, Mexico City. José de Celi, Indian solicitor, on behalf of the Indians of the town of Tamos, province of Pánuco, complains that the alcalde mayor of Pánuco gave a fishing site they have used from time immemorial to a Spaniard, and the two men try to hinder their fishing. The Indians' catch from the large stream flowing by their town both supports them and pays their tributes. On the advice of his assessor, the viceroy orders the alcalde mayor to allow the Indians of Tamos freely to fish in their river and not to let any Spaniard hinder them, under pain of payment of any damages suffered and the further penalty that an agent will be sent to enforce the order of amparo at the alcalde mayor's expense.[69]

38. May 22, 1629, Mexico City. At the petition of the Indians of Tula and on advice of his assessor, the viceroy issues an order of amparo, forbidding a Spaniard to settle in the district of the town.[70]

39. March 8, 1630, Mexico City. Don Baltasar Gómez, captain of the Chichimec Indians of San Luis de la Paz, states that he has served God and the king for twenty years in pacifying and congregating Guachichil Indians, and has served with Jesuits and royal governors. He petitions for an order of amparo so that none of his enemies may bring complaint against him for the killing of an Indian in the Río Verde thirty years ago, when he was helping the Spanish in his office of captain. The petition is reviewed in the General Indian Court. On the advice of his assessor, the viceroy issues an order of amparo to the justices of San Luis de la Paz and elsewhere for the protection of Don Baltasar against any complaint based on the old homicide. If there is any reason for complaint, it is to be heard only in the General Indian Court and nowhere else.[71]

40. March 20, 1630, Mexico City. Melchor López de Haro, Indian solicitor, on behalf of Melchor de los Reyes, *indio chino*, born in Manila, petitions for an order of amparo to protect his client from

68. Ibid., 10, cuad. 1 : exp. 7.
69. Ibid., exp. 21.
70. Ibid., exp. 97.
71. Ibid., exp. 265.

molestation by any justice in New Spain in his occupation of making and selling the maguey liquor calld *agua ardiente de maguey*. On the advice of his assessor, the viceroy issues the order of amparo.[72]

This document is notable because a Filipino, as a "Chinese Indian," is held to be entitled to the services of the court, and because the reference to the "burning water from the maguey" is one of the earliest references to distilled liquor from the fermented juice of the maguey. We cannot be sure just which species of agave was used, but the order of amparo certainly refers either to an early version of tequila or mezcal or to something similar.

41. March 22, 1630, Mexico City. On behalf of Antonio Marrero, widower of Angelina Sánchez, cacica and principal of Tehuacán, a petition relates that she inherited lands and rights in water granted to her parents and these have now passed to Marrero. Spaniards try to intrude. On the advice of his assessor, the viceroy issues an order of amparo to the alcalde mayor of Tehuacán for ensuring that Marrero enjoys full and quiet possession.[73]

42. October 19, 1630, Mexico City. Melchor López de Haro, Indian solicitor, on behalf of Don Gabriel de los Angeles, cacique of Atlacomulco, petitions for an order of amparo to ensure protection in his share of goods and land left by his father, and that all six legal heirs divide the burden of debts to be paid. Creditors try to collect all from him alone. On the advice of his assessor, the viceroy issues the order of amparo as petitioned for.[74]

A sequel to this case occurred a month later, when the same solicitor petitions for enforcement of the order already issued. On the advice of the assessor, a second order is issued with the date of November 29, 1630.[75]

43. April 16, 1633, Mexico City. José de Celi, Indian solicitor, on behalf of the Indians of Comanja, Cocupao, and other towns of their district in the province of Michoacán, complains that their ejidos and pastures have been seized by Don Juan de Haro, a Spaniard, and others, who seize the Indians' crops and livestock in order to pasture their own animals. Haro has no estancia of his own. Celi petitions that the justice of the province of Michoacán, without delay or excuse, see that the Indians' lands are returned to them, and that Haro, if he has anything to plead, do so in the proper tribunal with written evidence; further, that the justice expel all invading people from the lands, keep them out under proper penalties, and that he both determine the extent of damages and see that they are paid. On the advice of his as-

72. Ibid., exp. 212.
74. Ibid., exp. 308.
73. Ibid., exp. 215 (LBSF, 7:fols. 142–144).
75. Ibid., exp. 328.

sessor, the viceroy issues an order to the justice of Michoacán, granting amparo and ordering payment of damages done.[76]

44. September 2, 1676, Mexico City. Juan López, Indian of Coyotepec, province of Yanhuitlán, petitions for protection for himself and his wife in a small house they have on the town plaza near the royal buildings. He also asks that he and his wife be protected from levy of taxes for sales on market day, since they support themselves by selling chocolate, tamales, and vegetables. Certain persons threaten to seize the house and want to levy o/1 each market day for the right to sell. The viceroy issues an order of amparo.[77]

45. December 27, 1720, Mexico City. The Indians of Nueva Tlaxcala petition for protection against abuse by the *teniente* of the nearby mining center of Chalchihuites (Zacatecas). He mistreats and imprisons them and threatens to have any Indian of Nueva Tlaxcala caught in his jurisdiction given 200 lashes. The viceroy issues a decree of amparo. Involved in the case are the rights of the descendants of Tlaxcaltecan settlers in the North, who were guaranteed special privileges in perpetuity, and the rivalry between the Audiencia of Mexico, in which Nueva Tlaxcala lay, and that of Nueva Galicia, governed from Guadalajara, in which lay Chalchihuites. The viceroy was asserting his prerogatives to govern in the first audiencia and intervene, when he thought it desirable or necessary, in the other.[78]

46. March 23–30, 1805, Mexico City. Various Indians of Santa Ana Jilotzingo, province of Tenango del Valle, protest to the viceroy that they have been expelled from the Parián (a building and market in the central square of Mexico City) on the ground that they do not pay fees for selling articles of *hilillo* and *pita* (agave fibers). The viceroy orders the senior regidor of Mexico City to report; until the court reaches a decision, the Indians are not to be molested. The regidor reports that the space is needed for the regular vendors. The viceroy orders that a copy of the answer be furnished to the complainants. The docket ends at this point.[79]

2. Mistreatment and Exactions by Non-Indians

a. Spanish Provincial Governors, Their Subordinates, and Other Spanish Officials

Although substantially less numerous than cases affecting land, complaints against Spanish provincial governors, their subordinates,

76. Ibid., cuad. 3:exp. 161 (LBSF, 8:fols. 18–22).
77. Ibid., 25:exp. 147.   78. Ibid., 44:exp. 99 (LBSF, 11:fols. 55–60).
79. AGN-Civ, vol. 2140:exp. 6 (LBSD, vol. 15).

and other Spanish officials nevertheless constituted an appreciable proportion of the total business that came before the General Indian Court. Under the Spanish colonial system, the alcaldes mayores exercised both administrative and judicial authority in their provinces. So did the corregidores, who held equal power in the smaller areas they governed, and the lieutenants the alcaldes mayores appointed for districts within their provinces since the territories were too large to be administered directly. A shift to subdelegados under the Ordinance of Intendants of 1786 did not bring any real change. Accordingly, the Spanish provincial and local governors were vested with wide powers which permitted easy abuse of authority. At the same time, they were so poorly paid that they were easily led to use those powers to make up deficits in their revenues and from there go on to make their fortunes. The problem lay in the fact that the formal salary, no more than one to several hundred pesos a year for an alcalde mayor or corregidor, did not even cover the cost of papers of appointment, the required bonds, and the expense of reaching the locality. True, salaries were supplemented by levy of fees and costs for providing services and hearing cases, all in accordance with existing schedules. However, even such additional revenue could not provide well for a gentleman and his family, nor pay off his creditors. In an age when popular belief and prevailing custom held that office existed as a means for enrichment, temptation was almost irresistible. Their lieutenants, whom they appointed at will and who were usually local people, drew no salary but were entitled to the fees and costs set out in the schedules. They too had had to secure their posts and needed to recover their expenses, support themselves, and, if possible, add to their capital.[80]

The standard instructions for alcaldes mayores, evolved during the course of the sixteenth century, contain many clauses enjoining good behavior. The provincial governors were to collect only the tribute assessed and to levy no other contributions. They were to see that the Indians were not forced to sell below proper prices. They were to inspect community accounts only once, and then without charge. They were not to take money or anything else from the communities, even as a loan. They were not to accept gifts or food in any way, even if given voluntarily. They were to keep no livestock, to have no estancias, nor were they to engage in trade in their provinces. They were not to

80. See the comments of Velasco II in Chapter IV of this study. See also the royal cédula of August 12, 1649, to the Conde de Alba de Liste, in Konetzke, 2:439–440, no. 291; Ortega Montañés, sects. 22–26, pp. 67–69, dated March 4, 1697; Ortiz de la Tabla Ducasse, 25–28; and Pietschmann, *Die Einführung*, 91–105. See also Beleña, 1, part 5:197, no. 355, summarizing a royal provisión of the audiencia, Mexico City, August 17, 1784, forbidding provincial governors to appoint lieutenants for money or gifts before or after the appointment.

take part of the fees and salaries of notaries and other officials in their province, nor make under-the-table arrangements. They were to see that damages to the Indians from livestock of non-Spaniards were settled promptly. Further, Indians were to pay no jail charges except to the Indian bailiffs and jailor. The provincial governors were not to take money or anything else on plea of violation of rules on pulque, nor were they to enter Indian houses without formal cause. Finally, they might not acquire land, directly nor indirectly, nor any other possession in their territory during their terms of office and for six years afterwards.[81]

Unfortunately, most of these injunctions were circumvented or ignored. Perhaps the most common violation was the *repartimiento de mercancías*: a provincial governor, on entering his province, arranged a distribution of livestock and merchandise among the Indian families, at prices he set, the Indians having to pay in coin or merchandise at a somewhat later date. The practice was regarded as a means of bringing the Indians into more active commercial life; of getting them to buy merchandise, livestock, and tools; and of encouraging the production of desirable export crops such as cochineal. The debate over the repartimiento de mercancías went on throughout the colonial period. The practice was legal in Peru, illegal in Mexico, but crept in. In 1751 the crown legalized it in Mexico, but with orders for fixed schedules of amounts and prices for each province. The dilemma remained until the Wars of Independence, for without something like the repartimiento de mercancías, provincial governors could not earn enough to make their posts worth the effort; with it, there was possible vast abuse since the merchandise usually was something the Indians neither wanted nor needed, and payment was enforced by the same official, sitting as judge, who had foisted the merchandise upon them.[82]

A moderate amount of extortion does not seem to have brought the Indians to complaint; but when the fleecing reached proportions they deemed intolerable, they would protest either to the viceroy or the audiencia. Their complaints were organized in a series of charges, called *capítulos* (chapters), whence the terms *capitular* (to bring them)

81. Montemayer y Córdova de Cuenca, part 2:fols. 24v–28f, no. 58, and Beleña, 1, part 1:37–44, no. 58. See also the auto acordado of May 11, 1671, summarized as no. 57 in both works.

82. See the references cited in note 80 above; also Hamnett, passim, and Stein. The royal cédula legalizing the repartimiento in Mexico, dated Buen Retiro, July 17, 1751, is in AGN-RCD, 102:fols. 122f–124v. Although the Real Ordenanza de Intendentes of 1787 abolished the repartimiento (art. 12), the practice proved impossible to suppress. By royal order of June 13, 1798, the viceroys were given private jurisdiction to try complaints of repartimiento de mercancías (Azanza, 47), the crown thus ratifying what they had been doing.

and *capitulado* (to have them brought against oneself). Such charges were supposed to be attended to at once, without deferring hearing on them to the residencia, the investigation of conduct in office that every provincial governor had to undergo at the end of his term.[83] So long as the provincial governor and the parish priests were on good terms, it was unlikely that the Indians of the local towns would bring charges. When, however, the governor and the priests fell out, the Indians were likely to be persuaded by the priests or took courage from the mutual animosity to move their case. In time, the Spanish authorities in Mexico City learned further that they must make sure that such charges were truly brought by the town and the people signing for it, and demand guarantees that the charges were neither false nor frivolous.[84] Capítulos were a potent arm, if one judges from the outrage they provoked in Hipólito Villarroel, a bitter critic of the General Indian Court.[85]

47. December 15, 1612–January 4, 1613, Mexico City and Teposcolula. The Indians of Teposcolula sue in the General Indian Court to stop Pedro Maldonado Zapata, the alcalde mayor of the province, from forcing them to spin cotton into thread at low prices. They complain further that he forces them to sell him cochineal at low values. The viceroy orders the alcalde mayor to govern justly. On presentation of the decree in Teposcolula, the alcalde mayor in a notarial statement declares that he makes only one distribution of cotton, as is the custom. He gives out 3 arrobas 8 pounds of cotton for each arroba of thread required back, and pays the Indians 4/5/6 per arroba of thread. His trade in cochineal occurs outside the province. He orders the town regidores to declare what is the truth. Their testimony follows and agrees with the alcalde mayor.[86]

This docket, from the archives of Teposcolula, illustrates what might happen even after a viceregal decree was obtained and presented. Whatever the truth of the allegations, the Indian regidores were unlikely to gainsay the alcalde mayor to his face.

48. February 5, 1616, Mexico City. José de Celi, for the Indians of Nochixtlán, complains that Diego Ladrón de Guevara, corregidor

83. Montemayor y Córdova de Cuenca, part 2: fols. 35v–38f, no. 98, and Beleña, 1, part 1:59, no. 98, summarizing an auto acordado of May 4, 1656, issued on express royal order and repeating previous royal orders.

84. Croix, September 1, 1771, 56–57, sect. 17. See also the relación de mando of Revillagigedo I, Mexico City, November 28, 1754, clauses 33–34, in *Instrucciones*, I:303–304.

85. Villarroel, 495–496.

86. AJT-Crim, leg. 2.

of the town, interferes in the production of pulque and levies heavy fines. Production of *pulque blanco*, expressly permitted by the ordinances, is a major industry of the town. It uses local magueyes and the pulque is sold in public markets. The viceroy orders that the corregidor not interfere with the production or trade in pulque blanco, since it is legal, nor levy fines in connection with it, on pain of punishment.[87]

49. May 11, 1616, Mexico City. José de Celi, on behalf of the principales and other Indians of Huautla, declares that they came to Mexico City to complain of mistreatment by their corregidor and now fear to return home, lest he punish and mistreat them for complaining. They ask for remedy. The viceroy orders that they are not to be molested. The justice of the area is given commission by this order to protect them and send a report on any infraction directly to the viceroy.[88]

50. August 5, 1619, Mexico City. This is a follow-up decree. The Indians of Hueytepec, Huajolotipac, Istula, Elotepec, and Totomachapa (all part of Los Peñoles) presented a memorial listing exactions and mistreatment on the part of the corregidor of Ixcuintepec, Francisco Montaño Sotomayor. On order from the viceroy of June 3, 1619, Juan de Arialgabrán Velasco, corregidor of Teozacoalco, investigated the charges. He was to see that the Indians were repaid any sums extorted and report back to the court within thirty days. The viceroy now orders Montaño Sotomayor to appear before the General Indian Court in forty days, on pain for noncompliance of suspension from office and 200/ fine. He is to be notified of the order by anyone who can read and write.[89]

51. October 6, 1628, Mexico City. The Indians of Teticpac complain that their alcalde mayor levies chickens and rations of foodstuffs from them, uses them as *tamemes* (bearers), etc. The viceroy, on review in the court, orders the alcalde mayor to cease any levies, to pay for all foodstuffs obtained from the Indians, not to use them as tamemes, and to end all other improper practices.[90]

52. April 6, 1633, Mexico City. José de Celi, for the Indians of Atorpay and Chicuasontepec, province of Veracruz, presents a series of complaints against the local alcalde mayor. In a series of decrees, all of the same date, the viceroy orders reform: (1) The alcalde mayor has carried out an excessive number of community inspections with excessive fees for them and for confirming town elections. He is ordered not to do so, and to return what he has collected on penalty of fourfold

87. AGN-I, 7:exp. 20.   88. Ibid., exp. 50.
89. Ibid., 9:exp. 158.   90. Ibid., 10, cuad. 1:exp. 19.

restitution. (2) He uses Indians on his private business and fines them if they resist. He is to use them only on royal business. (3) Some residents of Veracruz prevent the Indians from marketing their produce and seize it, paying lower than market price. The alcalde mayor is ordered not to permit this and to fine anyone violating the order 100/. (4) The alcalde mayor forces the Indians to fish for him and to make available horses and mules without pay. He is not to use the Indians in his own business and is to pay them for any service rendered. He is to send evidence of compliance with this decree to Mexico City. (5) The alcalde mayor's use of the Indians for fishing has not allowed them to finish the town church. He is to desist and let them finish the church. (6) The alcalde mayor and his friends force money on the Indians and demand chickens and eggs in return, but at low prices. A chicken is worth 0/5, but the Spaniards pay 0/2. The alcalde mayor is reminded of the royal cédula on these practices and the penalties prescribed. (7) The alcalde mayor sends Indians with loads to Mexico City, Puebla, and other places, without pay. He is ordered not to do so.[91]

53. November 16, 1639, Mexico City. José de Celi, for the governors and towns of Astapa, Xaguacapa, and Xalapa, in Tabasco, declares that the Indians come freely to work for their encomendero, Lucas de Barros, on the reed houses he lives in. They are paid, but the alcalde mayor tries to stop them. He asks that the alcalde mayor be forbidden to interfere, so long as the work is voluntary and paid. The viceroy so orders.[92]

54. February 7–May 11, 1643, Mexico City and Cuernavaca. Officials of the villa of Cuernavaca vs. Francisco López, official for fruit sold in the main square of Mexico City, for seizing all fruit and selling it himself. February 7, in Cuernavaca, the town officials petition the alcalde mayor of Cuernavaca (in the Marquesado del Valle) for license to issue a power of attorney to Lucas de Santillán, of Mexico City, so that he may act as their agent in placing their complaint before the viceroy. The alcalde mayor grants the license, and the same day the town officials execute a power of attorney. On March 10, Santillán petitions the viceroy for summary investigation, punishment, and restitution. The court decrees that information be given to its notary and brought before the viceroy, and on March 18 four witnesses make their depositions via Pedro Vázquez, the interpreter of the audiencia. At this point the docket contains an undated petition by Santillán for the jailing of Francisco López and a Spaniard named Don Luis. On April 10 Francisco López makes a statement on the com-

91. Ibid., cuad. 3 : exps. 142–148 (LBSF, 8 : fols. 5–8).
92. Ibid., 11 : exp. 371 (LBSF, 8 : fols. 93–95).

plaint before the court notary, on order of the viceroy; April 15, the court orders that the parties be notified and given six days to present evidence leading to conclusion of the case; April 17–18, the parties are notified.

The docket at this point contains an undated petition for the town, through one Agustín Franco, that López be arrested and his staff of office taken away. April 24, the court orders that the parties be notified of the decree of April 15. Agustín Franco, on behalf of the town, asks for penalties and restitution. April 29, the court orders that the other party be given notice and witnesses be examined; its bailiff is to force witnesses to appear. On the same date, Cuernavaca presents six witnesses who give testimony before the court notary and interpreter. Lucas de Medina, attorney for López, petitions the court for ten more days; on April 30, the court allows six more. May 4, notice is given to López via his attorney. An undated plea by Medina and Lic. Alonso de Alavés, as attorneys for López, asks for twenty days more to give evidence. They plead that the charges are false, the form in which they have been made is incorrect, and the town officials are not genuine plaintiffs. May 11, the court orders that a copy of the pleading be furnished the Indians and both parties be allowed ten days for presenting answers and evidence. July 16, both parties are notified.

At this point the docket contains copies of two viceregal orders, dated January 26 and January 30, 1643, undoubtedly filed by López in his defense. The first orders López, as official for vagabonds and protector of the Indians who sell fruit in the main square of Mexico City, to store the fruit in one house, which is to seve as shelter for the Indians and their animals. The order was proclaimed in Mexico City, Coyoacán, and San Mateo Teopachic. The second, issued at the petition of López, who claims men and women of San Mateo Teopachic and San Agustín de las Cuevas intercept Indians bringing fruit to Mexico City, authorizes appointment of two men to stop this practice. Both viceregal orders are presented in notarial transcripts dated May 8, 1643. The docket ends here with a notation that Juan de Palafox examined it in his general inspection of New Spain on June 26, 1646.[93]

If López did not actually seize and sell fruit, his actions almost certainly would be upheld by the court since he was acting under express viceregal appointment and order. The case illustrates the extent to which Spanish court procedures were adopted by the court, but with abbreviated preparation of pleadings and records and without fees.

55. September 2, 1654, Mexico City. Francisco de Rosales and María, his daughter, complain that the alcalde mayor of Yanhuitlán

93. AGN-Crim, 46:exp. 6 (26 fols.) (LBSD, vol. 26).

employed them to sell chocolate, tobacco, sugar, soap, and other items. In fifteen days they turned over to him 450/, but he would not pay them their wages of 13/. When they refused to continue working for him, he threw them in jail, where they have been for four months, and seized their houses, 3 petticoats, 1 blouse, and 2 pounds of silver. They ask for release, payment of their wages, and protection against further molestation. The viceroy orders the alcalde mayor, if the story is true, to pay and release the petitioners and their goods. He is to send a sworn account to the court.[94]

56. March 7, 1655, Mexico City. Ignacio de Meneses, Indian of Teposcolula, complains to the court that the local alcalde mayor wanted his house for a Spanish resident named Marcos Pérez. Meneses refused and was kept in jail eleven days until he agreed to turn over the house without rent. Marcos Pérez has seized some images, metates, chests, etc., which were in the house. Meneses petitions for remedy. The viceroy orders the alcalde mayor to return the house and other goods to Meneses "without providing cause that he again complain."[95]

57. November 7, 1695, Mexico City. The Indians of San Mateo Calpulalpan vs. the alcalde mayor of Ixtepeje. This is the town we have already met in suit with Ixtlán. On November 29, 1694, it filed capítulos filling eight small books. The charges included trading in cochineal, engrossing all trade in the province by force, paying 0/2 to 1/2 the pound while cochineal sold in Antequera for 3/ the pound; extortion of other kinds, including charging for permitting Indians to go to Antequera; placing repartimientos de mercancías of goods not needed and at excessive prices, all to be paid in cochineal; mistreatment, brutality, and homicide. The last charge is supported by a detailed account of the alcalde mayor's beating an Indian with a firebrand and so injuring the latter that he died.

Investigation supports the charges. The fiscal protector recommends suspension from office, four years' service in the Philippines, perpetual exile from New Spain, full payment to the Indians for all taken from them, monetary compensation for the death of the principal at the hands of the alcalde mayor, and 1000 ducats' fine. The viceroy so decrees.[96] His sentence was undoubtedly appealed to the audiencia, but those papers are not here.

58. December 29, 1714, Mexico City. Gerónimo de Trejo and his wife, Indians of Tecozautla, province of Jilotepec, petition for redress and protection. They have a ranch, rented from Pedro Gómez Rojo. Three months ago soldiers from the presidio of San José came to

94. AGN-I, 17:exp. 199.   95. Ibid., 18:exp. 118.
96. Ibid., vol. 33: no numbering (LBSF, 10:fols. 98–107).

search the ranch for a piece of cloth they claimed the wife's brother had stolen. The search found nothing. Thereupon the soldiers took the family to jail in Tecozautla, seizing 130 goats and sheep, 2 milch cows, 2 calves, 2 horses, 3 saddles, 1 halter, 1 ounce of silk, 1 ball of cotton, 1 length of woolen cloth, and 1 of cotton. After three days in jail, the family was sent to a workshop for eight more. The husband was then taken to the presidio to guard livestock and strip the fibers from maguey blades; he fled. His wife was kept three months grinding corn and doing other domestic work. The couple went to see Gabriel Guerrero de Ardila (the commander at the presidio?) on his hacienda, asking for redress and return of their property. They were threatened with return to the workshop. When they went to their house, they found their two small daughters gone and their milpa ruined.

The couple ask that Guerrero de Ardila and his corporal be summoned to account for all property, pay for losses and damages, and be required to prove the charge of complicity in theft brought against the wife, and that they be given protection. The viceroy orders an investigation. The docket ends here.[97]

59. March 11, 1724, Mexico City. Santa María Aunvilla charges that the alcalde mayor of San Cristóbal Ecatepec extorts money from the Indians and keeps them prisoner without just cause. The viceroy orders the nearest justice to investigate, take testimony, and report back. The alcalde mayor of Ecatepec may file charges against those jailed but is not to molest any Indian, on penalty of 500/ fine. At the same time, the viceroy sends a letter of *ruego y encargo* to the ecclesiastical judge of the district, calling for any information he may have.[98]

60. February 25, 1761, Mexico City. Through Joaquín Antonio Guerrero, the Indians of Nuestra Señora de los Remedios de la Sábana, province of Ixmiquilpan, petition for redress. The town continually has quarrels with the employees and guards of the hacienda of Debode, owned by Francisco Xavier Paulín. At Paulín's petition, the alcalde mayor of Ixmiquilpan has kept 10 Indians in prison for three months. The Indians obtained a viceregal order for release, on pain of a fine of 400/, but it has not yet been served. Meanwhile, the alcalde mayor released the Indians but demanded costs and jail charges of 4/ to 6/ each. As guarantee, he kept 7 donkeys he had embargoed. The town lacks land, wasteland, etc. On the opinion of the fiscal protector that the earlier viceregal order should be observed at once unless the 10 Indians were in jail for seizing hacienda livestock, that the alcalde

97. Ibid., 39:fols. 156–157 (LBSF, 10:fols. 176–179).
98. Ibid., 48:exp. 112 (LBSF, 11:fols. 82–86).

mayor be ordered to explain why they were jailed, and that the Indians must not be kept from access to water they need for drinking, the viceroy so orders. Penalty for noncompliance is set at 200/. Service of the decree may be by any person who can read and write.[99]

61. June 10–September 13, 1769, Mexico City, San Cristóbal Ecatepec, and Guadalupe. Manuela Nopalatlán et al. vs. the alcalde mayor of San Cristóbal Ecatepec for forced unpaid service. The complaint is an unsigned petition prepared by someone other than the complainants. The court orders the *teniente* of Nuestra Señora de Guadalupe to take testimony in Ecatepec as special judge. The decree is to serve as dispatch, with a copy in the register of the General Indian Court. In Ecatepec the teniente takes testimony, all incorporated in his report to the viceroy. The alcalde mayor does use unmarried women and free widows, whom he pays 0/2 a week, the usual rate. The court sends all papers to the relator for ordering and summary, but requires the teniente to make another trip to Ecatepec in order to find out what is truly the usual wage. In Ecatepec, the Indians claim that the usual wage is 1/ to 1/4; the local vicar, giving testimony in the absence of the cura, says that an unmarried woman earns 1/ a week and a *"mujer hecha"* 1/4. The docket closes with the order of the teniente to send a report to the viceroy. Included is an affidavit that no fees were charged.[100]

62. June 30, 1774, Mexico City. Bernardo Martín, Indian of Teozacoalco, petitions the viceroy for release from prison, where he is kept as bondsman for the delivery of 10½ arrobas of cochineal at 1/2 the pound. The debt is not just since cochineal is worth 3/4 the pound, so that the quantity of cochineal has a real value of over 1000/. The alcalde mayor demands either the cochineal or the full money value. The petition further objects that it is improper for a creditor to sit as judge. The viceroy orders that the royal justice nearest Teozacoalco go to the town and, if the allegations are true, release the Indian.[101]

63. November 6, 1798, Mexico City. San Agustín Almoloya, province of Zacualpan, vs. the teniente of Teloloapan, for levy of improper fees when Indian officials take their staffs of office and on the delivery of tribute. The docket opens with execution of power of attorney, which is transferred to José María Ramírez, salaried Indian solicitor. November 6, 1798, he petitions the viceroy on behalf of the town, listing fees charged and asking that their levy be forbidden. The teniente charges 2/3 and 3 hens each third of the year for registering

99. Ibid., 59 : fols. 210–212 (LBSF, 12 : fols. 107–113).
100. AGN-Civ, vol. 2119 : exp. 5 (LBSD, vol. 15).
101. AGN-I, 44 : fols. 297f–299v.

tribute payment; for the August installment, he levies 1/ more. On election of town officials, he charges 2/4, and on the day of delivery of staffs of office, 2/ and 3 hens. For auditing community accounts, the charge is 6/ and 3 hens. The same day, on the advice of his assessor, the viceroy orders an immediate report from the subdelegado of Zacualpan, the superior of the teniente, and forbids further levy of any fees until the court decides. The next day the dispatch is given to the solicitor for delivery to his clients. The docket ends here.[102]

64. October 17, 1801, Mexico City and Actopan. Alejandro Bernardino, Indian of Tepetitlán, vs. Don Eusebio Corona, tax collector of the main square, for seizing Bernardino's stock of shoes. Corona brings a countercomplaint of refusal to pay a half-real tax for the new water supply. At viceregal instruction, the subdelegado takes testimony and reports back to Mexico City. The court rules in favor of Corona, but also instructs the subdelegado to return money charged as costs.[103]

65. June 15, 1803, Mexico City; a long case, 1800–1803. Francisco Xavier, governor of Teloloapan, vs. the subdelegado of Zacualpan, protesting a fine of 20/ for delay in delivering tribute and other abuses.[104] February 7, 1801, José María Arellano, for the governor, protests exactions by the subdelegado in charging fees as alleged in the case summarized above as no. 63 for delivery of tribute: 6/ on delivery of staffs of office, retaining the 1% of the tribute supposed to pay the governor for his work in collecting it, and levying a 20/ fine for slowness in delivery. The viceroy by letter and decree orders the justice of the district to report, and meanwhile not to molest the governor. March 4, Zacualpan, the subdelegado gives formal obedience and reports that delays in delivering tribute are long, that no fees are charged, but the Indians do give gifts of lesser amount than alleged. The governor has not yet presented his copy of the viceregal order. March 27, the court's assessor orders that the Indian be informed of the answer; this is done through his solicitor. September 9, 1801, another petition by the town with the same and more complaints. The viceroy orders the petition to be handled by the General Indian Court.

On November 12, 1801, the second petition is sent to the fiscal protector, who recommends joining all papers, and on November 17 renders opinion, upholding the governor and the town but also urging sending the matter to the royal treasury officials for audit of accounts. November 18, the assessor sends the papers to the relator for ordering

102. AGN-Civ, vol. 2179: exp. 2 (LBSD, vol. 6).
103. Ibid., 1261: exp. 10 (LBSD, vol. 2).
104. Ibid., 2182: exp. 3 (LBSD, vol. 7).

and summary, and on November 26 the viceroy and his assessor accept the fiscal's recommendations. Appropriate decrees are sent to the subdelegado and the royal treasury officials. On December 21, the latter report that the subdelegado has never presented for inspection and audit the accounts of the community treasury nor deposited any surplus, although his predecessor during his term deposited 11,000/8/9. The accounts presented by the governor have many irregularities and improper charges; furthermore, the town does not maintain the required school. On January 31, 1802, the fiscal protector urges that both the subdelegado and the governor be ordered to amend their accounts and their ways; they are to observe the procedures recommended by the royal treasury. On February 8 the court accepts the fiscal's recommendations and so orders.

The case does not end here. February 15–16, 1802, Zacualpan, there takes place the review of accounts and payments. The governor is paid his 1%, and voluntary gifts are returned. On February 18, the subdelegado in a letter to the viceroy declares his own purity and denounces the vices of the Indians, as should be clear from the treasury audit! February 22, Zacualpan, Emeterio Galán, the local administrator for royal revenue, reports that he could not finish his inquiry into improper exactions. March 13, the court sends all to the fiscal. March 20, the solicitor for the governor asks for and is granted permission to see the documents in the possession of the fiscal, so that he may pursue his client's rights on advice of a letrado. May 10, the solicitor presents a new pleading, a reply, and the text of a formal questionnaire to be sent to the administrator for royal revenue in Zacualpan, gathering testimony in the investigation. On May 5 the fiscal protector recommends asking the royal treasury officials for a report on the latest audit since the subdelegado was ordered to turn in accounts; June 1, the court so orders.

June 22, 1802, the royal treasury officials report: the subdelegado has not sent in his accounts; they have seen the comments and complaints of both parties, which they summarize and comment on in turn. They have audited a long series of receipts and corrections, filed after their first audit. These show perhaps 87/ due the governor, but probably the accounting is not complete. Since the public finances of Zacualpan are in disorder, it is difficult to propose an appropriate model for handling community property and funds as ordered in the viceregal decree of November 26, 1801. They have prepared a provisional model, a copy of which is attached, to serve until one is issued as required by the Ordinance of Intendants of 1786. July 31, the fiscal protector urges implementing the recommendations of the royal treasury officials and adding the new papers to the file on possible excesses of the subdelegado. August 7, 1802, the court orders all sent to the relator for ordering and summary.

On June 15, 1803, the assessor, acting for the viceroy, signs the decree accepting the fiscal's opinion. The docket closes with a notation June 28, 1803, Mexico City, by the court notary, that the appropriate dispatch had been prepared and turned over to the party for delivery.

66. July 9, 1804–August 14, 1806, Mexico City, Cuautla, etc. The town of Cocoyoc, province of Cuautla Amilpas, vs. its subdelegado, because he wishes to appoint a teniente for the town. The town petitions that there be no teniente. The subdelegado answers that one is needed, because there are so many mulattos in the town and it is on the border of the Marquesado, with much evasion. After the fiscal recommends that a local deputy justice is needed, the Indians ask that the person appointed not be Manuel de Porras, as the subdelegado proposes, since Porras is a local hacendado and merchant. Thereupon the fiscal urges that the subdelegado be ordered to appoint someone else. The viceroy so orders. This order evokes a protest from the subdelegado that Porras is not a merchant and that he is merely administrator of an hacienda, in which no Indian of the town is employed. His protest is countered by the attorney for the Indians, who cites the law on who may be appointed: an administrator or majordomo falls within the legal prohibition. The court then repeats its previous order, signed by the assessor acting for himself and the viceroy. In March 1805 the subdelegado reports compliance. Since there is no other suitable person available, there will be no teniente in the town.[105]

67. February 23–March 14, 1812, Mexico City and Chimalhuacán. The town of Chimalhuacán complains to the General Indian Court that its subdelegado forces them to bear arms against the enemies of the state, and some of its people abandon their homes in consequence. At viceregal order, the subdelegado reports that the military service demanded is necessary and not excessive. The court instructs the subdelegado to make the Indians understand by kindly methods their obligation to help preserve tranquility.[106]

68. December 11, 1817–January 7, 1818, Mexico City and Ayotzingo. María Manuela, of Ayotzingo, complains that the subdelegado of Chalco has jailed her husband and seized the family maize because they have not paid 60/, the value of two mules forced on them in the repartimiento de mercancías. The court orders the Indian released if the sole cause of jailing is as alleged. The subdelegado sends

105. Ibid., 2161:exp. 11 (LBSD, vol. 3).
106. Ibid., 2260:exp. 17 (LBSD, vol. 16).

the decree to the encargado de justicia in Ayotzingo, who explains that he has embargoed only the maize. The subdelegado forwards the report to the viceroy. The docket ends here.[107]

69. April 27–June 5, 1820, Mexico City and Coatepec-Chalco. The ranchería of Ríofrío, province of Coatepec-Chalco, complains to the court that the military force them to do work and collect money from them for use of the royal highway. Ordered to report, the subdelegado agrees that most of the charges are true. The fiscal protector renders an opinion that the local military commander should not force the Indians to bring in firewood. With the concurrence of the assessor, the viceroy so orders.[108]

b. Clergy

Much fewer in number than suits and petitions over property and complaints against local Spanish governors, complaints against clergy nevertheless comprised a very important segment in the business of the General Indian Court. Whereas a royal or viceregal appointee to local governorship normally served for from one to five years, the local friars and parish priests served for long periods. Parish priests with proprietary title (*curas colados*) held their parishes until they chose to leave for a more attractive post, accepted retirement, or died. Accordingly, the clergy, in far longer-term residence in the district and with detailed knowledge of their parishioners from the normal routine of the year, catechism, and perhaps most of all confession, usually exercised a strong influence that might become dictatorial and tyrannical. In their functions they were assisted by a staff of aides (to assemble the people for instruction or church services, to care for the church, to sing, to provide for their needs), who might easily be put to uses beyond those contemplated in proper practice, for controlling and even fleecing the Indian parishioners.

Royal and viceregal exhortations and prohibitions notwithstanding, many of the clergy forced Indians to serve them in private undertakings; interfered in town elections and administration; usurped many of the functions of royal justice, even to ordering Indians whipped and jailed; and levied fees and tithes beyond the official schedules. They were accused further of fomenting suits by the Indians. When the local parish priest and Spanish governor were on good terms, they could easily keep any extortion and abuse from being reported to Mexico City. If they fell out, the parish priest was likely to influence his parish-

107. Ibid., 2197:exp. 15 (LBSD, vol. 9).
108. Ibid., 2185:exp. 12 (LBSD, vol. 7).

ioners to complain of the governor, but sometimes the Indians would initiate complaints against their priest. One may guess that parishioners complained of their priests, in general, only after long abuse. Their irritation would then result in a demand for remedy of a single abuse or the larger series of charges moved as *capítulos*.[109]

The power of the royal and viceregal governments to hear and remedy such complaints was limited severely by ecclesiastical privilege, for the Church was a separate jurisdiction, with its own courts and its own administrators, protected by the formidable threats of excommunication and interdict. Complaints of abuse of lay people and improper activities and charges could be dealt with as an invasion of the royal sphere since the clergy were exercising jurisdiction beyond their purely ecclesiastical function and were not judging in matters of faith and morals. In the most extreme cases, of which there are none here, the audiencia could issue an order of *recurso de fuerza*, interposing the arm of the royal government. Any punishment or penalty against a priest could be inflicted only by an ecclesistical tribunal. Hence the viceregal government repeatedly was forced to refer the matter to the appropriate bishop or provincial in a letter of *ruego y encargo* (request and charge).[110]

70. March 12, 1616, Mexico City. José de Celi, on behalf of the Indians of San Juan Coscomatepec, province of Huatusco, complains that because his clients carried on a suit against their priest, the cura of Huatusco, in the archiepiscopal court and the episcopal courts in Puebla and Michoacán, which resulted in the Bishop of Puebla's sending a judge, who sentenced the curate to various penalties, the curate now demands that the Indians reimburse him for all costs and penalties of the suit; further, the curate demands that a special judge be sent to the town, all costs of the judge and his aides to be borne by the Indians, for dealing with them and exiling some of them. The Indians of the town, poor and worn out by burdens, ask for an order to prevent such mistreatment, with appropriate penalties; otherwise they will be forced to abandon the town and their lands. Upon the opinion of his assessor, the viceroy orders the alcalde mayor of Huatusco to

109. Ricard, *La "conquête spirituelle,"* 181–185; ordinance of the Conde de Priego, Mexico City, January 13, 1622, in Zavala, *Ordenanzas*, 278–279; royal cédula to the Dominican provincial in New Spain, Madrid, September 22, 1649, in Konetzke, 2:443–444 (no. 294); auto acordados of May 4, 1656, clauses 4 and 10, and of September 27, 1677, both in Beleña, 1, part 1:56–59 and 33–34 respectively; RLI, 1.12.5 and 1.13.6–13 and 23. See also the opening discussion here of complaints and suits against Spanish provincial governors.

110. RLI, 1.12.8–11 and 18. See also *recurso de fuerza* in Escriche y Martín, *Diccionario*, and Maldonado.

protect the Indians; he is not to allow vexation or mistreatment in the matters above, but he is also admonished not to enter into controversy with the cura nor with any other ecclesiastic.[111]

71. March 6, 1621, Mexico City. The Indians of San Juan Posto-can, all tenants new to the area (*terrazgueros advenedizos*), and a su-jeto of Santa María de la Redonda, near Mexico City, complain to the viceroy that their Franciscan doctrineros force them to provide guards for the doctrineros' livestock at Tepapalula, to sell cheeses for them, and perform other work. They ask that this practice be forbidden and that they be placed in the *doctrina* of San Francisco de Cetealpan, an-other division of the general Franciscan parish of Santa María de la Redonda. On the advice of his assessor, the viceroy orders the local justice to see that the Indians are not molested nor required to perform any of these services. On their plea that they be placed in the doctrina of San Francisco de Cetealpan, he orders that there be no change.[112]

72. April 11, 1633, Mexico City. The Indian officials of the towns of San Juan Teticpac and of San Dionisio and San Pablo, its su-jetos, province of the mines of Chichicapa, present testimony and de-crees forwarded from the Bishop of Oaxaca on molestation by the Do-minican friars who are their vicars. The friars exact improper levies and payments, specified in the capítulos presented. The Indians ask that they not be forced to give or pay anything not properly due. On the opinions of the fiscal protector and his assessor, the viceroy issues an order to the alcalde mayor of the mines of Chichicapa neither to allocate nor permit allocation of Indian workmen for the friars, nor to permit their majordomos to force labor by the Indians. The alcalde mayor is to punish any infraction with the full rigor of the law, power being expressly granted for this purpose. Within two weeks the vice-roy issues three letters of ruego y encargo. The first asks the titular vicar of Teticpac to observe the terms of the order and the ordinance of December 31, 1632, ending the repartimiento de indios in agricul-ture. He is to restrain his fellow friars from the abuses complained of. The second, to the Provincial of San Hipólito Mártir, the Dominican superior, seeks his cooperation in ending the abuses. The third, to the Bishop of Oaxaca, repeating all the charges, requests him to conduct a formal investigation.[113]

73. October 5, 1638, Mexico City. On the petition of the town of Cuautinchan, province of Puebla, asking that the local clergy not

111. AGN-I, 7:exp. 31.
112. Ibid., 9:exp. 305.
113. Ibid., 10, cuad. 3:exps. 150, 158, 159, and 164 (LBSF, 8:fols. 50–64).

interfere in town elections, the viceroy issues a letter which incorporates the text of the viceregal ordinance of January 13, 1622, on the subject.[114]

74. July 15, 1639, Mexico City. José de Celi, on behalf of the town of Aranza, province of Michoacán, first petitions for a copy of the royal cédulas of May 26, 1609, and March 12, 1622, and of the auto acordado of the audiencia, all ending the repartimiento de indios. He then complains that the vicar of Aranza, Lic. Juan de Covarrubias, in reprisal for the town's refusal to provide indios de servicio, forces them to pay exorbitant fees for his services: 8/ for a burial, 6/ for a marriage, and other services on the same scale. Previously the fee for a burial was 3/ for an adult and 1/4 for a child; that for a marriage, 4/5; and so on. The Indians cannot pay such charges. The petition asks that the vicar be ordered to keep to custom and not allege a new schedule of fees from the bishop. They ask that a letter of ruego y encargo be issued, with a certified copy for themselves to retain for use in any plea they choose to pursue in other courts. The viceroy issues the letter and orders that the town be given an additional certified copy.[115]

75. May 8, 1640, Mexico City. Don Baltasar Martín, cacique and Indian governor of Querétaro, complains that despite the Indian privilege on tithes, established by royal cédula and confirmed many times, he is being molested to pay tithe on maize raised on a farm he bought from Spaniards, which the tithe collector claims does not fall within Indian privilege. The tithe of the maize in dispute, 96 fanegas, has been put in deposit. He asks for its return and confirmation of the royal cédula of August 8, 1544. The viceroy so orders.[116]

The Church position was that the land when owned by Spaniards had paid tithe on its crops, and that rental or sale to Indians did not alter its status; the Indians, of course, claimed that the exemption was personal and followed them to any land they farmed for themselves. In the eighteenth century, when the increase in Indian population forced many villagers to rent or buy land previously held by Spaniards, the controversy grew much more widespread. During the colonial period it never came to a general settlement.[117]

76. January 26, 1654, Mexico City. Bernardo López de Haro, Indian solicitor, on behalf of Santa María Asunción Ocelotepec, prov-

114. Ibid., 11:exp. 8. See also the *cartas de ruego y encargo* for Pátzcuaro and Xochimilco, October 8 and November 4, 1638, in ibid., exps. 19 and 51 (LBSF, 8:fols. 28–30).

115. AGN-I, 11:exp. 250 (LBSF, 8:fols. 50–64).

116. Ibid., 12, part 2:exp. 85 (LBSF, 8:fols. 138–140).

117. See Borah, "The Cathedral Archive of Oaxaca," 644, for the claim of the diocese of Oaxaca.

ince of Miahuatlán, presents capítulos against the parish priest. In 35 charges, the Indians complain that the priest extorts money and cochineal, forces them to work without pay, seizes their property, and beats and imprisons them. The solicitor asks for a letter of ruego y encargo to the cathedral chapter of Antequera, *sede vacante* (governing for want of a bishop), or to any competent ecclesiastical judge. In a forceful opinion, the fiscal protector declares the abuses shameful. A parish priest should hold to the formal schedule of fees and give good treatment to his flock. He recommends that the viceroy issue the letter asked for and order the local justice to see that the Indians are well treated, on pain of a 500/ fine for noncompliance. When his assessor agrees, the viceroy issues the letter and order.[118]

77. September 11, 1691, Mexico City. The Indians of Tlaxcala de la Frontera, province of San Luis Potosí, file capítulos against their Franciscan doctrineros. Since Fray Jacinto de Quixos came as *guardián*, he has kept the town in turmoil. He is an inflexible man who demands unconditional obedience, as he did earlier in Colotlán, with the result that the Indians of that town applied to the Bishop of Guadalajara, the local justicia mayor, and the military *teniente de capitán general*, for his departure. Inter alia, the charges allege that the guardián appropriates the water from the local dam for the convent garden, refusing to let the Indians use it for their milpas, and that he has beaten savagely boy assistants, in one instance for coming to the friar's cell wearing a dirty serape. He forces two other boys to work in the convent garden without pay; and when they protested, had them flogged at the church door. Upon investigation by the fiscal protector, which finds the charges to be true, the viceroy issues a letter of ruego y encargo to the Franciscan provincial.[119]

78. October 14, 1712, and March 2, 1713, Mexico City. The Indians of Tenango, province of Tulancingo, rioted against their cura, Fray Juan de la Rea, against whom they had filed capítulos and asked the Bishop of Puebla for another parish priest. At the viceroy's order, the alcalde mayor carries out an investigation and sends to jail in Mexico City those Indians involved in the riot who can be found. The viceroy then orders the papers, together with the declarations of the Indians in the royal jail, sent to the fiscal. Some Indians are yet to be found. Furthermore, the town officials are to be required to explain their role in the riot—and if they are guilty in any way, are to be sent to the royal jail in Mexico City. Upon trial, two Indians are found guilty and sentenced to four years of exile from the town; others await sentencing or trial in Mexico City and Tulancingo.

118. AGN-I, 17:exp. 28 (LBSF, 9:fols. 91–114).
119. Ibid., 30:exp. 449 (LBSF, 10:fols. 78–81).

Upon petition from the Indians and review by the fiscal protector and his assessor, the viceroy decrees that the Indians are to be warned to keep the peace. Those in the royal jail and in jail in Tulancingo are to be sent to their houses and warned that for any breach of the peace or want of respect for their cura they will be sent to a workshop or bakery for four years of forced service and will become perpetually ineligible for office. The two Indians sentenced to four years of exile from the town are to begin their sentences at once, and for any breach of the sentence are to be sent to a workshop or bakery for four years.[120]

The docket has no statement on the disposition nor truth of the charges against the cura; the issue here was orderly town government and keeping the peace.

79. January 8, 1721, Mexico City. Antonio José de Ardariare, for the town of San Esteban del Saltillo (Coahuila), protests the attempt of the Bishop of Guadalajara to collect tithes on maize, frijoles, etc., and first fruits of one half-fanega for any kind of grain. He cites the royal cédula of August 8, 1544, on collecting tithes from Indians. The viceroy issues a letter of ruego y encargo to the Bishop of Guadalajara to observe the custom. Any differences on liability to tithes are to be brought to the Audiencia of Guadalajara for decision.[121]

This case has the additional interest that the viceroy gave judgment for territory in the Audiencia of Nueva Galicia or Guadalajara. Of course, the letter to the bishop was innocuous and the judicial rights of the Audiencia of Nueva Galicia carefully preserved.

80. March 16, 1745, Mexico City. The town of Actopan vs. the ecclesiastical judge of the diocese and its cura, over the right to elect the local *fiscal de doctrina* (the Indian town official who brought people to church and children to instruction). Upon the opinion of the fiscal—who defines the duties of the fiscal de doctrina and holds that they do not lie in the sphere of either the ecclesiastical judge or the cura, so that the Indians should elect the fiscal de doctrina as they do any other civil official—the viceroy so holds.[122]

81. April 24 and December 17, 1754, Mexico City. Santa María Yolotepec, province of Teposcolula, vs. its cura.[123] In a dispute between the town alcalde and the cura, the agents of the cura tried to arrest the alcalde. That attempt unleashed a riot in which the town women put the cura in his bedroom and the townfolk arrested all the cura's agents

120. Ibid., 38: fols. 110–112 (LBSF, 10: fols. 164–169).
121. Ibid., 45: exp. 3 (LBSF, 11: fols. 63–65).
122. Ibid., 55: fols. 268–271 (LBSF, 12: fols. 268–271).
123. Ibid., 57: fols. 125f–v, 183v–184v, and 220f–221f.

but one. The next day, at the governor's orders, the agents were flogged
and expelled from the town. Upon learning of these events, the alcalde
mayor on November 11, 1752, sent a commissioner, soldiers, an interpreter, and the governor of Ixcatlán to arrest the governor and town
officials of Yolotepec and embargo their property. When the culprits
could not be found, since they had gone to Mexico City to lay their
case before the viceroy, the commissioner seized their property, including 114/.

Upon petition of the governor and town officials, the viceroy on
December 17, 1753, orders the alcalde mayor to send all papers in the
case to Mexico City within fifteen days, on penalty of a fine of 200/ for
noncompliance. Notification may be by any person who can read and
write. That same day, the viceroy issues another order to the alcalde
mayor, based on the recommendation of the fiscal protector. The latter
points out that the guilt of the Indian town alcalde is insolence to the
cura, regardless of circumstances, and that the governor should have
controlled the town women. Since the term of office of both is over,
they cannot be deprived of office, but they can be ordered to show respect to the cura. Similarly, the women should be ordered, on penalty
of a term in an obraje, to apologize to the cura and to behave in the
future. All must go to the cura to give satisfaction, and he is to receive
them with paternal love. A subsidiary offender, a messenger from the
town who opened and read a letter denouncing the culprits, must be
found, since he fled jail, and be punished. The viceroy accepts the
recommendation.

Upon compliance with the viceroy's orders to forward all papers
to Mexico City, the alcalde mayor has them returned with a peremptory injunction to put them in order, pronounce provisional sentence,
and again forward them to Mexico City. In his comments, the fiscal
holds that four women and the two officials appear to be guilty. Their
testimony and that of other witnesses should be taken. The messenger
must also be found and punished. The docket ends here.

82. July 29, 1775–June 30, 1776, Mexico City and Actopan.
Mariano Pérez de Tagle, attorney for the Indians, petitions the viceroy
on behalf of the governor of San Salvador, province of Actopan. The
petition complains that the cura has arrested the governor unjustly
and keeps him imprisoned. The cura persecutes all the Indians. The
viceroy upon the recommendation of the fiscal orders that the alcalde
mayor of Actopan question the cura as to why he puts people in jail on
his own order without asking for intervention of the royal authorities,
and report back to the court. In the docket there follow the papers of
the proceedings in Actopan. The alcalde mayor reports that the cura
maintains a private jail, which at that time has no one in it, and never

requests intervention of the royal authorities, as he is supposed to. The Indians' attorney asks for a copy of the alcalde mayor's report, which upon the recommendation of the fiscal is given to him. At this point the docket ends.[124]

83. August 6, 1786, Mexico City. Juan Tomás, Indian of Ixcatepec, province of Ixcateopan, and mayordomo of the cofradía of Santiago, vs. the parish priest, for abuses, extortion, etc.—a long complex case running from 1778 to 1786.[125] Juan Tomás complains to the General Indian Court that he and another Indian formed a partnership to handle all the business of Ixcatepec, which gave them a power of attorney, but the town divided on the question whether fees and charges for the priest should be according to custom or schedule. For this reason the two men appealed to the fiscal protector in an expediente which is in the General Indian Court. Decision was rendered in favor of charging fees by the schedule.

The parish priest refused to accept the schedule, and refuses to summon the townfolk to pay according to the schedule. Again, Juan Tomás appealed to the General Indian Court and obtained a letter of ruego y encargo directed to the priest, enjoining him to observe the legal schedule. As a result, the priest hates Juan Tomás with an "*odio invencible*" and hatches various schemes to ruin him. In one, the priest left a baby on his doorstep, saying it was the daughter of Juan Tomás and a cousin. The baby was saved by Juan Tomás' wife, but the charge was sent to the General Indian Court with evidence cooked up by the priest. In 1783 the cousin was arrested for immorality and given 25 lashes, although she was not involved with Juan Tomás. On August 30, 1784, the priest had Juan Tomás jailed in Acapetlahuaya on the same charge and given 50 lashes. At every sixth lash he asked Juan Tomás questions of doctrine. According to the priest, the flogging was because Juan Tomás ruined a marriage.

On November 23, 1784, Juan Tomás, still in jail, petitions the priest for release, pleading the harm done his family by his long incarceration. Thereupon, the priest demands the account book of the brotherhood of Los Ranchos, which Juan Tomás does not have and has never seen. December 6, 1784, the wife of Juan Tomás pleads on her knees with the priest for his release because of the family's need. The priest repeats his demand for the account book and throws her out. Seeing that the priest's purpose is to have him die in jail, Juan Tomás breaks from jail in order to appear before the General Indian Court.

124. AGN-Civ, vol. 2241:exp. 7 (25 fols.) (LBSD, vol. 15).
125. AGN-Crim, 3:exp. 15 (LBSD, vol. 16).

The next move of the priest is to force the son and wife of Juan Tomás to live apart from him. "It was for this reason on May 21, 1786, in the presence of his fiscal and topiles, he had me given 75 lashes," merely because the Indian refused to consent to the separation. Juan Tomás is convinced that the priest plans his death. He has been obliged to pay 150/ in proceedings as well as 400/, losses attributable to his imprisonment. He petitions the court for damages as well as rectification of all charges against him.

On the recommendation of the fiscal, the viceroy orders the justice of the district to notify the priest of the letter of ruego y encargo, issued on the same date, requiring the latter to treat Juan Tomás and all Indians of his class with the benevolence prescribed by law. He may not proceed against any except through the appropriate royal officials. Notice is to be given to Juan Tomás. All other questions are left open, presumably for decision in ordinary civil tribunals.

84. October 19, 1795–March 31, 1796, Mexico City and Coyoacán. The parish priest of Coyoacán complains to the viceroy that the town Indians resist learning doctrine, taking communion, and marrying properly, and that the Indian town officials do not force them to do so. He proposes that the delinquents be jailed. The fiscal protector recommends that the governors of the parish be brought to the court for instructions on compelling church attendance. The penalty for failure to attend services should be six to eight lashes, instead of jail as proposed by the cura. The court accepts his recommendation, but turns also to the dean of the cathedral chapter for an opinion, and orders the corregidor of Coyoacán to report on the matter. The report of the corregidor supports the substance of the fiscal's recommendation, but urges that notice to the Indians be by the notary of the juzgado for better effect. In defense of the Indians, the corregidor reports that the priest is much absent from the parish. A second recommendation by the fiscal, based on the corregidor's report, accepts the changes and urges that the priest be advised to stay in his parish.[126] At this point the docket ends, but we may be certain that the final order and a letter of ruego y encargo were drawn in the terms of the fiscal's second recommendation. The matter was formally aired in the General Indian Court, although it might have been handled by simple administrative hearing.

85. October 24, 1797–June 11, 1798, Mexico City and Ixmiquilpan. The new town of Santiago de Mapete, doctrina of Cardonal, province of Ixmiquilpan, vs. the Garcías, for insisting upon serving as

126. AGN-Civ, 2279:exp. 4 (LBSD, vol. 19).

singers in the parish church. The town complains that the cura appoints his own singers, who are the Garcías. Upon the opinion of the assessor that the Indians have the right to select the singers, the court issues an order to the subdelegado of Ixmiquilpan, upholding the Indians. The cura then protests that the Garcías have served as singers for forty years, but the subdelegado reports that the men are insolent and refuse obedience. In the end, the court insists upon its earlier order and the cura agrees to obey it.[127]

86. August 17–18, 1798, Mexico City and Xochimilco. Salvadora Manuela, widow, of Milpa Alta, province of Xochimilco, vs. her parish priest, for keeping her in custody. José Manuel Vallarta, Indian solicitor, petitions on behalf of Salvadora Manuela: Her cura refuses to abide by the schedule of fees in charging for her husband's funeral. The dispute is over 21/ additional. The priest keeps her in custody. The inference is that she is in jail. After hearing the petition, the court orders the widow's release if she is in jail only for not paying the full charge, and that the archbishop be notified of the complaint. Vallarta is given the signed order for delivery to the local justice.

In Xochimilco, the subdelegado receives the order from the local administrator of royal revenue. He sends word to his encargado de justicia in Milpa Alta, who reports back that the cura, on being notified by the local interpreter, stated that he would forward documents explaining the case. The cura refuses further reply. As for the widow, she asked for refuge and has not been in jail. In Xochimilco, the administrator of royal revenue takes testimony from the widow which shows that she has had to stay in the royal office buildings but has never been in jail. She is sent back to Milpa Alta with a kind of amparo, a *papel de resguardo* that she is not to be molested by the cura for funeral costs. Inspection of the jail register shows no entry that she has ever been kept in the jail. The report of the subdelegado to the viceroy is sent to the Indian solicitor for his information on behalf of his client. At this point the docket ends.[128]

87. July 28, 1801, Mexico City. The towns of San Martín Huamelulpan, Santiago Nundiche, Santa María Ocotepec, San Pedro Yosotaco, and Santiago Nuyóo, in the province of Teposcolula, complain that since 1795, when Don Martín Gutiérrez y Barquín became tithe collector, he has gradually changed the old schedule to higher rates. He also forces the Indians to feed him, his servants, and his horses without payment. They ask that they not be molested further. The

127. Ibid., 2179:exp. 5 (LBSD, vol. 6).
128. Ibid., 2203:exp. 9 (LBSD, vol. 10).

viceroy issues an order citing Gutiérrez y Barquín to come to the court in person or send an agent for answer to the complaint. The docket contains only this order.[129]

According to the cathedral records in Oaxaca, the tithe-collecting system underwent considerable change in 1794, the Mixteca Alta being divided into two districts for more efficient collection.[130] This order furnishes a perception of the reaction from the Indians.

c. Private Spaniards and Other Non-Indians

Many of the categories of grievances already listed deal with the activities of private Spaniards and other non-Indians as agents, partners, or cooperating friends of officials and clergy. Those involving land and other property may have private non-Indians as direct principals. The category now to be examined brings together three major sources of complaint arising from relations between the two republics. As in other categories, grievances tend to overlap and may fit elsewhere; the basis for complaint to the General Indian Court may be the one the complainants considered most likely to move the court to action rather than the true motivation, but that kind of selective handling of motive and evidence is not confined to the colonial period nor to Mexico.

i. Settlement of Non-Indians in Indian Towns

Royal policy, formulated early in the sixteenth century, was to limit or forbid entirely the settlement of Spaniards and other non-Indians in Indian towns. A complete prohibition was obviously impossible, since a number of functions regarded as necessary to the existence of society and the state required the presence of Spaniards, official and private, among the Indians; but the Spanish authorities objected especially to the temporary or permanent residence of unmarried men, vagabonds, young people without occupation, mestizos, and Negroes. All such were regarded as dangerous for the Indians, almost certain to oppress them and teach them loose, disorderly ways. Mestizos and people with any Negro genetic admixture were regarded as particularly given to licentiousness, violence, and dishonesty. As a further measure for protecting the Indians, legislation prescribed minimum distances that non-Indian ranches or farms were to be from Indian lands. In general, the policy was a failure,[131] but it and its im-

129. AGN-I, 70:fols. 210v–211v.
130. Borah, "Tithe Collection," 508.
131. Mörner, passim, is the most thorough and comprehensive study, covering

plementing legislation did afford the Indians a means of attacking non-Indians they regarded as obnoxious.

88. July 8, 1594. On January 28, 1594, Velasco II, at the complaint of the Indians of Teposcolula, issues an order to the alcalde mayor of the province to expel Luis de Montesinos, a Spanish resident of the town, from the town and ten leagues around it. He may not return without express viceregal license, on pain of two years' exile from New Spain and a fine of 300/. The alcalde mayor is to report back to the viceroy within twenty days of receiving the order. On July 8, 1594, the viceroy issues a second order to the alcalde mayor that his earlier order be carried out. He is to send to Mexico City within fifteen days of receipt of the new order a sworn affidavit of compliance.[132]

89. December 11, 1596. In mid-1595, the town of Teposcolula complained to Velasco II that Juan Bautista—a mestizo, unruly, seditious, a thief and murderer—causes much trouble among them. He is the provincial interpreter, despite many orders to the contrary, and lives among them, despite orders for expulsion. He is favored by the alcaldes mayores because he is very useful to them. On June 14, 1595, Velasco II orders that, unless Juan Bautista is married to a local Indian woman, he is to be expelled. Whatever the reason or pretext, the mestizo remains in the town. Late in 1596, the town again complains to the viceroy, now the Conde de Monterrey. On December 11, 1596, he confirms the decree of Velasco II and orders it enforced. Even if Juan Bautista is married to an Indian, should he be causing trouble, he is to be exiled from the town and province.[133]

90. October 30, 1602–April 12, 1603, Mexico City, Ixcatlán, and Teposcolula. The Indians of Ixcatlán, province of Teposcolula, complain to the General Indian Court that a mestizo, Cristóbal de Acuña, living in the town, mistreats and beats the Indians. The viceroy orders the alcalde mayor of the province to investigate and punish appropriately. Since the docket is in the provincial archive, we have the follow-up. Upon presentation of the viceregal decree and investigation by the alcalde mayor, Acuña is jailed and tried in the provincial court. After a long trial with much testimony, he is sentenced to two years' exile from the province and thereafter may live in the neighboring town of Yolotepec, but not in Ixcatlán.[134]

---

the whole of Spanish America. See also comments in previous sections of this chapter, and Gibson, *The Aztecs*, 272–299.

132. AGN-I, 6, part 1:exp. 823.
133. Ibid., part 2:exp. 1085.
134. AJT-Crim, leg. 2.

91. July 12–13, 1649, Mexico City. The Indians of Xochimilco vs. Cristóbal Pérez, a Spaniard settled in their town; they demand expulsion.[135] The case begins May 15–June 12, 1649, in hearings before the corregidor of Xochimilco on the complaint of the town that Pérez seizes lands, goods, etc., and mistreats the Indians. Although arrested and put on trial, Pérez produces witnesses on his behalf and is acquitted. Before the conclusion of the local proceedings, the town officials of Xochimilco, through Bernardo López de Haro, Indian solicitor, bring their complaint to the General Indian Court, then presided over by the audiencia, governing in the absence of a viceroy. The court decrees that the local justice, the corregidor, gather information for transmittal to Mexico City. If there is evidence of guilt on the part of Pérez, he is to be arrested and sent to the royal jail in Mexico City and his property is to be embargoed. Upon presentation of the decree in Xochimilco, nothing is done. Thereupon the solicitor complains to the court, which by summary order of June 17 requires compliance and commissions a relator to take testimony in Xochimilco. Although the corregidor, notified by the bailiff of the court on June 19, indicates that he will comply, the further proceedings in Xochimilco are carried out by a relator under a third order of July 5. When the testimony indicates probability of guilt, Pérez is ordered arrested, and after some search is found and put in the royal jail in Mexico City. His property and that of his housekeeper are embargoed. On July 9, the court orders that Pérez may be released on bond, but he is to leave Xochimilco within fifteen days after notice, on pain of four years' service in the Philippines. His statement under oath is taken on July 10. He thereupon petitions for release from jail under warning, but on July 13 he is again ordered to leave Xochimilco, this time on pain of two years' service in the Philippines. That same day Pérez is given notice of the second order and is released.

Meanwhile, on the complaint of the Indian solicitor on the corregidor's behavior in the early stages of the case, the court orders the complaint and any pertinent evidence added to the file. On July 5, 1649, in the same order which commissions a relator to take testimony in Xochimilco, the corregidor is fined 50/ for disobedience. After four demands for payment of the fine, the relator seizes the corregidor's silver, which is then claimed to be the property of another. The relator adds the claim to the file. On July 6, the corregidor formally appeals the fine, on the ground that the case was being tried before him. On July 12 the court lowers the fine to 10/, but otherwise confirms its decree against the corregidor. He is further liable for all costs and fees in connection with his disobedience and appeal. Pre-

135. AGN-Crim, 49:exp. 12 (LBSD, vol. 26).

sumably, also, the papers in the case would be reviewed at the time of his residencia.

The case illustrates two important features inter alia. It shows that under the *audiencia gobernadora* the court functioned in exactly the same manner and with the same procedures as under a viceroy, and it illustrates the coercive power of the court upon failure of a provincial authority to carry out its decree. The docket bears the notation that it was reviewed in the general inspection carried out by Pedro de Gálvez, who arrived in Mexico in 1650 to complete the inspection begun by Juan de Palafox.[136]

ii. Damage to Indian Crops

Under Spanish law, the right to pasture livestock on land, once the crop was harvested, was common to all until the next planting. Brought to Mexico,[137] that rule led to many disputes and easy abuse, since the Indians almost never fenced in their milpas, which were easily invaded by the nearly feral livestock of non-Indians, roaming with little if any supervision until roundup. Where there was supervision, as happened more often with swine and sheep, the shepherds frequently were negligent or maliciously let their flocks invade the milpas. Even the rule of distance for grants of Spanish estancias, designed to help avoid this abuse, was far from successful. The Spanish authorities in Mexico were under strict injunction to see that damages to Indian milpas were paid promptly and in full.[138] Most such cases were dealt with by local courts,[139] but many came to the viceroy when remedy was slow or denied.

92. December 16, 1611–April 4, 1612, Mexico City and Teposcolula. The Indians of Tlaxiaco, province of Teposcolula, sue Juan de Cisneros and his son, Bernardo de Carpio, for damage done by their livestock, both ganado mayor and menor. They also ask pay of 1/4 a

136. Priestley, 113–114.

137. Chevalier, *La formation*, 105–108. See also Beleña, 1, part 2:110, no. 135, summarizing legislation of April 6, 1576, and May 25 and December 6, 1635, requiring that sowings be fenced during growing time; otherwise the owners of livestock were not liable for damages. The requirement placed a heavy burden on the Indians, and may have led to the widespread practice of growing agave hedges around milpas. Once the harvest was completed, the stubble was to be common pasture.

138. Clauses 8 and 9, royal cédula, Madrid, May 20, 1649, in AGN-RCD, 52: fols. 124f–128f.

139. Judicial provincial archives are full of complaints of damage on the part of the Indians, who very often counted their losses in exact ears of maize. They were almost invariably ordered paid by summary process.

week for three indios de servicio and one woman for grinding maize, all of whom they were forced to furnish to the Spaniards. They protest that the local justice does nothing on their complaints. The viceroy orders the local justice to perform his duty. On presentation of the order in Teposcolula, the alcalde mayor prepares an affidavit that all claims already have been paid in full, and issues an order for the jailing of the governor and alcaldes of Tlaxiaco for profanation of the royal justice.[140]

93. March 4, 1616, Mexico City. José de Celi, on behalf of the Indians of the towns of Jecalpa, Huauchinantla, Mitepec, and Tamazula, province of Teotlalco, complains that the Spanish farmers of the valley of Atlixo let their cattle invade the Indians' lands. The cattle eat fruit trees and crops, so that many natives abandon their lands. They ask that the provincial governor be ordered to stop this, that their claims for damages be paid promptly, and that they be given license to kill with arrows any cattle invading their lands. The viceroy orders the local alcalde mayor to force the Spanish farmers to pay for the damages their livestock have done to the Indians, and to warn them that they are to keep only such numbers as their lands and available pasture can maintain, under notice that the Indians will be given license to kill any livestock invading their lands in the future, and the offenders will be liable to a fine of 100/ for the expenses of the General Indian Court. The alcalde mayor is to send testimony of compliance within twenty days.[141]

94. January 18, 1633, Mexico City. José de Celi, for the Indians of Tixtla, complains that the sheep and shepherds of the Society of Jesus do much damage to Indian crops, and that the shepherds steal hives of honey. The viceroy orders the alcalde mayor of Tixtla to investigate. If the charges are true, he is to see that damages are paid at once, even selling the livestock to the extent necessary. This order is to be enforced against the Society of Jesus and any other religious order. This order came close to infringing the *fuero eclesiástico* since suits against Church entities should have been carried on in Church courts. Presumably, the fact that it was an Indian complaint brought into operation an overriding concern of the royal government to see that Indians were protected.[142]

95. June 30, 1642, Mexico City. The Indians of San Lucas and of Malinaltepec, province of Teposcolula, complain that Bartolomé Sánchez, a Spaniard, invades their lands with horses and burros, which

140. AJT-Crim, leg. 2.
141. AGN-I, 7:exp. 30.
142. Ibid., 10, cuad. 3:exp. 101 (LBSF, 7:fols. 186–188).

destroy their crops. His sons enter their houses and seize fowls, eggs, and other food. They beat and stone any Indians who object in any way. Juan de Palafox, as viceroy, orders the justice of Teposcolula to see that the livestock is removed, on pain of a 200/ fine. He is also to notify the Spaniard and the Indians that the latter are to be paid for damage done and are to be protected in enjoyment of their lands and houses. He must report back to the viceroy within one month.[143]

96. March 15, 1785, Tulancingo. Manuel Martín Hernández, an Indian, sued the widow of Vicente Oliver for damage by her livestock to his milpa. He gained a decree of the General Indian Court in his favor, and upon its presentation in Tulancingo, the alcalde mayor verified the nature and extent of the damage. A copy of the proceedings was then given to Hernández for transmittal to the court.[144] Although the notation in the provincial archive goes no farther, whatever damage the alcalde mayor uncovered in his investigation undoubtedly was paid.

97. July 1–17, 1788, Mexico City. Luis and Mateo de la Cruz, two Indians of Jilotepec, province of Huichapan, vs. Don Mariano Páez. The two are in jail for damage to Páez' burros, which were eating their milpas. One cut out the eyes of a female donkey. The Indians take their case to the General Indian Court, which sends the papers to the fiscal protector for his opinion and so notifies the Indians' procurador. At this point the docket ends.[145]

98. September 24, 1799, Mexico City. José María Arellano, for the town officials of Santa María de la Asunción Acaxochitlán, province of Tulancingo, complains that in the town there reside many *gente de razón* who have many hogs, sheep, chickens, etc. The animals roam the town streets and squares, doing much damage to Indian sowings, especially the hogs. To avoid the trouble of much litigation, they petition for an order to the local justice that the gente de razón keep their animals confined. On September 24, 1799, on the advice of his assessor, the viceroy orders the justice of the province as petitioned. The latter is to force the gente de razón resident in the town to keep their animals under proper care so that there is no damage to the Indians. He is to report back to the viceroy. The document consulted here is a notarial copy, dated September 25, 1799, sent to the alcalde mayor of Tulancingo.[146]

143. Ibid., 14:exp. 9.
144. Notations of expedientes surrendered from the juzgado of the alcalde mayor of Tulancingo, July 27, 1776–March 18, 1778, in AT.
145. AGN-Civ, 2158:exp. 14 (LBSD, vol. 5).
146. AT.

iii. Labor Disputes and Debts[147]

In the earlier colonial period, the Spaniards in Mexico derived the bulk of their labor from the Indians. In the later colonial period—as the non-Indian population increased very rapidly, so that there came into being large contingents of mestizos, pardos, and poor whites—the source of labor for the upper classes became more varied, but the Indians always furnished a substantial proportion. By the decade in which the General Indian Court was formally established, earlier legal forms for recruiting or drafting labor, such as slavery, the encomienda, and the repartimiento de trabajo, had either become illegal or had lost importance. The major form of recruitment already was so-called free labor, but actually the recruitment of wage labor bound by debt.

Under Castilian law, a debtor unable to pay his debt might be held to work for his creditor until his debt was paid off. That law, carried over to New Spain, was the legal basis for the extensive system of debt peonage that developed during the sixteenth century. Although recent studies indicate that debt peonage was not everywhere and in all

147. The paragraphs of introduction to this section are based upon the following: Borah, *New Spain's Century of Depression*, 19–21 and 34–42, which gives a brief outline of forms of labor; Zavala and Castelo, Introductions to vols. 3–8, giving a running history of repartimiento and debt-peonage forms of labor; Gibson, *The Aztecs*, 220–256 et passim; contributions in Frost, Meyer, and Vázquez, by Riley, Kagan, and Tutino, plus commentaries on Kagan, 215–221, and by Enrique Semo, on Tutino, 393–397; Semo, *Siete ensayos*, passim; Brading, *Haciendas and Ranchos*, 76–77 and 97–113; and AGN-I, 61:fols. 150–153 (LBSF, 12:fols. 117–133). For a general discussion and further bibliography, see articles by Grieshaber and Nickel.

The complex of legislation governing debt labor may be found in Beleña, vol. 1, part 1:37–44, no. 98 (par. 2 of instructions for alcaldes mayores, January 11, 1611), and nos. 89, 93, 96–98, 126, and 127 (regulations on advances, seizing Indians for debt, forced service for crime, pp. 55–60 and 69); part 2:75–89, no. 92 (ordinance of Velasco II, October 13, 1595, on Indian labor); part 3:15, no. 46 (regulation of September 15, 1755, limiting advances to Indians to 6/, but allowing a subsequent advance of 6/ at the expiration of the first); and part 5:208, no. 374 (a royal cédula of October 15, 1713, that Indians not be held to personal service, but were to work voluntarily and for wages); vol. 2:no. 45c (printing clauses of a royal cédula of March 23, 1773, an ordinance of June 3, 1784, and an auto acordado of March 22, 1785, regulating hacienda labor, pp. 193–199), and no. 54 (ordinances of obrajes of June 11, 1777, reissued October 4, 1781, pp. 298–306).

Further legislation may be found in AGN-I, 7:exp. 317 (forbidding turning Indians in the jails of the *parcialidades* over to Spanish masters without proper order; LBSF, 7:fols. 70–71); and the following royal cédulas, all in AGN-RCD:March 15, 1639, limiting the power of the viceroy and the alcaldes del crimen to punish Indians for serious offenses (vol. 61:fols. 34f–36v; BLT); May 20, 1649, clause 5, on abuses of debt labor (vol. 52:fols. 124f–128f); 1687, ordering enforcement of the ordinance on debt peonage of Viceroy Albuquerque, but lowering the proper amount of debt from 6/ to 5/ (vol. 34:fols. 367v–368v; BLT); and September 1620, forbidding the seizure of Indians for debt at the doors of the church (vol. 153, cuad. 3:exp. 162).

instances the oppressive system of near-slavery that it had been thought by scholars, there was enough complaint and regulation during the colonial period to show that it was readily subject to abuse. During the colonial period, an elaborate series of regulations came into being to organize its usage and prevent excesses. An Indian might be held to labor for debt, but only to the extent of one month's wages and by the original creditor. The monetary meaning of one month's wage rose with increase in monetary wages from 4/ in the time of Palafox to 6/ by the time of Albuquerque, until it was reduced to 5/ in 1687 by royal cédula and in 1773–74 was reinterpreted as the customary wage in money, a highly flexible formula. Employers easily circumvented the rule by advancing additional money as the original debt was paid off, or simply ignoring the limitation on advances. They did so, of course, at the peril that the debt, under inspection by a court, might be reduced to the legal limit or annulled as a further advance in violation of it; but cases on accounting indicate that the courts were not always willing to enforce the full letter of regulations against the employer.

Indian laborers, held under debt, were supposed to be allowed to return to their houses and families each night. They might not be confined, nor could punishment go beyond the moderate correction that custom allowed and the courts upheld. Only Indians under sentence to a term in a workshop, bakery, or other establishment receiving convicts were excepted, and their treatment and rations were subject to another set of regulations for insuring reasonable nourishment and not-too-inhumane conditions. Furthermore, only a court had the legal authority to deliver a debtor to his creditor for service; that is, the creditor legally could not simply seize the person of his debtor. Once delivered to the creditor, the debtor was legally bound to serve out his debt and, if he fled, could be seized and returned. Only the viceroy and alcaldes de crimen had the authority to sentence Indians to terms in workshops or similar establishments, although that rule seems to have been much evaded.

By the middle of the seventeenth century, custom began to distinguish between two groups of workmen on Spanish haciendas. Those who came from nearby villages and towns, called *tlaquehuales* in the region of Tlaxcala, were indeed bound by debt, but the courts would uphold their right to return to their homes and defend their rights to remain members of their communities. Those born on the hacienda, called gañanes, were bound to the estate and could be brought back if they fled. Only in unusual circumstances would the courts give permission for a move from the hacienda. By the eighteenth century, both groups of workers carried little booklets recording advances and debts, which might be checked against the hacienda records. *Sonsaque*, or luring away another's workers, was strictly forbidden. The new system found elaborate regulation in an ordinance on hacienda labor issued by Viceroy Matías de Gálvez in 1784.

Most complaints and suits arising from relations between Spanish employer and Indian worker were handled in the provincial courts, whether questions of debt or complaints of mistreatment; but a good many did reach the General Indian Court. Most involved work on haciendas. In general, mining labor was well paid, relatively well informed, mobile, and scarce enough so that it took care of itself. To be sure, questions arising under the remnants of the old system of labor draft for mines might reach the viceroy because the repartimiento represented an obligation enforceable on a town for delivery of workers.

The extent to which provincial tribunals and the General Indian Court enforced the legislation on the books or custom is a fascinating aspect of labor cases. A recent study of disputes between hacendados and their labor in Tlaxcala during the years 1654–1750, based on the archives of Tlaxcala and the records of the General Indian Court, arrives at the conclusion that the Spanish courts essentially acted as mediator and enforced both custom and law. Labor was coerced but not enslaved, for the possibility of access to the courts protected Indian workers against extreme abuse. On the other hand, while upholding the Indians' rights to reasonable treatment, the Spanish courts had no disposition to destroy haciendas or to punish the hacendados overseverely for abuse. Deprivation of labor force was in itself severe punishment, to be used sparingly. Even gañanes, by the later colonial period, regarded as *adscriptos ad glebam* (bound to the soil), the medieval term for serfs, could obtain a judicial sentence of release on ground of ill treatment or the failure of the employer to deliver customary pay and rations.[148]

99. May 30–September 16, 1616, Mexico City. José de Celi, on behalf of the town of Turicato, province of Michoacán, complains that his clients are held to service in copper mines 46 leagues from their town. The journey is difficult, and the distance means that three shifts are always involved. Since a recent epidemic in which the town lost 130 tributaries, it has only 250 left. The Indians ask reservation from the labor draft on ground of their low number, illness, hardship, and the need to finish their church. They complain that the administrator of the labor draft also uses them in cacao orchards. On May 30, 1616, the viceroy revokes the repartimiento for the time being and commissions his assessor to investigate and report. In July the Indians of

148. Riley.

Sevina Aranza, province of Michoacán, present a similar petition, with the same result on July 5. The proceedings are carried on as a civil suit with the administrator of the copper mines, which by September is in the stage of presenting evidence. The Indians of Sevina Aranza ask for a formal order for taking testimony by a receptor. On September 16, with the agreement of his assessor, the viceroy issues the order, addressed to the alcalde mayor of the province in which Sevina Aranza lies. The docket ends here.[149]

100. October 24, 1618, Mexico City. José de Celi, on behalf of Tejupilco and Ixtapan, province of Temascaltepec and Sultepec, states that his clients are occupied in collecting salt from November to May and deliver over 600 fanegas to the mines of Temascaltepec and Sultepec. They ask relief from direct labor draft, or the right to sell the salt freely in open market. A first order from the viceroy to the alcalde mayor went astray; so the Indians petition for a second one. On the advice of his assessor, the viceroy decrees that without express viceregal order the Indians are not to be held to service in the mines, nor need they obey local orders for such service. They may sell salt freely to the miners at any price they wish. Furthermore, they may transport salt to the mines on their own.[150]

101. June 18, 1629, Mexico City. Melchor López de Arco, Indian procurador, on behalf of the Indians of the Villa de los Valles, province of Valles, complains that his clients, who live among Spaniards since they are in a frontier zone, are kept at service and on haciendas without being allowed to return to their homes. They petition that the local justice be ordered to return them to the villa. On the advice of his assessor, the viceroy orders the justice of Valles to give full support and aid to the Indian authorities for the purpose petitioned for, on pain of 100/ for the royal treasury and the costs of a commissioner who will be sent to enforce the order in event of noncompliance.[151]

102. February 20, 1633, Mexico City. Gaspar Hernández, Indian of Tetzicapa, province of Jonotla and Tetela(?), complains that Gaspar Díaz, vecino and miner of Tetela, for whom he works, makes him work Sundays and feast days, puts him in fetters or in the stocks if he misses a day, and has seized his wife and son. He owes Díaz nothing, but the latter has falsified accounts. Hernández petitions for an order that the local justice free his wife and child and return them,

149. AGN-I, 7:exps. 61, 76, and 105 (LBSF, 7:fols. 28–33, 36, and 43–44).
150. Ibid., exp. 315 (LBSF, 7:fols. 67–70).
151. Ibid., 10, cuad. 1:exp. 105 (LBSF, 7:fols. 108–110).

so that all may go to their town. He asks that Díaz be forbidden to force them to work or to molest them, under severe penalties. The viceroy issues the order petitioned for.[152]

103. April 8, 1633, Mexico City. José de Celi, on behalf of Juan Miguel and his wife, Indians of the barrio of Santa Ana of Puebla, complains that his clients are wronged by Alonso Moreno, obrajero of Puebla, in that he has kept them prisoner in his textile workshop for over two years for a debt of the expenses of their marriage, which could not be as much as 10/. He will not let them go home, on the claim that the husband owes 55/ and the wife 60/, although they have received neither money nor goods from him. The couple are made to work day and night, as well as feast days, without being allowed to leave or being given food. In the course of work, they are mistreated by word and deed. The petition asks for an order to the alcalde mayor of Puebla to set the couple free and protect them. The viceroy orders the justicia mayor of Puebla to free the Indians and not allow them to be held on any pretext.[153]

104. June 26, 1635, Mexico City. Ana Clara, an Indian widow of Nativitas, province of Texcoco, complains that upon the death of her husband, a gañán of Jacome Pasalli, a resident, farmer, and obrajero of Texcoco, Pasalli set her and her sons to service on an estancia in order to pay off a claimed debt of her husband. Further, their clothing and metates were seized. Since Pasalli is favored by the justices of Texcoco, she turns to the viceroy for freedom for herself and her children and for the return of the clothing and metates. The decree of the viceroy quotes clause 3 of the ordinances on obrajes of March 10, 1633, that Indians are not to be put to work willingly or unwillingly in obrajes or sugar mills, nor to be locked up in them, on pain of death and loss of goods, with no appeal except on the loss of goods, and that the presence of Indians in such places is to be proof of guilt. The justice of Texcoco is ordered to enforce clause 3 and to see that the relief petitioned for is given.[154]

105. July ?–August 23, 1651, Mexico City and Texcoco. Agustina Micaela, Indian woman of Coatepec, vs. Capt. Francisco Monrroy, resident and farmer, for exacting forced labor from the Indians, including her husband, Juan Luis, who is not allowed to return to his home. The petition to the viceroy in the name of Agustina Micaela complains that Monrroy has seized her husband for service on his ha-

---

152. Ibid., cuad. 3 : exp. 131 (LBSF, 8 : fols. 1–2).
153. Ibid., exp. 149 (LBSF, 8 : fols. 8–9).
154. Ibid., 12, part 1 : exp. 223 (LBSF, 8 : fols. 119–123).

cienda, does not let him go home, and has paid no attention to previous orders of the General Indian Court on seizing Indians for labor. The corregidor of Coatepec does nothing to force Monrroy to obey the law. The viceroy orders the alcalde mayor of Texcoco, a neighboring province, to see that the husband is freed; that Monrroy complies with the law, on pain of 200/ fine for the new donation to the king; and that formal testimony is taken on Monrroy's past excesses. The alcalde mayor is ordered to report within eight days of receiving the order, on pain of payment of salary and costs of the commissioner who will be sent out in case of noncompliance. Upon presentation, the alcalde mayor forwards the order to the corregidor of Coatepec, who replies that the man is free, since he fled Monrroy's hacienda.

The testimony gathered fully substantiates the charges of seizing Indians, keeping them prisoner, beating them, not giving them enough food, and general abuse by Monrroy and his employees. The investigation further discloses the details of eight previous criminal complaints against Monrroy. Before the case is concluded, the viceroy issues a decree that Monrroy is not to imprison any Indian on his haciendas nor have his employees and sons seize Indians, on pain of a fine of 2000 ducats and loss of any right to use Indians at all on his haciendas. The alcalde mayor of Texcoco is to notify Monrroy and to send an affidavit to the court within eight days. At this point the docket ends.[155]

106. September 1, 1685, Mexico City. Five Indians, their wives, and the officials of the town of San Matías Tepetomatitlán, province of Tlaxcala, complain that for ten years they have worked for Juan Bernal Bejarano on his farm. He is now dead, and his son molests them and refuses settlement of accounts. They ask for payment and protection through an order to the justice of Tlaxcala. They also ask that his lieutenant in the town of San Agustín Tlaxco release a man he has in jail. The viceroy issues the order petitioned for: the Indians are not to be forced to work against their will, accounts are to be settled, there is to be no molestation, and the man jailed is to be released without costs. The penalty for noncompliance with the decree is a fine of 200/.[156]

107. October 21, 1712, Mexico City. On June 27, 1712, a petition on behalf of Felipe Mauricio of Santiago Ayapango, province of Tlalmanalco, who works for Juan Bautista de Etchegaray, a farmer in the province, complains that the Spaniard beat him cruelly with a whip because the livestock entrusted to him was not well fed. He asks for protection and adjustment of accounts. July 2, the fiscal protector

155. AGN-Civ, vol. 2186:exp. 13 (LBSD, vol. 8).
156. AGN-I, 29:exp. 83.

recommends granting the petition. Thereupon the viceroy orders the alcalde mayor to report. On July 11, the alcalde mayor reports that the Indian's offense was neglect in taking the livestock to pasture, that the flogging was not so brutal as alleged, and that the reckoning of accounts shows that the Indian owes 41/4. October 19, the fiscal renders opinion that even though the Indian was guilty of negligence, his punishment should have been more merciful. Accordingly, the Spaniard should forfeit the debt due him and be fined 100/, to be collected by the local justice and applied to construction of the royal palace. The Indian should not be held to service to the Spaniard. On October 21, 1712, the viceroy so decrees.[157]

108. June 10, 1722, Mexico City. Juan Francisco de Córdoba, on behalf of seven Indian gañanes of the hacienda of San Bartolomé Xonacula, province of Tlaxcala, owned by José Hernández, complains that Hernández owes his clients wages but will not pay. Instead, he mistreats them; his majordomo beats them cruelly and works them longer hours than customary. As a result, one girl is at the point of death. The petition asks for court permission to go to live in a town of their choosing. Upon the recommendation of the fiscal protector, the viceroy orders the governor of Tlaxcala, on pain of 200/ fine, to see that accounts are settled and to inform the hacendado that he is to give good treatment in future.[158] The Indians obviously were using the plea of bad treatment to break their tie to the hacienda. Equally, neither the Indians nor the courts objected to moderate chastisement.

109. February 22–August 12, 1777, Mexico City and Cuautitlán. The Indians of the town of San Martín, province of Cuautitlán, vs. the administrator of the hacienda of La Lechería. The town sues, through Fernando de Galves, Indian solicitor, complaining that the administrator of the hacienda, which is owned by the Marqués de Guardiola, has lengthened the hours and cut the pay of the gañanes. On the recommendation of the fiscal, the court orders the alcalde mayor to report. His report upholds the Indians in their complaint. The solicitor then asks for an order of amparo and for wages, damages, and costs where due. Upon the further recommendation of the fiscal, the court so orders. Costs are then assessed by the *tasador y repartidor general* of the audiencia at 10/5/6. When execution is made in Cuautitlán by the teniente of the alcalde mayor, the administrator announces that he is appealing. All papers and the teniente's report then go back to the court.[159]

157. Ibid., 38:fols. 112–113 (LBSF, 10:fols. 169–171).
158. Ibid., 45:exp. 139.
159. AGN-Civ, vol. 2217; exp. 8 (16 fols.) (LBSD, vol. 12).

110. September 16, 1785, Mexico City. Various Indian workers on the hacienda of Don José Chagaray, district of Tacuba, petition, through Manuel María de Arellano, Indian procurador, for payment of weekly wages due them and freedom from molestation by the majordomo and administrator when the Indians enter and leave the hacienda. September 7, 1785, the court orders an investigation by the justice of the district. If wages are due, they are to be paid at once. As for entering and leaving the hacienda, the administrator and majordomo are to observe the latest regulations. The decree is to serve as formal dispatch. September 9, the decree is presented to the teniente-general of the justice in Tacuba. The next day he questions the administrator and majordomo, both of whom swear that the wages due have already been paid, that the allegations about preventing free movement are false, and that the real reason for them is that the Indians want to drink. The Indians, when questioned, confirm that they have been paid, but late. On September 13, the teniente general, the alcalde mayor being ill throughout, reports to the viceroy. September 16, the court decrees that, since its order has been carried out, the papers are to be filed.[160]

111. April 2–29, 1786, Mexico City and Tulancingo. Manuel María de Arellano, on behalf of Pedro Antonio, Indian tributary of Cuautepec, province of Tulancingo, and a gañán on the hacienda of Cuautengo, rented by Lorenzo de la Rosa, petitions the court, complaining that his client is forced to labor with poor treatment and violence. He asks for freedom from service for his client and permission to repay the 5/ he owes after the present calamity [crop failure and epidemic] has passed. The court orders an investigation to be carried out by the alcalde mayor of Tulancingo. On April 29 the decree is presented to the alcalde mayor in Tulancingo, who certifies formal obedience and carries out his investigation. De la Rosa, notified and questioned, states that his measures are to prevent workers from stealing extra food beyond their rations in the present shortage. The local custom has been to steal maize from the storage *troje* in order to buy pulque "*por feriar su maíz*." He refused an extra advance to Pedro Antonio, and in spite the Indian carries false tales. De la Rosa asks for further hearing and review by the viceroy, since he will be unable to get workers and his crop will be lost. The docket in the provincial archive ends at this point with the report of the alcalde mayor.[161]

112. April 15–May 11, 1790, Mexico City and Apan. Tomás Antonio and Juan Antonio, Indian tributaries of Otumba, vs. Don Mi-

160. Ibid., vol. 2300:exp. 3 (LBSD, vol. 21).
161. AT.

guel de Añis, Spaniard and owner of the Hacienda de la Alaguna, over abuse and debt. The petition for the two Indians, through José Manuel Vallarta, Indian solicitor, states that they are gañanes with debts of 30/ and 21/ respectively. In the crop failure of the last year, Añis threw them off his hacienda. which is near Apan; but now that he needs them again, has had them seized for his service. Añis has violated the royal cédula of June 4, 1787, limiting debts to 5/ and forbidding involuntary labor. He has advanced up to 60/, despite the ordinances, publicly proclaimed, of June 3, 1774, and March 23, 1775. The petition asks that the justice of Apan go to the hacienda, free them, and further that they be released even from the 5/ debt that is legal, because of their loss of time through imprisonment. April 15, 1790, the viceroy orders the *encargado de justicia* in Apan to go to the hacienda, investigate, free the Indians if their tale is true, and notify the owner that each Indian owes only 5/ for advances that may be made legally. If there is further abuse, he will be punished.

Upon receipt of the decree in Apan, the encargado de justicia investigates and prepares his report, dated April 22, 1790. The complaint is not true, since the Indians are only shut up at night with the approval of the justice, because the wife of one sleeps with the other man. As to action in the past year, the owner had no maize, and so gave his workers money to buy it or urged them to work where maize could be gotten. The owner will report to the viceroy on the suit. The affidavit of the owner repeats what is in the report of the encargado de justicia. April 30, 1790, the papers are received at the General Indian Court on transmittal through the weekly courier by the subdelegado of Apan. On May 11 the court orders the docket kept on file for use if there is further complaint.[162]

113. August 5–September 24, 1802, Mexico City and Tulancingo. Máximo Nolasco, Indian tributary of Tulancingo, in jail, vs. the majordomo of the hacienda of Caltengo.[163] José Manuel Vallarta, Indian solicitor, presents a petition for Nolasco, who is in jail after a quarrel with and beating by the majordomo of the hacienda of Caltengo. The Indian complains that he is held for debt without an accounting and without a chance to earn money elsewhere. He asks for release and damages in the form of wages for time lost. On August 5, the General Indian Court orders the justice of the district, if the petitioner is in jail for the reason given in the petition, to free him at once, and to report to the court by return of the weekly messenger. On August 9 the subdelegado orders compliance but apparently not the Indian's release, and on August 11 holds a formal accounting, according

162. AGN-Crim, 10:exp. 23 (LBSD, vol. 22).
163. AT. The arithmetic is that of the subdelegado.

to which Nolasco received advances to April 18, 1802, of 67/8/6; thereafter he asked for and got 11/, so that he owes in all 78/5/6. He worked 60 days at 0/2 a day and a ration, for a net credit of 15/1/6, so he owes 63/4. His son owes 1/3 for money and 0/5 for a coa, or a net debt of 2/. Accordingly, the total debt is 65/4.

On August 13 the subdelegado reports to the viceroy that the jailing is as reported, but the majordomo was not at the fight. One of his aides was threatened by Pedro Antonio. The Indian worked out the day, then went to the Indian town governor, who ordered him to return to work. The subdelegado has inspected the Indian for any sign of a wound, finding none, and has questioned witnesses. He then asked for payment of the debt under the viceregal order of June 30, 1801. He found that the Indian did not want to change masters but did want to remain in his town and make occasional payments.

On August 18, the court orders that the report be shown to Nolasco's attorney, who on August 21 files a new petition for his client, again asking for freedom, an indemnity, and a careful accounting of his debt. He denounces the practices of hacendados. All papers then go for review to the fiscal protector, who says that the report of the subdelegado shows partiality and does not contradict the complaint. He recommends issuance of an order for release and careful accounting. If the Indian owes over 5/, he should pay on the official accounting but need not work at the same hacienda, in accordance with current legislation. On September 16, 1802, the assessor and the viceroy, accepting the fiscal's recommendation, give order for the necessary decree.

When the new decree reaches the subdelegado in Tulancingo, he orders the Indian released and a new accounting. The hacienda records show a net debt of 65/4, but the Indian admits only to 62/4, for burials, baptisms, clothing, and food. The administrator of the hacienda accepts this figure. With credit for 62 days of illness and jail, the net debt is 44/6/6. Upon being asked to work or give bond for the debt, the Indian gives bond for fifteen days in which to find a new master.

114. September 14–December 3, 1804, Mexico City and Ixtlahuaca. Seven Indians, claimed by the hacienda of Sila as its gañanes, appeal, since they are willing to pay their debts and tributes. The subdelegado of Ixtlahuaca had summoned them and ascertained that they want to live in the town of San Bartolomé. Six of the men confess that they are registered on the hacienda, in debt, and are very well treated. The subdelegado orders that they live on the hacienda and avoid evil ways. The General Court orders all papers sent to it, an order the sub-

delegado obeys. The gañanes are to be informed that they may have copies for further action if they so wish.[164]

3. Indian vs. Indian

One of the major purposes of the establishment of the General Indian Court was to handle disputes of Indian with Indian. The court was to settle such matters with as little litigation and as expeditiously as possible, reducing costs and fees or even eliminating them entirely. Many disputes among Indians have already been covered here under other headings, especially that of land and other property; others will be summarized under later headings—for complaints and disputes tended to concentrate a variety of grievances and pick up old irritations. Many of the complaints against Spanish officials and clergy included Indians, either as agents or partners and even as allies, for towns might split into factions over their priest, their Spanish justice, or a resident non-Indian. Furthermore, our categories here are hardly mutually exclusive.

a. Caciques and Indian Town Officials

A long series of sixteenth-century royal cédulas and viceregal ordinances attest to both the existence of, and attempts to curb, abuses by caciques and by the Indian officials in the new governmental system the Spaniards instituted. Later royal cédulas, ordinances, and reports testify to the prevalent and continued abuse of power throughout the seventeenth century and to the end of the colonial regime. There were, to be sure, changes, in that the power of the caciques as a group steadily declined, even more than might be easily apparent, for less and less did they occupy the foremost posts of town government. These increasingly came to other men who had or acquired wealth and prestige. But the newcomers proved equally adept at using their posts for personal profit and for burdening and mistreating their fellow Indians within the town. One avenue of seeking remedy lay in the Spanish custom that permitted complaint or suit before the Spanish authorities. So the famous capítulos came to be applied also to caciques and Indian town officials.[165] Upon establishment of the General Indian

---

164. AGN-Civ, vol. 2161:exp. 12 (LBSD, vol. 3).

165. See the discussion in Chapter III; ordinances of the Bishop of Yucatan as viceroy, Mexico City, July 4, 1648, confirmed in royal cédulas of May 20, 1649, and March 2, 1690: AGN-RCD, 52:fols. 124f–128f and 54:fols. 134f–135f. On Indian town government, see Gibson, *Tlaxcala*, 89–123 et passim, and *The Aztecs*, 166–193 et passim. On caciques, the judgment is mine, based on examining archival materials at length.

Court, many of such complaints and suits were brought before it. From the available records of such cases, it is clear that Indian townfolk, on the whole, did not approach the court frivolously or on light abuse. They were more likely to raise issues only after mistreatment and exploitation had reached what they regarded as intolerable levels. The chance of complaint rose as the people to be complained of lost sufficient power that the possibility of reprisal diminished accordingly. Many of the complaints and suits were imbedded in local politics and factional quarrels, at which a present-day reader of the record can only guess; sometimes much dirty linen came to light in the court-ordered investigation that any complaint was certain to bring about.

115. April 26–June 17, 1600, Mexico City and Chalcatongo. The town of Chalcatongo, province of Teposcolula, vs. its cacique, Don Antonio de Arellano.[166] Pedro Díaz Agüero, Indian procurador, brings three complaints to the General Indian Court on behalf of Chalcatongo. The first alleges that when Tristán de Luna y Arellano was alcalde mayor, he three times through the cacique had each woman spin 1½ pounds of cotton into thread. The present alcalde mayor has had the women each spin a similar amount once. Such spinning, worth 0/1 per 1½ pounds, has been paid for by the two alcaldes mayores, but the cacique kept all the money. On April 26, 1600, the court orders the current alcalde mayor, Francisco de las Casas, to see that the Indians receive their pay.

The second complaint alleges that the same cacique two years before levied a derrama of 0/1 per macehual and with the proceeds bought 200 sheep for the community. However, the community gets no profit from the sheep, and the macehuales are held to much work in order to care for them. The petition asks that the sheep be sold and the proceeds divided among the macehuales. Another court decree of April 26, 1600, orders the alcalde mayor to investigate.

The third complaint files a long list of the cacique's wrongs against the town: (1) For twenty years he has gotten five women and two men for service without pay. (2) For ten years he has gotten five herders for his estancias without pay. (3) Nine years before, when he married, he levied an assessment of 0/6 in money per macehual and additional clothing. (4) Three years before, he levied an assessment of 0/1 per macehual for the visit of the bishop, who never came. (5) Two years before, in a lawsuit between himself and Tecomaxtlahuaca, he levied an assessment of 0/2 per macehual. (6) He has twice levied the tax of *real servicio*, of 0/2 and then 0/4, two times in the same year. (7) Three years ago he levied a derrama of 0/0/6 to fight imposition of

166. AJT-Crim, leg. 2.

the new tax of real servicio. (8) The previous year, 1599, he levied an assessment of 0/2 per macehual to go to Mexico City on matters of the proposed concentration of Indian settlement (congregación). On May 2, 1600, the viceroy decrees that the cacique is to collect and be provided only with what is in the formal schedule for his office.

On June 14, 1600, Francisco de las Casas begins the investigation ordered by the General Indian Court. It undoubtedly finds much improper behavior and abuse by the cacique, but rather than punish him by criminal penalty, all agree to a concierto before the alcalde mayor: (1) The cacique agrees to pay 300/ to the macehuales within six months, in settlement of monetary claims. (2) He is to levy no further derramas. (3) He is to sell his livestock, apparently cattle or horses. (4) People assigned to his service in the future are to receive 0/3 a week, both those in the formal schedule and those in excess. (5) No men or women are to be assigned to the service of the principales. (6) Public posts in the cabecera and its estancias are in the future to go to the principales in both by fair election of the principales and overseers. (7) One Indian a week is to be assigned without pay to the church for its guard and custody. (8) The macehuales are to be held to no contributions for economic activities of others, obviously the cacique and the alcalde mayor. All swear compliance before the alcalde mayor and formally abandon their suits.

The complaints here obviously cover a range beyond the cacique's activities, even though most arise from them. Assessments of labor and money for the church and the principales, as well as distribution of posts between cabecera and estancias, fair elections, and selection of appropriate people are all handled in the agreement; equally, the clause on economic activities of others covers the Spanish governors as well. The case also illustrates unusually well the policy of the General Indian Court, evident as soon as it began functioning, to proceed as much as possible by discussion and compromise among the parties. Francisco de las Casas obviously served as arbiter and negotiator in what must have been a complicated and fairly lengthy process.

116. January 27, 1616, Mexico City. Dr. Galdós de Balencia, fiscal protector, for Bartolomé García, Indian of Cuistla, province of Miahuatlán, complains that Don Martín de Almaraz was the lover of García's wife before the two were married, and seeks to have her continue as his mistress. Although the ecclesiastical judge of the bishopric of Oaxaca has ordered him to desist, on pain of 100/ fine and exile, Almaraz, who is an Indian alcalde and a friend of the lieutenant of the alcalde mayor of Miahuatlán, and hence a man of power, has seized five mules García uses to earn his livelihood, to cover the expenses of

the suit in the Church court. Almaraz was town alcalde last year and is again so this year, and thus justice is impossible except from outside.

On the advice of his assessor, the viceroy orders the alcalde mayor of Miahuatlán, if the story is true, to go in person to Cuistla and force return of the five mules; if Almaraz has any claim against García, the alcalde mayor is to hear the case by summary procedure; if Almaraz has been alcalde the past year, he is not to hold office in the current year; and he is to be ordered not to molest García or his wife, under suitable penalties to be assigned by the alcalde mayor. Furthermore, Almaraz is to be forced to comply with the sentence pronounced against him by the ecclesiastical judge.[167]

117. December 22, 1617–January 31, 1618, Mexico City. José de Celi, on behalf of the principales and commoners of Tepeji (de la Seda), has filed charges against Francisco Motezuma, governor of the town. The court has entrusted investigation to the corregidor of Ahuatlán[168] and Zoyatitlanapa. Motezuma, through his attorney, asks for a copy of the charges and that he be permitted to file his answers with a nearby justice, since the corregidor is prejudiced. On December 22, 1617, on the advice of his assessor, the viceroy orders that Motezuma be given a copy, that he is to file answers before the new corregidor of Ahuatlán and Zoyatitlanapa within twenty days for transmittal to the court, and that during this twenty-day period he is not to exercise the powers of governor. On January 17, 1618, on a further petition by Celi for the town, the viceroy orders that an elected governor is to serve until Motezuma's case is decided. Shortly thereafter, on January 31, the viceroy orders the new corregidor of Ahuatlán and Zoyatitlanapa to go in person to Tepeji, to receive Motezuma's answers to the charges and to examine witnesses within thirty-six days, in accordance with the questionnaire that Motezuma has filed for approval, with due notice to the principales that they may either attend in person or send an agent for the swearing-in and recognition of the witnesses; otherwise, the proceedings will be void. The signed originals of the testimony are to be given to Motezuma, without levying any fee. At this point the docket ends.[169]

118. July 14–November 9, 1625, Mexico City and Teposcolula. Chalcatongo, province of Teposcolula, vs. its alcaldes, for excess levies. José de Celi, for the town of Chalcatongo, petitions the viceroy for relief. Rafael Sánchez, alcalde of the town, has levied such heavy de-

---

167. AGN-I, 7: exp. 19.
168. The name in the documents is Aguacatlán, but Gerhard, *A Guide*, 160–163, gives it as present-day Ahuatlán.
169. AGN-I, 7: exps. 240 and 252.

rramas that the town appealed to the preceding viceroy, the Marqués de Gelves, for an order of amparo, which was granted. Nevertheless, Rafael's son, Diego Sánchez, continues exactions. The petition asks for an order to the alcalde mayor for protection and restitution. On July 14, 1625, the viceroy so orders. Upon presentation of the order in Teposcolula, the alcalde mayor opens an investigation, which discloses that Rafael Sánchez is dead but that he, his son, and three other alcaldes have levied derramas on pretexts of suits, church costs, tributes, etc., raising over 800/, which has been spent on mules, harquebuses, clothing, and food and drink for themselves, as follows:

Rafael Sánchez, d. 1618	200/ derramas
	240/ extra tribute at 80/ a year
Pedro de Galicia, 3 years	240/ extra tribute at 80/ a year
Diego de Bejarano	120/ extra tribute at 80/ a year
Baltasar de Castro	80/ extra tribute at 80/ a year
Total	880/

The three alcaldes yet alive, and Diego Sánchez, are arrested, and their declarations recorded. On November 9, 1625, they post bond for the sum in Chalcatongo. The docket ends here. This case should be related to the complaint against the cacique of Chalcatongo in 1600 (no. 115).[170]

119. August 12–September 26, 1639, Mexico City. The principales and commoners of Pátzcuaro, province of Michoacán, vs. Don Francisco Ramírez, its governor for 1639, and his father, Don Gabriel Ramírez. José de Celi for the town of Pátzcuaro petitions the viceroy to have capítulos against the two men received and investigated. The two are mestizos, not Indians, and have committed many abuses. The Indians, although wanting to complain earlier, have been afraid to do so. The capítulos allege: (1) The governor levies tribute by the old, not the new count, and pockets the 600/ difference. He also charges the delegates who bring the tribute, money and gifts that come to 5/ each, and insists on payment of maize in kind at his measure, or in money at 0/5 the fanega above official commutation. He keeps the Indians for his service and insists on comida, ostensibly for the alcalde mayor. The women recruited for service in the house of the alcalde mayor, to avoid molestation by a mulatto, pay 0/5 a week each for release from service; the repartimiento for this is 8 women and 8 chickens, at 0/0/6 each. Other drafts for service for the alcalde mayor are several times the number needed; to escape them, people pay 0/2 to 0/4 each. All foodstuffs are taken at official values far below real values. (2) The governor forces payment of 5/ each for giving varas to barrio officials,

170. AJT-Crim, leg. 3.

alleging as his reason that he must recover 500/ paid to the alcalde mayor for arranging his election as governor. (3) The governor forces the barrios to pay 4/ to 5/ for repairing the fountain in Pátzcuaro, although the alcalde mayor collects a tax for this purpose. (4) The governor levies 3/ on each sujeto, 0/3 from the Indians in the cabecera, 10/ from each of three hospitals, and 100/ from that of Santa María to carry on suits and for other purposes. (5) The governor on his own order has had flogged over 70 men and women, has put others in jail, and keeps the boys from church instruction. And (6) he makes the rounds of the town at night and breaks into houses.

The capítulos are sent in Spanish, because the official interpreter in Mexico City is a friend of the two Ramírez men, who lodge in his house when they visit the capital. The petition asks an investigation and expulsion of the two men from the town. On August 12, 1639, the viceroy orders an investigation through a special judge, since the alcalde mayor is implicated.[171]

Six weeks later, José de Celi, acting for Juan Bautista Guasasco, the governor for 1638, petitions the court on the same matter. Upon receiving word of the capítulos and the investigation ordered, Don Francisco Ramírez, in alliance with the alcalde mayor, tried to arrest the chief complainants and to intimidate Guasasco. They demand an accounting of community property for his term of office, and have proceeded similarly for other principales. All such accounting lies within the function of the special judge the viceroy has appointed. The petition asks an order of amparo and that the alcalde mayor be instructed not to impede the complainants in proving their case, nor is anyone else allowed to do so. On September 26, 1639, the viceroy so orders.[172]

120. February 10, 1640, Mexico City.[173] The Indians of the town of Teposcolula file capítulos before the viceroy against two present alcaldes, Pedro de la Cruz and Mateo Ortiz, and two of past years, Domingo Osorio and Raymundo Belasco. To investigate, the viceroy sends Juan de Meras, receptor of the audiencia, who consults the local friars and the alcalde mayor, the latter declaring in shocked surprise that he was unaware of the abuses. Meras holds sessions with both sides, and on December 13, 1639, brings about a concierto.

The concierto is a long agreement on permissible charges and services: (1) The extra two reales over the royal tribute is not to be collected, on penalty of fourfold refund. (2) The Indians are not to be held to furnish 140 lengths of cloth for Maundy Thursday; the 12

171. AGN-I, 11:exp. 276 (LBSF, 8:fols. 68–78).
172. Ibid., exp. 323 (LBSF, 8:fols. 85–87).
173. Ibid., exp. 489.

lengths given to the poor are to be paid from community funds. (3) For the feast of St. Peter, for which the Indians were assessed 165 lengths of cloth, they are to give only 50, to be distributed among the friars of the local and other convents. The cloth is to be at fair price, and the Indians are to receive the cotton for it from the community. (4) Each Indian tributary is not to be held to give 600 loads of fodder a year, nor in default thereof o/6. If fodder is asked for, it is to be bought at fair price, since the Spanish justice and others pay for it. (5) For the feast of St. Peter, the Indians are not to be held to contribute 40 turkeys at o/3 and over 100 chickens at o/1, since they have to pay more to get them. Any fowls needed are to be bought at fair price. (6) Since the Indians say they ask for no change in the weekly labor draft for the friars, justices, and other persons, that is to remain at 10 men and 1 woman for the convent, 2 men and 1 woman, plus 2 *topiles*, for the justice, 2 men and 2 women for the notary, 1 man and 1 woman for the interpreter, 1 man for the royal notary, 2 men and 1 woman for each of the 2 caciques, 1 woman for the community, 1 woman for the town hospital, and 1 woman for Francisco de Salazar: in all, 22 men and 10 women weekly, all of whom are to be paid at customary rates. Penalty for infraction of the agreement is set at 500/, half for the other party and half for the royal treasury, plus two years of exile from the province. The original of the agreement is to be left in charge of the local notary public, and each sujeto and the cabecera is to get a copy.

After review by his assessor and upon his advice, the viceroy on February 10, 1640, confirms the concierto with the amendments that the Indians are not to be held to provide 50 lengths of cloth for distribution at the feast of St. Peter since it is not a proper public charge, nor are they under obligation to provide the men and women for weekly service, since that is contrary to royal legislation.

121. November 2, 1640, Mexico City. Juan Francisco, Indian of the barrio of Acoyac, of the parcialidad of Santiago Tlatelolco, complains that, despite his having been exempted from personal service by the Marqués de Cadereita when viceroy, because of a crippled leg, the overseer of his barrio makes him pay 2/ whenever it would be his turn to serve. He petitions again for exemption and protection. The current viceroy, the Duque de Escalona, grants the exemption again and orders amparo.[174]

122. February 6–October 22, 1723, Mexico City and Tultitlán.[175] Don Francisco Ximénez, cacique and governor of Tultitlán, district of Tacuba, on February 6, 1723, via Lic. Bazoa, defends him-

174. Ibid., 13:fol. 34 (LBSE, 8:fol. 173).
175. AGN-Civ, vol. 2154:exp. 8 (LBSD, vol. 4).

self before the General Indian Court against a complaint by an Indian that he interferes with Indian children who wish to go to school. His defense is that he insists that the children go to the town school, conducted by a Spanish teacher, and not to one "in the passageway" with an Indian teacher. The court asks the local parish priest to report. On February 25 the cura reports that the governor is carrying out the royal will for schools in Spanish, and that the Indians resist. On February 26 the court decrees that the local parish priest and justice are to assist the governor.

The case then takes on a new aspect when on August 18, 1723, the Indians of the barrio of San Francisco Chilpa of the same town try to replace the Indian teacher with a mulatto in order to avoid sending children to the cabecera's school. The governor again appeals to the General Indian Court, asking that, should the Indians go to another tribunal, the court issue a decree vacating the proceeding. The court orders that earlier records be brought to it, and on August 20 decrees that the mulatto is not to meddle in the matter and the justice is to carry out its previous order, on pain of a fine of 100/. Upon notification of this decree, the teniente of the town certifies obedience on August 27.

Meanwhile, on August 18, the barrio of San Francisco Chilpa petitions the audiencia for the right to have its own school and for an order to end the governor's opposition, alleging inter alia that he has jailed four people. That same day the audiencia issues a royal provisión to the alcalde mayor on the school and orders that the Indians, if jailed only on this issue, be released. On August 20 the order is received by the general deputy of the alcalde mayor in Tacuba and an order issued to the teniente in Tultitlán. That same day it is received by the teniente, who notifies the governor. The situation in late August 1723 is that there are two conflicting sets of orders and the teniente has agreed to obey both.

The governor, on notification, states that the Indians are in jail for other reasons, and the matter of the school has been decided in the General Indian Court. On September 4 the barrio petitions the audiencia for an order of punishment against the governor, asking that the file go to the fiscal protector. Upon referral of the docket to the fiscal protector, the latter recommends that the Indians in jail be released and that the barrio be protected in its school. The audiencia, however, in consultation with the viceroy as its president, on September 11 decrees that if the matter is not in the General Indian Court, judgment is to be rendered as the fiscal recommends; if it is in the court, all papers are to go there. On October 22, 1723, the viceroy, for the General Indian Court, orders that its decree of August 20 is to be enforced.

This case is notable as an instance of the resolution of resort by

Indians to two tribunals, and for the unusual circumstance that the recommendation of the fiscal protector differs from the decision of the General Indian Court.

123. March 30, 1745–June 9, 1746, Mexico City, Tlayacapan, and Chalco. The Indians of Tlayacapan, province of Chalco, through two Indian procuradores and one other, complain to the General Indian Court that their governors collect 4/ a year per tributary in two installments on the plea of *cuatequil* (public works). The court asks the local parish priest for a report, which states that such a levy has been immemorial custom. Investigation uncovers a decree of Viceroy Valero of March 24, 1719, forbidding the levy. The court orders the alcalde mayor of Chalco to stop all levy for cuatequil.[176]

124. August 14–October 9, 1794, Mexico City and San Cristóbal Ecatepec. Francisco Pasarán, of the rancho of San Simón, vs. the governor of Tolpetlac, province of San Cristóbal Ecatepec, for improper imprisonment. Pasarán petitions the General Indian Court, explaining that he is a muleteer who transports pulque and has been jailed illegally by the governor for refusing to work on the road. The viceroy orders the alcalde mayor of San Cristóbal Ecatepec to see that justice is done. In Ecatepec, the alcalde mayor, holding that Pasarán is not Indian and therefore that the governor has no jurisdiction over him, jails the governor for exceeding his authority and sends all papers to the viceroy. In turn, the governor appeals to the General Indian Court. Upon recommendation of the fiscal protector, the two parties see the papers in the case and file pleadings. Upon further referral to the fiscal, that official holds that if Pasarán is a Spaniard, the guilt of the governor is greater; if not, his resistance to community roadwork was excessive, but the governor abused his authority. The governor should be given warning and released. The court accepts the fiscal's recommendation without ruling on the racial and fiscal status of Pasarán.[177]

125. November 21, 1800, Mexico City. José María de Arellano, Indian solicitor, on behalf of Francisco Toribio, Indian of Santa María Nativitas, province of Tulancingo, petitions the viceroy for release of Toribio's wife, who has been jailed by the town's governor because Toribio left the town to find work, there being none locally. He asks for release of Toribio's wife and that the governor be ordered to explain. Upon the advice of his assessor, the viceroy issues a decree that, if the matter is as alleged, the woman is to be released and the governor is to explain his action.[178]

176. Ibid., 2229:exp. 8 (LBSD, vol. 13).
177. AGN-Crim, 10:exp. 2 (LBSD, vol. 21).
178. AT.

b. *Indios Revoltosos*

Just as the Spanish idea of a harmonious Indian body politic was opposed to extortions and misgovernment by caciques and town officials, it also censured members of Indian towns who withheld proper obedience and refused to live in peace with their neighbors. *Indios revoltosos*, or unruly Indians, flouted the authority of the proper officials of the town, conspired to seize the posts of town government, or operated as a lawless group, preying upon the community. If the town authorities found themselves unable to deal with their own scofflaws, in exasperation they might call upon the local Spanish governor for assistance or appeal to the viceregal government. Behind the complaints very often lay a more complex story of factions within a town, the settlement of new people, or changes in the town structure of power.

126. July 20, 1612–January 12, 1613, Mexico City and Teposcolula. José de Celi, on behalf of the governor and alcaldes of Malinaltepec, province of Teposcolula, complains to the viceroy that four macehuales revoltosos will not work on the church or pay derramas levied for the work. The petition asks that the viceroy order the alcalde mayor to investigate and punish the guilty. On July 20, 1612, the viceroy issues the decree. Presentation of the decree and hearings by the alcalde mayor take place almost six months later, January 9–12, 1613, in Teposcolula. The town officials of Malinaltepec present the decree with a parallel petition to the same effect. In the hearings, witnesses testify that the men are from Tlaxiaco and have settled in Malinaltepec. The four have levied derramas to fight the principales and will not assist in the milpas for the community. In their defense, the four men declare that all the trouble began four years ago at the instigation of the town cacica. The docket ends here.[179]

127. March 20, 1613–April 10, 1617, Mexico City and Teposcolula. A long suit by Don Pedro de Sotomayor, cacique of Ocotepec, province of Teposcolula, to secure recognition of his position and service from the officials and principales of the estancia of Santiago Nuyóo.[180] On March 20, 1613, the viceroy approves a schedule of payment and service for Sotomayor as cacique. Upon the failure of Santiago Nuyóo to comply with its share, the cacique sues in the provincial court. The estancia officials are imprisoned various times for refusal to obey orders on complying with the schedule, are released on agreeing to do so, and imprisoned again as they fail to comply. In the hearings, the officials present evidence that the macehuales refuse service be-

179. AJT-Crim, leg. 2.
180. AJT-Civ, leg. 2.

cause Sotomayor either pays nothing or only a half-real a week. One macehual, Marcos de Guzmán, apparently the leader, advised his fellows not to appear for work unless paid in advance. Guzmán collects 2 to 3 reales a week for the suit. Another macehual testifies that he did report for work twice, receiving o/o/6 the first week and o/1 the second. A definitive sentence by the alcalde mayor of Teposcolula threatens sentence to an obraje for further disobedience. At that moment the estancia officials are again in jail.

Worsted in the provincial tribunal, the estancia resorts to the General Indian Court. Through José de Celi, it presents a petition, asking for amparo and investigation by another Spanish justice. On April 27, 1616, the viceroy orders release of the imprisoned Indians under bond and an investigation by the corregidor of Tilantongo. May 25, the order is presented to the corregidor of Tilantongo, and shortly thereafter in Teposcolula. The imprisoned Indians are released under bond, but must return within fifteen days. On June 20 they are ordered under arrest. Meanwhile, the corregidor of Tilantongo has carried out his investigation and reported to the viceroy, who on July 21 orders all prisoners in the case released without bond and all papers sent to him. September 2, 1616, in Teposcolula, the alcalde mayor complies with the viceregal decree, but Sotomayor files formal notice of appeal. On February 20, 1617, the court decrees execution of its previous orders; recognition of Sotomayor as cacique; observance of the viceregal schedule for the cacique of March 20, 1613; and punishment of anyone guilty of improper behavior. On April 10, 1617, the viceregal decree is presented in Teposcolula to the alcalde mayor.

Ostensibly an affair of rebellious commoners, this case clearly has elements of resentment of the estancia's dependent status upon the cabecera and reaction against traveling a long distance for work (the macehuales claimed 6 leagues) with inadequate pay or none.

128. September 30, 1632, Mexico City. The town officials of Teposcolula complain that Juan Francisco, Pedro del Valle, and Juan de Zárate, who know Spanish and sing in the church, have caused much trouble in the town. The town secured a viceregal decree dated August 3, 1632, for their arrest and trial, but the three fled to the hills and then to Mexico City. With false stories, they got a decree of amparo from the General Indian Court. They then returned to Teposcolula and stirred up more trouble. The town asks for enforcement of the order of August 3, and the court orders the alcalde mayor to carry out the order, arrest the three, judge the case, and send on the papers, all within a month.[181]

181. AGN-I, 10, cuad. 3:exp. 76.

129. July 5—September 18, 1745, Mexico City and Cuautitlán. Ventura Francisco vs. Don Pedro Pablo, ex-governor, and Sebastián de la Cruz, current alcalde, all of Tultepec, province of Cuautitlán.[182] Ventura Francisco, a principal, appeals to the General Indian Court, complaining of verbal abuse and beatings. On July 5, the court orders the justice of the district to investigate and settle the matter within three days upon presentation of the decree. On July 9 the decree is delivered to the lieutenant of the alcalde mayor in Cuautitlán by the plaintiff's wife.

Once formal obedience is recorded, the proceedings get under way. Witnesses testify that Francisco objected to a derrama for the expenses of a suit with San Miguel, and in the ensuing quarrel was beaten. The lieutenant orders the arrest of the ex-governor and alcalde and reports to the viceroy. On July 10, the ex-governor and alcalde present a petition to the lieutenant in Cuautitlán, declaring that Francisco was drunk and late in reporting for community work. According to local custom, he was whipped, but only with 6 lashes. They ask for a medical examination of the complainant. Carried out by a doctor, the examination finds three to four weals made by a whip on the man's buttocks, and no other marks. The doctor infers a light beating of 4 to 6 lashes with a *disciplina* (a whip with several lashes, usually of hemp), but no signs of violence elsewhere, and certainly no evidence of danger to the man's life. Later testimony on behalf of the town officials discloses that in the quarrel over collection of the levy, Francisco threatened the ex-governor with a sickle. He was then seized by four men, held on the ground, his *calzones* lowered, and beaten on the bare rump. On July 13, in Mexico City, a petition is filed before the General Indian Court on behalf of the town, asking that the two men in jail be released on bond. On court permission, that is done.

The next stage of the case is a series of attacks and counterattacks. The town files two petitions with the court. On July 20 it petitions for an order that Ventura Francisco and his family be expelled from the town as unruly people, and in another petition that the family be forced to live in nearby Tlalnepantla, district of Tacuba, where they have land. Those petitions elicit further petitions on the part of Francisco: one asking for protection, since the town is trying to exile him and his family, and the other—on the ground that the beating was worse than the town declared, since a month later he still has scars—asking for a new formal inspection of the stripes, and punishment of the two men. Faced with this barrage, the court orders all files joined; that the town gather evidence on the bad character and evil life of Ventura Francisco, but only through testimony of Spanish witnesses; that

182. AGN-Civ, vol. 2300:exp. 5 (LBSD, vol. 21).

the town prove that the family has land in Tlalnepantla; that Francisco may make use of its earlier decree for his protection; and that both he and the town should go to the local justice and not to the General Indian Court. The court also asks the parish priest for a report on the life of Ventura Francisco and his family. In reply, the priest declares that there is in the town one unruly family of mulattos, that Francisco's wife is from this family, and Ventura Francisco follows their ways: the man is a drunkard and a poor Christian who should be expelled from the town.

The last papers in the docket are dated September 1745. Faced with the requirement of Spanish witnesses, the town files an affidavit that no Spaniards or near-Spaniards live in the town and that the only non-Indian family is mulatto. On September 18 the lieutenant of the alcalde mayor of Cuautitlán reports that, as ordered, he summoned the town officials of Tultepec and required them to justify their demand for expulsion. They have announced that they will do so within two days. The docket ends here.

This case well illustrates the problems of Spanish officials in sorting out testimony. The requirement that the town officials of Tultepec produce Spanish witnesses was in accordance with the general reluctance to accept Indian testimony, but posed an almost insuperable problem for the town officials of Tultepec. For their side of the case, the report of the parish priest was massive support, whatever the priest's motives. The case further illustrates the fact that infliction of moderate punishment by authorities and employers was accepted by the courts, provincial and superior.

c. Disputed Elections

Indian town officials were elected around the New Year for one-year terms, which had to be confirmed either by the local Spanish justice or by the viceroy. The officials were to be pure Indian on both sides and ineligible for reelection until after three years, but the rules were widely violated as non-Indian genetic stock entered the higher ranks of Indian society. As the Indians quickly grasped the fact that control of the town machinery meant power and possibilities of revenue, factional fights within the town between groups in the cabecera, or between cabecera and sujetos, became a rich source of disputes. Furthermore, local Spaniards, the parish priest, and the local Spanish governor frequently manipulated the factions to their own wish and advantage.[183] The resulting disputes over elections became so frequent

183. Gibson, *The Aztecs*, 175–181. Much of this comment is based upon the cases themselves, since the rules and detail of administration show up in them very clearly. See also RLI, 6.5.15; the order of Viceroy Gelves, Mexico City, April 5, 1622

that for some years a large part of the records of the ramo of Indios concerns them.[184] Confirmation of elections was an administrative matter and, if handled by the viceroy, properly lay outside the function of the General Indian Court. Nevertheless, many of the disputes were heard in the court, and the resulting decrees issued as court decisions. The intention may have been to vest the decision with greater solemnity as a means of discouraging appeal or suit before the audiencia, but the measure also illustrates a general viceregal policy of channeling all Indian matters to the court—which was, after all, the part of the viceregal staff most experienced in Indian ways. However, the proprietary right of the two secretaries of gobernación to handle such business was always respected, in that, if the decree issued from the court, it still was drawn up and registered by them. In 1664, Viceroy Mancera specifically reconfirmed this right on petition of the two secretaries, who complained that in the previous year third parties had begun to act as intermediaries in bringing the papers to the viceroy.[185] One can only wonder if the third parties were private people, the judicial secretaries, or the viceroy's personal secretaries.

130. July 27, 1628, Mexico City. Melchor López de Haro, Indian solicitor, on behalf of the Indians of Uruapan, province of Michoacán, complains on behalf of his clients that after they held the town election of 1628, and the alcalde mayor and viceroy confirmed the results, the alcalde mayor, to please the ex-guardian of the convent, Fray Andrés Medrano, declared that the election had to be held again. Thereupon the encomendero took away the document of confirmation, and the friar and a lieutenant of the alcalde mayor held a new election, the results of which were forwarded to Mexico City; but there confirmation was refused, because the first election had been approved. Then a third election was held, which by inadvertence was

---

(AGN-I, 9 : exp. 78f–v; BLT), that the elections of officials of Indian towns be approved only on his express order, and not as a routine function of the secretaries of gobernación; the viceregal ordinance of August 23, 1642, that the officials of Indian towns must be pure Indian on both sides of their descent; the royal cédula of June 4, 1687, confirming this rule, applying it to interpreters in Indian towns, and ordering that there be no reelection of the same person for three years; and the circular instruction of January 12, 1777, that Spanish provincial authorities levy no fees or costs for approving the annual elections or for formally giving the staffs of office: all in Beleña, 1, part 2 : 25, no. 49, and part 5 : 206–207, nos. 380 and 381; royal cédula of 1682, antecedent to that of June 4, 1687, in DCLI, 1 : 152–154 (no. 118). See also articles 12–14 of the Ordinance of Intendants, 1786, in Beleña, 2 : app., vii–ix. Most of the legislation codified rules already in effect.

184. LBSF, 12 : fols. 94 and 113.
185. Mexico City, November 8, 1664, AGN-RCD, 20 : fol. 114f–v (BLT).

confirmed in the viceregal administrative secretariat. Since the new governor does not represent the will of the principales, the town asks that the first election be enforced, since it was legally and properly carried out and represents the true will of the principales and commoners. On the advice of his assessor, to whom all papers were sent, the viceroy orders the alcalde mayor to assemble the principales of Uruapan and all others customary, hold a new election, and send the results to the secretaries of gobernación.[186]

131. December 25, 1629, Mexico City. Upon the petition of the town of San Mateo Atengo, province of Metepec, asking that a first election for 1630 of Don Juan Luis as governor be confirmed, rather than a second one of Don Pedro Cipriano, the viceroy ordered the alcalde mayor of Ixtlahuaca to investigate and report. That report revealed that Cipriano is a mestizo and was governor for 1629; accordingly, he cannot be reelected without a special dispensation. (He was, of course, ineligible at all times as a mestizo.) Moreover, his administration in 1629 was marked by many quarrels and suits. Upon review of the papers by the assessor of the General Indian Court, the viceroy confirms Don Juan Luis as governor for 1630.[187]

132. April 12, 1630, Mexico City. Melchor López de Haro, on behalf of the alcaldes, regidores, and community of Jonotla, complains that Andrés Ponce, a macehual, has been governor twice through the favor of the corregidor, despite the fact that there are eligible caciques and principales. Ponce has governed ill, levying derramas and excess payments for royal tribute; he lives scandalously, mistreats the principales and other residents, denies justice, insists upon a labor draft of workmen for sowing his crops, and carries on illegal dealings in other towns. He has worked hand in glove with Leonardo de Cervantes, an Indian of the town who is an unruly person, leads a bad life, and foments suits and dissension. The complaints ask that the local Spanish justice, under heavy penalties, be forbidden to allow reelection, and that the two men be punished and forced to make restitution. Ponce at once files a denial of all charges.

Upon the advice of his assessor, the viceroy orders the justice of the district of Jonotla to see that the governor is not reelected and that the two men are punished for any misdeeds and forced to make restitution of whatever they have taken improperly from the Indians. Penalty for noncompliance is set at a fine of 100/, half for the royal treasury and half for the Hospital Real de los Indios, plus the costs of

186. AGN-I, 10, cuad. 1:exp. 4.
187. Ibid., exp. 184.

sending another person for enforcement. If there is no notary in the town, notification may be made by anyone who can read and write.[188]

133. February 6, 1673, Mexico City. Juan López de Pareja, Indian solicitor, for Don Gerónimo Ortiz de Tapia, cacique and principal of the town of Teposcolula, complains that his client was elected alcalde for 1673 but that the governor of 1672, Don Francisco Pimentel, in order to get reelected, held a second election at night with the help of the alcalde mayor, Ortiz being excluded from the meeting and not elected. The petition asks that the second election not be confirmed and the papers of the first be examined. The viceroy orders the alcalde mayor of the province to hold back all papers on the town election and send them to the General Indian Court for further review. Until the court decides, the oldest regidor is to serve as governor.[189]

134. December 22, 1713, Mexico City. Indians of Santiago Tillo, province of Yanhuitlán, complain to the General Indian Court that on November 22, 1713, the town electors assembled and elected a slate for 1714, with Domingo Victoria as governor by 40 votes; but the governor of 1713, Miguel de la Cruz, then held a new election with fewer people present and presented the slate chosen there to the lieutenant of the alcalde mayor in Yanhuitlán, who approved it. When the lieutenant was informed of the first slate, he advised an appeal to the General Indian Court. The petition asks for an order installing the first slate. The court issues a letter of ruego y encargo to the parish priest, asking for a report on the dispute.[190]

135. June 4–July 21, 1772, Mexico City. Cuautempan, sujeto of Tlayacapan, province of Tlalmanalco, vs. its alcalde, Luis de Santiago, protesting his continuance in office, because he is bondsman for repartimientos and so carries out extortions. Upon petition of the town to the General Indian Court, the viceroy orders that if the facts are as alleged there be a new election, and requires a report in six days. The lieutenant of the alcalde mayor, upon recording testimony of Santiago's misdeeds, reports to the viceroy that all is false and the alcalde honest. The alcalde arrests a number of the complainants.

Thereupon the court orders its previous order enforced, and upon petition of the attorney for the sujeto to see the report, gives permission. The sujeto next petitions for enforcement of the earlier order and punishment of the lieutenant, since the election of Santiago is a mere appointment by him. Upon the recommendation of the fiscal and opinion of the assessor, the court issues two decrees. The first, to the

188. Ibid., exp. 220.   189. Ibid., 24:exp. 454.
190. Ibid., 38:fols. 304v–305v.

alcalde mayor, sets a penalty of six years' service in an obraje for Luis de Santiago for molestation of the petitioners or their families. The second orders that the earlier decree be sent for enforcement to the alcalde mayor, who is to make a summary investigation, return all goods seized, release all prisoners, and do justice.[191]

d. Internal Relations of Towns and Questions of Dependency

The Indian town frequently was a complex entity, with a nucleus called the *cabecera*, and a number of dependent villages, called *estancias* or *sujetos*. The cabecera might be divided in turn into *barrios* as might the estancias and sujetos. In such towns, the distribution of burdens, offices, and civic enterprises in equitable form, so regarded by all, was not easy at best, and might be so arranged that the cabecera profited at the expense of its dependent villages. Furthermore, barrio might quarrel with barrio or sujeto with sujeto. All such disputes could move from the provincial tribunal to the General Indian Court. Another frequent cause of dissension was the attempt of sujetos to become cabeceras, and so independent of any other Indian town.[192] Although recognition of independent status was an administrative matter, such disputes often came to the General Indian Court. If there was physical distance between the sujeto and its cabecera, the basis for decision was usually the number of Indian families in the sujeto, that is, whether it had enough people for an independent life.[193] As the Indian population began to increase, sujetos began to have suitable numbers so that in the eighteenth century many petitioned for and secured independent status.[194]

136. December 7, 1628, Mexico City. The two parcialidades of Santiago Matlatlán, province of Mitla and Tlacolula, have been quarreling, and appeal to the viceroy to establish order. At his commission, the alcalde mayor arranges a pact of peace and harmony between the two parcialidades, the document being forwarded to the viceroy for confirmation. Upon the advice of his assessor, the viceroy confirms the agreement.[195]

137. September 19, 1629–May 16, 1630, Mexico City. José de Celi, on behalf of the town of Carácuaro (Michoacán), complains that

191. AGN-Civ, vol. 2285:exp. 2 (LBSD, vol. 19).
192. See Gibson, *The Aztecs*, 34–57.
193. RLI, 6.3.15, summarizing a royal cédula of October 10, 1618, allowing a settlement of over 40 families, 1 alcalde and 1 regidor; over 80 families, 2 alcaldes and 2 regidores; and if very large, up to 2 alcaldes and 4 regidores.
194. LBSF, 13:fols. 10–11.
195. AGN-I, 10, cuad. 1:exp. 33.

its sujetos of Santa Catarina Purungeo and San Lucas seek to shift dependency to Nocupétaro, another town of the same encomendero, to the damage of the old cabecera. The petition asks for an order compelling the two sujetos to remain obedient to Carácuaro and to fulfill their obligations. On the opinion of his assessor, the viceroy orders the justice of the district of Turicato to enforce previous dependence.[196] On the same day, the viceroy, on petition of the Indians of Carácuaro, issues an order of the General Indian Court removing the lieutenant of the corregidor in the town.[197] One suspects a connection with the previous order, but it may be no more than irritation on other counts and the opportunity of a delegation in Mexico City.

The next year, José de Celi, on behalf of the town of Turicato, complains to the General Indian Court that Nocupétaro, Carácuaro, Santa Catarina Purungeo, and San Lucas Carácuaro are all its sujetos, as shown in the documents presented; but the officials of Carácuaro, claiming that Santa Catarina Purungeo and San Lucas Carácuaro are its sujetos, demand that the two villages obey their orders. Turicato asks the taking of testimony by the justice of La Huacana and an order that the two sujetos do not assist Carácuaro in building its church, etc. On the opinion of his assessor, the viceroy orders the taking of information within six days of presentation of his decree. He also appoints Melchor López de Haro as attorney for Carácuaro if the town wishes to give evidence. When the information is gathered and received in the court and reviewed by the assessor, the viceroy orders the justices of the district and the officials of Carácuaro to enforce and obey his decree of September 19, 1629, that previous custom be enforced. Santa Catarina Purungeo, San Lucas, and their dependent villages are to observe obedience to their true cabecera. Carácuaro is not to ask anything of them; and if it does, a commissioner will be sent to enforce the court's order at the expense of the guilty.[198]

138. December 14, 1638, Mexico City. José de Celi, for Chilacachapan, sujeto of Coatepec, province of Ixcateopan, with 25 tributaries out of a total of 90 for the entire town, complains that the cabecera exacts two Indians a week for work in the mines of Taxco. The petition asks for an order that the official in charge of the local labor draft protect them, see that they are held to provide only one worker a week, and require the cabecera to contribute its fair share. On the advice of his assessor, the viceroy orders the local justice and asks the parish priest for reports, and orders the last tributary count and tribute assessment to be brought to the court. The documents show that

196. Ibid., exp. 147.
197. Ibid., exp. 150.   198. Ibid., exp. 241.

the last count, dated January 15, 1572, came to 90 tributaries. Thereupon the fiscal protector renders opinion that the petition is justified; and the viceroy, upon the supporting opinion of his assessor, orders the official in charge of the local labor draft to protect the Indians of Chilacachapan and see that they are held to furnish only one Indian worker a week for the mines of Taxco.[199]

It may seem astonishing that this case was decided on the basis of a tribute count made 66 years before; but in the long population decline that was coming to an end at the time of this controversy, the Spanish authorities preferred not to inquire further, lest they have to reduce tributes and the numbers required in labor drafts.

139. March 16–December 30, 1658, Mexico City. The town of Tiltepec, province of Nochixtlán, protests to the General Indian Court that its sujeto, Santiago Nejapillo, attempts to elect its own governor and alcaldes, i.e., to set itself up as an independent cabecera. Tiltepec asks that the justice of Yanhuitlán, who is nearer to Tiltepec than the alcalde mayor of Nochixtlán, investigate, and that thereafter an order be issued to keep to custom. March 16, 1658, the viceroy so orders.[200]

The next order, November 26, 1658, is that the justice nearest Santiago Nejapillo—but not those of Yanhuitlán and Nochixtlán, who have been challenged as prejudiced—carry out the investigation on whether or not Santiago Nejapillo is a sujeto of Tiltepec and on its right to elect town officials. There are to be allowed twenty days from public proclamation of the inquiry for approval of questionnaires and presenting evidence, and all papers are to be sent to Mexico City within eighty days. The order is issued at the request of the fiscal protector, in order to settle the suit.[201]

On December 30, 1658, at the petition of Santiago Nejapillo, an amended order is issued. It allows thirty days instead of twenty for presenting proof since some witnesses are in Antequera and elsewhere, but preserves the period of eighty days for delivery of the completed papers in Mexico City. The available records end here, and we do not know the result of this suit. Ultimately, Santiago Nejapillo became an independent cabecera.[202]

4. The Proper Ordering of Indian Society

Many of the orders and decisions summarized to date fall in this category as well, but we here deal with disputes and complaints that do not fit easily into previous categories. The royal government and its

199. Ibid., 11:exp. 77 (LBSF, vol. 8, fols. 31–39).
200. Ibid., 23:exp. 63.
201. Ibid., exp. 208.   202. Ibid., exp. 242.

officials had a clear idea of a well-run hierarchical society in which each order had a place and a role. Social justice meant that each order kept to its place and fulfilled its function. It is an idea that would not be called social justice in accordance with twentieth-century ideas on the subject.

a. The Proper Ordering of Towns

140. September 26, 1617, Mexico City. Fray Melchor Quijada, prior of the convent of Santa Cruz in Mexico City, complains that Indians in the houses of Spaniards do not come to religious services, receive the sacraments, etc., because the bailiff charged with bringing them is afraid to enter Spanish houses since he has no order giving him authority to do so. The prior asks that one be issued. The viceroy issues the order, and empowers the bailiff to cite anyone hindering him in his duties before the General Indian Court.[203]

141. June 9, 1618, Mexico City. The town of Chichicapa, province of Zimatlán and Chichicapa, sues the town of Zimatlán, to force the return of residents who have moved to Zimatlán and lived there a long time. On the advice of his assessor, the viceroy rejects the complaint, since Indians have the right to move and settle where they will, so long as they fulfill the requirements of orderly living and paying tribute.[204]

142. May 7, 1619, Mexico City. José de Celi, on behalf of the town officials of Tlapa, petitions that they be paid wages from the community treasury, since their posts take up so much time that they cannot attend to sowing crops or otherwise earning the money for tributes. Upon viceregal order, the alcalde mayor of the province reports that the community treasury of the town has income of 500/ a year, a surplus of 1500/, and owes no arrears of tribute to the king or the encomendero. The officials are 1 governor, 4 alcaldes, 6 regidores, 1 notary, and 1 jailer. On the opinion of his assessor, the viceroy sets a schedule of annual salaries of 100/ for the governor, 25/ for each alcalde, and 20/ for each of the other officials. The viceroy is to be kept informed of the state of the community treasury so that he may provide what is proper.[205]

A decree of this nature should have been strictly administrative; but since this one is issued on the advice of the assessor, it must be considered a decision of the General Indian Court. Again, the viceregal policy was to concentrate decision on Indian matters in the court and its experienced staff.

203. Ibid., 7:exp. 228.
204. Ibid., exp. 286.   205. Ibid., exp. 381.

143. November 29, 1628, Mexico City. The Indians of Cholula petition the local corregidor to allocate the yield of the annual monopoly on furnishing meat for the repair of roads and two bridges ruined in storms, as was done once before. The town has no revenues of its own. The corregidor forwards the petition to the viceroy who, upon consulting his assessor, orders the corregidor to report on the advisability of granting the petition. Again, what should have been a purely administrative decision moves through the court.[206]

144. March 5, 1785, Tulancingo. The alcalde mayor forwards to the audiencia gobernadora the proceedings ordered by the General Indian Court on the petition of Vicente Ferrer Ortiz that his accounts be accepted for the time he was majordomo of the religious brotherhood of Nuestra Señora de Guadalupe. The proceedings are in 10 folios.[207]

145. February 15–March 20, 1793, Mexico City and Xochimilco. The parish priest of Xochimilco complains to the subdelegado that three Indians and their wives have fled to Mexico City, and upon recommendation of the subdelegado appeals to the viceroy, who summons the Indians to the General Indian Court. The docket ends at this point.[208]

146. January 6–February 7, 1798, Mexico City and Santiago Tlatelolco. The parish priest of Cuautitlán writes to the governor of the parcialidad of Santiago Tlatelolco, asking for the return of 30 Indians who have left the town. Apparently the governor refers the matter to the General Indian Court, for the absentees are summoned before the court. Some answer the summons; some do not. At this point the docket ends.[209]

b. Tributes, Debts Associated with Them,
and Community Finance

147. June 23, 1628, Mexico City. Juan Patiño de Avila vs. the towns of Tlachichilpa and Almoloya, province of Metepec. Patiño de Avila petitions the General Indian Court for an order for collection, stating that he bought the unpaid arrears of maize tributes of the two towns for the harvests of 1620 and 1623 at public auction on July 27, 1627. On December 15, 1627, the town officials petitioned the viceroy, stating that since the maize had not been sent for, they asked for release from obligation to provide it. Their statement is false, since the

206. Ibid., 10, cuad. 1 : exp. 32.
207. Notation in list of expedientes surrendered from the juzgado of the alcalde mayor of Tulancingo, July 27, 1776–March 18, 1785, in AT (17 fols.).
208. AGN-Civ, vol. 2218 : exp. 3 (LBSD, vol. 12).
209. Ibid., 2224 : exp. 3 (idem).

document Patiño de Avila presented for collection clearly stated that he was the purchaser. On the Indians' petition, the case was admitted to presentation of evidence in the General Indian Court, with a limit of twenty days and the obligation of public notice, but the Indians proved nothing and only initiated the suit to hinder collection. Patiño de Avila, pointing out that it is just that royal tributes be paid, asks for an order to enforce collection. The court orders a copy of the petition to be furnished the Indians, with a limit of three days for exhibiting papers in the case to date. Upon their filing a reply, the docket is reviewed in the court and decision rendered against the two towns. The viceroy orders that Patiño de Avila may use his right and power to collect, forcing the Indians to pay. The justice of the province is to give him all necessary help in this.[210]

148. August 31, 1628, Mexico City. The town of Cholula petitions the viceroy, stating that it has filed papers on the demand of Manuel Pérez de Luján for 1400/ as the value of the tribute maize that he bought in royal auction 25 years ago, but made no move to collect for 20 years. The local justice is moving to sell communal property to meet the demand. The town asks for viceregal review since the case is hindering collection of royal tribute currently due; it further asks that the royal comptroller report on the matter. Upon calling for the royal comptroller's report and examining it, and upon the opinion of his assessor, the viceroy orders the alcalde mayor of Cholula to forward all the papers in the case to his office and not to do anything further until a viceregal decision.[211]

149. June 22, 1629, Mexico City. José de Celi, on behalf of Tlaxiaco, province of Teposcolula, petitions the viceroy for an order reaffirming a money value of 1/1 the fanega for tribute maize. The town has been paying in coin at this value, but the agent of the encomendero now asks for more. The viceroy orders that the maize be commuted at a money value of 1/1 the fanega. Should the encomendero or his agent object, they are to appear before the General Indian Court for this purpose.[212]

150. April 12, 1630, Mexico City. Don Diego de la Cueva, cacique of Malinaltepec, province of Atlatlauca, through José de Celi,

210. AGN-I, 10, cuad. 1:exp. 1.
211. Ibid., exp. 8.
212. AJT-Civ, leg. 2. An aftermath of this case is a case of November 28, 1634, in the court of the alcalde mayor, in which the town of Tlaxiaco protests that Felipe de Andrada Montezuma, as agent for his brother, Juan, the encomendero, is demanding higher prices for two years back. Upon being ordered to abide by the viceregal decision, Felipe announces that he will protest to the viceroy, presumably by suit in the General Indian Court. Alas, we do not know what then took place.

petitions the court, explaining that he received money from some merchants of Antequera for buying cochineal from the Indians for later delivery. When the cacique began to collect the cochineal, the corregidor, Domingo de Morga, arrested him and released him on bond; Morga then died, leaving all of the cochineal embargoed. The cacique finds himself without recourse or possibility of relief, since Morga left no goods to levy on and there is no one else from whom to collect. Furthermore, since it is prohibited to advance money to Indians, they are free of any civil debt. He asks that he be declared free from liability also, or at the least be given four years in which to pay, and that he be given an order of amparo against molestation. Upon the opinion of the assessor, the viceroy issues an order of amparo to the justice of Malinaltepec and all others that the cacique is not to be molested for the debts. If anyone wishes to sue, he must do so in the General Indian Court and nowhere else.[213]

151. December 21, 1630, Mexico City. Melchor López de Haro, on behalf of Don Francisco Sánchez and Don Luis de los Reyes, brothers, caciques, and principales of Atlacomulco, province of Metepec, explains that their father, Don Domingo de Peralta, lent the town of Jocotitlán 500/ to meet the royal tribute, repayable from community property and income. Their father having died, they as his heirs have asked for payment, but the governor and principales of Jocotitlán refuse. The two caciques ask for an order to enforce payment. Upon the advice of his assessor, the viceroy orders the governor and principales of Jocotitlán to pay, or file reason within one month why they should not; otherwise, proper action will be taken.[214]

152. December 12, 1634–April 28, 1637, Mexico City and Teposcolula.[215] The town of Tequixtepec, province of Huajuapan, petitions the viceroy. Since the town has no land for agriculture, it paid no tribute in maize, before the Conquest or after. It lives on maize brought from Teposcolula, which "is the granary and source of food for all the Mixteca Alta and Baja." In lieu of the 10 brazas of sowing for the community, each tributary pays 0/1/6 in cash, the maize due the priest being bought from Teposcolula. But Teposcolula, on the plea that harvests have been bad, no longer wishes to sell maize at customary prices. Actually, it seeks higher prices. Tequixtepec asks for an order that sale and delivery continue as in the past. The viceroy orders the alcalde mayor of Teposcolula to investigate and report, which although he could not find the governor and principales of Teposcolula[?], he does. On the basis of this report, the viceroy, after consult-

213. AGN-I, 10, cuad. 1:exp. 321.
214. Ibid., cuad. 2:exp. 4.   215. AJT-Civ, leg. 2.

ing his assessor, on February 14, 1635, orders Teposcolula to furnish maize for the current year as in the past, but Tequixtepec is to make the normal community sowing so that next year it can itself provide for its priest.

On August 22, 1636, the town of Teposcolula petitions the court for release from the obligation to provide maize as required by the decree of February 14, 1635. November 1, in Huajuapan, the Indians of Tequixtepec are notified of the petition and ask for adherence to previous custom. December 10, 1636, the viceroy confirms his earlier order. January 31, 1637, the town of Teposcolula asks for a notarial copy of the proceedings and decree. In the petition, it explains that the problem arose when the viceroy ordered a general commutation of tribute maize at 1/1 the fanega. Teposcolula used to supply the friars of Tequixtepec with 100 and those of Teposcolula with 150 fanegas. On April 28, 1637, the Indians of Tequixtepec are notified of the petition of Teposcolula.

153. February 16, 1639, Mexico City. Baltasar Pérez, of Nochixtlán, petitions the General Indian Court, explaining that the previous year he and the other town officials borrowed 60/ for necessary town expenses from a woman in the town, Luisa, there being no other resource. The money was spent carefully and properly; but when the time came to pay, Luisa sued only him, although it was a town debt. He was thrown in jail, where he nearly died. One day he found the doors open and fled to Mexico City to seek justice. He asks that he not be punished for breaking jail since it was to appear in court in Mexico City; that the debt be collected from all of the officials of that year; and that he be given a year's grace for paying his share. The viceroy so orders the justice of Nochixtlán.[216]

154. August 29–October 23, 1788, Mexico City and Tlalmanalco.[217] Nicolasa María, wife of Domingo Felipe, Indian of Ayotzingo, province of Chalco, petitions on behalf of her husband who, as alcalde for the past year, is in prison for debt on the royal tribute. The failure to pay the sums due arises because of the general poverty caused by famine and epidemic, the loss of tributaries therein, and the borrowing of money to complain to the ecclesiastical judge of the archbishopric about brutal floggings administered by order of the parish priest. Her husband has no property from which to pay. The petition asks that the alcalde mayor take the sum due from community funds, leaving the accounting to be settled as the money is collected.

216. AGN-I, 11:exp. 107.
217. AGN-Civ, vol. 2163:exp. 5 (LBSD, vol. 4).

No solicitor signs the petition, and the petitioner is stated in it to be illiterate. The viceroy sends the petition for opinion to the fiscal of the royal treasury, then acting as Indian protector, who recommends getting a report from the alcalde mayor on the amount due, the time the man has spent in jail, and the state of community funds. Meanwhile, the Indian may be freed under special admonition to collect the sum due. On September 13, the viceroy so decrees.

On October 1, the alcalde mayor reports that the Indian's story is as alleged, he owes 98/6, and the community treasury holds 615/. On October 7, the viceroy forwards the report to the fiscal for another opinion, and on October 17 it is rendered, to the effect that the Indian clearly cannot pay; the money should be taken from the community treasury, and the Junta Superior de Hacienda so informed. On October 23, 1788, the viceroy orders a decree of the court to this effect.

155. July 9–31, 1799, Mexico City, Atotonilco el Grande, and Tulancingo.[218] Dionisio Sótano, cacique of Atotonilco el Grande, province of Tulancingo, petitions the General Indian Court, stating that he has fled from jail, where he was put by the alcalde mayor's lieutenant for his town, for a debt of 71/4 arising from his father's funeral. His father, although governor for seven years, owes the royal treasury nothing. The father sold a house and left the money for his funeral. The petitioner is stated in the petition to be illiterate. On July 9, 1799, the viceroy orders that the subdelegado be instructed that, if the story is true, justice is to be done and the man released from jail.

On July 15, in Tulancingo, the subdelegado files formal statement that he had previously had a verbal report from his lieutenant that the sum belonged to the community, but the lieutenant is now to send a written statement. The cacique is to be jailed in Tulancingo since the facts are not clear. On July 31, the lieutenant in Atotonilco el Grande orders his report forwarded to the subdelegado, who sends it to the viceroy. In it the lieutenant explains that he carried out an order to collect from the ex-governor's property and the community revenues. The latter come from town lots rented out to non-Indians for a total of 90/ a year, less parish charges for the festivals of Corpus Christi and the town's titular saint, St. Augustine, so that the net sum is 61/4. The cacique's father, who was governor in 1797, owed the sum but did not pay. In February he was to be put in jail, but then declared he had sold a house and other property to cover the debt.

When the collection of a royal *donativo* (a gift to the king for extraordinary need) was under way, the lieutenant found that the ex-governor had died, that his son had seized all property from the widow,

218. AT (4 fols.).

his stepmother, and that the funeral expenses were paid from community revenue. When summoned to the local court, the cacique said his stepmother, not he, was liable. He was then jailed; and when he asked for release on bond, the people who came forward as bondsmen were unsuitable. The subdelegado ordered release on proper bond and assistance in listing debts owed the cacique, but the man then fled. On May 27, an alcalde of 1797 paid 11/ of the 12/ due from him. The docket ends here.

c. Pulque Concessions and Other Taxes

The crown derived substantial revenue from taxes on pulque, which were farmed out via concessions for territories for periods of years.[219] Since the concessionaires collected on all pulque brought into their town for sale, the Indians usually objected. Sometimes they were successful. During the wars of independence, 1810–1821, the royal government financed its war expenses by a series of new taxes, many of which brought appeals to the General Indian Court for relief.

156. June 11, 1748–July 7, 1750, Mexico City and Tlayacapan.[220] A suit before the General Indian Court seeking establishment of a pulque concession in the district of Tlayacapan, province of Chalco, to be sold at auction for nine years at 200/. The case opens with a petition by Francisco Sánchez de Sierra Tagle, a licensed solicitor, no principal named, for establishment of the concession. Upon examining the petition, the fiscal protector recommends citing the royal treasury officials and the parties. On June 11, 1748, the viceroy accepts the recommendation. Upon being notified, the Indians of Tlayacapan promptly object and cite a decree of Viceroy Valero of 1722 declaring that there shall be no pulque concession in the district.

Sierra Tagle then asks issuance of a *carta creencia* with which the viceroy should (1) send a receptor to take testimony on the purported lack of water and lack of trade in pulque, and (2) reimburse in-lieu charges already assessed. The opposition, declares the solicitor, is the work of the justice who will lose the in-lieu charges now being paid. On August 1, 1748, the viceroy issues the carta creencia, addressed to the royal justice and judges of the province of Chalco. August 3–4, testimony is recorded in the district. It is voluminous in nature, contradictory on the adequacy of water supply, and in agreement that the Indians pay in-lieu charges of 0/0/6 a week per pulque-gatherer.

219. See the long discussion in Fonseca and Urrutia, 3:338–428; LBSF, 11:fol. 69.

220. AGN-I, 56:fols. 72v–104f (LBSF, 12:fols. 48–71).

At this point, the attorney for the Indians, Jacobo Ramírez, files a protest and a demand for testimony on a questionnaire to be submitted by the Indians to cover (1) the lack of adequate supplies of water; (2) the misdeeds of Negroes in sugar mills, and their mistreatment of the Indians; (3) the fact that the pulque produced in the area is consumed there, so that granting the proposed concessions means thirst and more trouble; and (4) the allegation that the o/o/6 paid by each pulque-gatherer is to put *palo guapatle*, a fortifying agent, in the pulque in order to preserve it. The viceroy issues the decree as requested, testimony is again taken by questioning witnesses in terms of the questionnaire, and the local springs are surveyed and measured.

With all papers then brought together in Mexico City, the fiscal protector renders his opinion that pulque is clearly indispensable in the district, for lack of water, and that therefore the viceregal decree of 1722 is fully justified. As for the use of palo guapatle, that practice is forbidden and can never be justified. The levy of contribution of o/o/6 should be used for the local church. On July 7, 1750, the viceroy so orders.

157. January 21–June 17, 1779, Mexico City and Tlayacapan. This case represents a revival of the same issue for the same town in a slightly different form. The Indians of Tlayacapan, province of Chalco, petition the court that they not be required to work for an hacienda and that there be no introduction of the pulque concession of Cuernavaca since the town is Indian. The recommendation of the fiscal protector points out that by royal cédula of January 20, 1778, questions concerning revenue from pulque must go to the superintendent of the tax. The court so orders, and further decrees that the Indians be notified. The decree is issued by the judge of the audiencia gobernadora acting as judge of the court. Meanwhile, the lieutenant in Tlayacapan of the alcalde mayor of Chalco takes testimony on exactions of alcabala from the Indians and their relation to the use of pulque. June 2, 1779, all is incorporated in a petition to the court presenting evidence of the order of Viceroy Revillagigedo I on June 7, 1750, forbidding a pulque concession in Tlayacapan, and a later one of August 11, 1761, by Viceroy Cruillas, both on the ground that the area has insufficient water. On this evidence, the assessor, acting as judge of the court for the audiencia gobernadora, issues an order of amparo on behalf of the Indians of Tlayacapan.[221]

158. July 3–September 7, 1818, Mexico City and Guadalupe. The governors of the sections of Náhuatl and Otomí speakers in Tlal-

221. AGN-Civ, vol. 2175:exp. 17–18 (LBSD, vol. 6).

nepantla, district of Tacuba, petition the General Indian Court for a lowering of the military contribution of o/o/6 a week per tributary. Upon recommendation of the fiscal protector that others than Indians should carry the burden, the viceroy so orders the local military commander.[222]

d. Licenses and Exemptions

By his general ordinance of January 15, 1597, the Conde de Monterrey attempted to end the flood of Indian petitions for special licenses. Requests regarded as reasonable were not to require license in the future; others, such as for carrying firearms, were not to be granted in any circumstances, and so would not be heard in the future.[223] The system was confirmed in somewhat altered form in the ordinances of the Bishop of Yucatan as Viceroy of New Spain on July 4, 1648, these in turn being given force of royal legislation by royal cédula of May 20, 1649.[224] Nevertheless, Indians continued to petition for viceregal licenses in situations in which local justices illegally pressed for penalties, or the standard prohibitions manifestly had an element of injustice that the viceroy might be persuaded to remedy. Indian need for special licenses became much more acute in the area of the capital in 1692, when the riots of that year led the viceregal government on July 18 to order that the Indians of the Mexico City region wear Indian mantles and not use stockings nor have long hair, so that they might easily be recognized.[225]

159. October 5, 1616, Mexico City. Alonso Ximénez de Castilla, Indian solicitor, petitions on behalf of Doña María Castelán Xochitl, of Tlaxcala, who has a textile workshop in her house to support herself and her children. It makes coarse colored woolens, skirts, blouses, blankets, and cloaks, and is equipped with apparatus to dye and spin as well as weave. Doña María employs Indians, who are well paid and work of their own free will. Now the local judge of textile workshops tries to interfere, on the ground that she is married to a Spaniard. That is so, but she is an Indian and as such petitions the court. The viceroy licenses Doña María and her husband to manufacture the wares described. Production must be carried on in her house, nor may she sell outside Tlaxcala. The register carries a marginal notation that the license was reissued in 1632.[226]

222. Ibid., 2231:exp. 8 (LBSD, vol. 13).
223. See Chapter IV.
224. AGN-RCD, 52:fols. 124f–128f.
225. AGN-I, 32:fols. 60v–61f.
226. Ibid., 7:exp. 108 (LBSF, 7:fols. 44–45).

160. January 17, 1618, Mexico City. Upon petition, the viceroy issues a license to Diego de Mendoza, cacique and governor of Tepeji de la Seda, to wear Spanish dress, carry arms, and ride a horse.[227]

161. May 23, 1622, Mexico City. Feliciano de Velasco, cacique of Huajuapan, petitions for license to own and trade with 12 pack mules. On the opinion of his assessor, the viceroy grants the license.[228]

162. September 30, 1629, Mexico City. José de Celi for Don Gabriel de los Angeles, principal of Atlacomulco, province of Metepec, petitions for a license for his client freely to have livestock on his estancias with guards. Don Gabriel has four haciendas, with 200 cows and many mules and horses. Justices hinder his having them and impose penalties; the petition asks for an order to stop them. The viceroy grants license in the form of an order to the justices not to hinder Don Gabriel.[229]

163. June 15, 1632, Mexico City. Don Juan Vizcaíno, cacique of Xichú, petitions for license to have an harquebus, leather armor, and from three to four Indians as guards on horseback with saddle and bridle. He needs all this for protection against the wild Chichimecs, against whom he, his father, and his grandfather have served the king. After asking for a report from the alcalde mayor of the mines of Xichú and receiving one favorable to the petition, the viceroy grants the license.[230]

164. April 18, 1693, Mexico City. Don Miguel Osorio, cacique, petitions for exemption from the order that Indians wear native dress in the capital. The viceroy grants the license in the form of an order of amparo.[231]

5. Criminal Cases

The General Indian Court exercised jurisdiction in criminal cases in two quite different ways. In what must have been a substantial segment of its activity, it tried Indian offenders in the Indian jails of the two native parcialidades attached to the capital through weekly review and sentencing. On audiencia mornings, the governors of the two parcialidades reported to the assessor of the General Indian Court with a list of offenders, and the court notary and abogados for criminal matters attended the weekly review of all prisoners in each jail. Unfortunately, we know nothing beyond the regulations for such review and

227. Ibid., exp. 247.
228. Ibid., 9:exp. 371 (BLT).
229. Ibid., 10, cuad. 1:exp. 157.
230. Ibid., cuad. 3:exp. 6 (LBSF, 7:fols. 172–173).
231. Ibid., 32:fols. 112v–113f.

inspection of records, for the archives of the Indian parcialidades have not yet come to light; and in view of the destruction of their facilities, upon the assertion of authority over them by the city government under the Constitution of 1812 and subsequent Mexican constitutional instruments, those records may no longer exist. Accordingly, we cannot examine cases, even less attempt any quantitative measure.[232]

The second way in which the General Indian Court exercised jurisdiction of criminal nature was in the regular viceregal audiences in which the viceroy sat as judge of the court. In such audiences, he and his assessor heard cases in which criminal penalties were demanded and sometimes imposed. They came, in general, from the provinces, through removal of the case from the local tribunals, or they might be brought directly before the court by private petition. In yet others, what began as a civil action might disclose reason to impose criminal penalty. Many of the summaries of cases and complaints presented thus far show such features, and no attempt has been made in those cases to separate criminal from civil actions.

Procedures did not differ in the two kinds of cases, particularly if the action began on private petition to the court. Spanish law and judicial practice at this time still left the initiation of most criminal cases to the aggrieved party, who approached a tribunal directly with his complaint, asking for a criminal penalty, and conducted the prosecution directly or through his own attorneys. The much sharper distinction characteristic of our time has developed in the changes of the nineteenth century in Hispanic countries. Nevertheless, Spanish and Indian authorities in some of the cases heard by the General Indian Court in its viceregal audiences did prosecute cases directly.

165. April 15, 1619, Mexico City. Don Miguel de Mendoza, Indian governor of Huatusco, province of Córdoba, was charged by Sergeant Alonso de Losano Guzmán, commissioned to hunt down fugitive Negroes, with hiding and not reporting them. Apparently Don Miguel petitioned for trial before the General Indian Court, which called for the papers and proceedings. They were then reviewed by the assessor. Upon his recommendation, the viceroy issues a formal decision absolving Don Miguel.[233]

166. May 25, 1619, Mexico City. Some Indians of Actopan complain to the General Indian Court that, with license of the alcalde mayor of their province, they took 8 pack animals loaded with honey

232. See the discussion earlier in this chapter. See also clause 8, public regulation on the General Indian Court, December 5, 1785, in Beleña, 2:199–203, no. 47.
233. AGN-I, 7:exp. 367.

to Texcoco and there sold the honey. On their return, they were stopped by the lieutenant of the bailiff of Chiconautla, who demanded 30/ on the ground that such sales were forbidden. In lieu of the money, he seized their two best mules and equipment. They ask for arrest of the official. The viceroy orders that the bailiff of the General Indian Court go to Chiconautla, arrest Juan Andrés, the offending lieutenant bailiff, and bring him to the royal jail in Mexico City. All papers are then to be given to the assessor.[234]

167. October 2, 1632–October 24, 1633, Mexico City and Teposcolula. Pedro López, Indian of the estancia of Santa Catalina, sujeto of Achiutla, province of Teposcolula, stabbed Agustín de Barrios when he caught the latter with María López, his wife. When Barrios died of a deep wound in the back above the kidneys, the alcalde of Achiutla arrested López for trial before the alcalde mayor in Teposcolula. Thereupon the father of the accused, Antonio Ruiz, went to Mexico City and through José de Celi petitioned the General Indian Court to take jurisdiction so that his son may be found innocent. The viceroy orders all papers sent to him so that the case may be reviewed in the General Indian Court. On October 24, 1632, the decree is presented in Teposcolula and formal compliance recorded. The proceedings in Teposcolula fill 14 folios. The docket ends at this point.[235]

168. November 24–December 19, 1648, Mexico City and Jojutla.[236] Don Juan Esteban, governor of Tetelpa, province of Cuernavaca, is denounced to the teniente in Jojutla of the alcalde mayor for selling a 9-year-old boy to the operator of a sugar mill and for other crimes. The teniente in Jojutla promptly opens a criminal trial, taking testimony from an Indian principal and four other people. On November 28 the teniente issues an order of arrest against Don Juan Esteban, which is certified as executed on December 9. Meanwhile, since there is no notary in Jojutla, he summons one from Cuernavaca, receiving an answer on December 9 that the notary will appear as soon as his business allows. On December 11 Esteban's declaration is recorded: He is 35 years old, beat the boy lightly, and sent him to serve for a theft of 20/ until the sum was repaid. The boy is 10 years old. On December 12, the teniente allows the governor and others three days for pleading and sets six days of proof for the taking of testimony. Sentence is then to follow. There follows an affidavit of notification to the governor.

Meantime, Juan Esteban has arranged that a petition for re-

234. Ibid., exp. 399.
235. AJT-Crim, leg. 3.
236. AGN-Crim, 38 : exp. 3 (LBSD, vol. 24).

moval of the case be presented to the General Indian Court. The petition by Agustín Franco on his behalf protests that the teniente is the governor's enemy, because Esteban is suing the teniente in Mexico City for restitution of 140/ taken from the Indians. The petition also prays for release from jail. On December 14, 1648, the General Indian Court sends a peremptory order to the teniente halting proceedings. All papers are to be sent to Mexico City within eight days. If Esteban is in jail for an offense not punishable by corporal punishment, he is to be released on bond to the General Indian Court by suitable bondsmen. On December 19, the court's order is presented to the teniente, the affidavit of reception being signed by him and Don Juan Esteban. All papers are then sent to the General Indian Court. The docket ends here.

This case has the additional interest that in it the General Indian Court operated in first instance in the Marquesado del Valle, despite the latter's seigneurial privilege. The court behaved as though Cuernavaca were a royal province.

169. February 3–9, 1650, Mexico City and Mexicaltzingo. Juan Antonio, governor of San Mateo, province of Mexicaltzingo, vs. Diego Hernández, principal of Coyoacán, for breaking the staff of justice of the local bailiff. On complaint by the governor, the corregidor of Mexicaltzingo orders testimony taken; and when that discloses an offense and probability of guilt, Hernández is ordered arrested. He is then required to name a defender and is tried and found guilty. Meanwhile, his wife petitions the General Indian Court then functioning under the audiencia gobernadora for removal of the case. The court orders the corregidor to report, but he carries the case to conclusion and then sends on the papers. On February 9, the General Indian Court orders that Hernández receive 50 lashes, but pay no costs; the corregidor is warned not to try cases without Spanish witnesses and is fined 4/ for continuing the case after notice of supersession. A final affidavit certifies that the bailiff of the General Indian Court has had the order executed in all terms in Mexicaltzingo.[237]

170. August 6, 1701, Mexico City. Punishment of Indians of Ucila, province of Teutila, for riot and sedition on November 21, 1699. The viceroy sent a special judge to try the rioters, who in anger at the excesses of the local alcalde mayor stoned the royal offices and wounded the alcalde mayor. What we have here is the review by the assessor and the sentence by the viceroy. The assessor criticizes the fact that the investigating judge charged each rioter separately and did

237. Ibid., 29:exp. 3 (LBSD, vol. 2).

not look into the excesses of the alcalde mayor, although these were the basic cause of the riot. The viceroy decrees that the rioters are to be fined and exiled for from two to three years and are to be disqualified for town office. Their goods are to be embargoed to pay the fines. They already have been in jail for more than a year.[238]

171. December 19, 1758–August 17, 1759, Mexico City. The governor of Tlaxiaco, province of Teposcolula, had been guilty of oppression, drunkenness, wenching, etc., and was finally jailed. The townfolk then tried to break into the jail to seize him; and when they could not do so, assaulted the houses of Spaniards, striking a Spanish housewife. Thereupon the alcalde mayor called out part of the local Spanish militia to restore order and arrest the leaders. The men sought for arrest took refuge in the local church; instead, their goods were taken. The town then appealed to the viceroy for quick help to restore order.

The viceroy on December 19, 1758, commissions the alcalde mayor of Nochixtlán, on pain of 300/ fine for noncompliance, to collect the evidence and send on the papers to Mexico City within one month. In the summer of 1759, the town of Tlaxiaco again petitions the viceroy, claiming that the extent of public disorder had been much exaggerated, and that the alcalde mayor of Nochixtlán is in collusion with the one of Teposcolula, merely signing papers of an investigation the latter was carrying out. On August 17, 1759, the viceroy commissions a third man, Domingo Nieto, to take over the hearings, conclude them, and send the papers to Mexico City.[239]

172. March 23–September 13, 1768, Mexico City and San Cristóbal Ecatepec. Isidro Felipe, Indian of San Pedro, province of San Cristóbal Ecatepec, vs. Juan Cayón and Francisco Cabello, two Spanish employees of the hacienda of San Juan de Riesco, for whipping him. Isidro Felipe complains to the viceroy that the two employees of the hacienda beat him with a whip. Attached to the petition is a surgeon's certification of whip stripes on the man. The viceroy orders the alcalde mayor of San Cristóbal Ecatepec to investigate, jail the administrator of the hacienda if he is guilty, and report quickly. During the investigation, Cabello declares that Isidro Felipe was stealing *agua miel*, the unfermented juice of the pulque agave. He is jailed; the other man cannot be found. The alcalde mayor then reports the circumstances of the quarrel and the whipping; he further reports that the hacienda is in steady difficulties with two Indian towns over the steal-

238. AGN-I, 33:exp. 59 (LBSF, 10:fols. 135–136).
239. Ibid., 59, fols. 97v–98f and 148v–149v.

ing of agua miel. Upon petition by Felipe through his solicitor, the viceroy orders the owner of the hacienda to pay the costs of treatment and other expenses of Isidro Felipe. Investigation sets the following expenses and costs:

Cure and food, by days	6/4
Costs and paper, by schedule	10/6
	17/2

On August 8, 1768, the sum is paid in Mexico City.[240]

173. December 29, 1774–January 4, 1775, Mexico City, San Cristóbal Ecatepec, and Totolcingo. Pedro Pablo, Indian of Totolcingo, province of Teotihuacán, vs. Don Blas de Olvera, for beating him and his daughter. On December 29, 1774, Pedro Pablo and his daughter appear at the house of the assessor of the General Indian Court to complain of beatings by Don Blas de Olvera. They show the whip-marks on the girl. That day and the following, two affidavits that the wounds are serious are filed by the *"ministro de cirujano"* of the General Indian Court and the Parcialidad of San Juan, and by another surgeon. December 31, 1774, Pedro Pablo formally petitions the viceroy for justice. An order is at once issued that the nearest justice investigate and report quickly, without fees for the time being, on pain of 200/ fine. January 3, 1775, the order is presented to the alcalde mayor of San Cristóbal Ecatepec, an affidavit of obedience prepared, and testimony of witnesses recorded. The girl had taken a *manta* from a shepherd girl. In his report to the viceroy, the alcalde mayor points out that Don Blas de Olvera has always been kind to the Indians and helped them, but he admits the truth of the testimony here. January 4, 1775, Pedro Pablo presents a document to the alcalde mayor suspending his complaint on the ground of the provocative words of his daughter and the previous good character of Olvera.[241] On January 5, 1775, all is sent to Mexico City, where it is filed. Obviously the town urged dropping the case, and probably Olvera bought off Pedro Pablo and his daughter.

6. Supervision of the Indian Barrios and Parcialidades of the Capital

The Indian barrios around Mexico City lay largely within a zone governed directly by the viceroy and audiencia. They were organized into the two parcialidades of San Juan Tenochtitlán and Santiago Tlatelolco. A number of barrios within adjacent districts and prov-

240. AGN-Crim, 8:exp. 12 (LBSD, vol. 21).
241. Ibid., exp. 19 (idem).

inces, with local Spanish governors, also had special relations to Mexico City and to the General Indian Court as the administrative and judicial arm of the viceroy for dealing with them. Although not a part of Mexico City and not under the jurisdiction of its municipal council, the barrios provided the labor and many of the supplies without which, in the existing ordering of society and economy, the Spanish city could not have lived. Even at the beginning, the sharp distinction proposed between the two republics was blurred through the presence of numbers of Indian servants domiciled within the city in Spanish houses. With the passage of time, and the further interpenetration of the two ethnicities, Mexico City acquired substantial numbers of mixed-bloods and Hispanized Indians, the former technically non-Indian, both a transitional group between the two republics.

The dependence of the Spanish city upon the barrios created a special relationship recognized in law and custom. The city and the barrios cooperated in an enormous annual observance of Corpus Christi, a vast procession organized under the responsibility of the Spanish municipal council, with the participation of the city guilds. The role of the Indians was to build an archway of reeds and wood covered with mats the length of the route of the procession, so that the marchers would be protected from the June sun. For that purpose, the governors of the two parcialidades and the interpreter of the General Indian Court organized a work draft from the Indians within the city and its native barrios.[242] There were probably other occasions for such cooperation within the year, with the governors of the parcialidades and the interpreter of the court serving as supervisors of the natives and intermediaries between the Spanish city and their own people.

Since the barrios mostly lay in the zone of special government by the audiencia and viceroy, the famous five leagues, they were supervised much more directly by the viceroy, to whom some of the judicial functions of the audiencia were delegated, i.e., criminal judgment of Indian cases in first instance. The viceroy also had to assume other responsibilities that in the provinces were discharged by the local Spanish governors, most notably the supervision and audit of the community treasuries in their revenues and expenditures. At some time as yet unknown, the viceroy relieved himself of what was a relatively routine and ceremonial chore of minor consequence, but time-consuming to a very busy official, by delegating it to the assessor of the General Indian Court. We know nothing of the process, except that toward the end of the colonial period the governors of the parcialidades and each of the Indian barrios reported on finances to the assessor, were audited under his supervision, and required his permission for expenditures in

242. Estrada, 325.

celebration of the feasts of saints and other activities that required disbursement from the community till.

Our fullest information as yet comes for the period immediately after the incorporation of the barrios and parcialidades into an enlarged Mexico City, when the municipal council seized the communal treasuries for municipal application and left the former Indian barrios and parcialidades, who despite their lack of legal existence still had strong communal consciousness, without means of financing their religious celebrations. We do know that the assessor rendered an annual report to the viceroy on the audit of the finances of the parcialidades.[243] The assessor in his supervision of the parcialidades and barrios, and intervention in their affairs, relied heavily upon the services of the interpreter and notary of the General Indian Court. This latter functionary enjoyed the exclusive right to prepare the papers on the elections of officials of the two parcialidades and certain of the barrios. His fees, set in formal schedule, represented a substantial addition to his salary.[244] Presumably the elections were confirmed by the assessor, acting for the viceroy.

All of this function represented the use of the court as a convenient instrument for relieving the viceroy in person of fairly routine administrative chores. Supervision of the barrios and parcialidades seldom had truly judicial aspects, but cases undoubtedly did occur.

174. February 18–April 24, 1820, Mexico City and Coyoacán. Lic. Ignacio Flores Alatorre, general attorney for the parcialidades, petitions the General Indian Court for exemption of the Indians of Mexicaltzingo, Churubusco, and Culhuacán from the tax on rural properties levied to pay the royal expenses of suppressing the insurgents. The petition is backed by an opinion of the royal tax collector for Coyoacán that, since the Indians of Ixtapalapa have been exempted, the request is just.

The court sends the papers to the fiscal protector, who recommends getting a report from the general administrator of municipal revenues. That report is somewhat contradictory, in that in an earlier opinion on the similar petition in 1819 the official recommended denial since the tax is moderate. On the renewed petition, he now supports exempting the houses of the truly wretched and poverty-stricken. On a second referral, the fiscal protector agrees that the hovels of the truly wretched should be exempted since the legislation establishing the tax so provides. The court so decrees and notifies the parties.[245]

243. Mexico: AGN, *La secretaría de cámara*, cuad. 3; AGN-I, vol. 100, passim; and Lira González, "La ciudad de México."
244. Schedule of permitted fees for the General Indian Court, Mexico City, October 3, 1741, in AGI-M, leg. 1286, no. 342, fols. 23f–26f.
245. AGN-Civ, vol. 2259:exp. 10 (LBSD, vol. 16).

C. Some Answers

Now that we have concluded our somewhat lengthy examination of specific cases in summary, let us return to further consideration of the jurisdiction of the General Indian Court. Within the colonial political structure, the court afforded a special channel of relief for one estate of the society, namely, Indians; but at no point, with the exception of certain administrative attributes such as supervision of the Indian parcialidades and barrios of the capital, did the court exercise exclusive jurisdiction. Rather, it exercised concurrent but supersessory competence in relation to Indians, in that, if they so chose, they could apply to the local tribunal, either the provincial justice or his lieutenant (should the province be divided into districts), for exactly the same relief. The lower court legally at least was bound to the same simplification of procedure and elimination or reduction of fees and costs as obtained in the viceregal audience. However, if an Indian applied to the General Indian Court, the local court could not continue to hear the case except by express viceregal order; and for any case before a local court, the matter could be taken to the General Indian Court, superseding the local proceedings. Such a removal technically did not constitute an appeal, but rather supersedure; the effect was often the same.

If a civil case went ill in a lower court, whether through delays, prejudice on the part of the local justice, failure on the part of the plaintiff to substantiate the complaint, or weakness in the defense, it might well be removed to Mexico City. The General Indian Court then took over, examining the matter as a new case. The Indian charged in criminal cases also could have his case removed to Mexico City for hearing. In many instances, the removal meant a change of venue to a more impartial tribunal; in many others, the effect must have been flight from a probably unfavorable verdict—so that the viceregal hearing, though legally in first instance, meant a review that had many features of an appeal. The one limitation on the provincial courts in criminal proceedings was that they could not punish serious offenses by Indians, jurisdiction in those being reserved to the viceroy and the alcaldes del crimen of the audiencia. The meaning of the prohibition was that only the viceroy and the alcaldes del crimen could impose sentences of death, mutilation, and sale for forced service to obrajes or other workshops.[246] In practice, the provincial justices could pronounce provisional sentences, which were suspended while the papers in the case were sent to the alcaldes del crimen for review and definitive judgment.

246. Royal cédula of January 27, 1632, in AGN-RCD, 59:fols. 34f–36v. This is summarized in Montemayor y Córdova de Cuenca, 1:5.7.56 (fol. 232f).

Although the competence of the viceroy acting within the General Indian Court permitted such sentences, his verdicts too went to the alcaldes del crimen for review. The one check on the competence of the viceroy in Indian criminal cases came in the eighteenth century, through the establishment of the Acordada, a special tribunal and police force with jurisdiction over robbery and murder on roads and highways. It was distinguished by abbreviated procedures and speedy, drastic punishments. Its jurisdiction overrode that of any other tribunal.[247]

In relation to provincial courts, the General Indian Court had the advantage of the prestige and powers of coercion inherent in the viceroy, who was after all the administrative superior of the local governors and the military head of the colony. In relation to the audiencia, the General Indian Court exercised a competing jurisdiction of a much more delicate nature, for viceroy and audiencia operated in a tension of nearly equal status and much conflict of competence, the administrative and military powers of the former and his function as president of the audiencia suffering serious limitation through the latter's right to entertain appeals and its steady reports to the crown. Examination of Indian complaints and of cases brought to the audiencia and handled by it clearly demonstrates that the audiencia heard as an alternate channel all matters that might be brought to the General Indian Court.

The audiencia dealt in first instance as well as second and third with disputes over land; inheritance; complaints of debt peonage and mistreatment of Indian workers by Spaniards; charges of excesses, extortion, improper levy, denial of justice, or abuses of power by provincial governors and their lieutenants; equally, charges of abuse and extortion brought by Indians against parish priests and other clergy; the almost endless bickering that resulted from disputes in Indian town government, and the relations of caciques and town officials to commoners; and all manner of criminal charges against Indians (this last clearly a matter of concurrent jurisdiction, as were most of the other categories). The audiencia issued writs of amparo and incitativas[248] in as wide a range of matters as the viceroy. Such issuance could be justified as being as much a judicial as an administrative function.

Although elections in Indian towns were clearly within the viceroy's private competence as chief administrator in the colony, the audiencia intervened in matters of electoral disputes or competence either directly or on the plea of appellate jurisdiction. In other instances,

247. On the nature and functioning of the Acordada, see MacLachlan, passim but esp. 88–101. See also Beleña, 1, part 5:72–74, nos. 15–20.

248. See the autos acordados of January 7, 1744, and June 7, 1762, in Beleña, 1, part 3:nos. 84 and 85 (pp. 31–33).

it intervened in purely administrative matters without judicial pretext, as in 1714 when it took advantage of the absence of Viceroy Linares from Mexico City to order payment of the garrison in Veracruz on its own responsibility. Viceroy Linares complained bitterly to Madrid about this invasion of viceregal prerogative, commenting that his hands were so bound that he could do only what judges and lawyers permitted. His letter enclosed a notarially certified list of 74 Indian cases handled as administrative matters, all of which had been appealed to the audiencia. They involved tax collection, difficulties in Indian administration and disputes among Indians, claims of caciques, repartimiento assignments of Indians to mines, elections of town officials, complaints of forced personal service, and exactions by provincial governors. Linares conceded the propriety of appeal for most cases, but held a number to be clearly administrative matters not subject to audiencia review. Two appeals he had thought so outrageous that he attempted to prevent them—one as manifestly unjust, a position upheld by the audiencia's fiscal; the other on the ground that only the sovereign could decide. The viceroy asked for a return to the custom that appeals could only move forward with viceregal permission. In 1715, on the recommendation of the Council of the Indies, the crown rebuked the audiencia and ordered it to abide by custom; as a gesture to the audiencia, the viceroy also was urged not to delay proper appeals.[249] That the royal cédula made much difference may be doubted.

The possibility of conflict was eased by some accommodation on the part of the audiencia. When it became apparent that one party to a case was suing in the audiencia and the other in the General Indian Court, or that what were essentially parts of a single case were being pursued in separate actions before the audiencia and the viceroy, the audiencia very often referred the entire matter to the viceroy for judgment in first instance.[250] Similarly, when the audiencia governed in the absence of any viceroy (audiencia gobernadora), it scrupulously preserved the institution of the General Indian Court, the only change being that the functions of assessor and judge were merged in a single member of the audiencia who served as delegate of the whole.

As between audiencia and General Indian Court, hearings before the audiencia, regardless of considerable simplification of procedures

249. Linares to the king, Mexico City, July 30, 1714, in AGI-M, leg. 486B; Croix, clause 16 (pp. 55–56); Azanza, clauses 24–25 (pp. 48–50). See also the cases, all before the audiencia, analyzed in Coy. All cases are for the area of Texcoco.

250. See, for example, the defense of Don Francisco Ximénez, cacique and governor of Tultitlán, district of Tacuba, February 6–October 22, 1723, Mexico City and Tultitlán (AGN-Civ, vol. 2152:exp. 8; LBSD, vol. 4), summarized in this chapter as case no. 122.

and reduction of costs for Indians, were more complicated and expensive. Either option was open to an Indian, who in consultation with his legal adviser—a solicitor, procurador, or abogado, chosen from among the Indian agents of the medio real, or one selected from the roster of the audiencia—decided where to initiate his suit. What became much more difficult for him was to maneuver between viceroy and audiencia; for once started in the General Indian Court or the audiencia, the complaint remained there until decided or sent elsewhere for decision. The other party involved might, of course, take the case from the audiencia to the viceroy. Most decisions by the viceroy could be appealed to the audiencia, in exercise of its undoubted prerogative of hearing in second instance.

The entire system afforded the natives much ground for maneuver which they were quick to use to their advantage; for if it is true that the imperialists study their colonial charges, it is equally true that the charges study their masters—with great care and much cunning. Who shall say which understands the other more?

CHAPTER VI

The Court:
Functionaries, Procedures,
and Policies

LEGALLY, the broad jurisdiction of the General Indian Court lay in the viceroy, but that official was the head of a considerable organization, increasingly a bureaucracy, the parts of which developed their own esprit de corps, their own procedures, and their own policies. As a man, the viceroy was a peninsular noble of long service, usually in the European realms of the crown of Castile, tending to be elderly, and considered worthy of a post of great honor and profit. Appointed for a term of years supposed to be five, but sometimes longer, he rarely had been in Mexico or any other part of America before his appointment. He arrived knowing little of the colony, and only toward the middle or end of his term acquired the experience that might permit him to administer the court judiciously and well. Almost invariably a noble *de capa y espada*, trained to govern and wage war, he lacked the legal knowledge to function as judge without the expert counsel of a legal adviser. Furthermore, he was the official in the colony to whom in the end all decisions came for making, review, or forwarding to Spain—*de despacho universal*, to use the phrase of the time—and with no regard for the slackening energy of elderly years, was kept too busy with administrative cares and ceremonial functions to handle the business of the court without large measures of assistance—in short, staff.[1]

1. See the eloquent statement of Manuel de Flon, Intendant of Puebla, to Miguel Cayetano de Soler, Minister of Hacienda, Puebla, December 21, 1801, in Pietschmann, "Dos documentos," 436–438; and Villarroel, 27–28. For sample lives of the viceroys, see Calderón Quijano, *Los virreyes de . . . Carlos III* and *Los virreyes de . . . Carlos IV*,

Continuity in functioning and policy, easily detectable in the cases dealt with by the court, clearly came from the staff, whose members continued through the administrations of several viceroys; for they held permanent appointments, subject only to the normal requirements of good behavior, professional and physical capacity, and desire to continue in their posts. Within the staff, the linchpin was the assessor, who after some experimentation in the first years[2] was always a judge of the audiencia with long experience in the colony and in Indian matters. As Juan de Palafox commented for an incoming viceroy, the Conde de Salvatierra, in 1642:

> The protection of the Indians lies in the viceroy's having an assessor seasoned through long experience . . . ; that is why His Majesty commands by cédula that he not be replaced nor the system changed without substantial reason.[3]

With the exception of the two crown attorneys attached by the audiencia in the civil and criminal divisions, both of whom by royal command were protectors of the Indians, the staff received salaries from the fund of the medio real, whence their collective name *ministros del medio real*—that is, salaried Indian legal agents. (The term *ministros* has no easy equivalent in present-day English, since in the Spanish meaning it has become archaic or even obsolete.) Chapter VII will deal with the functions and functioning of the Indian agents, but some listing and discussion of them is necessary here.

The first table of organization for the Indian agents, instituted by Luis de Velasco II and the Conde de Monterrey, was already fairly elaborate, as the two viceroys tried to arrange for necessary functions to be covered and important bureaucratic interests placated by shares in the medio real.[4] Some increase took place in the following years, most probably during the administration of the Marqués de Guadalcázar (1612–1621), whose genius in organizing the colony for thoughtful plunder, and getting the *gente de bien* to like it, has not been fully appreciated by later writers. By the time of the general inspection of Juan de Palafox in the 1640s, the table of organization had the general shape it was to maintain with relatively minor changes until the end of the Spanish regime.[5]

passim; Aiton, passim; Sarabia Viejo, passim; and the brief indications in Bancroft, vols. 2–4, passim.

2. See the discussion in Chapter VII.
3. Palafox y Mendoza, 2:144–146.
4. See Chapter IV; also Díez de la Calle, 116–117, 120–122, and 126–127.
5. List of tributaries and charges upon the medio real before and after 1643, n.d., in AGI-M, leg. 469. On Guadalcázar, see Bancroft, 3:28–32; and Borah, "Un gobierno provincial de frontera," 548–549.

Such comparative stability in size of staff is of some interest, for obviously the volume of business to be handled did not remain constant over more than two centuries. We may guess that it followed in a general way the fluctuation in Indian numbers in central Mexico, which at the time of establishment of the court were moving downward and reached their nadir in the first half of the seventeenth century. Thereafter, despite some fluctuations, the tendency was steadily upward, even though the indigenous element participated somewhat less in the general upsurge that characterized the Mexican population in the later colonial period. Accordingly, the eighteenth century was a time when an increasing village population pressed upon resources in land and disputed its possession with neighbors, whether other villages or private holders.[6] It was also a time when—if other conflicts and crime approximated the proportion to numbers of people of the early seventeenth century—there would have been a steady increase in absolute but not in relative terms.

The volume of Indian business, which put pressure upon the court in its early years, must have slackened for a few decades in the early and middle seventeenth century and then have begun a steady increase. At the beginning of the Bourbon regime, the crown received reports of a heavy backlog of cases, including Indian matters, in the audiencia,[7] which it met by adding new judges. It was not until the 1740s that the backlog disappeared so that the extra judges could be removed by attrition.[8] We do not have similar information on the General Indian Court, but would be justified in holding that there was a similar increase in volume, met in part by relatively small increases in staff in the eighteenth century. Since the increases were modest, there were only two ways of adjusting the flow of business to a relatively inelastic staff. The court either had to restrict the number of cases coming before it, or somehow achieve greater efficiency in dispatch so that more cases could move through it. Let us keep this question in mind.

Under the supervision of the assessor, the Indian agents discharged four basic functions. Three—assistance at the viceregal audience; dispatch of criminal cases at the Indian jails of the parcialidades of the capital; and supervision of those divisions—have already been discussed in other contexts and now must be examined in new terms.

6. Taylor, *Landlord and Peasant*, 83–89. See also Florescano, 140–197, which stresses the conflict, although it assigns another cause.

7. Albuquerque to the king, Mexico City, March 31, 1703, in AGI-M, leg. 475 (BLT).

8. Duque de la Conquista to the king, Mexico City, February 27, 1741, and Conde de Fuenclara to the king, Mexico City, May 25, 1745, in AGI-M, legs. 507 and 509 respectively.

The fourth function—serving as legal agents for Indian cases on appeal before the various parts of the audiencia, and further representing natives before ecclesiastical courts and other tribunals, obviously only in the area of Mexico City because of their small numbers and the problems of distance—lay outside the General Indian Court, although within the pledge of the medio real.[9]

Supervision of the two Indian parcialidades and their constituent barrios within the neighborhood of Mexico City required the services of the assessor, the notary, and the interpreter. As already stated, this function was administrative rather than judicial. Each year the elections for officials of the barrios and parcialidades had to be recorded in proper form and the resulting documents brought for approval to the assessor, acting for the viceroy. Preparation of the documents was the prerogative of the notary of the court, who, even at the official schedule, reaped a generous harvest of fees.[10] Each year also, the accounts of the treasuries of the parcialidades and their constituent barrios were presented to the assessor for audit and approval—for which the assessor must have had the assistance of someone skilled in bookkeeping, since his training was in law, not accounting. In addition, the auditing must have been essentially routine and time-consuming. Permission to barrios and parcialidades for expenditures from community treasuries, especially for celebrations of the festivals of patron saints, also had to be secured from the assessor, again acting for the viceroy. The court notary, of course, prepared the formal documents. Each year the assessor rendered formal report to the viceroy on his audits and permissions for expenditures.[11]

In all this the official court interpreter assisted whenever Nahuatl had to be turned into Spanish; perhaps for Otomí as well, since it too was much used in the vicinity of Mexico City. He came into his own as a court official in the preparations for observance of Corpus Christi in the Spanish capital, one of the great annual religious festivals whose celebration, under the aegis of the city council, brought together almost all Spanish dignitaries, members of the city guilds, and a huge concourse. Together with the governors of the two parcialidades, the court interpreter organized work drafts of Indians from all communities within a radius of something like 30 miles for the construction

9. See tabulation of the declarations of the two solicitadores of 1784, in AGI-M, leg. 1286, no. 342, in the appendix. The abogados and procuradores among the Indian agents had the same obligation.

10. Schedule of fees for the notary of the General Indian Court, Mexico City, October 3, 1741, in Testimonio del expediente sobre arreglo de las obligaciones de los solicitadores de indios y demas dependencias del Juzgado General de Naturales, December 14, 1785, fols. 21–24, in ibid.

11. Mexico: AGN, La secretaría de cámara, cuad. 3. See also Chapter V.

of archways of reeds and wood, covered with mats, to keep the blazing sun from the long, slow procession.[12]

All these practices were well developed by the last decades of the colonial period, but as yet we have no evidence of how or when they came into being. Inasmuch as some of the Indian barrios lay within provinces adjacent to the capital, such as San Cristóbal Ecatepec and Tacuba, and the assessor discharged functions of audit and supervision normally the prerogative of provincial governors, harmonious relations between the court and the administrators of those provinces must have required some measure of tact.[13]

A second function of the General Indian Court—dispatch of criminal cases for prisoners held at the Indian jails of the two parcialidades—can only be dealt with sketchily here, since no records of the actual cases have yet come to light. That it was separate from the operations of the viceregal audience is apparent from the listing of papers by the two solicitadores in 1784, since no case that can be ascribed to the Indian jails appears there. This function consisted both of assisting in the weekly inspection of the jails conducted by judges of the audiencia in formal procession and the actual judging of the cases in first instance, with appeal to the alcaldes del crimen. The necessary services from the Indian agents were those of assessor, abogado and procurador for criminal cases, notary, interpreter, and bailiff.[14] That the solicitadores participated in any way is uncertain; they probably did not. In the eighteenth century, the *procurador de lo criminal* was raised to the dignity of abogado, so that there were two *abogados de lo criminal*.[15]

The weekly inspection of the Indian jails, as well as all others of the secular government, was a formal ceremony of considerable dimension. Each Saturday the appropriate dignitaries of the city and the parcialidades—judges, corregidor, governors or alcaldes, bailiffs—formed at 11 a.m., in the palace chamber appointed for the purpose, to wait for the audiencia to rise from its session. With them were the Indian agents listed above, except for the assessor, who was sitting with the audiencia. Present also were the attorneys for the poor and the crown attorney for criminal matters. They waited however long, hoping that the inspection would not have to be deferred to the afternoon so that, even though they carried out the spirit of the law, they

12. Lira González, "La extinción," 309–316, and "La ciudad de México y las comunidades indígenas"; Estrada, passim.

13. See the cases in Chapter V for Indian barrios within the two parcialidades. See also the listing of towns for elections in which the court notary had a monopoly of preparing papers, as in the schedule of fees cited in note 10.

14. See discussion later in this chapter.

15. Testimonio de auttos fhos [on the medio real], December 1, 1703, in AGI-M, leg. 474; and Fonseca and Urrutia, 1:551.

did not carry out its exact letter, specifying the morning. This somewhat peculiar statement is that of the auto acordado of January 9, 1786, regulating such inspections. Actually, the inspections usually took place in the afternoon.

Once the audiencia rose, the two oidores on weekly turn headed the company in formal procession to the *carcel de corte*, the audiencia jail in Mexico City, and then divided to inspect the two Indian jails. At the carcel de corte the two oidores, and at each Indian jail one oidor, examined the registers to see who had been admitted, who released, and for what reason, and inspected the facilities to see that the prisoners had food, water, and bedding and were kept in clean cells, with adequate provision of religious and medical care. The terms in which these injunctions were observed were, of course, those of the time, not ours. Each prisoner on the premises was looked at to determine if he was there with adequate reason, whether detained for trial, serving sentence, awaiting punishment, or held on other sufficient order.[16] Assistance by the appropriate Indian agents was necessary at the carcel de corte, for some of the prisoners there were held on order of the General Indian Court.[17] Their major assistance, obviously, was at the Indian jails, for the court notary was responsible for maintaining the registers; and the prisoners, all Indian, were in one way or another the responsibility of the General Indian Court.[18]

Disposition of the charges against prisoners at the Indian jails brought the assessor into the function, unless he had served as oidor on weekly turn. Each business day except Saturday, between the hours of 11 and 12 a.m., the governors of the Indian parcialidades, or in substitution of them Indian alcaldes, plus one abogado for criminal matters, the interpreter, and the bailiff, waited upon the assessor. The governors or their substitutes presented detailed reports of the arrests made since the previous report, together with evidence and testimony,

16. Autos acordados, no. 57 of January 7, 1744, reworking that of October 30, 1642, caps. 12 and 34; nos. 123 of March 22, 1714, and April 9, 1744; 124 and 125 of May 31, 1747; 128 of September 10, 1755; and 130 of January 9, 1786, all in Beleña, 1, part 3:18–23 and 48–50. The governing royal instructions were legislation of 1480, 1518, and 1554, incorporated in the *Nueva recopilación* as 2.9.1–2, repeated in the Novísima recopilación as 12.39.1–2; and the extensive provisions in RLI, 7, títs. 6–7. The permission for the two oidores to divide, one each to a jail of an Indian parcialidad, is in 7.7.12. On the *visita de cárcel* as a general custom, see Escriche y Martin, *Diccionario*, 712.

17. Non-Indians, Indians from the provinces in some cases, and Indians approximating noble status would be held at the carcel de corte on order of the viceroy and the General Indian Court.

18. See note 10 above; auto acordado no. 198 of December 22, 1676, in Montemayor y Córdova de Cuenca, part 2:62f.

so that the assessor might determine which prisoners should be released and which detained for judgment.[19] In general, prisoners under
arrest for drunkenness and other light offenses were released with a
warning and without trial. For other offenses regarded as light enough,
the entire matter was handled verbally, as far as the culprits were concerned, and without formal trial. Youths arrested for gaming seem to
have fallen into this category. Those held at the request of their families or communities for dissolute or incorrigible misbehavior underwent no trial beyond formal establishment of cause for detention.[20]

In terms of our concepts and those brought into vogue by the
Enlightenment, the criminal trials exhibited grave defects, for they
were held without the presence of the accused. What he had to say on
his own behalf, the charges against him, testimony by witnesses for
and against, and any other evidence were recorded at the jail by the
court notary or a delegate acting for him. Determination of guilt or
innocence was made by the assessor on the basis of the written record,
in consultation with the abogado de lo criminal, acting for the accused, and with the crown attorney for criminal affairs, acting in such
instances both as attorney for the state and as Indian protector. The
assessor furthermore decided on the sentence. It was this procedure
that permitted relatively speedy dispatch by a busy official.[21] Legally,
the assessor acted merely as adviser to the viceroy in each case, so that
the viceroy's rubric was necessary on the document of judgment, but
that was a formality. Toward the end of the colonial period, the assessor acted as delegate of the viceroy for settling Indian affairs, a final
step releasing the viceroy even from the ceremonial participation of
affixing a rubric.[22]

The court had formidable powers of punishment, for it could
sentence to terms of forced service in textile workshops, bakeries, and
other establishments glad to receive convicts; it could order flogging,
branding, and mutilation, although mutilation was rare; and finally, it
could sentence to death. All punishments for Indians had to be corporal, since they were exempt from pecuniary penalties such as fines and

19. Clause 8, public ordinance on the General Indian Court, Mexico City, December 5, 1785, in Beleña, 2:202, no. 47.
20. Schedule of fees for the notary of the General Indian Court, Mexico City,
October 3, 1741, clause 7, in AGI-M, leg. 1286, no. 342.
21. Ibid., clauses 7 and 8. The same practice of taking evidence on the spot but
sending the testimony elsewhere for determination of guilt and sentence may be found
in Alejandro O'Reilly's instructions for posts in Louisiana under Spanish rule: see the
discussion in Baade, "Marriage Contracts," 37–39; a brief summary may be found in
Torres Ramírez, 123.
22. See the discussion later in this chapter.

seizure of property. From the General Indian Court, appeal lay to the alcaldes del crimen of the audiencia.[23]

The major functioning of the General Indian Court was centered in the viceregal audience, the core of the court. It required the services of the assessor; the two secretaries of gobernación and the two of cámara, in alternating teams of one each; two abogados, in teams of one for civil and one for criminal cases; the two procuradores; the two solicitadores; the relator; the notary; the interpreter; and the bailiff. In addition, other receptores from the approved audiencia list, and the crown attorneys, were called on as needed, but received no salary from the medio real. The increase in personnel between the administration of Monterrey and the inspection of Palafox doubled the number of solicitadores, procuradores, and abogados to two each.[24] In the eighteenth century, the number of attorneys for criminal cases increased further. Whether or not the volume of business justified the increase in the seventeenth century, it certainly did in the eighteenth. The *porteros*, doorkeepers or ushers whom Luis de Velasco II wished to put on salary from the medio real, do not appear in the seventeenth-century table of organization but do in the eighteenth-century one.[25]

At this point, explanation of the meaning of some of the professional titles is required, for the old Spanish legal system differed not merely from ours but also from the English one, then and now, and perhaps from the present-day continental ones.[26] The *abogados* were *letrados*—that is, they had studied the full course of law in a university and had been examined and admitted formally to practice before the audiencia.[27] They were *de número*, i.e., licensed for practice in set

23. Montemayor y Córdova de Cuenca, part 1: fol. 157v, sum. 8, and fol. 232f, sum. 56, summarizing paragraphs of royal cédulas, Madrid, May 30, 1594, and March 15, 1639; the latter is given in full in AGN-RCD, 61: fols. 34f–36v. That such sentences were executed on Indians may be seen from Gemelli Carreri, 1:91 and 2:177–178. On the prohibition of pecuniary penalties against Indians, see Chapters III and IV above. In the eighteenth century, this prohibition was extended to embargoing or seizing property of Indians; their property had to be turned over to heirs or relatives: auto acordado no. 16 of the Sala del Crimen, Mexico City, April 29, 1765, in Beleña, 1, part 4:59.

24. Compare the table of organization given in Chapter IV with the list of tributaries and charges upon the medio real before and after 1643, n.d., in AGI-M, leg. 469 (analyzed in Table 7.1).

25. Fonseca and Urrutia, 1:547 and 551.

26. Robson, 1–6 et passim. The French system had *avocats*, *procureurs*, and *praticiens*, whose functions were analogous. Old Regime France did not have a unified legal system, but this triple division was true of the area of the Coutume de Paris, which included French North America: Baade, "Marriage Contracts," 7–11 and 14–15.

27. The discussion which follows is based upon the description of function in the auto acordado, Mexico City, July 28, 1580, in Montemayor y Córdova de Cuenca, part 2: fol. 1, no. 1; that of October 30, 1642, in Beleña, 1, part 1:70–76 (also in Montemayor y Córdova de Cuenca); Escriche y Martín, *Manual*, 264–265, 279, 282–284,

number, and in the later colonial period organized in a corporate body with its own charter, the local *colegio de abogados*.[28] Only they might authorize or prepare in final form complaints, demands, answers, questionnaires, pleadings, and petitions for conclusion; in short, all papers held to be substantive in content and to require proficiency in the law for adequate statement.

The *procuradores* were held to a lesser knowledge of law, but also were examined and admitted to practice by the audiencia, again in a set number. Their relation to the abogados was made clear by the requirement that when an abogado spoke in judicial hearing, the procuradores must keep respectful silence. Their function was to prepare and file with the courts papers of a procedural nature, asking for extensions or limits of time, pointing to failure to answer by the other party (*rebeldía*), petitioning courts to reach interlocutory or final decisions on pleadings, etc. They might draft papers of substance, but these had to be reviewed and signed by the abogado. They had to have a power of attorney from the client or clients, and theoretically they sought out the abogado. In the provinces, where abogados were scarce or not present at all, the procuradores usually assumed without protest all the functions of legal representation, very like the county attorneys of England.[29]

The *solicitadores* were men-of-all-work with little legal standing in the courts. They frequently were the persons to whom the prospective client first turned; they advised on the appropriate procurador, secured the indispensable power of attorney so that the procurador and abogado could function, gathered evidence, ran errands, secured and served legal papers, etc. Although there were no legal requirements of training, most must have acquired experience through service with older practitioners or even in the offices of procuradores and abogados. In practice, the solicitadores, invading the sphere of the procuradores, began to prepare procedural papers and to draft legal documents of substance for review and reworking by the abogados or procuradores. Their invasion received partial sanction by royal cédula

---

and *Diccionario* (1837), passim; the descriptions of functions in the Testimonio of December 14, 1785, cited in note 10 above; Parry, *The Audiencia*, 154–162; and Soberanes Fernández, "La administración," 177–178. The next few notes will indicate additional references.

28. Mexico (Viceroyalty): Real Colegio de Abogados, passim. The Real Colegio de Abogados was organized under a royal cédula, Buen Retiro, June 21, 1760; examination and admission to practice in the Mexico City area continued to be handled by the Audiencia de Mexico (clause 2).

29. The AT, passim, indicates that for most of the colonial period there was no abogado in the province. In many provinces there may not even have been a trained and examined procurador.

of June 19, 1685, which permitted the solicitador to sign pleadings, together with the abogado, in the absence or refusal of the procurador.[30] In the General Indian Court, the two salaried solicitadores were full-time, hard-working employees, who saw more of the Indian clients than any other category of employee, and because of the special nature of the court were allowed far more leeway and function than in other tribunals. Because of this, Beleña proposed, toward the end of the eighteenth century, that the two solicitadores of the General Indian Court also be examined by the audiencia, like abogados and procuradores.

The *relator* was a trained lawyer who organized and reviewed the docket, pointed to missing papers and pleadings, and summarized the main points of the case for the judge, who thus was spared much reading. The function as such is unknown to Anglo-Saxon procedure, except to the extent that a judge's law clerk may fulfill it today.

Two functions discharged by necessary officials not drawing salary from the medio real were those of the *receptor*, outside of Mexico City, and the crown attorney or *fiscal*. The receptor was a trained notary, formally examined and admitted to serve with the audiencia, within a set number, who heard and recorded testimony, usually in the form of answers to a set questionnaire. Within Mexico City the notary of the General Indian Court discharged this function; but if testimony had to be taken at a distance from the tribunal, the services of one of the receptores attached to the audiencia, assigned in turn, became indispensable, since this official traveled to the witnesses' location, asked the questions formally set forth in the *interrogatorio*, and recorded the qualifications and answers of the witnesses. Payment of fees and travel came from the party asking for the service or the one losing the case.

The crown attorneys were by royal order protectors of the Indians, without additional stipend for such service, and entered cases before the General Indian Court as a matter of official obligation. The *fiscal de lo civil* usually advised in formal written opinion, reviewing the complaint, the answer if any, and the evidence, in what amounted to assessment by an additional legal mind on the matter. If the case was considered criminal, the function was discharged by the *fiscal de lo criminal*. In the last decades of the eighteenth century, the entire function of Indian protector fell upon the fiscal de lo criminal. In the event of incapacity of either or both through illness, vacancy, or recusation, the crown attorney for the treasury filled in. If the royal treasury had an interest in the case, an opportunity for him to enter an opinion was mandatory.[31]

30. AGN-RC, 20:exp. 100; Konetzke, 2:764–766, no. 519.

31. On the crown attorneys, see Chapter III above and the cases summarized in Chapter V. See also Rodríguez García; and Brading, *Miners and Merchants*, 57–58.

Let us now trace the movement of petitions and complaints from their first appearance, in the viceregal palace of Indians seeking relief, to the final decision of the viceroy. Obviously, cases differed in complexity and accordingly in the number of steps required. Equally, very real differences in procedure distinguished judicial from truly administrative cases, even though the difference might not follow the fictitious distinction that extended the jurisdiction of the General Indian Court to areas otherwise forbidden. Nevertheless, all steps may be subsumed under four major categories: (1) formulation and presentation of the petition or complaint; (2) the hearing, whether following judicial or administrative procedure; (3) the decision; and (4) enforcement of the decision.[32]

1. *Formulation and presentation of the petition or complaint.* In general, even though the court had express jurisdiction in cases in which the Indians were sued by others, Indians were the petitioners or complainants. They might appear as individuals on their own behalf or as representatives of a community or part thereof, whether a barrio or cofradía. Since they had to appear in person or through a properly authorized deputy before the court sitting in Mexico City, distance from the capital became an important winnowing agent determining frequency of resort to the court and the method. For Indians living within a radius of perhaps 100 miles from the capital, a distance of five to seven days' journey, travel to the court was relatively easy. The shorter the distance, the greater the ease of using the court in preference to other governmental entities.

At greater distances, travel and the necessary stay in Mexico City became far more of a burden. For an individual, cause for complaint must have appeared grave indeed, and the chance of local remedy slight, before he would undertake the long trip to the capital and the expenses of maintenance there. For a community or corporate group, the cost of sending a delegation could be spread among all members, and the expense of maintenance in Mexico City and along the road reduced by carrying provisions, but that meant sending representatives, women to care for them, and porters. It is undoubtedly the matter of travel time and cost that led to the bunching of petitions and complaints which shows up clearly in the viceregal registers. A town would use the occasion of a complaint so driving that it felt it had to

---

32. This division is based upon Escriche y Martín, *Manual*, 258–259. I have added to it the category of enforcement. The discussion following is largely taken from papers of cases before the General Indian Court in AGN-I, -Civ, and -Crim, a number of which are summarized in Chapter V. For the next several pages, notes refer only to additional material from other sources.

approach the court as an occasion for pressing all other needs for relief which had not been raised, although very real. The result shows up as a series of decrees of the same or nearly the same date for one town: a good example is the eight decrees secured by Tepeaca at one time in 1630.[33]

This need to send delegations, which might have relatively large numbers of people, and to maintain them in the capital, raised some concern among the Spanish authorities that their presence in Mexico City meant the removal of laborers from milpas and the care of their families. Monterrey attempted to handle the problem by limiting the number in any delegation to two, and providing food and lodging for them as a matter of royal grace; but since this last measure cost the royal treasury money, it soon lapsed.[34] Neither were the Indians likely to be content with sending merely two people for any voicing of complaint by a town.[35] There was a partial return to the Monterrey plan in 1662, when delegations from Oaxaca, complaining of the distinctly arbitrary new tribute assessments made by Montemayor y Córdova de Cuenca in his inspection as special judge, brought so many natives to the capital that the audiencia issued a special order that each town send no more than one or two of its officials, upon threat of sentence of the surplus to service in an obraje; for

> . . . on this pretext they leave their towns and do not carry out their duty of tilling their fields, coming to Christian instruction, and taking care of their property, so that they become unable to pay their tributes and bring offerings to their churches, as is their obligation. . . .[36]

One doubts the success of this measure, as of all others like it. In the end, the limit on the size of a delegation and its length of stay must have been the burden on the town.

Upon arrival in Mexico City, the Indian complainants sought out an Indian agent, usually a solicitador. They might find him at home or, on business days, at a desk in the corridor outside the viceroy's offices from 8 to 11 in the mornings and from 2 or 3:30 to 4 or 5:30 in the afternoons. Each solicitador was supposed to be well removed from

33. AGN-I, 10, cuad. 1:exps. 262–267.
34. See Chapter IV above.
35. The comment of Mendoza, quoted in Chapter III, should be kept in mind.
36. Mexico City, September 25, 1662, Testimonio de autos y padrones quel oidor Montemayor, 1661–62, fol. 365f–v, in AGI-P, leg. 230A, ramo 8. The restriction may have been less innocent than its stated reason, for the Bishop of Puebla charged that when Indians of Oaxaca came to Mexico City in order to protest legally Montemayor y Córdova de Cuenca's new tribute assessments, "no letrado or procurador was willing to take their cases, for fear of the oidor, until the Indians secured special decrees coercing the letrados and procuradores to act for them": Bishop of Puebla to the king, Puebla, December 6, 1662, in AGI-P, leg. 230B, ramo 13.

the other, so that neither could hear what was transacted at the other's desk.[37] The complainants discussed their cause for grievance with the solicitador, who must have given a good deal of unofficial advice on what had a chance of success before the viceroy and what did not, thus winnowing out the most trivial and preposterous matters. Others might be sent elsewhere, on the ground that their cases were outside the competence of the General Indian Court.

If the solicitador accepted the case, as in the end he was legally bound to do, he asked for a formal power of attorney either for himself or for one of the procuradores de indios. Usually the solicitador prepared the instrument and wrote the complaint in the form of a petition to the viceroy, in as simple language as possible. Sometimes the complaint was written by other people, occasionally by the complainant; but one of the minor mysteries is that some complaints on file, not written by a solicitador or procurador, end with the statement that the petitioner could neither read nor write.[38]

Either at the formulation of the written complaint or in filing it for presentation at the earliest viceregal audience, the solicitador or procurador was supposed to make sure by strict questioning, if necessary through an interpreter, that the Indians were truly who they said they were; that they were Indians; that if they came on behalf of a corporate body, they truly were authorized to speak for it; and that they had not been incited to complaint by outside parties seeking to stir up trouble. Since Indians were not held to post bond for calumny nor were they punished for perjury, except perhaps by penance at church confession, they were free from the ordinary barriers that restrained non-Indians in such instances. Spanish authorities, throughout the colonial period, testified to the need for making very sure that the complainants were who they said they were; if they appeared as representatives of a town or its officials, that they had proper authorization and were not self-appointed; and that if they brought charges against clergy or local administrators, Spanish or Indian, the charges had some basis in fact.[39]

37. Nuevo reglamento para el Juzgado de Indios, Mexico City, May 6, 1598, in both AGN-I, 6, part 2:exp. 1004, and AGI-M, leg. 24; public ordinance on the General Indian Court, Mexico City, December 5, 1785, in Beleña, 2:202, no. 47, clauses 6 and 7. The 1598 reglamento specifies 2 to 4 p.m.; that of 1785, 3:30 p.m., presumably continuing for two hours. The change probably reflects the movement into the afternoon of the principal meal of the day (comida). On compliance with these hours, see Chapter VII.

38. These show up in cases referred to the provincial administration of Tulancingo and the originals deposited in the AT.

39. Auto acordado no. 49, Mexico City, September 27, 1677, in Beleña, 1, part 1:33–34 (also in Montemayor y Córdova de Cuenca); relación de mando of Revillagigedo to Amarillas, Mexico City, November 28, 1754, in Mexico (Viceroyalty), *Instruc-*

2. *The hearing*. Presentation of the petition or complaint was made to the General Indian Court at one of the thrice-weekly viceregal audiences, held Monday and Wednesday mornings and Friday afternoons. In the earlier years of the court, the petitioner appeared in person with his petition or complaint and, accompanied by his solicitor or procurador, for a personal hearing by the viceroy or his assessor. Luis de Velasco II saw the Indians himself; Monterrey substituted his assessor as much as possible, in a change that was more efficient but less immediately satisfactory to the Indians, who as in Mexico today undoubtedly wanted to get to the top man. So long as the petitioner appeared in person, the portero was also an important subordinate functionary, since he controlled access. By the eighteenth century, as movement of papers took over in increasing measure, presentation of the petition became more a matter of filing by the Indian agent and examination without the plaintiff's presence, his agent appearing for him. The petitioner obtained personal audience only in unusual circumstances, when clarification was needed or the case indicated need for the reassurance of a personal audience.

The nature of the complaint and the remedy asked for automatically indicated the course of the proceedings. If the complainant demanded justice for seizure of lands or other property, the court had to follow judicial procedures. If the complaint alleged misdeeds by parish priest, Spanish governor, or an Indian town official, the court had to proceed by investigative procedures that were essentially administrative. Cases in which non-Indians were the defendants, involving land, labor relations, and debt, were legally administrative but in practice followed either set of procedures as seemed appropriate. In many instances, the petitioner merely asked that the court order a Spanish provincial governor to hear or to expedite his hearing of a matter; and the desired remedy, a simple order for hearing the matter expeditiously, called an *incitativa*, was considered an administrative action, even though the audiencia too issued them.

In cases handled by judicial procedures, the first determination concerned whether to hear the matter directly or to send it for hearing to a provincial tribunal, with instructions then to remit all papers to the General Indian Court for either decision or review. Here the criteria were, on the one hand, distance from Mexico City and the expense of summoning and keeping all parties in the capital and, on the other, the preference of the complainant. The case might be remitted to the

ciones, 1:303–304; Croix (September 1, 1771), 56–57. The exemption apparently began as an act of the Audiencia of Lima, ratified by the crown, and then was extended elsewhere: Viñas Mey, 203–204. It carried out the royal injunction to spare the natives any pecuniary penalty.

tribunal of the province in which the parties lived; or, if the complaint alleged partiality or improper behavior on the part of the local Spanish justice, might be sent to the tribunal of a neighboring province, the judge of which might hold the hearing at his seat or come to the province of the parties as judge on commission.

Whether the hearing took place on order in a provincial tribunal or in the viceregal palace, the course of the suit was essentially the same; for, despite all attempts at simplifying procedures in Indian litigation, the formal parts of the case remained those of Spanish legal procedure, the parties themselves resisting abbreviation. Simplification did occur, but in the preparation of papers, the keeping of records, and the movement of papers, the Indians being given summonses and writs for presentation instead of the papers' moving as formal dispatches through the weekly messengers who tied the provincial seats to the capital or through court officers on fee.

In Spanish legal procedure, the formal parts of a suit were the demand or complaint; the summons to the other party; his answer, which might involve presentation of a countercomplaint (*reconvención*); the formal presentation of evidence by both sides (*prueba*), which might turn into a lengthy matter; and the judicial decision or sentence. In the General Indian Court, the summons to the other party was issued as a document usually delivered to the plaintiff for presentation to the defendant. Upon the defendant's choosing his procurador, providing him with formal power of attorney, and filing an answer through him, whether simple denial or countercomplaint, the case was ready to move to the presentation of evidence. That might consist of the exhibition of documents, even to Indian pictographic manuscripts (*pinturas*); if appropriate, the testimony of physicians on medical examination; and almost invariably, the testimony of witnesses.

This last was carried out in a way which is odd in the extreme to our eyes. Each side had the right to present to the court for approval an *interrogatorio*, a formal questionnaire for answer by up to 30 witnesses presented by that side—although for Indian cases, the court, in common with other Spanish tribunals in the colony, objected to anything approaching that number as excessive. The questionnaire was administered by either the notary of the court or a receptor, chosen in turn from those admitted for practice before the audiencia. As needed, the court interpreter or others assisted. In the provinces, the local notary discharged the function, unless a receptor was sent out from Mexico City. In answering the questionnaire, each witness, upon being duly sworn, first established his competence and objectivity by answering the general questions required by Spanish law. Then, one by one, he replied to the questions, with which he might either agree, disagree, or state that he did not know. He usually declared on what ground he knew, i.e., whether direct knowledge or hearsay; but he could not add additional information, nor was he questioned further or subjected to cross-examination. So the possibility of ferreting out the gaps and contradictions through cross-examination, which is so important an element in Anglo-Saxon legal procedure, was largely surrendered.

The determination whom to believe as between two opposing panels of witnesses, each swearing stoutly that they knew of their own direct experience the truth of questions in direct contradiction, undoubtedly tested the skill of a seasoned judge, who might well have sighed for a Solomon. The witnesses most likely to gain credence from a Spanish court were Spaniards of substance and long residence in the area; other non-Indians of substance and long residence; and last of all, lower-class non-Indians and Indians, in that order. Testimony by the village priest, if he was not a party or somehow embroiled in the dispute, received special weight. Presumably, long residence in the area and deep acquaintance with the natives, through religious administration and hearing their confessions, made him especially knowledgeable, while his cloth made him more disposed to tell the truth. The attorneys for each side were given opportunity to file comments and objections to the other side's questionnaire and witnesses when the taking of testimony had been completed, and in this way brought to the proceedings an element of substitution for cross-examination.

Throughout the proceedings so far, there might well have been a running accompaniment of motions and countermotions at all stages after the initial presentation of the complaint: *rebeldía*, or failure to answer, with a plea either for infliction of a penalty or a decision in favor of the other party; pleas for more time or less time for some stage in the proceedings; pleas that the testimony offered on behalf of the other side was false, perjured, or calumnious; and finally, *recusación*, complaints of partiality or improper behavior or attitude on the part of any officers of the court not directly attached to a client, with the demand that some other person discharge the function. Recusación was a formidable legal weapon. Its use was limited as to judges of the audiencia, including the viceregal assessor, and the crown attorneys, by a requirement that the allegation must be substantiated by "conclusive evidence and with witnesses worth full faith and credit,"[40]

40. Royal cédula, Madrid, August 28, 1641, in DCLI, 2:218, no. 494. In one case of disputed election in Zacatlán in 1629, the assessor was recused and the viceroy had to send the papers to Lic. Matías de Palacios, abogado of the audiencia: mentioned

but it might more easily be used to discredit local Spanish judges and such officials of the General Indian Court as the interpreter.[41] The court sought to avoid even slight suspicion of taint by turning to other officials, as may be seen in the notable instance of the suit of Ixtlán vs. Calpulalpan and two of its sujetos, 1631–1634, in which a fair compromise arranged by the alcalde mayor of Antequera was delayed in implementation for nearly three years until a report by the corregidor of Tecocuilco, as new judge, confirmed the justice of the earlier arrangement.[42]

At each stage, as appropriate, the pleadings would move to the crown attorneys for civil or criminal matters for an independent opinion, which amounted to a careful review of the entire case to that point, with a recommendation on the action to be taken by the court; then to the assessor, for his recommendation; and to the viceroy, who merely approved what the assessor recommended, and by the middle years of the eighteenth century simply stamped his rubric, rather than writing a half or full signature, on an order already prepared for him and bearing the rubric of the assessor.

If the proceedings followed an essentially administrative form, the court, upon receipt of the complaint, might send out an order for immediate remedy unless the local official reported that the complaint was specious, or the court might initiate a longer process of investigation: the local official would be informed of the complaint or petition, and ordered to carry out an investigation to ascertain the truth of the allegations. If the complaint referred to actions of the local Spanish administrator, or his impartiality was impugned, a nearby Spanish official might be commissioned to carry out the investigation and report back to the court. The order usually set a time limit for compliance, varying with distance but most frequently thirty days, and a penalty that might include a fine of from 100/ to 200/ and an additional threat of removal from office, or recording the dereliction for use when the

---

in decree, Mexico City, March 6, 1629, in AGN-I, 10, cuad. 1: exp. 63; but this case was before 1641.

41. Capítulos of the town of Tetepango against Don Alonso de Aguilar Cervantes, alcalde mayor of Hueypoxtla, April 2–July 20, 1639, but not concluded, in AGN-Crim, 34: exp. 12 (132 fols.) (LBSD, vol. 24). On April 9, 1639, the interpreter for Otomí, Francisco de Orozco, was recused as an enemy of the plaintiffs, and Luis de Aranda appointed for the case in his stead. In another case, in 1771, against Vicente García of Teposcolula, for excesses in town government, the procurador of the court and the provincial interpreter and notary of Teposcolula were recused. The procurador de pobres in Mexico City replaced the recused procurador: decree, Mexico City, May 2, 1771, in AGN-I, 63: fol. 92v.

42. Summarized as case no. 2 in Chapter V.

official came up for his residencia or consideration for a new appointment. Transmission and delivery of the decree were left to the complainant, who was given the formal signed version carrying in its text the statement that it was to serve as the official dispatch and that it might be served by anyone who knew how to read and write.

If the local official, despite the threat of penalties, did not comply, he might again be required to carry out the order, sometimes under threat of increased penalty, occasionally under threat of reduced penalty. This last element is striking, but the reason for it unknown. On further recalcitrance, an order might be sent to a nearby official for investigation and report, or an official might be sent out from Mexico City at the expense of the erring party. In the end, if the complainant persisted, a report would be secured. Upon its appearance in the court, it passed through a formal, meticulous review. It was made available to the complainant or his representative; the appropriate crown attorney as protector was asked for his opinion, which again usually consisted of a careful review of the evidence and the ruling law, with specific recommendations either for further investigation or for immediate remedy; the assessor had prepared a decree for one or the other step, to which he affixed his rubric and brought the document to the viceroy for the latter's rubric.

Possible actions varied considerably. The report might be returned for amplification as unsatisfactory, and in more extreme instances another official near the locality or from Mexico City might be sent for further investigation. If essential evidence was lacking, but there was no sign of dereliction on the part of the local Spanish official, he might be ordered to gather the additional evidence and forward it to the court. If there was reason to presume guilt on the part of the local Spanish official or any other people, the presumed culprits might be ordered tried locally or sent to Mexico City for trial by the General Indian Court. A Spanish provincial governor might be summoned to appear before the court within a definite term of days or to send a representative for answer in his stead.

3. *The decision.* The final decision or definitive sentence, whether the proceedings had followed a judicial or an administrative pattern or some mixture of the two, was issued after careful review of the docket. At this point the docket might be put in order and summarized by the court relator. After the first decades of the court's existence, the docket almost variably went to a fiscal protector for his opinion and recommendation. That opinion, occasionally modified but usually accepted by the assessor, became the basis for the final or-

der prepared at the instruction of the assessor, given his rubric, and taken to the viceroy for the final rubric.

The decision might be a clear victory for one side or the other, but most often it was not. The court was interested in calming passions, avoiding further expensive litigation, and keeping the Indians at their proper role of production, care of their families, support of the church, and payment of royal tribute.[43] Accordingly, its efforts and those of its agents and emissaries in the field were directed more to arranging compromises (conciertos) that might bring enough satisfaction to all to have a reasonable chance of enduring. If the dispute was over land, and each party could show some evidence of right, the land was likely to be divided and the parties bound to perpetual peace.[44] If the complaint was extortion and improper levy, whether by town officials or a Spanish administrator, the settlement made partial restitution or some payment to settle the claims, promised good treatment in the future, and attempted to clarify in writing the obligations of the Indian commoners. The settlement arranged by Francisco de las Casas in the suit of Chalcatongo in 1600 against its cacique, for extortion, is a clear illustration of court policy.[45] Perhaps even more notable is the settlement of the suit by Teposcolula against its Indian alcaldes in 1640, in which local Spanish officials and clergy, both resident in the town, protested complete ignorance of years of extortion, and the agreement for settlement negotiated locally provided for a payment in settlement of much greater claims. A striking feature of the Teposcolula concierto, as of many others, was that the macehuales were prepared to be levied upon well beyond legal limits; so that, when the arrangement came to the court for approval, it deleted some of the agreed-upon levies and obligations as contrary to royal cédula.[46]

A similar policy of limiting exploitation of the Indians to levels regarded as normal and reasonable—tolerable, if one wishes the term—but at the same time of not interfering with government and production, was apparent in cases of labor and debt peonage. An employer guilty of abuse of his employees would be admonished to mend his ways or he would be deprived of Indian labor. The Indian peons similarly were admonished to good behavior, and their debts carefully reviewed to establish the true amount, but rarely were they released

43. The policy is stated clearly in the decree of appointment of Manuel María de Arellano as Indian solicitador, Mexico City, December 15, 1781, incorporating the recommendation of the assessor, November 20, 1781, in Testimonio, in AGI-M, leg. 1286, no. 342, fols. 39f–40v. The policy dates back to the beginning of the court.

44. Tuxtla vs. Tamazulapan, 1617, summarized as case no. 1 in Chapter V.

45. Summarized as case no. 115 in Chapter V.

46. Summarized as case no. 120 in Chapter V.

from service on the hacienda. Even a certain amount of beating or other punishment, to the extent of moderate correction, was accepted as reasonable by the court and, it must be admitted, by the Indians themselves. The basic policy was to interfere with agricultural and other production only to the minimum that could not be avoided,[47] just as the policy in regard to Indians in towns was to keep them at work in orderly polity, meeting their town obligations, their tributes, and service to the church. In a very real sense, the General Indian Court was not so much a court of law as a court of compromise and accommodation. It may in this respect have dealt more in justice than do courts of law.

4. *Enforcement of the decision.* Once the General Indian Court issued its decision—again usually in the form of a decree given to the complainant or petitioner, which he served on the other party—the losing party had two choices: appeal or compliance. Appeal lay to the audiencia. If the case was regarded as administrative in nature, appeal could only be filed with the consent of the viceroy, a consent usually granted.[48] Once appeal was filed, the case moved out of the viceregal jurisdiction, although the Indian agents of the medio real still had the obligation to act for their clients in the appellate jurisdiction. If no appeal was filed, the decision was supposed to be implemented.

One may raise the question: To what extent were the decisions of the General Indian Court enforced? There are certainly recorded instances of long defiance of its orders. Capt. Francisco Monrroy, hacendado of Coatepec, paid little attention to orders of courts, local or the General Indian Court, in seizing Indians for labor and mistreating them; yet in 1651 the General Indian Court, then under the audiencia gobernadora, caught up with him.[49] Such long-term defiance must have been relatively rare, for the court had at its disposal in enforcing its interlocutory and final orders a formidable array of punitive measures. It might assess fines to be collected forthwith. It might send out other officials, at the cost of the recalcitrant party, for enforcement of its decision. In the instance of Indian officials, it might order removal during their terms of office and immediate accounting; for Spanish of-

47. See the discussion and case summaries in the section on complaints arising from labor disputes and debts in Chapter V; Riley, 237–241; and the suit of Ventura Francisco of Tultepec in 1745, summarized as case no. 129 in Chapter V.

48. Linares to the king, Mexico City, July 30, 1714, in AGI-M, leg. 486B; Croix, 55–56, clause 16; Azanza, 48–50, clauses 24–25. On the other hand, the royal cédula issued as a result of the inspection of Lic. Francisco Garcerán, 1716–1720, contained a stern reproof to the viceroy for not allowing appeals to the audiencia: Lerma, December 13, 1721, in DCLI, 2:231, no. 504.

49. Summarized as case no. 105 in Chapter V.

ficials, it might order removal, an accounting at the time of residencia, and a recording of the disobedience and transgression, to be raised whenever the official was considered for appointment to a new post. It might order seizure and sale of goods to pay fines and other forms of judgment.

Though limited by the prohibition against levying pecuniary penalties upon Indians, a judgment for payment of damages and the expenses of collection against a recalcitrant town might come to a formidable sum, as may be seen in the enforcement of judgment for Tlatlaya and other towns against Acapetlahuaya and its allies in 1808–09. Even the village priest's mule was swept up by the commissioners sent out to enforce collection, in the process racking up a heavy load of additional costs.[50] The court further might order arrest and imprisonment in either the provincial jail or the carcel de corte of the audiencia, exile, or forced service of some kind. For Spaniards, it might be service in the Philippines, or in a presidio; for an Indian, a term in an obraje, bakery, or some other workshop using forced labor. Finally, in the instance of Spanish grantees or employers, it might annul the grants and void the right to use Indian workers.

The major weakness in its armament showed up through the ecclesiastical fuero; for in dealing with clergy, it could only remit the case to the ecclesiastical superior with a letter of ruego y encargo. Yet, perhaps on the plea of an overriding concern for the Indians and alleging the matter to be administrative, the General Indian Court did entertain suit in 1640 against the Jesuits of San Luis Potosí over the lands claimed by San Miguel Mezquitepec, rendering verdict against the Society of Jesus.[51] Similarly, in another suit, in 1633, by Tixtla against the Jesuits for damages to crops, the court ordered immediate payment of damages.[52] In effect, in these as in similar cases, the court came close indeed to breaching the ecclesiastical fuero. It is tribute to the general good sense of the Society of Jesus that in the Mezquitepec case it arranged a compromise with the town, and in the Tixtla case, in which its agents were clearly in the wrong, paid the damages.

Our discussion thus far has dealt with the procedures and policies of the General Indian Court as changing little from its establishment in 1592 to its abolition under the Spanish Constitution of 1812 and Mexican independence. A careful reading of the cases summarized in Chapter V will make it clear that this view is essentially justified. By 1592, the nascent bureaucracy around the viceroy and audien-

50. Summarized as case no. 15 in Chapter V.
51. Summarized as case no. 4 in Chapter V.
52. Summarized as case no. 94 in Chapter V.

cia had had nearly 60 years of probing Indian needs and their relation to the royal government and the Spaniards. The staff of the court inherited these ideas and views. Nevertheless, no institution can exist for more than 200 years without some change. There were obviously the necessary adjustments to new royal legislation and to the evolution of Indian life in Mexico. The entire group of cases on fundo legal could have existence only when royal legislation created the concept, in the second half of the seventeenth century. Similarly, pleas by sujetos for autonomous or separate community existence could arise or hope for success only when the increase in Indian population provided sufficient numbers to justify separation or autonomy. Let us now look at the court in terms of change as well as continuity, and in terms of implementation of the declared royal policy on Indians.

Certain changes occurred in the roles of personnel within the functioning of the court, namely, the assessor and the crown attorneys. In the first years of the court under Luis de Velasco II, the assessor acted as legal adviser to the viceroy, who sat in audience and gave orders for the appropriate decrees in accordance with his advice. The next viceroy, Monterrey, already began to shift much of the burden of interview, decision, and preparation of decrees to his assessor. Thereafter the details of the shift are not clear. The division of work and authority may well have shifted back and forth according to the personal vigor, conscientiousness, and burden of the individual viceroy and the zest for responsibility of his assessor. In the middle decades of the seventeenth century, the assessors were given stamps of the viceregal rubrics for use at their discretion, but later and perhaps more vigorous viceroys more actively intervened in the court. By the later eighteenth century, the shift was nearly complete. By then the assessor presided over the audience, decided on the appropriate decrees, had them prepared, placed his rubric on them, and had them taken to the viceroy for the second and final rubric. The viceroy usually was not consulted in advance, and merely stamped papers brought to him by a private secretary. By the administration of Azanza (1798–1800), the practice was so customary that no one could put a date to its origin.[53]

The final step in this shift probably arose from a decision of the audiencia when it governed in the absence of a viceroy. Since one of its members, a man of extensive legal training and long judicial experience, functioned as legal assessor, it made little sense to have the full

53. Appointment of Dr. Diego de Barrientos de Ribera as assessor, Mexico City, May 5, 1641, and that of Juan Francisco Montemayor y Córdova de Cuenca, October 2, 1662, in AGN-I, 13:exp. 264 and 19:exp. 544 respectively; Azanza (San Cristóbal, April 29, 1800), 45–46, clause 15; and relación de mando of Marquina, Tacubaya, January 1, 1803, in Mexico (Viceroyalty), Instrucciones, 2:644–646.

audiencia or the senior judge review the decrees, even less so at a time when the audiencia was carrying an extra and heavy load. Hence by the second half of the eighteenth century the audiencia gobernadora designated the legal assessor as the delegate judge of the General Indian Court during its interim government.[54] The step was completed almost at the end of Spanish rule, perhaps by the administration of Branciforte (1794–1798), certainly by the administration of Iturrigaray (1803–1808), when the viceroy, recognizing that his role increasingly had become formal and nominal, designated the assessor his delegate for Indian affairs.[55] The viceroy then covered the functioning of the court with his name and the prestige of his office, but the court had become a virtually autonomous bureaucracy in which he intervened only in unusual instances or when its authority came into question.

Concomitant with the change in the role of the assessor came change in that of the crown attorneys. In the seventeenth century, they rendered opinion when called on as protectors of the Indians or when there was a crown interest somehow involved. By the eighteenth century, as the assessor took over most of the role of the viceroy in the day-to-day functioning of the court, the fiscales began to assume much of the former role of the assessor. The papers were submitted to them for evaluation of the complaint, pleas, and evidence, and at the close of their evaluations they made detailed recommendations on the action or decision the court should take. Except in unusual circumstances, the assessor then simply accepted the recommendation of the fiscal.[56] "*Como pide el Sr. Fiscal*" ("as the crown attorney asks") be-

54. The case (summarized as no. 157 in Chapter V) of Indians of Tlayacapan petitioning that they not be required to work for an hacienda and that there be no pulque concession in their town, Mexico City and Tlayacapan, January 21–June 17, 1779, in AGN-Civ, vol. 2175: exps. 17–18 (17 fols.) (LBSD, vol. 6), was heard by Diego Antonio Fernández de Madrid, "Juez del Juzgado General de Naturales por comisión de la Real Audiencia Gobernadora" (Judge of the General Indian Court by commission of the Royal Audiencia Gobernadora). Before the coming of Bernardo de Gálvez in June 1785, Beleña functioned for the audiencia gobernadora with similar title: preface to decree of Bernardo de Gálvez on General Indian Court, Mexico City, December 5, 1785, in Beleña, 2:199, no. 47.

55. The suit of the Indians of Tonatico, province of Zacualpan, over being forced to contribute personal services for rebuilding the royal houses, Mexico City and Zacualpan, April 23, 1789–March 21, 1798, in AGN-Civ, vol. 2292: exp. 1 (15 fols.) (LBSD, vol. 21), was heard in 1797–98 by Lic. Quijada as assessor and delegate of the viceroy. In the case of Francisco Xavier, governor of Teloloapan, vs. the subdelegado of Zacualpan, Mexico City and Zacualpan, 1800–June 15, 1803 (summarized as no. 65 in Chapter V), in AGN-Civ, vol. 2182: exp. 3 (76 fols.) (LBSD, vol. 7), Lic. Quijada continued to function as assessor and delegate of the viceroy.

56. The change is clear in the cases summarized in Chapter V.

came the formula. The change may well have come about because of the increasing burden on the assessor. Both changes meant improvement in orderly and efficient movement of papers in a system that increasingly came to reduce everything to paper.

The intent of the crown in the first half of the sixteenth century in setting up a special legal regime for Indians was that the "good usages and customs of the Indians shall be observed so long as they are not contrary to our Christian religion . . . ," and further, that Indian cases be decided as much as possible by oral rather than written testimony, quick determination of the facts, and summary decision. Even by the 1590s that intent no longer corresponded to the realities of New Spain,[57] but the General Indian Court did attempt to implement as much of it as was feasible.

The use of oral rather than written testimony became almost impossible from the start, since the court sat in one place but its cases came from all over the administrative territory of the Audiencia of Mexico. If the proceedings took place in the provinces, they had to be written down for remission to the viceregal palace; if they took place in the palace, they had to be reduced to writing at some stage, so that there might be some kind of record and a formal decree might issue. Since, furthermore, appeals were possible, and often probable, there had to be enough written record for the hearing in second instance to function properly. It is these needs which explain, in part at least, the drift in the court from relatively laconic decrees based on oral proceedings to much fuller decrees based on written pleas and proceedings. Adjustment to Indian needs took the form of reduction of the potential volume of paper and quicker, more nearly summary, procedural and final decisions. Other measures of simplification were discouragement of using the full number of witnesses allowed by Spanish legal procedure—although if the parties insisted upon their full quota, there was no way of refusing them; abbreviation of the procedures of transmission and notification; and attempting to restrict access to the court except through the salaried staff of Indian agents, who had less interest in prolonging disputes than did attorneys and other agents drawing their livelihood from fees and full costs.

Simplified, shortened pleading by a trained staff, and summary decision by officials experienced in Indian matters, were undoubtedly important in relatively rapid and fair decisions or compromises. A further, notable reduction of procedural burden was the way in which the General Indian Court carried out its paperwork. The initial petition or complaint was written on a single sheet of paper, or as few as possi-

57. See Chapters III and IV above.

ble, in direct, unlegal phrasing. Much of the time it was drawn up by an Indian agent, but sometimes by the complainant, sometimes by a friend. Upon the same sheet, the officials of the court entered their comments and the court decree, usually on the bottom half, reverse, or the margin. Very often the sheet was given a quarter turn, to set off the court decree from the complaint. The fiscal protector and the assessor entered their opinions in the margins, unless they required more space and had to add leaves.

That the intention was to spare the Indians expense is clear from the practice itself and from the regulations on the use of stamped paper. When the crown in December 1638 instituted the requirement that after January 1, 1640, all legal instruments be written on stamped paper bought from a royal concessionaire—the beginnings of a stamp tax that still endures in the Mexican Republic—Indians were held to use double sheets of the lowest cost, a quarter-real. All instruments not prepared on stamped paper were to lack legal validity and possibility of enforcement in court or administrative office. Nevertheless, ran the royal order,

> . . . even in such case, if paper without the royal stamps should be used [in Indian legal instruments], that lack shall not void the instrument, for our intention and will always has been, and is, to mitigate any load or burden upon them.[58]

To the end of the Spanish regime, petitions and proceedings often were on plain paper without any impairment of validity or refusal of the court to accept them.

Abbreviation of paperwork and procedure were also manifest in the transmission and serving of summonses and writs, for the petition with the viceregal order at the bottom or on the reverse side usually was returned to the Indian for delivery. He or any person who could read and write served it, and if necessary, prepared an affidavit to that effect. A copy of the order was entered in chronological, running form in the central registers kept by the judicial and administrative secretaries. The procedure was beautifully simple and inexpensive, but it did have drawbacks, for the Indians might lose the document and have to apply for a copy of the order;[59] or, as happened much more fre-

58. RLI, 8.23.18. The requirement was instituted in the Audiencia of Mexico in 1640–41: Fonseca and Urrutia, 3:32–36. An attempt in Guatemala in the early 1680s to insist that the Indians use stamped paper for suits, schedules of fees, and titles of governors instead of ordinary paper met with flat rejection by the crown, which ordered the terms of its cédula of 1638 to be observed: royal cédula to Jerónimo Chacón Abarca, oidor of the Audiencia of Guatemala, Madrid, March 14, 1686, answering a letter of July 28, 1683, in Konetzke, 2:775, no. 527.

59. Decree exempting the Indians of Tejupilco and Iztapa from furnishing work-

quently, they held it until they decided to serve it,[60] so that there might be a considerable period intervening between issuance of the decree and its service.

The nature of the paperwork and recording explains one phenomenon that has caught the attention of scholars, namely, that in the remains of the central registers as they have come down to us there are few instances in which the Indians lost their cases. That circumstance has given rise to the idea that Indians lost few of their cases before the General Indian Court[61]—an attractive idea but probably not true, even though we have no means of determining proportions of cases won and lost. The phenomenon is easily explained in that a decree would issue only on establishment of probable cause for investigation or judicial suit or in the event of further interlocutory or final decision. If the General Indian Court rejected the complaint as flimsy or unjustified, no decree would issue to be recorded in the central registers.

So drastic a simplification of preparation, transmission, and recording of legal papers carried with it very real danger of confusion and even chaos. That danger was apparent to the thoughtful scrutiny of Monterrey, who in his reglamento of May 6, 1598, for the General Indian Court established a series of controls. The interpreter had to prepare a list of what was turned over to him at each audience, for delivery to the viceroy at the next session. The procurador de indios was to distribute all papers to the appropriate secretaries, but with receipts, so that there would be a record; he was further to keep a list of all Indian cases on appeal to the audiencia, whether heard or not, and to keep a list of all appellate sentences in Indian cases, both for the viceroy's scrutiny on Wednesdays. The notary of the court was to keep a list of all movement of papers and orders at each viceregal audience, to be placed before the viceroy at the next audience. Furthermore, he was to keep a book recording all petitions and other papers presented to the viceroy, decision on them, or what happened to them, until the conclusion of each matter.[62]

These measures provided a considerable degree of control, especially if the viceroy or his assessor carefully reviewed each list at the appropriate times, but it was still possible, although much less so, for items to slip through chinks. One such slip-up, almost impossible to

men for the mines, Mexico City, October 24, 1618, in AGN-I, 7:exp. 315 (LBSF, 7:67–70), issued because the first order had been lost.

60. In the long case of Juan Tomás, Indian of Ixcatepec, province of Ixcateopan, vs. his parish priest, 1778–1786 (summarized as no. 83 in Chapter V), it took from August 17 to October 1, 1785, for the plaintiff to deliver an order issued in Mexico City: AGN-Crim, 3:exp. 15 (LBSD, vol. 16).

61. LBSF, 8:137 and 10:68–70.

62. AGN-I, 6, part 2:exp. 1004; also in AGI-M, leg. 24.

avoid under the system, occurred in 1630 when the Indians and the Spanish miners of San Luis de la Paz each obtained viceregal decrees favoring their interests, but in direct conflict.[63] Both were administrative decrees, one entered in the court register, the other in a formally administrative one. Another kind of chink resulted from the tactic on the part of Indians dissatisfied with the final decision, especially if the plaintiffs were communities, of waiting until memory of the case had been lost and then reviving the issue in a new suit. The tactic could be detected by search of the registers—but there was no easy access to their content, since they were kept in running, chronological order with no index beyond marginal notations. A search was not likely unless the other party protested on the ground of *cosa juzgada* (matter already judged) or produced its copy of the earlier judgment.[64]

The preservation of Indian custom and law in court procedures was really a lost cause by the time the General Indian Court came into being. From what has been discussed so far, and from the summaries of cases in Chapter V, it is clear that the procedures used in the court were essentially those of Spanish law and administrative practice, somewhat simplified to be sure, but with virtually no remnant of native custom or usage. It may be doubted that the question of the use of Indian procedure in any form even arose in the court. Further, the drift toward reliance on written documents obliterated whatever chance there may have been of respect for native forms, since all documents, except occasionally the first petition, were prepared by Spanish officials. Whatever the Indians said appeared in proper Spanish form and according to prevailing Spanish norms.

Neither was there any substantial preservation of Indian law. The court, like other Spanish tribunals in New Spain, respected inherited boundaries and customary relations to the extent that they had not become manifestly obsolete or been modified through conquest, Christianization, and Spanish appropriation, as in the distribution of temple holdings and lands set aside for the Triple Alliance in tributary towns or in the recasting of tributary relationships. The Spanish, moreover, had an interest in preserving Indian dress as modified by the missionaries, and until well into the eighteenth century restricted Indian access to European technology in the form of horses and firearms. For the rest, the decisions of the General Indian Court enforced

63. Decree of May 10, 1630, Mexico City, in AGN-I, 10, cuad. 1 : exp. 234.
64. See the comments of Mendoza in his relación de mando, as quoted in Chapter III. The tactic continues to be used in Mexico to this day, as I found when working in the archive of Coixtlahuaca. The papers of a suit over lands in dispute with the neighboring town of Suchixtlahuaca, together with the record of a compromise dividing the lands in 1813, lay forgotten in one of the legajos. The suit was revived in 1949–51, with Suchixtlahuaca claiming the rest of the land, and was settled by another acuerdo.

Spanish rules and ideas on ownership of land, inheritance, organization of towns and subordinate parts thereof, trade, labor, taxation, personal conduct, and crime.

But what it enforced was not the law of Castile in its entirety and as it was evolving in the Iberian Peninsula by the early eighteenth century as the law of united Spain. During the sixteenth century the crown tried to maintain the unity of law for Castile and America, even though that effort encountered serious difficulties. Early in the seventeenth century, recognizing that its American possessions had special needs that could not be met by legislation for the Peninsula, the crown decreed that only legislation passed through the Council of the Indies thenceforth should be valid for the New World. The decision, in effect, gave preference to a body of special decision and legislation for America which had had to be issued because of peculiarly New World conditions in such fields as mining, tributary arrangements, land grants, and labor. It also tacitly accepted differentiation in legislation for the various parts of America, a differentiation that already had been imposed by local circumstance.[65]

For the Audiencia of Mexico, the ruling law in the seventeenth and eighteenth centuries was a composite body of royal and local legislation. It was, of course, law in the sense of the Civil Law, that is, specific enactment by a competent authority. Judicial precedent and previous case decision determining appropriate custom, as in the Anglo-Saxon system, played no role, except to the minimal extent that there might be an attempt to determine what had been Indian custom. Each decision was based upon specific enactment or codified clause. If one was lacking, the crown by royal cédula, the audiencia by auto acordado, or the viceroy by ordinance of good government supplied the deficiency.

From Spain came the legislation of Castile as it existed in the late sixteenth century and had been incorporated in the *Nueva Recopilación . . . de Castilla* of 1567; royal legislation and orders for the Indies, as they were published by Vasco de Puga in the 1560s and codified by Encinas in the early 1590s; later royal orders not codified until the *Recopilación* of 1680; and royal orders issued after 1680. Much of the material had to be consulted in manuscript registers or local compilations or might be summarized in local printed compilations. Local legislation consisted of autos acordados of the audiencia and ordinances issued by the audiencia and viceroy in various forms. They might be found in the compilations of Montemayor y Córdova de Cuenca (1678) and Beleña (1787), or in manuscript compilations

65. García Gallo, "La ley," 607 and 614–618; Baade, "The Formalities," 666–669; RLI, 2.1.39–40.

which were kept up to date on laws issued since the last printed compilations. For the General Indian Court, the most important groups of legislation were the royal and viceregal regulations on land grants; rights of Indian villages to wood, water, and fundo legal; allocation of labor; enforcement of debt, especially through service; and criminal punishments, including forced service in obrajes, bakeries, and other such establishments. What it enforced was essentially royal legislation for Mexico and local ordinances, very often issued with prior or subsequent royal approval—in effect, a body of Mexican law. For the matters that came before the court, the law was relatively simple; what caused prolonged controversy was more often questions of fact.

Within this body of Mexican law, it should be emphasized, the Indians remained a separate group, distinguished by payment of tribute and the medio real de ministros; right to the services of Indian agents and the General Indian Court; and exemption from a number of other taxes. The place of Indians in colonial Mexican society may be seen in the preference, even in the General Indian Court, for Spanish as against Indian testimony, and the fact that Indians were not held to post bond for calumny nor were they prosecuted for perjury. It was taken for granted that they were so likely to lie that prosecution would touch too many. This attitude is further manifest in the fact that moderate correction, even to four to six blows with a whip on the bare rump, was regarded as proper and not worth notice.[66]

A similar attitude prevailed in regard to the non-Indian poor and wretched, who had special legal agents and were entitled, at least in theory, to particular consideration within Spanish courts. The elements held to characterize natives, such as proneness to lying, general untrustworthiness, gullibility, drunkenness, laziness, filth, etc., were thought to be equally characteristic of the non-Indian poor. They have been charged against the lower orders in most societies for centuries, or even millennia, without regard to race. The convergence indicates that with the passage of time, and the formation of a large body of non-Indian poor, the two groups were moving to form a common lowest order, a process not yet complete by the end of Spanish rule.

66. See case summary no. 129 in Chapter V.

CHAPTER VII

The Indian Agents of the Half-Real, Their Rivals, and Their Clients

WITHIN the growing governmental bureaucracy of New Spain, the Indian agents of the medio real formed a group set apart. Limited in access to fees, the major source of revenue for most officials, and even forbidden them, they drew salaries from a special fund collected and administered by the viceregal government—but that fund was a royal trust, not a royal revenue. In their relations with other members of the notarial and legal professions and practitioners with less formal license, they tried to assert an even more monopolistic claim than their brethren licensed to practice before the Audiencia of Mexico; for the Indian agents attempted, although unsuccessfully, to require exclusive use of their services by Indians seeking redress in Mexico City, whatever the tribunal. Their relations with their clients, presumably paternal and protective, embodied a tension—at times low, at times high—as on the one hand the clients turned out to run the gamut from innocent, illiterate victims clearly worthy of redress to surprisingly sophisticated manipulators of Spanish governmental organs; and on the other hand, the Indian agents at times fulfilled their functions punctually and honorably, and at times tried to improve their revenues by improper practice and illegal charges. The more than 220 years of the court's existence provided opportunity for human behavior in a wide variety of forms. Let us examine the Indian agents, their rivals in legal practice, and their clients, in that order.

Table 7.1 shows the organization of the Indian agents at various times from the late sixteenth to the late eighteenth centuries. Since it is

based mostly upon reports of expenditures in specific years, it is a series of soundings rather than a complete history of changes and development. Nevertheless, much of that history can be reconstructed. The
totals of the table represent the sum of charges upon the medio real.
Its revenue was supposed to cover the charges, but might come to surplus or deficit, according to the number of tributary Indians and the
efficiency of collection. Its yield, moreover, was subject to charges for
collection and some extraordinary disbursements which do not appear
in the table.[1]

As the table indicates clearly, the initial appointments by Viceroy
Velasco II were cautious and experimental. Velasco's plea for compensation from the medio real for the porteros, based upon their undoubted services in handling the flow of Indian petitioners, went un-
heeded until the second half of the eighteenth century. Instead, they
were assigned salaries from penas de cámara, the crown's share of
court costs and fines.[2] Velasco's provision for legal services in Indian
criminal cases before either the alcaldes del crimen or the viceroy himself for offenses committed within the audiencia's jurisdiction in first
instance—that is, within five leagues of Mexico City—was a small additional payment to the staff already provided for cases of the poor,
and a further payment to the notary of the General Indian Court for
assuming this additional function. The arrangement was makeshift
and inadequate, but inexpensive. All of Velasco's appointments set
modest salaries whose total was least likely to upset a bankrupt monarch while the viceroy, hunting for a means of funding, began collection of the medio real. All salaries were additional payments for an
added function; they did not aim at furnishing the complete revenue
of any official, nor were the functions envisioned as taking any official's full time. In short, to use present-day Mexican terms, rather than
puestos de tiempo completo and even *de dedicación exclusiva*, they
were a series of *chambas*.

Revision of Velasco's table of organization into the form it was
to maintain with few changes throughout the seventeenth century and
well into the eighteenth came in the administrations of Monterrey,
Montesclaros, and Guadalcázar. By then, the system of salaried Indian
agents had operated long enough for the viceroys to perceive adjustments needed for greater efficiency. Perhaps the greatest impulse for
revision came from the audiencia secretaries and legal staff, as the true
yield of the medio real became clear and they understood that if they
could not collect fees and costs, they could at least achieve far better

1. For this, see Chapter VIII.
2. See Chapter IV above and the discussion later in this chapter.

TABLE 7.1 Salaries Paid from the Medio Real de Ministros

Title	Velasco II	To 1642	1643	1703	1738	1759	1768	1788
Asesor[a]	1,654/3/3	1,654/3/3	942/5/11	994/	994/	994/	994/	994/
Protector de indios					128/	128/	128/	300/
Agente fiscal de indios					448/	447/7	447/7	
Chancillor de la audiencia	135/	135/	76/7/5	139/4	139/	139/	139/	139/
Registrador de provisiones	120/	120/	68/3					
Escribano mayor de gobernación	1,000/	3,308/6/6	1,885/4	1,712/	1,712/	1,712/	1,712/	1,500/
Escribano mayor de gobernación	1,000/	3,308/6/6	1,885/4	1,712/	1,712/	1,712/	1,712/	1,500/
Escribano mayor de cámara	650/	1,985/2/4	1,131/2/4	1,160/	1,160/	1,160/	1,160/	1,000/
Escribano mayor de cámara	650/	1,985/2/4	1,131/2/4	1,160/	1,160/	1,160/	1,160/	1,000/
Escribano de la sala del crimen	1,100/	1,100/	626/6/6	536/	1,160/	1,160/	1,160/	1,060/
Escribano de la sala del crimen	1,100/	1,100/	626/6/6	536/	1,160/	1,160/	580/[b]	500/[b]
Relator de lo civil		350/	199/3/6	150/	250/	250/	250/	250/
Relator de lo civil		250/	142/3/8	150/	250/	250/	250/	250/
Relator de lo civil		250/	142/3/8	150/	250/	250/	250/	250/
Relator de lo civil		250/	142/3/8	150/		250/	250/	250/
Relator de lo criminal					250/	250/	250/	250/

Relator de lo criminal	200/				250/	250/	250/	250/
Relator del juzgado general de indios	400/} 100/}[c]			234/	78/4	234/7/6	234/7/6	400/
Escribano del juzgado general de indios		400/	237/7/5	365/3/6	400/	400/	400/	(400/)[i]
Abogado de indios de lo civil	700/	784/3	446/7/8	447/7	448/	447/7	447/7	447/7
Abogado de indios de lo civil		584/3	332/7/9	311/	448/	447/7	447/7	447/7
Abogado de indios de lo criminal	100/	206/2	117/4/2	311/	448/	447/7	447/7	216/
Abogado de indios de lo criminal								216/
Procurador de indios de lo criminal	200/	125/	71/1/10		178/	178/	178/	178/
Procurador de indios	400/	337/4	192/2/6	178/				
Procurador de indios	400/	337/4	192/2/6	178/				
Solicitador de indios	300/	100/	56/7/10	58/	58/	100/	100/	200/
Solicitador de indios		100/	56/7/10	58/	58/[e]	100/	100/	200/
Interprete de indios	300/	300/	170/7/7	164/6 200/	?[f]	364/2	364/2	364/2
Interprete de la audiencia								
Interprete de la sala del crimen					100/			

Table 7.1 (*continued*)

Title	Velasco II	To 1642	1643	1703	1738	1759	1768	1788
Alguacil/ministro ejecutivo	250/	250/	242/3/8	120/1	129/3	129/	129/3	129/3
Porteros of audiencia and sala del crimen (6)								1,800/
Archivero de la secretaría del virreinato								800/
Portero de la secretaría del virreinato								300/
Procurador de pobres					178/[g]	178/[g]		
Propinas de ministros					500/			
Administrador del medio real/ tesorero/ receptor	300/	496/2/8	496/2/8	500/[d]				
Contador general de tributos						616/	750/	600/
Oficial mayor of medio real					600/	900/	900/	800/[k]
Asesor de la contaduría de tributos					500/	500/	100/	100/
Oficial segundo de la real caja					400/	400/	400/	400/

Glosador (auditor) oficial del libro y cuenta						400/	400/	100/
Gasto de escritorio (paper and ink)					31/2	31/2	31/2	31/2
Adjustment (nature not stated)							86/5/10	
Totals	11,059/3/3	19,818/7/7	11,516/7/11	11,675/5/6	15,978/1	16,047/7/6[h]	16,194/2/2[i]	16,823/5[i]

[a] Equivalent to 1,000/ oro de minas (450 maravedís to peso, instead of 272). The raise of 400/ oro de minas reported as given in 1616 by Díez de la Calle (part 7, chap. 2; 126–127) either did not continue or never happened.

[b] Title reduced to Teniente Escribano (deputy notary), and salary to half.

[c] Additional payment for work on Indian criminal cases.

[d] Report of charges on medio real, 1703 (AGI-M, leg. 474) gives amount as 500/. The royal cédula ordering abolition (Madrid, April 28, 1702, in AGN-RC, 31: fols. 39f–40v (BLT)) states 600/. The office was suppressed in 1703, and administration turned over to the Contador General de Tributos. By royal cédula of December 19, 1703, Madrid (AGN-RC, 31: fol. 469f–v (BLT)), the crown approved the action.

[e] Salary given at annual rate of 29/, probably because of special circumstance; undoubtedly regular rate was 58/.

[f] No salary indicated for the interpreter of the court, but such an official was indispensable. The salary for the interpreter of the sala del crimen was far too low for a joining of the functions.

[g] Since there is no payment for a second procurador de indios, and the procurador de pobres was paid the same salary, one suspects a joint function funded from the medio real de ministros. The charge was transferred to a new tax on pulque entering Mexico City.

[h] This is the total of salaries and charges reported by Amarillas, Mexico City, April 2, 1759. He states the annual charges as 16,748/2/6. The difference is probably 400/ paid for audit but not listed here, and a fee based on the number of tributaries in assessments paid to the Oficial mayor de Contaduría de Real Hacienda y Caja.

[i] Total of royal accountants. The true total is 16,204/2/3.

[j] The salary of the notary (400/), not listed in Fonseca and Urrutia, was probably omitted inadvertently; I add it.

[k] Post continued until 1787 when holder died. The contador-general de tributos then suggested distributing the stipend among the other officials of his staff who had taken over the duties. In February 1791 the proposal was still under consideration.

Sources: Velasco II to Philip II, Mexico City, March 2, March 25, May 20, and June 15, 1592, and October 4, 1593, in VC, fols. 116r–117v, 117v–118r, 120r–v, 130r–v, and 143v; Díez de la Calle, 126–127; statement of salaries from medio real, ca. 1654, copy of report on medio real and salaries paid from it, 1703, papers in suit of oficiales mayores of the Contaduría de Real Hacienda, 1714–1755, report of Viceroy Amarillas to the king on the medio real de ministros, Mexico City, April 2, 1759, and consultas of the Council of the Indies on the report, September 9, 1763, and December 20, 1764; all in AGI-M, legs. 469, 474, 798, 520, 1124, and 1324, respectively; Razón de lo librado . . . del medio real de ministros, 1768, in AGN-Tr, 2: exp. 2; and Fonseca and Urrutia, I: 551.

compensation. In a series of suits and petitions, the audiencia and its officials pressed their case, securing provisional arrangements finally ratified by royal cédula in 1621.[3] The *escribanos mayores de gobernación* and *de cámara*, i.e., the secretaries for administrative matters and civil suits, increased their salaries from the medio real more than threefold. Salaries of their counterparts in the sala del crimen were judged adequate and left unchanged; they had been set relatively generously from the start. The 4 relatores for civil cases had their function recognized through award of salaries. The abogado for Indian civil cases received a modest increase and was given a colleague at lesser salary. The staff for criminal cases in first instance was revised much more drastically, as the abogado received a more-than-doubled salary and the procurador's compensation was cut substantially, from 200/ to 125/. Unfortunately, we have no way of knowing whether these changes meant new officials for Indian matters or better payment to the staff provided for the poor, for assuming the additional load. In view of the continuing intertwining of the handling of cases for Indians and the poor in this judicial division, it is perhaps more probable that the payments augmented the stipends of the staff for the poor.

Those who fared worst in the readjustment were the staff most directly affiliated with the viceregal audience, for the court notary lost his additional payment for handling documents in criminal cases arising in the audiencia's jurisdiction in first instance; the 2 procuradores de indios suffered a reduction of approximately 12.5%; and the 1 solicitador de indios, at an annual compensation of 300/, became 2 at 100/ each. This last change involved a division of case load as well as reduction in pay. Of the lower officials directly attached to the viceregal audience, only the interpreter and alguacil came through the revisions without change. So did the assessor, though not for want of trying; but an attempt by Guadalcázar in 1616 to raise his salary by 400 pesos de minas failed, probably through rejection by the crown.[4] A final change in the roll was a raise to 496/2/8 for the new administrator or treasurer of the medio real, from the 300/ set by Velasco. In accordance with the custom of the time, the charge was laid to the revenue rather than paid from some other source. Through the changes, the total charge upon the medio real, which had been 11,059/3/3 in Velasco's table of organization, rose to 19,818/7/7.

At the time the changes were made, the revenue was easily able to defray the charges;[5] but as the Indian population continued to de-

3. Díez de la Calle, 122 (cap. 2, part 5); see also the copy of the report on the medio real and the salaries paid from it, 1703, in AGI-M, leg. 474.

4. Díez de la Calle, 126–127 (cap. 2, part 7).

5. Royal cédulas to Montesclaros and the Audiencia of Mexico, Valladolid, July 1, 1603, AGN-RCD, 4:exps. 28 and 41.

cline, the medio real, which was directly geared to tribute counts, decreased upon each recount of a town, establishing the official number liable to tribute.[6] By the 1620s and 1630s, the drop in yield through recounts and through arrears in payments by towns no longer able to meet a too-high official schedule must have brought the total of the medio real well below the charges upon it. By the 1640s, the annual amount due under prevailing assessments, if all were paid and there were no expenses of collection, would have brought into the fund something under 13,000/. Not all amounts due were paid on time or sometimes paid at all, so that the true yield could not have been more than between 11,000/ and 12,000/.[7] In the general inspection of Palafox y Mendoza in the 1640s—one of the main purposes of which was to reorganize the finances of the colony so that local costs might be reduced and more revenue made available for transmission to Spain—the fund of the medio real and the charges upon it underwent careful scrutiny. The two were brought into balance by a drastic downward revision of salaries by about 44%, from which only the administrator of the fund escaped unscathed. The total of the revised list came to 11,516/7/8 a year.

Our next information in Table 7.1 is for the year 1703. The list for that year indicates that the table of organization of the time of Guadalcázar, as revised by Palafox, endured with only slight change. Some salaries, to be sure, were raised by small percentages; some were lowered. The other changes in the list at some time during these 60 years were that the *registrador de provisiones* (the official recorder of audiencia writs) was dropped, never to be returned to the list; a relator for the General Indian Court, an office instituted by Velasco II but dropped by his successors, was restored to the list; one procurador for Indian criminal cases was dropped; and the interpreter of the audiencia received a salary of 200/, a perquisite shortly thereafter removed. In 1703, by royal order, the office of administrator of the fund, by then with title of treasurer, was abolished, and the administration of the fund turned over to the royal Contaduría de Tributos, the treasury staff handling all Indian tributes.[8] As the entries for subsequent years in the table indicate, the change did not bring economy, but rather greater expense, even to a new charge for the paper and ink used in keeping the accounts.

6. See Cook and Borah, *Essays*, 3:1–128.
7. Ibid., esp. 95–102 and 118–124.
8. By royal cédula of April 28, 1702, Madrid, which reached Mexico City in January 1703: copy of the report on the medio real and the salaries paid from it, 1703, in AGI-M, leg. 474. See also the royal cédula to Viceroy Alburquerque approving his suppression of the office of treasurer of the medio real, Madrid, December 19, 1703, in AGN-RC, 21:fol. 469f–v (BLT).

Our later benchmarks of 1738, 1759, 1768, and 1788 in the table record the changes of the Bourbon era. In general, they involved some expansion of the number of Indian agents as the increasing number of Indians brought a steady increase in the business the agents had to handle. The protector of the Indians, i.e., the crown attorney for civil affairs, received a small stipend for the enlarging official role he played in court proceedings. His delegate, who really did much or most of the work, received a larger stipend, which was abolished at some time after 1768 in favor of raising the protector's stipend to 300/, still a nominal sum for the service. He may have compensated his delegate in a private arrangement. At some time after 1759, one of the 2 secretaries of the sala de crimen was reduced to the rank of assistant secretary (*teniente escribano*) and his salary to 580/, and then 500/, a year. The relatores fared well under the Bourbons. In 1738, one in the civil division of the audiencia does not appear on the list, but that was more probably through death or some other reason for vacancy, for the office reappears thereafter. The group was raised to 250/ a year each, and strengthened by the addition of 2 relatores for criminal matters. The relator of the General Indian Court appears in the 1738 list at a salary of 73/4, but that amount reflects payment for only part of the year, as subsequent entries show. Between 1768 and 1788, the office of abogado for criminal matters was divided into 2 appointments at slightly less than half-salary each.

A notable change in salaries, but not in function, concerned the solicitadores and the court interpreter. For virtually full-time employees, as the solicitadores were, a stipend of 58/ a year constituted respectable poverty. By 1759 the salary was raised to 100/, and in the Beleña reform of 1784–86, as evidence showed clearly that even 100/ was inadequate compensation, the salary was raised with royal approval to 200/. In the adjustment between 1738 and 1759, the interpreter's salary rose to 364/2, there to remain for the rest of the colonial period.

Another notable change arose through the plight of the porteros of the various chambers of the audiencia. The arrangement forced upon Velasco II and his successors worked so long as the fund derived from court costs and fines had enough to defray the salaries. In 1765, the yield had sunk so low that the porteros went without salary; the total that entered the fund that year was 8/2/8, and the following year nothing.[9] On the other hand, the medio real de ministros by then yielded a steadily rising amount with substantial surplus, upwards of 20,000/ a year, as against charges of little more than 16,000/. With the

9. Fonseca and Urrutia, 1:546–547 and 3:487–488 and 519–520.

well-founded plea that they rendered services to Indian litigants and petitioners, the porteros appealed to the audiencia and viceroy, who in turn referred the petition to the king, since by royal cédula of December 20, 1763, any additional charge upon the fund of the medio real required express royal approval. Discussion of the matter in Spain took nearly eight years, until 1773. The Council of the Indies and its crown attorney were agreed that the porteros should be paid, but held that the medio real was not the proper source for the funds. Their solution was to order payment from a surplus in the Mexico City sala del crimen from the sale of convicted criminals to obrajes. The king agreeing, the appropriate royal cédula went to the viceroy in Mexico. Since that solution did not solve the problem, the Council of the Indies and the monarch reluctantly returned to the original suggestion in the petition. A royal cédula of November 10, 1773, approved payment of salary of 300/ a year to each of the 6 porteros of the audiencia, with the exception of the last to be appointed, who received 8/ less.

Rather than increase the charges upon the medio real, the king decreed that the sum be made up by reducing the secretaries of gobernación 212/, those of cámara 160/, and of the sala del crimen 160/ each; the Contador General de Tributos 150/, and his assessor 400/. Another 178/ was to be gained by removing the procurador for the poor, who had been placed upon the list at some time before 1738, the ground for removal being that his salary was not a fair charge upon the Indians. The reductions came to 1,792/; the lacking 8/ was made up at the cost of the most junior appointment.[10] Actually, since the second secretary of the sala del crimen held junior rank and received only 580/, the royal command had to be adjusted. The teniente escribano lost only 80/ in salary, and the difference plus the lacking 8/ came from further charge upon the medio real. The changes appear in the table in the 1788 column.

Removal of the procurador for the poor broke the long arrangement made by Velasco II for the handling of Indian criminal cases arising within audiencia jurisdiction in first instance, but it led to further anomaly. In 1777, by royal order, an elaborate system of legal aides for the poor replaced the older, much less amply staffed one. It raised the necessary funds from a tax of one half-grano on each arroba of pulque entering Mexico City. The procurador, with a salary of 178/ a year, became 4 abogados with annual salaries of 600/ each. The same arrangement provided for 2 abogados for the assistance of Indians in

10. Ibid.; consultas of Council of the Indies and annexed documents, September 26, 1763, and December 20, 1764, in AGI-M, legs. 1324 and 1124 respectively. A request of the porteros in their petition for a rise in salary to 600/ a year met with flat refusal.

civil cases arising in audiencia jurisdiction in first instance. They were paid 450/ each annually from the tax on pulque.[11] The royal order thus created Indian agents not paid from the medio real. Accordingly, they do not appear in the table.

Other changes of the later Bourbon period added the portero of the viceregal audience to the list at the same salary as other porters and the archivist of the new state-paid viceregal secretariat. The administration of the medio real placed more officials upon the roll, reaching a climax in our listing for 1768, with substantial reduction thereafter. There were furthermore heavy losses, commissions for collection and administration, and loans for state purposes, all of which will be dealt with in Chapter VIII.

One last item worth notice is the charge for *propinas* in the 1738 column. This was a bonus of 500/ distributed among the Indian agents annually, in what proportions we do not know. The practice began in 1722, when Viceroy Valero ordered a distribution of 500/ from the fund of the medio real to the Indian agents, on the occasion of the marriage of the Prince of Asturias, heir to the throne, and continued as an annual custom until 1747, when a new viceroy, Revillagigedo I, suppressed it as an abuse.[12]

The listing for 1788 gives the Indian agents in the form they were to keep until the end of the colonial period and the abolition of the system. Aside from the changes in amounts of salary and the varying listings for payment for administration of the fund, the table indicates a surprisingly stable organization from the early seventeenth century to the first decades of the eighteenth. The changes thereafter mostly concerned the officials handling Indian criminal cases from the parcialidades, those charged with collection and administration of the medio real—not really Indian agents—the porteros, and the viceregal secretariat, which came into being as a state-funded entity in the second half of the eighteenth century.

Appointment to all stipends throughout the entire period of existence of the system fell into two categories: those attached automatically to another office and those named directly, presumably in the viceroy's fee. Another method of classification would be to divide the posts into those which were put up at public auction, although sold only to persons meeting the necessary professional qualifications, and

11. Beleña, 1, part 4:64, advertencia.
12. Report of Viceroy Amarillas to the king on the medio real de minstros, as ordered by royal cédula of April 28, 1758, Mexico City, April 2, 1759, in AGI-M, leg. 520.

those to which appointment was made without purchase. Let us examine the posts in terms of the first method of classification.

A substantial number of salaries were paid to officials for handling Indian matters with reduced or no fee, but their appointments and most of their duties fell outside the scope of the system of Indian agents. Of this nature were the chancellor of the audiencia, who had responsibility for issuing formal decrees under royal seal; the registrar of writs, during the time this office was on the roll; the 6 escribanos mayores of gobernación, cámara, and the sala del crimen; the 6 relatores; the fiscal protector and his deputy; and the officials of the Real Contaduría de Tributos. Equally, the porteros of the audiencia and the sala del crimen were appointed by vote of those bodies, even after their entire salary came from the medio real. The remaining functions were discharged by appointees of the viceroy. Lesser posts, such as interpreter or solicitador, and even abogado and procurador, probably were filled upon the recommendation of the assessor, who in turn may have been influenced by the advice or urgings of members of the staff.

The key appointment for any viceroy undoubtedly was his assessor, for under an able, judicious legal adviser the court and staff could function with little direct intervention by the viceroy, whereas an inept or injudicious man could either wreak havoc or force the viceroy to assume a much larger and time-consuming role. A further problem lay in the need to avoid or minimize friction with the audiencia and the sala del crimen, a possible source of serious dissension best avoided by naming a junior or senior judge (i.e., an oidor or alcalde del crimen) as assessor. Velasco II and Monterrey both appointed judges to the post, and a royal order ratifying the arrangement directed that all future appointments be of the same nature; but the next viceroy, Montesclaros, found grave inconvenience in the arrangement—for, as he reported to the king, the hearing of Indian matters required the full time of the assessor, yet the hours of the audience coincided with those of the audiencia and its sala del crimen. A judge could not handle both functions without skimping one or the other or both. After some discussion, the decision in Madrid was that the viceroy might name anyone he wished to the post, despite the earlier order, the only caution being that the salary be kept as low as possible.[13] This decision came to Mexico in the form of two royal cédulas, one signed at Valladolid, April 19, 1605, and the other at El Escorial, October 5, 1606, directing that the assessor not be a judge but instead a letrado. In 1621, Philip IV reinforced the earlier cédulas with a new one that for-

13. Montesclaros to the king, Mexico City, October 25, 1605, and marginal comments of the Council of the Indies and the king, ibid., leg. 26.

bade any viceroy to use an oidor as assessor or to ask for an opinion from one.[14]

From the receipt of the cédulas of 1605 and 1606, the assessor for some years was an abogado; but the advantages in relations with the audiencia of having one of its judges fill the post led viceroys to ignore or somehow circumvent the royal prohibition. At his death in 1641, Dr. Luis de las Infantas y Mendoza, an oidor, was serving as assessor of the court. He was replaced by Dr. Diego Barrientos de Ribera, an abogado.[15] How the appointment of Infantas y Mendoza was explained to Madrid is an interesting question, at this point without answer. In 1653 the incoming viceroy, the Duque de Albuquerque, named to the post Dr. Manuel de Sotomayor y Pantoja, then an alcalde del crimen;[16] and in 1654, when Sotomayor could not serve because of absence from Mexico City, Albuquerque replaced him with Juan de Valcárcel Soto, another alcalde del crimen.[17] In 1660 the next viceroy, the Marqués de Leyva, appointed Francisco Calderón Romero, an oidor, and so reported to Philip IV in a letter of November 28, 1660. The reply, dated March 26, 1662, ordered that the rule enacted in 1605 and 1606 be observed and a new assessor, who could not be a senior or junior judge of the audiencia, be named. Nevertheless, the next viceroy, the Marqués de Mancera, upon taking office found Dr. Juan Francisco de Montemayor y Córdova de Cuenca, an oidor, serving as assessor. As Mancera reported to Madrid, although he realized the inconvenience of detaching judges from their many duties, he left Dr. Montemayor in the post, since the appointment was one made by his predecessor. He asked the queen-regent, then governing during the minority of Carlos II, to decide what to do.[18] The royal decision apparently was to rescind the cédulas of 1605, 1606, and 1621 either directly or tacitly, for thereafter the assessor of the General Indian Court was always either an oidor or an alcalde del crimen. Harmony of relations with the audiencia—as in the then-evolving post of juez conservador of the Marquesado del Valle, a post also filled

14. Mancera to the queen-regent, Mexico City, December 19, 1666, ibid., leg. 41.

15. Appointment of Barrientos de Ribera as replacement for Infantas y Mendoza, Mexico City, May 20, 1641, in AGN-I, 13:exp. 264; Schäfer, 2:475.

16. Alburquerque to the king, Mexico City, November 14, 1653, in DIE, 104: 394–395; Schäfer, 2:457.

17. Order of appointment, Mexico City, October 22, 1654, in AGN-I, 17:exp. 250; Schäfer, 2:456 and 461.

18. Mancera to the queen-regent, Mexico City, December 19, 1666, in AGI-M, leg. 41; Schäfer, 2:456, 466, and 493; appointment of Montemayor y Córdova de Cuenca as assessor, Mexico City, October 2, 1662, in AGN-I, 19:exp. 544.

by an oidor[19]—apparently was worth the inconvenience of having a judge who was not able to function within the audiencia a good deal of his time. For the audiencia, there were the twin advantages of having one of their own number administer a competing jurisdiction and secure an additional salary.

Our second method of classification—namely, purchase of office or appointment without it—gives a somewhat different distribution of posts. Between 1559 and 1581, all notarial offices became subject to public auction and sale at the most favorable price to an otherwise qualified person. So the posts of the 6 escribanos mayores de gobernación, cámara, and the sala del crimen, and that of the notary of the General Indian Court, were subject at the outset to sale, and carried with purchase the right to resign in favor of a designated successor at a price.[20] The power of the viceroy to choose the notary was thus illusory, for he could only appoint the highest qualified bidder. In one sale on June 20, 1644, after public bidding, the post brought 3,100/.[21] The offices of the escribanos mayores were worth much higher prices. In 1615, two of those of the sala del crimen brought 18,000/ and 20,000/ respectively. The posts of escribanos mayores de cámara for the civil division brought higher prices:

1615	30,000/	(two sales each)
1617	63,000/	
1622	65,000/	
1627	42,500/	(two sales each)
1645	44,000/	

The highest price for any post in the first half of the seventeenth century came in 1644 for the post of escribano mayor de gobernación: 67,000/.[22] These values give some idea of the probable yield of the posts from fees and charges for costs, and explain the holders' anger at the limitation of fees for Indian documents. They also explain much of the drive for more generous compensation in the early years of the court. Unfortunately, we do not have data on the value of these offices in later years.

Of the non-notarial posts, very few were subject to sale. The chancellorship of the audiencia was subject to sale as long as it remained an independent post. In 1620 it brought 6,400/ to the crown at auction. However, in 1623 all chancellorships for the American au-

19. García Martínez, 102–110 and 122–123.
20. Parry, *The Sale of Public Office*, 6–20.
21. Díez de la Calle, 122 (cap. 2, part 5).
22. Ibid., 120–121.

diencias were merged into that of the Grand Chancellor of the Indies, which Philip IV granted to his favorite, the Conde-Duque de Olivares. The grand chancellor's functions in the colony were discharged by deputies appointed by Olivares.[23] At a later time, the chancellorships of the audiencias again became independent appointments. Similarly, the posts of procurador in the Audiencia of Mexico also became subject to sale, even before a royal cédula of 1622 declared them subject to purchase. In the first half of the seventeenth century, they brought the crown:

1615	2,000/	for one	
1626	3,000/	"	"
1639	2,727/	"	"
1643	2,400/	"	"

The system affected the 12 procuradores licensed to practice before the Audiencia of Mexico.[24] The procuradores appointed as Indian agents may have been of their number, or may have been yet other qualified people. There is no evidence of purchase of their appointments as Indian agents. The remaining posts were either regarded as judicial at audiencia level and hence not subject to purchase,[25] or as too small for sale.

On the whole, the sale of offices affected the operations of the Indian agents within and without the General Indian Court only insofar as it governed selection of the recording secretaries and the notary and may have made them more determined to recover their investment with full return. Accordingly, they might be led to slight Indian business in favor of better-paying non-Indian parties, or as much as possible to assign the handling of Indian matters to deputies.

Appointment secured, whatever the exact means, each Indian agent went through a formal procedure before he officially took office and could begin to earn salary from the medio real. For the recording secretaries, the chancellor of the audiencia, and the court notary, the formalities were longer and attested in the documents ratifying accession to office and appointment. For lesser officials among the Indian agents, the procedure was less lengthy and less wrapped in ceremony, but equally formal. First, a document of appointment was issued over

23. Ibid.
24. Ibid.
25. In the 1670s, governorships of provinces began to be sold. As far as is known, only one post of oidor of an audiencia was given for money: in the Audiencia of Mexico in 1695, to Lic. José de Luna y Arias for 16,000/, offered as a gift to the royal treasury: Parry, *The Sale of Public Office*, 54–58; Schäfer, 2:191 and 458. In 1707, Luna y Arias became assessor of the General Indian Court: appointment, January 12, 1707, Mexico City, in AGN-I, 36:fols. 358v–360v.

viceregal signature. Many such appointments are preserved in the Indios section in the Mexican national archive.[26] Second, the document
of appointment had to be taken to the royal officials charged with collecting *media anata*—that is, a tax of one-half of a year's salary and
one-third of estimated emoluments and profits, payable half upon receiving the document of appointment and half at the beginning of the
second year in the post. This tax was instituted in 1631.[27]

During the middle years of the seventeenth century, the Indian
agents regularly paid the media anata, as notations on the copies of
documents of appointment certify.[28] At some time in the later seventeenth century, the Indian agents won a ruling that since the medio
real was not a royal revenue, no tax was due. Nevertheless, the officials
of the media anata continued to record the appointments, certifying
that no tax was due, both on the original documents and on the entry
in the viceregal register.[29] So transfer of the porteros to the medio real
not only assured them of regular delivery of their salaries, but also
freed them from payment of the media anata. The ruling saved the Indian agents from yet another difficulty, for in 1787 the crown ordered
that no royal employee in America might receive two royal salaries
without express royal license, even if for different posts, both fully discharged.[30] Since the medio real was not a royal revenue, the Indian
agents were free from this new restriction.

The third step in entering upon office was to take the oath of office. We are fortunate in having the affidavit of the oath taken by a
solicitador in 1782. Appearing in the audiencia chambers before a
deputy secretary of cámara, acting for the presiding officer of the audiencia, he swore "to discharge well and faithfully the said post, in

26. Several appointments of assessor have been cited in previous footnotes to
this chapter. Scattered throughout AGN-I are also those for interpreter, alguacil or ministro ejecutor, solicitador, procurador, and abogado.

27. A careful historical discussion of the tax will be found in Fonseca and Urrutia, 2:487–533.

28. For example, appointment of Montemayor y Córdova de Cuenca as assessor, Mexico City, October 2, 1662; of Dr. Fernando Guerrero as abogado for criminal
cases, Mexico City, November 8, 1663; of Juan Domingo as alguacil, Mexico City, October 19, 1663; of Lic. José de Cabrera as abogado, Mexico City, July 1, 1661; and of
José de Ribas as alguacil, Mexico City, November 1, 1664: all in AGN-I, 19:exps. 544,
657, and 683 bis, and 24:exps. 2 and 67, respectively.

29. Appointment as solicitador of Gregorio de Cárdenas, Mexico City, September 16, 1681, with the certification, October 8, 1681, that he owes nothing old or new
for media anata; and of Manuel María de Arellano, Mexico City, March 4, 1765: AGN-I,
26, cuad. 2:exp. 52, and 60:fols. 144f–145v, respectively. The registry copy of Arellano's appointment carries the statement, dated March 5, that since the medio real is
not a royal revenue, no media anata is due, but that the appointment has been copied in
the register of the accounting office for that revenue.

30. Royal order, San Ildefonso, August 1, 1787, in Beleña, 2:378–379, no. 71.

accordance with the laws, autos acordados, ordinances, and official schedules; not to charge excessive fees, and for Indian tributaries, the poor, and on business of his Majesty and his royal hacienda, none; and to defend the mystery of the pure and immaculate conception of Our Lady."[31] Enforcement of the requirement of taking the oath may have been negligent at times, for in 1782 another solicitador was found to have been serving and receiving salary since 1765 without having taken the oath. He rushed to remedy the deficiency, once disclosed, but without a promise on fees.[32] Thereafter, the zeal of the Bourbon reforms probably kept enforcement fairly tight.

Once the formalities of filing the requisite documents were completed and the oath taken, the new appointee entered upon his duties. He received his salary every four months—the Spanish system of *tercios*—from a special official in the Contaduría Real de Tributos. Notwithstanding the salary assigned that official from the medio real, he deducted a small sum from the payment as a further emolument.[33] The practice probably dated from the inception of the medio real. (No salaries shown in Table 7.1 allow for this deduction.)

Let us now consider the Indian agents as a functioning bureaucracy. The meaning of the titles and the professional divisions of labor has been sketched in previous chapters. So too have all of the categories of the agents' functions except one, their operations outside the viceregal palace and the viceregal audience. The salaries paid the escribanos mayores de cámara reimbursed them for limitations and even prohibitions on levying fees and costs upon Indians, not merely in the viceregal audience but also in the operations of the audiencia in both chambers and in full session. They had to attend the audiencia in turns in person or by deputy, since they could not be in all places simultaneously; record all papers, and issue all audiencia decrees and royal writs, charging only half-fees from Indian caciques and corporate bodies and none from all other Indians. Similarly, the recording secretaries for the sala del crimen, by accepting salary from the medio real, were under the same obligation to perform all duties for Indians fairly and promptly, either without fee and costs or under the reduced rates

31. Affidavits of appointment of Bartolomé Díaz Borrego as solicitador and of registry with office of media anata, Mexico City, December 15 and 19, 1781, and of his taking oath of office, January 10, 1782: Testimonio del expediente sobre arreglo . . . del Juzgado General de Naturales, Mexico City, 1784–86, in AGI-M, leg. 1286, no. 342, fols. 39f–42v.

32. Affidavits of appointment of Arellano, and registry for media anata, March 4 and 5, 1765, and of his taking oath of office, January 11, 1782: ibid., fols. 34f–39f.

33. Report by Díaz Borrego and Arellano on their salaries, Mexico City, August 7, 1784, ibid., fols. 42v–44v.

allowed for caciques and corporate bodies. We should note here that, in spite of its name, the sala del crimen also exercised civil jurisdiction in first instance for the audiencia within five leagues of Mexico City, the senior judges exercising purely appellate jurisdiction in their two chambers and jurisdiction in third instance as a united body (*unión de las dos salas*). Hence Indians living within Mexico City and its parcialidades who chose not to turn to the General Indian Court could take their cases to the sala del crimen and enjoy the privileges of the services of the Indian agents without fee—or, if a cacique or corporate body, at half-fee.

The relatores in the two chambers of the audiencia and in the sala del crimen, since they too received compensation from the medio real, were obligated to perform their functions of ordering and summarizing papers upon the same terms. The abogados, procuradores, and solicitadores paid from the medio real were obligated to serve Indians in their cases before all parts of the audiencia, so that a considerable proportion of their work appears in the audiencia records.[34] For the purpose of facilitating service, each of the 2 solicitadores was assigned in the earlier years of the court to an abogado, both to discharge lesser tasks and to turn to him for legal help in drafting papers and other matters. A few of the early appointments of solicitadores also assigned the new appointee to a specific procurador,[35] but that practice lapsed in the later seventeenth century as the solicitadores came to encroach increasingly upon the functions of the procuradores. In the later period also, the assignment to a specific abogado lapsed in favor of an instruction to use the counsel of one of the letrados, i.e., abogados, on the medio real.[36]

This obligation of the abogados, procuradores, and solicitadores receiving salary from the medio real to serve in cases outside the viceregal audience extended beyond those heard in the various parts of the audiencia to all tribunals in the area of Mexico City. The Appendix, summarizing the reports of the two solicitadores serving in 1784, lists cases in which they, and with them other Indian agents, were involved, before the *Juzgado de Intestados* (a court for handling estates of persons dying intestate); the special royal court administering the customs and sales taxes and tax on pulque; the seigneurial court of the Marquesado del Valle, with formal seat in Mexico City; the special

34. Ibid., passim; and instructions in the registries of papers of appointment in AGN-I, passim.

35. For example, the instructions in the appointment as solicitador of Antonio de Castro, Mexico City, February 13, 1617, and of José de Celi, December 10, 1620: AGN-I, 9:exps. 26 and 289 respectively.

36. For example, appointment of Diego de Castilleja Guzmán as solicitador, Mexico City, January 19, 1692, ibid., 32:fols. 95v–96v.

court for awarding royal grants of lands and settling faulty titles to lands not in dispute; and the court of the Archbishop of Mexico City, for cases arising within the archbishopric under Church law and within ecclesiastical jurisdiction. The obligation of the Indian agents presumably did not extend to courts, royal or Church, outside the area of Mexico City. It would have been impossible for so small a staff to spread itself so thin or spend so much time in travel.

Except for cases before the senior judges of the audiencia, the working of the Indian agents is impossible to trace in detail through case records, since such records are either lacking or not available to the public. For Indian cases heard by the senior judges of the audiencia, for which ample documentation survives in the Mexican national archive, there can be no doubt that the Indian agents operated widely. Their names and their affidavits appear in many dockets. Moreover, they could be forced through petition to the viceroy to provide legal aid outside the viceregal audience. A notable instance of this occurred in 1662, when the abogados and procuradores de indios, for fear of reprisal from Oidor Montemayor y Córdova de Cuenca, refused to serve as legal agents in the appeals of the Indian towns of Oaxaca against distinctly arbitrary new tribute counts he made during his trip of inspection to that region. Upon petition of the contador of the royal treasury in Mexico City, the viceroy ordered the abogados and procuradores to take the cases, under penalty of 500/ fine for the abogados and loss of office for the procuradores. The new counts were voided.[37] (Ironically, a few months later, in October 1662, Montemayor y Córdova de Cuenca became assessor of the General Indian Court.)[38] So we know from this and the documents of many other cases that the Indian agents afforded legal aid in a wide range of matters outside the viceregal audience. With what dispatch and probity they operated remains to be seen.

The Indian agents were held to duty on the days and during the hours of judicial and viceregal dispatch of business, which probably did not differ from ordinary office hours. The days were working days, i.e., all except Sundays and religious holidays—the variety and number of the latter reduced effective work substantially, to around 200 days a year.[39] Working hours officially were no more than five a work-

37. Testimonio de los autos, padrones y otros documentos relativos a la actuación del oidor Montemayor y Córdova de Cuenca en Tehuantepec, y de pleitos resultantes, 1661–62; and the Bishop of Puebla to the king, Puebla, December 6, 1662: AGI-P, leg. 230A, ramo 8, and leg. 230B, ramo 13, respectively.

38. Appointment, AGN-I, 19:exp. 544.

39. If one allows for Sundays, holidays, and the three periods of official vacations, Mexican federal employees today work perhaps 280 days a year. Political independence and official neutrality or hostility to the Church have lengthened the working year considerably.

ing day, but their occurrence changed somewhat during the colonial period, as the time of the principal meal moved from high noon into the early afternoon. In the opening years of the court, the hours were from 8 to 11 a.m. and from 2 to 4 p.m., the periods when the audiencia and viceroy officially transacted business. In the later colonial period, the morning hours remained unchanged, but the afternoon sessions began at 3:30 p.m.[40] (By the later nineteenth century, afternoon sessions would have begun at 5 p.m.)

Working in turns, the recording secretaries, the relatores, the abogados, procuradores, and solicitadores were supposed to be present either at the sessions of the audiencia and the sala del crimen or at the viceregal audience, as appropriate. Porteros were present at all of these during business hours, for regulating the flow of traffic and ushering in petitioners in appropriate order. At the sessions of the audiencia and the sala del crimen, the recording secretaries functioned continuously in turn, but on all business. Their obligation as Indian agents required them merely to handle Indian cases as they appeared; so equally did the obligations of the relatores and the members of the legal professions. At the viceregal audience, where all business related to Indian matters, the recording secretaries, abogados, and procuradores took their turns entirely as an obligation of their salaries from the medio real. The assessor, court relator, notary, interpreter, alguacil or ministro ejecutor, and the viceregal portero were needed at all sessions.

Viceregal audiences for Indian affairs were held on Mondays and Wednesdays in the morning and on Friday afternoons. Most of the sessions were presided over by the assessor, the viceroy appearing in person only for part of the time, perhaps an hour or two, if at all. If the viceroy did come, the escribanos mayores up for their turns had to appear in person; if the session was to be presided over entirely by the assessor, they might discharge attendance and their duties through deputies.[41] Presumably the superior dignity of the viceroy relative to the audiencia required that degree of deference, for an escribano mayor supposed to serve in a chamber of the audiencia on the same day he attended the viceregal audience would have to send a deputy to the audiencia session. The arrangement, however, also required that there be some means of knowing when the viceroy planned to attend

40. Nuevo reglamento para el Juzgado de Indios, Mexico City, May 6, 1598, clause 1, in AGN-I, 6, part 2:exp. 1004; reform rules for the General Indian Court, Mexico City, December 5, 1785, clause 6, in Beleña, 2:202, no. 47; instruction in appointment of Castilleja Guzmán as solicitador, January 19, 1692, in AGN-I, 32:fols. 95v–96v.

41. Nuevo reglamento, May 6, 1598, clause 1 and passim; order of Guadalcázar on attendance and discipline at the General Indian Court, Mexico City, January 30, 1617, in AGN-I, 9:exp. 24.

and when he would not. That in turn indicates the existence of communication on such matters in advance among the escribanos mayores, the assessor, and the viceroy. In all probability, the assessor served as guide, in effect as chairman of arrangements.

On working days and during business hours, the solicitadores, when their presence was not required in the viceregal audience, were supposed to sit at tables or benches in the corridor outside the audience chamber, dressed in formal legal robes, including the high Spanish legal ruff (*golilla*). Equally, the procuradores were supposed to spend business hours in rooms in the palace set aside for them, unless their presence was required at the audience. The official intent of these requirements was that Indians might find the solicitadores and procuradores easily, in order freely to initiate petitions and suits and to prepare papers. The two solicitadores were supposed also to sit far enough apart so that whatever was said at one table or bench could not be heard at the other.[42] Although the solicitadores usually were proficient in Nahuatl,[43] they could call upon the court interpreter[44] or other interpreters if their prospective clients spoke other Indian tongues. The procuradores presumably had the same access to interpreters.

Obviously, the entire system depended upon reasonably prompt discharge of functions and probity among the staff. Adherence to such prompt discharge was enjoined by a formidable system of reporting and fines initiated by the Conde de Monterrey in 1598, embodied in his *Nuevo Reglamento para el Juzgado de Indios* (New Rules for the General Indian Court).[45] The clauses may be summarized briefly:

1. On viceregal audience days, all agents supposed to be present must be there for the duration of the audience, under penalty of a fine of 1/ for lateness and 2/ for absence—the fines to be applied by halves to the poor in the jail and the royal hospital for Indians.

2. Business dispatched in the viceregal audience must be written down on the same day by the interpreter, who must immediately de-

42. Nuevo reglamento, clause 9, and reform rules, clauses 6–7; appointment as solicitador of José de Celi, December 10, 1620, and of Castilleja Guzmán, January 19, 1692: AGN-I, 9:exp. 289 and 32:fols. 95v–96v.

43. For example, the statement in the appointment of Antonio de Castro as solicitador, February 13, 1617, in AGN-I, 9:exp. 26.

44. The interpreter could be a person of learning and distinction. Fernando de Alva Ixtlilxóchitl, 1568–1648, one of our most important sources of pre-Conquest culture—a descendant of the rulers of Texcoco, a grandson of Cuauhtémoc through his mother, and not merely writer on Texcocan tradition, but also possessor of a notable library of books and native pictorial manuscripts—was in his last years interpreter of the General Indian Court: see Chavero's Foreword to Ixtlilxóchitl, 1:6.

45. AGN-I, 6, part 2:exp. 1004; also in AGI-M, leg. 24, no. 22.

liver it to the procurador, so that in the next audience he might report to the viceroy. The penalties for omissions were o/4 for each item from the interpreter, if he failed to record, and from the procurador if he failed to report to the viceroy, the money to go to the Indian whose petition or suit suffered delay.

3. All matters assigned in an audience to the assessor, procurador, solicitador, recording secretary, or any other official must be entered in a list to be kept by the court notary and placed upon the viceroy's table ready for him when he entered the following audience for Indians, so that at the close he might take account whether or not his instructions had been carried out and the necessary documents prepared for delivery to the petitioning Indians. The purpose was that they not suffer more delay than from one audience day to the next. Penalties for omission on the part of any official were to be 4/ for each item, the fine to be divided between the poor of the jail and the Indian who suffered delay.

4. Petitions for grants or licenses already agreed to were to be read first in the audiences and taken immediately to a recording secretary of gobernación, so that the viceroy might sign the document before leaving the audience. The solicitador was to see to carrying out this clause; failure to do so by him or by the recording secretary was to be punished by a fine of 1/ each, the money to be applied to the royal hospital for Indians.

5. The procurador must prepare a list of all writs ordered issued in Indian cases in second instance on Tuesdays, in the audiencia's public session, when they would be announced, to be brought to the viceroy on Wednesday, so that he might give appropriate orders to the escribanos mayores de cámara and see to prompt implementation without excuse. The penalty for failure to comply was a fine of 1/ from the procurador, to be applied to the royal hospital for Indians.

6. At the entrance of the viceroy, the procurador must present a list of the suits whether being appealed or not in second instance to the audiencia, so that the viceroy might immediately give appropriate orders that the relatores take to the audiencia the documents of suits yet to be heard, and notice of those already heard be given to the judges and the viceroy before his meeting with them as president of the audiencia, so that the audiencia would be led to act quickly. Penalty for failure or omission on the part of the procurador or his aide was a fine of 1/ for the royal hospital for Indians.

7. On the same day that in the audiencia or the General Indian Court an order was issued to give a copy of a complaint against an Indian or to accept a case for presentation of evidence, the procurador must take the papers to the abogado so that, with one day for prepara-

tion, the latter might answer or present a list of questions in defense in the hearing immediately following. The penalty for omission was a fine of 1/ for the royal hospital for Indians.

8. The procurador must distribute papers coming to him, and presented in the viceregal audience, to the appropriate recording secretary, obtaining receipts for all. He must keep records and obtain receipts for the papers of suits sent on appeal, or in some other manner, to the audiencia. The penalty for omission was a fine of 1/ for the royal hospital for Indians. The procurador was also to be liable for the loss caused to any Indian by delay, or at the least was to pay the costs of reopening or returning the case to its original state.

9. The procurador was to keep business hours by the clock in the room assigned to him from 8 to 11 a.m. and from 2 to 4 p.m., except for the time he was either in the viceregal audience or in that of the audiencia, so that the Indians coming to the city might have easy access to him and not fall into the hands of mestizos and other unqualified persons. Failure to comply was to be punished by a fine of 4/ for each day of omission, the money to be divided equally between the poor of the jail and the royal hospital for Indians. Long-continued omission would lead to removal from office.

10. To make sure that there was a written record of all business at all times, the court notary was to record in a book notice of all petitions and other documents that might be presented in the viceregal audiences, and the viceregal decisions. The penalty for omission was to be 1/ per item, the money to go to the royal hospital for Indians. Long-continued delinquency would lead to removal from office.

At the time these rules were promulgated the staff was small, but could easily be stretched to cover larger numbers, especially in instances in which two agents discharged a function formerly handled by one. Under the regulations, the fines were to be collected forthwith in public audience. They were so heavy that a fairly small number of delinquencies and absences through a year could consume all or the greater part of the stipend of a lesser official, and their infliction be resented accordingly. In any office, especially a governmental one, the question always arises: Who will enforce discipline; who will tattle upon his fellows; in short, who is willing to incur the dislike of people with whom he must work for the sake of a principle or an instruction? The reluctance of fellow employees to bear witness against one another or to call attention to omissions and failures has long been notorious, as can be seen in the extraordinary difficulty of dismissing for cause a civil service or unionized employee today. There is no reason to suppose that bureaucracies in the seventeenth and eighteenth centuries differed substantially from those in the present day. One suspects that Monterrey's *reglamento* may have been enforced from time to time in an exemplary and momentary display of virtue, but did not really work. By 1617, laxness among court officials reached such a point that the then-viceroy, the Marqués de Guadalcázar, issued a new order that the assessor, Luis de Villanueva Zapata, enforce the reglamento, and as a further measure for enforcement appointed one of the solicitadores, José de Celi, *multador*, or levier of fines, with the obligation to denounce infractions of the rules among the staff and report to the viceroy every four months how much should be discounted from each agent's stipend. For this function he was to receive 30/ a year from the yield of the fines.[46] The same problems of enforcement and the quiet resistance of the agents undoubtedly nullified the measure.

As a bureaucracy, the Indian agents were beset by a series of basic difficulties. Some were inherent in the way the system was organized, some in the nature of Spanish and Indian cultures as they then existed, and some derived from human nature itself are still with us in bureaucratic systems in our time. They may be classified as (1) part-time employment; (2) additional function, which led to the use of deputies and substitutes; (3) negligence; (4) collusion; and finally, (5) further corruption, in the form of excessive and improper charges.

The problem of part-time employment was built into the structure of the court and the entire system of Indian agents. When not meeting their clients or appearing in sessions of the audiencia, sala del crimen, the General Indian Court, or some other tribunal in discharge of their duties—a matter of perhaps five hours a working day—or drawing up papers and completing work assigned in the sessions—a matter of an indefinite amount of time, but one that could be handled flexibly—the staff were free to take on additional clients or other employment, so long as their doing so did not conflict with their obligations as Indian agents. Most Indian agents managed very well, in part through the use of deputies and substitutes, but some could not except by neglecting their duties as agents of the medio real. The solicitadores and the porteros were held to such continuous service that it is difficult to see how they could find much time for other clients or other employment. In fact, the impossibility of finding enough free time from their duties as Indian agents to supplement their stipends was the

---

46. AGN-I, 9 : exp. 24. Guadalcázar may have been moved as much by the insult to his dignity through attendance at his personal audience of oficiales mayores of the recording secretaries. An order for personal attendance when the viceroy appeared in person is included.

major complaint of the solicitadores in the 1780s, and held to be justified in the official investigation at the time.[47] Further, the two increases in salary accorded them during the eighteenth century indicate that their plight was patent enough to bring official remedy, once between 1738 and 1759 and the second time as a result of the investigation of the 1780s.[48]

It was possible in the less-busied earlier days of the court for one solicitador to combine his post with the additional one of interpreter to the audiencia[49]—though one wonders how he managed, since the hours of sessions were the same. But as Indian petitions and suits increased during the eighteenth century, that kind of supplementation became far more difficult, if not out of the question for a conscientious solicitador, and such testimony as we have indicates that the solicitadores were the hardest-working, most conscientious Indian agents, the ones most acceptable to Indian clients.[50] The temptation, though, for them, as for other Indian agents, would be to augment inadequate or unsatisfactory salaries by practices falling within our other categories.

The difficulty arising from the use of deputies and substitutes was inherent in appointment as an additional function, for most of the Indian agents—most notably the escribanos mayores, the abogados, and the procuradores—were required to function in several places at the same time. For the escribanos mayores of cámara and of the sala del crimen, their principal obligation as officials lay in their service in the various parts of the audiencia. Further, all the escribanos mayores and the court notary headed staffs they had to pay from their salaries and revenues, for the writing and copying of documents requiring employment of scriveners and attendance at simultaneous sessions could only be discharged through the use of deputies and substitutes. Resort to deputies was common. The reglamento of 1598 issued by Monterrey expressly mentions an agent of the procurador who helped him discharge his duties. Guadalcázar's order of January 30, 1617, refers to the *oficiales mayores* of the escribanos mayores, a term that suggests a large, well-organized staff for each. The Grand Chancellor of the Indies, residing in Spain, obviously had to discharge his duties as

47. The assumption of part-time work is implicit in the documents of appointment, which bind the new officials not to assume cases in conflict with their obligations under the medio real. In Beleña's inquiry into the duties and obligations of the solicitadores, the point of income from other employment was gone into at some length. See the discussion later in this chapter.

48. See Table 7.1.

49. Andrés Hernández, who held both posts, was replaced on February 13, 1617, by Andrés de Castro: AGN-I, 9 : exp. 26.

50. See the discussion of complaints by the province of Tlaxcala later in this chapter.

chancellor of the audiencia in Mexico City through a deputy. In a very real sense, the assessor of the court often stood in as deputy for the viceroy.

There was nothing wrong in the practice, so long as it did not impair service or lead to corruption. Unfortunately, it quickly did both. In its sale of offices, the crown soon discovered that it could obtain a better price if the appointment carried with it the right to discharge the duties through a deputy.[51] The officeholder then pocketed most of the salary and perquisites, assigning some to a lieutenant who, because he was much less well paid, in turn would not compensate his staff adequately. Even without formal royal license, a less-than-conscientious officeholder could discharge his obligations through deputies, pocketing much of the revenue of the office and keeping his time free. Those Indian agents who used deputies did not assign them part of their stipend in the medio real, but on the other hand expected them to perform duties paid for by that stipend. The results were sure to be negligence in performance and attempts to collect fees in one way or another. After all, the deputies and substitutes had not taken the oath as agents of the medio real. A proposal to assign deputies stipends in the medio real, as a means of avoiding the problem of illicit fees, was rejected by the crown.[52] Difficulties arising from the use of deputies were compounded by a further abuse, namely, that officeholders frequently appointed men who had few or none of the professional qualifications necessary for proper discharge of their duties.[53] So to venality was added incompetence, and the Indian clients suffered.

Negligence always appears in any human society, and in the more leisurely, easy-going society of New Spain, it may have been present to a particularly large extent. While in great measure it derives from innate human factors, the system of Indian agents on stipend, working part-time, and the use of deputies and substitutes, encouraged its appearance. Since the stipend was assured, and one's fellow employees were not likely to blab, one need not hurry. If one had to earn additional income to supplement an inadequate stipend, or wished to earn more, that earning might well come first, and the duties attached to the stipend a poor second. The Indians complained repeatedly that the escribanos mayores let the documents of their cases rest

51. See Díez de la Calle, 120–121 (cap. 2, part 5).

52. Linares to the king, Mexico City, December 15, 1712, and September 15, 1715, in AGI-M, legs. 484 and 487 respectively; royal cédula to Linares, Madrid, December 3, 1714, in AGN-RC, 37:exp. 116 (BLT).

53. Royal cédula to the Audiencia of Mexico and the judges of the sala del crimen, Lerma, December 13, 1721, on the substance of charges resulting from the visita of Francisco Garcerán, 1716–19, in DCLI, 2:228–232, esp. 229–230 (no. 504).

while they attended to the business of non-Indians, who could be charged full fees and costs.[54] For the deputies and substitutes, held to perform duties for which their principals received stipend, but did not share it with them, the temptation was even greater.

From negligence to collusion was an easy step. An Indian agent might impede or even prejudice the movement of a petition, complaint, or defense in order to favor a party who would show gratitude by a suitable gift. Possibilities of bribes, and accordingly temptation, must have been particularly strong in cases involving either Indian towns or a wealthy non-Indian. In other instances, the attempt to influence the movement of a case may have occurred as a personal favor to a friend, a compadre, or a relative. One major Indian complaint was that Indian agents either tried to dissuade them from filing complaints, particularly against provincial governors, or temporized until the time limit for making the complaint had passed. Some agents simply refused to accept complaints.[55] If negligence was deplorable, collusion was illegal, and punishable by severe penalties, at least in theory; nevertheless, it was much complained of.

Corruption in the further forms of assessing undue costs; diverting to personal use money entrusted for paper, ink, and proper legal costs; demanding fees where none were due, or large sums as against moderate, legally proper amounts; taking bribes and gifts; and requiring unpaid service for handling cases—all of these appeared so frequently that one suspects they were endemic. The problem was complex and by no means one-sided. Part of the difficulty lay in the fact that the Indians themselves were accustomed to give gifts for government services and tended to be suspicious of any made available without charge. Our most explicit evidence is in the account of pre-Conquest culture in Yucatan prepared by Gaspar Antonio Chi for the Spanish governor in 1582. Chi declared that no Indian appeared before a cacique or any person of rank without bringing a gift, even though the best he could manage might be of slight value. Judges received presents, as a matter of custom, from both parties to a complaint, without any suggestion of impropriety.[56] To be sure, Yucatan lies outside the Nahuatl area, although within Mesoamerica; but the difference was more linguistic than cultural in this matter, if one judges by an episode related by the Neapolitan traveler Gemelli Carreri. On March 4, 1697, as he left the audience chamber in the viceregal palace after paying his respects to the viceroy, the Conde de Moctezuma, he saw arriving deputies from Indian towns, accompanied by numerous

54. See the discussion later in this chapter.
55. See the discussion later in this chapter.
56. Landa, trans. and ed. by Tozzer, app. C, 231.

delegations. As was their custom when presenting a petition or memorial, they brought a large tree covered with flowers, which they left with the viceroy.[57] We should remember also the normal suspicion of peasants and laborers, and indeed most people, when presented with an offer of services without demand for some kind of counterpart return: "What's in it for you?" In colonial Mexico, the suspicion would be intensified by the deep cultural and socio-political differences dividing Indians from Spaniards.

Corruption resulted in part also from the very attempt to shift to salaries from a system based upon fees, in a society largely functioning on fees—a society, moreover, organized on the basis of estates, with firm views on the right of the upper estates to maintenance by the lower one, and the obligation of each person enjoying power or opportunity to provide for himself and his relations. To some extent, the government, royal and viceregal, itself was to blame. The original idea in organizing the General Indian Court and the levy of the medio real had been to spare Indian commoners all costs; but shortages in revenue led to imposition of moderate levies for paper, ink, filing costs, and such.[58] With the introduction of stamped paper, a further charge, moderate but still a charge, became necessary.[59] The practice was for the Indian client to deposit with the solicitador enough money to cover all such charges. In addition, if the client was a cacique or corporate entity, the solicitador became responsible to the procuradores, abogados, relatores, and escribanos mayores, etc., for the half-fees and costs that accrued to them. Since many Indian clients failed to pay upon the conclusion of their case, the solicitadores tended to collect such money in advance.[60] One complaint on the part of the Indians was that money deposited was spent or simply disappeared without an accounting.[61]

Complaints of Indian agents' illegally levying fees from Indians, demanding gifts, and delaying suits, as a means of extorting further payment, arose almost as soon as the relatores and escribanos mayores managed to secure much more generous salaries from the medio real.

57. Gemelli Carreri, 42.

58. Beleña's inquiry in 1784–86 accepted such charges as proper. See the discussion of his reform campaign and measures later in this chapter.

59. See the discussion in Chapter VI.

60. Declaration by the two solicitadores, Mexico City, August 7, 1784, in Testimonio del expediente sobre arreglo . . . del Juzgado General de Naturales, 1784–86, in AGI-M, leg. 1286, no. 342, fols. 42v–44v. See the further declaration of Díaz Borrego in fol. 67f–v.

61. Report of the crown attorney for civil matters, charged with care of criminal ones and the general protection of Indians, Mexico City, June 22, 1785, ibid., fols. 77v–81f.

By 1623, reports reaching the Council of the Indies were sufficiently serious so that the fiscal of the council reported to the king, and the king in turn sent a royal cédula to the viceroy, the Marqués de Gelves, ordering an investigation and remedy.[62] That much was done is doubtful, since the Mexico City riots of 1624 effectively paralyzed the viceregal government for some time. In the 1640s, the visita of Palafox raised charges that the escribanos mayores of cámara and gobernación were levying fees where none were due, or were charging too much, and were forcing the Indians to go to the officials' houses in order to obtain properly executed documents. One item in the charges really involved a dispute over fees to be charged caciques and Indian communities, since the notaries claimed that they were entitled under an ordinance of Velasco II to charge 1/ for preparing a dispatch. Again, political disorder in the form of the dispute of Palafox and the Jesuits delayed completion of the visita.[63] Only in 1661 did the first royal cédula ordering reform arrive. It was promulgated in 1663 by an auto acordado reiterating the rule of no fees for Indians and expressly declaring that caciques and Indian communities were included within its scope.[64] A further rebuke to the escribanos mayores de cámara of the sala del crimen and those of gobernación, based upon the charges raised in the visitas of Palafox and Pedro de Gálvez, came in a royal letter dated June 27, 1670, and in November was communicated to the officeholders[65] (one hopes still those guilty in the 1640s).

During the last quarter of the seventeenth century, abuses aroused an Indian counteroffensive. The complaints were brought to the attention of the Council of the Indies and the king by the Indians of the province of Tlaxcala, a well-organized corporate body with claims to Spanish respect for their services during and after the Conquest. Their most serious accusations, duly incorporated in a royal cédula of June 19, 1685, charged that the two abogados of the court were so busy with cases of Spaniards and other powerful people that they could not

---

62. Madrid, June 13, 1623, in Konetzke, 2:276–277, no. 176. An earlier royal cédula on the recording secretaries for cámara is summarized in Montemayor y Córdova de Cuenca, part 1:fol. 111v, sum. 2. The obedecimiento is in fol. 217f, sum. 50. The royal cédula of 1623 is in the RLI, as 6.6.4.

63. Formal approval of the charges did not take place until 1669, when the Council of the Indies declared them valid. They were communicated to the viceroy through a royal dispatch of June 27, 1670. He acknowledged receipt and assured implementation in two letters to the queen-regent, Mexico City, November 13 and 29, 1670, in AGI-M, leg. 44.

64. Summarized in Montemayor y Córdova de Cuenca, part 1:fols. 63v–64f, sum. 55, and 111v, sum. 3; part 2:fol. 10f–v, auto 1. They may also be found in Beleña, 1, part 1:11–17. The audiencia set an official schedule of fees.

65. See note 63 above.

handle Indian cases within legal time limits. In cases of extortion and abuse by alcaldes mayores and curas, both the abogados and procuradores among the Indian agents, while expressing sympathy for the Indians, delayed presenting the complaints to the General Indian Court and the audiencia until the legal time limit for complaint had passed. If they presented the complaint, they did not move the case, on the ground that they were disqualified, the reason as alleged by the Indians being that they held powers of attorney from the parties on the other side. The result of such delays was that, after great expense in Mexico City, the Indians let their complaints drop. The Indians of Tlaxcala expressly excepted the solicitadores from these charges, petitioning that the latter be permitted to act as procuradores in drawing up legal petitions and pleas, subject only to the normal requirement of the signature of an abogado. The royal cédula ordered reform.[66]

Thereafter the solicitadores had royal permission for the enlarged role they already were assuming. By their applications to the viceroy and directly to the Council of the Indies, the Indians of Tlaxcala won the formally established right for all Indians in New Spain, at their own choice, to use the agents of the medio real or resort to private legal representatives of their own choosing, even before the General Indian Court. Of course in the second instance, though the private legal representatives were under the same restrictions on levy of costs and fees as the Indian agents, few were so altruistic, one suspects, as to take on a case without some arrangement for better compensation. The audiencia, moreover, continuing to uphold the monopoly of its examined and appointed staff, interpreted the royal will to mean that Indians were free to choose whom they wished in the provinces, but that in petitions and suits before tribunals in Mexico City, Indians must select from the abogados and procuradores formally admitted to practice before it.[67] Nevertheless, the Indians gained some field for maneuver, and by choosing with care might at least gain more assurance that their attorneys truly acted on their behalf.

Complaint and investigation continued through the 1690s. In 1693 more complaints reaching Madrid on the misdeeds of procuradores and abogados of the medio real led the crown to order further investigation. The order was received formally in Mexico City on Au-

66. Konetzke, 2:764–765, no. 519); Viceroy Conde de Paredes to the king, Mexico City, January 23, 1686, on measures for implementing, in AGI-M, leg. 56.

67. In its formal act of obedience to the royal cédula, on October 25, 1685, the audiencia ordered that the Indians might use any procurador on the official list, paying his fees. That order, ambiguous in the light of earlier legislation, might be interpreted as giving permission for charging Indians full fees if they resorted to legal aides other than those of the medio real. See the discussion later in this chapter.

gust 20, 1695, and registered with the secretaries of gobernación.[68] The latter, in turn, were the subject of continued complaints that they evaded the official schedules of fees, alleging that no such official list existed. In 1698 the viceroy, the Conde de Moctezuma, reported that he had instructed them to observe the schedule of fees brought by Montemayor y Córdova de Cuenca in the 1660s. Only then did the secretaries of gobernación end their charge of 1 peso for a viceregal decree, but primarily because the Conde de Moctezuma issued decrees through his own private secretary, who was paid from the viceroy's own pocket, neither fees nor gifts being allowed.

Moctezuma's report to the crown commented that a bad custom had come into being of permitting the recording secretaries of gobernación to charge fees from the poor and Indians. As a remedy, he dispatched decrees as soon as he received a petition in order to avoid delays and charges. As a further precaution, he had the decrees prepared in his personal secretariat. Delays, excessive legal formalities in order to increase charges, and the charges themselves, he commented, had reached the point at which the costs of most suits came to a large part of the value in dispute. In the audiencia, "winners emerge as poor as losers."[69]

The Bourbon dynasty's accession to the throne of Spain at the opening of the eighteenth century brought, on the one hand, a culmination both of the burden of charges for legal services and attempts to wring compensation from Indians; and on the other, stricter measures for enforcing the rules. Costs of litigation relative to the values involved apparently reached a high point at the beginning of the eighteenth century. The Cortes of Catalonia, in one of its last sessions before being merged into the general cortes of united Spain, laid before Philip V the grievance that charges by abogados had reached such sums that many subjects preferred to suffer unjust damage rather than sue.[70] That a similar situation obtained in Mexico is clear from the Conde de Moctezuma's report in 1698. The first important move to remedy abuse in Indian cases began in 1712, when Viceroy Linares reported to Madrid that in the offices of the recording secretaries for civil judicial affairs, the lieutenants and other lower officials collected fees from Indians on the ground that the proprietary officeholders did not share with them any of their stipends from the medio real, and it was unfair that they serve with no pay. "It does not sit well with me to

68. Royal cédula to the viceroy, Madrid, November 1693, and acts of obedience in Mexico City, in AGN-RC, 25 : exp. 68 (BLT).

69. Letter to the king, Mexico City, May 14, 1698, in AGI-M, leg. 472.

70. Lalinde Abadía, 251–252.

let this evasion pass," wrote Linares, "for the Indians by providing salary to the proprietary secretary pay for all the work of his office without making a distinction between him and his subordinates; let the latter turn to the man who appointed them for pay." Yet the political weight of the recording secretaries in the audiencia was such that Linares reported the abuse to the king for remedy rather than enforce local legislation long established.[71] Upon receipt of the letter, the Council of the Indies promptly recommended that remedy and punishment of the guilty be ordered. By royal cédula of December 3, 1714, the crown ruled that lieutenants and other subordinate officials of escribanos mayores not charge fees, and instructed the viceroy to apply any remedy he thought desirable, the king approving in advance through his order whatever might be done. Punishment there was none, but there was an admonition to mend ways. At the viceroy's order, the royal cédula was read to all escribanos mayores and copies of it posted in their offices. Formal notification took place from August 8 to 14, 1715, and in January 1717 affidavits were prepared, probably for transmission to Madrid.[72]

The measure taken seems to have ended this one abuse, or reduced it to tolerable levels, for complaints on this issue no longer appear in viceregal correspondence and audiencia autos acordados. Other abuses undoubtedly present during the episode of 1712–15 came to light through a general inspection of the audiencia and all courts in its district, carried out by Lic. Francisco Garcerán, inquisitor in Mexico, between 1716 and 1720. As his findings were sifted through the Council of the Indies and returned to Mexico by royal cédula of December 13, 1721, Garcerán found great disorder in the legal professions and the courts. Most of his findings need not concern us here. In regard to Indians and their cases, he reported that court officials and legal agents delayed the movement of cases, were slovenly and remiss in wearing proper legal attire, and had their offices in remote and distant sites, where papers were stored in confused heaps, so that those relating to a single case became separated and could not be located except after expensive search and delays. The relatores and recording secretaries of the audiencia divisions charged excessive fees. Worst of all, abogados, procuradores, recording secretaries, and others, all with salary in the medio real, demanded as the price of carrying out their functions that Indians perform unpaid work of the dirtiest kind for them at their houses, like washing coaches, cleaning out stables, and

71. AGI-M, leg. 484.
72. AGN-RC, 37:exp. 116, with acts of obedience (BLT); Linares to the king, Mexico City, September 15, 1715, in AGI-M, leg. 487.

emptying cesspools. Instead of protecting the Indians from repartimientos de mercancías, personal service, and other extortions, all prohibited by law, the Indian agents tried to dissuade the natives, delayed filing complaints, or postponed them for consideration at the time of residencia.[73]

The response of the audiencia came in an elaborate series of regulations issued in 1721 and 1723. All Indian cases were to be heard promptly by summary procedure. Indian agents of the medio real might not charge fees. Any and all Indian debts arising from repartimientos de mercancías were to be held void, nor was any other form of extortion to be permitted. The official protector of the Indians was to watch carefully.

In effect, existing rules were reenacted. Similarly, the more general abuses in matters of assessing and recording fees were remedied by reenacting the existing rules in more stringent forms. In each case the judge or his assessor was to indicate appropriate fees, which the abogados, relatores, and notaries must list on the documents. That requirement was much strengthened in 1723 by a new regulation that all legal agents and justices must record on the documents of any case their fees and charges, using the formula, "I have charged ____ so much for this item according to the official schedule, and no more; so I swear by God, our Lord, and the Holy Cross." The penalty for noncompliance or lapse was set at 500/ fine for justices, "y del interés de las partes," and in general fourfold restitution and a report to the king. Thereafter, legal documents carry the required formula and list fees and charges in detail.[74] The new system probably had considerable effect.

Our discussion so far has dealt with corruption and abuse at various levels, but to a much greater extent at the level of the higher, better-paid Indian agents, their delegates and subordinates, and the abogados and procuradores. That kind of abuse was sufficiently prominent to call forth attempts at remedy in a term of years, although with indifferent success. A much more modest kind of levy, largely unreported and uncomplained of, probably went on in the form of small charges by the solicitadores and perhaps other lower agents, among them the porteros. Since the charges were low indeed, the Indians paid them without complaint, reconciled to them by the fact that they re-

73. DCLI, 2:228–232; Beleña, 1, part 5:97–102.

74. Beleña, 1, part 5:97–102; part 3:17 (autos acordados nos. 51, October 10, 1722, and 52 and 53, June 1 and 21, 1723). The rule was specifically reenacted for relatores, abogados, notaries, receptores, etc., on December 15, 1783: auto acordado 54. In no. 53, the exact meaning of "del interés de las partes" is not clear; it probably meant that if the overpayment helped one of the parties, that party also should be fined.

ceived immediate legal help, clearly visible to them. Like the better and most acceptable aspects of the *mordida* in Mexico today, the charges supplemented inadequate salaries and, in return, brought prompt or even extraordinary services.

One pervasive but moderate abuse arose from the development of a new group of low-level legal aides, the *llevadores*, whose function was to carry legal papers from the solicitador or procurador to the abogado, to bring them back, and to deliver the official final court decree to the client. Their charges were low, a few reales for each act. Since they did not exist in the time of Velasco II, their function then being discharged by the solicitadores, there was no provision for them in the medio real, nor an explicit prohibition against their charges. In time, apparently, the solicitadores of the General Indian Court recaptured this function, since it carried fees, and continued to charge them. When discovered by Beleña in 1784, the charges were a regular, modest levy, grown into long-established custom.[75] They may well have existed unnoticed and unreported through all the scandals over other charges and abuses in the previous century and a half. Yet it was this custom that precipitated a shake-up in the court and the reform of the 1780s.

The reform was the work of Eusebio Ventura Beleña, whose name is best known today as the compiler of a published two-volume compendium of royal cédulas, autos acordados, and viceregal ordinances for the Audiencia of Mexico, a work fundamental for the study of colonial Mexican law. He was also oidor and assessor of the General Indian Court. Born in Imón in the bishopric of Sigüenza, Spain, around 1730, he studied at Sigüenza and Alcalá, receiving the degree of doctor in canon law. After a few years in Madrid as abogado, he went to Mexico in the train of the Bishop of Puebla, whom he served as judge for wills, chantries, and pious foundations. From 1765 to 1771 he worked with the energetic and formidable José de Gálvez during the latter's visita-general, distinguishing himself as an unusually vigorous, able administrator and helping in the expulsion of the Jesuits.[76] Beleña clearly formed one of the new group of officials who took prominent part in the reforms of Carlos III and Gálvez. Like Gálvez he must have been competent, steeped in the Spanish Enlightenment, and thoroughly regalist. For his services in the visita-general, and to Viceroy Croix thereafter, Beleña was rewarded with judicial ap-

75. On charging small fees, see the entire expediente on the General Indian Court, 1784–86, in AGI-M, leg. 1286, no. 342. The function of the llevadores is mentioned in the reform rules for the court and its officials, Mexico City, December 5, 1785, clause 2, in Beleña, 2:200, no. 47.
76. Torre Revello.

pointment, quickly becoming oidor of the Audiencia of Mexico.[77] He soon served as interim assessor of the General Indian Court, succeeding to the post as proprietary occupant shortly thereafter.[78] Both as interim assessor and proprietary assessor, he attempted to enforce discipline on the Indian agents and see that rules were observed.

The storm burst in March and April 1784.[79] Early in March Beleña and the viceroy, Matías de Gálvez, brother to José, learned that the solicitadores must be sought in their houses by would-be clients, causing delay and extra expense. On March 18 they issued an order that the solicitadores and other agents be present punctually at their posts in the palace. Late in March, an Indian of the province of Querétaro complained to the regent of the audiencia that Manuel María Arellano, one of the two solicitadores, had asked for money for carrying on a suit in the General Indian Court. Arellano, when rebuked by the regent, replied that he was merely following the custom, which set charges of o/2 for carrying papers to an abogado, o/4 for bringing them back, and o/2 for securing a decree of the court. In terms of the legal costs of the time, the charges were modest indeed. On March 30, at the regent's order, an affidavit of what had taken place was prepared and sent to Beleña, who signed a receipt for it on April 20, but must have been aware of its contents earlier.

The following day, Beleña ordered preparation of a series of affidavits, establishing his efforts to enforce proper behavior on the officials of the court and recounting his interview with Arellano on April 14 about the reported complaint. In the interview, Arellano told Beleña that he did not come daily to the General Indian Court (i.e., the viceregal palace) because he had no matters in his care, and that only from afternoon to afternoon did he sign or prepare a few documents, which only yielded 2 to 4 reales; and that matters pertaining to communities were not entrusted to him, because he always refused to sign for solicitadores or legal agents not licensed to practice in the Corte de México. Asked by Beleña who were the *intrusos*, Arellano replied, various people. Asked what fees he charged tributary Indians, the solicitador answered, only 2 to 4 reales. Beleña then forbade him to

77. *Diccionario Porrúa*, 1:245. González's Preface to Beleña, 1:ix–xvii, affords the best biography of Beleña written to date. Beleña died in 1794.

78. Opening statement of reform rules for the court and its officials, Mexico City, December 5, 1785, in Beleña, 2:199, no. 47.

79. What follows is based on the Expediente sobre el arreglo y reforma del Juzgado General de Indios, 1784–86, in AGI-M, leg. 1286 (100 fols.). The full expediente contains the sworn testimony and documents sent from Mexico, the correspondence of the viceroy and of the Minister for the Indies (who was José de Gálvez, under his title of Marqués de Sonora), and some of the proceedings of the Council of the Indies; the rest are in ibid., leg. 1132.

charge tributaries anything, and ordered him to be present in the palace for punctual discharge of his duties. To that, Arellano replied that his salary of 100/ a year was not enough, for it did not cover a quarter of his living costs, and that taking the small sums he did had been custom when he took up his post. Upon Beleña's pointing out that Arellano's oath of office forbade him to take fees, Arellano answered that he had never taken the oath of office.[80] Nevertheless, the assessor forbade him to take fees or to take as costs more than half a real for paper. If the salary was not enough, he and his fellow solicitador should petition the viceroy for adequate pay. Preparation of affidavits and forwarding reports to the viceroy took until June; on June 21 the viceroy ordered Arellano committed to the royal jail.

In the interim period of April and May, further evidence of levying illegal charges came to light. On April 24, 1784, Eugenia Micaela, an Indian housewife of Apan, presented a paper in the General Indian Court; and when Beleña inspected it, he found that the procurador, Juan de Dios Velasco, who had prepared it—not an Indian agent— had charged 20 reales. The next day the assessor ordered Velasco committed to the royal jail. After he returned the money, Velasco was severely warned against repeating the offense, and released. On May 13, Beleña, while examining a paper presented in the General Indian Court by Anselmo Rodríguez Balda, procurador of the medio real, on behalf of Juan Alonso, tributary of San Martín Atexac, Molango, found noted on the document that the abogado co-signer of the document, Lic. Manuel de la Bandera, had charged 1/. Summoned to the court and questioned in the presence of the two solicitadores, Bandera admitted the charge and admitted knowing that he should not charge fees, but declared that the peso was for paper and the services of a scribe. Beleña ordered the peso returned, as was done at once, and warned the abogado not to repeat the offense.

In that month of May, the aroused assessor ordered the official schedules of fees copied into the docket he was having prepared. To be included also were affidavits of a viceregal order of January 10, 1782, reiterating rules on fees and unlicensed legal agents for the General Indian Court, and of an auto acordado of December 15, 1783, reenacting existing rules that all fees levied in connection with any legal instrument must be noted on it.

In July the docket reached the two crown attorneys for civil and criminal matters for their recommendations. In regard to Arellano, the erring solicitador then in jail, they suggested that as an act of mercy he might be released with a warning. On the operations of the court, they

---

80. Appointed in 1765, he took the oath belatedly in 1782, two years before this statement, but in it swore nothing on fees.

pointed out that there ought to be rules for avoiding arbitrary administration of the duties of solicitadores. They therefore asked for a general review of the appointments of the solicitadores and their duties, so that they might examine the papers and suggest rules needed.

The resulting investigation incorporated instruments of appointment, certifications by treasury officials, oaths, and the remarkable reports on all legal papers before the General Indian Court which provide us with our appendix on legal business. In the investigation, the two solicitadores reported on the amount of time they gave to their functions as Indian agents, which did not permit earning much additional revenue, and the inadequacy of their stipends. Their salaries were supposed to be 100/ a year each, but they actually received 96/2 in three installments, since the notary of the disbursing office deducted 3/6 for his fees. Their duties as Indian agents were essentially the same as those of the procuradores licensed to practice before the audiencia—namely, to be present in the General Indian Court and other tribunals of the audiencia and the viceregal government on audience days, and on other business days to receive clients and prepare legal papers. At other times, "*en las horas irregulares*," they were to move petitions and cases in the lesser courts of Mexico City and before those of the archbishopric and the Marquesado del Valle. In whatever time remained on business days and on holidays, they were to move papers in cases through the hands of relatores, abogados, and others by going to their houses; and further, "in those hours that people devote to rest," they were supposed to prepare statements of fact, declarations of refusal to plead on the part of the other party, petitions to set time limits, and any other documents that did not have to be prepared by a licensed abogado.

"[T]hus the informants can assure Your Lordship," ran the statement of the solicitadores, "that our duties are so time-consuming that they do not allow us opportunity for work of any profit." As clinching notes in their petition for a raise in pay, the two solicitadores pointed out that they had to handle most cases without fee and that, in addition, they had to advance the costs for paper, services of a scribe, fees for affidavits of failure to respond by the opposing party, and payments for the movement of documents from one legal aide to another and to the judges, etc. Oddly enough, the two solicitadores did not advance one of the more telling reasons for a raise—that is, the sharp increase in prices in Mexico City during the second half of the eighteenth century, a movement reported by José de Gálvez some years earlier and the basis for his recommendation that the judges of the audiencia be granted substantial raises.[81]

81. Gálvez, 10.

In December 1784—when, the viceroy having died, the audiencia governed pending arrival of a new one—Beleña, with the title of "Judge Assessor of the General Indian Court by Special Commission of the Royal Audiencia Gobernadora," proposed new rules for the court and issued judgment on Arellano. Since the rules were subject to revision by the crown attorneys and had to be promulgated by the holder of the viceregal authority, we shall examine them in their final form. In the matter of Arellano, the evidence clearly showed guilt that would justify removal from office. (His excuse that he had not taken the oath was disproved by the affidavit which demonstrated that he had taken it belatedly in 1782, although without the clause on fees.) Nevertheless, the assessor, moved by sentiments of clemency, allowed him to continue in office with the hope of better behavior. That there was a basis for the complaint of inadequate pay is evident in a further recommendation that the two solicitadores have their stipend doubled to 200/ a year each.

Upon inspection of the proposed reform measures by the crown attorney for civil affairs, charged with the protection of Indians, a number of important additions and changes emerged. One urged that the solicitadores of the court, since they were taking on the functions of procuradores, needed a knowledge of law and procedure, their competence in which could only be ensured by examination before the full audiencia; furthermore, taking the oath of office there would avoid lapses like the long delay in the instance of Arellano. Another pointed out the abuse in handling money entrusted by Indian clients for covering costs, and urged that all such money be deposited in an appropriate office. It should be disbursed only on proper accounting in writing, which should be recorded on the documents of each case and filed in an additional statement with each docket. A further review by the crown attorney for the royal treasury agreed with the recommendations of his counterpart for civil matters, and added that the raise of 100/ a year for each of the solicitadores, although fully justified, must go to the king for approval. In addition, the rules in their final form should be sent to all offices of escribanos mayores, to all abogados and other legal aides, and a copy posted on the door of the General Indian Court.

In the leisurely processes of eighteenth-century administration, the various steps took ten months before, on October 5, 1785, a new viceroy, the Conde de Gálvez, nephew to José, signed the redrafted rules. On October 31, he and Beleña ordered that they be printed for wide distribution, the costs to be defrayed through pro-rata assessment on community treasuries with surplus funds. In November, all Indian agents were formally notified of the new rules. In December, copies of the broadside of the rules were posted in the viceregal offices and in the General Indian Court, and others sent to the audiencia and the sala del crimen for posting in the office of each recording secretary; one was sent to the judge of the Marquesado del Valle, and one each to the crown attorney, the assessor, and the viceregal military judge; 100 to the rector of the Colegio de Abogados for distribution among its members; and one to every solicitador, procurador, and licensed legal agent in Mexico City. Finally, the court notary was ordered to post a copy in each notarial office in the capital. Surplus copies were to be preserved in the viceregal archive for future use. Clearly, no one was to be able to plead ignorance of the new rules.

The reform rules, dated December 5, 1785, in the broadside and in Beleña's published legal compilation,[82] represented ad hoc legislation, provisions for dealing with specific problems rather than a comprehensive body of rules. There were nine clauses:

1. A copy in clear, easily legible hand of the section of the official schedule of fees dealing with the General Indian Court must be posted in the public part of the main court chamber for all to read.

2. All Indian agents and all others, including delegates of the crown attorneys and the men who carried papers for them, must list under oath on each document what they charged, those charges to be in accord with the official schedule. No petition or document of any kind would be received in the court without such certification. The penalty for infraction by the subaltern Indian agents was to be a fine of 2/ for the first offense, 4/ for the second, and loss of office for the third, this in addition to further penalties provided by the audiencia in the schedule of fees and the promulgating auto acordado of December 15, 1784. Money derived from the fines was to be spent on the welfare of Indian prisoners in the two jails of the parcialidades and Indian women under confinement at the House of St. Mary Magdalene.

3. The two solicitadores were to place their benches in the corridor outside the General Indian Court at a suitable distance from each other, so that business transacted at one could not be heard at the other. If the Indians had no procurador, the solicitadores were to take on the cases in alternation, handling them promptly and energetically. If a case required a power of attorney which was lacking, one must be executed on the spot.

4. If Indians came with a paper not signed by a known legal agent on the licensed list, the author was to be investigated by verbal questioning, arrested by the ministro ejecutor of the court, placed in

---

82. Copies of the broadside are in AGI-M, legs. 1132 and 1286; it is published in Beleña, part 2: 199–203, no. 47.

the royal jail, and notice given to the assessor, so that he might take appropriate measures for ending *agentes intrusos*. The staff of the General Indian Court were not to reveal the contents of any matter except to a proper legal aide of the parties. Furthermore, procuradores, licensed legal aides, and solicitadores might not prepare legal documents other than those within the legal competence of procuradores, namely, "petitions for decrees and time limits, notice of failure to respond, and others leading only to the bare and pure procedural movement of matters"; no others prepared solely by them would be received in the court.

5. Procuradores and solicitadores in the court and in other tribunals must write on the legal documents they presented sworn statements of sums received for costs. The sums would be administered by the court on written voucher; in addition, receipts must be given to the parties. The assessor or any judge in another tribunal might require an accounting at any time, but must do so on issuing final judgment. The least violation of this rule would bring the corresponding citation.

6. On audience days, the office of the General Indian Court must be open in the mornings from 8 to 11 and in the afternoons from 3:30 (presumably for two hours). The solicitadores must be present for business, and in the mornings wear formal legal dress, including the legal ruff.

7. On audience days, two abogados among the Indian agents, one for civil and the other for criminal matters, must be present from 11 a.m. to noon, taking turns in pairs. The interpreter and the ministro ejecutor must also be present at these hours.

8. The governors of the two parcialidades—or in their absence for justifiable cause, the presiding alcaldes, or those on weekly turn—must come to the court at 11 a.m. to report on Indians arrested in the previous 24 hours, so that prompt decision might be reached whether to continue detention or order release.

9. Solicitadores might be appointed only after examination before the full audiencia and upon taking oath of office.

A full report, incorporating certified copies of all testimony and documents, including a copy of the broadside of the new rules, was sent under date of December 31, 1785, to Madrid, directed to José de Gálvez as Minister of the Indies. He submitted the matter to the Council of the Indies, which reviewed the docket in mid-1786. On the recommendation of its own fiscal, it urged that all measures, including the increase in salary for the two solicitadores, be approved by the crown. Sometime late in 1786 or early 1787 the letter bearing the

royal approval must have reached Mexico City,[83] and the two solicitadores then received their long-awaited raise. Their new salary shows
up in Table 7.1 in the column for the year 1788.

The Beleña upheaval in the General Indian Court sheds interesting light on the nature of later Bourbon reforms in general. Upon clear
evidence that one grievance of the erring employees had a basis in fact,
the viceregal government moved to remedy it, and generously, through
a 100% raise in pay. The new regulations were directed at specific
abuses and needs rather than any theoretical model for recasting the
entire system, but the head officials also were determined to enforce
the rules and devote the necessary vigilance for securing that end. The
dockets of Indian cases of the last decades of Spanish rule show far
greater order and contain notations indicating careful compliance
with the rules. That the notations were reviewed is also evident from
one case before the General Indian Court in 1800, a suit of an Indian
of Huicuiltepec, province of Zacualpan, against the local justice, for
sequestering his goods. The solicitador and procurador charged no
fees, as was proper. One abogado listed "half-fees 20 reales and no
more; I so swear." The crown attorney, pointing to the charge, recommended that the abogado be ordered to refund it, "since the Indian as
a tributary owes no fees," and the court in its judgment so ordered.[84]
The cases of the last decades give a firm impression of a staff that functioned much more efficiently and perhaps in a better-knit fashion. It
had a much better-developed esprit de corps in serving the Indians.

During the entire colonial period, in the view of many viceroys
and the legal agents attached most directly to the General Indian
Court, the ideal arrangement would have been reliance solely upon
them for legal services before tribunals in Mexico City—in short, a
monopoly, to be enforced by prohibitions against resort to other legal
agents. Had the Indian agents constituted a perfectly functioning bureaucracy, operating promptly and without corruption in Indian interests, they might have had a better chance to enforce such a monopoly;
but as our discussion of corruption and the clauses of Beleña's reform
rules indicate, that was hardly the case. Their claims were sure to
arouse opposition, even if they had operated as an incorruptible body
without taint of partiality or inefficiency, simply because the parties to

83. The new rules were approved by royal cédula of October 1, 1786: Beleña, 1,
part 5:211, no. 346. The same cédula may have carried approval of everything as a
package, or there may have been separate ones for various items, but they would have
been issued about the same time. Transmission to Mexico City would take six weeks or
more, probably longer.

84. AGN-Civ, vol. 2163:exp. 7 (5 fols.) (LBSD, vol. 2).

cases themselves were not prepared to accept adverse judgment without complaints and charges of unfairness. In the end, they would resort to other legal aides in the hope that, whatever the rights or wrongs, another team would better advance their cause. The parties were much less interested in justice or fairness than in winning.[85]

As the Indian agents really functioned, the tributaries were even more moved to insist upon a right to choose other legal aides if they so wished. As reasonable and prudent people, they wished as much ground for maneuver as possible. Presumably, other legal aides who agreed to serve Indians lay under the same prohibitions and limitations on fees and costs as the Indian agents; but it seems unlikely that many lawyers would accept and carry forward cases without considerably more compensation, although that might be given surreptitiously or less directly in the form of gifts, services, or perhaps political power of some kind.

The issues appeared in three forms: the matter of *agentes intrusos*, the related one of clergy serving as attorneys and legal aides, and the right to use before the General Indian Court and elsewhere other legal aides licensed to practice before the audiencia. In a legal sense, the matter of agentes intrusos was the simplest; for the viceroy, audiencia, and licensed legal professions were all agreed that intrusos should not be allowed to function before the administrative and judicial organs of the viceregal government. Even prior to establishment of the General Indian Court, a series of autos acordados and ordinances forbade any person not on the list of licensed procuradores of the audiencia to serve as procurador or solicitador before the organs of the viceregal government, except with express permission of the viceroy. For Spaniards, the penalty for violation of the rule was two years' banishment from Mexico City; for all others, 200 lashes and similar banishment.[86]

In addition to defending the monopoly of duly licensed abogados and procuradores, this rule aimed at ending the abuse by unauthorized and usually rascally volunteers who met Indians coming to the capital for suits or petitions and persuaded them to accept the interlopers as their legal agents. They then delayed and prolonged negotiations or pleadings, if they started them, and when they had exhausted the ability of their clients to pay further, abandoned them and their cases. This abuse was closely linked with another one that equally

85. The summaries of cases in Chapter V make the truth of these statements clear.

86. Beleña, 1, part 2:93–94, no. 100, summarizing legislation of January 13, 1575, March 10, 1588, and December 11, 1590. See also the discussion in Chapters III and IV above.

aroused the viceregal government—namely, that these rascals, usually identified as "mestizos and mulattos," persuaded Indians coming to Mexico City with foodstuffs for sale to turn all over to them as agents. Here the governmental objection was to diversion from the normal public market—"regrating," in the medieval conception—as well as to defrauding the peasants. Both abuses were rampant in the sixteenth century, that of intrusive legal representation being one of the main reasons for establishment of the system of Indian agents and the General Indian Court. However, although the measures of the 1590s probably reduced the frequency of the abuse, they were unable to end it.

A major part of the problem arose from the gullibility and suspicions of peasants confronting a strange system, very often conducted in a language they could not understand, in an unknown, frightening city. In their fears and timidity, many fell easy prey to smooth-talking confidence men. In 1656, the audiencia found it necessary to reenact its prohibitions against unauthorized people meeting Indians on the road to Mexico City and representing themselves as legal aides or agents for the sale of foodstuffs.[87] In 1682, the audiencia by special instruction to the alcalde mayor of Chilchota ordered enforcement of the enactments of the sixteenth century forbidding unlicensed people to serve as legal aides.[88] Almost exactly 100 years later, Viceroy Mayorga again moved against agentes intrusos in the General Indian Court, through an order of January 10, 1782, that any found preparing petitions and pleas or otherwise operating be arrested at once by the court bailiff and placed in the royal jail for trial. The reform rules of 1785 incorporated this injunction, instructing that any signatures be examined to determine if they were of licensed legal aides or someone else other than the party, any agente intruso so detected to be incarcerated immediately in the royal jail for decision on prosecution by the assessor.[89] Since detection operated through the inspection of signatures of legal aides, the new method had a chance of success that might be rated as fair to excellent. All depended upon the vigilance of the solicitadores and procuradores of the medio real, spurred by their vested interest in warding off intruders.

A special aspect of the agentes intrusos was the appearance of clergy as legal aides. Their motives must have varied widely, from genuine concern with people who either were their charges or might be so considered; through a wish for approval, popularity, and influence

87. Montemayor y Córdova de Cuenca, part 2:fols. 35v–38f, no. 98, and Beleña, 1, part 1:59, no. 98, giving the text of an auto acordado of May 4, 1656; the pertinent clause is no. 6.

88. Mexico City, November 27, 1682, in AGN-RCD, 67:fols. 13v–14f.

89. Reform rules of 1785, clause 4, in Beleña, 2:201, no. 47.

among the lower classes; to simple venality. Throughout the colonial period, friars and secular priests in the parishes stirred the Indians to suits: so ran the suspicions and accusations of many administrators reporting to Madrid.[90] It was a simple step for some of the priests, especially seculars, who might acquire legal training perhaps for other purposes related to their own needs and those of the diocese, to take and promote Indian cases, even though they may have held no license from the audiencia or viceroy.

Perhaps the most celebrated instance of violation of the rule, one that secured temporary royal license, concerned a secular priest, Antonio Laynez, who attempted to practice in Indian cases before the tribunals of Mexico City and did so for many years in the mid-seventeenth century. He was able to persuade many Indians that he could gain more for them than other legal aides. When warned to desist by the audiencia and the archbishop, Laynez, in alliance with a mestizo, Gaspar de Santiago, who was then governor of San Juan Moyotla, secured signatures from members of the government of that and other communities on a petition directed to the crown, asking that Laynez be named their defender. Sent secretly without any of the required permissions, the petition reached Madrid and received favorable result in a royal cédula of May 24, 1668, authorizing Laynez to use the power of attorney issued by the Indians, but also asking for a report from the viceroy whether there might be reason or evidence to the contrary.[91]

By the time the cédula reached Mexico, Gaspar de Santiago and a number of the members of his group were in jail on charges of spending money they had collected as royal tribute. Notwithstanding their circumstances, they arranged to have a petition, signed by them and claiming to be in the name of all the Indians of New Spain, presented to the viceroy, asking that the royal cédula be recorded and implemented. This was done, but the new governors of the two parcialidades and other principales then petitioned the viceroy to have the cédula withdrawn, on the ground that it had been secured on false evidence; that they did not wish Laynez to be their attorney or defender, and that indeed his acting as such would be their "total ruin." In the light of such a petition, the viceroy did what he had to—i.e., consult the audiencia; institute an investigation, which confirmed the validity of the opposition to Laynez; order the cédula recalled; charge the archbishop to punish his cleric; and report to the Council of the Indies. Laynez was placed in jail by his Church superiors; and upon review of all the documents sent to Madrid by the Council of the Indies,

90. See the discussion in Chapters III and V above.
91. AGN-RC, 10:exp. 42 (BLT).

the crown by royal cédula dated Madrid, August 10, 1670, approved the revocation of its earlier cédula, charging the archbishop to punish Laynez severely for causing the "upsets and seditions proved in the certified copy of the papers" sent to Madrid.[92]

One might think that Laynez had shot his bolt. Not so; for in a letter dated May 26, 1674, sent to the Conde de Medellín, president of the Council of the Indies, he complained of the discredit brought upon him and of the sorrow of the Indians that he no longer was allowed to work for the defense of people so continually subject to mistreatment. His letter was reviewed together with the other papers in the case— unfortunately for him, the Spanish government was most efficient at keeping files—and by royal cédula of December 10, 1675, the viceroy, by then the archbishop, was instructed to enforce the cédula of 1670.[93]

Laynez may have been a rascal; he certainly worked with a rascally governor. On the other hand, he may have been a sincere defender of the Indians, who surely were oppressed and mistreated, as he stated. The evidence we have does not justify too firm a judgment. Clearly, the viceroy, judges, and legal professions united to oppose him; and although their opposition involved a defense of legal monopoly, they accumulated a weighty dossier against the man. Perhaps more telling a point, the new governors of the parcialidades violently objected to him as defender. At this point, a fair estimate would be that Laynez was either too impetuous to be effective, or a rascal.

A second instance, which occurred a few years later, concerned Lic. Luis Ximénez de Mendoza, a secular priest and cacique of the city of Tlaxcala, a rare case of an Indian who was trained in law and may even have been admitted to practice as an abogado. An affidavit of his competence, reliability, and zeal was filed with the Council of the Indies in 1680. Ximénez de Mendoza acted as legal representative for the province of Tlaxcala before the Audiencia of Mexico in a successful proceeding for gaining a lower tribute from the province. He further acted in proceedings for remedying and curbing the exactions of alcaldes mayores, and in suits for keeping offerings to the Church down to the official schedule. His activities aroused the Bishop of Puebla, the cathedral chapter, and the alcalde mayor of the province of Puebla, all of whom combined to have the provisor and vicar-general of the diocese arrest Ximénez de Mendoza on the ground that he promoted upset among the Indians. His property was embargoed and he himself imprisoned in fetters in the episcopal prison for over three months. When finally released, he was admonished to take no further

92. The royal cédula is incorporated in that of December 10, 1675, cited in note 93.

93. AGN-RC, 14:exp. 147 (BLT).

part in Indian petitions and cases. As he told the story, he emerged from prison so crippled that he had to spend more than two years in bed, all for having worked for the relief of his poor fellow Indians.

Ximénez de Mendoza must have enjoyed considerable backing in the province of Tlaxcala, for among the petitions from the province to the crown in the early 1680s appeared one from him, appealing to the Council of the Indies and the king for license to serve freely as Indian legal procurador for the province of Tlaxcala, with title of defender-general, as had been conceded to Laynez (by then a thoroughly unfortunate reference). He asked further that the crown issue a royal cédula enjoining the royal and Church authorities to recognize his title and not hinder him on any pretext in exercising it. As was customary, the crown referred the petition back to the viceroy for substantiation of the allegations and a recommendation, all to be sent to Spain as quickly as possible for royal decision.[94] Although we do not have further records on the affair, the report must have urged against such an appointment.

The two affairs of Laynez and Ximénez de Mendoza make evident the amount of trouble that a clergyman, and especially one with legal training, could stir up, should he champion Indian complaints. For an administration which aimed at tempered exploitation in a system of estates, merely curbing abuses that went too far, and ever fearful of Indian upheaval, such intervention was sure to be obnoxious. Under the relatively pro-clerical later Hapsburgs, people in holy orders could practice law. Under the Bourbons, devoutly Catholic but thoroughly regalist, any such intervention became less tolerable. In the reworking in 1744 of the auto acordado of 1642 on lawyers, clergymen were specifically limited to practice in specified categories of cases.[95] In 1757, by royal cédula, the crown expressly ordered that henceforth no clergyman might be admitted as abogado, and that those already licensed might plead only in defense in their own cases, those of the church where they held benefice, those of their parents and other persons of whom they were heirs, and in those of the poor and miserable.[96] Under that regulation, no person in holy orders eventually would have had license to practice as abogado before a lay tribunal, through

94. Royal cédula to the Conde de Paredes, Viceroy of New Spain, Madrid, June 17, 1682, and affidavit of obedience, Mexico City, December 20, 1682, in AGN-RC, 19:exp. 26 (BLT).

95. Montemayor y Córdova de Cuenca, part 2:fols. 44f–48f, no. 129; auto acordado of October 30, 1642, on officials and lawyers of the audiencia, has nothing on qualifying or on clergy. The reworking of this auto acordado by a new one of January 7, 1744, in clause 13 expressly enacts limitations on men in holy orders received as abogados: Beleña, 1, part 3:20, no. 57.

96. Beleña, 1, part 3:2, note.

a process of natural extinction. Unwilling to wait even that long, the crown by royal cédula of November 25, 1764, passed by the Council of Castile, but extended to the Indies, ordered that no clergy, secular or regular, might serve as agents or procuradores for persons or communities in lay affairs.[97] So the prohibition became absolute for all direct forms of legal aid.

The issue of the right of Indians to choose licensed legal representatives other than the agents of the medio real was far more difficult for the lower Indian agents and the viceregal government—for, although it did not affect the notaries, it brought the interests of the other legal professions into the fray on the side of the Indians seeking choice. The dispute really was limited to representation in Mexico City, since the Indian agents obviously could not function in the provinces, so that natives with petitions or cases had to turn to local persons. Presumably the local representatives found themselves bound by the standard restrictions on charging Indians fees and costs. Some unusually honorable ones may have done so, but many or most would be unlikely to. Direct fraud, quid pro quo in the form of barter or favor, and under-the-table arrangements are hardly inventions of the twentieth century. Some Indian communities, to be on the safe side, petitioned for legal license from the viceroy to appoint a legal representative in their suits, presumably in the provincial court.

Even in Mexico City, it would have been impossible for the Indian agents to have served in all Indian cases. For perhaps three-quarters of a century, a somewhat uneasy informal compromise or truce existed, in that natives could employ legal representatives of their own choice in cases before the audiencia and other tribunals, if they chose not to ask for representation by the Indian agents; but in the General Indian Court, they were required to use the Indian agents. What broke the truce came as attempts by the province of Tlaxcala to sue for redress of the highly illegal repartimiento de mercancías and other exactions by its governor, as well as excessive charges by curas. The Tlaxcaltecans were directed to use the Indian agents as representatives; but found them, as they stated, to be spies for the other parties, and at best given to long delays. They were usually so busy that they could not handle the complaints, or turned them over to bumbling, incompetent substitutes. In 1678, the province secured from the viceroy, Archbishop Fray Payo de Ribera, permission for all Indians to employ any licensed abogado, paying his fees themselves, particularly in complaints of exactions by alcaldes mayores and curas. They took their complaint of corruption and demanding fees against the abogados

97. Ibid., part 5:175, no. 290.

and procuradores of the medio real to the crown in Madrid, and secured a royal cédula, dated June 17, 1682, ordering investigation, reform, and the punishment of culprits.[98]

Perhaps equally useful to the natives of New Spain was another royal cédula of the same date, also secured on petition of the province of Tlaxcala, that all Indians be allowed freely to pursue all matters proper in law, and at all proper times, without any requirement of bond of any kind, since all were to be held poor and miserable. The concession applied to matters before the audiencia and viceroy, but not to appeals to the Council of the Indies.[99] This second cédula confirming an existing privilege, perhaps not always enforced, meant that charges could be filed freely against provincial governors, curas, and others without need for posting bond against falsehood or calumny.[100]

The province of Tlaxcala, with its strong corporate sense, had active representatives in Madrid through some years of the 1680s. Returning to the offensive, perhaps strengthened by corroboration of their previous charges, they petitioned the crown for royal confirmation of their right to employ legal representatives of their own choosing, should they wish. The abogados and procuradores of the medio real were too busy with Spanish business to attend to Indians, they explained, or worked for the other parties. Their petition expressly exempted the solicitadores from the complaint, declaring them to be hard-working public officials who truly attended to their Indian clients. Accordingly, they asked also for explicit royal permission for the solicitadores to perform all legal duties normally reserved for procuradores in judicial and administrative matters. The royal cédula that was issued incorporated the previous one of June 17, 1682, ordering investigation of Indian agents, which was again to be enforced, but repeated the substance of the Tlaxcaltecan petition.[101] After receipt of each royal cédula, the viceroy ordered investigation, punishment of the guilty, and reform.[102]

98. Konetzke, 2:744–745, no. 502.

99. Beleña, 1, part 5:205–206, no. 378; full text in 2:188–189, no. 44.

100. Philip III, Lisbon, July 20, 1619, in RLI, 7.1.12; Viñas Mey, 203–204; auto acordado of September 27, 1677, in Beleña, 1, part 1:33–34, no. 49.

101. Konetzke, 2:764–766, no. 519.

102. The copies of the two royal cédulas, in AGN-RC, 19:exp. 32 and 20:exp. 100, carry affidavits of obedience. That of 1685 carries also an affidavit of the viceroy's order for investigation and enforcement. In a long letter to the king from Viceroy Conde de Paredes, Mexico City, January 23, 1686, the measures for enforcement are given in detail. Essentially, these were notification to the legal aides and notaries and publication so that the Indians would know. The audiencia ordered that the Indians might use any procurador on the official list, paying his fees. The exact meaning of that permission is not clear, since the audiencia and the viceroy did not revoke Velasco II's restrictions, which were being enforced in the later eighteenth century.

The far more important and enduring results arose from the implied royal permission to choose any licensed abogado, enlargement of the legal powers of the solicitadores, and the royal confirmation of release from the need to post bond. The royal confirmation of Indian rights as free subjects in these cédulas merely empowered them to choose at will among abogados and procuradores licensed to practice before the audiencia. Their representatives still remained bound by the standard legal limitations on charging Indians fees and costs, and still had the same possibilities for illegal arrangements. In 1787, after renewed measures for ending the operations of agentes intrusos, the viceroy again defined the limitations on Indians and their rights in legal representation. They were free to choose their own agents for cases in courts outside Mexico City, namely, those tried before alcaldes mayores, corregidores, and other provincial and local judges. They had to resort either to the Indian agents, or to other proper legal officers licensed to appear before the audiencia, in any cases heard in the General Indian Court or any other superior tribunal, either in first or second instance.[103] Presumably, existing legislation covered the matter of fees.

The energetic and successful battle of the province of Tlaxcala, in conjunction with the steady employment by Indians of other legal representatives before the audiencia, indicates unmistakably that the natives objected to exclusive reliance upon the Indian agents and the General Indian Court. That point raises the question of the Indian approach to the court and the Indian agents and of their reasons for use of them; for clearly they sometimes used them, and at other times shunned them. Consideration of the question is made difficult by the fact that our knowledge comes almost entirely from documents prepared by Spaniards and so influenced by Spanish cultural patterns that the Indians tend to disappear behind a series of formulas. Moreover, we are dealing with millions of people and more than two centuries, with all the variety possible in such masses and such stretches of time. Nevertheless, we can arrive at some ideas.

In the Indian approach, as one may detect it from legal records, the General Indian Court and its agents provided an additional opportunity for maneuver in their battles against enemies and opponents and in maintaining rights they claimed. Hence their strenuous objection to making the court and its agents the only channel for redress of grievances and legal defense. Their own preference lay in jockeying from one channel to another, seeking the one likely to be most favor-

103. Beleña, 2:201, note.

able to their case. If the Indian complaint concerned a Spaniard, or if a Spaniard initiated suit in a local court or in the audiencia, the Indians were likely to move the case to the General Indian Court.[104] A characteristic pattern was that a Spaniard sued before the audiencia, which tended to be more sympathetic to his interests, whereas the Indians began their defense or countersuit in the General Indian Court, which was apt to be more favorable to them. Similarly, in a suit between Indian communities or in a quarrel that pitted a barrio against town authorities or against another barrio, one party very often would sue in a provincial tribunal or the audiencia and the other take the case to the General Indian Court. In such instances of multiple suits on the same grievance, the General Indian Court took jurisdiction in first instance.[105] A natural extension of this practice of choosing the most favorable jurisdiction for hearing was that, should a case in a provincial court begin to turn out unfavorably for one party, or be likely to, the affected litigant took it to the General Indian Court, hoping for a more favorable hearing there, or at the very least for postponing the unhappy day of defeat.[106] In criminal cases against Indian nobles and town officials—which very often involved feuds within the town, with the provincial governor siding with the prosecuting group—removal of the case to the General Indian Court was frequent, and perhaps the only way of securing a fair hearing.

Resort to the court was much promoted by a feature of Spanish procedure, even more pronounced than in our own—namely, that the solicitors and the court were dependent upon the allegations and testimony brought to them by the petitioner.[107] In Spanish law, the protection against tendentious testimony and charges lay in a requirement, in charges against officials and curas, that bond be posted to cover penalties for *siniestra relación* should the charges be disproved; but that requirement of bond came to be waived for Indians, who were declared free of it en masse as poor and miserable persons. Ultimately, of course, the other party would have a chance to answer, but might be put to great expense on ill-founded or false complaints.

The viceroy and the audiencia found themselves caught between, on the one hand, the royal desire to favor the natives and make sure

104. See, for example, case no. 18 in Chapter V, in which the Spaniard wished removal to the audiencia; Manuel González vs. Cuantillán, 1781, in AGN-Civ, vol. 2158, exp. 10 (5 fols.) (LBSD, vol. 5); Acatempa vs. Juan Antonio Romano, 1801, in AGN-Crim, 3:exp. 31 (5 fols.) (LBSD, vol. 2).

105. For example, cases no. 2 and 122 in Chapter V.

106. For example, cases no. 2, 62, 83, 97, 127, 153, 155, 167, 168, and 169, in Chapter V.

107. See, for example, cases no. 5, 14, 30, 86, 102, 103, 137, and 155 in Chapter V.

that they were encouraged to bring just complaints for early remedy; and on the other, a flood of complaints, many of which proved to be frivolous or malicious. To revoke freedom from bond or limit resort to the viceroy and audiencia was unthinkable. Accordingly, they ordered that any Indian appearing on behalf of a group or community be questioned closely, if necessary through an interpreter, to establish his true motive in coming to file complaint; whether he had been induced to do so and, if so, by whom; whether he had power from the community or group, or acted as a private person; in short, to investigate all circumstances that might shed light on the probable validity of the complaint.[108] Eventually, both the audiencia and the viceroy were forced to order that in disputes over land and water, any initial orders of amparo should be considered merely instruction to the provincial governors for investigation and report.[109]

One early case illustrates the problem. In 1611, the town of Tlaxiaco sued two Spaniards for damages by livestock and for the pay of Indian men and women working for them. The local Spanish justice, they complained, did nothing. A viceregal order was issued at once for full justice to be done; but upon its presentation in Teposcolula, the provincial capital, the alcalde mayor in great indignation prepared an affidavit that all claims had been paid in full. He then ordered the governor and alcaldes of Tlaxiaco arrested for contempt of the royal justice.[110] Many Indians had just complaints—perhaps most of them, but not all, by any means. Enough of them used or tried to use the court for causing trouble, pursuing enemies without proper legal cause, or avoiding punishment for their own misdeeds, to create serious problems in sifting testimony. As the viceroy and assessor declared in one case in 1806, the court was not to serve as a safeguard for delinquents.[111]

For us, reading the dockets, there is another problem, in that the standard reasons alleged by the natives for objecting to labor levies, petitioning for protection and extension in their lands, protesting new taxes, or complaining of exaction and oppression by their alcaldes mayores and curas was that they needed to build or repair their church, maintain divine worship and religious instruction, pay the royal trib-

---

108. See the discussion of release from requirement of bond, earlier in this chapter; auto acordado of September 27, 1677, in Beleña, 1, part 1:33–34, no. 49; royal cédula of the king to the Audiencia of Mexico, Madrid, July 12, 1695, in DCLI, 1:89–90.

109. Autos acordados of January 7, 1744, and June 7, 1762, in Beleña, 1, part 3:31–33, nos. 84–85.

110. Case no. 92 in Chapter V.

111. Pío Quinto José, of Istapaluca, province of Chalco, vs. the encargado de justicia, for arrest and beating, 1806, in AGN-Crim, 2:exp. 9 (20 fols.) (LBSD, vol. 1).

utes, and cultivate their fields in order to secure revenue for all of these purposes and to support their wives and children. How sincere they may have been, from petition to petition, is a matter for reflection in the light of legal pleas today. For higher Spanish officials, such arguments had strong persuasive power, since all of these activities fitted well with their conception of the natives' role in a well-ordered colonial society. The arguments themselves probably came from the Spaniards, for official Spanish orders and regulations are couched in the same terms.[112] They undoubtedly were incorporated in petitions and pleas on the advice of the Spanish and Hispanized legal aides who prepared the documents for their clients. Anyone who has had a lawyer prepare a legal instrument and has seen the translation of his intent into legal terminology will understand. One may doubt that there was massive hypocrisy in the colonial documents—for the natives, who lived in a society of estates and knew no other, were prepared, in general, to accept the terms and conditions of that society, even to the extent of a considerable amount of correction and abuse. Only after, and frequently long after, abuse reached limits regarded as intolerable did most of them seek remedy.

Two features that show up prominently in petitions and cases before the General Indian Court shed much additional light on the ways in which the Indians made use of its facilities. One is the large number of failures to press petitions and cases, once initiated. They appear in the Appendix with the term *suspenso* (in abeyance). The reason might be the technical one of failure to sign a power of attorney, so that the solicitador might proceed; but in many such instances, the client never again appeared to execute the necessary power. In many others, the client at any point in the proceeding might leave Mexico City with no further interest in his case.

Changing one's mind about a lawsuit, especially at the beginning, is hardly unknown today; but behind most of these occurrences lay something else, which is even clearer in the second feature, *apartamiento*. The complaining parties would announce by formal statement in court that they withdrew (*se apartaron*) from the case.[113] In a number of instances, they gave their reason, namely, that their claims had been satisfied in a private settlement. That must have happened in vir-

112. Ordinances issued by Montemayor y Córdova de Cuenca as judge of inspection, Tehuantepec, July 19, 1661, and Nejapa, October 19, 1661, in AGI-P, leg. 230A, ramo 3; and auto of the Audiencia of Mexico, September 25, 1662, in Testimonio de autos y padrones que el oidor Montemayor, 1661–62, ibid., ramo 8.

113. For example, cases no. 115 and 173 in Chapter V. A typical case is the capítulos filed by the governors of Mazatepec, Guasitlán, Tetecala, and Agueguexotzingo, province of Cuernavaca, vs. Don Antonio Santibáñez, alcalde mayor, in AGN-Crim, 45 : exp. 4 (52 fols.) (LBSD, vol. 24).

tually all instances of apartamiento and, one suspects, in many cases left in suspense. Complaint and suit arose when redress was refused or the settlement offered was less than the prospective complainant wanted. Beginning action in the General Indian Court, as in other tribunals, forced the prospective defendant to reconsider his position, weigh the costs of defense and the possibility of victory, and in many instances either offer a settlement or improve the terms of one already offered. The tactic would work particularly well if the complaint or suit might damage the reputation or public standing of the prospective defendant.

In short, the Indians of New Spain came to the court with ideas and motives that must have varied widely in the course of more than two centuries and among millions of people. Nevertheless, in general, they perceived the General Indian Court as another opportunity in a complicated game of defense, redress, and even offense. They fought to maintain their access to other avenues of redress, preferring as broad a range of choice as possible, but they also made wide and varied use of the resources provided by the court and the agents of the half-real.

CHAPTER VIII
The Fund of the Half-Real

THE General Indian Court and the fund of the medio real constituted two complementary parts of a whole. The yield of the fund, after the expenses of collection, supported the bureaucracy of Indian agents, in return for their pledge to provide legal services at reduced fees, or none at all, to their Indian clients. The court and its Indian agents could not have existed without the fund or some substitute for it not easily conceivable in the circumstances of colonial Spanish America. The fund endured as long as the General Indian Court, but with a separate existence more marked by hazard. Among the revenues administered by the royal officials in Mexico City, the medio real de ministros enjoyed a peculiar and almost unique status. It constituted an annual payment of legal insurance, an unusual concept during all the life of the fund. Linked to the royal tribute, it was not part of it. Collected and administered in the king's name, it was not a royal revenue, but rather a royal trust.[1] Until the expulsion of the Jesuits added a number of new funds regarded as trusts to royal administration,[2] the medio real de ministros was paralleled only by the *medio real de hospital*, the half-real each Indian tributary paid for the right to free care in the royal Indian hospital in Mexico City, should he or any member of his family present themselves, sick, at its gate.[3]

1. Fonseca and Urrutia, 1:536–552, give a history of the medio real de ministros which has been corrected and augmented in this chapter. On the relation of the medio real to royal revenues, see Testimonio de autos, 1703, in AGI-M, leg. 474.
2. Most notably the ramos of Temporalidades and the Fondo Piadoso de Californias: Fonseca and Urrutia, 5:91–242 and 6:303–320.
3. Ibid., 6:199–302.

Begun in 1592 by Viceroy Luis de Velasco II as a means of financing his new staff of Indian agents, the levy of a half-real per tributary was planned as a subtraction from the portion of the annual tribute reserved for the needs of the Indian community, i.e., the *caja de comunidad*. In practice, it quickly became an addition to this tribute, since the Indian communities steadily resisted any reduction of their portion. When by royal cédula issued in Valladolid on April 19, 1605, the General Indian Court received indefinite royal approval, the levy of the half-real was approved as well. The royal cédula also contained the pious wish that if any surplus arose in the yield, it be applied to the needs of the next year, and the levy be reduced correspondingly.[4] In the next two centuries that never happened.

Despite the initial plan, then, the medio real de ministros became a supplementary tax linked to the tribute. Each whole tributary, defined as a married Indian couple, paid annually one half-real, or a sixteenth part of the standard silver peso, in addition to their tribute. Half-tributaries, defined as widows, widowers, and unmarried adult men and women, paid half that amount.[5]

However, just as the tribute system was not truly uniform,[6] the levy of the medio real also developed variations. Some arose from the levy of tribute itself. In frontier zones in the north, the Indians were for many years exempt from tribute as an additional incentive to be loyal Spanish subjects. In general, the medio real was not collected in the same zones; that is, San Luis Potosí, Nombre de Dios, Guanajuato, Guadalcázar, San Miguel, and San Felipe. Even when the provincial governors began to levy tribute, the medio real usually was not collected. Throughout the Audiencia of Mexico, the tribute system began as a levy upon Indians in towns and spread somewhat slowly to Indian workers living on Spanish agricultural holdings without affiliation to a town (the *gañanes* or *laboríos*). Except in a few provinces such as Celaya and Salvatierra, payment of the medio real was not extended to them, perhaps because of the difficulty of collection. Where it was levied on laboríos, the alcaldes mayores received a premium of 9% on the collection. In general, the laboríos were more prominent in the north than in central and southern Mexico.[7]

Another anomaly arose from the presence in the Audiencia of Mexico of the Marquesado del Valle, the seigneurial estate conferred

4. See Chapter IV above. The royal cédula was entered in the RLI as 6.1.47.

5. For a brief history of changes in tribute classification and the categories within it, see Cook and Borah, *Essays*, 1:17–25; Fonseca and Urrutia, 1:411–518.

6. Cook and Borah, *Essays*, 3:102–104.

7. Fonseca and Urrutia, 1:539–540; report of José Rafael Rodríguez Gallardo, Mexico City, September 19, 1759, in AGI-M, leg. 520.

upon Hernán Cortés and his descendants in gratitude for the conquest of the country. The marquesado had the right to primary Indian tribute and adjudicature in first instance in the seven provinces of its grant. By royal cédula issued in Toledo on May 25, 1596, the crown ordered that the Indians within the seigneurial jurisdiction nevertheless pay the medio real for the salaries of legal aides, even if they should not be royally appointed ones. The terms were vague enough to contain an offer of compromise and some suggestion that the marquesado offer the same kind of service to its Indians, for the practice quickly formed that the seven provinces collected the medio real, but delivered only half to the royal treasury officials in Mexico City. The other half, retained by the Cortés holdings, maintained the marquesado's own staff of Indian agents. This arrangement lasted through a century and a half of bickering and adjustments between the viceregal administration and that of the marquesado. As a series of compromises came into being by which the judicial privileges of the Cortés estate were confirmed, but administered under the supervision of a *juez conservador*, who was always a judge of the audiencia, the issue of the medio real again arose in 1748. It was resolved by an agreement of the viceregal government, including the audiencia, that all of the medio real from the Indians of the marquesado should be retained in the coffers of the estate, to be spent on a parallel system of Indian agents within its jurisdiction. From 1748 on, the Indians of the seven provinces within the estate paid the medio real, but collection and administration lay outside viceregal and royal control.[8]

What the royal treasury officials in Mexico City considered a further anomaly concerned five western provinces, the so-called subaltern *alcaldías mayores* of Amula, Autlán, Izatlán and La Magdalena, Tuxpan and Zapotlán, and Sayula. Although administratively subject to the viceroy in the Audiencia of Mexico, for judicial matters they were part of the Audiencia of Guadalajara. Indian judicial matters arising within them, therefore, went to Guadalajara for decision. They were probably exempt from payment of the medio real from the beginning. The question of payment was raised during the administration of the Marqués de Casa Fuerte and was settled by him through a decree of February 14, 1731, to the effect that the Indians of the five subaltern alcaldías mayores should not be liable.[9] Since the General Indian Court and the Indian agents operated in both administrative and judicial spheres, the question had not been simple. Decision might have gone either way, but probably was dictated by previous usage.

8. Fonseca and Urrutia, 1:538; García Martínez, 115–116. See also Chapter IX for a fuller account.

9. Fonseca and Urrutia, 1:540; report of Rodríguez Gallardo, September 19, 1759, in AGI-M, leg. 520.

A final change in the classification of Indians subject to tribute and hence to medio real concerned unmarried women 18 years and over and widows. Originally they were included in the counts as half-tributaries, a practice that lasted for more than two centuries after the Conquest. Meanwhile, in a codification of categories of Indians subject to tribute, Philip III in 1618 decreed that no woman be held to pay, a provision that entered the *Recopilación de leyes . . . de las Indias*, promulgated as a general code for the Spanish possessions in America in 1680.[10] In the early decades of the eighteenth century, a series of local suits began to gain exemption for Indian women on the basis of this provision. The audiencia rendered judgment in 1731 that the royal will in the code must govern, but implementation was held up by a series of appeals to Madrid and royal orders for more information.[11] Finally, by royal cédula signed in Villaviciosa on November 4, 1758, the crown decreed total exemption from tribute for all Indian women.[12] That exemption carried automatic exemption from payment of the medio real. Implementation of the royal cédula was rapid for most of the country, but as late as the 1790s in some towns Indian women with land were being held to payment of tribute, and presumably of the medio real.[13]

To summarize a discussion that could easily become even more complicated, the medio real as a levy followed the definition of Indian tributary and changed with it, the major exception being the laboríos and other Indians living outside town control. In terms of territory, it was levied in less than the entire Audiencia of Mexico, in that frontier zones and the five subaltern alcaldías mayores did not pay at all, and the seven provinces of the Marquesado del Valle paid under special arrangements. Of the 150 provinces in the Audiencia of Mexico in the later eighteenth century, 132 delivered the medio real to the royal treasury officials in Mexico City. Of the 1,181 town cabeceras in the audiencia district around 1790, Yucatan not included, approximately 1,000 paid the medio real.[14]

In the towns and provinces, the system of assessment and collection was also closely linked to the tribute. Each recount and reassessment of a town or province for purposes of tribute also automatically

10. Royal cédula, Madrid, October 10, 1618, in the RLI, 6.5.19. The significant clause is "Las mugeres de cualquiera edad que sean no deben pagar tasa."

11. Royal cédulas, El Pardo, March 14, 1728, and Buen Retiro, December 21, 1748, in AGN-RCD, 90: fols. 200–202, and 102: fols. 61v–62v.

12. Fonseca and Urrutia, 1: 434–435.

13. Double expediente on forming new matrículas de tributos and implementation of the Ordenanza de Intendentes, 1788–1793, in AGN-Tr, 3: exp. 1–2 (151 fols.).

14. Fonseca and Urrutia, 1: 428, table between 450–451, and 540; report of Rodríguez Gallardo, Mexico City, September 19, 1759, in AGI-M, leg. 520.

adjusted liability for the medio real in the proportion of one-sixteenth of the new number of tributaries. Collection, like the tribute, began with town officials, who every four months had the obligation to collect the appropriate amount from their town members for delivery to the local provincial governor. Each alcalde mayor and corregidor, as part of the oaths and bonds required for taking office, had to execute a bond that he would deliver the yield of the medio real "in accordance with the amount indicated by the tributes of the towns and no more . . . ," the sums to be delivered promptly every four months to the appropriate agent for the fund in Mexico City, without being held back for the use of the provincial governor.[15]

Like the tribute, then, the medio real usually was paid in three installments a year through the town officials to the provincial governors, who, in turn, were supposed to forward the sums to Mexico City. Like the tribute, the system turned out to be subject to much delay and difficulty. Many towns were unable to pay the full amount due on time, and so built up large sums in arrears. That was particularly likely to happen during the late sixteenth and first half of the seventeenth centuries when Indian population was falling, so that the tribute assessments were adjusted to the lowered town populations only late and reluctantly. The accounting was also faulty in that the provincial governors tended to hold back the sums which they used for their local operations, so that delivery in Mexico City was late, very often completed only in the final adjustment of accounts during the required residencia. Neither the Indian town officials nor the provincial governors were supposed to receive any pay for collecting and remitting the medio real, beyond the formal salaries attached to their posts,[16] the only exception being that alcaldes mayores in the north might deduct 9% from collections from laboríos and vagos, that is, Indians not registered in towns.[17] The matter of payment for collection resurfaced toward the end of the Bourbon period with the changes brought by the Ordinance of Intendants.

In contrast to the essential machinery of local collection, which never changed during the entire colonial period, central receiving and disbursement in Mexico City did vary. In the second half of the eigh-

15. Royal provisión appointing Pedro de Salazar alcalde mayor of the mines of San Luis Potosí, Mexico City, November 22, 1612, in Cerralvo Papers (4 fols.); printed general instructions for alcaldes mayores by Velasco II, Mexico City, January 11, 1612, clause 49, in AJT-Civ, leg. 8; general instruction for alcaldes mayores, Mexico City, January 11, 1611, clause 33, in Beleña, 1, part 1: 37–44; relación de mando, September 1, 1771, in Croix, 58.

16. See citations in note 15; report of Rodríguez Gallardo, Mexico City, September 19, 1759, in AGI-M, leg. 520.

17. Fonseca and Urrutia, 1: 539–540.

teenth century, as tribute and viceregal officials tried to analyze the history of collection for the crown, they indicated four periods, i.e., four changes in system. During the first, which lasted throughout the Hapsburg period and until 1703, central collection for the medio real remained separate from that for the tribute. At the very beginning of the levy of the medio real, Velasco II appointed a treasurer, with the formal title of receptor and a salary of 300l. That office was continued on May 21, 1596, by his successor, Monterrey, either through reappointment of the same man or appointment of another. In the general adjustment of salaries under Montesclaros and Guadalcázar, the stipend of the receptor-treasurer rose to 496/2/8 (see Table 7.1). Instructions regulating the duties and obligations of the post were issued on September 16, 1596, by Monterrey, and on November 26, 1620, by Guadalcázar. Under them, the treasurer was responsible only for the sums actually delivered to him by the alcaldes mayores, and nothing more. He had an obligation to press the provincial governors to deliver their quotas, but in no way might he be held liable for their failures to comply.[18]

In the fiscal systems of the time, there were two basic methods of collection: direct administration, and rental or farm. In the first, royal officials undertook collection directly, exacting the sums due, moving the money if necessary to Mexico City, and maintaining detailed accounts of amounts due, paid, and in arrears. In the second method, the tax-farm, the crown in public auction sold the right of collection to private bidders, who might be invited to bid for a specific tax over the territory of the entire audiencia, or by district. The contract awarded to the highest bidder might be for one year or a term up to perhaps five. The successful bidder was then obligated to pay the crown the sum agreed upon, in installments also agreed upon; in short, the crown could count upon the stipulated amount, which had to be delivered regardless of the success or failure of collections by the tax-farmer. The latter counted upon the difference between what he paid and, hopefully, the larger sum he collected, to provide him with a substantial profit. As a private individual, he could substitute his own efforts and those of less well-paid agents for the clumsy, slow-moving, expensive operations of royal officials; moreover, since his own well-being was at stake, he would look closely to receipts and seek to avoid pilfering and malversation of funds which now belonged to him.[19]

18. Report of Rodríguez Gallardo, Mexico City, September 19, 1759, in AGI-M, leg. 520. Rodríguez Gallardo could not trace the collection system back of May 21, 1596. See also Díez de la Calle, 126–127 (cap. 2, part 7). Since collection began in 1592–93, there must have been a receiving official in Mexico City at that time.

19. Colmeiro, 1:547–560 and 2:1145–1156; see also Borah, "The Collection of Tithes," 393–397, and "Tithe Collection in . . . Oaxaca."

As the Bourbon historians of the royal treasury in Mexico surveyed what records they could locate, it seemed to them that the "medio real was rented from time immemorial in five-year contracts, with public announcement and auction, the successful bidders posting bond to the satisfaction of the royal treasury officials."[20] The instructions of 1596 and 1620 to the treasurer would indicate, to the contrary, that the first system was direct delivery by the provincial governors to the treasurer. That the system worked well may be doubted, since, despite the fact that his liability was limited to sums actually delivered to him, the treasurer for the years 1607–1619 owed 70,542/0/9, a huge deficit uncovered in a visita of 1620. Presumably that sum represented the surplus of collections over disbursements for those years, put to his own uses by the treasurer, since there was no call upon it. Apparently the crown could recover nothing, for all of this deficit entered into the far larger deficit found in the mid-eighteenth century.[21] The change to tax-farms, divided on a territorial basis and running for as long as five-year terms, may have come about as the viceregal government tried to remedy matters.

We have almost no data on the operations of the collection system of the medio real in Mexico City for the long stretch of time from 1620 to 1702. The shrinkage of the Indian population, which lowered tribute accounts, brought the yield of the medio real below a point at which it could cover the generous salaries of the early seventeenth century. In accordance with the custom of the time, failure in the revenue meant failure to pay the full charges upon it, normally in pro-rata reduction. The redoubtable Palafox adjusted salaries to revenue in 1643 (see Tables 7.1 and 8.1). Thereafter, the fund of the medio real and the people drawing stipend from it rocked along in reasonable adjustment for the rest of the seventeenth century. During the second half of the century, the beginning of increase in the Indian population, showing up in tribute counts and schedules revised upward accordingly, eased the pressures upon the fund and even permitted some extremely modest adjustments of salaries. In the absence of specific records, it is difficult to arrive at any firm statement on the presence or absence of scandals in the administration, but one may make an argument from absence: namely, that since there are no royal cédulas among the many of the seventeenth century in the Mexican national archive demanding reports on misuse or loss of funds, whatever did take place was too insignificant to reach the notice of Madrid.[22] The system of tax-

20. Fonseca and Urrutia, 1 : 538–539.

21. Report by Rodríguez Gallardo, Mexico City, September 19, 1759, in AGI-M, leg. 520.

22. The Real Contaduría de Tributos, in the same years, was involved in a series of scandals: Cook and Borah, *Essays*, 3 : 8–9; Fonseca and Urrutia, 1 : 442–443. Ac-

farming very much reduced the chance for pilfering, so far as the royal treasury was concerned.

The change to what the Bourbon historians of the royal treasury considered the second period and system in administration of the medio real came in response to a royal cédula signed at Madrid, April 28, 1702. The ministers of the new Bourbon king, searching for revenues to finance the War of the Spanish Succession, were examining the finances of the monarchy in a desperate effort to locate revenue. The royal cédula, reciting that Don José de Bustos had been appointed treasurer of the fund of the medio real by the previous viceroy, with a salary of 600/ a year, ordered immediate and unconditional abolition of the office, and return to administration by the royal treasury in Mexico City, as before.[23] Although the royal cédula clearly was in error as to the history of administration, it could not be ignored, and set in motion a long inquiry duly reported to Madrid.[24]

Investigation at that time into the archives, at viceregal command, could not locate any evidence on when the office of treasurer had been established, nor how the revenue had been administered before there was a treasurer. A request for a report from the royal court of audit (the *Real Tribunal de Cuentas*) brought a somewhat embarrassed answer that the court of audit never had checked the accounts of the fund, because it was not considered a royal revenue. Asked for its opinion, the royal tribunal of central accounting for royal revenues (*Real Tribunal de la Contaduría Mayor*) suggested that administration be entrusted to the *Real Contaduría de Tributos*, the central administration of Indian tributes; that under suitable bonds, the provincial governors deliver sums collected to this body for accounting, administration, and disbursements, in the form specified in the royal cédula of August 9, 1690, for the medio real levied for construction of the cathedral in each diocese. When the contador de tributos, in turn, asking for copies of all documents, pointed to the difficulties of getting the provincial governors to keep funds for the medio real separate in their accounts, since they delivered sums at intervals and often made a large settlement after their terms were over, he suggested the royal treasury

---

cording to the latter source, the royal ramo of tributes lost 346,000/ under direct administration after the year 1694 to some unstated date early in the eighteenth century. The bankruptcy of Antonio Salamanca added a loss of 6,536/, for a total sum of 352,536/ by the end of 1735. In view of these losses and difficulties in collection of tributes, the parcialidades were farmed out, beginning in 1736, for some decades thereafter. The tributes of other provinces apparently were handled by direct administration.

23. AGN-RC, 31:fols. 39f–40f (BLT).

24. Testimonio of inquiry resulting from the royal cédula of April 28, 1702, and consulta of the Council of the Indies, 1703, in AGI-M, leg. 474. The following account is based upon these documents.

officials as the appropriate parties for administration. At this point, the crown attorney for the treasury urged further inquiry.

We may be grateful for that further inquiry, since it furnishes us with a list of the annual charges on the fund as of April 24, 1703 (see Table 7.1). Upon further discussion, the contador de tributos reluctantly agreed to administer the medio real for the time being, but continued to object to taking on the charge without a supplementary stipend for himself or anyone in his office. The minimum, he argued, was appointment of a special official in his office, paid from the fund, and a supply of the stamped paper needed for accounts, also to be paid from the fund. These conditions met the approval of the crown attorney, who further recommended that the notary of the General Indian Court do the notarial work without charge, since he already was paid, and that the contador get no salary, since the king had the right to readjust his duties at will. On April 16, 1703, the viceroy accepted the terms as an interim arrangement and ordered Bustos to turn over all papers within fifteen days. Apparently he did so, but the transfer ran into the obstacle that the Real Tribunal de Cuentas, now spurred to audit, could not finish its task quickly enough for rapid transfer. Meanwhile, the contador de tributos, after another and equally unsuccessful attempt to secure additional stipend, in July nominated Juan Fernández de Valdivia Cartagena, who had formerly held a post in one of the escribanías mayores de gobernación, as the paid official. After careful report on the man's antecedents and the amount of work involved in the new post, salary was set at 400/ a year.

Valdivia Cartagena took up his duties in August 1703 with considerable bureaucratic vigor and imperialism. One of his first moves was to ask for copies of all pertinent documents on the medio real; copies of all new tribute assessments from 1702 on, from the secretaries of the audiencia; and copies of the bonds of all provincial governors, from the notary of the General Indian Court. Somewhat upset at the quantity requested, the crown attorney suggested that copies of the bonds be supplied as needed. The contador de tributos, on behalf of his new official, also asked for a report from the governor of the Marquesado del Valle listing what salaries his officials received from the medio real and what was turned over to the royal administration. He wished copies of the specific documents on which all of the marquesado's actions in regard to the medio real were based, for examination by the viceroy. This, too, the viceroy conceded through an order to the governor of the marquesado, duly delivered and accepted. All reports and actions, copied into a notarial *testimonio*, were sent to Spain.

In Spain, the Council of the Indies had been notified through two letters from the viceroy antecedent to the long dossier sent in December 1703. The crown attorney of the council recommended approving suppression of the office of treasurer, but nothing else, since there were no documents to show why the office had been established. On December 1, 1703, the council agreed on formal approval in these terms.[25] Whether the Council of the Indies and the monarch approved the new system or not, it became indispensable once the office of treasurer was suppressed. The change probably meant a major shift in central administration, in that the Real Contaduría de Tributos administered the revenue directly, without tax-farms, the provincial governors being required to deliver sums they collected directly to the royal office for tributes, along with their remittances and accounting for the royal tributes.

That the new system would save money proved illusory from the start, as is quickly apparent from Table 7.1, for by 1738 four officials within the office received stipends to a total annual charge of 1,900/, in addition to a cost of 31/2 a year for a ream of stamped paper. By 1768, officials within the royal office for tributes were drawing 2,650/ annually, the ream of stamped paper continuing as a steady annual cost.

With a steadily rising Indian tributary population, held to increasing total tributes through recounts every five years, this increase in stipends was negligible. Unfortunately, however, the change to direct administration quickly brought more serious problems and costs that handling of the revenue by tax-farms had either concealed or left for the tax-farmers to struggle with at their own expense. First in order of magnitude was undoubtedly the matter of uncollected arrears and deficits in the accounts of the provincial governors. Between the beginning of direct royal administration on August 11, 1703, to mid-1720, an amount of 71,251/5/2 remained due under the tribute assessments but undelivered. From mid-1720 to the end of 1734, the arrears rose to 130,884/4/3, and from 1735 to the end of 1744 they rose yet further to 153,447/4/11. In over 40 years of royal administration, failure to collect an average sum of 3,788/6/8 a year piled up impressive arrears.[26] Not all of the deficit could be laid to negligence or malversation, since epidemic and crop failure made it impossible for some villages in some years to meet their quotas, and the country-wide epidemic of *matlazáhuatl* in 1736–37 made it impossible to collect from many towns.[27] Despite rising arrears, it should be noticed that the fund

25. Embodied in royal cédula to Viceroy Alburquerque, Madrid, December 19, 1703, in AGN-RC, 21:fol. 469f–v (BLT).

26. Report of Rodríguez Gallardo, Mexico City, September 19, 1759, AGI-M, leg. 520.

27. Fonseca and Urrutia, 1:435; Gibson, *The Aztecs*, 448–451, lists epidemics during the colonial period. The epidemic of *matlazáhuatl*, which began in 1736, lasted until 1739.

nevertheless yielded a steadily rising revenue, minus the costs of collection, during these years (see Table 8.1).

Second among the costs was a new one brought by direct administration. Since the medio real was based upon the tribute counts and reassessments, the officials in the Real Contaduría de Hacienda—most notably two oficiales mayores, Pedro Telles and his successor Laburu—raised the claim, in a series of petitions and suits that lasted from 1714 until 1758, that they should be paid additionally from the medio real for revising the counts. Telles was successful in securing orders for payment at intervals, for a total sum of 11,615/; but then on the ground that such revision of the tribute assessments was a function of his office and had not previously been given additional compensation, the crown by royal cédula of July 28, 1739, ordered that all sums be returned and that Telles pay a fine of 1,000/ for misrepresentation. Appeal on that decision lasted until 1758, when the Council of the Indies finally ruled in favor of Telles and his successors. Sums paid by the two men to the royal treasury and the 1,000-peso fine were to be returned to their heirs.

The settlement, enshrined in a royal cédula of April 28, 1758, awarded payment at the rate of 1/2 (10 reales) for every 100 tributaries, and 2/4 (20 reales) for every 1,000 Indians under tribute age. In 1791, the two historians of the royal treasury calculated that from 1728 until 1787 the award brought the officials concerned in revising tribute counts and assessments an average of 1,332/2/4 a year, or a total for the 60-year period of 79,937/6/10. For the eleven years from 1777 to 1787, the annual average ran 1,425/7/10, testimony to a slowly rising population. The charges continued until the end of 1787, when the Ordinance of Intendants assigned the entire cost of reviewing tribute counts and assessments to the Real Contaduría de Tributos. From 1788 and thereafter, the medio real de ministros was free of this cost.[28] The amounts shown in Table 8.1 are the net of these costs. As the fact of victory in the long suit suggests, there was neither impropriety nor unfairness in the cost, but it was a new one which lowered what would otherwise have been a higher annual yield.

A third possible problem, normally inherent in direct royal administration, does not show up in the official history nor in official reports on the medio real. It was direct fraud. The cost of this may be concealed in the huge sum of arrears in delivery that had arisen by the end of 1744; or perhaps the constant inspection of accounts, be-

28. Report of Rodríguez Gallardo, Mexico City, September 19, 1759, and papers in the suit of the oficiales mayores of the Contaduría de Real Hacienda, Mexico City, to collect for tribute counts, 1714–1755, esp. nos. 52 and 53 of the Testimonio, which deal directly with the medio real de ministros, in AGI-M, legs. 520 and 798 respectively; and Fonseca and Urrutia, 1:541–545.

TABLE 8.1   Yield of the Medio Real

Year	Amount	Source
ca. 1600	40,000/plus	Royal cédula to viceroy, Valladolid, July 1, 1603, in AGN-RCD, 4: exp. 28.
ca. 1643	11,500/	Estimate, based on maximum possible yield of 13,000/, less probable arrears: Cook and Borah, *Essays*, 3: 1–28, 95–102, and 118–124.
ca. 1680	20,000/plus	Royal cédula to viceroy, Madrid, June 17, 1682, in Konetzke, 2:744–745 no. 502. Probably too high.
1738	12,175/5/3	Testimonio in suit of officials of Con-
1739	10,467/6/11	taduría de Real Hacienda, Mexico City, in AGI-M, leg. 798, nos. 52 and 53.
1743	18,624/6/6	Report of Rodríguez Gallardo, Mexico City, September 19, 1759, in ibid., leg. 520.
1745	16,700/[a]	same
1747	16,600/[a]	same
1749	16,236/7/6[b]	same
1753	22,406/5/9	same
1754	22,576/1/6	same
1755	22,641/2/3	same
1756	23,599/5/9	same
1757	24,215/4/6	same
1758	24,610/1/9	same
1767	21,748/0/7[c]	AGN-Tr, exp. 1, fols. 41–42.
1768	19,409/4/5[d]	AGN-Tr, exp. 2.
ca. 1778–1782	21,332/1/6	Beleña, 1, part 5:232.
1788	23,400/0/3[e]	Fonseca and Urrutia, 1:349.
1805	29,904/0/9[f]	Estado general, Mexico City, December 5, 1805; original in AGN-Tr, 43: last exp.

[a] Revenue farmed out.
[b] Tax-farm lowered, since Marquesado was to collect from its tributaries and pay its own Indian agents.
[c] Uncollected for the year: 699/4/7, or a total due of 22,214/7/11. Amount shown as yield includes 231/5/6 arrears of previous years.
[d] Uncollected for the year: 2,986/5/8, or a total due of 22,396/2/1.
[e] Uncollected for the year: 1,161/1/4, or a total due of 24,561/1/7.
[f] Amount due according to tribute schedules after deducting Yucatan and the Marquesado. The latter came to 1,500/4/9 due. Collections probably ran less by perhaps 10%, so that the yield for the year was nearer 26,914/.

cause of the long suit of the oficiales mayores of the tribute office, may have made pilfering, except on a very small scale, too dangerous.

In 1744, the towering total of arrears led the royal treasury officials to review the collection system and embark upon a sharp change. They decided to revert to handling by tax-farms, the rental to be at public auction for annual contracts for the entire territory. The successful bids came to 16,700/ for 1745 and 16,600/ for 1747, a distinct reduction in net yield, which had been 18,624/6/6 in 1743. For 1747, because of the subtraction from the tax-farm of any revenue from the Marquesado del Valle, the highest bid came to 16,236/7/6. These yields, though, were certain, and came with none of the headaches of direct administration.

The years 1745–1752 constituted the so-called third period in systems of collection for the medio real.[29] The impulse to change back to direct administration, the fourth period, came with the appointment of a new contador general de tributos, José Rafael Rodríguez Gallardo, who took office in 1752. When the best bid for the tax-farm of the medio real came only to 18,150/, Rodríguez Gallardo and the royal committee on tax-farms decided to return to direct administration. Under the direction of the new, energetic contador, who insisted upon regular audit, the medio real yielded 22,406/5/9 in 1753. For the five-year period 1753–1757, the annual average yield came to 22,730/1/3.[30] There was a slow but steady rise until 1761–64, when a countrywide epidemic of *matlazáhuatl* again made it impossible for many towns to pay and forced cancellation of the sums due. The annual yield fell to 19,409/4/5 in 1768 and rose slowly thereafter until the calamitous crop failures and epidemics of 1784–87[31] (see Table 8.1). Even so, the annual yields were not too much lower than those of the 1750s, but did reflect the relative trough in the movement of population. By 1805 they were considerably higher than the best yields of the 1750s,[32] and probably continued high until 1810, when the outbreak of the Wars of Independence brought turmoil and either inability or refusal to pay on the part of many towns affected by propaganda and devastation.[33]

29. Report of Rodríguez Gallardo, Mexico City, September 19, 1759, in AGI-M, leg. 520.

30. Ibid.

31. Fonseca and Urrutia, 1:435; Gibson, *The Aztecs*, 450–451; see values and sources in Table 8.1. See also the proceedings for release from tributes because of the epidemic of 1788 for towns in the Mixteca Alta, 1792, in AGN-Tr, 6:exp. 19.

32. "Estado General de tributos y tributarios, 1805," second table, 28–37.

33. See, for example, the expediente on the petition of Coixtlahuaca and San Miguel Tequixtepec for release from the medios reales de ministros y de hospital and the pulque tax for 1812–13, because of the ravages of rebels, 1815, in AGN-Tr, 30: exp. 26.

What might have been a fifth period in the history of collection of the medio real, or a subperiod of the fourth period, showed signs of coming into being upon the application to Mexico in 1787–88 of the system of intendants. In the general considerations of how to apply the enacting ordinance, there were discussions covering tribute and medio real. The ordinance legislated a new, simpler definition of tributary— namely, that all adult males within the ages liable to payment be counted as full tributaries, thus holding unmarried males and widowers to full rather than half payment. The effect would have been an increase in yield of the levy, and accordingly in the yield of the medio real. However, although much discussed and investigated, that definition never was implemented. Similarly, the viceroy and audiencia discussed at some length finally conceding compensation for collection to the provincial governors—renamed subdelegados under the ordinance—and to town officials. They decided upon a 6% deduction from the total collected, 5% to the subdelegados and 1% to the town officials, but also decided to suspend granting it so long as the new definition of tributary should not be put into effect.[34] In practice, the delay turned out to be permanent, since abolition of the entire levy came sooner.

Change to direct administration in the fourth period did not affect the problem of arrears, which had led to tax-farming in 1745. The problem of additional arrears did not arise under the system of tax-farms in the third period, and the more energetic fiscal administration under the later Bourbons was able to prevent substantial increase in the amount. Rodríguez Gallardo, who served as contador de tributos from 1752 to 1770, seems to have been an unusually able and energetic official.[35] There remained, however, the arrears of the past.[36] A

34. Double expediente on forming new matrículas de tributos and implementation of the Ordenanza de Intendentes, 1788–1793, in AGN-Tr, 3 : exps. 1–2 (151 fols.); arts. 132 and 137 of the ordinance, Madrid, December 4, 1786, in Beleña, 2 : 39–40 and 41–42. For the entire viceroyalty, including Yucatan and Tabasco, the new classification would have increased the number of full tributaries by 11.7% through reclassifying half-tributaries as full ones: "Estado general de tributos y tributarios, 1805," 6–27, esp. 27.

35. Estado y razón de la renta del medio real de ministros, Mexico City, September 6, 1769, in AGN-Tr, 2 : exp. 1.

36. The paragraphs which follow are based upon the report by Rodríguez Gallardo, Mexico City, September 19, 1759, Viceroy Amarillas to the king, Mexico City, April 2, 1759, and annexed documents and consultas of the Council of the Indies in the docket, in AGI-M, leg. 520; consulta of the Council of the Indies, September 26, 1763, and annexed documents, ibid., leg. 1324; royal cédula of the king to the viceroy and Audiencia of Mexico, Madrid, September 19, 1790, incorporating the earlier royal cédulas of December 20, 1763, and November 10, 1773, in AGN-RCD, 159 : fols. 23v–27v; and Fonseca and Urrutia, 1 : 545–547.

substantial sum, 70,542/0/9, represented a deficit in accounts going back well over a century to the time of Montesclaros and Guadalcázar. By the mid-eighteenth century, the royal treasury could not be sure who the responsible heirs were. Even for towns in arrears in the eighteenth century, collection proved difficult; sums owing from provincial governors were even more so. At the time of the change to tax-farms, Viceroy Fuenclara, in an attempt to spur collection of arrears, ordered that the bailiff of the Real Contaduría General de Tributos be paid 2/ a day for work on such collections. Between 1745 and 1759, he managed to recover 40,000/ at a charge of 5,826/, but the still-uncollected arrears stood at 223,000/.

In 1759, Rodríguez Gallardo wrote a long report on the history of the medio real, charges upon it, and problems of collection. Duly appended to a letter from Viceroy Amarillas to the king, that report served as the basis for much of the account of the fund in the late-eighteenth-century history of the royal treasury in Mexico, and for additional material incorporated here. The report by Rodríguez Gallardo became the subject for a long review in Madrid, where the royal government for the first time had a detailed, clear picture of the state of the fund and what had been happening. Decision was not embodied in a royal cédula until December 20, 1763, but embodied sweeping reform and readjustment when it came.

In the matter of arrears, the royal government decided upon a payment of 5% of any sum collected, and in accordance with that decision ordered that the bailiff of the Real Contaduría General de Tributos receive 5% of the 40,000/ he had managed to recover—that is, 2,000/, instead of the 5,826/ paid him at the rate of 2/ a day. He was to return to the royal treasury all in excess, and the remaining arrears were to be collected to the extent possible. Some small amounts could be recovered in later years, but in general the arrears turned out to be lost, something on the order of 220,000/.

Upon review of the stipends paid from the medio real, the royal government declared that some, such as the payment to the procurador de pobres, should be suppressed as improper. Other stipends were reduced or raised (see Table 7.1). Most important of all, no change might be made in stipend or charge without express royal approval, and the fund must be audited rigorously each year, a report on the exact state of accounts to be sent to Madrid. The result was to force to Madrid for royal approval the addition to the charges of the porteros and a raise from 100/ to 200/ in the stipend of the two solicitadores; but cumbersome as the procedures for change were after 1763, it is also true that the administration of the fund operated under regular, careful supervision without scandals. Such deficits and arrears as occurred were most often due to natural disasters no one could avert.

A major effect of the royal cédula of December 20, 1763, was to end the ability of the viceroy to direct payment from the fund. Since the medio real was not a royal revenue—and hence until 1745 not subject to regular audit, nor until 1763 to limitation of the viceroy's right to order disbursement at will—the eighteenth-century viceroys turned to it as a source of revenue for extraordinary disbursements. With the rise in yield in the early Bourbon period, the fund had a surplus over stipends that otherwise would have built up to a comfortable amount.

The practice had begun with Viceroy Valero, who in 1720 ordered 2,000/ delivered as a loan to the head of the special tribunal and police force for safety on the highways, the Acordada, the sum to be repaid from fines. For over 50 years that was not done. In 1722, the viceroy further authorized payment of a bonus of 500/ for distribution among the Indian agents, on the occasion of the marriage of the Prince of the Asturias, who became the short-lived Luis I. Thereafter, 500/ a year was distributed as a bonus to the agents of the half-real in unknown proportions until 1747, when Viceroy Revillagigedo I ordered an end to the practice. He may have considered it improper, or have found that the fund could no longer provide it, in view of his own disbursements from it. His orders for payment rapidly used up the surplus. They came to 4,000/ each to Manuel de Chinchilla, an alcalde de corte, for extraordinary work in the collection of arrears of tributes; to José Díaz de Celís, interim contador of tributes, for ten months spent also on collection of arrears of tributes; to Pedro Núñez de Villavivencio, previous contador of tributes, for similar effort; and to the royal treasury officials in Mexico City, for changing the old, cut coins for a new circular coinage. Since even the collection of arrears of tributes could not be considered a function of the fund of the medio real, Revillagigedo I's disbursements on matters other than the concerns of the medio real thus came to 16,000/.

Upon review in Madrid of Rodríguez Gallardo's report, the crown attorney of the Council of the Indies and the council itself held that at the very least the disbursements to the Acordada and the royal treasury officials must be repaid to the fund of the medio real; and, in strict legality, the grants for collections of arrears of tributes. In order to prevent similar raids by the viceroy, the royal cédula of December 20, 1763, instructed that not only should any increase in expenditure or new charge upon the medio real require express royal approval, but also that all surplus must be deposited in the royal treasury. If the surplus became substantial, the king must be consulted on what to do with it. The instructions were repeated in a royal cédula of November 10, 1773, and another of September 19, 1790. At that latter date, the 16,000/ of Revillagigedo I's grants still had not been returned to the fund, but equally no viceroy dared misapply any of the surplus.

Under the much stricter supervision of the fund through the royal measures, the careful limitation of expenditure, and the slow but steady rise in Indian numbers, the fund of the medio real did accumulate a substantial surplus. As of December 31, 1776, it stood at 53,707/0/4.[37] As a royal trust on behalf of the Indians, the royal cédula of April 19, 1605, instructed that any surplus in it either be used to reduce the levy in the succeeding year or be spent for the good of the native communities. There were three possible ways in which the royal will as expressed in 1605 might be implemented in the late eighteenth century. One was to apply the surplus to arrears of Indian tributes, a suggestion that elicited enthusiastic approval from the Council of the Indies when raised by Montesclaros in 1605.[38] By the 1770s, that kind of approach with its distinct note of hypocrisy was no longer possible among the enlightened ministers and officials of Carlos III. It does not appear to have been raised.

A second use for the surplus was to let it grow until it reached a sum sufficient for investment at interest with a return that would cover the charges upon the medio real. The levy could then be abolished. Since the charges came to between 16,000/ and 17,000/, the capital sum necessary, at the then-current standard rate of interest of 5%, was on the order of 320,000/– 340,000/.[39]

A third possible use was to apply the surplus to assist some institution established for the good of the Indians. The preference of the viceregal government, especially in the years of the frugal Viceroy Bucareli, and of the crown in Madrid, was creation of a capital sum and abolition of the annual levy. On the other hand, an interim measure which surely would have been used today—investment of the surplus at interest, as a means of assisting in increase in the capital sum— does not seem to have been considered. Since the money would have gone into the Banco de San Carlos or government obligations, all ill-fated, perhaps it was just as well. In the end, the viceregal government and the crown were forced to this third possible use, expenditure for the good of the Indians.

37. Fonseca and Urrutia, 1:547–548.
38. See Chapter IV above.
39. Such was the suggestion of Viceroy Amarillas: letter to the king, Mexico City, April 2, 1759, in AGI-M, leg. 520. Amarillas hoped that even the medio real de hospital could be ended, through return on a capital amount accumulated through the surplus of the medio real de ministros. See also Fonseca and Urrutia, 1:547.

The choice as to use of the surplus in the medio real de ministros was made, in effect, by the increasingly desperate need of the Hospital Real de Indios, the royal hospital for Indians in Mexico City, to which all Indians in the audiencia district were entitled to come for medical treatment and, should they die—as many did—for Christian burial. Toward the end of the eighteenth century, the hospital was treating from 2,500 to 3,500 Indians in a normal year, and many more in years of epidemic. It had a large building and staff, complete even to its own pharmacy for providing medicines. In the eighteenth century, the hospital enjoyed considerable provision of revenues in the form of a levy upon each Indian tributary of a half-real for the hospital, paralleling the medio real for the Indian agents; a permanent grant of 1,400/ a year from the crown, which might not be reduced or diminished in any way; the return from endowment funds invested at interest; the yield of the right to print and sell *cartillas*; and whatever profits might come from operation of the principal theater in Mexico City, the Coliseo. From 1786 to 1790, all of these revenues yielded an annual average of 36,265/6/9, substantially more than the yield of the medio real de ministros.

The problem of the hospital lay in the fact that, as against the Indian agents, with their unvarying annual set of charges, the hospital had to meet the emergencies of epidemics, which would bring more ill to its doors than it could handle; it also had to maintain a substantial, costly physical plant; and finally, it had to keep the Coliseo in repair and finance its operations, in order to get any revenue from it.[40] In 1779, an epidemic of smallpox brought the hospital to substantial deficit and need. Two suggestions of the administrator, for help from the $8\frac{1}{3}\%$ of the tithes assigned for hospitals, or from confiscated Jesuit properties, were rejected—the first on the ground that this portion of the tithes was already assigned for local hospitals, and the second for the reason that all had been assigned by then to suitable charitable purposes. There remained only the third suggestion of the administrator of the hospital, to apply the surplus of the fund of the medio real de ministros. Since assistance to the Hospital Real de Indios clearly was for the good of all the Indians in the audiencia district, and especially so in time of epidemic, there could be no legal or moral objection.

The viceregal administration approached the royal government in Madrid, royal approval being mandatory. Both agreed upon transfer from the surplus of the medio real through the device of a loan,

40. For accounts of the Hospital Real de Indios, see Borah, "Social Welfare and Social Obligation," 53–54; Muriel, 1:115–137; and Fonseca and Urrutia, 6:199–302.

payment being assured by assigning to the medio real the 1,400/ annual subsidy to the hospital from the royal treasury until the loan
should be liquidated. As events turned out, the first advance in 1779
from the surplus of the medio real had to be supplemented by another
in 1781. Massive crop failure and epidemics in the years 1784–1787,
perhaps the worst demographic disaster due to nature in the last three
centuries of Mexican history, forced other advances from the medio
real, the total of five years coming to 34,000/. That amount was partially offset by delivery to the medio real of the annual subsidy for the
hospital of 1,400/ for the years 1781–1786, a total repayment of
8,400/. In 1787, the immediate needs of the royal hospital reached
such crisis that the treasury subsidy had to be reassigned to it. In 1788,
the fund of the medio real lent the royal hospital an additional 5,625/.
At the end of 1788, the debt stood at 31,225/.[41]

Although detailed data have not been found for subsequent
years, it seems unlikely that the royal hospital was able to repay much
of its debt to the fund of the medio real, or perhaps any of it at all.
Because of the emergencies of the two natural disasters of 1779 and
1784–87, all loans had gone to ministering directly to the sick and
dying. There remained the badly needed repairs to the buildings of the
hospital and the Coliseo. On September 10, 1790, a royal cédula, reviewing the situation, ordered the viceroy to supply from the surplus
of the medio real funds for immediate repairs to the hospital buildings
and the Coliseo, and for other needs of the hospital.[42] From the royal
cédula, it was clear that application of the surplus of the medio real to
the needs of the royal hospital constituted appropriate and legitimate
use for the good of the Indians.

In 1797, a massive countrywide epidemic of smallpox brought
new emergency and renewed need for expenditure. A period of respite
after 1798 came to an end in 1806–1810 with epidemics in the districts around Mexico City of what were described merely as fevers.[43]
With the upheaval brought by the Wars of Independence, beginning in
1810, the load of patients for the royal hospital grew, at the same time
that its finances fell apart.[44] The viceregal government, with royal approval, probably made yet other advances from the surplus of the medio real, and the finances of the royal hospital never reached so favor-

41. Fonseca and Urrutia, 1:547–549; expediente on the needs of the Hospital
Real de Indios and deliberations in Madrid, 1782–1790, in AGI-M, leg. 1131; and audiencia gobernadora to the Minister of the Indies, Mexico City, December 27, 1784,
ibid., leg. 1283.

42. AGN-RCD, 159:fols. 23v–27v.

43. Gibson, The Aztecs, 451.

44. Muriel, 1:128–130.

able a state that it could make substantial repayment. There can be no doubt, nevertheless, that application of the surplus funds of the medio real to the needs of the Hospital Real de Indios was a worthy use, morally and legally in accord with the pious pledge of the royal cédula of 1605.

The fund of the medio real thus endured a somewhat checkered existence in which its status as a royal trust and not a royal revenue may have done it more harm than good. Despite the losses through dishonesty, carelessness, and unavoidable inability to pay, it probably fared better than its parallel royal revenue, the Indian tribute, which had a remarkably corrupt history in the seventeenth century and one of considerable arrears in the eighteenth. Whatever the turns and twists of collection policy and problems, the medio real, in general, met the charges upon it and met them with admirable promptness.

CHAPTER IX

The Special and Exempt Jurisdictions

WITHIN colonial Mexico—or within the Viceroyalty of New Spain, in the narrowest sense of that highly elastic term—there lay two audiencia districts: Mexico and Nueva Galicia (Guadalajara). The General Indian Court, its attached system of Indian agents, and the levy of the medio real de ministros operated within the greater part of the Audiencia of Mexico. The Audiencia of Nueva Galicia, as a separate audiencia district with its own high court—even though one subordinate in certain respects to the Audiencia of Mexico, and in even more to the Viceroy of New Spain—had a separate and different method of handling Indian cases.[1]

Within the Audiencia of Mexico, Yucatan constituted a separate, though subordinate, government under its own governor, appointed directly from Spain. He enjoyed considerable administrative and judicial autonomy, although appeal lay to Mexico City in both spheres, and his accounts were audited in Mexico City. A similar levy of half a real and a special judicial arrangement for handling Indian cases came into being in Yucatan as a separate, parallel system.[2]

1. On the early history of the Audiencia of Nueva Galicia and its jurisdiction relative to the Audiencia of Mexico, see the fine study by Parry, *The Audiencia of New Galicia*, passim, but esp. 162–163 and 167–184. The later period of Indian petition and litigation unfortunately lies beyond the temporal limitation of Parry's study.

2. Molina Solís, passim; Chamberlain, 275–345; royal treasury accounts for Yucatan, 1540–1650, in AGI-C, leg. 911A–B; Ancona, 2:148 and 189–190; García Bernal, *La sociedad*, 76–77, 104–105, 125, and 128–129; and Cogolludo, 1:205, 406–409, and 561–582 (lib. 4:cap. 10; lib. 7:caps. 12 and 13; and lib. 10:caps. 8–13).

Within the Audiencia of Mexico, in the narrower sense of excluding Yucatan, furthermore, there existed the seigneurial estate of the Marquesado del Valle de Oaxaca, with a royal grant of jurisdiction in first instance over its vassals and residents. Its claims conflicted with those of the General Indian Court and the levy of the medio real de ministros during much of the colonial period.[3] All of these special or exempt jurisdictions, in relation to the General Indian Court and the levy of the medio real de ministros under the administration of the Viceroy of New Spain, should now be examined.

Surprisingly, one seigneurial jurisdiction in the Audiencia of Mexico, with privileges paralleling those of the Marquesado del Valle, did not constitute a special jurisdiction in terms of the General Indian Court or the medio real. The Duchy of Atlixco, created in 1706 by Philip V as a reward for support of the Bourbon cause in the struggle over the Spanish succession, erected the perpetual encomiendas of one branch of the descendants of Moctezuma, the last Aztec emperor, into a seigneurial jurisdiction with the right to appoint the alcaldes mayores in the provinces of Atlixco, Ixtepeji, Tepeaca, and Tula. Its first holder was José Sarmiento Valladares, Conde de Moctezuma y del Valle de Atlixco through his wife, the true holder of the encomienda and its titles. Despite a royal privilege which paralleled that of the Cortés estate, the Dukes of Atlixco never opposed the General Indian Court's jurisdiction in their four provinces nor the levy of the medio real de ministros by royal officials.[4] Their estate, therefore, did not constitute a special jurisdiction for our purposes.

A. The Marquesado del Valle de Oaxaca

The Marquesado del Valle de Oaxaca[5] came into being in 1529 through royal grant of 23,000 vassals in a series of enumerated towns, with seigneurial rights to tribute and to justice and administra-

---

3. We are fortunate in having the fine study of the marquesado as a seigneurial jurisdiction in New Spain by García Martínez, passim but esp. 101–116.

4. *Diccionario Porrúa*, 1:167–168; Gerhard, *A Guide*, 57, 139, 279, and 333; royal cédulas of March 3, 1706, November 30, 1711, September 15, 1772, and February 16, 1775, summarized in Beleña, 1, part 5:88, nos. 59 and 60. Unfortunately, no study like that of García Martínez for the marquesado has yet been done for the Duchy of Atlixco. The records of the viceregal administration and those of the General Indian Court indicate no difficulties in exercising jurisdiction over Indian cases for the four provinces in the duchy.

5. The account which follows is based upon García Martínez, passim but esp. 33–90 and 101–116; for maps and a detailed description of the territories of the marquesado, see pp. 131–144.

tion. The first holder was Hernán Cortés, the first marquis, as reward for his role in bringing Mesoamerica under the rule of the Crown of Castile. So spectacular a service to the monarchy required the equally spectacular reward of a title and large seigneurial estate. On the other hand, the long-term policy of the crown was to reduce seigneurial privilege and prevent feudal alienation of crown control. In consequence, there resulted a long struggle as Hernán Cortés and his successors sought the widest possible interpretation of the royal grant, at the same time that the viceregal government in Spain was trying to restrict the terms as much as possible. In the interests of the centralizing policy of the monarchy, the viceroy and audiencia would have liked to bring the grant down to a permanent encomienda of 23,000 Indian tributaries, without rights of justice and administration. The marqueses, on the other hand, sought full rights of administration and justice within the towns designated in the grant, without interference of royal officials except for limited use of appeal.

Most prominently at issue were a count of the vassals and removal of all over 23,000 from the grant; delimitation of the towns—no easy matter, since that meant determining complex claims to others as dependencies; the rights of royal judges and agencies to operate directly within the territory of the marquisate in first instance in matters considered special royal obligations, such as inspection of obrajes and Indian suits and complaints; and the right of the viceregal government to set tributes and to exercise supervision over the administrators appointed by the Cortés family. The viceroy and audiencia were aware that within the marquisate there were considerably more than 23,000 Indian tributaries, and they and the king quickly learned that the enumerated towns included Tehuantepec, a port, so that the grant violated a long-standing royal policy of keeping all ports under direct royal control. An initial compromise in the early 1560s restored Tehuantepec to royal control, in return for a perpetual grant of money and maize equal to the tributes of those years and for the crown's agreement that, whatever the number of Indian tributaries in the enumerated towns, they might be held as vassals by the Cortés estate. The long decrease in Indian population unleashed by the Conquest brought the number of vassals within the 23,000 before the end of the sixteenth century. They were grouped for administration into seven provinces: Coyoacán, Cuernavaca, the Cuatro Villas in Oaxaca, Tuxtla, Toluca, Charo, and Jalapa del Marqués. Each was governed by an administrator appointed by the marquis and reported to a governor of the estate in Mexico City.

Tensions were resolved for a time in 1567 when the second marquis, Martín Cortés, was arrested on a charge of conspiracy against the king, the estate sequestered, and its holder shipped back to Spain for trial. Whatever the truth of the charges, the marquis paid a heavy fine and had to surrender the rights of administration and justice to the crown. In effect, the grant became a perpetual encomienda, receiving tribute from Indians resident within its towns, but with no other rights. This loss of seigneurial privilege lasted until 1593, when upon the marriage of the third marquis to Doña Mencia de la Cerda, sister of the Conde de Chinchón and lady-in-waiting to the Princess Isabel, Philip II restored to the marquisate civil and criminal jurisdiction, high, low, and mixed, as it had been before 1567. The royal will received implementation in 1594 and early 1595 through replacement of royal governors by ones named by the marquis and the governor of his estate.

Return of seigneurial jurisdiction meant a resurgence of the disputes over its meaning, with all the additions that the extending scope of viceregal intervention and inspection had brought in the second half of the sixteenth century, most notably the inspection of obrajes and the system of Indian agents based on the medio real de ministros which came into existence in 1592–93. Although faithfully carrying out the royal will, Velasco II was equally diligent in pointing out the problems that ensued. Once returned to seigneurial jurisdiction, the Indians of the marquesado began to refuse payment of the medio real from which came the salaries of the General Indian Court and the other Indian legal aides. Further, they advanced the claim that they were no longer subject to labor draft under viceregally-ordered repartimientos. Third, the administrators of the marquesado objected to viceregally-appointed inspectors of obrajes within the estate, on the ground of seigneurial privilege. Giving way on the first point, commented Velasco II, would mean that the Indians of the marquesado would be the prey of unscrupulous rogues, exactly the evil the system of Indian legal aides was designed to prevent. Yielding on the second would mean that Indians would migrate to the marquesado, to the gain of the estate and the loss of the crown and other encomenderos. Accepting the marquesado's claim on the third would mean much fraud and perpetual prison for Indians held in obrajes within the boundaries of the estate. Velasco II asked for a royal order that Indians living within the marquesado be treated as Indians held in the crown and by other encomenderos, despite the right of seigneurial jurisdiction.[6]

By royal cédula of May 25, 1596, Philip II ruled in favor of the views of his viceroy. The marquis and his administrators were ordered

6. Greenleaf, "Viceregal Power," 366–367, citing a letter of Velasco II to the king, Mexico City, January 21, 1595. The same arguments are advanced in a letter of April 6, 1595, in VC, fol. 188f–v.

to collect the medio real de ministros, even though the legal aides paid from the proceeds might be other than those of royal appointment. If the Cortés estate collected less tribute from its Indians or gave them any other advantage over Indians elsewhere, ran the royal cédula, the latter, "since Indians are averse to labor, would all move to the said marquisate, and the towns of my royal crown and those of encomenderos would become deserted." The cédula tried to distinguish between rights of seigneurial jurisdiction and an overriding obligation of the crown to protect Indians:

> I order and decree that, beyond what touches the jurisdiction I have commanded be returned to the said marquis, which he will enjoy in accordance with my grant, the Indians of his estate be subject in other matters to the same measures that govern those of my towns and the towns of encomenderos, as has been done until now, without difference in any matter of those listed above nor in others that may affect their conservation and increase. On these matters, my viceroy and audiencia must have very special care, as I have charged them; for if they do not, there may follow many undesirable consequences, and all that has been provided in favor of the Indians may be upset. . . .[7]

The cédula was received in Mexico City with formal act of obedience on September 11, 1597, and an order of implementation was issued.[8] A generalized version of the one clause on the medio real de ministros, rephrased to apply to all Indians under seigneurial jurisdiction, entered the *Recopilación de leyes . . . de las Indias*.[9]

The cédula of 1596 gave royal approval to the concept of a royal obligation to protect the Indians that overrode seigneurial privilege, a concept advanced by Velasco I in defense of his invasions of the privileges of the Cortés estate[10] and undoubtedly learned by the son from his father. Again, the marquesado displayed considerable powers of resistance through interpretation. When the viceroy appointed an inspector of obrajes with a commission to examine those within the boundaries of the estate, the marquesado protested, managed to have the commission revoked, and appointed its own inspector. Through repeated use of this tactic, it was able to forestall any meaningful royal inspection of obrajes for nearly a century, with the result predicted by Velasco II that the marquesado became a refuge for obrajes and the scene of flagrant abuse of the Indians within them.[11]

The royal provision on the collection of the medio real de minis-

---

7. The royal cédula is quoted in part and summarized in part in García Martínez, 115–116; the text he consulted is in AGN-J, leg. 318, exp. 15, part 2.

8. Montemayor y Córdova de Cuenca, part 1:216f, sum. 61.

9. RLI, 6.6.11.

10. García Martínez, 96–98; Chevalier, *La formation*, 172 and 420–421.

11. Greenleaf, "Viceregal Power."

tros was flexible enough for compromise. Its wording might be met by accepting full royal jurisdiction and administration for Indian suits or by setting up a seigneurial one, using the proceeds of the medio real within the marquesado, or by some mixed arrangement. We do not know what negotiations took place nor how long they were carried on. In the end, an arrangement came into being under which the marquesado collected the medio real de ministros and delivered half the proceeds to the royal treasury in Mexico City to help in covering the salaries of the royal Indian legal aides, but retained half for payment of stipends among its own staff—also in Mexico City—for their services in handling Indian complaints and suits in a similar way.[12]

This arrangement created a dual, competing system. Indians living within the marquesado and paying tribute there with its annexed levies had the right to apply to the legal aides designated by the marquesado for their protection and paid by stipends from its half of the medio real. They could sue or petition for adminstrative relief with the same abridgement of process and summary decision that marked the General Indian Court, and pay no fees or, if a cacique or community, half fees. They had an equal right to ignore the seigneurial machinery and apply to the audiencia or viceroy, who would use the same procedures, with the services of the royal Indian legal aides supplied on the same legal basis. In either instance, the application might come directly or through supersession of the jurisdiction of a court in one of the seven marquesado provinces. The two systems were in direct competition, but the royal one had the advantage that it could assume jurisdiction in supersession of the seigneurial one, and that formal appeals from seigneurial decisions came to the audiencia and the viceroy under an audiencia order of 1599.[13] For their part, the Indians used the two systems as they thought their advantage lay. On occasion they may have erred, but it was not for want of a considerable amount of knowledge and careful thinking.

A more durable compromise came into being during the course of the seventeenth and eighteenth centuries. It did not take final form until the years 1748–1769. The driving force through the earlier years was the virtual bankruptcy of the marquesado, which found its revenues unable to meet the charges upon them arising from the bequests and endowments of the first three holders of the estate. When the creditors embargoed the revenues of the estate, the Council of Castile pro-

12. Fonseca and Urrutia, 1:538.

13. See the cases summarized later in this chapter. In 1599, the marquis was expressly forbidden to exercise jurisdiction in second instance of any kind: García Martínez, 102, citing AGN-J, leg. 299, exp. 30, fols. 34–38. An eighteenth-century notarial copy of the papers of the suit is in ibid., exp. 29.

posed a special judge to administer the revenues; and upon nomination by the fourth marquis, the king, by royal cédula of June 9, 1613, appointed one to be in complete charge of the marquesado's finances and its remissions of funds to Spain. The special judge also took over management of the judicial jurisdiction of the estate, and by another royal cédula of August 31, 1616, gained the unusual privilege that no judges or other authorities might intervene in cases before him. Since the finances of the Cortés estate remained in precarious state for most of the seventeenth century, the office of *juez privativo* continued. By the second half of the seventeenth century, the title began to be *juez conservador*. The holder of the post was always a judge of the audiencia, appointed by the crown on nomination of the marquis, but serving the estate and drawing an additional salary from the estate for his services. In effect, the crown had the assurance that one of its judges exercised the judicial functions granted to the marquesado; the marquesado had the assurance that a man high in the viceregal government, and accordingly able to smooth over disputes, drew salary from it and saw to its interests. As events turned out, the juez conservador was usually the defender of the interests of the estate, so that the marquesado gained greatly from the arrangement.[14]

Development of the institution of the juez conservador gained concessions of considerable importance for the marquesado. The judge could act as inspector of obrajes, so that the viceregal government had the satisfaction of seeing the function discharged in the marquesado by a royal judge, and the marquesado equally knew that it was discharged by a judge it could trust and who drew salary from it. In 1680, the crown made decisions of the juez conservador appealable only to the Council of the Indies, and by a sobrecédula of 1681 cut off the protests of the audiencia. That concession, which removed hearing in second or third instance from the audiencia, led to continued protests from the viceroy and the audiencia. A royal cédula of August 22, 1742, reiterated the privilege and imposed perpetual silence, a command that did not stop the viceroy and audiencia from yet more protests. Another cédula of September 16, 1747, repeated the royal command. In obedience to the royal will, Revillagigedo I in 1754 was forced to threaten royal officials infringing the jurisdiction of the marquesado with a fine of 2,000/.

The accession to the throne of Carlos III reopened the question but led to an acceptable solution. By royal cédula of November 25, 1760, the king suppressed the office of juez conservador and its privileges; thereupon the audiencia again asserted its right to hear appeals. The marquesado then sued in the Council of the Indies and won a fa-

14. García Martínez, 80–81, 101–110, and 122–124.

vorable decision, embodied in first and second sentences of November 23, 1767, and November 22, 1768, and a definitive decision of February 4, 1769. The office of juez conservador held by a judge of the audiencia was restored. The judge was to serve as appellate judge in second instance for cases originating in the provincial courts of the marquesado, but his decisions in turn might be appealed to the audiencia in third instance before appeal to the Council of the Indies. The restored juez conservador was a more powerful official in the marquesado than the governor, for he had exclusive control over the finances of the estate and served as head judicial official. In the absence or incapacity of a governor, the juez conservador even discharged those functions.[15]

The calming effect of the intertwining of seigneurial and royal appointments in the same person, which extended to lesser officials within the government of the estate, may be seen in the sequestrations of the eighteenth and nineteenth century. In 1629, when the fourth marquis died, the title passed to his niece, who was married to the Duke of Terranova. At the end of the century, it passed through the female line again to the Pignatelli family, Dukes of Monteleone, resident in Naples. In the War of the Spanish Succession, the then-holder of the title sided with the Austrian claimant, and the Bourbon occupant of the Spanish throne on December 14, 1707, decreed seizure of the estate. It remained embargoed until March 30, 1726—but in an unusual form of confiscation in which the estate remained under separate administration by its own officials, none of whom were removed. All of its privileges were respected. The same treatment prevailed in the short sequestration of May 4 to November 28, 1734, and the longer one of October 12, 1809, to August 1, 1816, this last when the holder of the title sided with the Bonapartes.[16] Clearly the monarchy regarded the marquesado as sufficiently domesticated that it presented no threat to royal power.

The slow evolution of administrative arrangements which satisfied both the monarchy and the marquesado also led to resolution of the competing jurisdictions in Indian cases and the services of legal aides. The first settlement dealt with the medio real. No records yet have been located that shed light on the method of collection and division before 1703, beyond the statement that the yield was divided by halves between the fund administered by the royal treasury officials and the estate, nor did a search by the contador of the estate in 1802

15. Ibid.; Beleña, 1, part 5: 224–225, no. 422, summarizing the decision of the Council of the Indies; and Croix, 67, clauses 40–41, September 1, 1771.
16. García Martínez, 81–86 and 101.

find any.[17] Since the marquesado followed royal administrative and judicial procedures in its own practices,[18] the medio real undoubtedly was collected by its provincial governors along with the Indian tribute for delivery to the central financial offices of the marquesado, either in its entirety or the half retained by the estate. The share designated for royal administration may have been delivered to the treasury official or tax-farmer holding royal warrant by the provincial governors, or have been turned over by the central financial offices of the marquesado.

At some time early in the eighteenth century, probably 1703–05, the governor of the marquesado agreed that the estate would deliver the half of the yield of the medio real designated for royal administration to the royal treasury in Mexico City. Its responsibility would begin with the medio real collected for 1703. The year 1703 is the one in which by royal cédula the office of treasurer of the medio real was suppressed in favor of direct administration by the Real Contaduría de Tributos, and the governor of the estate ordered to report on collection and the legal basis for the existing system. At some time after 1731, the crown attorney for treasury matters initiated suit against the marquesado in the matter of the medio real, but unfortunately we do not know whether for control of all collection or for payment of the half that was designated for royal administration. The royal claim held the marquesado fully liable for all sums due, whether collected or not, to the end of 1731. The dispute continued until November 8, 1748, when the viceroy, after consultation with the audiencia, issued a decree declaring that the medio real must be collected, but should remain in the marquesado in its entirety, to be kept completely separate from other revenues of the estate. The decree specifically enjoined that the yield of the levy must be spent on the juez conservador and his staff, for the purpose of relieving the Indians resident in the marquesado from legal fees and costs. As for the royally administered fund of the medio real, which maintained the royally appointed staff of Indian legal aides, the marquesado need not contribute to it and owed it nothing. The viceregal decree of 1748 was in accord with the royal cédula of May 25, 1596, but beyond that neither the various entities of the royal treasury nor the royal historians of the

17. Fonseca and Urrutia, 1:538 and 540; reports of the contador of the estate revenues to the juez conservador, Mexico City, April 26 and May 17, 1802, in AGN-J, leg. 331, exp. 55.

18. García Martínez, 114–115. See also Instrucción librada por el Señor Marqués de el Valle para los justicias de el territorio de su estado en esta Nueva España, n.d., in AGN-J, leg. 448, exp. 3, which is clearly modeled on royal instructions. Although here an eighteenth-century copy, the instructions are more probably from the sixteenth or early seventeenth century.

treasury could find documents giving the detailed reasoning on which it was based. Neither could the chief financial officer of the marquesado in 1802, when he searched the archives available to him for information.[19]

Independence from the royal treasury was confirmed on June 20, 1755, by a junta of estate officials, acting on an opinion of the Real Contador de Tributos. Both agreed that administration of the medio real within the marquesado should be completely free from any ties to or supervision from the royal treasury, and that the yields must be spent for one purpose and that only, namely, support of the legal aides of the marquesado who served the Indians.[20]

Settlement of the dispute over the medio real in 1748, and the decision of the Council of the Indies on the scope of the judicial competence of the marquesado, embodied in a final decision dated February 4, 1769, led to settlement of the second point in dispute over Indian cases, namely, the claims of both the marquesado and the crown to adjudicature in first instance. The terms of the royal ejecutoria of 1769 aroused a further claim by the estate that the General Indian Court no longer entertain suits by Indians resident within the marquesado, but that these be heard by the juez conservador of the estate. After a good deal of consultation within the organs of the viceregal government, Viceroy Croix in 1771 ordered that "'the General Indian Court neither take jurisdiction of nor handle the petitions and suits of Indians and other residents within the provinces of the estate and Marquesado del Valle.'"[21] Thereafter such petitions and suits were referred to the *Juzgado Privativo del Marquesado* for adjudicature—no great problem for the petitioners and litigants, since it lay across the central square of Mexico City, in what is now the Monte de Piedad, facing toward the royal palace.[22] From the decisions of the juez conservador, as for the General Indian Court, appeal lay to the audiencia. For the half-century remaining to the Spanish regime, the viceregal government followed the decision of 1771 faithfully.[23] Although the Ordinance of Intendants of 1786 contemplated a change by which the provincial governors of the marquesado were to become royal subdelegados under the supervision of the newly established intendants,

19. Reports of the contador of the estate revenues to the juez conservador, Mexico City, April 26 and May 17, 1802, AGN-J, leg. 331, exp. 55; report of Rodríguez Gallardo, Mexico City, September 19, 1759, in AGI-M, leg. 520; Fonseca and Urrutia, 1:538 and 540.

20. Reports of the contador of the estate revenues, April 26 and May 17, 1802.

21. García Martínez, 110–111, citing AGN-J, leg. 299, exp. 13, penultimate folio.

22. Ibid., 123.

23. See the cases summarized later in this chapter.

TABLE 9.1   Marquesado del Valle de Oaxaca: Salaries Paid from the Medio Real de Ministros, 1755–1805

Title	1755	1770	1805
Judge of estate	250/	125/	125/
Governor of estate	250/	125/	a
Abogado of estate court	200/	200/	200/
Comptroller of estate revenues	100/	100/	100/
Chief clerk of estate revenues	50/	75/	75/
Chief clerk of offices of estate	25/	50/	50/
Notary	125/	100/	100/
Interpreter	20/	20/	b
Bailiff	20/	20/	20/
Procurador c	100/	75/	75/
Abogado for Indians and the poor		200/	200/
Second chief clerk of offices of estate			25/
Third chief clerk of offices of estate			50/
Second chief clerk of estate court			30/
Totals	1,140/	1,090/	1,050/

a Office vacant at time of report in 1805.
b No explanation given in report, but probably a temporary vacancy in post.
c In 1755, for Indians only; in 1770 and thereafter, for Indians and the poor.
Source: Report of Estate Office of Revenues (Contaduría de Rentas), Mexico City, December 14, 1805, in AGN-J, leg. 331, exp. 54.

that change was never implemented, and thus whatever consequences might have ensued from it never occurred.[24]

In accordance with the decision of 1748 on the medio real, the Cortés estate established a new table of stipends for its legal aides serving the Indians. Whether at the same time there was a reorganization of the staff for that purpose, we do not know. Essentially Indian petitions and suits were handled by assigning additional functions to officials already on the payroll, who in this respect served with no fee or the half-fees permitted in the instance of caciques and communities. The officials and stipends for the years 1755, 1770, and 1805 are listed in Table 9.1 The judge was, of course, the juez conservador and always an oidor of the audiencia. The abogado of the estate court (abogado de cámara) served as legal assessor, apparently in a manner approaching the services of the legal assessor of the General Indian Court. By 1770 the abogado and the procurador who directly helped Indians in their suits served in the joint function of legal aides for both Indians and the poor. Since the marquesado dealt with far fewer cases

24. García Martínez, 129–130; Beleña, 2:app., ix–x.

TABLE 9.2   Salaries of Marquesado Officials

Title	1714	1771
Judge of estate	1,315/	4,500/
Governor of estate	350/	4,000/
Abogado of estate court	200/	200/
Comptroller of estate revenues		525/
Chief clerk of estate revenues		200/
Notary	250/	380/
Notarial chief clerk		50/
Bailiff	75/	100/
Solicitador	100/	100/
Procurador	50/	50/
Supervisor of construction		50/
Supervisor of paving		75/

Source: García Martínez, 124.

than the viceregal government, the joining of function corresponded to the amount of business.[25] Both the abogados and the procuradores were admitted to practice before the audiencia and were legally officials of that body[26]—again, part of the happy intermingling of viceregal and seigneurial functions in the same people which resolved many of the disputes between the two jurisdictions.

The meaning of the additional stipends paid from the medio real to some members of the marquesado staff may be inferred from Table 9.2, which lists salaries for some of the officials as they have been found by Bernardo García Martínez and published in his fine study of the seigneurial regime of the Cortés estate. These salaries were better than the table indicates, in that they were not subject to the subtraction of media anata, as were royal appointments, and the officials in some years received bonuses that might run to two months' salary—as García Martínez comments, "a juicy bonus."[27] For the juez conservador and the governor of the estate, the stipends were relatively small, although not contemptible. It should be noticed that the juez conservador received from the estate in form of salary and other perquisites considerably more than his salary as a judge of the audiencia, which in 1771 was still 3,000/.[28] That difference may explain the tena-

25. Report of the Estate Office of Revenues, Mexico City, December 14, 1805, in AGN-J, leg. 331, exp. 54.

26. García Martínez, 122.

27. Ibid., 124. The list in Table 9.2 is selective; a fuller list is in García Martínez, 121.

28. Gálvez, 10 (December 31, 1771). The salary had not been raised for centuries, but rather was lowered by the levy of the media anata. Díez de la Calle, 116—

cious defense of the privileges of the marquesado by an official who was always a royal judge, sworn to the royal interest. For the abogado who served as attorney for the marquesado and assessor in Indian cases, the stipend from the medio real meant a doubling of salary. For the procurador, the stipend meant more than a doubling of salary; for the abogado, a fairly generous payment for forgoing fees; for yet others, lesser but still substantial increments to salary. The puzzling exception is the solicitador, on the payroll of the estate with an annual salary of 100/ but who does not appear at all on the list of stipends from the medio real. In the marquesado tribunal of the juez conservador, the procurador may have handled functions that in the General Indian Court devolved upon the solicitadores.

The history of the fund of the medio real de ministros in the marquesado after the viceregal decision of 1748 parallels the story of the royally administered fund but differs somewhat from it, for the officials of the marquesado had a more favorable agreement. Table 9.3 lists the number of tributaries on the rolls under prevailing assessments for various years, and the amount of medio real that such a number should have yielded if the levy were paid in full. Both values must be subject to certain corrective reflections. In the first place, the year given is that of prevailing assessments, which were all made at preceding dates that might range a considerable number of years back. Even under the much more efficient and careful later Bourbon administration, the first value for 1805 contains counts made between July 4, 1793, and December 6, 1800; that is, the latest in effect was already five years old.[29] In earlier years, the lag was much greater. In the second place, the totals for some years omit either one or both of the small provinces of Charo and Jalapa del Marqués. Accordingly, the true total may be from 75 to 525 tributaries more, or values in terms of the medio real of from 4/5/6 to 32/6/6—not large sums. In the third place, the values for the medio real are for the full amounts due; but in practice, arrears, failure to pay due to natural disaster, defalcation, and whatever expenses were deducted for collection would bring down the yield by perhaps as much as 10–20%. The disaster years of the 1760s and 1780s were reflected not merely in drops in number of tributaries but also in larger amounts that could not be collected.

One clue to attrition due to collection, perhaps an extreme instance, may be found in the adjustment in the royal contract for tax-farming in the 1740s. In consequence of the decision of 1748, which

---

117 (cap. 2, part 3), gives the salary at 800,000 maravedís, a sum that at 272 maravedís to the silver peso comes to 2,941/2/9; it had been rounded for convenience to 3,000/. Perhaps as a result of Gálvez' efforts, the salary was raised to 4,500/: Brading, *Miners*, 57.

29. "Estado general de tributos y tributarios, 1805," 28–34.

TABLE 9.3   Medio Real Legally Due by Assessment in the
Marquesado[a]

Year	Total Number of Tributaries	Medio Real
1620	17,642	1,102/5
1636	12,741	796/2/6
1706	15,941	996/2/6
1746	18,021	1,126/2/6
1756	20,169½	1,260/4/9
1771	18,125	1,132/6/6
1785	21,231	1,326/7/6
1794	20,968	1,310/4
1800	24,353½	1,522/0/9
1805[b]	24,009½	1,500/4/9
1805[c]	24,537½	1,533/4/9
1809	25,689	1,605/4/6

[a]The figures for tributaries are from assessments prevailing in the year at
the time the total was reported. The actual counts were made earlier,
and may represent lags of from a few years up to 20; see the dates of
formal assessment in "Estado general." Similarly, the medio real de
ministros due is based on the prevailing assessment. It represents a
maximum figure often not achieved because of arrears, natural disaster, and deduction of some costs of collection. For 1746, 1771, 1800,
and 1809, either Charo or Jalapa del Marqués are not included; for
1785 and 1794, both small provinces are excluded. The discrepancy
ranges from perhaps 75 tributaries to 525, or 4/5/6 to 32/6/6 of the
medio real.
[b]Value of Real Contaduría de Tributos, December 5, 1805: "Estado
general."
[c]Value in report of contaduría of estate, December 14, 1805. It probably
takes into account a new assessment or two.
Sources: García Martínez, 166–168; "Estado general de tributos y tributarios, 1805," 28–39; report of contaduría of marquesado to juez
conservador, Mexico City, December 14, 1805, in AGN-J, leg. 331,
exp. 54.

meant that the tax-farmer could not collect the half of the medio real
previously due from the Indians of the marquesado, the royal treasury
in Mexico City agreed to a reduced price, which discounted 363/0/6
(see Table 8.1). If we double the amount, that would suggest a value of
726/1 as the yield of the medio real within the marquesado under the
tax-farm. The sum due in 1746, as the value is given in Table 9.3, was
1,126/2/6, or a difference of 400/1/6. At half that value, or 200/0/9,
the tax-farmer would have remained with a handsome profit of 55.1%
on the royal share. This would have been too large to escape the notice
of the royal treasury officials. When they resumed direct collection,

they were able to raise the yield by no more than 40%. The inference is that there was also an element of arrears, failure to collect, and perhaps some retention by the provincial governors in the yield of the tax-farm. The marquesado collected its levy directly through its provincial governors, with small arrears except in times of natural disaster. Table 9.3 indicates the times of difficulty by the decreases in number of tributaries in the succeeding value shown. Except for those fluctuations, the table indicates the normal course of Indian population in central Mexico: a continuing decrease into the seventeenth century and a steady, if fluctuating, increase thereafter.

Disbursements from the medio real under the arrangements of 1748 and 1755 differed from those of the royal administration in that the entire sum collected in the marquesado had to be spent on the juez conservador and his staff for service of the Indians, whereas the royally administered fund was a trust to be spent for the benefit of the Indians; but after receipt of the royal cédula of December 20, 1763, no change in disbursement or additional disbursement might be made without express royal approval. The royal Indian legal aides, paid from a broader territorial base, on the whole received their salaries promptly, but those salaries were inflexible in a time of rising prices. It took years of delay to add the porteros to the list and to increase the salary of the solicitadores, because of the need for consultation with Madrid.[30] The marquesado staff, whose fund came from a much smaller territory, was in some ways on a more precarious base, but its administration could react more flexibly both in reducing and in adjusting salaries upward.

Downward adjustment, due to the drop in revenue resulting from the *matlazáhuatl* epidemic of the early 1760s, may be seen in the lower schedule of stipends of 1770 relative to 1755.[31] To their credit, the juez conservador and the governor of the estate took most of the brunt. The schedule remained at the same level through the natural disasters of the 1780s until 1805. If one adds the stipends of the two officials on the list but not receiving payment in 1805, the true total would be 1,195/ rather than 1,050/; the small increase came about through small payments to three additional officials.

Upward adjustment required building up a surplus. Until 1790 there was none that could be used for such a purpose, because the governors of the marquesado used whatever medio-real funds were available, after paying salaries, for ad hoc grants to sick and destitute employees and their families. Not all of these may have been serving the Indians, as the settlement with the crown required. In 1790, when

30. See Chapters VII and VIII above.
31. See Table 9.1.

the Marqués de Sierra Nevada assumed office as governor, he found the sum of the fund insufficient to meet the scheduled stipends of the staff for the first half-year and ordered that all ad hoc grants cease. Thereafter a surplus was built up. By the spring of 1802 the surplus reached 3,817/6/1, and the contador of the estate reported that even with a slight deficit in collections over the payment of salaries for the half-year, there would remain 3,798/7/7.[32] His report came in obedience to an inquiry from the juez conservador, who in April 1802 received a petition from his staff pointing out that the fund of the medio real was supposed to be spent entirely on them, that costs had risen over the years so that their salaries brought less real value, and that there was a substantial surplus in the fund. They asked that as much of it as possible be distributed to them pro-rata as an additional payment. After careful inquiry of the financial office of the estate and discussion, all of it supporting the employees, the juez conservador—who also discharged the functions of governor, since none had been appointed up to that time—directed the contador to distribute 2,100/, the equivalent of two years' salaries, to the employees, in accordance with the schedule and upon due execution of receipts. By May 19, 1802, that was done.[33]

In July of 1803 the employees returned to the matter of surplus with a new petition to the juez conservador. By then the surplus amounted to 2,130/5/5, in spite of the distribution of the previous year, and was sure to rise, since Indian tributaries were increasing in number. Again the employees pointed to the terms of the compromise with the crown and pleaded their right to all of the medio real. Since precedent had been set the previous year, the juez conservador ordered another distribution of the equivalent of two years' salaries as a bonus, another 2,100/. That was done on July 30, 1803. Thereafter distribution of the year's surplus, in the form of a bonus pro-rata according to stipend, became custom. On February 6, 1806, the juez conservador, noting that the surplus was 540/, ordered it distributed pro-rata; it was done the same day. By then, annual distributions had disposed of accumulated surplus, so that all that could be paid out was each year's surplus as it accrued.[34] The distribution constituted a varying but most welcome augmentation of stipend for the Indian legal aides of the marquesado in a time of rising costs. During those same years, the Indian legal aides on the viceregal staff were locked into stipends that had been set much earlier and were steadily falling in real value.

Let us turn now to Indian petitions and cases arising within the

32. Reports of April 26 and May 17, 1802, AGN-J, leg. 331, exp. 55.
33. The entire docket is in AGN-J, leg. 331, exp. 55.
34. Ibid.

marquesado. Since the judicial records of the seigneurial jurisdiction of the marquesado have not yet been found, we are dependent upon the records of the General Indian Court. Before 1771, the two exercised competing authority in Indian matters. After 1771, the General Indian Court relinquished competence in first instance, for Indians resident in the marquesado, to the seigneurial jurisdiction. Even then the Indians of the marquesado still had the right to invoke the assistance of the legal aides associated with the General Indian Court, despite the fact that their payment of the medio real did not contribute to the latter's support.

1. December 14, 1641, Mexico City. Final judgment in a suit of the town officials of Cuernavaca vs. Melchor Arias Tenorio, vecino of the same town and owner of a sugar mill. Bernardo López de Haro, procurador de indios, had sued in the General Indian Court on behalf of the town officials of Cuernavaca for the unpaid rent of 1 caballería of community land at 70/ a year and damages to trees removed; Arias Tenorio, the tenant, had not paid rent. López de Haro asks for an order to the local justice, since the land is under an embargo by the special judge of the marquesado, Oidor Agustín de Villa Vicencio. Notice to Arias Tenorio elicits no answer; so he is declared to be in *rebeldía*. It turns out that he is in jail in Cuernavaca at the order of Villa Vicencio. Further inquiry discloses that Villa Vicencio is willing to lift the embargo and that Arias Tenorio is willing to pay five years' rental at 60/ a year (probably the correct figure). José de Celi, another legal aide attached to the General Indian Court, on behalf of the Indians accepts all items in the declarations in their favor. The viceroy issues an order to pay and for execution and collection of costs on the property and person of Arias Tenorio. The bailiff of the General Indian Court is to enforce the judgment.[35]

On the whole, the two jurisdictions cooperated well in this case, demonstrating the utility of the appointment of a judge of the audiencia as juez privativo of the marquesado.

2. May 16, 1642, Mexico City. The principales and town officials of San Luis Amatitlán, province of Cuernavaca in the marquesado, report that the town is down to 8 households but nevertheless is held to provide one Indian workman a week for the mines of Taxco. The official in charge of labor levy assigned the workman to a secular priest, who sold his right to Francisco de Urquiza in the province of Cuernavaca. The Indian sent each week is forced to work hard and more than his week. The town asks for reservation from the work levy,

35. AGN-I, 13:exp. 433.

because of the low number of inhabitants and the fact that three of the households are of the rank of principales. The petition is reviewed in the General Indian Court. Upon the opinion of the assessor, the viceroy orders the justice of the town of Cuernavaca and the official in charge of labor levy for the mines of Taxco to report on the petition, giving the number of tributaries in the town, so that he may provide what is fitting.[36]

3. November 24–December 19, 1648, Mexico City and Jojutla. The trial of Don Juan Esteban, governor of Jojutla, for selling a 9-year-old boy for service in a sugar mill. (This case is no. 168 in Chapter V.)

4. September 12–14, 1652, Mexico City and Coyoacán. Juan Nicolás and other Indians of Coyoacán vs. the bailiff of the town, for seizing their pulque and jailing them. A petition by the Indians, obviously written by someone else, is presented to the viceroy, who on September 12, 1652, issues an order to the corregidor of Coyoacán that, if the Indians are in jail only for having pulque, they are to be released at once without costs. Two days later the order is presented in Coyoacán, where the corregidor takes testimony, releases the Indians, and sends the documents to the viceroy for decision of the General Indian Court.[37]

5. December 4, 1696, Mexico City. The Indians of the towns of Tecali, Tecalcingo, Jojutla, and Nexpa, all in the province of Cuernavaca, sue in the General Indian Court, complaining that Don Martín Rodríguez Mariscal, teniente in Jojutla, has served in that post for 14 years and should not be allowed to continue in it. The viceroy issues a decree that Rodríguez Mariscal is to be removed at once and the governor of the marquesado is to appoint someone else.[38]

6. September 9, 1740–June 15, 1747, Mexico City, Cuernavaca, Jonacatepec, etc. The Indians of Tetelilla and Talistac, province of Cuernavaca, vs. Don Juan Coutiño, teniente of Jonacatepec, for exacting improper fees and services. The case is heard by the juez conservador of the marquesado. The Indians use as their procuradores Pedro de Vargas Machuca, a viceregal Indian legal aide, and Lic. José Francisco de Aguirre Espinosa y Cuevas who is abogado defensor of the marquesado. Repeated pleas over a six-year period go first to the governor and justicia mayor of the Cortés estate, who uses his abogado de cámara as adviser, but quickly pass to the juez conservador, at this time Lic. Francisco Antonio de Echavarrí, judge of the audiencia, with

36. Ibid., 14:fol. 1 (LBSF, 9:4–6).
37. AGN-Crim, 29:exp. 2 (LBSD, vol. 22).
38. AGN-I, 33:exp. 372.

the marquesado's abogado de cámara acting as assessor. The juez conservador names a commissioner to take the testimony of the Indians in Mexico City, with the help of the audiencia interpreter, who holds the same function for the sala del crimen, the viceregal government, and the tribunal of the bulls of the Crusade. Testimony is also taken at length in Jonacatepec.

As the case proceeds, what had been initially a complaint against the teniente for exacting fees and services becomes a fight over fiestas and relations with other towns. The parish priest, an Augustinian friar, in his testimony upholds the teniente. Finally, a compromise is arrived at and issued as an order of the governor of the marquesado, ratifying the terms and setting penalties for violation. The Indians continue their protest. No fees were charged throughout.[39]

This case is an interesting example of the cooperation of people attached to various judicial entities. It also took place entirely within the marquesado's facilities.

7. October 22, 1764–June 4, 1765, Mexico City and Yautepec. Various Indians of San Miguel, a barrio of Tepoztlán, province of Cuernavaca, vs. their cura, for giving them cows and forcing payment in excess of the products of the cows. The case opens in Yautepec, where the teniente, an official of the marquesado, takes testimony on the complaints of the Indians. They then petition in the General Indian Court, rather than the court of the marquesado, complaining that their parish priest assigns them cows, collects annual rent on them, and forces replacement if anything happens to a cow. The viceroy issues a letter of ruego y encargo to the parish priest and a decree to the governor of Tepoztlán on January 31, 1765. On February 8, it is given formal obedience by the alcalde mayor of Cuernavaca. On February 9, the necessary proceedings take place and an affidavit of an order for observance by governors past, present, and future is prepared. A formal report of compliance is sent to the viceroy. On April 20 the Indians petition the viceroy again, complaining of persecution because of their suit. They ask that a receptor be sent to take testimony, at the expense of the alcalde mayor. On June 4, 1765, the viceroy orders that a certified copy be prepared of all previous documents and orders in the case. The docket ends with that copy.[40]

8. March 22, 1773–April 16, 1774, Mexico City, Cuernavaca, Tlaquiltenango, Cuautla, Jonacatepec, etc. The Indians of Tetelpa and nearby towns, province of Cuernavaca, protest an order of the alcalde mayor of Cuernavaca that they furnish a squad of 20 Indians for ser-

39. AGN-Civ, vol. 2229:exp. 1 (LBSD, vol. 13).
40. Ibid., 2182:exp. 13 (LBSD, vol. 7).

vice in draining the mines of Cuautla, in the royal province of Cuautla-Amilpas, changing personnel every 15 days. The order was issued on the petition of a mine owner dated March 22, 1773, to the teniente-general of the alcalde mayor of Cuernavaca. It derives its legal basis from an order of Viceroy Cruillas of January 18, 1765, on petition of another mine owner of Cuautla for an allocation of Indian workmen to be completed from the town of Jolalpan in the province of Cuernavaca. The viceregal order is directed to the alcalde mayor of Cuautla-Amilpas. Upon presentation of the order of the teniente-general of Cuernavaca to the teniente of Jonacatepec for implementation, the latter refers it to the juez conservador for an opinion. The juez conservador, in turn, asks for an opinion from the abogado de cámara of the estate, whose deliberations take more than a year.

Meantime, on January 25, 1774, a mine owner in the mining district of Cuautla petitions the alcalde mayor of Cuernavaca for an allocation of Indians for drainage operations, and the requested order is issued. It is promptly appealed to the juez conservador by the Indian towns in three sets of petitions, their arguments in all being that such labor never before had been required of them, that the mines were in another province with a different and for them highly unhealthful climate, that making them work in drainage would damage the interests of the marquesado, and that the mines were so poor as to be of little possible profit. Their petitions pass to the abogado de cámara, who renders his opinion February 11, 1774, that royal laws permit Indian labor for use in mines, but that allocations must be by the justice of the district concerned and must not be for personal favor. He recommends asking that the alcalde mayor of Cuernavaca be ordered to report on the reasons for the allocation, the utility, and the legal basis. On February 18, 1774, the juez conservador issues a decree to that effect. In the interim, the Indians are to be left in peace.

On March 4 the order is received by the alcalde mayor, who orders that it be carried out. That same day he prepares a report, appending a copy of Viceroy Cruillas' order, defending his allocation of workmen on the ground that the matter of mines is exclusive to the royal jurisdiction, so that the marquesado has no voice in it, and that each Indian worker is to be paid 0/2/6 a day, a good wage. His report passes from the juez conservador to the estate abogado de cámara, who on April 16, 1774, signs an opinion pointing out that the viceroy's order applies to Totolapan (province of Chalco) and not to towns in the marquesado. (The difference in town name between the text of the viceroy's order and the abogado de cámara's opinion is baffling, but worked to the advantage of Tetelpa and its allies.) The order of the alcalde mayor, therefore, must be voided. That same day the juez conservador issues an order as the abogado de cámara recommended.[41]

This case is an excellent example of the careful procedures, which copied those of the royal courts, and especially the General Indian Court. The juez conservador always asked for and always followed the opinion of his abogado de cámara. All pleas, decisions, and inquiries took place within the administrative and judicial facilities of the marquesado, so that lodging of the docket in the audiencia records is puzzling. That may have occurred through appeal by the mine owners to the audiencia.

9. November 18, 1788–January 27, 1789, Mexico City, Jonacatepec, and Yecapixtla. The Indians of the town of Xochitlac (Xochitlán?), province of Cuernavaca, vs. their cura, for forced, unpaid work on the parish houses, etc. On November 18, 1788, José Manuel Vallarta, solicitador of the General Indian Court, presents in the court a complaint on behalf of the town, alleging unpaid work required of 90 persons and asking for an accounting and payment. The petition is signed also by Lic. Blas Ochoa Abadiano, procurador of the court. The court decrees that a copy be issued, to serve as a dispatch for the justice of the province and from him to the parish priest. The cura is to be instructed not to levy unpaid work. A notarial affidavit of November 20 certifies that the copy has been given to the Indians. On January 4, 1789, the copy is presented in Jonacatepec to the teniente of the alcalde mayor and is received with formal, written act of obedience. Three days later, the parish priest is notified in the chief town of the parish, Yecapixtla, and an investigation carried out, all of which is duly written down for transmission to the General Indian Court. The priest swears that all work is voluntary, the Indians have not been forced to furnish materials, and the tale of 90 persons is false. The docket, in the records of the court, ends at this point. According to the papers, the solicitador received 1/ and the procurador 1/2[42]—proper half fees, since the action was on behalf of a community.

The interesting point of this case is that, despite the viceregal decree of 1771, it was brought in the General Indian Court, undoubtedly because it concerned a member of the clergy and so required an authority stronger than that of the marquesado. Matters affecting the Church lay in the royal jurisdiction.

10. October 19, 1795–March 31, 1796, Mexico City and Coyoacán. Petition of the parish priest of Coyoacán for forcing atten-

41. Ibid., 2199:exp. 14 (LBSD, vol. 9).
42. Ibid., 2182:exp. 11 (LBSD, vol. 7).

dance at church services by his parishioners (summarized as no. 85 in Chapter V). In this case, a parish priest turns to the viceroy and the General Indian Court, with the cooperation of the corregidor of Coyoacán, an official of the marquesado. The authority of the General Indian Court is invoked as more likely to bring obedience.

11. March 30–August 30, 1798, Mexico City, Cuernavaca, and Jonacatepec. The governors and Indians of the towns of Jonacatepec and Tepatzingo, province of Cuernavaca, vs. their teniente, Don Antonio Montoto, alleging illegal fees for approving elections and carrying out inspections. The suit begins with a petition to the viceroy, via a solicitador and procurador with full power of attorney. The petition is heard by the assessor as delegate of the viceroy. His decision on April 21, 1798, is that all be sent to the juez privativo conservador of the marquesado. That is done, with a letter of transmittal from the assessor. Upon receipt of the documents, the juez conservador on April 25 orders that the alcalde mayor of Cuernavaca take testimony and report. In Cuernavaca, the alcalde mayor receives the dispatch, carries out the required investigation, and reports in writing on May 5. He has never given orders for such exactions; if they have been levied, the teniente has done so without authority and must take the blame. An interrogatorio on behalf of the Indian plaintiffs is challenged on the basis of signatures and ordered redone. On May 11, the contador and notary of the marquesado each file an affidavit that all titles issued to alcaldes mayores and their tenientes have a clause ordering that no extra charges be levied. The docket, which is lodged in the records of the audiencia along with many of the General Indian Court, ends at this point. According to the documents in it, no fees were charged the Indians.[43]

As far as the record in this case goes, the General Indian Court scrupulously observed the viceregal decision of 1771 on jurisdiction, and the juez conservador equally scrupulously carried out his function.

12. March 5–30, 1819, Mexico City. The natives of Santa María Alpuyeca, province of Cuernavaca, complain that the tithe collector does not abide by custom in his collections. The case is heard in the General Indian Court, where the docket opens with a power of attorney given by the officials of the town to solicitador Joaquín Pérez Gavilán, who makes formal complaint on their behalf that the tithe collector for that district is introducing new charges and demands, contrary to long-established custom, requiring that they declare their pigs and other products on which they never have paid tithe. He asks that the

43. Ibid., 2130:exp. 4 (LBSD, vol. 15).

tithe collector be ordered to abide by established custom. On March 5, 1819, the court orders the papers reviewed by the fiscal, who on March 20 recommends that reports be ordered from the provincial governor, the parish priest, and the tithe collector, for further examination of the matter and decision by the court. On March 29 the court accepts the opinion, and the next day the dispatches are sent.[44] The docket ends here.

Once again, a dispute affecting Church rights and privilege comes to the General Indian Court rather than the juez conservador. Decisions affecting the Church, its personnel, and its revenues clearly were held to be a matter of royal jurisdiction.

These summaries of cases indicate that in the earlier period of competing judicial competence, the Indians could secure relief from the viceregal court, and did. Rivalry between the two jurisdictions did not impede much cooperation in providing relief. In the later period, under the settlement of 1771, the two jurisdictions cooperated well. The one area in which Indians of the marquesado had to continue to apply to the viceroy involved complaints against parish priests, tithe collectors, and other arms of the Church. These matters fell within the royal jurisdiction. Whatever the rivalries of the two sets of officials and competing judicial authority, even in the earlier period, the Indians, provided they had a legal basis, received the relief they sought.

B. Yucatan

Isolation from central Mexico, and the accidents of a history of conquest separate and markedly more prolonged and difficult, dictated for Yucatan and its dependency of Tabasco a substantial degree of administrative autonomy that gave it peculiar status within the Audiencia of Mexico.[45] In aboriginal times Yucatan was part of southern Mesoamerica. Mayan in speech and culture, and indeed the seat of many of the cities of Mayan high culture, it never was subject to the Triple Alliance. In terms of geography and culture, it might well have fitted better into the Audiencia of Guatemala, and for a time in the middle sixteenth century was attached to the territory of that body.

44. Ibid., 2199:exp. 13 (LBSD, vol. 9).
45. The paragraphs which follow are based on Cook and Borah, Essays, 2:1–7 et passim; Gerhard, The Southeast Frontier, 6–20 et passim; Hunt, passim; Molina Solís, passim. See also the other references in note 2 of this chapter. It was only in 1782 that by royal cédula Yucatan was brought to the same degree of review in criminal cases as other parts of the Audiencia of Mexico: Beleña, 1, part 5:197, no. 353.

Nevertheless, isolated though it was from central Mexico by the Isthmus of Tehuantepec and wide stretches of swamp and tropical rainforest, it was assigned definitively to the Audiencia of Mexico in 1560. Thereafter its governors were subordinate in matters judicial and fiscal to Mexico City. The audiencia heard appeals from the area; the royal fiscal authorities audited accounts sent forward from the royal treasury in Mérida, reporting on its collections and disbursements and those of the subcajas in Campeche and Tabasco. In administrative and military affairs, the governor of Yucatan was accountable to the viceroy but enjoyed a wide degree of discretion and even autonomy from 1561 until 1787. Then the reorganization of Yucatan as an intendancy, subordinate to the viceroy as superintendent-general, knitted it more firmly to Mexico City and probably ensured its presence in the Mexican federation.

The Spanish governors of Yucatan administered a large territory, embracing the present Mexican federal entities of Quintana Roo, Yucatan, Campeche, and Tabasco, with lieutenant-governors in Valladolid, Campeche, and the capital of Tabasco (successively Santa María de la Victoria, Villahermosa, and Tacotalpa). From 1561 to 1565, the governor bore the title of alcalde mayor; in 1565 the title became governor, and in 1617 governor and captain-general. Appointed by the king and Council of the Indies in Spain, he reported to them directly, a degree of freedom denied other provincial governors in the Audiencia of Mexico. Difficulty of communication with Mexico City (solved only in the 1930s, through the construction of a railroad completing linkage of Mérida, Campeche, and Mexico City), and the steady military danger of persistent foreign attack, forced an autonomous, essentially self-reliant administration that the governors made full use of.

In European settlement, economy, and Indian administration, Yucatan differed considerably from central Mexico during the colonial period. The peninsula is essentially a low-lying limestone formation close to sea-level. To the west, this gives way to other geological formations covered by swamp and tropical rain-forest, as in Tabasco and western Campeche. To the east is the high bush of Quintana Roo. In between lie the drier areas of lower bush. A dense aboriginal population soon dwindled to a much smaller one, with survival best in the drier zones around Mérida. Although lured to the region initially by hopes of great wealth, the Spanish found that there were no mines of precious metals and little production of crops that might be traded for European goods. Until late in the colonial period, foreign trade as well as communication was at very low levels. The peninsula produced cotton cloth, wax, maize, and fowls—items useful for subsistence, but not of great demand in trade outside the region, and too bulky to warrant the costs of transportation over long distances. Climate and topography also discouraged European settlement, and with it the development of other forms of economic endeavor.

In consequence, throughout the earlier colonial period, European settlement remained sparse, and the major supports of the Spanish community were encomiendas and the profits of administration. However unwilling, the crown found itself forced to agree to steady regranting of encomiendas until the eighteenth century, long after almost all had been allowed to lapse elsewhere in New Spain, simply as a means of keeping enough Spanish population in the peninsula to ensure a source of militia for policing the Indians and for protection against foreign attack. The entire Spanish community continued to rely upon labor drafts of Indians for constructing and maintaining churches and convents, buildings of civil administration, private dwellings, and roads, and for the ordinary service of households. Repeated orders from Spain forbidding the practice met steady resistance from all Spaniards in the peninsula, clergy included.

Even the missionary history of the peninsula added to its peculiarity, for conversion to Christianity was almost exclusively the work of the Franciscans, who in consequence for a long time enjoyed a dominance in Yucatan that in central Mexico was far less evident, because of the presence of various orders and a much more powerful secular clergy. The demands of the clergy in Yucatan for labor and payments of various kinds became a heavy burden upon the natives.

All of the peculiarities of economy and society in colonial Yucatan relative to central Mexico added up to much more direct exploitation of the native population throughout most of the colonial period. It resembled the early history of Spaniard—Indian relations in central Mexico in the sixteenth century, with far less of the mitigation that the presence of a viceroy and audiencia brought to the core of New Spain. In this system of *mise-en-valeur*,[46] the role of the governor was central. He appointed district administrators; he was judge—subject indeed to appeal, but to the remote audiencia in Mexico City. So long as he managed to maintain reasonably harmonious relations with the bishop and clergy, he was almost invulnerable during his term, normally of five years. At the end of the term, to be sure, each governor had to endure a residencia, but that could be handled if the residents and clergy backed him, in preparation for equal cooperation with his successor.

In Yucatan, then, a small Spanish upper-crust derived its support from a much more numerous Indian lower-crust in a relationship that,

46. The French term is preferable to the English *exploitation*, since the latter carries a pejorative connotation that the former does not. Cultivating a field is *mise-en-valeur*; exploiting a field suggests destroying it.

relative to central Mexico, changed far less from its earliest form until late in the colonial period. The Spaniards were increasing slowly but steadily, while, during much of the period, the natives were losing numbers. What strains may have resulted from the divergent trends, and how these strains showed up, has yet to be studied.

The Indians do not appear to have objected to a substantial degree of exploitation in the form of support of the Spanish community, the Church and its clergy, and their own native superstructure. All of that they were accustomed to from aboriginal times. Most Spaniards equally aimed at a continuing, long-term *mise-en-valeur*. The problem was to ensure a regular and moderate form—in short, on the one hand, to restrain excess on the part of unusually greedy individuals, or actual violence and crime; and on the other, to see to it that the Indians did contribute in what was regarded as proper proportion. Attempts at a solution to this problem led in the sixteenth century to development of a system of protectors of the Indians, who could bring excesses against Indians or by Indians to the attention of the governor.[47] A further measure, very much like the development in central Mexico, was the use of administrative orders by the governor, in resolution not merely of administrative questions and disputes but also of matters that were essentially judicial.[48] The aim, as in central Mexico, was to minimize suits and quarrels among the natives—perhaps most of all, to alleviate the costs of such activity—and to provide a relatively quick and effective measure of redress in cases in which the complainant clearly was entitled to it, whether from Indian or Spaniard.

The events and decisions that led to the creation of a special Indian court in Yucatan centered in part upon developments in the Audiencia of Mexico and the negotiations of Velasco II with Philip II, and in part upon local institutions, most notably the office of protector of the Indians. That function was discharged at times by the local bishop, and the royal intention in general was that the function be entrusted to the bishop. Nevertheless, in 1569 Governor Luis de Céspedes appointed a vecino of Mérida, Francisco Palomino, *Defensor de los Naturales destas Provincias*, with a yearly salary of 150/ of fine gold (248/1/11 in the silver of colonial Mexican coinage). Palomino took office on January 8, 1569; his appointment received royal approval in a *real cédula ejecutoria* of January 13, 1572. Palomino served until November 11, 1577, when he was suspended from office by the then governor, Guillén de las Casas. Las Casas then appointed Diego Briceño,

47. Cogolludo, 1:404–405 (lib. 7:cap. 12); royal treasury accounts for Yucatan, 1540–1650, in AGI-C, leg. 911A–B.
48. Velasco II to the king, Mexico City, September 28, 1591, in VC, fols. 100v–101v.

another vecino of Mérida. Thereafter the two men alternated in the office, as incoming governors replaced one with the other.

The protector of the Indians was helped in his functions by two other officials: an interpreter-general, paid 80/ of fine gold a year (132/2/8 of silver), and an interpreter-general of the governor's tribunal, paid 200/ of silver a year. During the 1580s, the general interpreter was the redoubtable Gaspar Antonio Chi,[49] an Indian born in Maní the son of a priest of the aboriginal cult. Chi became a skilled bilinguist, organist, and most useful ally of the Spaniards. He helped his own people in their suits, writing petitions and other documents, and pleaded their cases most effectively in the governor's tribunal[50]— which, since the governor was a military man without formal legal training, was actually guided by a legal assessor, the *teniente letrado*.[51]

Meanwhile, the post of protector was under discussion in Madrid. On October 4, 1579, a royal cédula ordered the removal of Palomino and discharge of the function of protector by the bishop. Although the royal order reached Yucatan, it was not carried out. Three years later, a royal cédula, signed in Lisbon on May 7, 1582, ordered that all protectors of Indians be removed and the office abolished. That order equally was not carried out in Yucatan until another royal cédula of March 20, 1586, specifically directed to the governor of Yucatan, peremptorily ordered compliance and the restitution of many sums extorted from the natives. On October 30, 1586, the governor finally complied with the first part of the royal order, removing Palomino, who once again was in office. However, abolition of the office led to enough difficulty for Indians seeking hearings that the Franciscan provincial wrote a letter, dated May 18, 1590, reporting the worsening situation and asking for a restoration of the office. The king in a reply of April 9, 1591, advised the provincial that he had ordered the office restored and other measures taken for the relief of the natives.[52]

A royal cédula of the same date, directed to the governor of Yucatan, ordered restoration of the office of protector, but went much farther than that. This date is also that of the royal cédula and royal letter to the Viceroy of New Spain which provided the legal basis for the General Indian Court in the Audiencia of Mexico.[53] This coincidence of date must mean that the imperial authorities in Madrid, very

49. Royal treasury accounts for Yucatan, 1567–1590, in AGI-C, leg. 911A; Cogolludo, 1:402–405 (lib. 7:cap. 12).

50. Sánchez de Aguilar, 144–145; Landa, 44–46, 230–232. Gaspar Antonio Chi also wrote many of the relaciones geográficas of 1577–1585 for Yucatan: Cline, "The Relaciones Geográficas," 225.

51. See the discussion later in this chapter.

52. Cogolludo, 1:404–406 (lib. 7:caps. 12 and 13).

53. See Chapter IV, above.

much aware of the plight of the Yucatecan Indians and seeking measures of relief that would work, decided upon essentially common measures for the Audiencia of Mexico and virtually autonomous Yucatan.

The royal cédula sent to Yucatan paralleled the provisions of the one sent to Mexico City. The governor of Yucatan was to appoint a protector, letrado, and procurador for the Indians, who were to see that the latter obtained justice in whatever matters might arise. These officials were to receive proper salaries from fines or from the Indian communities, and were in no way to accept or ask anything from the Indians for their services. In suits of Indian against Indian before the governor, the protector was to act as legal aide for one party and the letrado and procurador for the other. In order to eliminate or limit costs to Indians, no notary, relator, or procurador might charge Indians fees, except for communities and caciques, who might be charged half the schedule for Spaniards. Further to limit or eliminate costs, the governor was to issue dispatches to Indians signed only with his rubric and countersigned by the appropriate notary. Such dispatches were to be received by all as formal judicial sentences in the royal name. To avoid having the Indians leave their lands to seek remedy in Mérida, the governor was to see that the local administrators sent the dispatches and court papers to the protector, so that they might be decided by the governor and his lieutenant (i.e., judicial assessor), for return as soon as decided. Again, as in the orders sent to Mexico City, the royal injunction was abbreviated process, rapid decision, resolution by administrative order even in judicial matters, elimination of costs, and keeping Indians in their villages, so they might till their fields and maintain their families and community as well as the state. The royal cédula reached Yucatan late in the summer, was given formal obedience by the governor, and proclaimed publicly in the central square of Mérida on September 9, 1591.[54]

In prompt compliance with the royal will, Governor Antonio de Vozmediano appointed officials for the new court: a protector or defender, a letrado, a procurador, interpreters, and a bailiff. The key official of the viceregal system, the legal assessor, was not on the list—probably because, in the simpler arrangements of Yucatan, where the governor presided over a tribunal, he already employed an assessor with title of lieutenant. Equally, the governor already had an Indian interpreter for dealing with the natives in their languages, as well as

54. Cogolludo, 1:406–407 (lib. 7:cap. 13), quoting the cédula in part and summarizing the rest. The full text may be found in the acts of appointment of legal aides in the eighteenth century; it was almost invariably incorporated in full in the appointments of the protector-defensor, abogado, and procurador: AGI-M, leg. 1021.

another attached to his tribunal; but he preferred to attach both, as well as his bailiff, to the new Indian court.[55]

The three other officials were new. Of these, the protector was regarded as the most important. For this office, Vozmediano named Juan de Sanabria, a crony but also one of the relatively small number of Spaniards available in Mérida, and issued a long instruction—incorporated in quotation and summary in Cogolludo's history—which is a mixture of general royal concerns for the Indians, such as helping in Christianizing them and detecting idolatry, seeing that they planted crops in proper amount, and detecting outbreaks of disease among them; and of specific injunctions related more directly to the new court. The protector might not leave Mérida without express permission of the governor. He was to carry out the provisions of the royal cédula and all protective legislation, seeing that the Indians received the benefit of the new provisions in their favor. He might not ask for nor accept presents, fees, nor anything else from the natives, however small the amount, under penalty of suspension from office. He might not engage in trade nor in business deals with Indians in any way, nor might he use his office to collect debts for Spaniards dealing with the natives. Any complaint by an Indian must be brought immediately to the governor for remedy. Furthermore, he must place great care in seeing that the royal will on fees and costs was obeyed. In civil and criminal cases of Indians, as they might arise before any justices in the territory of Yucatan, he might act for the Indians. He might "provide the Indians with all forms of defense, recusation of judges, petitions, and appeals that the laws allowed and that operated in favor of the natives." He was to serve the Indians faithfully and diligently "against any persons whatever . . . so that through his fault or negligence no damage or prejudice might accrue to the causes of the said Indians. . . ." For help and advice he was to turn to the letrado.[56]

As in Mexico City, one of the first problems to arise came from the protest of the notary most involved. In the much smaller world of Yucatan, that was the *secretario de gobernación y de guerra*, the official notary attached to the governor for all purposes, both administrative and judicial. There does not seem to have been a *secretario de cámara*; apparently the flow of business did not justify nor could it support the division of function that obtained in the viceregal seat. Under the royal order of 1591, the governor's notary thenceforth was to charge all Indian commoners no fees, issuing their dispatches with-

55. Cogolludo, 1:205 (lib. 4:cap. 10) gives a partial list. The full one was found by Hunt (p. 356) in the residencia of Governor Juan Bruno Tello de Guzmán, 1688; it is in AGI, Escribanía de Cámara, leg. 321B, pieza 1. See Table 9.4 in this chapter.

56. Cogolludo, 1:407–408 (lib. 7:cap. 13); Molina Solís, 1:233.

out cost, and might levy only half fees on Indian communities and caciques. The secretary promptly appealed to the Audiencia of Mexico on the ground that the royal cédula applied only to matters of justice, for there was no official schedule of fees for Spaniards in administrative matters, since Spaniards never petitioned for orders like those sought by the natives. We have no information on the course of the suit, save that the viceroy, in reporting the matter to Madrid, suggested that a further royal cédula cut short the appeal by directing that administrative dispatches must conform to the new rules.[57] Undoubtedly such a cédula was sent. On the other hand, as in Mexico City, a compromise was reached quickly, probably with explicit royal approval, for the payment of an annual stipend to the secretary in lieu of fees. It was set at approximately 2,000/ in silver,[58] a more generous amount than the initial arrangement of Velasco II with his notaries, but less than the more generous allocation of his immediate successors (see Table 7.1).

The approximately 2,000/ a year allocated to the secretary was by far the largest stipend of the new costs. An annual salary of 200/ in fine gold (330/7/1 in the silver of ordinary circulation) was assigned to the protector.[59] Under existing arrangements, one interpreter, the Indian Gaspar Antonio Chi, received 80/ in fine gold (132/2/8 in silver); the other, a Spaniard with the resounding title of *Interprete general del juzgado mayor destas provincias* (Interpreter-General of the High Court of These Provinces), received 200/ in silver.[60] Either at this time, in view of the greater responsibilities to be placed upon Chi, or early in the seventeenth century, the two salaries were set at the equal rate of 200/ in silver. We have no information on the salaries assigned to the letrado and procurador. In the later seventeenth century, they were 396/6 for the abogado and 300/ for the procurador, both in silver. The odd amount for the abogado would indicate a salary set at 240/ in fine gold. By then, the protector had been raised to 300/ in fine gold (496/6

57. Velasco II to the king, Mexico City, September 28, 1591, in VC, fols. 100v–101v.

58. Cogolludo, 1:205 (lib. 4:cap. 10). Cogolludo gives the amount in silver; the stipend was more probably 1,200 pesos of fine gold, not quite 2,000 silver pesos. See Table 9.4.

59. Ibid., 407 (lib. 7:cap. 13). Until the middle of the seventeenth century, the treasury accounts of Yucatan were kept in pesos of fine gold, worth 450 maravedís, but actual dealing was conducted in silver pesos worth 272 maravedís. Conversions here may differ slightly from those of the royal treasury officials, in that those here have been calculated on an electric calculator, hopefully with greater accuracy. The silver coinage in actual use was silver pesos, reales at 8 to the peso, and *granos* at 12 to the real. More important officials had their salaries stated in pesos of fine gold; less important officials merited merely a statement in silver. Both, of course, got silver.

60. Royal treasury accounts of Yucatan, 1540–1650, in AGI-C, leg. 911A.

in silver). At that proportion, the abogado's initial salary in the 1590s would have been 160/ in fine gold (264/5/8 in silver). By the early eighteenth century, both protector and abogado were brought to nearly equal salary at 500/ in silver, a rounding of 300/ in fine gold. The bailiff—at a salary of 100/ set in silver, as became a lesser official, rather than the money of account in fine gold used for more prestigious posts—probably enjoyed that already, and merely was transferred to the new court.[61]

The total of these salaries added up to a large sum, perhaps 3,500/ in silver, for which a source of revenue had to be found. One source indicated in the royal cédula of April 9, 1591, the yield of fines, probably had no unallocated surplus that could be used. It was a chancy fund, since the intake varied widely from year to year and the charges on it were numerous.[62] Accordingly, in Yucatan as in the viceregal system, the solution consisted of a new levy of half a real per tributary added to the amount that each community had to deliver to collectors. In Yucatan the levy took on the Maya name *holpatán*.[63] As in the viceregal system, it was not a royal revenue, but rather a royal trust. As such, receipts and disbursements for it do not appear in the accounts of the royal treasury officials until late in the colonial period. The officials of each Indian town delivered the holpatán to a trustee for community funds in Mérida, directly in the districts of Mérida and Valladolid, more likely indirectly in Campeche and Tabasco through the subcajas in those dependencies. In Mérida, the trustee—described by Cogolludo as a competent person acting as a mayordomo—received revenues and disbursed payments, neither function being extensive nor onerous, and was paid 500/ a year for his work. He seems to have had no connection with the royal treasury officials, but rather to have been accountable only to the governor.[64] The post was held by one family for most of the colonial period. In 1683 the mayordomo was a woman, Doña Magdalena Magaña, with the title of *depositaria general*; it was most unusual for a woman to hold such office.[65]

A determination of the balance of receipts from the holpatán and expenditures is not easy to arrive at for much of the first century of the Indian court in Yucatan. Most of the colonial records retained in the

61. See Table 9.4.

62. Royal treasury accounts of Yucatan, 1540–1650, in AGI-C, leg. 911A–B.

63. The meaning is additional tax or levy, from *hol* or *h'ol*, additional, and *patan*, tax or levy: *Diccionario de San Francisco*, 145 and 287; *Diccionario de Motul*, 398 and 753; and Swadesh, Álvarez, and Bastarrechea, 54–73.

64. Cogolludo, 1:205 (lib. 4:cap. 10); Bolio and Echánove.

65. Hunt, 356 and 629, note 110; AGI-M, leg. 2100, fols. 409f–418f, 485f–491v, and 515f–516v, all of the latter royal cédulas of appointment and orders of suppression of the office in 1777.

peninsula have been lost, either through the ravages of insects and other enemies in a moist, warm climate, or through repeated domestic tumults in the nineteenth and twentieth centuries. Neither have parallel records yet been found in Spain. Accordingly, we are forced to estimate. Stipends during the early period of the court must have come to a sum between 3,500/ and 4,000/ in silver. In 1606, a year for which there is a good summary of prevailing tribute assessments in most of Yucatan, there were approximately 47,654 tributaries in the districts of Valladolid, Mérida, and Campeche.[66] Tabasco had perhaps 1,440 tributaries, who should be added to the number contributing holpatán,[67] for a total of 48,994—in round numbers, 49,000 tributaries. The yield would have been 3,962/4. Since we deal here with estimates and approximations, I am forced to add a much-used Mexican phrase, *poco mas o menos*. If all of the officials serving the Indian court in Yucatan were paid from the holpatán, the fund could not have covered their salaries in full at the beginning of the century. Not until well into the eighteenth century, with substantial recovery of native population, could yield at the quota of half a real per tributary and charges have come into balance.

The deficit could have been handled in a number of ways. Spanish custom in such contingencies was to distribute the money available in a fund pro-rata to the people entitled to payment, making them bear the deficit in the same proportion. That may have been done part of the time. A second possibility is that the surplus of native town revenues over town disbursements, which had to be sent to Mérida for administration by the same trustee who administered the holpatán, was regarded as applicable to the needs of the court and used to meet the charges to the extent that the holpatán could not. A third possibility, and the one probably put into practice, is that the levy was increased from a half-real to perhaps as much as a real until revenue equaled charges. Such a possibility receives distinct support from official statements in the seventeenth and eighteenth centuries in which the holpatán is described both as a half-real and as a real.[68]

By the later seventeenth century, the yield of the holpatán un-

66. Cook and Borah, *Essays*, 2:70–72. See also García Bernal, *Población*, 79–87.

67. Gerhard, *The Southeast Frontier*, 42.

68. See for example the appointment of Seferino Pachecho as protector-defender, Madrid, September 25, 1704, and that of his successor, Bernabé Antonio Mezquita, Zaragoza, February 13, 1711, which specify payment from the "medio real o real de holpatán": AGI-M, leg. 1020. For community assessments, see Molina Solís, 2:405–406. See also the royal cédula of appointment of Bernardo de Magaña as depositario, which calls the holpatán a real. Madrid, December 12, 1649, in AGI-M, leg. 2100, fols. 409f–410f.

TABLE 9.4   Annual Charges on the Holpatán (in silver pesos)

Post	1683	ca. 1740[a]	1767
Secretario de gobernación y guerra/Notary	1,993/4	2,000/	1,985/5
Protector-defender	496/6	500/	646/5
Abogado	396/6	500/	496/5[b]
Procurador-general	300/	300/	500/[b]
Interpreter	200/	200/	200/
Interpreter	200/	200/	200/
Alguacil	100/	100/	100/
Depositario of fund	500/1	500/	496/5
Deputy-governor in Campeche			150/
Assessor in Campeche			400/
Interpreter in Campeche			200/
Totals	4,187/	4,300/	5,375/4

[a] Figures for ca. 1740 are taken from reports and correspondence of governors, 1720–1759. The figures undoubtedly represent roundings of salaries in pesos of fine gold converted to the silver in use.
[b] Raises granted by the king in 1763.

Sources: Hunt, 356, citing the papers of the residencia of Governor Juan Bruno Tello de Guzmán, 1680, in AGI, Escribanía de Cámara, leg. 321B, pieza I; report of Tómas de Ortiz Landazuri, Madrid, July 6, 1770, on a report (n.d. but 1768–69) of the Governor of Yucatan on the holpatán: AGI-M, legs. 1020–1021 (1720–1759) and 2100, fols. 482f–484v; Cogolludo, 1:205 (lib. 4, cap. 10).

doubtedly was sufficient to meet charges. The question is the quota that each tributary paid. In 1683 the charges came to 4,187/ (see Table 9.4). The yield of the holpatán in that year came to 4,525/; in 1687, it was 4,424/4.[69] At the rate of a half-real per tributary, the yield for 1683 would indicate collection from 72,400 tributaries; and that of 1687, from 70,792.[70] These are values that fall in the range of reports of numbers of tributaries for the Intendancy of Yucatan in the early nineteenth century. Even at the lower family number of the later seventeenth century, they imply an Indian population for all Yucatan and Tabasco of around 272,000, estimates that are far too high.[71] The solvency of the fund came about through a higher levy than a half-real, probably as much as a whole real.

69. Hunt, 355.

70. I use the conversion factor of 3.8 indicated as appropriate for 1690–1700 in Cook and Borah, Essays, 2:50.

71. Gerhard's estimates, which for these years are somewhat higher than those in Cook and Borah, still are well below such values: Gerhard, The Southeast Frontier, 25; Cook and Borah, Essays, 2:114. García Bernal, Población, 115–145, arrives at even lower estimates for Yucatan without Tabasco.

The yield of the holpatán relative to charges upon it may explain why the governor's lieutenant and legal assessor never was assigned a share in it. He was important enough so that the governor and the viceroy vied for the right to name him, until the crown in 1645 decreed that the appointment be the prerogative of the king and the Council of the Indies. His annual base salary was 500 ducats,[72] in Yucatan another money of account, with a value in silver of 689/2/8. It is also true that, since he was paid to be legal assessor to the governor, he had no just claim for further compensation. In that respect, his situation differed from that of the assessor of the General Indian Court in Mexico City, who took on a new function not otherwise part of his duties.

The regretable loss of most colonial records within Yucatan has removed all case records that might give detailed information on the functioning of the Indian court in Mérida. We have general but sparse indications for the seventeenth century, and somewhat better ones for the eighteenth. All Indians wishing redress from the governor had to bring their grievances and complaints to Mérida, where the officials of the court were under obligation to assist them in preparing necessary documents and to move them in hearing and decision. Although the royal cédula of 1591 to the governor of Yucatan ordered that the papers be brought to Mérida for review and decision, but that the Indians remain in their towns, the Indians and Spaniards in Yucatan were in agreement in refusing compliance. If the matter was a civil one, the Indians came; in criminal matters, the Indians were sent to Mérida for trial.

Perhaps the most serious departure from the royal will lay in the fact that the Indians brought their wives and children, with supplies for the trip and their stay in the capital, and with gifts for the officials whose services they would need and the judge whose decision they hoped to influence. The officials and judge, of course, were expressly forbidden to accept bribes, gifts, or offerings in any way. Furthermore, they were forbidden to charge for their services, except for the half fees permitted in the instance of Indian communities and caciques. Nevertheless, Indians and Spaniards in Yucatan entered into continuous open conspiracy to violate the express royal legislation. Accustomed by aboriginal practice to bring gifts to their judges and other officials, the Indians continued to do so throughout the colonial period, and the officials of the Indian court in Mérida accepted the offerings.[73]

72. Díez de la Calle, 186–187 (cap. 2, sec. 18).
73. Ancona, 2: 189–190; Bolio and Echánove; Sierra O'Reilly; relación of Gaspar Antonio Chi, March 20, 1582, in Landa, app. C, 231.

Despite the express royal prohibition, a custom developed of small fees being charged by the officials of the court. According to a letter to the crown from one of the few reforming governors in the history of Yucatan, Antonio de Cortaire, writing from Mérida on July 2, 1723, the two interpreters, by then each paid 200/ a year to translate for the Indians without fee, charged 0/2 and a chicken for each translation. The protector and defender of the Indians, by then paid approximately 500/ a year, charged 0/3 for signing the translation and 0/6 for his assistance with or signature on any other document. Presumably the other officials also levied charges, although the governor does not mention them. His letter comments, in regard to the legal aides of the court:

> All the officials of the Indian court are under obligation to discharge their functions in every way without fee. The Indians know this very much, but nevertheless they insist upon bringing what they should not. I know that they do not do so with me, since they are aware from experience that I give them protection. What happens is that sometimes in gratitude the Indians bring to the officials a gift of a chicken or a little honey. The officials of the court should explain their behavior to Your Majesty.[74]

The basic problem, virtually insoluble, lay in the nature of the Yucatecan society and economy of the time. A relatively small group of Spaniards in a relatively primitive society depended upon the Indians for support. That support they derived in the form of tribute and fees, either directly, or indirectly via salary and subsidy from the royal treasury.[75] The secretario de gobernación attached to the governor, who received approximately 2,000/ from the holpatán in lieu of fees, had bought his office. Early in the seventeenth century, one family purchased the office in perpetuity for its descendants.[76] They had both to recover the original price and maintain a social position of great prestige in the community. The more important among the other officials of the court were appointed by the king and Council of the Indies in Spain, probably after purchase. They too had to recover those costs. All officials after the 1640s paid media anata on their posts, even after the legal aides of the medio real in Mexico City secured a ruling that, since their stipends came from a revenue merely a royal trust, they were not liable to the tax. For example, Cayetano de Cárdenas, appointed protector and defender of the Indians on August 21, 1726, on a salary by then 500/ a year paid media anata of 256/2, calculated as half a year's salary plus 18% for the cost of insurance and moving the

74. AGI-M, leg. 1020.
75. Hunt, passim.
76. Cogolludo, 205 (lib. 4, cap. 10).

silver to Veracruz for shipment to Spain. Lucas de Gorrástegui, appointed procurador-general of Indians on February 15, 1731, with an annual salary of 300/, paid media anata of 177/—150/ for half salary and 28/ for freight, i.e., the cost of shipping and insuring it.[77] As one governor commented in the 1740s, a salary of 300/ was not enough to support a procurador and his family decently.[78]

The key official in the system of *mise-en-valeur* was, of course, the governor, who made and unmade district officials, authorized or permitted drafts of labor for the Spaniards, both lay and clerical, for Indian dignitaries, and for what were considered community needs, such as official buildings, churches, and roads. So long as the Spaniards cooperated with each other and the governor, they could resist attempts at reform directed from Spain. If they fell out, the governor became vulnerable.[79]

One notable instance occurred in 1629–30, when Governor Juan de Vargas Machuca, resisting a royal cédula forbidding the appointment of special judges and military captains in Indian towns, found himself confronted by charges brought before the Audiencia of Mexico through Melchor López de Haro, procurador of the General Indian Court, acting for Diego García Montalvo, vecino of Mérida and encomendero of Tixcocob, Hunacamá, Ixil, and Pencuyut. The special judges and captains, one surmises, were draining off too much revenue and depriving the other Spaniards of what they regarded as their share. The Audiencia of Mexico sent a special judge to Yucatan, an oidor, who met determined resistance from the governor and was finally forced to flee to the Dominican convent in Mérida. He found an ally in the bishop, who was under explicit royal injunction to help preserve order in the colony. Under threat of excommunication, the governor gave way, and was taken as a prisoner for trial to Mexico City, where he died. Despite another royal cédula again forbidding such judges and military captains in Indian towns, the interim governor appointed by the viceroy restored them, reverting to the former arrangement.[80]

The inability of the crown to impose unwanted reforms on the Spanish community in Yucatan was well illustrated in a series of attempts in the first half of the eighteenth century, aimed at reducing the allocations of Indian workers for personal service to laymen and clergy and moderating levies for the parishes and dioceses. In these efforts, largely ordered from Spain, the Yucatecan aides of the local Indian court played a double role, in that they reported on many of the exac-

77. Appointments, in AGI-M, leg. 1021.
78. García Bernal, *La sociedad*, 76–77.
79. Hunt, 142–151, 488–502, et passim; see also Molina Solís, 2:222–227.
80. Cogolludo, 1:561–582 (lib. 10:caps. 8–13); Hunt, 269–270 and 461.

tions and were themselves reported on for their own abuse of office. In 1704, the procurador-general denounced to the king the *musil*, a levy on the Indians for covering costs of the bishop's pastoral inspections. By royal cédulas of May 5 and August 29, 1704, the crown ordered the charge ended. In 1720, the Spanish *villa* of Valladolid protested against the exactions of the deputy of the governor and captain-general, who functioned as private judge in Indian cases, civil and criminal, superseding the jurisdiction of all district officials, and appointed special judges for collection of levies. Despite the marked exactions upon the Indians, no one dared protest to the governor until the villa did so. Again, the dispute represented a heightened levy by one party which interfered with the revenues of the Spanish community in the area. It may have been as a result of this protest that the crown, by royal cédula of November 28, 1722, gave to the Bishop of Yucatan a special commission as judge, with private and exclusive jurisdiction to proceed against people guilty of excesses against Indians. Although the bishop duly promised compliance and proclaimed his commission, his broom left little trace.

Probably as part of its intention to bring about reform, the crown sent out a new governor, Antonio de Cortaire, to whose pressure we owe a series of reports from the legal aides of his Indian court amply documenting the extent and nature of levies in labor, coin, and kind upon the Indians. In 1722 they reported on increases in customary levies. They also denounced to a diocesan synod on June 25, 1723, the excessive number of servants demanded by the local clergy. Larger Indian towns furnished 100 to a convent; smaller ones, 50. Such service found favor among the Indians because it was easier than working for laymen. In a long report of July 2, 1723, to the crown, Cortaire reported upon the abuses of office by his own Indian legal aides, and in multiple appendixes documented the case against much of the Spanish community in Yucatan. His letter virtuously protested that he had made no new allocations of labor—although he had changed none in existence, since they had been ordered by his predecessors. Clearly the perquisites of the Spanish community, lay and ecclesiastical, constituted a hornet's nest he preferred not to touch.

A new group of legal aides, appointed to office after these light sweeps of the broom of reform, continued to document the nature and extent of levy on the Indians in Yucatan. In 1735 they reported at length to the crown on the use of Indians as workmen in construction of roads, walls, churches, convent buildings, and so on. In 1738 they returned a collective report on personal services required from the Indians of the peninsula in a long statement to the governor, which was duly forwarded to Madrid. The one bright note in their report was a reduction in the levy of cloth and wax for the bishop. In the years

1756–1759, the crown returned to its inquiries. The then governor, Melchor de Navarrete, in a letter of July 4, 1757, defended his legal aides as zealous and active in the protection of the Indians. All proceedings began with documents submitted in Maya, translated for review and decision, and all decisions were translated into Maya for the benefit of the Indians. All of his legal aides, he commented, had had their appointments confirmed by the crown.[81]

By 1759 a new king, Carlos III, was ready to launch a much more vigorous effort at reform, so that in the years of his reign the broom of reform began at long last to show some results. One of the moves of the late 1750s from Madrid was to inquire into the administration of the holpatán. It may be remembered that a parallel inquiry was under way in Mexico City. The answers to this inquiry from Yucatan may have been the first time that the imperial administration in Madrid conducted a careful examination of the holpatán and its fiscal administration.[82] By the opening years of the second half of the eighteenth century, the salaries assigned to the legal aides of the local Indian court were given in current pesos of silver rather than in the old money of account in fine gold. There had been some increase in pay as well. Table 9.4 lists the offices and salaries for the 1740s and 1767. In terms of change, Yucatan continued to be a backwater.

The changes of the high Bourbon era in the end were relatively minor in the Indian court of Yucatan.[83] By royal cédula of December 5, 1770, the crown ordered that the office of notary of the court be removed from that of the secretario de gobernación y guerra and sold separately, but that the removal not take place until the death of the actual holder. On his death in 1774, that change took place over the protests of the secretary's son and hereditary successor in the main post. The office of depositario, held in hereditary succession for a century and a half, was a genuine anomaly, sure to be offensive to a centralizing monarch; yet only on January 15, 1777, did the crown order reform of the administration of the holpatán. Collection and disbursement were entrusted to the royal treasury officials, who were to handle both community surplus and the holpatán without additions to their salaries. The office of depositario was abolished. In compliance with

81. AGI-M, legs. 1020–1021; García Bernal, *La sociedad*, 95–99, 104–105, 125, and 128–129.

82. The documents fill most of AGI-M, leg. 2100.

83. The paragraphs that follow are based upon Bolio and Echánove; "Estado general de tributos y tributarios, 1805," 34–35; report of Diego de Lanz, contador real in Mérida, to the Minister of the Indies, Mérida, January 26, 1784, in AGI-M, leg. 2100, fols. 879f–882v; royal cédula, Madrid, December 5, 1770, and report of Tomás de Ortiz Landazuri, Madrid, December 20, 1774, in ibid., fols. 442f–443v and 510f–510v respectively.

the royal decree, the depositario turned over 4,623/3/6 for both funds, but presented only current books and no further accounting for an administration that stretched back to the early seventeenth century. Equally remarkably, the royal treasury officials took no steps to compel formal accounting.

Under the more careful supervision of the treasury officials of the later Bourbons, both funds prospered. Careful books were kept for the 230 communities involved. In each community, the local caciques and officials collected the holpatán and community levy semi-annually, disbursed from the community portion what was needed locally, and delivered the holpatán and community surplus to the district Spanish official. Within the first six years of royal administration—that is, by the summer of 1783—the cumulative surplus rose from 4,623/3/6 to 45,099/4/6. In 1787, with the organization of Yucatan and Tabasco as the Intendancy of Mérida, the local Spanish officials became the subdelegados. The Indian officials received 2% of the community portion for their work; the subdelegados, nothing. They remitted the funds, without deduction, to the royal treasury officials.

With the continuing increase in Indian population in Yucatan, the yield from the levy increased at the same time that the charges remained relatively fixed. By 1805, under counts carried out in 1803, the Intendancy of Yucatan with 16 districts (*subdelegaciones*) had 81,295 tributaries, from whom 5,080/6/6 annually was due for holpatán. By early 1813, according to a report of April 22, 1813, to the intendant, the surplus in the holpatán was in excess of 58,000/. At the time of the report, not all sums due for 1812 had been collected. The surplus might have been higher had not it been tapped for relief and maintenance of Indians in jails, and had not the stipend of the notary been raised. Sad to say, most of the surplus—some 50,000/— was turned over to the national Spanish treasury, and vanished in the Wars of Independence. Although Indian tribute was abolished on May 26, 1810, by the Cortes of Cádiz, the holpatán continued to be levied. The report of 1813 recommended that it too be ended as no longer necessary. Although the return to the throne of Ferdinand VII, who restored all of the old levies, undoubtedly preserved it for a few years more,[84] it disappeared in 1820–21 with separation from Spain.

To the somewhat jaundiced eye of a writer in the middle nineteenth century, reviewing the Indian court of Yucatan, it had numerous faults; for 400,000 Indians in over 280 towns had to come to the court, regardless of distance, to seek remedy. Although forbidden to accept gifts, the officials of the court nevertheless did so, and the Indians gave them in attempt to win favorable judgment. By the last years

84. See Chapter X below.

of the colonial period, the holpatán yielded so much that the officials of the court promoted conflicts and suits among Indians, Indian towns, and haciendas so that they might profit. However minor the matter or slender the plea, the Indians involved had to go to Mérida for hearing and decision with loss of time, cost to them for travel and maintenance, and provision of items for gifts. So charged the writer, who also objected to the unified jurisdiction of the governor, the special procedures, and perpetual guardianship of the Indians. Of this last, although he regarded it as obsolete, he was inclined to hold that it should have been abolished gradually, so that the Indians might become accustomed to life as free citizens.[85]

If one makes allowance for the radical change in perspective and view of the proper organization of government between the colonial period and the years after the French Revolution, the writer's comments yet are testimony to wide use by the Indians of Yucatan of the special facilities for quick legal redress placed at their disposal. It is hard to see how fomenting discord would have benefited the legal aides, the assessor, and the governor, except through increase in bribes and gifts, for they could not increase their shares in the holpatán. The complaint in all likelihood reflected the annoyance of the Spanish community in Yucatan, which found that the Indians used one of the very few avenues of remedy available to them in uncomfortable measure. Despite the role of the governor as chief exploiter, and the selection of his legal aides from among local Spaniards, the special Indian court thus played a very real role in mitigating fleecing of the Indians. Its function never was to end exploitation—an end far from Spanish imagination and the realities of society, then and now—but to restrain excesses; in short, to keep exploitation within measure. That it may well have done.

C. The Audiencia of Guadalajara

A sketch of the adjustment to Indian judicial needs in the Audiencia of Guadalajara—or of Nueva Galicia, as it was first called—is included here because it lay within colonial Mexico. As an audiencia presided over by a president who exercised overall powers of administration, but without the force of a viceroy or captain-general, it was more nearly typical of most audiencia districts of the Spanish empire in America such as Guatemala, Panama, Quito, and even Bogotá and Buenos Aires until the Bourbon changes.[86] None of these developed a

85. Sierra O'Reilly.
86. See Muro Romero, passim.

system of legal insurance for Indians, with attendant legal aides and extraordinary jurisdiction supported from the yield. Nevertheless, royal directives required that all make special provision for adapting Spanish law and legal procedures to Indian needs; that lawsuits between Indians, or with an Indian as party, be handled by speedier and less costly procedures than those customary in Castilian practice; and that their complaints, if justified under official Spanish rules, receive rapid relief. Although audiencias and their practices varied from one district to another, and the Audiencia of Guadalajara, because of its relations with that of Mexico, tended to copy the procedures of the senior and more prestigious body,[87] this sketch illustrates Spanish arrangements for Indian legal needs in the absence of a system of legal insurance.

The Audiencia of Nueva Galicia came into existence in 1548[88] as a separate high court within a territory detached from the jurisdiction of the Audiencia of Mexico. It remained subject to the appellate jurisdiction of the senior body, although protected from much appeal by distance and costs. It served as an appellate court for the provinces within its territory, and exercised civil and criminal jurisdiction in first instance within a circuit of five leagues of its seat. In overall administration, military matters, and audit of the royal finances, it was supposed to be subordinate to the authority of the viceroy, royal fiscal officials, and audiencia in Mexico City; but in the course of the sixteenth century it won effective autonomy except in matters of audit.

Because of resistance by the Audiencia of Mexico and the viceroy to detachment from their jurisdiction of any lands of value, the territory assigned to the new audiencia showed marked peculiarities. The eventual audiencia seat, Guadalajara, lay near the boundary with the older jurisdiction. A minor rectification in 1574 added even more anomaly, since five provinces—Amula, Autlán, Izatlán and La Magdalena, Sayula, and that of Tuxpan and Zapotlán—were placed in the judicial sphere of the northwestern audiencia, but remained under the administrative and fiscal supervision of the viceroy. They became the *provincias subalternas*. The effect was to give the Audiencia of Guadalajara more judicial territory south of its seat, but the distribution still remained very much skewed and received adjustment only late in the colonial period.

The authority of the audiencia extended far north and east of its seat, into the whole of the northwest of Mexico as we know it and

87. See the discussion later in this chapter.
88. The paragraphs which follow are based upon Parry, *The Audiencia*, passim; Simmons, passim; notarial copy of docket accompanying Audiencia of Guadalajara to the king, Guadalajara, May 11, 1787, in AGI-G, leg. 351; Muro Romero, 59–71, 122–172, 203–209, and 222–223; and Soberanes Fernández, *Los tribunales*, 61.

much of the southwest of what is now the United States. Toward the end of the colonial period, the organization of the Provincias Internas and the extension to Mexico of the system of intendants brought further changes, in that Coahuila and Texas were transferred to the Audiencia of Guadalajara, so as to place all of the Provincias Internas within the one audiencia, and the provincias subalternas were placed within the Intendancy of Jalisco and so brought within the administrative district of the audiencia, while entrusting administration to an official reporting directly to the viceroy in Mexico City. In the later eighteenth century, appeals from as far away as California, New Mexico, and Texas had to come to Guadalajara. In terms of square kilometers, the Audiencia of Guadalajara ultimately exercised jurisdiction over a larger territory than its senior in Mexico City; in terms of population, the coverage of its jurisdiction was far less.

Most of the Indians, all of those in the farther reaches, either accepted no Spanish authority or were administered by provincial governors, like that of New Mexico, with wide-reaching powers and substantial autonomy. Indian matters were dealt with locally, without reference to the audiencia and almost invariably without appeals. Appeals would have had to be carried enormous distances across arid wastes; the effort and cost threw up substantial barriers. In practice, the effective judicial jurisdiction of the audiencia extended to the Indians in the provinces closer to the tribunal's seat, those in Jalisco, Nayarit, Aguascalientes, Querétaro, and southern Zacatecas. In 1548 the Indians in these provinces numbered upwards of 250,000; around 1650, at the nadir of the native population, they numbered perhaps 25,000. Within the core area of the Audiencia of Guadalajara, natives were far fewer than in the Audiencia of Mexico, and with a steady drop in numbers became almost negligible, except for certain village concentrations. Even with the demographic recovery of the eighteenth century, Indian numbers remained relatively small, some 65,000 in 1760 and 125,000 in 1805. Nueva Galicia and its associated provinces were lands for European and mestizo settlement.[89] In the sixteenth century, the Indian villages were assigned in encomiendas or paid tribute directly to the crown. In the seventeenth and eighteenth centuries, as Indian population fell to its lowest point and began to recover, the encomiendas gave way to direct payment of tribute to the crown. Throughout these centuries, there were enough natives to require special measures of protection and judicial adjustment.[90]

Even before Nueva Galicia was detached from the Audiencia of

89. Cook and Borah, *Essays*, 1:303–311, and in general all of Chapter 5, and 2:197–198; "Estado general de tributos y tributarios, 1805," 30–34.
90. Borah, "Los tributos y su recaudación," passim but esp. 39.

Mexico,[91] it had a protector of the Indians, but that post was allowed to lapse. In 1582, after the audiencia received a royal cédula ordering the removal of all protectors, the audiencia to assume this function, that tribunal wrote to the king that there had never been such an official in Nueva Galicia and that the fiscal, an office initiated there in 1568, discharged this function in suits and other matters. With considerable unction, the judges assured the monarch that they were always careful to see that the Indians received protection, and that the abuse of trading by provincial governors and other administrative officials was unknown.[92]

The substantial body of special, protective directives for Indians issued in the sixteenth century and later, applied directly or indirectly to the Audiencia of Guadalajara. Those sent to the Audiencia of Mexico prior to 1548, and those issued for general application in Spanish America or sent to the Audiencia of Guadalajara, bound that audiencia through immediate injunction. Those sent to the Audiencia of Mexico after 1548 and those sent to other districts, most notably the Audiencia of Lima, became binding when they were incorporated in the compilation of Diego de Encinas, published in 1596. Other royal legislation, issued later for other districts, became binding, if not known earlier, through the Recopilación de leyes . . . de las Indias, promulgated in 1680 and published in 1681. Most of that legislation, virtually all of it issued in the sixteenth century, has been analyzed already in the earlier chapters of this book in the discussion on the Audiencia of Mexico.

Under that legislation, Spanish judges were to respect Indian laws and customs so long as they were not clearly unjust or contrary to Christianity.[93] They were not to allow prolonged litigation in ordinary Castilian form between Indians or with them; but once the facts of the matter were evident, were to decide them by summary, abbreviated process.[94] In matters of little importance, decisions were to be by administrative decree and not by judicial provisión real, "so that the Indians may be relieved of damages and costs to the greatest possible extent." Such decrees, signed with the rubric of the president of the audiencia and countersigned by the appropriate notary, were to have

91. Probanza on the services of Cristóbal Pedraza, protector de indios for the province of Nueva Galicia, Compostela, January 11, 1536, and the Bishop-elect of Nueva Galicia to the king, Guadalajara, December 15, 1547, in AGI-G, legs. 46 and 55 respectively.

92. Guadalajara, October 17, 1582, in ibid., leg. 6; Parry, The Audiencia, 127. The fiscal's work, according to Parry, was substantially that of public prosecutor in criminal cases.

93. RLI, 2.1.4, 2.15.83, and 5.2.22.

94. Ibid., 2.15.83 and 5.10.10.

the validity of formal *provisiones reales* under royal seal. The purpose was to remedy Indians' remaining for long periods away from their homes in order to secure dispatches and provisiones reales, at much cost and trouble to them.[95] For small matters, notarial receptores might not be sent to Indian towns for gathering testimony.[96] Further to ease the burden of Spanish law and procedures on the Indians, they might not be tried nor punished for blows with the bare hand nor of mere words, but were merely to be rebuked by the judge.[97] In the weekly inspection of Indian jails by oidores, the judges were to examine the testimony of witnesses and not accept summary accounts by others.[98] Indians jailed for debt might be turned over to their creditors for service only after careful examination of the circumstances of the debt, their abilities, and the setting of a proper rate of pay; further advances were automatically void, and no Indian might be transferred to someone other than the original creditor.[99] Indians in jail for drunkenness might not be held to costs, fees, or jailor's charges, and might not be condemned to involuntary service.[100]

This legislation added up to substantial protection, to the extent that it was observed. To ensure rapid dispatch of Indian matters, the audiencia was enjoined to devote two days a week and Saturdays, so far as suits of the poor did not fill that day, to the dispatch of suits among Indians and those between Indians and Spaniards.[101]

Since proceedings before a court required legal advice and even legal aides, the legislation also sought to make provision for them in districts without legal insurance. Where there were protectors of the Indians, the arrangement had a checkered existence, since the post was authorized and abolished at various times.[102] Finally, in 1589, the crown authorized continued existence of the protectors where they had functioned previously.[103] By then the institution was long extinct in the Audiencia of Guadalajara. The royal legislation authorized a substitute in the fiscal or crown attorney attached to the audiencia, who was to act as protector, to help the natives in all proper matters, and to plead for them in all civil and criminal suits, those of government interest, private, and with Spaniards. Only in suits among Indians over money matters (hacienda) must he remain neutral.[104] If the fiscal on behalf of the crown carried on suit against an Indian, and there was no other protector or procurador who might act in his behalf, the audiencia was to name the most suitable person for the In-

95. Ibid., 2.15.85 and 5.10.12.   96. Ibid., 2.15.84.
97. Ibid., 5.10.11.   98. Ibid., 7.7.13.
99. Ibid., 7.7.14.   100. Ibid., 7.6.21.
101. Ibid., 2.15.81.   102. Bayle, "El protector," 83–102, esp. 93.
103. RLI, 6.6.1.   104. Ibid., 2.18.34 and 87.

dian's defense.[105] In grants of land, when interested parties were cited to determine possible conflict, the crown attorney must be summoned on behalf of the Indians.[106]

An attorney for one side obviously was not enough for many Indian cases. The royal legislation recognized the need by providing that in each audiencia district, the viceroy or president name a letrado and a procurador who would defend and handle Indian cases and complaints. They were to receive salaries from fines or the funds of Indian communities, and in no case were to accept fees. In suits between Indians before the audiencias, the fiscal was to represent one party and the protector (if not the fiscal), and the procurador, the other. If the case began before a provincial governor and then moved to the audiencia, the papers were to be sent to the audiencia "without giving basis for the Indians to leave their lands, so far as the quality of the matter may allow." Once the audiencia reached decision, it was to be sent back to the provincial governor for implementation.[107] The reader will recognize provisions of the royal cédulas which established special Indian tribunals in the Audiencia of Mexico and in Yucatan, extended to all of Spanish America and amplified by subsequent royal instruction. Some of the later legislation considerably extended the obligations of the protectors and the restrictions upon them. They were to send detailed reports to the viceroys or presidents on the state of the Indians and treatment of them; these reports had to be sent on to Spain.[108] In each audiencia district, the chief administrative officer was enjoined to give immediate and ample audience to the protectors.[109] Finally, the protectors might not function through substitutes.[110] That rule did not apply to the crown attorneys in their automatic capacity of protectors.[111]

One provision which has caused some confusion is the royal cédula of rebuke signed in Madrid on June 13, 1623, and sent to Mexico City. Its statement that the Indians of New Spain paid a half-real for the salaries of legal aides and relief from fees has been construed to mean that the levy operated in the Audiencia of Guadalajara as well.[112] The confusion lies in the ambiguities of the term New Spain, but the reference is to New Spain in the narrowest sense of the Audiencia of

---

105. Ibid., 2.18.35.
106. Ibid., 2.18.86.
107. Ibid., 6.6.3 and 13.
108. Ibid., 6.6.12.
109. Ibid., 6.6.10.
110. Ibid., 6.6.6.
111. As is evident from the circumstance that in the Audiencia of Mexico the fiscales did use deputies, called *agentes fiscales*.
112. See Chapter VII above. The cédula was entered in the RLI as 6.6.4. See also Parry, *The Audiencia*, 163, and Simmons, 189–190.

Mexico. The half-real for legal aides never was collected in the audiencia district of Guadalajara (Nueva Galicia in its widest sense).[113]

The royal cédula of 1623 does give rise to one question, however: To what extent were the Indians in the Audiencia of Guadalajara charged legal fees and costs? In the latter half of the sixteenth century, notaries in documents for Indians were ordered to abide by the schedule of fees in force in Castile, without the fourfold adjustment for the higher costs of the Indies.[114] That rule met bitter opposition from the escribano mayor of the audiencia, a post held through a substitute by Turcios, the secretario de gobernación in Mexico City. Royal confirmation of the order in 1583 did not settle the matter, since the notaries sued in the audiencia, and when they lost the suit there, in 1583, appealed to the Council of the Indies.[115] Despite repeated petitions from the fiscal of the audiencia, Lic. Pinedo, that appeal still was pending in April 1602, when Pinedo wrote:

> I beg your Majesty that he command that the case be concluded, for the Indians live in such great misery that without further investigation all could be declared to be paupers. The worst is that no Indian carries on a suit of any importance except in the name of all, and thus they pay twelvefold.[116]

Even if an Indian had sued as an individual and qualified as a pauper, i.e., was entitled to free notarial and legal service, he had the problem of getting notaries and members of the legal fraternity to perform work without pay. An Indian community, however poverty-stricken and without resources, could not qualify as a pauper.

The royal cédulas of April 4, 1591, severely limiting the fees of notaries and all kinds of lawyers, in that none could be charged Indians as individuals and only half fees might be charged caciques and native communities, applied within the Audiencia of Mexico. No royal order specifically directing extension to the Audiencia of Guadalajara has yet been found. It might be held that none was issued; certainly the complaint of Lic. Pinedo would indicate that as late as 1602 none had been. Nevertheless, the complaints and reports of the eighteenth century suggest that they had been applied in Nueva Galicia,[117] although how and when they were transmitted are questions yet to be resolved.

113. See the discussion later in this chapter.

114. Royal cédula, Madrid, January 23, 1569, and letter from Audiencia of Guadalajara to Ovando, Guadalajara, n.d. but March 1570, in AGI-G, leg. 5.

115. Audiencia of Guadalajara to the king, Guadalajara, March 25, 1583, and Lic. Pinedo to the king, Guadalajara, March 25, 1584, in ibid., leg. 6.

116. Lic. Pinedo to the king, Guadalajara, April 10, 1602, ibid.

117. See the discussion of the eighteenth century later in this chapter.

The high tribunal which administered the territory and enforced this protective legislation consisted early in the seventeenth century of a president-governor, four oidores, and a fiscal. Subordinate officials included a relator, a chief bailiff, and a secretary or escribano mayor. The two latter posts were held for life, through purchase at prices of 4,000/ and 12,000/ respectively.[118] There were further lesser officials paid from the proceeds of fines and costs of justice. According to the treasury accounts for 1595–96, among them were a procurador de pobres at 100/ a year, an abogado de pobres at the same salary, and four interpreters, two at 110/2/6 a year, one at 110/0/4, and one at 36/ a year.[119] The only special arrangements for handling Indian matters were the interpreters, their number testimony to the variety of languages the tribunal had to deal with. Indian cases probably were handled by the abogado and procurador de pobres, there being no other special provision except for the fiscal's function as protector. This sparse and unsatisfactory provision lasted until the eighteenth century.

It must be said that the tribunal functioned in a seat and district that throughout the seventeenth century was poor and bore the signs of the frontier. Guadalajara at the start of the seventeenth century had 173 Spanish vecinos, with a total Spanish population of perhaps 500 persons. It had an additional Indian population of unknown but probably modest number. Within the city lived 26 encomenderos, testimony to the general lack of sedentary Indians. The city had three rich vecinos with fortunes of at least 100,000/; some 22 merchants had capital of 4,000/ to 20,000/. The other Spanish families each had less than 2,000/ in total wealth.[120] Such affluence as there was really lay in the mining city of Zacatecas. For the rest, the entire audiencia district had a sparse settlement of Spaniards, i.e., people of Spanish culture, and few sedentary Indians under Spanish control to provide workers and wealth.[121] It was not an economic environment that could support notaries, abogados, procuradores, and solicitadores in any number or well, and there were correspondingly almost none. The professional distinctions and formal titles that meant so much in Mexico City became very much blurred in the much poorer, smaller world of Guadalajara.[122]

The effort to extract support from the Indians led to considerable abuse by provincial administrators and justices in Nueva Galicia

118. Díez de la Calle, 201–202 (cap. 3); Mota y Escobar, 45.
119. AGI-C, leg. 859B.
120. Mota y Escobar, 46–47.
121. Vázquez de Espinosa, 175–176 (nos. 527–529); Mota y Escobar, passim; Cook and Borah, *Essays*, 1:301–344.
122. Parry, *The Audiencia*, 155–156 et passim.

(in the narrow sense) and Nueva Vizcaya, effectively the present-day states of Jalisco, Nayarit, Durango, Aguascalientes, and Zacatecas. A letter from Lic. Pinedo to the king in 1598 sheds much light upon their practices and upon the extent to which the audiencia actually enforced protective legislation. Since the provincial governors and justices received their salaries and additional sums for costs from fines and court costs, they levied heavy fines and imposed severe sentences to see that the fund remained full. It was illegal for a judge to receive a share in the fines he himself imposed, complained Pinedo, but it was universal practice. For any offense, however trivial, Indians were sentenced to fines and then sold to employers for working off their fines and the costs. Local justices and employers were in league for ensuring a supply of labor and fines. Once sold into service, the Indians never regained their freedom, for they were advanced money for clothing and other items, so that they never could work off their debts. Although the audiencia had forbidden imposition of fines on Indians except in cases of damage to persons, the provincial judges ignored the rule.[123]

Most Indian cases never got beyond provincial courts. Luis Páez Brotchie, who spent so much time rummaging in the remaining records of the Audiencia of Guadalajara, found only one from the late sixteenth and early seventeenth centuries, the trial for homicide of one Indian at the complaint of another, the widow being considered the prosecuting party. The case was remitted to the audiencia from Nochistlán (Zacatecas), where it originated and where the culprit was in jail. As usual, the tribunal judged from the documents. On April 3, 1601, it issued sentence that the culprit receive 100 lashes and be sold into forced service for four years. The proceeds of the sale were to be divided one half to the widow, her children, and relatives of the dead man; one quarter to the royal treasury; and part of one quarter for 20 masses for the soul of the dead man, the remainder to be applied to bringing water to Guadalajara.[124] Two other criminal cases appear in the report of Lic. Gaspar de la Fuente on his inspection in 1608–1610. In the province of Tlaltenango and the villa of Jérez (Zacatecas), he reported that an Indian had been tried and convicted of rape of a 6-year-old Indian girl. "Since he was a pauper and in these matters the Indians are weak," he was condemned to 100 lashes and eight years of personal service, the price received to be given to the girl. In the same province, a Spaniard, his two sons, and a slave were tried for murdering an Indian. They were twice condemned to the gallows; but on

123. Pinedo to the king, Guadalajara, April 15, 1598, in AGI-G, leg. 6.
124. Páez Brotchie, 29–30.

third hearing, to two years of service in the Philippines, presumably at their expense, and the payment of 50 days' salary to the officials of the inspection. Normally these cases would have gone to the audiencia, but Lic. De la Fuente on his tour of inspection exercised both supersessary and appellate jurisdiction.[125]

In the later seventeenth century and throughout the eighteenth, the Indian population of the audiencia district steadily increased, and extension of the zones under Spanish control brought new numbers within the jurisdiction of provincial authorities,[126] if not always the effective jurisdiction of the tribunal. In the more remote provinces, there were sometimes local protectors. One such official functioned in New Mexico during the later seventeenth and early eighteenth centuries, but the post then lapsed. It was revived just before the end of the colonial period.[127] We do not know the extent to which protectors functioned in other provinces. Only studies in detail of government in the provinces on the northern frontier could give that information. Exploitation of Indians undoubtedly continued, and with their rise in number would become more widespread. The audiencia, in general, either was unable or unwilling to interfere. In 1716, the Bishop of Durango complained to the crown that Indians were being put to work in Spanish ore-grinding mills, contrary to regulations, and that the audiencia, knowing of the practice, did nothing. The letter brought forth an immediate royal rebuke to the audiencia, a weak one, that Indians were to do such work only of their own free will and for pay.[128]

The somewhat sketchy concern of the tribunal with the sedentary Indians in the territories nearer Guadalajara may be inferred from an exchange in 1739–40. On July 12, 1739, at Buen Retiro, Philip V signed a royal cédula, general to all officials and prelates in the Spanish Indies, requiring reports on the treatment of the Indians. It was a shotgun affair asking about communities, observance of laws for Indian defense, freedom, religious training, increase or decrease, the extent to which there were protectors-general, protectors, and other special officials for Indian aid, and how all of these carried out their duties. The cédula inquired especially into the functioning of the crown attorneys attached to the audiencias in Indian civil and criminal cases, "since they are the principal defenders of the Indians." In answer to the copy sent to Guadalajara, the fiscal of the audiencia, the historian Lic. Matías de la Mota Padilla, replied on July 19, 1740, in a cautious let-

125. AGI-C, leg. 874, ramo 2.
126. Cook and Borah, *Essays*, 1:309–356.
127. Simmons, 189–191.
128. Bayle, "El protector," 40–41, citing a ms. in AGI-G, leg. 76.

ter that gave little information. The audiencia had ordered that Indian communities make communal sowings, wrote Mota Padilla, but the greater part of his letter discussed the mixed-bloods and suggested that Spaniards be permitted to live freely among the Indians.[129] In a sense the letter constituted an answer, if the staff of the Council of the Indies chose to read between the lines, but whatever they thought they kept to themselves.

By the second half of the eighteenth century, as the Bourbon broom swept deeper, the somewhat easy-going administrative and judicial ways of the tribunal became more difficult to sustain. Moreover, the imperial administration in Madrid, intent upon tightening the bonds of empire and improving yield to Spain, began to insist upon implementation of more of the clauses in the *Recopilación de leyes . . . de las Indias*. For the Audiencia of Guadalajara, one result was a long-drawn-out series of inquiries and reports on Indian legal aides and means of supporting them that at times was a comedy of errors, illustrating both the virtues and the faults of the highly organized Spanish bureaucracy in Spain and the Mexican audiencias. The series began innocently enough with discussion within the tribunal in Guadalajara on how to finance rebuilding of the royal offices and the jail in the city. On June 13, 1757, the audiencia wrote to the crown, recommending a tax on mezcal and urging that the medio real for legal aides, which it thought was collected in the subaltern provinces—those administratively within the Audiencia of Mexico, but subject judicially to the Audiencia of Guadalajara—be applied for the buildings rather than spent on the support of Indian legal aides in Mexico City. In their letter, the judges also recommended that the levy of the medio real be made general within the audiencia district.[130]

In Spain, the letter rested for 16 years until receipt early in 1774 of another letter from the audiencia, dated October 15, 1773.[131] Large numbers of petitions and memorials from Indians and Indian communities, it reported, were coming to the tribunal and its officials. They arrived almost daily, and all were defective in that they were drawn without proper formality and knowledge of law by untrained persons. The Indians received notable damage in the costs, and the public even more, since the tribunal's time was filled with these inept complaints. As a remedy, the audiencia appointed an abogado protector, appar-

129. AGI-G, leg. 104.
130. Consulta of the Council of the Indies, Madrid, August 9, 1777, in ibid., leg. 242.
131. The account which follows is based on the docket, 1773–1777, in ibid., leg. 341.

ently the first, to help in such cases. For this role it chose Lic. Casimiro de Aguilar, who the year before had been defender of pauper criminals and had done well. Although the audiencia had no funds to pay Lic. Aguilar, since Nueva Galicia levied no medio real de ministros, he had been willing to take on the function in order to acquire merit. In the six months he had been in the post, he had so expedited the movement of Indian petitions and complaints that the natives received much more relief, and the audiencia found itself freed of much minor business. The judges urged that Lic. Aguilar be given formal royal appointment as abogado protector and a salary. Alas, the audiencia, on June 10, 1774, had to report that it had suspended Aguilar from functioning as an abogado in any capacity for four years, because of disrespect in open court.

In Spain, the letter of October 15, 1773, led to long deliberations in the Council of the Indies. The first reaction was to ask for more information, as it did by royal cédula of February 21, 1774. In the summer of 1774 the council came to a decision. The audiencia should be instructed to name an abogado and procurador for Indians, in accordance with the provision in the *Recopilación de leyes . . . de las Indias* ordering that there be such posts, but must find the salaries in the crown's share of fines or in the goods of the Indian communities, since the provision so stated.[132] At the same time, the viceroy should be ordered to report on the desirability of extending the levy of the medio real de ministros to the audiencia district of Guadalajara. Both decisions were issued as royal cédulas on August 18, 1774.

On February 10, 1775, the Audiencia of Guadalajara both acknowledged receipt of the royal cédula and reported its compliance. It had appointed a procurador de indios as ordered, but found no money available in either the yield of fines or Indian community treasuries that could be applied as salary. Abogados and procuradores accepted the new function as part of their professional duties. Accompanying the letter came extensive copies of proceedings in Guadalajara as evidence of prompt obedience. In the documents is the appointment on January 7, 1775, of Lic. Rafael Ignacio Vallarta as procurador de indios for a term of one year, the other procuradores to take annual turns at this post as at those of procurador for paupers and defender of paupers in jail. Another document, dated January 12, 1775, appointed Lic. Vicente Fernández Lechuga to the post of procurador de indios, on the ground that no appointment had been made earlier with the same provisions. Perhaps Vallarta refused to serve. Both men were

132. RLI, 6.6.3.

fully qualified professionally, since both had law degrees and had been admitted to practice before the tribunal. The copies of proceedings in Guadalajara made it amply clear that there was no surplus revenue in the two existing funds for use in salaries for legal aides.

In Mexico City, the royal cédula directed to the viceroy came to that able but arch-bureaucrat, Viceroy Bucareli y Ursúa. As instructed, he at once asked for opinions from the committee then engaged in drafting new regulations on Indian tribute, and from the contador de tributos and one of the crown attorneys. This last urged first asking opinions from Eusebio Sánchez, judge of the audiencia, and from Domingo Arangoiti, fiscal of the sala del crimen, since both men had served in Guadalajara. Both agreed that the many Indian cases in the Audiencia of Guadalajara were poorly handled by badly trained notaries and legal people, and that the levy would be very useful and would permit maintaining in the neighboring audiencia a staff of legal aides for Indians, as in the Audiencia of Mexico. The contador found in his office only information on the five subordinate provinces, which had 9,417½ tributaries. For data on the number of tributaries in the provinces administered by the Audiencia of Guadalajara, he had to turn to the court of audit in Mexico City, which reported 14,684½ tributaries, or a total of 24,102 and potential yield from a medio real de ministros of 1,506/3, more than enough to maintain a modest staff. From it might even come a surplus that would permit formation of a capital fund and eventual end of the levy. With these reports in hand, Bucareli convoked a meeting of representatives from the audiencia and the royal fiscal offices on April 6, 1775. All agreed with the previous recommendations. In a long letter dated April 26, 1775, accompanied by the usual notarial copies of all reports and proceedings, Bucareli sent on the recommendations to the crown.

All of these reports came under consideration in the Council of the Indies in the summer of 1777. The Council was reluctant to extend the medio real de ministros to all of the Audiencia of Guadalajara, but agreed that the officials serving the Indians were entitled to pay. Their solution was to urge the king that the medio real presumably collected in the subaltern provinces be applied for that purpose, since it was not fair that the Indians in those provinces pay for legal help in Mexico City outside of their judicial district. Any further action on legal protection for the Indians in the Audiencia of Guadalajara was suspended, since it had been decided that the fiscal of the audiencia there continue to discharge the function. Finally, the suspension of Lic. Aguilar for four years was too harsh; the audiencia should be ordered to end it, and Aguilar should be warned to be more respectful before the tribunal. The decision on the medio real de ministros was accepted by the king and embodied in a royal cédula of December 4, 1777.

The royal cédula of December 1777 arrived in Guadalajara early in 1778.[133] It received formal obedience on April 1, 1778, and on May 11 was ordered carried out. To secure transfer of the medio real purportedly collected in the subaltern provinces, a notarial copy of the cédula, with a request for implementation, should be sent to the viceroy. Actually, the viceroy received a parallel royal cédula, also dated December 4, 1777, direct from Spain, probably before the one sent to Guadalajara arrived there. In Mexico City, the royal instruction set off a long series of directives for implementation and inquiries. The net result lay in the answer of the contador de tributos on June 4, 1778, that the office in his charge never had collected the medio real de ministros in the five subaltern provinces and, of course, had nothing to do with tribute collection in the provinces administered from Guadalajara. After much discussion by the judges of the audiencia, the crown attorneys and Bucareli reported to Madrid and informed the Audiencia of Guadalajara that there was no such revenue as the medio real de ministros in the subaltern provinces. Upon receipt of this letter, the Audiencia of Guadalajara on May 10, 1779, ordered that a summary of all be prepared by its relator and be brought to it.

From May 1779 until October 1784, discussion and proceedings, as far as the written record goes, were suspended, rather a longer lull than was customary even in the leisurely proceedings of the high court in Guadalajara. On October 11, 1784, the tribunal resumed consideration of the matter with an order that the secretaries of gobernación and of cámara, the relator, and its receptores report on any emoluments they received beyond the fees set by the official schedule. That order unleashed a series of affidavits that took from October 14, 1784, until April 29, 1785. All officials testified that little of their work brought fees, since most of it either was official, and so without fees, or for Indians, and so equally without fees. They were even forced to pay for the paper used in such work out of their own pockets. Legal work which did provide fees came to so little that they were forced to live on loans in unusually lean periods. The affidavits are interesting testimony to at least one aspect of the life of the legal profession in what was still a modest capital not too far removed from the frontier. Upon examining all of the testimony, as well as the papers preceding, the crown attorney for civil affairs wrote a relatively lengthy opinion pointing out the plight of the legal profession, the

133. The account which follows is based on the docket, 1777–1789, in AGI-G, leg. 351.

great utility that the medio real and the staff of legal aides supported from it brought the Indians in the Audiencia of Mexico, and the fact that there was no such revenue either in the subaltern provinces nor elsewhere in the Audiencia of Guadalajara. To impose it in the subaltern provinces, whose Indians had to resort to Mexico City for administrative relief and to Guadalajara for judicial relief, might create an unfair burden. On March 27, 1787, the Audiencia of Guadalajara ordered that a copy of all papers be sent to the crown—one cannot be sure whether with the hope of securing something like the medio real throughout its territory, or as a simple means of washing its hands of the whole business. The formal letter to the crown and the accompanying notarial transcripts bear the date May 11, 1787.

Upon arrival of the letter and accompanying copies in Spain, the course of response was equally deliberate. On November 12, 1788, the fiscal of the Council of the Indies rendered his opinion on the file. He agreed that the Audiencia of Guadalajara had proceeded properly in suspending the royal cédula transferring the medio real of the subaltern provinces, since that was based on misinformation; he found it deplorable that the audiencia had not informed itself of the circumstances more exactly before the entire affair began; but most of all, he found fault in the long delay in reporting back to Spain. As for the suggestion of extending the levy of the medio real to the entire audiencia district, that would add to the burdens upon an already heavily burdened people. The Council of the Indies deferred consideration of the entire matter until it could consider it jointly with the need to repair the jail in Guadalajara, not yet rebuilt in 30 years. A last notation dated April 1, 1789, still deferred consideration. As late as 1805, there was still no decision to be communicated to the audiencia in Guadalajara—in effect, decision by default to continue the existing state of affairs.[134]

The entire series of inquiries and deliberations constituted considerably less than a tempest in a teapot; at most, the teapot came to a slightly higher temperature. One effect was to force the audiencia to appoint legal aides for Indians, whether paid somehow or serving to acquire merit in official eyes. Equally, one fiscal—for by then the increase in legal business had led to appointment of more than one— thenceforth discharged the duties of protector with more vigor. The willingness with which the function was assumed may be gauged by the fact that it fell upon the fiscal with less seniority. Since implementation of the Ordinance of Intendants in 1787–88, and creation of a

134. The inventory of royal cédulas for the Audiencia of Guadalajara, 1670– 1774, extended to 1805, shows no further action.

new military and administrative command of the northern provinces, the Provincias Internas, truncated the audiencia's administrative authority while leaving its judicial jurisdiction intact, the fiscal charged with protection of the Indians found his duties affected by the changes. In the Provincias Internas, some of the districts were given provincial protectors, largely autonomous, but whose appointments were cleared with the fiscal, since they were nominally subordinate to him.[135] The effect of the change upon the sedentary Indians in the north has yet to be studied. As regards the nomadic and unsubdued Indians, the creation of the Provincias Internas meant a unified military command and much more effective mobilizing of resources to wage war against them.

For the audiencia district of Guadalajara, the eighteenth century was a period of substantial and relatively steady growth in population among the Indians, and even more among the Hispanic elements. Guadalajara, the audiencia seat, developed steadily into a substantial center of wealth and authority, with considerably more professional resources than it had had earlier.[136] These changes show up in the records of the tribunal, of which far more survive than for the earlier colonial period. Páez Brotchie has found and listed a relatively substantial number of cases, some of which involved Indians. All are of a civil nature, except for one of 1730–1739 by the alcalde mayor of Parras (Coahuila) against the Indian governor of the town, for abuse of office. For some reason, even that was considered civil. The rest of the cases relate overwhelmingly to disputes over lands, very often with Spanish neighbors; in much lesser proportion to payment of tribute, declaration of privileges, and disputed town elections.[137] These listings indicate similarity to the general proportions of Indian cases in the Audiencia of Mexico, but with much less of the smaller categories, as befitted a far smaller Indian population spread over a much larger area. The major difference is that none relate to labor—a most interesting discrepancy, since mines, workshops, farms, and ranches in many parts of the audiencia district used Indians as so-called free wage laborers held by debt. Presumably, none of the disputes went beyond provincial courts; and the audiencia, although it had the right, seldom exercised supersessive jurisdiction—or perhaps more accurately, seldom was petitioned to do so. The larger number of listings is testimony not merely to the better survival of records, but undoubtedly in part as well to the larger number of cases reaching the tribunal

135. Simmons, 189–191. The Ordinance of Intendants meant that administration was under intendants who reported to the viceroy in Mexico City as superintendent-general.

136. Cook and Borah, *Essays*, 1 : 309–356; Cook, "Las migraciones," 355–367.

137. Páez Brotchie, 129–131 et passim.

from an increasing Indian population, and one by then much more accustomed to living in Spanish civilization. Probably as well, the tribunal was able to exercise somewhat more effective judicial control over the outer provinces of its territory. Whether the natives fared better or worse in the absence of the elaborate system of legal aid and the special viceregal competence of the Audiencia of Mexico is an interesting and crucial question yet to be answered.

CHAPTER X

The Coming of the New

During its long existence, the General Indian Court was certain to arouse antagonism and give rise to a considerable amount of criticism. Attacks came from many and diverse groups; some already have been discussed: from those who lost fees but drew no stipend from the medio real, and from those who complained of inefficiency and corruption.[1] Doubtless there were many others whose animadversions remain unknown because they were not committed to paper or, if written, have disappeared with the letters and documents containing them. Other complaints have reached our time. They indicate that in the later decades of the eighteenth century criticism became more vigorous, and the volume of it probably rose. It ranged from the bitter, private attack of Hipólito Villarroel, a career bureaucrat in Mexico, through suggestions for change as part of the centralizing reforms of Carlos III and IV, to visions of another organization of society and government in which estates and special jurisdictions would become obsolete. In the later Bourbon period, steadily intensifying dissatisfaction with the traditional structures of government and society undermined confidence in them and eventually brought about replacement. In that replacement, the General Indian Court, the medio real de ministros, and the entire special protective system for Indians met their demise.

Villarroel may be regarded as representative of one major school of the large and varied older group who made their living through ad-

1. See Chapters IV and VII above.

ministration, especially provincial administration. They were strongly in favor of the repartimiento de mercancías, the forced sale of animals and merchandise to the natives by the provincial governors, which constituted a profitable business and was defended as making the Indians active participants in the economy. Equally, the members of this group frequently came into conflict with the clergy.

We know little of the life of Villarroel. He had legal training and was formally admitted to practice as an abogado. He served in the administration of the royal tobacco monopoly and as inspector of the handling of royal revenues in Puebla and Acapulco. He supervised the expulsion of the Jesuits from their college for novitiates at Tepoztlán.[2] These functions all suggest that he was one of the reformers around José de Gálvez, and may well have been born and educated in Spain. Villarroel served eight years as alcalde mayor of the province of Cuautla Amilpas.[3] In the later 1770s he was alcalde mayor of the province of Tlapa in the Mixteca Baja, where in 1777 he was cited before the General Indian Court on formal charges (capítulos) brought by the Indians with the assistance of the local clergy. The charges were essentially improper levies, misuse of local officials for private gain, and repartimiento de mercancías. Oddly enough, they did not include the one charge he mentions in his writing, the forced raising of cochineal. In 1778, Villarroel was found guilty by the General Indian Court and promptly appealed to the audiencia, which did not get around to review of his case until 1782. While the appeal lay before the audiencia, Villarroel completed his term as alcalde mayor, so that the charges against him were incorporated in the customary residencia. In 1790, that was still under judicial consideration. Meanwhile, in 1784, Villarroel was named legal assessor for the Acordada; and although promotion to the office as proprietary holder was delayed because of his residencia, he was permitted to serve before it was completed.[4] He was evidently well-educated, energetic, and imbued with the ideas of rationality and efficiency of the earlier phase of the Spanish Enlightenment, an able though perhaps venal official of the enlightened despotism of Carlos III.

Between 1785 and 1787, Villarroel wrote a long manuscript, only published after his lifetime, entitled "Political infirmities which the capital of this New Spain suffers in almost all the bodies of which it is composed, and remedies which should be applied for healing, if it

2. Note by Vito Alessio Robles, in Villarroel, 509.
3. Ibid.
4.. Ibid., 321–322; secret report on Hipólito Villarroel to the king, Mexico City, Tlapa, and Madrid, 1785–1790, in AGN-Civ, vol. 2176:exp. 1 (22 fols.).

is to be of use to the king and to the public."[5] It is a slashing attack on much of what went on in government and society in late colonial Mexico, with special attention to the Indians, the General Indian Court, the Indian agents, the local clergy, and the crown attorneys, among many other topics treated. The true nature of the Indians could scarcely be believed, he wrote: they were lazy, extremely malicious, enemies of truth, untrustworthy, given to riots and disturbance, superficially Christians but really idolaters, outwardly humble but inwardly deceitful, prone to drunkenness, robbery, homicide, rape, incest, and all manner of suits, few justified. Unfortunately, their outward humility and lies moved some agents to help them carry on ruinous litigation in the courts against provincial governors, clergy, and hacendados. Lawyers fresh from school, knowing little of the true nature of the Indians, were ready to lend them an ear and out of mistaken pity assist them in usually unfounded prosecutions.[6] Equally, clergy qualified as abogados were allowed on the plea of defense of the poor to meddle in the suits of Indians and move them against hacendados, alcaldes mayores, and other Spaniards. So the Indians were led to additional levies upon themselves and were forced to sell themselves into service in order to obtain the money necessary for endless litigation.[7] The protection of the Indians by the crown attorneys and the audiencia, who knew nothing of them, merely protected them in idleness, to the ruin of agriculture.[8]

Villarroel found the General Indian Court especially prejudicial and useless. The brief dispatch by the assessor and viceroy prevented proper examination of matters that often should have been aired in other tribunals. Indian suits with each other were usually over land. The natives did not really care where they were heard, and brought many such suits before provincial governors and the audiencia. Worst of all, in defiance of explicit royal command, the court extended its competence to charges against provincial governors even though the latter were entitled to hearings before the audiencia and might be removed only after such hearing. He found the assessors of the court ignorant of the true nature of the Indians, and the court bound in a

5. A copy of a large part of this manuscript was found in Mexico City and published in 1830 as a supplement to *La voz de la Patria*, a Mexico City newspaper, by Carlos María Bustamante, and in 1831 was issued in book form. The full manuscript was discovered in the Bancroft Library, and was published in 1937 for the Bibliófilos Mexicanos in an edition of 50 copies, with an introduction by Genaro Estrada. The 1979 edition used here is a facsimile of that edition.

6. Villarroel, 85–87, 90–92, and 451–452.

7. Ibid., 133–135.

8. Ibid., 299–300.

"blind, vicious, unwise, and self-serving practice that benefited the no-tary, relator, and other lower officials."[9] As for the viceroys, they were basically military men, but nevertheless wasted four to six hours a day in the dispatch of essentially judicial business laid before them by the two secretaries of gobernación. All they could do was decree that the matters be passed to the crown attorney or to the assessor, and so the dockets became interminable with review and counter-review, all to the loss of litigants and enrichment of the notaries. Villarroel sug-gested delegation to the assessor for quick dispatch,[10] a measure being adopted even as he wrote. The crown attorneys, he declared, were the real deciders of cases since the viceroy and audiencia merely agreed to what they recommended; but the fiscales prolonged suits endlessly, and often wrote opinions quickly and in ignorance.[11]

As remedies, Villarroel suggested a long series of measures, some of which frankly favored the group of provincial administrators, oth-ers of which looked to improving the efficiency desired by the reform-ers of Enlightened Despotism. The Indians should be taught to live in Christian, useful society, in proper obedience to the king and his of-ficers, through the application of more punishment and less misdi-rected piety. As an additional means to that end, non-Indians should be permitted to live among them.[12] The only way to bring about good government was to restore the jurisdiction of the provincial governors, which should be respected by the audiencia, the crown attorneys, and the local clergy. A further desirable measure was to legalize a moder-ate, carefully applied repartimiento de mercancías, with previously fixed limits, so that the provincial governors would bring their Indians to industry and life within a commercial market.[13] The General Indian Court should be abolished, and presumably with it the entire system of salaried agents of the half-real.[14]

Villarroel's strictures and remedies bear the stamp of both old and new ideas. On the one hand, he would have permitted, under some restrictions, the exploitation of Indians by provincial governors and other Spaniards, a view reminiscent of the earlier colonial period. On the other hand, his reasons bore the stamp of the Enlightenment, for he held that the Indians must become civilized, industrious, well-behaved members of an essentially unified society of which they would be the lowest class. Many of his comments and remedies aimed at more efficient, more uniform ordering of society and government, but nowhere did he suggest equality before the law or in access to of-ficial posts.

9. Ibid., 85–87 and 495–496.   10. Ibid., 71–73.
11. Ibid., 109–115.   12. Ibid., 485–487.
13. Ibid., 452–453 and 492–495. 14. Ibid., 495–496.

Some of Villarroel's dissatisfaction with the anomalous jurisdiction of the General Indian Court showed up also in the major reform of administration embodied in the Ordinance of Intendants of 1786, one of the principal results of the endeavors of José de Gálvez as inspector-general and as minister of the Indies. The ordinance not merely interposed an intermediate layer of authority between viceroy and audiencia, on the one hand, and the provinces, on the other, but also aimed at instituting a much more unified and rational system of administration. For the first time, Yucatan and the territories of the Audiencia of Guadalajara were firmly knit into the administrative structure of New Spain since all intendants reported to Mexico City. Further, the ordinance gave the intendants jurisdiction over the collection of Indian tributes and the supervision of Indian community treasuries. Reports were to go to the Junta Superior de Real Hacienda in Mexico City, and all disputes were to move through the ordinary courts. According to the language of the ordinance, supervision of the cajas de comunidad of the parcialidades of Mexico City, a special attribute of the General Indian Court, should have moved to the intendant of Mexico, and the court should have been inhibited from hearing cases on Indian tributes and communal revenues. In practice, the court and its officials resisted the changes; and upon consultation with the crown, a royal command of February 21, 1788, ordered that there be no change in the jurisdiction of the court.[15]

A further idea on the court, arising out of the new system of intendants, came in 1794 in the instructions for the newly appointed viceroy, the Marqués de Branciforte. He was to study the possibility of carrying the reform farther by giving the intendants jurisdiction in Indian cases, to be exercised with legal assessors. The General Indian Court would be abolished. In the discussions between Branciforte and the minister of grace and justice on this point, the minister raised the additional idea that, if the court was abolished, the revenue raised for it should not end with it, but should be used to endow local courts staffed with trained lawyers.[16] Whether or not Branciforte in Mexico carried out this study cannot be determined, in the absence of any evidence; the one thing certain is that nothing came of the project. So all reforms associated with the system of intendants failed to affect the court. However, it is clear that administrators in Spain were aware of the anomalies, and uncomfortable with them.

15. Lira González, "La extinción," 304–309, citing a gloss to art. 6 of the copy of the Real Ordenanza de Intendentes in the Biblioteca Nacional, Mexico City, (FR/D344, 872/Mex. 1).

16. María del Pópulo Antolín Espino and Luis Navarro García, "El marqués de Branciforte," in Calderón Quijano, Los virreyes . . . Carlos IV, 1:381.

Inherent in the Ordinance of Intendants was the conception of improving administration by decreasing the load on the viceroy, but it was a reform that the viceroys themselves fought to a standstill. Invasion of the intendants' sphere by the viceroy brought forth in 1801 an eloquent remonstrance to the royal administration in Madrid from the veteran and able intendant of Puebla, Manuel de Flon. His reasoned statement went far beyond the original provocation to become an assessment of the nature of government by a viceroy in Mexico. The post of viceroy, the "first in the kingdom . . . in dignity, power, and emoluments," was usually given to men of elder years and distinguished service, but they knew nothing of the vast territories they were to administer, which they saw for the first time. They came lacking the strength to handle the vast array of duties and charges, deprived of honest advice through the flattery of interested aides, and were required through centralization of authority to settle matters brought hundreds of leagues to Mexico City for determination. In practice,

> these matters passed through crown attorneys, through assessors, through secretaries, and other aides that the viceroys have at their side; but even these men do not suffice for handling the flow of business, and must make use of delegates, substitutes, and officials who are so many additional enemies of those who to their misfortune have recourse to the courts. Some write opinions; others support them; and the viceroy signs all. Since the decisions, however burdensome, bear the seal of the viceroy's authority, they are carried out at all cost. He who would appeal is brought to silence by force or by the difficulties and expense of recourse to the throne.[17]

Flon wrote his eloquent, well-reasoned attack upon the centralization of authority in the viceroy merely to protest a failure to delegate to the intendants. Moreover, he wrote in full loyalty to the monarch he served; but his attack could apply equally as searching criticism of the concentration of function in an all-powerful sovereign. There inhered in Flon's representation an underlying knowledge and partial acceptance of arguments in favor of the division of government into three branches which would render the old form obsolete, and with it obviously the General Indian Court. One suspects that Flon had read Montesquieu.

Within New Spain, there came other assaults on the jurisdiction of the court from the city of Mexico—which pursued no high theory, but naked self-interest, as it attempted to extend the competence of its municipal judges to the Indian parcialidades. The city could plead that

17. Manuel de Flon to the king, Puebla, December 21, 1801, in Pietschmann, "Dos documentos," 437–438.

conditions had altered greatly by the later eighteenth century, whereas the political arrangements dated from the early sixteenth. In the earlier colonial period, a relatively small group of urban Spanish-speakers lived in the so-called *traza*, centered around the viceregal palace and the cathedral, kept free of Indians at night except for servants, and ready for defense in case of siege by Indians from without. This was the city of Mexico. The Indians who once occupied the central core had been resettled in the barrios on the outskirts, grouped in two parcialidades. They had their own languages, their own society, and their own special government. But during the succeeding centuries, the two republics steadily began to merge. The Spanish city expanded beyond the original streets toward the barrios, and the barrios toward the city. The Indians increasingly began to use Spanish and take on Hispanic ways. Increasingly, both city and barrios had large groups of mixed-bloods, who might know an Indian language but for the most part lived in Hispanic culture and spoke Spanish. In short, less and less did the boundaries and institutions of the sixteenth century reflect the reality of the later colonial period.

The zeal of the city officials for change is easily understandable, for jurisdiction meant revenue. (That it would be spent on the Indians was unlikely.) Apparently there were repeated encroachments by the city, until in 1800 a dispute over judicial competence arose in the arrest and trial of some Indians of Ixtacalco in the parcialidad of San Juan Tenochtitlán. Thereupon the abogado for the two parcialidades petitioned the viceroy for a declaratory ruling that civil and criminal cases of Indians within the parcialidades lay within the exclusive jurisdiction of the General Indian Court and that the municipal government of Mexico City lacked all competence in the matter. In his formal opinion to the viceroy, the crown attorney upheld the abogado's position, specifying an exclusive viceregal jurisdiction in civil and criminal matters, elections of local officials, and community finances. In minor matters, the Indian governors had jurisdiction and reported directly to the viceroy. Accordingly, the government of Mexico City had no legal authority of any kind in the Indian barrios. In support of his opinion, the crown attorney cited royal orders of 1787, 1788, and 1789—a citation that is interesting as evidence of recent disputes over the viceregal competence. As was to be expected, the viceroy ruled in October 1800 in favor of the General Indian Court—that is, himself, operating through his assessor.[18] For the time being, the city was rebuked, but it was certain to return to the attack.

The situation of Mexico City was paralleled in many Indian

18. Lira González, "La extinción," 308–309.

towns, which, though settlement of non-Indians was formally forbidden, nevertheless contained substantial numbers of long-resident families of non-Indians. Whatever their wealth and influence, they were excluded from the town government and any share in communal
finance.[19] They lived with the latent danger that in disputes with Indians of influence or the entire community they could be haled before
the General Indian Court as intruders. By the later colonial period,
that danger admittedly was slim and the device little used, but the
presence in growing proportion of non-Indian elements within sup-
posedly purely native communities was adding to the anomalies of existing institutions.

Criticism and opposition to the special protective system for Indians—of which the General Indian Court was a major part—obviously came from two different groups, which frequently overlapped,
but in the end had distinctly different approaches. Villarroel, in his
plea for a legalized repartimiento de mercancías and strengthening the
authority of provincial governors, and the city of Mexico, in its attempts to extend its authority to the Indian barrios, displayed ideas
and purposes of an archaic cast in which the natives were the appropriate object of unabashed exploitation by a Spanish upper class. The
other ideas of change aimed at a more efficiently operating, less hetero-
geneous administration and a more rational approach to the organization of society. We deal here with the reception of the Enlightenment
in the Hispanic world. In that world the attack upon religion came late
and was greatly muted. Nevertheless, the new came as essentially another way of viewing the universe and man's place within it that meant
a radical change from older conceptions and approaches. Any all-
encompassing definition of the Enlightenment is difficult, for it meant
many things and resulted in diverse ideas and programs, even to dog-
mas as fiercely dependent upon faith as the older ones it decried. Perhaps its essence lay in the ascendance of reason as the principle governing thought and action. Anything traditional must be tested by
reason since mere existence from the past could not be held adequate
ground for continued acceptance. Joined to the primacy of reason was
an immense faith in its regenerative and transforming power as a
source of reform and the guide and promoter of progress.[20]

The Enlightenment as a body of ideas and writing took shape in

19. The presence of large numbers of long-resident non-Indians became particularly evident when the Indian town governments were reorganized as constitutional
ayuntamientos, especially in 1820, and this hitherto disenfranchised element voted in
the elections and held municipal office.

20. Aldridge, 4–9 et passim; Miranda, *Humboldt y México*, 11–12 et passim;
and Dominguez Ortiz, 476–477.

the late seventeenth and early and middle eighteenth centuries in France, Germany, and Italy. Its reception in Spain came in three stages, linked to generations. The first, in the middle of the century, is associated with the writings of Feijóo, a Benedictine monk. The second, from perhaps 1770 to 1790, witnessed a far wider diffusion of writing from abroad and much Spanish writing. It is associated with the names of such men as Moñino, Campomanes, and Jovellanos, and found major agencies of diffusion in the societies of friends of the country and a new daily press. A number of the principal figures, prominent in the government of Carlos III, promoted what has been called Enlightened Despotism. Basically, the new ideas were held by a small elite, who attempted to apply them in education, government, and economic life as loyal servants of the crown and devout, if regalistic, Catholics.

In the third period, 1790–1821, under the shattering force of the French Revolution, the wars it brought, the Napoleonic invasion of Spain, and the virtual collapse of the monarchy, the new ideas spread much more freely and began to take on radical aspects. The ideas of Locke, Montesquieu, and Rousseau, spread both by direct reading and by absorption in the writing and discussion of others, increasingly became articles of faith. They may be summarized as follows: Sovereignty resides in the people, from whom monarchs receive authority through a social compact rather than the irrevocable act of delegation asserted in Roman and medieval thinking. The proper form of government is division into three branches, the executive, legislative, and judicial, of which the monarch should exercise only the power of the executive; the branches should be kept separate and not encroach upon each other. Lastly, all men should be equal before the law and eligible for all posts. Seigneurial rights and jurisdiction should be abolished. The people of a country constitute a nation, within whose political boundaries there should be one law for all and a uniform set of institutions. In short, the random, haphazard jumble of laws and jurisdictions of the late medieval and Renaissance states should be brought to a single system of administration and taxation, with no internal barriers.[21] In a program based upon these ideas, there could be no place, of course, for a special protective system for Indians nor for the General Indian Court.

21. Herr, 37–85, 154–200, 348–375, et passim; Elorza, 69–118; Sarrailh, 573–611; Spell, 13–200; Dominguez Ortiz, 477–519; Álvarez de Morales, 50–119; Maravall, "Las tendencias de reforma," 71–76, and "Cabarrús y las ideas de reforma"; Polt, 51–66; and Martínez Marina, 1:38, 109–111, and 244–245, and 2:199–220 and 248–260. For a statement of earlier prevailing political philosophy, see Maravall, *La philosophie politique espagnole au XVIIe siècle,* passim.

To Mexico, the Enlightenment came even more slowly than to Spain. Its carriers were merchants, travelers, educated clergy—most notably the zealous, able bishops of the later colonial period—military people from Spain, private people of leisure, the small foreign colony, and perhaps most important of all, government officials, including the viceroys. Forbidden books entered private libraries either by special permission or in defiance of the Inquisition. The ideas contained within them were discussed in fashionable gatherings, and most notably in the receptions and parties held by the viceroys and vicereines in the viceregal palace.[22]

The crumbling of the old was fundamentally an inner erosion and replacement, in which the higher royal officials and clergy in Spain and Spanish America administered traditional structures which they themselves were questioning, and in many of which they had lost faith. One can point in Spain to Vicente Alcalá Galiano, a high treasury official and faithful servant of Carlos IV, who was a republican in his private thinking; or to Jovellanos himself.[23] In Mexico, one can point to the unease with the procedures of the General Indian Court in Viceroy Azanza's relación de mando for his successor. He was concerned both with abdication of the power of decision by the viceroy to his assessor and by the exercise of an indiscriminate jurisdiction in all civil and criminal cases of Indians, even if they were plaintiffs. "In not a few instances, the court has accepted and rendered sentence in charges against alcaldes mayores, corregidores, and subdelegados. The royal audiencia has protested in my time against this abuse."[24] His successor, Marquina, repeated Azanza's comments in his relación de mando for Iturrigaray. "Your Excellency will notice that the General Indian Court handles business in a way that is hardly compatible with a system of clarity and obedience to its own instructions. . . ."[25]

Perhaps the most extreme position among the loyal ministers of the old order was found in Manuel Abad y Queipo, Bishop-elect of Michoacán. In a long memorandum to the crown upholding the personal immunity of the clergy—his ox threatened with goring—Abad y Queipo made a reasoned plea for the abolition of tribute from Indians and castas, of all restrictions upon them, and of the infamy of their status; a declaration of their legal eligibility to all posts; and the distribution to them of community and other lands. He urged further an

---

22. Miranda, *Humboldt y México*, 22–33; Pérez-Marchand, 95–105; and Mora, *México*, 1:82–85.

23. Elorza, 92–93.

24. San Cristóbal, April 29, 1800, in Azanza, 45–46, clause 16.

25. Tacubaya, January 1, 1803, in Mexico (Viceroyalty), *Instrucciones*, 2:644–646, clauses 50–53.

end to all restrictions on the settlement of non-Indians in Indian communities. In effect, he recommended full legal equality for Indians and castas, with endowment of lands and freeing of economic development. Tribute would be replaced with a moderate head tax on all.[26] Clearly in the opening decade of the nineteenth century, and probably before, opinion among the educated elite was turning against the traditional ideas embodied in the General Indian Court.

The extent of the erosion of older, traditional ideas of society and government became manifest in Mexico in the storms brought by the Napoleonic invasion of Spain. That is a long story that can only be summarized in a few lines here. In 1808, Napoleon induced both Carlos IV and the latter's son, Fernando VII, to abdicate in his favor, and in their stead attempted to impose his brother Joseph as king. A popular revolt receiving aid from the English found leadership in regional juntas that soon merged into a central council of regency. That, in turn, summoned the cortes, which met in Cádiz and drafted the Constitution of 1812 for all the dominions of the monarchy. The new constitution was strongly influenced by the French Constitution of 1791.[27]

In Mexico, the first events in Spain brought a replacement of the viceroy and much uncertainty and unrest. Underlying tensions broke through the surface in the revolt headed by Miguel Hidalgo, which found its major support among the peasants of the west and the Bajío. The intendant of Guanajuato, Riaño, attempted to calm public unrest by proclaiming the abolition of Indian tribute on September 25, 1810.[28] That was followed on October 5 by viceregal proclamation of a decree of the council of regency of May 26, 1810, which abolished all Indian tribute throughout America. Viceroy Venegas in his proclamation extended the abolition to the tributes levied upon castas who remained loyal and aided the royal cause. The proclamation, published in Spanish and Nahuatl, did not affect either the medio real de ministros or the medio real de hospital since these were not tribute, but directed the intendants, town governors, and corregidors to report on town resources and possible measures for abolishing the two levies.[29] That the decree had much effect upon the revolt is doubtful. Nevertheless, Hidalgo was defeated, captured, and executed. The

26. "Representación sobre la inmunidad personal del clero," Morelia, December 11, 1809, in Mora, *Obras sueltas*, 173–213, esp. 208. See also Mora, *México*, 1: 65–73 and 168–174, for an opinion after Mexican independence.

27. Latimer, 9–96; Alamán, 1: 149–165; Suárez.

28. Alamán, 1: 165–419 and 4: 1–135; Hamill, 53–215, esp. 139 and 168.

29. The proclamation is reproduced in Spanish and Nahuatl in Hernández y Dávalos, 2: 137–141 (nos. 70 and 71); Mexico: AGN, *La constitución*, 2: 79–82 and 287–290. The Spanish is in Armellada, 104–107; an original of the Spanish version is in AGN-Tr, vol. 7.

rebellion continued under Morelos and other leaders, but by 1815 largely had been suppressed, opposition continuing as a series of isolated guerrilla enclaves and forays.[30]

Meantime, while fighting raged in Mexico and on the Peninsula for different quarrels, the Cortes of Cádiz enacted into legislation the political ideas of much of the Enlightenment. Many of its laws concerned the Indians in Mexico and in America in general. On January 5, 1810, it ordered that Indians be protected in their rights and property; protectors and priests were to be vigilant in reporting infractions.[31] That might have looked like the special protection of the traditional system, but subsequent legislation quickly proved the new trend. On October 15, 1810, the cortes pledged equality of rights to the people in America and the Peninsula and promised amnesty if the areas in revolt came to obedience.[32] A few months later, on February 9, 1811, the promise of equality was extended in another resolution, assuring all natives of America that they were free to cultivate whatever crops they wished—an end to any restrictions in the interests of the Peninsula—and promising them full equality in appointment to public posts.[33] On March 13, 1811, the cortes ratified the decree of the council of regency of May 26, 1810, and the proclamation of Viceroy Venegas on abolition of tribute, the end of the special tax being made applicable to all Indians and castas in America. As further measures, communal lands in Indian towns were to be distributed to Indians but not to castas, and the repartimiento de mercancías was rigorously forbidden.[34] In August 1811 the cortes discussed the legal status of the Indians. Although a majority of the members were in favor of full equality and ending the legal status of Indians as minors, no resolution was adopted.[35]

That same month, on August 6, 1811, a long enactment returned to the Spanish nation all rights of seigneurial jurisdiction, but not property derived from them. Upon promulgation of this law in Mexico on December 31, 1811,[36] the Marquesado del Valle and the Ducado de Atlixco should have gone out of existence as seigneurial entities. On November 9, 1812, the cortes ordered the abolition of *mitas*

30. Hamill, 180–220; Alamán, vols. 1–4, passim.
31. Armellada, 91–92; Spain, Laws, etc., *Colección*, 1:45–46; Mexico: AGN, *La constitución*, 2:82–83.
32. Armellada, 103; Spain, Laws, *Colección*, 1:10–11.
33. Armellada, 92–93.
34. Ibid., 98–99; Spain, Laws, *Colección*, 1:89–90; Mexico: AGN, *La constitución*, 2:87–88.
35. Armellada, 66–68.
36. Spain, Laws, *Colección*, 1:193–196; Mexico: AGN, *La constitución*, 2:93–95.

(labor drafts) and personal services of all kinds by Indians, except for municipal labor levies binding upon all citizens without distinction. This law was promulgated in Mexico on April 28, 1813.[37] A long enactment of January 4, 1813, ordered the distribution of communal and royal vacant lands to Indians and castas.[38] Finally, on September 8, 1813, flogging as punishment was abolished throughout Spanish territory.[39]

The crowning achievement of the Cortes of Cádiz was planned to be the Constitution of 1812, promulgated on March 19, 1812.[40] It envisioned a sweeping new system of government for the Peninsula and the overseas territories, in which all inhabitants were to be citizens of a common nation.[41] All were to be equal before the law and for purposes of taxation.[42] The government was to be a limited monarchy, organized in three branches, with the king exercising the executive, the cortes the legislative, and an independent judiciary the judicial function.[43] All local government was to be organized uniformly into town ayuntamientos and provincial diputaciones, with provision for election of members.[44] Application of the laws in civil and criminal matters was to be exclusively a function of the courts, the king and cortes being forbidden expressly to interfere.[45] All courts were to be organized on a uniform system of justices of the peace; district courts presided over by trained lawyers, with appeal to appellate courts replacing the old audiencias; and final appeal to a supreme tribunal in Madrid.[46] Equality and the end of special privilege and jurisdiction were enshrined in three clauses: "Laws shall set the order and formalities of procedure, which shall be uniform in all tribunals, and neither the cortes nor the king may give dispensation."[47] "No Spaniard shall be judged in civil or criminal cases for any act except by the competent tribunal, as determined beforehand by law."[48] "In common, civil, and criminal matters, there shall be but one code of law for every

37. Armellada, 95–96 and 313; Spain, Laws, *Colección*, 3:161–162; Mexico: AGN, *La constitución*, 2:108–109.

38. Armellada, 97–100; Spain, Laws, *Colección*, 3:189–193; Mexico: AGN, *La constitución*, 2:109–110.

39. Armellada, 100–101; Mexico: AGN, *La constitución*, 2:129–130.

40. A careful analysis of the Constitution of 1812 and its meaning for New Spain may be found in Alamán, 3:104–135.

41. Art. 1, in Tena Ramírez, 60; but persons with Negro ancestry could become citizens only by special concession of the cortes: art. 22, ibid., 63.

42. Arts. 248 and 339, ibid., 89 and 100.

43. Arts. 14–17, ibid., 62.

44. Arts. 309–337 (Title 6), ibid., 95–99.

45. Arts. 242–243, ibid., 89.

46. Arts. 242–308 (Title V), ibid., 89–95.

47. Art. 244.   48. Art. 247.

class of persons."[49] The only exceptions were to be Church tribunals for offenses of clergy under Church law, and military courts for infractions of military law by soldiers and sailors.[50] In this instrument, the former arrangement of councils, viceroys, and audiencias went by the board, as did their mixed functions. Indians became full Spanish citizens with all legal rights, but equally without any special protection, and their town governments were abolished in favor of a uniform local and municipal organization in which all Spanish citizens voted in the first tier of elections.

The Constitution of 1812 was promulgated in Mexico City on September 30, 1812.[51] In the midst of rebellion and civil war, it was impossible for the viceroy to become merely the chief administrative officer of a group of provinces; but as regulations for putting specific sections of the constitution into effect reached Mexico City, most were implemented.[52] Indian town governments were reorganized as constitutional ayuntamientos, with suffrage for all free male citizens of appropriate age and appropriate race (Negroes and part-Negroes being excluded). Around Mexico City, the barrios and parcialidades went out of existence, and at long last the council of Mexico City took jurisdiction. Tribunals were reorganized in terms of the constitution, so that the General Indian Court ceased to function as a court, just as abolition of the Indian barrios and parcialidades ended its territorial administration.

Although the constitutional clauses on lands received an implementing ordinance in Spain on October 15, 1812, promulgated in Mexico City on April 28, 1813, it was inexpedient to enforce it. So Indian communal lands and the community treasuries were left intact, except for the barrios and parcialidades around Mexico City.[53] No clause touched the medio real de hospital or the medio real de ministros; accordingly, these levies continued to be made and the funds passed into the respective treasuries.[54] In Yucatan and the marquesado the special Indian courts also ceased to operate; but the private jurisdiction of the juez conservador in the marquesado remained undisturbed, on the plea that since the holder of the post was always a

---

49. Art. 248.
50. Arts. 249–250.
51. AGN, *La constitución*, 1:1–33; Alamán, 3:277–280.
52. AGN, *La constitución*, 1:34–326; Alamán, 3:281–303.
53. Lira González, "La extinción," 313–314.
54. See the petitions of Teposcolula and Coixtlahuaca for release from payment because of rebel occupation in 1812–13, and the subsequent proceedings in Mexico City and Spain, Teposcolula, and Mexico City, January 16, 1815–October 29, 1817, in AGN-Tr, 30:exps. 26–27; copy of expediente on establishing schools, which also contains much of the same matter, Madrid, Mexico City, and Oaxaca, June 4–December 31, 1817, in AJT-Civ, leg. 18.

THE COMING OF THE NEW

judge of the audiencia, the jurisdiction was not exercised by a seigneurial appointee, but rather by a royal one, as required by the new
constitution.[55]

Suppression of the Indian barrios and parcialidades around Mexico City as formal political entities had consequences that soon became manifest, for the new constitutional council of the city appropri-
ated the funds of the legally extinct entities but did almost nothing for
the people in them. One instance occurred when an epidemic of "ma-
lignant fevers," perhaps typhus, reached Mexico City in 1813 after
devastating Puebla. Since the city council found itself without funds, it
set up a General Treasury of Charity to collect and distribute contributions toward relief of the needy. It also petitioned Viceroy Calleja,
under his new title of *jefe político superior*, for permission to take possession of the funds in the communal treasuries of the former parcialidades, on the ground that under the new constitution, Indian communities were no longer to remain separate from the general municipality.
With Calleja's permission, the council took over the balance of 6,000/
in the treasury of the two parcialidades. Thus annexed to the general
municipality, the Indians outside the custom gates marking the old
Spanish city found that the money was spent on the needy within the
gates, so that unfortunates outside the gates had to depend, to the extent that they received aid, upon a separate charitable commission
which received no municipal funds.[56]

Further consequences arose in the financing of the parcialidades'
religious celebrations and policing, which had been paid for by small
disbursements from communal funds. In 1813, as the feast of Santiago
was approaching, the Indians of the parcialidad of Santiago Tlatelolco
asked for the funds customary to celebrate July 25 and 26 and invited
the higher authorities of the capital to be present at the celebration of
the feast of their patron saint. The superior political executive, the former viceroy, upon being consulted by the city council, replied that old
custom should not be changed until decision had been reached on disposition of the property of the parcialidades. Accordingly, he directed
that money be given for the celebration of the saint's cult, but none for
the banquet and gifts formerly offered the viceroy. The money was to
come from the municipal treasury, as the recipient of the funds of the
former parcialidades, but it was found that no funds were there. Somehow money was found for the celebration.[57] Clearly, despite legal sup-

55. García Martínez, 122–123, but the Marqués del Valle lost the right to call
himself lord of vassals, to govern through his appointed deputy, and to name judges:
ibid., 86.

56. Anna, 163–169; Lira González, "La extinción," 310–311; Bancroft, 4:
504–505.

57. Lira González, "La extinción," 312.

pression, the parcialidades continued to function, but had to turn to the city council or the royal administrator of their property for any money.

Despite the reasonable compromise on funding the celebration of the feast of Santiago, other functions of the parcialidades fared worse. In September and October 1813 the governor of San Juan Tenochtitlán twice complained to Calleja, under his extinct title of viceroy,[58] that since May the administrator of the funds of the parcialidades had refused to deliver the 22/6/6 a month, plus the expenses of masses on feast days of obligation, that funded much of local communal functioning. The governor detailed part of the monthly expenditure: 12/ for the local sickhouse; 8/ in stipends to the eight alcaldes who spent alternate weeks patroling the territory; 4/ in stipends to the Indian council members, the chief bailiff, and the official notary; and 10/6/6 for the cost of food for prisoners in the jail of the parcialidad. The amounts add up to 34/6/6 monthly, of which the administrator furnished 22/6/6 plus whatever was spent on masses of obligation. Clearly, the parcialidad had another source of revenue than its property and revenues in official custody; but equally clearly, despite their official suppression under the Constitution of 1812, the parcialidad and its barrios continued to elect officials, arrange street patrols, and house prisoners in its jail. The governor's petition made two further points: (1) the patrols recently had been extended, at the express direction of the viceroy to this governor; and (2) the parcialidad of Santiago Tlatelolco had a similar organization, discharged similar functions, had received a parallel sum of 22/6/6 monthly from the administrator, and must be in the same need.

When asked by Calleja for an explanation, the administrator replied that since the parcialidades no longer had legal existence, and accordingly any rules and observances carried out by them ceased equally to have legal reason, he could do nothing without express direction from higher authority. The ball having been returned neatly to him, Calleja then referred the matter to the crown attorney for his opinion, and early in January 1814 received a recommendation that the administrator first be required to furnish copies of his letter of appointment and the instructions governing his exercise of his post. On that demand, the petition and inquiry ground to a halt, for as late as the first days of June the Indians had not picked up the order for delivery to the administrator. In despair of early relief, they probably had made some arrangement for other financing.[59] That the city planned to

58. AGN-I, 100:fols. 216v–218v and 224f–233v, containing the letters and subsequent documents.

59. Lira González, "La extinción," 312–313.

undertake policing or any other service in these territories was a vain, if pious, hope.

By then the feast of their patron saint was approaching, and the parcialidad of San Juan Tenochtitlán petitioned Calleja for 30/4, the sum customary for defraying the celebration. Calleja, thus appealed to, ordered the city council—whose treasury by then had received the funds of the parcialidades—to deliver the customary amount. Putting the best face on the affair, the council agreed to payment, since the amount was small and was to be spent on religious celebration. Without Calleja's order, it is unlikely that the council would have been moved.

The meaning of legal equality and the suppression of special protection and avenues of appeal became further clear in the matter of passports for entering and leaving the central area of Mexico City within the old custom gates. Because of the revolts and war in Mexico, passports were required. Residents within the old traza, who were well-known to the authorities, had no trouble securing permanent papers. Indians, since they were not personally known to the authorities, had difficulty securing papers of any kind. If they attempted to pass without papers, they were arrested and put to public work deemed beneficial. The old viceregal authorities, who established and supervised the requirement, were responsible. Although the city council complained that the inspection kept out people bringing supplies of foodstuffs, the higher authorities could not be moved,[60] nor were the Indians able as in the past to appeal through the General Indian Court. In this instance, the Indians were the victims of their cultural difference and poverty, but their future role as the lowest class in a common culture was delineated unmistakably.

In 1814, the taste of the new proved temporary. The defeat of Napoleon's armies led to release of Fernando VII, who returned to Spain amid great rejoicing. On May 4, 1814, at Valencia he issued a decree annulling all the acts of the cortes and restoring absolute monarchy in Spain and its dominions. He met almost no resistance, and entered Madrid in triumph.[61] On December 4, 1814, Calleja in Mexico City proclaimed the nullity of all decrees of the Cortes of Cádiz, abolition of all changes emanating from them, and restoration of the old order and forms as they had existed on May 1, 1808. He placed special emphasis upon reestablishment of Indian communal governments and special tribunals. So Mexico City and other Spanish municipal bodies shrank to their former limits and powers. The repúblicas de indios, including those in the barrios and parcialidades of Mexico

60. Anna, 80–83.
61. Latimer, 99–101; Alamán, 4:124–144.

City, resumed control of their property and revenues and began to function in the traditional way. The entire machinery of administration, countrywide and provincial, which had not had the time to change fully in the face of the emergencies of rebellion, discarded the forms of the Constitution of 1812 and returned to the customary organization and procedures.[62] With no hesitation, the General Indian Court resumed its functions as tribunal and as administrator of the parcialidades of Mexico City.[63] Since the medio real de ministros continued to be collected and disbursed during the years 1810–1814, the staff dependent upon it remained intact. Lest there be any doubt about the return to the old, Fernando VII by royal cédula of March 1, 1815, restored the tribute as a tax on natives and castas throughout his dominions in America and the Philippines.[64]

For the next six years, the General Indian Court returned to a perhaps more lethargic functioning. In the general dispersal and loss of many records during these years, it is impossible to estimate the volume of business that passed through the court. These were relatively peaceful years, since the more severe and widespread fighting of the rebellions—or civil wars, as one may prefer to call them—was over for the time being. They left a legacy of cases of *infidencia* (disloyalty or sedition), which lay outside the court's jurisdiction, and exactions of labor and supplies by military commanders, which the viceroy and his assessor, upon complaint by the Indian peasants, tried to explain and mitigate as best they could, for they could not give genuine relief so long as the viceroyalty remained upon a war footing.[65]

The six years of comparative tranquility came to an end in 1820. On January 1, 1820, part of an army assembled at Cádiz for embarkation to South America, to suppress independence movements there, mutinied under the leadership of Lt. Col. Rafael del Riego y Núñez, proclaimed the Constitution of 1812, and marched upon Madrid. Faced by insurrection in Madrid, Fernando VII in March accepted the constitution and on March 9, 1820, swore to observe it.[66] Once again instructions went out to Mexico for restoration of the administrative and judicial system implanted in 1812–13.[67] The General Indian Court

62. Alamán, 144–165; Mexico: AGN, *La constitución*, 2:145–162. containing the proclamations of Viceroy Calleja and his orders for reestablishment of the traditional institutions and forms.

63. As may be seen by the cases of the later years and the evidence, later in this chapter, of administration of the parcialidades. See also Lira González, "La extinción," 314.

64. AGI-M, vol. 2100, last item.

65. See cases of 1816–1819 in Chapter V above; Alamán, 4:639 et seq.

66. Latimer, 109–116; Alamán, 5:1–13.

67. AGN, *La constitución*, 2:169–188 publishes some of the more important

again ceased to function, and the parcialidades of Mexico City again came under the jurisdiction of a revived constitutional ayuntamiento.

In August, the intendant of Guanajuato inquired of the viceroy whether all Indian local government and posts were to give way to the new constitutional ayuntamientos. His legal adviser thought they should, but suggested delaying change until there was a viceregal proclamation. The answer was yes.[68] So distinctive Indian institutions and forms were to end, but the experience of the first constitutional years had suggested the need for caution in dealing with the funds of the parcialidades of Mexico City. As legal entities, the parcialidades had lost legal existence, and the new constitutional ayuntamiento on June 10, 1820, approached the viceroy under his new title again of *jefe político superior*, asking that all funds, revenues, and records of the parcialidades be delivered to it. In reply, at the suggestion of his assessor for Indian matters, the viceroy ordered that the existing administrator of their funds, José Joaquín Romanos, appointed in 1815, continue to collect and disburse the funds, which were to be spent for the benefit of the Indians, but that custody of the money and accounting were to be in the municipal treasury. Romanos was also to continue as general attorney for the parcialidades until further decision, and was to turn over the papers in his possession to one of the four newly organized offices of the superior tribunal (the old audiencia). In acknowledging the viceroy's order, Romanos reported that he disbursed annually 330/4 for various celebrations through money given on each occasion to the governor. (He may have meant payments for only one parcialidad, since the detail cannot be reconciled with the needs of the two parcialidades.)[69] The wisdom of the viceroy's measure quickly be-

---

documents; Alamán, 5 : 14–22 and 33–49. Many more of the documents may be found in AGN-Jus, vol. 8.

68. AGN-I, 100:fols. 641f–644v.

69. Lira González, "La extinción," 314–315; AGN-I, 100:fols. 654f–656v. The breakdown of the 330/4 disbursed annually by Romanos as administrator was:

90/	divided among the 6 barrios of the parcialidad
10/	first-class mass on the day of the patron saint
6/	fees for the license on the pallium and for exposing the sacrament
50/	fireworks and illuminations
8/	4 masses of 10 and 11 reales each
40/	*tlapalolixtli* [?]; this term means the soaking of bread in broth or soup
50/	cost of mules in the parish of Santa Ana when the sacrament was brought forth
25/	purchases in the parish of Santa Ana
51/4	8-day feast in the parish of Santa Ana for the patron saint

---

330/4

came clear when on July 10 the Indians of the parcialidad of Santiago Tlatelolco protested to him that the city council member in charge of markets was trying to take over collection of payments for rental of stalls in the marketplaces of Santiago, Santa Ana, and Los Angeles during the feast of Santiago on July 25 and 26. The rentals provided funds for community celebration of festivals. For that year, the city council gave way.[70]

In January 1821, the constitutional ayuntamiento of Mexico City reported to the viceroy, as *jefe político superior*, on the funds of the legally extinct parcialidades. The money was then in the city treasury, and the council had asked the administrator of the parcialidades, Romanos, for a copy of his instructions on handling them and information on the functions of the assessor of the old General Indian Court in governing the parcialidades and their finances. In reply, the council had received a copy of the instructions issued on March 24, 1807, by Guillermo de Aguirre as assessor and viceregal delegate. Article 2 required that all funds be kept in a strongbox with three keys, one each to be held by the administrator of the funds of the parcialidades, their general attorney, and the relator of the court, a requirement difficult to meet in changed circumstances. So the ayuntamiento asked whether two keys might not be enough, so long as the money was in its possession.[71]

Further dismantling of the protective apparatus embodied in the General Indian Court and the ministros del medio real, and distribution of the assets of the Indian parcialidades of Mexico City, was speeded up by the coming of Mexican independence from Spain in 1821. On February 24, 1821, Iturbide proclaimed the Plan of Iguala; and in July, with an army composed of old rebels and former royalist soldiers, entered Mexico City in triumph. Control of the government was assumed by a sovereign provisional commission of government headed by Iturbide.[72] A more bureaucratic approach, more fully in accord with the theory of division of governmental powers among branches, at once became apparent. In December 1820, under royalist constitutional government, it was still possible for the Indians of Ríoverde to petition the jefe político superior, the former viceroy, for return of lands seized by the town governor, on the plea that the local

---

The use of the term *parcialidad* rather than *parcialidades*, the number of parishes (6), and the concentration on the expenses of Santa Ana suggest that this list is but a small part of what the parcialidades and its constituent barrios and parishes really spent. It is probably a list of part of the expenses of Santiago Tlatelolco.

70. AGN-I, 100:fols. 621f–636v; Lira González, "La extinción," 314–315.
71. AGN-I, 100:fols. 715f–717v.
72. Alamán, 5:50–380.

judge refused all relief, and to secure an order to the subdelegado that justice be done at once, "promptly and fully, without giving rise to complaints or further claims."[73] Under the rule of the provisional junta, similar petitions were returned with the notation that the petitioner apply to the jefe político in his province or to the appropriate judge. A petition for relief from the gañanes of the town of San Gabriel Tezayuca, complaining of bad treatment and withholding of wages, received the unusually full reply: "Let the people concerned apply to the judge of the district; and if they consider themselves wronged, they may complain to the local tribunal, which has jurisdiction." The orders bear the rubric of Iturbide.[74]

Early in 1822, the provisional junta took up consideration of special levies on Indians, that is, the medio real de ministros, the medio real de hospital, and the real and a half paid for community functions. The junta's commission on finance urged abolition of all. In considering the report, the junta agreed with the justice of abolition of such special levies, but was concerned about the expenses they had defrayed. Finally, the junta agreed to abolition. It also agreed to make further provision for support of the School of Anatomy and the General Indian Hospital, which had been supported from the medio real de hospital; that in future, Indians should be received in all hospitals; and that it would provide for other services covered by the levies. Although not mentioned, the future of the ministros del medio real obviously was in play. On February 21, 1822, the junta issued the decree of abolition.[75] So the medio real de ministros went out of existence, after over two centuries of supporting much of the special Indian protective system.

The juxtaposition of the conception of monarchy, with its element of the reserve power of the monarch to concede relief as an act of royal grace, and the conception of the republic, in its new sense of an egalitarian society ruled by a government divided into three branches, each held carefully to its sphere, became manifest through the political changes of the years 1821–23. The provisional junta governed as though it headed a republic of the new kind, even though Mexico was technically an empire. In May 1822 Iturbide was proclaimed emperor and on December 18, 1822, a provisional constitution for the new empire echoed the by then standard clauses that the government should be organized in three branches; that all Mexicans were equal before

73. AGN-I, 100:fol. 637.

74. The petitions and replies may be found scattered through AGN-Jus, vol. 13½. The petition from the gañanes of San Gabriel Texayuca is in fols. 147–148.

75. Mexico (Empire, 1822–1823): Junta, 315–318 and 329–331; Dublán and Lozano, 1:596; Alamán, 5:298–299.

the law; that there should be no exceptions to the laws; that, save for clergy and military, there should be uniform tribunals, which alone might judge; and that there should be a uniform system of city and town governments.[76]

Nevertheless, the new emperor, in reversal of his unsympathetic responses as chairman of the provisional junta, began to give more favorable answers to petitions for relief. In October 1822, for example, Tomasa Gertrudis of Huaquechula, province of Atlixco, complained to the emperor that the constitutional alcalde of Atlixco and others had seized 20/ which the religious association honoring the patron saint of the town had collected for the church. The money, she pointed out, should therefore be delivered to the church. From her name, she was obviously Indian, and the association Indian as well. In reply, an order from the private secretariat of the emperor directed the jefe político of Puebla, the *jefatura* or intendancy in which Atlixco lay, to investigate the matter and take whatever action was necessary.[77] Agustín I obviously was displaying the imperial grace appropriate to monarchy in a manner reminiscent of Antonio de Mendoza and other viceroys. When in April 1823 his empire dissolved, to be replaced by a federal republic organized under the Constitution of 1824,[78] the new government returned to the practice of answering petitioners with recommendations that they take their complaints to the local administrative officer or court, as appropriate.

Complete dismantling of the colonial system of special protection for Indians, as it was embodied in the General Indian Court and the ministros del medio real, turned out to be a complex process that took place over some years. it involved doing away with the court and analogous institutions elsewhere, the administrative functions of the court, the levy that supported it and its officials, the staff of officials, and that inevitable residue, their records. As we have seen, the judicial functioning of the court came to an end when the provisions of the Spanish Constitution of 1812 were once again implemented in Mexico in 1820. That implementation removed as well the special Indian courts in Yucatan and the marquesado. It seems less likely that the marquesado was able to salvage its general judicial jurisdiction, as it had in 1813; if it had, such temporary success vanished in the ongoing triumph of the new order through Mexican independence. The means of support of the special protective system, the medio real de minis-

76. Reglamento provisional del Imperio Mexicano, in Tena Ramírez, 125–144, esp. clauses 6–7, 23–24, 55–57, and 91–92; Alamán, 5:601 et seq.

77. AGN-Jus, 14:fols. 157f–159v; petitions are scattered through vols. 14–20.

78. Alamán, 5:686–815. The Constitution of 1824 is published in Tena Ramírez, 167–195, the important articles for our purposes being 6, 123, 143, and 154.

tros, was abolished by the regency which took control upon the entrance of the Army of the Three Guarantees into Mexico City. That left to be handled the officials deriving support from the medio real, the records of the General Indian Court, and its administrative supervision of the parcialidades and their finances.

Some of the staff drawing revenue from the medio real probably solved matters by departing to Spain in the general exodus of loyal upholders of the House of Bourbon. That exodus removed many of the higher administrative and judicial figures. Lesser ones, especially those born in Mexico, preferred to stay. They were provided for by reassignment to the supreme court of the new national judicial system—and when that had to be divided between the states and the federation in the new federal system, by allocation to the supreme court of the newly created state of Mexico. In November 1824, the federal congress decided that the national capital should be Mexico City, in a district 4 leagues in diameter centered on the Zócalo. Accordingly, the state of Mexico gradually was to move itself to another capital of its choosing, and government functions were to be sorted out by mutual agreement. In that sorting-out and move, which was completed in 1827, the former employees of the General Indian Court became the responsibility of the state and were assigned to its supreme court.[79]

Perhaps the last echo of this assignment occurred in 1830–31, when Vicente de la Rosa y Saldívar, interpreter of the former court, petitioned the federal minister of justice for his salary, which had not been paid since 1827. He had, his petition declared, served as general interpreter without complaint for more than 40 years. Now 78, he had a large family to support and was too old for a new career. He asked for payment of arrears and future salary. Upon investigation, De la Rosa showed his appointment signed on September 28, 1789, by Viceroy Flores, acting for the king. When the federal treasury was asked for a report, it answered that the interpreter's salary had come from the medio real de ministros, and by the division of revenues and responsibilities between the state and the federation, responsibility passed to the state of Mexico. Accordingly, the federal treasury had sent De la Rosa a notice of termination; the petition should be referred to the state. On May 27, 1831, all documents were turned over to the interpreter's son for pursuit in the new state capital of Toluca.[80]

Disposition of the files of the General Indian Court was a small matter, but in government few matters are small in terms of paper-

79. Report of federal treasury officials, Mexico City, 1830, AGN-Jus, vol. 129 (BLT); decree of federal congress of November 18, 1824, Dublán and Lozano, 1:743–744.
80. AGN-Jus, vol. 129 (BLT).

work. The records of the court had been moved into the viceregal and audiencia archives as cases were decided and orders issued. Those papers, in the very large mass that does survive, are lodged in the national archive. In addition, the court had dockets of cases under consideration or filed pending disposition. Upon the abolition of the court in 1820, those papers were placed in the custody of the senior judicial notary for criminal matters and lodged in a cell of the local jail. There they remained, subject to the depredation of rats and deterioration through damp. On April 22, 1825, the notary appealed to the supreme court of the state of Mexico, asking that the governor of the state inform the federal government of the existence of the archive, to publicize its existence and allow people who had filed papers to reclaim them, should they wish. His letter worked its way from the state supreme court to the governor to the federal minister of justice and ecclesiastical affairs and on to the president. The president's decision was that the papers be moved to the federal or national archive and that notices be posted throughout the states, so that people might reclaim their papers. Investigation on why the papers were suffering damage, and posting of proclamations inviting people to claim their papers, took a good deal of time, during which the state and federal governments were in uneasy coexistence in the same city. In January 1827, as the date for removal of the state government from the federal district became imminent, the federal ministers of foreign affairs and justice agreed that removal of the remaining papers was urgent.[81] The papers probably were moved, but where they lodged in the national archive cannot be determined with assurance. They may be in the last volume of the section of Indios, in some volume of the sections of Civil and Criminal, or have rested in the famous Casa Amarilla in Tacubaya until the recent incorporation of those documents into the general corpus of the archive.

Disposition of the property of the parcialidades was even more complex and an even longer process. The end of the royal regime meant the end of restrictions upon the jurisdiction of the city government of Mexico during the Iturbide period. Two sets of events thwarted it in part. On November 18, 1824, the federal congress designated the city as its capital and erected a federal district with boundaries that left much of the territory of the parcialidades in the state of Mexico.[82] Secondly, on November 23, 1824, the federal congress decreed that the property of the parcialidades be turned over to the constituent Indian towns within them as their property. A commission of seven persons from the parcialidades was to prepare instructions on how to ad-

81. Ibid., 22; fols. 192f–201v.
82. Dublán and Lozano, 1:743–744.

minister or distribute the properties.[83] During 1825 and 1827, the Mexico City municipal authorities moved against the governors of the native towns and barrios and named commissions to distribute the lands, perhaps under the authority of this decree. In the next decades, the lands became private property or were put to uses alien to the original intention of supporting Indian communal life. Whatever the Indian attachment to a distinctive communal life, they were brought to the common culture and the mainstream of national life.[84] What it meant for them as absorption occurred, and for succeeding generations, is a complex problem in social and economic accounting.

So the institution and levy forged in the concerns for social welfare and social justice, as the sixteenth century conceived them, came to an end. Designed to ease the new status of the Indians in the Audiencia of Mexico as subjects of the Spanish crown, the General Indian Court came too late to preserve native culture as it had existed at the beginning of the sixteenth century, and became a means of further Europeanization. Yet, as institutions take on a mold of their own, and preserve it long after it may no longer be appropriate, the General Indian Court, the medio real, and the staff of special Indian legal aides held the Indians in the new forms of colonial native institutions long after the relentless process of ethnic and racial amalgamation had created new conditions in which non-Indians lived side by side with people formally held to be Indian because they paid tribute. Alongside the legally Indian proletariat and peasantry there had come into being masses of formally non-Indian proletariat and peasantry, distinguishable only by their freedom from payment of tribute and medio real, and with that denied the privileges of the General Indian Court. They had the right, to the extent that they could exercise it, to the privileges of paupers and the services of the small staff of legal aides for the poor; but the extraordinary use of administrative process that distinguished the General Indian Court was withheld from them. In that sense, there was unfairness in the protective system for Indians quite aside from the question of their continued status as minors. In another age and environment, it might have been possible for equity to be achieved through a general system of legal insurance and special protection for all the needy, but in the early nineteenth century such a possibility was a conception yet to come. The decision in the name of equity was to abolish the special Indian protective system.

83. Ibid., 744.
84. Lira González, "La ciudad de México," 50–52, and "La extinción," 316–317.

If one subscribes to the idea derived from the Enlightenment that a single Mexican nation should occupy the territory of the United Mexican States from southern to northern boundary and from sea to sea, obviously the Indians had to be absorbed within that common group. (Other multinational solutions theoretically are possible but alien to the thinking of the nineteenth century, and even today to twentieth-century Mexican thinking.) Accordingly, any special institution which set off Indians from other Mexicans had to go. There were, nevertheless, costs as well as perhaps ultimate advantages associated with the change. One set which we must examine concerns the value of the General Indian Court and its legal aides as a system of protection; that is, how effective was it? Let us start with the admission that the question is thorny and complicated, for how may we measure the efficacy of an institution and a system? Today, with the masses of statistics currently gathered, highly sophisticated formulas of analysis can offer answers, provisional and fraught with error though they may be. Despite wide margins of error, these can furnish at least some idea of the degree of impact and efficiency; but however tempered and provisional it may be, such elegance of treatment and hopeful assurance of result are denied to those who deal in historical materials of far lesser abundance and certainty of coverage. So we must resort to a much more general formulation of estimate.

The protective system supported by the medio real de ministros must be understood in the terms of its day, not ours. It was devised to moderate exploitation. At no point did the Spanish crown and its officials hold to any view other than that the Indians should provide support for their own upper strata, for the Spanish, and for the Church, but that this support was to be kept to levels which would favor the survival of the Indians and even their increase.[85] Further, they were to have their own institutions and cultural life, as remade in a Christian mold. Viewed in this light, the protective system may be judged as to efficacy in three ways: as contemporaries saw it; through comparison with the somewhat differing but parallel system in Peru; and through the benefits, or lack of them, that may be ascribed to abolition.

Contemporaries complained loudly and eloquently of the corruption and inefficiency of the General Indian Court and the aides of the half-real. Nevertheless, the bitter polemic of Villarroel does indicate that the court did have a role in restraining depredations by the provincial governors. The number of cases brought by Indians, despite the sometimes long trek to Mexico City, is equally testimony to its substantial use by them. True, they had available alternate channels

85. Riley, 240–241.

for airing complaints or suits, in the provincial courts and in the audiencia, which many of them used to an extent and in a relative proportion which we cannot gauge, but which must have been substantial. Nevertheless, a considerable number of natives found in the
General Indian Court a preferred channel. Since they were on the
scene and, in general, aware of possibilities, they must have found in
the General Indian Court a channel of redress more likely to be favorable than the others.

Comparison with the protective system in Peru indicates very
real differences in impact, on the whole suggesting much greater Mexican efficiency. The Viceroyalty of Peru developed a far more elaborate
apparatus, with legal aides and special judges in each province, termi-
nating in a staff in the viceregal capital of Lima, and all supported by a
tax that was double the one in Mexico. Comparison with Mexico is
rendered difficult by a tribute system that was far heavier,[86] although
tempered by price and wage levels that also were higher. Furthermore,
it was made much more burdensome by truly oppressive exploitation
on the part of the provincial governors through an official repartimiento de mercancías and unofficial excesses that went far beyond it.
Nevertheless, with all caveats entered, the elaborate protective system
did not have as much effect as the simpler one in Mexico. A remarkable letter written by José Antonio de Areche, who was sent to Peru as
visitador-general to carry out a mission similar to that of José de Gálvez in Mexico, makes the comparison. Areche, who had served in
Mexico, wrote in 1777 to Fernando Mangino, superintendent-general
of the royal treasury in Mexico City:

> This land is not like Mexico in any way. There, in general, one finds
> justice; here, daily tyranny. There, the Indians buy what suits them;
> here, what the corregidor allots them. There, they deal in a free market;
> here, in forced sale. . . . The bishops protest this abuse; everyone knows
> that it exists; but all look at each other without attempting remedy or
> correction. The absence of upright judges, the [presence of] Indian
> labor drafts, and [the nature] of provincial trade keep this region of
> America moribund. The corregidores deal only in what is in their own
> interests. . . .[87]

Whatever his failures in his mission, Areche was a well-informed man
and his testimony too striking to be ignored. The marked differences
in treatment of the Indians in the two viceroyalties undoubtedly derived from many causes, among which must lie the inherited aboriginal base, so that the difference in efficacy of protection should not be

86. Escobedo, passim.
87. Vargas Urgarte, 3:379–380.

ascribed solely to the protective systems. Nevertheless, Areche's statement clearly indicates a markedly greater degree of efficacy for Mexico (unless one wishes to ascribe it to the greater benevolence of Spaniards, lay and clerical, in Mexico). Some portion of this, and probably a generous one, must be ascribed to the General Indian Court and the legal aides of the medio real.

Third, we should look at what the disappearance of the protective system meant for the Indians—or as they rapidly were becoming, Mexican peasants. The legal equality that came with independence and the new constitutions quickly turned out to carry with it very real loss. One may defend the destruction of a distinctive communal life as the necessary prerequisite for construction of a nation; but the loss of peasant lands, the seizure of their persons, for labor and war, and the substitution of the tyranny of caciques and generals for the far more orderly administration of the colonial authorities—all of these are much less easily defended. An end to legal tutelage meant exposure to far greater exploitation and simple ravage. The plundering of the communal holdings of the parcialidades, far from being unique, was paralleled by the plundering of communal holdings and resources over large parts of Mexico. Such massive destructive effects did not escape notice by Mexicans at the time, including some of the Liberals. Two distinguished spokesmen for the Liberals—Justo Sierra O'Reilly, writing on Yucatan, and María José Luis Mora, on Mexico as a whole—deplored the fact that a more gradual dissolution of the status of minors had not been devised, so that the Indians would have been permitted more opportunity for adapting to the new conditions.[88]

Perhaps the most telling argument testifying to the gap and the need is that in time a substitute has come into being. The great change is that it embraces all Mexican poor rather than a single group set apart by race, and so responds more fittingly to a national need. As peasant villages in desperation have turned to the Mexican executives, state and federal, for orders (of perhaps dubious constitutionality, but of real effectiveness) that would cut through red tape and compel unwilling local authorities and justices to render them what they have thought their due, or have petitioned for allocations of state and federal financial aid, the executives have been induced to the same kind of hearing and executive order that first gave rise to the precursor of the General Indian Court in the time of Antonio de Mendoza. Since the Mexican Revolution, and even more since the agrarian emphasis of Lázaro Cárdenas as president (1934–1940), village delegations again come to Mexico City so that they may petition the president for relief

88. Sierra O'Reilly; Mora, *México*, 1:67–73, but also 168–184.

and again gain a hearing. With the change of offices from the national palace to the presidential residence at Los Pinos, the locale has changed from the presidential patio in the palace to the outskirts of Chapultepec—but it still continues, and for some decades has been used as well by urban and labor delegates.

In effect, a kind of General Indian Court again functions, its range widened to the new national structure. All that is missing is legal insurance, but that is appearing in other countries as a bold new concept. Perhaps it is.

APPENDIX
Papers Handled by the Solicitadores of the Juzgado General de Indios, 1784

Comments on the Categories of the Appendix Table

CATEGORIES overlap in part. For instance, other property may have been lands, but merely stated as *bienes*; disputes over division of property and inheritance also may have been over, or included, land. Division of property may have been over inheritance. Disputes over money may relate to labor debt, ordinary commercial debt, or community accounts. The category of petitions for extension of time to pay debts may include labor debts as well as commercial ones.

In the category of petitions and complaints against Spanish provincial authorities are many that represent petitions to make sure that justices performed their functions in investigations, forwarding papers, and carrying out viceregal orders. The remainder are complaints over jailing, extortions and improper charges, mistreatment, and the like.

Town disputes and complaints may be of extortion and mistreatment by town officials or the cacique, their complaints against commoners, or demands for accounting for funds in trust for the term of administration.

Miscellaneous as a category includes petitions whose content is not stated; disputed elections (one case); *reducciones* (a resettlement of some sort; one case); expulsion of mulattos (one case); division of a town or separation of a sujeto (three cases).

Explanation of symbols used in appendix table:

C   *Corriente*, i.e., before the court or other Spanish
         authorities for decision.
F   *Fenecido*, i.e., completed or ended.
O   *De oficio*, a case handled without fee as part of
         the obligation of the office; almost invariably
         concerning private Indians.
P   *De parte*, a case usually involving an Indian
         community or cacique, and so handled at the half-
         fees permitted.
S   *Suspenso*, i.e., in abeyance.

Papers Handled by the Solicitadores of the Juzgado General de Indios

Parties	Town or Province	Subject of Dispute	State	O/P	Location of Papers
		Declaration of Bartolomé Díaz Borrego, August 26, 1784			
		Cases before the Juzgado General de Indios			
San Pedro Tlahuac vs. Misquic	Xochimilco	Money from use of a swamp	Appeal to aud.	P	Relator
María Gertrudis de Luna vs. stepmother	México	Division of property	S	O	
Isidro Sánchez, of La Montaña, vs. cura	Teposcolula	Return of two mules		O	With abogado to calculate costs
Santa Ana Necoxtla	Izúcar	Annulment of sale of lands		P	Relator
Juan de la Cruz, of Yenchu, vs. Taranco	Ixtlahuaca		S	O	
Diego Vital, etc., vs. Doña Josefa González	Tlalmanalco	Lands	Appeal to aud.	O	Relator
Antonio Francisco, of San Bartolomé de las Tunas, vs. Lorenzo Lucas	Huichiapan	Lands	Report asked for from justice	O	
Jorge and José de los Reyes, of Irapuato, vs. Juan López	Guanajuato	Lands	S	O	
Criminal - vs. Gregorio Antonio, of La Cruz Tillan, and María Asuncia, of Milpa Alta	Xochimilco	Adultery	To justice	O	
San Bartolomé Ozolotepec vs. teniente, Don José Egrediaga	Tenango del Valle	[Not given, but surely excesses]		P	Fiscal protector
San Juan Bautista Nogales vs. some vecinos	Orizaba	Lands and titles	S, no power of attorney	P	

Parties	Town or Province	Subject of Dispute	State	O/P	Location of Papers
Ignacio Ortega, of San Bartolomé Naucalpa, vs. Margarita de la Luz	Tacuba	Property	Sent to justice		
Dominga Antonia, etc., of Actopan, vs. justice	San Juan Teotihuacán	Excesses	S	O	
Pedro Pablo, of Atengo, vs. Candelaria María	Metepec	Lands		O	Abogado
Francisco Aziza vs. Don Antonio	Izúcar	Damages	Notice sent to other party	O	
Nopalucan vs. admin., Hac. of Tepalcatepec	Tlaxcala	Excesses		P	Abogado de parte
Chilcuautla vs. Antonio López	Ixmiquilpan	Lands		P	Juzgado G. de I.
Tecali vs. gov., Don José Reacón	Tecali	Excesses	Appeal to aud.	P	
Gov., alcaldes, etc., of Huehuetoca vs. teniente	Cuautitlán	Excesses		P	Fiscal
José Pérez vs. Teodoro Bravo	Actopan	Lands	S	O	
Cacique Gaspar de los Reyes	Santiago Tlatelolco	License to sell a town lot	To give information asked for by fiscal	P	
San Juan Tochatlaco vs. San Agustín Zapotlán	Cempoala	Lands	To justice for investigation	P	
Tomás Martín vs. Bernabé Marín, of Timilpa	Huichiapan	Lands		O	Relator
Silverio, of Santa María Actahuacán	Mexicalcingo	Seizure of his lands		O	Abogado
Mexo Martín vs. Patricio Pascual, of San Andrés Timilpa	Huichiapan	House and piece of land		O	Abogado

Case	Place	Subject	Status		Role
Bartola Luisa vs. Luis Gonzaga Alcántara, of San Antonio la Isla	Tenango	[Not given, but probably property]	Exchange of pleas	O	
Andrés Luis and Julián Francisca, of Los Santos Reyes	Chalco	[Not given, but probably property]	To general interpreter	O	General interpreter for transl.
Pedro de los Angeles, etc., of San Pedro Xalostoc, vs. Nicolasa Agustín	San Cristóbal Ecatepec	Inheritance	To justice for execution of sentence	O	
Pascuala Antonia	Santiago Tlatelolco	Protection for purchaser of land from her father		O	Relator
Pascuala Antonia	Santiago Tlatelolco	Protection for purchaser of land from her father		O	Fiscal
Manuel de la Cruz vs. Santos San Francisco	Zinacantepec	Lands		O	Abogado, to set fees
Santiago Cuautlalpa vs. Hac. of Tepetitlán	Texcoco	Use of a road	To justice for investigation	P	
Yolotepec vs. Hac. of Ocosar	Actopan	Demand that they work on hacienda	Awaiting answer to petition	O	Abogado
San Ildefonso vs. cura	Tula	Improper charges		P	Fiscal
Gañanes of Hac. of Acasonica vs. majordomo and aides	Antigua Veracruz	Mistreatment		[O]	Fiscal
Teoloyuca	Cuautitlán	Petition for land to pasture livestock		[P]	Fiscal
Santa Ana Necostla vs. San Mateo Ostolotla	Izúcar	Lands		[P]	Fiscal

Parties	Town or Province	Subject of Dispute	State	O/P	Location of Papers
Cacique Joaquín Daniel, of San Luis de las Peras, vs. Don Domingo Vázquez	Jilotepec	Lands		[P]	Abogado, to set fees

Escritos Sueltos [Documents] in Juzgado General de Indios

Parties	Town or Province	Subject of Dispute	State	O/P	Location of Papers
Leonardo Julián vs. Doña Ana Cerralvo	Tacuba	Money	Decree issued	O	
Marcelino Antonio, of Toyahualco	Xochimilco	Lands	Decree issued	O	
Pascuala vs. María Candelaria	Atzcapotzalco	Property	Decree issued	O	
Bartolomé Lorenzo vs. Felix, of Los Amoles	Celaya	Yoke of oxen	Decree issued	O	
Angela Sabina vs. alcalde	San Juan Teotihuacán	Excesses	Decree issued	O	
Catarina del Espíritu Santo, of Naucalpan	Tacuba	Jailing of husband	Decree issued	O	
Marcelo Jacinto vs. Francisca, of Tecoxpa	Xochimilco	Lands	Decree issued	O	
Felipe Nicolás vs. Don Agustín Ruedas, of San Luis de las Peras	Huichiapan	Damages	Decree issued	O	
María Asencia vs. justice, Tecomi	Xochimilco	Remitting papers of investigation	Decree issued	O	
Pascual de la Cruz vs. Don José Agreda, of San José de los Amoles	Celaya	Land	Decree issued	O	
Nicolasa María vs. Simón de los Santos, her son-in-law	San Martín Cuatlalpan	Land	Decree issued	O	
María de la Encarnación vs. María de Lino	Tacuba	Sale of magueyes	Decree issued	O	
Leonardo Julián vs. justice	Tacuba	Investigation	Decree issued	O	

Marcos Domingo vs. Don Miguel Vega, of Tepeji del Río	Tula	Money	Decree issued	O
Juan Crisóstomo vs. Don Ramón de Mata, of San Lorenzo Quautengo	Tenango del Valle	Money	Decree issued	O
Margarita Rosa vs. community, Tepetlaoxtoc	Texcoco	Accounting	Dispatch issued	O
Juan de la Cruz vs. majordomo, Hac. of Gotoluca	Apan	Mistreatment	Dispatch issued	O
Pedro de Jesús, etc., vs. Don José Guadalajara	Tenango del Valle	Return of papers	Decree issued	O
Francisco Javier vs. justice	San Miguel el Grande		Decree issued	O
Manuela María vs. Antonio Hernández, etc.	Chapa de Mota	Land	Decree issued	O
Margarita María vs. justice, of Naucalpan	Tacuba	Remitting papers of investigation	Decree issued	O
Bartolomé Vicente vs. majordomo, Hac. of Jesús María	Cuautepec	Liquidation of accounts	Decree issued	O
Laureano de la Cruz vs. justice	Santa Cruz Sultepec	Papers	Decree issued	O
Ventura Nicolás vs. justice, Jilotzingo	Tenango del Valle	Remission of papers of investigation	Decree issued	O
Felix Antonio vs. Mariano Francisco, of Tlatotepec	Tepeaca	Excesses	Decree issued	O
Diego de Santiago López, of Ocotlán	Chiautla de la Sal	Extension of time on debts	Decree issued	O
Isabel María vs. justice, Jilotepec	Huichiapan	Remission of papers of investigation	Decree issued	O

Parties	Town or Province	Subject of Dispute	State	O/P	Location of Papers
Manuela María vs. Juan Vicente, of Almoaya	Tenango del Valle	Land	Decree issued	O	
Atlacomulco vs. Ambrosio Sánchez	Ixtlahuaca	Excesses	Dispatch issued	P	
Villa del Carbón vs. Francisco Pedro, fiscal	Jilotepec	Excesses	Dispatch issued	P	
Manuela María vs. justice, Almoaya	Tenango del Valle	Remission of papers of investigation	Decree issued	O	
Andrés Lucas vs. Juan Agustín, of San Juan Huichicori	Tehuantepec	Money	Decree issued	O	
San Esteban Tlahuilacolco vs. Cipriano Onofre	Tacuba	Rental of land	Decree issued	P	
Florentino Alexo vs. Clemente Andrés, of Jiquipilco	Ixtlahuaca	Payment for mule	Decree issued	O	
Diego Solache, etc., of Chilpancingo	Tixtla	Payment of tribute	Decree issued	O	
Manuel Antonio Ramírez, of Chilpancingo	Tixtla	Excesses	Decree issued	O	
Mariano Serrano vs. admin., Hac. of Santa Clara, of Amosoque	Puebla	Excesses			
Antonio Juan, etc., vs. justice, Mimiapa	Tenango del Valle	Remission of papers of investigation	Decree issued	[O]	
Vicente González, of Nativitas	Salamanca	Extension of time on debts	Decree issued	O	
Manuel Antonio	Chiautla de la Sal	Petition for *incitatorio*	Decree issued	[O]	

Name	Place	Subject	Decree	P/O
Orizaba	Orizaba	Town lot	Decree issued	P
Felix Antonio vs. Vicente Martínez, barrio of Xolalpa	Tlalnepantla	Land	Decree issued	O
Juan García, etc., of San Antonio	Metepec	Freeing prisoners in jail	Decree issued	O
Pedro Pablo vs. Candelaria María, etc., of Atengo	Metepec	Land	Decree issued	O
María Gregoria, etc., vs. teniente, San Juan Teixcalpan	Tlalmanalco	Excesses		
Santa Ana Nopalocan vs. admin., Hac. of Tepalcatepec	Tlaxcala	Damages		P
Bernardino Antonio vs. Procopio José, etc., of Pipiltepec	Temascaltepec	Excesses		[O]
Domingo Antonia vs. justice, Actopan	San Juan Teotihuacán	Remission of papers of investigation	Decree issued	O
José Pérez, etc., vs. Teodoro Bravo	Actopan	Lands		O
Chilcuautla vs. Antonio López	Ixmiquilpan	Lands		P
Diego Hernández vs. Don Antonio Miranda, of San Lucas Ocotepec	Ixtlahuaca	Money	Decree issued	O
María Dolores vs. husband, Cuautepec	Tacuba	Ill treatment		
Félix Antonio vs. justice, Tlacotepec	Tepeaca	That he carry out an order		
San Esteban Aquilacalco vs. Cipriano Onofre	Tacuba	Excesses		
Diego Luciano	Jilotepec	Extension of time on debts		O
Lucas Sebastián, of Capulac	Tenango	License to pay creditors	Decree issued	O

Parties	Town or Province	Subject of Dispute	State	O/P	Location of Papers
José de la Cruz	Milpa Alta	Return of a deed	Decree issued	O	
Pedro Nolasco vs. Don Cristóbal García	Actopan	Excesses	Decree issued	O	
Ixtlacosacan vs. Haguican	Ameca	Land	Decree issued	O	
Vicente María vs. justice	Jilotepec	Remission of papers of investigation	Decree issued	O	
Antonio de los Santos vs. admin., Hac. of Caupilco, Xamimilolco	Huejotzingo	Accounting			
Gov. of Huehuetoca vs. teniente	Cuautitlán	Excesses	Decree issued	O	
Sebastián de la Rosa vs. Gertrudis González, of Quisyuca	Tepeji de la Seda	Damages	Decree issued	O	
Las Salinas [saline area]	San Juan Tenochtitlan	License to drain lands	Decree issued	P	
Feliciano Santiago vs. Juan Pérez	Actopan	Land			
Juan Antonio vs. Victoriano Velázquez, of Purificación	Texcoco	Land	Decree issued	O	
Simón Cano vs. Don José Hernández, of Tepetlaoxtoc	Texcoco	Liquidation of accounts		O	
Tepesayuca vs. justice	Tenango del Valle	Release		P	
Isidro Rafael vs. Francisco Morales, of Atzcapotzalco	Tacuba	Insults		O	
Lucas Pérez vs. Don Manuel de la Vega	Huejotzingo	*Dependencia indebida*		O	
María Vicente vs. mother-in-law	Sanctuary of Guadalupe	Lands	Decree issued	O	

424

Party	Location	Complaint	Outcome	
Bernabé Martínez vs. Tomás Martínez, of Timilpan	Huichiapan	Land		P
María Guadalupe vs. Tomás Juan, of Capulac	Tenango	Land		O
Silverio Luis vs. teniente, Aztahuacán	Mexicalcingo	Seizure of land		
Xicalco vs. Antonio Montes	Xochimilco	Land	Decree issued	O
María Rafaela vs. alcalde mayor, Milpa Alta	Xochimilco	Holding her in jail	Decree issued	
Cacique Francisco Páez Mendoza vs. gov., Amecameca	Tlalmanalco	Excesses	Decree issued	
Pedro José vs. alcalde mayor, San Martín Ocoyoacac	Tenango del Valle	*Apremiado por dependencia*		
Cipriano Antonio, of Santa María Magdalena de las Salinas	San Juan Tenochtitlan	Payment for a horse distributed in repartimiento	Decree issued	O
Juan Angel, alcalde of San Juan Tochatlaco	Zempoala	Seizure of his lands	Decree issued	O
Basilio José, etc., of Acotzingo and San Pablo	Tlalmanalco	Seizure of axes		
María Cecilia	Xochimilco	Exaction of 4/		O
Antonia Tello, widow of Francisco Bustamante, of Santa María Magdalena Tepetlaoxtoc	Texcoco	Land		O
Rosa María, wife of gañan, Hac. of San Nicolás Cuautengo	Tulancingo	Jailing		
Santa Cruz Montuoso vs. encomenderos	Celaya	Extortions, etc.		P
José Antonio, of Hac. of La Cañada	Celaya	Jailing for father's obligations		

Parties	Town or Province	Subject of Dispute	State	O/P	Location of Papers
María Manuela, wife	Tacuba	Jailing	Decree issued	O	
Vicente Antonio vs. majordomo, San Lorenzo Chausingo	Huejotzingo	Liquidation of accounts			
José Leonardo vs. corregidor, Santiaguito	Lerma	Molestation	Decree issued	O	
Francisco Imperial, of San Bartolomé Titlán	Tula	Debt of pesos and a horse	Decree issued	O	
Leonardo Julián, ex-gov. of Tacuba	Tacuba	Seizure of his lands	Decree issued	O	
Francisca Mexía, wife, vs. justice, San Francisco Tepeyaco	Cuautitlán	Remission of papers of investigation			
Vicente Antonio, of San Lorenzo Chausingo	Huejotzingo	Court order to be carried out by justice of San Salvador el Verde			
Ignacio Pérez vs. justice	Huejotzingo	Sending a despatch			
Lucas Martín vs. justice, San Pedro Cuaco	Huaquechula	Excesses and holding in servitude			
Cacique Don Blas de Andrade vs. alcalde	Santiago Querétaro	Sending papers of investigation on cacique's peons	Decree issued	O	
Agustina María, of Capulac	Tenango del Valle	Seizure of town lot			
Manuel de la Cruz vs. justice, barrio of San Francisco	Zinacantepec	Sending papers	Decree issued	O	

Petitioner	Place	Subject	Action	Code
Juan Mateo López	Mextitlán	Seizure of his lands	Decree issued	O
Pablo Monicario, etc., of Santa María Cuautepec, residing in Ixtapalapan, near Mexicalcingo, vs. corregidor of Mexicalcingo	Tacuba	Remission of papers of investigation		
Gov. of San Nicolás Xochicoatlán vs. justice	Xochicoatlán	Jailing	Decree issued	O
Andrés de Rivas, of Tlautla	Jilotepec	Debts	Decree issued	O
Luciano Ramos, etc., of Ixtapaluca, vs. Don Rafael Rivera Nolos	Chalco	Forced labor on hacienda	Decree issued	O
Antonio Esmenegildo vs. Acordada	Querétaro	Having corregidor force acordada to show cases	Decree issued	O
Felipe de la Cruz, of Nuestra Señora de la Concepción Calimaya	Tenango del Valle	Rental of land		
Miguel Aparicio, of Santa María Magdalena Tlatelolco	Tlaxcala	Payment of money due	Decree issued	O
Manuel de la Cruz vs. Santos de la Cruz, barrio of San Francisco	Zinacantepec	Remission of papers of investigation by justice	Decree issued	O
José Manuel vs. justice	Querétaro	Have justice perform function	Decree issued	O
María de la Cruz, of Tanepantla	Tlayacapa	Lands and magueyes		
Nicolás Miguel	Lerma	Jailing	Decree issued	O
Juan Lorenzo	Lerma	Jailing	Decree issued	O
San Miguel Istapa	Temascaltepec	Return of titles		P

Parties	Town or Province	Subject of Dispute	State	O/P	Location of Papers
Vicente Alfonsa, wife of Juan Ignacio, of Milpa Alta	Xochimilco	Bite by a dog	Decree issued	O	
Pedro Martín, etc., of Acapistla	Jonacatepec	Debts in money		O	
15 Indians of San Francisco Tepeyaco vs. Don Joaquín Diestro, Spaniard	Cuautitlán	Accounting	Decree issued		
Santiago Cuautlalpa	Texcoco	Road to woodlands not to be closed		P	
Nicolás de la Cruz vs. Don Pedro de la Maza, of Santa María Magdalena	Metepec	Lands		O	
Manuel de Santiago, of San Nicolás	Tehuacán	Debt in money		O	
Ex-gov., Santa Bárbara de la Lagunilla	Actopan	Accounting for livestock			
José Agustín, etc., of Santa Cruz Atizapan	Tenango del Valle	Lands	Decree issued	O	
José de la Cruz, of Milpa Alta	Xochimilco	Property	Decree issued	O	
María Marcela Sánchez, of San Miguel Chalmita, and San Juan Tenochtitlan	Tacuba	Sale of land			
Teresa de Jesús, of Milpa Alta	Xochimilco	Lands	Decree issued	O	
Domingo Miguel vs. Alexandro Antonio, of San Miguel Totomoloya	Sultepec	Land		O	
Bernabé Mariano, of San Juan Teocalco	San Juan Teotihuacán	Seizure of his lands	Decree issued	O	
Felipe de Santiago vs. justice, Silao	Guanajuato	Remission of papers of investigation	Decree issued	O	

Party	Place	Complaint	Disposition	P/O	Referral
Juan Antonio, of Silao	Guanajuato	Debts	Decree issued	O	
Catarina Andrea, of Santo Tomás Apipilhuasco	Texcoco	Jailing of husband	Decree issued	O	

Viceregal Government—Office of Soria

Party	Place	Complaint	Disposition	P/O	Referral
Gov. of Tacubaya vs. admin., royal powder mill	Tacubaya	Excesses	To fiscal	P	Fiscal
Dionisio Díaz vs. teniente, Miscahuala	Tetepango	40+/ owing	Assessor gen.	O	Assessor Gen.
Macehuales vs. caciques, Jocotitlán	Ixtlahuaca	Turns in official posts and functions	Dispatch for information	P	
Querétaro	Querétaro	Levy of money for community treasury	To contaduría de propios	P	Contaduría de propios
San Felipe and Santiago Chichicapa	Jalapa	On their new settlement	To fiscal		Fiscal
Santiago Temoaya	Lerma	Nullity of election	To justice for information		
Sichu vs. Miners of Real	San Luis de la Paz	Forced services	Dispatch issued	P	

Viceregal Government—Office of Gorráez

Party	Place	Complaint	Disposition	P/O	Referral
Aguas del Venado	México	Lands and that alcalde mayor not impede taking case to Mexico City	Fiscal de lo civil	P	
Sentlalpa vs. gov. of Amecacameca	Tlalmanalco	Rental of lands	Dispatch issued	P	

Parties	Town or Province	Subject of Dispute	State	O/P	Location of Papers
Chalchichilco	Tenancingo	Division of government	To assessor general	P	Assessor general
Quetzala	Tlapa	Jailing of governor	To assessor general	P	Assessor general
Quetzala	Tlapa	Expelling mulattos in town	To fiscal protector	P	Fiscal protector
San Marcos	Orizaba	Division of government	In cabecera	P	
Audiencia—Office of Medina					
María de la Trinidad vs. José de Santiago	Querétaro	Lands	F	O	
Acapetlahuaya vs. Totoltepec	Zacualpan	Lands	In proof	P	
Santiago Tepetlasco vs. Carmelite College of San Joaquín	Tacuba	Lands	In proof	P	
Ixcateopan vs. cacique	Tlapa	Lands	Dispatch to cacique for information		
Ixhuacán de los Reyes and Ayahualulco vs. heirs of Don Pedro Rincón	Jalapa	Lands	Sent to other party		
Tlahuac vs. Mixquic	Xochimilco	Money derived from swamp, appeal from Juzgado General de Indios	Seen and decided	P	

Tecali vs. cacique gov.	Chiautla de la Sal	Excesses, appeal from Juzgado General de Indios	To relator	P	Relator

Audiencia—Office of Mota

Huahuastla	San Juan de los Llanos	Fundo legal	To fiscal	P	Fiscal
San Francisco Jonacatlán vs. majordomo, Don Agustín Villanueva	Tenango del Valle	Lands	Sent to other party	P	
Tepemasalco vs. Conde de Santiago	Tenango del Valle	Lands and excesses	S	P	
Huisuco vs. Don Vicente Malbán	Taxco	Lands	To fiscal protector	P	Fiscal protector
San Gerónimo Acasulco vs. cura	Tenango del Valle	Excesses	To fiscal	P	Fiscal
Malacatepec vs. Hac's. of San Felipe and La Asunción	Metepec	Lands	Sent to other party	P	
Barrio of Nuestra Señora del Perdón Congregación San Pedro Piedragorda, vs. majordomo, cofradía of Jesús Nazareno		Lands	To abogado for answer	O	
José Antonio Camargo, etc., vs. heirs of Don Manuel Calvo Pintado	Salamanca	[Lands - Indians of Salamanca] appeal to audiencia	To relator	O	Relator
San Felipe vs. Jiquipilco	Ixtlahuaca	Money	To other party	O	

Sala del Crimen

Felipe Mendoza	Valladolid		To fiscal	O	Fiscal

431

Parties	Town or Province	Subject of Dispute	State	O/P	Location of Papers
Victoriano Vicente, dec., vs. Eugenio José, etc., of San Francisco Tlaltzapan	Tacuba	Money	To fiscal	O	Fiscal
Juzgado de Intestados					
Turicato vs. heirs of Don José Langarica	Valladolid	[Lands?]	To abogado to fix fees	P	Abogado
Royal Customs					
Santiago Tepalcatlapa	Xochimilco	Moderation of assessment for pulque tax	F	P	
Cuajimalpa	Coyoacán	Moderation of assessment for pulque tax	S		Abogado fiscal
Agustín Rojas	Querétaro	Exemption from alcabala as Indian tributary	Dispatch sent	O	
Estado and Marquesado del Valle					
Juan Ventura Jiménez vs. Don Manuel Prada, of Ocuituco	? / Ocuituco	Extension of time on debts	To abogado fiscal	O	Abogado fiscal
Vicente Antonio	Jonacatepec	Extension of time on debts, various creditors		O	

Juzgado Privativo de Tierras

			Dispatch sent	
Atlistlaca	Tlapa	Lands, in return for *donativo*	Dispatch sent	P
Totolsingo	San Juan Teotihuacán	Lands, in return for *donativo*	About to be considered	P

Secretariat of Archbishopric of Mexico

San Lorenzo Guichichilaqui vs. vicar	Lerma	Excesses	S	P

Declaration of Manuel María de Arellano, September 2, 1784

Papers Currently Before the Juzgado General de Indios

San Pablo Huatepec vs. Don Luis Mejía		Land	C	[P]
Tequanipa vs. Ameca		Land	C	[P]
Micaela Gregoria vs. Don Ramón de Mata	Cuautengo	Excesses	C	[O]
Felipe García vs. José García	San Juan Puruándiro	Land (town lot)	F	O
Pascuala Zacarias, of San Sebastián	México	*Dependencia*	C	O
Pedro Martín vs. José de la Cruz	Metepec	Land	C	O
Micaela Gregoria vs. Juan Crisóstomo	Cuautengo	Land	S	O
María Rafaela Hernández vs. Dominga de la Cruz	Metepec	Land	C	O
Marcos de la Cruz vs. Domingo Ramos	San Lucas	Land	S	O
Francisco Tirano vs. Domingo Antonio	Actopan	Land	F	O

Parties	Town or Province	Subject of Dispute	State	O/P	Location of Papers
Dominga Antonia vs. justice	Actopan	Excesses	C	O	
Dominga Antonia vs. Rita	?	?	S	O	
Papers and Decrees Sent to Justices					
Luis Martínez vs. Don Juan Ponce	Ozumba	Liquidation of accounts	F	O	
José Trinidad vs. corregidor	Querétaro	Excesses	F	O	
Sebastián Mateos vs. María Guadalupe, of Santorum		Property	S	O	
Rafael Antonio	Tepetlaoxtoc	?	F	O	
Sebastián Hernández vs. brother	Tlalpujahua	Division of property	S	O	
Ignacio Samaniago vs. justice	Calpuluac	Grant of land	F	O	
María de la Concepción vs. justice	Tacuba	Carrying out order	S	O	
Manuel Hernández vs. María Magdalena	La Laguna	Land	F	O	
Marcelo Antonio vs. Blas de la Candelaria	Santiaguito	Excesses	F	O	
Mauricio Martín vs. cousin	Tepetlaoxtoc	Division of property	F	O	
Antonio Alonso vs. Agustín Palas	Querétaro	Accounts	S	O	
José Alejandro vs. José García	Igualtepec	Division of property	F	O	
Luis Francisco vs. Juan	La Asunción	Maize	S	O	
San Francisco vs. justice	Oaxaca	Carrying out order	S	P	

Case	Place	Subject		
...María, etc. vs. Nicolás Juan	Tlaxcala	Land	S	○
Ignacia María vs. teniente	Metepec	Excesses	S	○
Juan del Carmen vs. Manuel Antonio	Atzcapotzalco	Excesses	S	○
Miguel Francisco vs. admin. of a mill	San Salvador el Verde	Accounts	S	○
Manuel Trinidad vs. sister-in-law	Ozumba	Division of property	S	○
Luis Bernardo vs. vicar	San Gregorio	Keeping his wife with caretaker	F	○
Miguel Fabián vs. cura	Tehuantepec	?	S	○
Juan Marcos vs. Tomás Valdés	Tenango del Valle	Land	F	○
Marcos de la Cruz vs. justice	San Lucas	Remission of papers	S	○
Andrés Antonio vs. town alcaldes	Tlayacapa	Improper levies	S	○
Manuel de Jesús vs. admin., Hac. of Mimiahuapa	Tlaxcala	Excesses	F	○
Felipe de la Cruz vs. justice	Capula	Jailing	F	○
Manuela María vs. Antonio	Chapa de Mota	Land	F	○
Seferino Millán vs. Don Lorenzo Espejal	Calpulalpan	Debt in money	S	○
Pedro Seferino, etc., vs. justice	Apan	Excesses	F	P
Jacinto Roque vs. gov.	Tacuba	Land	S	○
Juan Marcos vs. justice	Tenango del Valle	Carrying out order	F	○
Francisco Juan vs. Vicente	Capuluac	Land	S	○
Tomás de San Lucas vs. Marcelo	Tenango	Land	S	○
Antonio Cornejo vs. Pascuala	Tepetitlán	Land	S	○
Manuel Juan vs. Domingo	Ayotzingo	Land	F	○

Parties	Town or Province	Subject of Dispute	State	O/P	Location of Papers
Pedro Ramos vs. justice	Salvatierra	Embargo on goods	S	O	
María Rosa vs. justice	Ayacapistla	Jailing of man [husband?]	F	O	
José Hilario vs. teniente	Tlalnepantla	Improper levies	F	O	
Juan de la Encarnación vs. justice	San Miguel Amealco	Jailing	S	O	
Marcela María vs. justice	Tarasquillo	Jailing	F	O	
Domingo Crescencio vs. teniente	Tacuba	Payment for a mule	F	O	
Ignacio Pérez vs. majordomo, Hac. of San José	Huejotzingo	Excesses - beating	S	O	
Miguel Antonio vs. justice	Tacuba	Jailing	S	O	
Miguel Gerónimo	Tacuba	Property	F	O	
María del Carmen	Tacuba	Placing her daughter in custody of caretaker	F	O	
Antonio Cornejo vs. justice	Tepetitlán	Carrying out order	S	O	
José Caudillo vs. justice	Silao	Remission of papers of investigation	S	O	
Domingo García	San Bartolomé Actopan	Will	S	O	
Rita Asencia vs. Francisco	Capuluac	Land	S	O	
Manuel Francisco vs. Teresa	Cuautla	Property	F		

Case	Place	Subject		
Felipe Juan vs. Melchora María	Tenango	Land	F	O
Agustín Antonio vs. María Josefa	Capuluac	Land	F	O
Melchora de los Reyes vs. gov.	Tacuba	Land	S	O
Calistro Lucas	Tacuba	Land	F	O
Hilaria María	Tepeji del Río	*Dependencia* of dead husband	F	O
José Sandoval vs. alcalde of Pachivia [?]	San Cristóbal Ecatepec	Exhibit a dispatch	S	O
Juan Manuel vs. justice	Sahualco [Zacoalco?]	Jailing of mother	S	O
Viceregal Government—Both Secretaries				
Caciques of Jocotitlán vs. commoners	Jocotitlán	Governance	C	P
San Pedro Actopan	San Pedro Actopan	Jailing of governor	C	P
San Pedro el Alto vs. cura	San Pedro el Alto	Excesses	C	P
Tonalisco	Tonalisco	Separation of town government	C	P
Audiencia—Both Secretaries				
Caciques of Tula	Tula	Inheritance	C	P
Lucas Garibaldi vs. Juan Antonio Bautista	Querétaro	Land	C	O
Huichichilapan vs. vicar	Huichichilapan	[Excesses?]	C	P
Riofrío vs. Don Felipe Vega	Riofrío	Land—appeal from Juzgado General de Indios	C	P

Declaration of Money Held by Solicitors for Clients

Money on Deposit from Parties to Suits

32/, of which the following spent:

Petition to declare sentence	1/
Petition accusing recalcitrance	0/4
To porter for presentation	0/2
? for collection	0/2
Getting papers and taking them to abogado	1/2
Petition asking for limit of time	0/4
	4/7

[actually 3/6; one item probably omitted]

Arellano has 27/1 to pay relator, etc.

No other fees on deposit except for Riofrío, since "the parties pay their own."

Source: Declarations of the solicitadores of the Juzgado General de Indios, in the expediente on the juzgado, 1784–1786, fols. 45v–72v, in AGI-M, leg. 1286.

438

Glossary

Abogado. A professional lawyer, with a formal university degree in law, some years of apprenticeship, and formal acceptance to practice through examination and license by an *audiencia*.

Abogado de pobres. An abogado formally appointed to handle the cases and causes of paupers.

Agentes intrusos. Legal agents who without proper authorization of the authorities attempted to represent clients and frequently cheated them.

Alcabala. Sales tax.

Alcalde. A municipal official who served as justice of the peace or as judge in first instance.

Alcalde mayor. In colonial Mexico, the governor of a province (*alcaldía mayor*). He served as judge of appeals from town courts and as judge of first instance in more serious cases.

Alguacil. Bailiff; the *alguacil mayor* was the principal or head bailiff.

Amparo. Literally, protection; in colonial Mexico, an administrative or judicial order guaranteeing protection in the enjoyment of some right or privilege.

Apartamiento. Withdrawal; i.e., withdrawing from a suit or complaint.

Asesor. Assessor; in legal matters, the trained lawyer who advised a judge or governor, etc. By Spanish law, a man without legal training could not function as judge without an assessor, who actually indicated the decision to be reached, the nominal judge merely accepting and signing.

Audiencia. In colonial Spanish America, both a high court of appeal and the territory of its jurisdiction. In a viceregal capital, the court functioned as viceregal council as well as judicial body; where there was no viceroy, it functioned as governing body for the territory.

Audiencia gobernadora. The audiencia, exercising the powers of a viceroy upon the death of one without royal designation of a successor, until arrival of a royal appointee.

Barrio. A neighborhood within a town, usually with local religious institutions and a patron saint.

Braza, brazas. Literally, arm or arms; a unit of measure of two Spanish yards, slightly less than our fathom.

Brazo secular. The secular arm; i.e., the royal or viceregal administration upon which the Church was supposed to call for enforcement of its judgments.

Caballería. A land measure of approximately 105.4 acres.

Cabecera. Head; a term applied to the chief agglomeration in a *pueblo* of more than a single settlement, or to a town which was the seat of the parish church and parish priest.

Cacique. The title and post reserved for former native rulers under Spanish administration, with right to salary and revenues; treated as an entailed estate (*cacicazgo*) but, in Spanish-style, with women (*cacicas*) entitled to succeed as well as men.

Caja. A chest; also a royal treasury and the officials assigned to it.

Caja de comunidad. Community treasury, the name being derived from the treasure chest used to store funds under triple lock.

Calpisque. A native overseer.

Calzones. Trousers; in the colonial period, the trousers of unbleached, coarse cotton cloth introduced by the Spaniards for the Indians.

Cámara. Literally, chamber, but also court or of judicial nature.

Capa y espada. Cloak and sword, a term meaning of military rather than legal training.

Capítulos. Literally, chapters; in colonial Mexico, charges organized in paragraphs or chapters, presented against a government official or priest.

Carta creëncia. A judicial letter sent to another judicial district attesting to the validity of an order to be enforced there.

Cartillas. Notebooks; the first books of letters of children.

Casco. Literally, shell or outer structure; as applied to towns, the outermost houses.

Casos de corte. In Spanish law, cases which might be taken directly to the royal court of appeal or to the sovereign himself.

Cédula. See *Real cédula.*

Chambas. Multiple posts, held at the same time.

Cognitio summaria. Hearing in a case by abbreviated process.

Compadre. In medieval English, Godsib; a relationship of religious brotherhood created by common participation as sponsors for someone in a religious ceremony, such as baptism, confirmation, etc.

Composición. A settlement or compromise, usually of some delinquency in relation to the state, through payment of a sum of money in return for clear title or wiping out the offense.

Composición general. A general handling of delinquencies; in colonial Mexico, applied to royal examination of all land titles by a commissioner-general, and clearance of titles by payments.

Concierto. Agreement or compromise.

Concluso. Finished, completed; applied to cases that had been brought to completion in a court.

Congregación. Compact settlement of a previously dispersed population.

Corregidor. The Spanish administrator of a town or city, with the powers of an alcalde mayor in colonial Mexico.

Cura. Parish priest.

De oficio. Official business, or as an obligation of the state.

De parte. Business starting on private initiative.

Defensor de los indios. Defender or protector of the Indians, usually in lawsuits and complaints.

Dependencia. A relationship of servitude, whether wage or legal or both, toward another person.

Derrama. A levy upon Indian commoners in the name of the town for extraordinary expenses.

Despacho universal. Handling all kinds of business; a term applied to the viceroy as the highest official in the colony.

Doctrina. A parish in which the Indians were regarded as in process of conversion, more often administered by friars than by secular priests.

Doctrinero. The priest in a doctrina, but also applied to any missionary, even one without formal assignment to a parish.

Ducado. A ducat, a coin of account valued at 375 maravedís.

Encargado de justicia. An official administering justice by designation of a governor, but without formal viceregal confirmation.

Encomienda. The grant of Indians or their tributes to an individual by the crown; its holder was an *encomendero*.

Escribano. Notary or legal secretary.

Escribano mayor de cámara. A recording secretary and notary for judicial affairs, by formal appointment.

Escribano mayor de gobernación. A recording secretary and notary for administrative affairs, by formal appointment.

Estancia. A general term for a ranch used for raising livestock.

Estancia de ganado mayor. A grant of land for raising horses or cattle, of 1 square league, or 6.76 square miles.

Estancia de ganado menor. A grant of land for raising sheep, goats, and pigs, of 4/9 square league, or 3 square miles.

Expediente. A docket.

Fiscal. Actually a shortened form of *procurador fiscal*, i.e., attorney for the crown.

Fiscal protector. Technically, all crown attorneys in Spanish America were charged to act as protectors of the Indians, but in each audiencia district, usually one ordinarily discharged this function.

Fuero. A special set of laws of personal or regional application, but also the special privilege of having those laws applied, usually to one's benefit.

Fuero eclesiástico. The right or privilege of being sued or tried under Church law in a Church tribunal.

Fundo legal. The minimum of land around each legally recognized Indian settlement, guaranteed to it.

Ganado mayor. Large livestock, i.e., horses and cattle.

Ganado menor. Smaller livestock, i.e., sheep, goats, and pigs.

Gañan. A rural Indian wage laborer, very often held in debt, and if domiciled on an hacienda, bound to it.

Gente de bien. People of the middle and upper class; usually applied to non-Indians.

Gente de razón. Literally, "people of reason," a term applied to non-Indians in a broad sense, and in a more restricted one only to whites and *mestizos*.

Gobernación. Administration, as distinguished from the judicial.

Grano. A grain; in monetary terms, the 12th part of a *real* or the 96th part of a silver peso.

Guardián. Among the friars, the title given to the head of a convent.

Hacienda. A word of many meanings: a large agricultural or stock-raising estate; a business; a treasury; here usually used in the first meaning.

Huerta. A word of wide application which may mean an orchard, a kitchen garden, an irrigated plot, a cacao grove, etc.

Incitativa. A motion or order directing an official to undertake a hearing or proceeding.

Interrogatorio. In Castilian law, a formal questionnaire proposed by one party to a suit for administration to a set list of witnesses. Answers were limited to the questions and the basis for knowledge.

Intruso, intrusos. Intruder, intruders—terms applied to trespassers and usurpers.

Juez conservador. A judge who might be nominated or appointed for judging and conserving privileges and properties in special instances by royal consent; the powers of such a judge overrode those of ordinary judges.

Juez de letras. A judge trained in law.

Juez de residencia. The judge empowered to examine conduct in office and assess penalties at the conclusion of an official's term.

Juez privativo. A judge with exclusive jurisdiction in a special category or a special territorial jurisdiction.

Juzgado. A tribunal.

Letrado. A man trained in law and with formal law degree.

Licenciado. A university degree conferring license to practice law, subject to an audiencia's right to examine and admit to practice.

Llevadores. Messengers carrying legal papers.

Macehual, macehuales. Indian commoner(s).

Manta. A cloak or length of cloth; coarse muslin; also used for the small, slitted, cotton or woolen strip of weaving used as protection against cold.

Maravedí. An obsolete medieval Spanish silver coin, cited as a common denominator for Spanish money values.

Marquesado. Marquisate; in colonial Mexico, the seigneurial estate given to Cortés and his heirs, the Marquesado del Valle de Oaxaca, but actually seven provinces throughout central Mexico.

Matlazáhuatl. An epidemic disease, possibly a form of typhus.

Media anata. A royal tax of half a year's salary on new appointees.

Medio real. A half-real, an actual silver coin; also, a tax for legal insurance and for hospitals, levied on Indian payers of tribute.

Milpa, milpas. Fields, usually for maize.

Moriscos. Moslems converted to Christianity.

Obrage, obraje. A workshop, very often for cloth.

Oficial mayor, oficial mayores. Chief clerk(s) or executive officer(s).

Oidor. A judge of the audiencia.

Papel de resguardo. A document guaranteeing payment of a debt or fulfillment of a contract.

Parcialidad. A district within a town or city; in the specific instance of Mexico City, the two governmental units into which the Indian barrios around the Spanish city were organized, and which were independent of the Spanish municipal government, although subject to the viceregal government.

Peso. Literally, weight; the name of coins of account and circulation of varying values, the common denominator being the maravedí, an obsolete medieval Castilian silver coin. The peso of fine gold (*oro de minas*) was worth 450 maravedís; that of silver (also of *tepuzque* and *oro común*), 272.

Portero. Gatekeeper, usher.

Principal, principales. Indian noble(s) within a native town.

Probanza. Proof, evidence; a formal document adducing evidence.

Procurador. An agent, in fact or in law. The agent in law had to have legal training and be admitted to practice.

Procurador general de indios. An official appointed to act as general legal representative and defender for the Indians.

Propina. Tip.

Protector de indios. An official appointed to assist the natives in their suits and complaints and to prosecute or even punish directly cases of abuse of them.

Provisión real. A formal judicial order issued under royal seal.

Real. The 8th part of a silver peso; our bit as in two bits.

Real cédula. A formal royal administrative order issued under royal seal.

Real cédula ejecutoria. A formal royal order directing carrying out a sentence or decision, usually following a real cédula in dispute.

Real provisión. See Provisión real.

Real servicio. In Spain, a direct tax granted to the monarch by the Cortes; in colonial Mexico, where there was no Cortes, an additional tax on all Indian tributaries, whether in crown or encomienda, of o/4 a year.

Rebeldía. Contumacy; a formal accusation brought against a party for not filing an answer in a case.

Regidor. A councilman in the municipal council of a Spanish settlement.

Reglamento. Rules for carrying out an ordinance or law.

Relación de mando. The report which each viceroy was bound to prepare at the end of his term for guiding his successor.

Relator. A court official charged with examining the papers of a case to see that they were all there, putting them in order, and preparing a summary for the judge or judges.

Repartimiento. A distribution or allocation; sometimes applied to the labor draft in colonial Mexico, and even to the encomienda.

Repartimiento de indios. An allocation of Indians for work, tribute payment, etc.

Repartimiento de mercancías. The compulsory allocation of merchandise to Indian tributaries at set prices, usually by provincial governors, with the requirement of payment on a set schedule.

Residencia. A judicial examination of an official's acts during his term of office, carried out by a special judge at the conclusion of the term.

Ruego y encargo. Request and charge; the formula in which injunctions and commands went from the royal authorities to churchmen.

Sala del crimen. A junior chamber of the Audiencia of Mexico (or any other audiencia), with jurisdiction, civil and criminal, in first instance within the immediate territory of its seat.

Secretario. An alternate title for the principal recording notaries for judicial and administrative affairs.

Sede vacante. Governing in the absence of a bishop until one was appointed.

Señores naturales. Native rulers of Indian groups, with claim to sovereignty.

Sobrecédula. A real cédula repeating one already issued and ordering enforcement. If a real cédula was suspended pending appeal to the crown on grounds of fraud or misinformation in its issuance, a sobrecédula meant that the terms had to be implemented.

Solicitador. The lowest rank in a triple division of the legal professions; the solicitador dealt most closely with the client, secured powers of attorney, and moved papers, but ordinarily had to defer to the procurador and abogado, and might not be permitted to appear in formal hearings. The solicitadores of the medio real had far wider powers.

Subcaja. A branch of a royal treasury in another city of the same district.

Sujeto. A dependent town within an Indian town, owing obedience to the cabecera.

Suspenso. Suspended; usually applied to cases in which the complainant abandoned the suit.

Tameme. A Nahuatl term for porter or bearer carried over to colonial Mexican Spanish.

Tasador y repartidor general. An official of the Audiencia of Mexico charged with setting specific fees and with apportioning the business of the audiencia among various officials.

Teniente. Deputy or lieutenant, usually of a governor or other administrative official.

Teniente de capitán general. A military title borne by the deputy for a military commander, either as his immediate lieutenant or as his administrator for a district.

Teniente-general. General deputy; a formal office as deputy carrying the widest powers. Such appointments were supposed to be ratified by the viceregal government.

Teniente letrado. A lieutenant or deputy trained in law, who could act directly as judge or as legal assessor for the governor sitting as judge.

Tomín. The eighth part of a peso, its value varying with that of the parent peso.

Topil. A town or parish lower official.

Traza. The Spanish city of Mexico within which Indians were forbidden to settle.

Vara. A Castilian yard; in metric terms, 83.59 cm.

Visita. An inspection; carried out by a *visitador*, with the powers of a judge.

Visitador-general. An official charged with carrying out a general review and inspection of a colony, whose powers superseded those of all officials within the colony.

Volador. A Mexican Indian ritual observance in which four men, each attached to one of four cords wound around a high pole, descend in an unwinding that moves them outward from the pole.

Bibliography

Manuscripts

Mexico:
Archivo General de la Nación (AGN), Mexico City, ramos of
Archivo del Hospital de Jesús	Ordenanzas
	Reales Cédulas
Civil	Reales Cédulas, Duplicados
Criminal	
General de Parte	Tierras
Indios	Tributos
Mercedes	Vínculos

Archivo Judicial, Teposcolula, Oaxaca
Civil	Criminal

Archivo de la Secretaría Municipal, Puebla
Libros de cabildo

Spain:
Archivo General de Indias (AGI), Sevilla, sections of
Audiencia de Guadalajara	Indiferente General
Audiencia de Méjico	Justicia
Contaduría	Patronato

Biblioteca Nacional, Madrid
"Correspondencia de Don Luis de Velasco con Felipe II y Felipe III acerca de la administración de los

447

virreinatos de Nueva España y del Perú durante los años 1590 a 1601." Ms. 3636. 295 ff.
Real Academia de la Historia, Madrid
    Colección de Juan Bautista Múñoz

United States:
The Bancroft Library, University of California, Berkeley
    Documents Relating to the Juzgado de Indios, 1580–1826, selected by Lesley Byrd Simpson from the Archivo General de la Nación, Mexico, 1939–1940 (LBSD). A set of film enlargements of documents photographed in AGN, Civil, Criminal, and Historia. 26 vols.
    Simpson, Lesley Byrd. Field and Archive Notebooks, 1931–1940 (LBSF). 17 vols.

In private possession:
    Archivo de Tulancingo   Cerralvo Papers

Publications

Aegidius Romanus (Egidio Colonna). *De regimine principum libri III. Recogniti et una cum vita auctoris in lucem editi per F. Hieronymus Samaritanium.* Rome, 1607; facsimile ed., Aalen, 1967.
————. *Glosa castellana al "Regimiento de Príncipes" de Egidio Romano. Edición y estudio preliminar de Juan Beneyto Pérez.* 3 vols. Madrid, 1947.
Aiton, Arthur Scott. *Antonio de Mendoza, First Viceroy of New Spain.* Durham, N.C., 1927.
Alamán, Lucas. *Historia de Méjico desde los primeros movimientos que preparon su independencia en el año de 1808 hasta la época presente.* 5 vols. Mexico City, 1849–1852.
Aldridge, A. Owen, ed. *The Ibero-American Enlightenment.* Urbana, Ill., 1971.
Altamira, Rafael. "El texto de las Leyes de Burgos de 1512." *Revista de historia de América,* no. 4 (December 1938): 5–80.
Alva Ixtlilxóchitl, Fernando de. *Obras históricas,* ed. Alfredo Chavero. 2 vols. Mexico City, 1891–1892.
Álvarez de Morales, Antonio. *Apuntes de historia de las instituciones españolas (siglos XVIII y XIX).* Madrid, 1976.
Álvarez de Velasco, Gabriel. *De privilegiis pauperum et miserabilium*

personarum . . . Tractatus in duas partes divisus, 3rd ed. 2 vols. Lausanne and Geneva, 1739.

Ancona, Eligio. *Historia de Yucatán desde la época mas remota hasta nuestros días*, 2nd ed. 4 vols. Barcelona, 1889.

Anna, Timothy E. *The Fall of the Royal Government in Mexico City*. Lincoln, Nebr., 1978.

Arenal, Celestino del. "La teoría de la servidumbre natural en el pensamiento español de los siglos XVI y XVII." *Historiografía y bibliografía americanistas*, 19–20 (1975–1976):67–124.

Armellada, Cesáreo. *La causa indígena americana en las Cortes de Cádiz*. Madrid, 1959.

Arvizu y Galarraga, Fernando. "Especialidades procesales de la Recopilación Indiana." 4th Congreso Internacional de Historia del Derecho Indiano, Morelia, 1975, *Memoria*, pp. 23–61.

Ayala, Francisco Javier de. "El descubrimiento de América y la evolución de las ideas políticas (Ensayo de interpretación)." *Arbor*, 3, no. 8 (1945):304–321.

———. *Ideas políticas de Juan de Solórzano*. Sevilla, 1946.

Azanza, Miguel José de. *Introducción reservada que dio el virrey don . . . a su sucesor don Féliz Berenguer de Marquina*, ed. Ernesto de la Torre Villar. Mexico City, 1960.

Baade, Hans W. "The Formalities of Private Real Estate Transactions in Spanish North America: A Report on Some Recent Discoveries." *Louisiana Law Review*, 38 (1977–1978):655–745.

———. "Marriage Contracts in French and Spanish Louisiana: A Study in 'Notarial' Jurisprudence." *Tulane Law Review*, 53 (1978–1979):1–92.

Baer, Yitzhak Fritz. *A History of the Jews in Christian Spain*, trans. from Hebrew by Louis Schoffman. 2 vols. Philadelphia, 1961–1966.

Ballesteros, Pío. "Los indios y sus litigios, según la recopilación de 1680." *Revista de Indias*, 6, no. 22 (1945):627–633.

Bancroft, Hubert Howe. *History of Mexico*. 6 vols. San Francisco, 1883–1888.

Bayle, Constantino. "Los municipios y los indios." *Missionalia hispanica*, 7 (1950):409–442.

———. "El protector de indios." *Anuario de estudios americanos*, 2 (1945):1–180.

———. *El protector de indios*. Sevilla, 1945.

Beleña, Eusebio Buenaventura. See Mexico (Viceroyalty), *Recopilación sumaria*.

Bermúdez Aznar, Agustín. "La abogacia de pobres en Indias." *Anuario de historia del derecho español*, 50 (1980):1039–1054.

Biermann, Benno. "Die Anfänge der Dominikanertätigkeit in Neu-Spanien und Peru im Anschluss an einem neu veröffentlichen Brief von Fray Bernardino de Minaya, O.P." *Archivium Fratrum Praedicatorum*, 13 (1943):5–58.

Biondi, Biondo. "Summatim cognoscere." *Bullettino dell'Istituto di Diritto Romano*, Rome, 30 (1921):220–258.

Bolio, Pedro, and Policarpo Antonio de Echánove. "Resumen instructivo de los fondos de medio real de ministros y comunidades de indios de la provincia de Yucatán, en su tesorería principal de Mérida, Mérida, 22 de abril de 1813." *El Fénix*, Campeche, April 10, 1849.

Borah, Woodrow. "The Cathedral Archive of Oaxaca." *Hispanic American Historical Review*, 28 (1948):640–645.

———. "The Collection of Tithes in the Bishopric of Oaxaca during the Sixteenth Century." *Hispanic American Historical Review*, 21 (1941):386–409.

———. "European Cultural Influence in the Formation of the First Plan for Urban Centers That Has Lasted to Our Time." 39th International Congress of Americanists, Lima, 1970, *Actas y memorias*, vol. 2, pp. 35–54.

———. "Un gobierno provincial de frontera en San Luis Potosí (1612–1620)." *Historia mexicana*, 13 (1963–1964):532–550.

———. "Juzgado General de indios del Perú o juzgado particular de indios de El Cercado de Lima." *Revista chilena de historia del derecho*, no. 6 (1970):129–142.

———. *New Spain's Century of Depression*. Ibero-Americana, vol. 35. Berkeley and Los Angeles, 1951.

———. "Population Decline and the Social and Institutional Changes of New Spain in the Middle Decades of the Sixteenth Century." 34th International Congress of Americanists, Vienna, 1960, *Akten*, pp. 172–178.

———. "Social Welfare and Social Obligation in New Spain: A Tentative Assessment." 36th International Congress of Americanists, Barcelona, Madrid, and Sevilla, 1964, *Actas y memorias*, vol. 4, pp. 45–57.

———. "Tithe Collection in the Bishopric of Oaxaca, 1601–1867." *Hispanic American Historical Review*, 29 (1949):498–517.

———. "Los tributos y su recaudación en la Audiencia de la Nueva Galicia durante el siglo XVI." In Bernardo García Martínez et al., eds., *Historia y sociedad en el mundo de habla español: Homenaje a José Miranda* (Mexico City, 1970), pp. 27–47.

Borah, Woodrow, and Sherburne F. Cook. *The Aboriginal Population of Central Mexico on the Eve of the Spanish Conquest*. Ibero-Americana, vol. 45. Berkeley and Los Angeles, 1963.

———. "A Case History of the Transition from Precolonial to the Colonial Period in Mexico: Santiago Tejupan." In David J. Robinson, ed., *Social Fabric and Spatial Structure in Colonial Latin America* (Syracuse, N.Y., 1979), pp. 409–432.

———. "Conquest and Population: A Demographic Approach to Mexican History." *Proceedings of the American Philosophical Society*, 113, no. 2 (February 1969):177–183.

———. *The Population of Central Mexico in 1548: An Analysis of the suma de visitas de pueblos.* Ibero-Americana, vol. 43. Berkeley and Los Angeles, 1960.

—————. *Price Trends of Some Basic Commodities in Central Mexico, 1531–1570.* Ibero-Americana, vol. 40. Berkeley and Los Angeles, 1958.

—————. "La transición de la época aborigen al período colonial: el caso de Santiago Tejupan." In Jorge E. Hardoy and Richard P. Schaedel, comps., *Asentamientos urbanos y organización socioproductiva en la historia de América Latina* (Buenos Aires, 1977), pp. 69–88.

Born, Lester Kruger. "The Perfect Prince: A Study in Thirteenth- and Fourteenth-Century Ideals." *Speculum,* 3 (1928):470–504.

Bosch García, Carlos. *La esclavitud prehispánica entre los aztecas.* Mexico City, 1944.

Brading, David A. *Haciendas and Ranchos in the Mexican Bajío: León, 1700–1860.* Cambridge, 1978.

—————. *Miners and Merchants in Bourbon Mexico, 1763–1810.* Cambridge, 1971.

Calderón Quijano, José Antonio, ed. *Los virreyes de Nueva España en el reinado de Carlos III.* 2 vols. Sevilla, 1967–1968.

—————. *Los virreyes de Nueva España en el reinado de Carlos IV.* 2 vols. Sevilla, 1972.

Calle, Juan Díez de la. *Memorial y noticias sacras y reales de las Indias Occidentales,* new ed. Mexico City, 1932.

Cantù, Francesca. "Esigenze di giustizia e politica coloniale: una 'petición' inedita di Las Casas all'Audiencia de los Confines." *Ibero-Amerikanisches Archiv,* n.s. 3 (1977):135–165.

—————. "Per un rinnovamento della coscienza pastorale del Cinquecento: il vescovo Bartolomé de Las Casas ed il problema indiano." *Annuario dell'Istituto Storico Italiano per l'Età Moderna e Contemporanea,* 25/26 (1973–1974):5–118.

Casas, Fray Bartolomé de las. *Apologética historia sumaria,* ed. and with preliminary study by Edmundo O'Gorman. 2 vols. Mexico City, 1967.

—————. *Obras escogidas,* ed. Juan Pérez de Tudela Bueso. 5 vols.; Biblioteca de Autores Españoles, vols. 95, 96, 105, 106, and 110. Madrid, 1957–1958.

Caso, Alfonso. *Reyes y reinos de la Mixteca.* 2 vols. Mexico City, 1977–1979.

—————. "La tenencia de la tierra entre los antiguos mexicanos." *Memoria del Colegio Nacional,* 4, no. 2 (1959):29–54.

—————, Silvio Zavala, José Miranda, et al. *Métodos y resultados de la política indigenista en México.* Instituto Nacional Indigenista, Memorias, vol. 6. Mexico City, 1954.

Castañeda Delgado, Paulino. "La condición miserable del indio y sus privilegios." *Anuario de estudios americanos,* 28 (1971):245–335.

Castillo de Bovadilla, Lic. Jerónimo. *Política para corregidores, y señores de vasallos, en tiempo de paz y de guerra, y para prelados en lo espiritual, y temporal entre legos, jueces de comisión, regidores, abogados, y otros oficiales públicos; y de las jurisdicciones, preminencias, residencias, y salarios de ellos; y de lo tocante a las de órdenes, y caballeros de ellas*, new ed. 2 vols. Madrid, 1759.

Chamberlain, Robert S. *The Conquest and Colonization of Yucatan, 1517–1550*. Washington, D.C., 1948.

Chance, John K. *Race and Class in Colonial Oaxaca*. Stanford, Calif., 1978.

Chevalier, François. *La formation des grands domaines au Mexique: Terre et société aux XVIe–XVIIe siècles*. Paris, 1952.

———. "Les municipalités indiennes en Nouvelle Espagne, 1520–1620." *Anuario de historia del derecho español*, 15 (1944): 352–386.

Chiovenda, Giuseppe. *La condena en costas*, trans. Juan A. de la Puente y Quijano; notes and concordance with Spanish law by J. R. Xirau. Madrid, 1928.

Chipman, Donald E. *Nuño de Guzmán and the Province of Pánuco in New Spain, 1518–1533*. Glendale, Calif., 1967.

Circourt, Albert de. *Histoire des mores, mudejares et des morisques ou des arabes de l'Espagne dans la domination des chrétiens*. 2 vols. Paris, 1846.

Cline, Howard F. "Civil Congregations of the Indians in New Spain, 1598–1606." *Hispanic American Historical Review*, 29 (1949): 349–369.

———. "The Relaciones Geográficas of the Spanish Indies, 1577–1648." In *Handbook of Middle American Indians*, 12:183–242.

Los códigos españoles. See Spain: Laws, Statutes, etc.

Cogolludo, Fray Diego López de. See López de Cogolludo, Fray Diego.

Colección de documentos inéditos para la historia de España (DIE). 112 vols. Madrid, 1842–1895.

Colección de documentos inéditos para la historia de Hispano-América (DIHA). 14 vols. Madrid, 1927–1932.

Colección de documentos inéditos, relativos al descubrimiento, conquista y organización de las antiguas posesiones españolas de América y Oceanía, sacados de los archivos del reino, y muy especialmente del Indias (DII). 42 vols. Madrid, 1864–1884.

Colección de documentos inéditos, relativos al descubrimiento, conquista y organización de las antiguas posesiones españolas de Ultramar (DIU). 25 vols. Madrid, 1885–1932.

Colmeiro, Manuel. *Historia de la economía política en España*, new ed. 2 vols. Madrid, 1965.

Congreso Internacional de Historia del Derecho Indiano, 4th; Morelia, Michoacán, 1975. *Memoria*. Mexico City, 1977.

Cook, Sherburne F. "Las migraciones en la historia de la población mexicana: Datos modelo del occidente del centro de México,

1793–1950." In Bernardo García Martínez et al., eds., *Historia y sociedad en el mundo de habla española: Homenaje a José Miranda* (Mexico City, 1970), pp. 355–377.

Cook, Sherburne F., and Woodrow Borah. *Essays in Population History.* 3 vols. Berkeley and Los Angeles, 1971–1979.

———. *The Indian Population of Central Mexico, 1531–1610.* Ibero-Americana, vol. 44. Berkeley and Los Angeles, 1960.

———. *The Population of the Mixteca Alta, 1520–1960.* Ibero-Americana, vol. 50. Berkeley and Los Angeles, 1968.

———. "Quelle fut la stratification sociale au centre du Mexique durant la première moitié du XVIe siècle?" *Annales: Économies, sociétés, civilisations,* 18, no. 2 (1963):226–258.

Cook, Sherburne F., and Lesley Byrd Simpson. *The Population of Central Mexico in the Sixteenth Century.* Ibero-Americana, vol. 31. Berkeley and Los Angeles, 1948.

Cots i Gorchs, Jaime. "Textos de dret rosellonès: II. Els estils de la cort del verguer del Rossellò i Vallespir." *Estudis universitaris catalans,* 17 (2nd ép., 7; 1932):64–85.

Coy, P. E. S. "Justice for the Indian in Eighteenth-Century Mexico." *American Journal of Legal History,* 12 (1968):41–49.

Croix, Carlos Francisco de, Marqués de. *Instrucción del virrey . . . que deja a su sucesor Antonio María Bucareli,* ed. Norman F. Martin. Mexico City, 1960.

Cuevas, Mariano, comp. *Documentos inéditos del siglo XVI para la historia de México.* Mexico City, 1914.

———. *Historia de la iglesia en México,* 5th ed. 5 vols. Mexico City, 1946–1947.

Daniels, W. C. Ekow. *The Common Law in West Africa.* London, 1964.

Dávila Padilla, Fray Agustín. *Historia de la fundación y discurso de la provincia de Santiago de México de la Orden de Predicadores,* 3rd ed. Brussels, 1625; facsimile ed., Mexico City, 1955.

Denevan, William M., ed. *The Native Population of the Americas in 1492.* Madison, Wisc., 1976.

Derrett, J. Duncan M. "The Administration of Hindu Law by the British." *Comparative Studies in Society and History,* 4 (1961): 10–52.

Diccionario de Motul maya-español, atribuido a Fray Antonio de Ciudad Real, and *Arte de lengua maya, por Fray Juan Coronel,* ed. Juan Martínez Hernández. Mérida, Yucatan, 1929.

Diccionario de San Francisco, ed. Oscar Michelon. Graz, Austria, 1976.

Diccionario Porrúa de historia, biografía y geografía de México, 3rd ed. rev. 2 vols. Mexico City, 1970–1971.

Díez de la Calle, Juan. See Calle, Juan Díez de la.

Domínguez Ortiz, Antonio. *Sociedad y estado en el siglo XVIII español.* Barcelona, 1976.

Dozy, R. *Histoire des musulmans d'Espagne jusqu'à la conquête de l'Andalousie par les almoravides, 711–1110*, ed. and rev. by E. Lévi-Provençal. 3 vols. Leiden, 1932.

Dublán, Manuel, and José María Lozano, comps. *Legislación mexicana ó colección completa de las disposiciones legislativas expedidas desde la independencia de la república*. 44 vols. Mexico City, 1876–1913.

Elias, T. Olawale. *British Colonial Law: A Comparative Study of the Interaction Between English and Local Laws in British Dependencies*. London, 1962.

Elorza, Antonio. *La ideología liberal en la Ilustración española*. Madrid, 1970.

Encinas, Diego de. See Spain: Laws, Statutes, etc., *Cedulario indiano*.

Escobedo, Ronald. *El tributo indígena en el Perú (siglos XVI–XVII)*. Pamplona, 1979.

Escriche y Martín, Joaquín. *Diccionario razonado de legislación civil, penal, comercial y forense*, ed. Juan Rodríguez de San Miguel. Mexico City, 1837.

———. *Manual del abogado americano*. Paris, 1863.

Espinosa, Isidro Félix. *Crónica de la provincia franciscana de los apóstoles San Pedro y San Pablo de Michoacán*, ed. Nicolás León and José Ignacio Dávila Garibi, 2nd ed. Mexico City, 1945.

Esquivel Obregón, Toribio. *Apuntes para la historia del derecho en México*. 4 vols. Mexico City, 1937–1948.

"Estado general de tributos y tributarios, 1805." AGN, *Boletín*, 3rd ép., 1, no. 3 (October–December 1977): 3–43.

Estrada, Dorothy Tanck de. "La abolición de los gremios." In Elsa Cecilia Frost, Michael C. Meyer, and Josefina Zoraida Vázquez, eds., *El trabajo y los trabajadores en la historia de México* (Mexico City and Tucson, 1979), pp. 311–331.

Fernández y González, Francisco. *Estado social y político de los mudéjares de Castilla, considerados en sí mismos y respecto de civilización española*. Madrid, 1866.

Florescano, Enrique. *Precios del maíz y crisis agrícolas en México, 1708–1810*. Mexico City, 1969.

Fonseca, Fabián de, and Carlos de Urrutia. *Historia general de real hacienda*. 6 vols. Mexico City, 1845–1853.

Foster, George M. *Culture and Conquest: America's Spanish Heritage*. New York, 1960.

Friede, Juan. "Fray Bartolomé de las Casas, exponente del movimiento indigenista español del siglo XVI." *Revista de Indias*, 13 (1953): 25–55.

Frost, Elsa Cecilia, Michael C. Meyer, and Josefina Zoraida Vázquez, eds. *El trabajo y los trabajadores en la historia de México*. 5th Reunión de Historiadores Mexicanos y Norteamericanos, Pátzcuaro, Michoacán, October 12–15, 1977. Mexico City and Tucson, 1979.

Galanter, Marc. "Indian Law as an Indigenous Conceptual System."

Items (Social Science Research Council, New York), 32, nos. 3–4 (1978):42–46.

Gallegos Rocafull, José María. *El pensamiento mexicano en los siglos XVI y XVII.* Mexico City, 1951.

Gálvez, José de, Marqués de Sonora. *Informe general que en virtud de real órden, instruyó y entregó el Excmo. Sr. Marqués . . . al Excmo. Sr. Virrey Frey D. Antonio Bucareli y Ursúa, con fecha 31 de diciembre de 1771.* Mexico City, 1867.

García Bernal, Manuela Cristina. *Población y encomienda en Yucatán bajo los Austrias.* Sevilla, 1978.

———. *La sociedad en Yucatán, 1700–1750.* Sevilla, 1972.

García Gallo, Alfonso. "Las bulas de Alejandro VI y el ordenamiento jurídico de la expansión portuguesa y castellana en Africa e Indias." *Anuario de historia del derecho español,* 27–28 (1957–1958):461–829.

———. "La ciencia jurídica en la formación del derecho hispanoamericano en los siglos XVI al XVIII." *Anuario de historia del derecho español,* 44 (1974):157–200.

———. "El derecho común ante el Nuevo Mundo." *Revista de estudios políticos,* no. 80 (January–April 1955):133–152.

———. "La ley como fuente del derecho en Indias en el siglo XVI." *Anuario de historia del derecho español,* 21–22 (1951–1952): 607–730.

———. *Manual de historia del derecho español,* 2nd ed. rev. 2 vols. Madrid, 1964.

———. "Los principios rectores de la organización territorial de las Indias en el siglo XVI." *Anuario de historia del derecho español,* 40 (1970):313–347.

García Icazbalceta, Joaquín, ed. *Colección de documentos para la historia de México.* 2 vols. Mexico City, 1858–1866.

———. *Don Fray Juan de Zumárraga, primer obispo y arzobispo de México,* 2nd ed. 4 vols. Mexico City, 1947.

———. *Nueva colección de documentos para la historia de México.* 5 vols. Mexico City, 1886–1892.

García Martínez, Bernardo. *El Marquesado del Valle: Tres siglos de régimen señorial en Nueva España.* Mexico City, 1969.

Gemelli Carreri, Giovanni Francesco. *Viaje a la Nueva España,* trans. José María de Agreda y Sánchez, new ed. 2 vols. Mexico City, 1955.

Gerhard, Peter. "Congregaciones de indios en la Nueva España antes de 1570." *Historia mexicana,* 26 (1976–1977):347–395.

———. "La evolución del pueblo rural mexicano, 1519–1975." *Historia mexicana,* 24 (1974–1975):566–578.

———. *A Guide to the Historical Geography of New Spain.* Cambridge, 1972.

———. *The Southeast Frontier of New Spain.* Princeton, N.J., 1979.

Gibert y Sánchez de la Vega, Rafael. "El derecho privado de las ciudades españolas durante la Edad Media." In *La Ville: Troisième partie, Le droit privé* (Recueils de la Société Jean Bodin, vol. 8; Brussels, 1957), pp. 181–221.

Gibson, Charles. "The Aztec Aristocracy in Colonial Mexico." *Comparative Studies in Society and History*, 2 (1960):169–196.

———. *The Aztecs Under Spanish Rule: A History of the Indians of the Valley of Mexico, 1519–1810.* Stanford, Calif., 1964.

———. "Rotation of Alcaldes in the Indian *Cabildo* of Mexico City." *Hispanic American Historical Review*, 33 (1953):212–223.

———. *Tlaxcala in the Sixteenth Century.* New Haven, Conn., 1952.

———. "The Transformation of the Indian Community in New Spain, 1500–1810." *Cahiers d'histoire mondiale*, 2 (1955):581–607.

Giménez Fernández, Manuel. *Bartolomé de las Casas.* 2 vols. Sevilla, 1953–1960.

———. "La jurisdicción jeronimita en Indias." *Revista de la Facultad de Derecho* (Universidad Nacional Autónoma de México), 1 (1951):209–261.

Gómez Canedo, Fray Lino. "La cuestión de la racionalidad de los indios en el siglo XVI (nuevo examen crítico)." 36th International Congress of Americanists, Barcelona, Madrid, and Sevilla, 1964, *Actas y memorias*, vol. 4, pp. 156–165.

———. *Evangelización y conquista: Experiencia franciscana en Hispanoamérica.* Mexico City, 1977.

Góngora, Mario. *El estado en el derecho indiano: Epoca de fundación, 1492–1570.* Santiago, Chile, 1951.

González, Mario del Refugio. See Mexico (Viceroyalty): Laws, *Recopilación sumaria . . .* , ed. and with Preface.

Gratianus. *Corpus iuris canonici: Editio Lipsiensis secunda, post Aemilii Ludovici Richteri curas, ad librorum manu scriptorum et editionis Romanae fidem recognouit et adnotatione critici instruxit Aemilius Friedberg*, part 1. Leipzig, 1879; facsimile ed., Graz, Austria, 1959.

———. *Corpus iuris canonici . . .* , part 2: *Decretalium collectiones.* Leipzig, 1879; facsimile ed. Leipzig, 1922.

Greenleaf, Richard E. "The Inquisition and the Indians of New Spain: A Study in Jurisdictional Confusion." *The Americas*, 22 (1965–1966):138–166.

———. "Viceregal Power and the Obrajes of the Cortés Estate, 1595–1708." *Hispanic American Historical Review*, 48 (1968):365–379.

———. *Zumárraga and the Mexican Inquisition, 1536–1543.* Washington, D.C., 1962.

Grieshaber, Erwin P. "Hacienda-Indian Community Relations and Indian Acculturation: An Historiographical Essay." *Latin American Research Review*, 14 (1979):107–128.

Hakluyt, Richard. *The Principal Navigations, Voyages, Traffiques & Discoveries of the English Nation, Made by Sea or Over-Land to the Remote and Farthest Distant Quarters of the Earth at Any Time within the Compass of These 1600 Yeeres*, new ed. 12 vols. Glasgow, 1903–1905.

Hamill, Hugh H., Jr. *The Hidalgo Revolt*. Gainesville, Fla., 1966.

Hamnett, Brian R. *Politics and Trade in Southern Mexico, 1750–1821*. Cambridge, 1971.

Hand, G. J. *English Law in Ireland, 1290–1324*. Cambridge, 1967.

Handbook of Middle American Indians, ed. Robert Wauchope et al. 17 vols. Austin, Tex., 1964–1976.

Hanke, Lewis. *Bartolomé de las Casas, pensador, político, historiador, antropólogo*. Havana, 1949.

————. *The Spanish Struggle for Justice in the Conquest of America*. Philadelphia, 1949.

————, ed., with the collaboration of Celso Rodríguez. *Los virreyes españoles en América durante el gobierno de la casa de Austria: México* (HM). 5 vols. Biblioteca de Autores Españoles, vols. 273–277. Madrid, 1976–1978.

————. *Los virreyes españoles en América durante el gobierno de la casa de Austria: Perú* (HP). 7 vols. Biblioteca de Autores Españoles, vols. 280–286. Madrid, 1978–1980.

Hera, Alberto de la. "El derecho de los indios a la libertad y a la fe: La bula 'Sublimis Deus' y los problemas indianos que la motivaron." *Anuario de historia del derecho español*, 26 (1956): 89–181.

Hernández y Dávalos, Juan E., comp. *Colección de documentos para la historia de la guerra de independencia de México de 1808 a 1821*. 6 vols. Mexico City, 1877–1882.

Herr, Richard. *The Eighteenth-Century Revolution in Spain*. Princeton, N.J., 1958.

Höffner, Joseph. *La ética colonial española del Siglo de Oro. Cristianismo y dignidad humana*, trans. Francisco de Asis Caballero; Introduction by Antonio Truyol Serra. Madrid, 1957.

Hunt, Marta Espejo-Ponce. *Colonial Yucatan: Town and Region in the Seventeenth Century*. Doctoral dissertation, University of California, Los Angeles, 1974.

Innocentius IV. *Commentaria: Apparatus in V libros decretalium*. Frankfurt, 1570; facsimile ed., Frankfurt-am-Main, 1968.

Ixtlilxóchitl, Fernando de Alva. See Alva Ixtlilxóchitl, Fernando de.

Kagan, Richard L. *Lawsuits and Litigants in Castile, 1500–1700*. Chapel Hill, N.C., 1981.

Kagan, Samuel. "The Labor of Prisoners in the Obrajes of Coyoacán, 1660–1693." In Elsa Cecilia Frost, Michael C. Meyer, and Josefina Zoraida Vázquez, eds., *El trabajo y los trabajadores en la historia de México* (Mexico City and Tucson, 1979), pp. 201–214.

Kirchner, Walther. *The Rise of the Baltic Question*. Newark, N.J., 1954.

Konetzke, Richard. *Colección de documentos para la formación social de Hispanoamérica, 1493–1810*. 3 vols. in 5 parts. Madrid, 1953–1962.

Kubler, George A. *Mexican Architecture of the Sixteenth Century*. 2 vols. New Haven, Conn., 1948.

Kuttner, Stephan. "A Forgotten Definition of Justice." *Studia Gratiani post octava decreti saecularia collectanea historiae iuris canonici*, 20 (Rome, 1976): 75–109.

Lalinde Abadía, Jesús. "Los gastos del proceso en el derecho histórico español." *Anuario de historia del derecho español*, 35 (1964): 249–416.

Lallemand, Léon. *Histoire de la charité*. 4 vols. in 3 parts. Paris, 1902–1914.

[Landa, Diego de]. *Landa's Relación de las cosas de Yucatan*, trans. and ed. with notes by Alfred M. Tozzer. Peabody Museum of American Archaeology and Ethnology Papers, vol. 18. Cambridge, Mass., 1941; reprinted New York, 1966.

Las Casas. See Casas, Fray Bartolomé de las.

Latimer, Elizabeth Wormeley. *Spain in the Nineteenth Century*. Chicago, 1898.

Lea, Henry Charles. *The Moriscos of Spain: Their Conversion and Expulsion*. Philadelphia, 1901.

Lévi-Provençal, Évariste. *Histoire de l'Espagne musulmane*, new ed. 3 vols. Paris, 1950–1953.

Lewin, Julius. *Studies in African Native Law*. Cape Town, 1947.

Lira González, Andrés. *El amparo colonial y el juicio de amparo mexicano (Antecedentes novohispanos del juicio de amparo)*. Mexico City, 1971.

———. "La ciudad de México y las comunidades indígenas." *Razones*, March 24–April 6, 1980, pp. 49–52.

———. "La extinción del Juzgado de Indios." 4th Congreso Internacional de Historia del Derecho Indiano, Morelia, 1975, *Memoria*, pp. 299–317.

Llaguno, José A. *La personalidad jurídica del indio y el III Concilio Provincial Mexicano, 1585: Ensayo histórico-jurídico de los documentos originales*. Mexico City, 1963.

López de Cogolludo, Fray Diego. *Historia de Yucatán*, 5th ed. 2 vols. Madrid, 1688; facsimile ed., Mexico City, 1957.

MacLachlan, Colin M. *Criminal Justice in Eighteenth-Century Mexico: A Study of the Tribunal of the Acordada*. Berkeley and Los Angeles, 1974.

McNeill, William H. *Plagues and Peoples*. New York, 1976.

Maldonado, José. "Los recursos de fuerza en España: Un intento para suprimirlos en el siglo XIX." *Anuario de historia del derecho español*, 24 (1954): 281–380.

Maravall, José Antonio. "Cabarrús y las ideas de reforma política y social en el siglo XVIII." *Revista de Occidente*, 2nd ép., 6, no. 69 (December 1968): 273–300.

————. *La philosophie politique espagnole au XVIIe siècle dans ses rapports avec l'esprit de la contre-réforme*, trans. Louis Cazes and Pierre Mesnard. Paris, 1955.

————. "Las tendencias de reforma política en el siglo XVIII español." *Revista de Occidente*, 2nd ép., 5, no. 52 (July 1967): 53–82.

————. "La utopía político-religiosa de los franciscanos en Nueva España." *Estudios americanos*, Sevilla, 1, no. 2 (January 1949): 199–228.

Margadant S., Guillermo Floris. *Introducción a la historia del derecho mexicano*. Mexico City, 1971.

Martínez Marina, Francisco. *Teoría de las cortes, ó grandes juntas nacionales de los reinos de León y Castilla . . . con algunas observaciones sobre la lei fundamental de la monarquía española de 1812*. 3 vols. Madrid, 1813.

Medina, José Toribio. *La imprenta en México, 1539–1821*. 8 vols. Santiago, Chile, 1907–1912.

————. *La primitiva inquisición americana, 1493–1569: Estudios históricos*. 2 vols. Santiago, Chile, 1914.

Mendieta, Gerónimo de. *Historia eclesiástica indiana, obra escrita a fines del siglo XVI*. Mexico City, 1870; facsimile ed., Mexico City, 1971.

Mexico City. *Actas de cabildo del ayuntamiento de México*. 54 vols. Mexico City, 1884–1916.

Mexico (Viceroyalty). *Instrucciones que los virreyes de Nueva España dejaron a sus sucesores*. 2 vols. Mexico City, 1873.

————: Laws, Statutes, etc. *Provisiones, cédulas, instrucciones para el gobierno de la Nueva España*. Mexico City, 1563; facsimile ed., Madrid, 1945.

————. *Real ordenanza para el establecimiento é instrucción de intendentes de exército y provincia en el reino de la Nueva-España*. Madrid, 1786.

————. *Recopilación sumaria de todos los autos acordados de la real audiencia y sala del crimen de esta Nueva España, y providencias de su superior gobierno; de varias reales cédulas y órdenes que después de publicada la Recopilación de Indias han podido recogerse así de las dirigidas á la misma audiencia ó gobierno, como de algunas otras que por sus notables decisiones convendrá no ignorar: por el doctor don Eusebio Buenaventura Beleña*. 2 vols. Mexico City, 1787.

————. *Recopilación sumaria . . .* , ed. and with Preface by María del Refugio González. 2 vols. Mexico City, 1981.

————. *Svmarios de las cedvlas, ordenes y provisiones reales, que se han despachado por su magestad, para la Nueva-España, y otras partes; especialmente desde el año de mil seiscientos y veinte y ocho . . . Con algvnos titvlos de las materias, que nuevamente se añaden: y de los autos acordados de su real audiencia. Y algunas ordenanças del govierno. Que juntò, y dispvso el doctor d. Iuan*

Francisco Montemayor, y Cordova, de Cuenca. Mexico City, 1678.

Mexico (Viceroyalty): Real Colegio de Abogados. *Estatutos, y constituciones del ilustre, y r. colegio de abogados, establecido en la corte de México con aprobación de S. M. y baxo de su real inmediata protección, para el socorro de las personas y familias de los profesores de la abogacía.* Madrid, 1760.

Mexico (Empire, 1822–1823): Junta Provisional Gubernativa del Imperio Mexicano. *Diario de las sesiones de la soberana junta provisional gubernativa del imperio mexicano, instalado según previenen el plan de Iguala y tratados de la villa de Córdoba.* Mexico City, 1821.

Mexico: Archivo General de la Nación (AGN). *La constitución de 1812 en la Nueva España.* 2 vols.; AGN Publicaciones, vols. 4 and 5. Mexico City, 1912 and 1913.

———. *Documentos inéditos relativos a Hernán Cortés y su familia.* AGN Publicaciones, vol. 27. Mexico City, 1935.

———. *La secretaría de cámara del virreinato en México*; text by Linda Arnold. Mexico City, 1980.

Meza Villalobos, Néstor. *Historia de la política indígena del estado español en América: Las Antillas: El distrito de la Audiencia de Santa Fe.* Santiago, Chile, 1975.

Millares Torres, Agustín. *Historia general de las islas Canarias*, 2nd ed., ed. Agustín Millares Carlo. Havana, 1945.

Miranda, José. *Humboldt y México.* Mexico City, 1962.

———. "La *pax hispanica* y los desplazamientos de los pueblos indígenas." *Cuadernos americanos*, November–December 1962: 186–190.

———. *Vitoria y los intereses de la conquista de América.* Mexico City, 1947.

Molina Argüello, Carlos. *El gobernador de Nicaragua en el siglo XVI.* Sevilla, 1949.

Molina Solís, Juan Francisco. *Historia de Yucatán durante la dominación española.* 3 vols. Mérida, 1904–1913.

Montemayor y Córdova de Cuenca, Juan Francisco. See Mexico (Viceroyalty): Laws, Statutes, etc., *Svmarios.*

Montesquieu, Charles-Louis de Seconday, Baron de la Brède y de. *De l'esprit des lois*, new ed., ed. Gonzague Truc. 2 vols. Paris, 1961.

Monumenta Germaniae historica: Legum. 2 vols. Hanover, 1835–1837.

Mora, José María Luis. *México y sus revoluciones*, new ed. 3 vols. Mexico City, 1950.

———. *Obras sueltas*, 2nd ed. Mexico City, 1963.

Mörner, Magnus. *La corona española y los foráneos en los pueblos de indios de América.* Stockholm, 1970.

Mota y Escobar, Alonso de la. *Descripción geográfica de los reinos de*

Nueva Galicia, Nueva Vizcaya y Nuevo León, 2nd ed., Introduction by Joaquín Ramírez Cabañas. Mexico City, 1940.

Muldoon, James. *Popes, Lawyers, and Infidels: The Church and the Non-Christian World, 1250–1550*. Philadelphia, 1979.

Munch G., Guido. *El cacicazgo de San Juan Teotihuacán durante la colonia, 1521–1821*. Mexico City, 1976.

Muriel, Josefina. *Hospitales de la Nueva España*. 2 vols. Mexico City, 1956–1960.

Muro Orejón, Antonio. "Ordenanzas reales sobre los indios (las leyes de 1512–13)." *Anuario de estudios americanos*, 13 (1956): 417–471.

———. "Régimen legal de los indios de la Nueva España según el cedulario del doctor Vasco de Puga, 1563." 4th Congreso Internacional de Historia del Derecho Indiano, Morelia, 1975, *Memoria*, pp. 485–520.

Muro Romero, Fernando. *Las presidencias–gobernaciones en Indias, siglo XVI*. Sevilla, 1975.

Navarro B., Bernabé. *Cultura mexicana moderna en el siglo XVIII*. Mexico City, 1964.

Neuman, Abraham A. *The Jews in Spain: Their Social, Political, and Cultural Life During the Middle Ages*. 2 vols. Philadelphia, 1942.

Nickel, Herbert J. "Las deudas pasivas en favor de los gañanes en las haciendas de Puebla–Tlaxcala, epoca colonial." *Jahrbuch für Geschichte von Staat, Wirtschaft und Gesellschaft Lateinamerikas*, 16 (1979): 245–256.

Novísima recopilación. See Spain: Laws, Statutes, etc., *Novísima recopilación de las leyes de España, . . . hasta 1804*.

O'Gorman, Edmundo. "Sobre la naturaleza bestial del indio americano." *Filosofía y letras* (Universidad Nacional Autónoma de México), 1 (1941): 141–158 and 305–315.

———, ed. "Mandamientos del virrey d. Antonio de Mendoza, 1° dic. 1537 a 12 sep. 1538; 7 mar. 1550 a 25 mar. 1550." AGN, *Boletín*, 1st ép., 10 (1939): 209–311.

Oliveros, Martha Norma. "Construcción jurídica del régimen tutelar del indio." *Revista del Instituto de Historia del Derecho "Ricardo Levene,"* no. 18 (1967): 105–128.

Ollennu, N. M. "The Influence of English Law on West Africa." *Journal of African Law*, 5 (1961): 21–35.

Ortega Montañés, Juan de. *Instrucción reserva que el obispo-virrey . . . dio a su sucesor en el mando el conde de Moctezuma*, with Introduction and notes by Norman F. Martin. Mexico City, 1965.

Ortiz de la Tabla Ducasse, Javier. *Comercio exterior de Veracruz, 1778–1821; crisis de dependencia*. Sevilla, 1978.

Páez Brotchie, Luis. *La Nueva Galicia a través de su viejo archivo judicial: Indice analítico de los archivos de la audiencia de la Nueva*

Galicia o de Guadalajara y del supreme tribunal de justicia del estado de Jalisco. Mexico City, 1939.

Palafox y Mendoza, Juan de. *Tratados mejicanos*, ed. Francisco Sánchez-Castañer. 2 vols.; Biblioteca de Autores Españoles, vols. 217–218. Madrid, 1968.

Parry, John Horace. *The Audiencia of New Galicia in the Sixteenth Century: A Study in Spanish Colonial Government*. Cambridge, 1948.

———. *The Sale of Public Office in the Spanish Indies Under the Hapsburgs*. Ibero-Americana, vol. 37. Berkeley and Los Angeles, 1953.

Paso y Troncoso, Francisco del. *Epistolario de Nueva España, 1505–1818*. 16 vols. Mexico City, 1939–1942.

Pazos, Fray Manuel R. "Los misioneros franciscanos de Méjico en el siglo XVI y su sistema penal respecto de los indios." *Archivo ibero-americano* (Madrid), 2nd ép., 13 (1953):385–440.

Pérez de Tudela Bueso, Juan. *Las armadas de Indias y los orígenes de la política de colonización, 1492–1505*. Madrid, 1956.

———. "Ideas jurídicas y realizaciones políticas en la historia indiana." *Anuario de la Asociación "Francisco de Vitoria,"* 13 (1960–1961):137–171.

Pérez-Marchand, Monelisa Lina. *Dos etapas ideológicas del siglo XVIII en México a través de los papeles de la Inquisición*. Mexico City, 1945.

Pérez y López, Antonio Javier, comp. *Teatro de la legislación universal de España e Indias*. 28 vols. Madrid, 1791–1798.

Peru (Viceroyalty). *Gobernantes del Perú: cartas y papeles, siglo XVI, documentos del Archivo de Indias* (GP), ed. Roberto Levillier. 14 vols. Madrid, 1921–1926.

———. *Relaciones de los virreyes y audiencias que han gobernado el Perú*. 3 vols. Lima, 1867–1872.

———. *Tasa de la visita general de Francisco de Toledo*, ed. Noble David Cook. Lima, 1975.

Phelan, John Leddy. *The Kingdom of Quito in the Seventeenth Century*. Madison, Wisc., 1967.

———. *The Millennial Kingdom of the Franciscans in the New World*, 2nd ed. rev. Berkeley and Los Angeles, 1970.

Pietschmann, Horst. "Dos documentos significativos para la historia del régimen de intendencias en Nueva España." AGN, *Boletín*, 2nd ép., 12 (1971):397–442.

———. *Die Einführung des Intendantensystems in Neu-Spanien im Rahmen der allgemeinen Verwaltungsreform der spanischen Monarchie im 18. Jahrhundert*. Cologne and Vienna, 1972.

Polt, John H. R. "Jovellanos and His English Sources: Economic, Philosophical, and Political Writings." *Transactions of the American Philosophical Society*, n.s., 54, pt. 7 (1954).

Prem, Hanns J., with contributions from Ursula Dyckerhoff and Günter Miehlich. *Milpa y hacienda; tenencia de la tierra indígena y española en la cuenca del Alto Atoyac, Puebla, México, 1520–1650.* Wiesbaden, 1978.

Priestley, Herbert Ingram. *José de Gálvez, Visitor-General of New Spain, 1765–1771.* Berkeley, 1916.

Puga, Vasco de. See Mexico (Viceroyalty): Laws, Statutes, etc., *Provisiones.*

Ramos Pérez, Demetrio. "Los agentes solicitadores de Indias: Otra reforma de Carlos III." *Anuario histórico jurídico ecuatoriano,* 5 (1979):381–442; 5° Congreso Internacional de Historia del Derecho Indiano, Quito and Guayaquil, 1978, vol. 1. Quito, 1980.

Ricard, Robert. *La "conquête spirituelle" du Mexique: Essai sur l'apostolat et les méthodes missionaires des ordres mendiants en Nouvelle-Espagne de 1523–24 à 1572.* Paris, 1933.

———, ed. "Un document inédit sur la situation du Mexique au XVIe siècle." In *Miscelânea de estudos em honra de d. Carolina Michaëlis de Vasconcellos* (Coimbra, 1933), pp. 556–562.

Riley, James D. "Landlords, Laborers, and Royal Government: The Administration of Labor in Tlaxcala, 1680–1750." In Elsa Cecilia Frost, Michael C. Meyer, and Josefina Zoraida Vázquez, eds., *El trabajo y los trabajadores en la historia de México* (Mexico City and Tucson, 1979), pp. 221–241.

Roberts-Wray, Sir Kenneth. "The Adaptation of Imported Law in Africa." *Journal of African Law,* 4 (1960):66–78.

Robinson, David J., ed. *Social Fabric and Spatial Structure in Colonial Latin America.* Dellplain Latin American Studies, no. 1. Syracuse, N.Y., 1979.

Robson, Robert. *The Attorney in Eighteenth-Century England.* Cambridge, 1959.

Rodríguez García, Vicente. "El fiscal Posada: índice para una biografía." *Anuario de estudios americanos,* 34 (1977):187–210.

Romero, María de los Angeles. "Los intereses españoles en la Mixteca—siglo XVII." *Historia mexicana,* 29 (1979–1980):241–251.

Rosenblat, Angel. *La población de América en 1492: Viejos y nuevos cálculos.* Mexico City, 1967.

———. *La población indígena y el mestizaje en América.* 2 vols. Buenos Aires, 1954.

Rousseau, Jean-Jacques. *Du contrat social,* ed. Georges Beaulavon, 2nd ed. Paris, 1914.

Rumeu de Armas, Antonio. *Historia de la previsión social en España: cofradías, gremios, hermandades, montepíos.* Madrid, 1944.

———. "Los problemas derivados del contacto de razas en los albores del renacimiento." *Cuadernos de historia: Anexos de la revista Hispania,* 1 (1967):61–103.

Salvioli, Giuseppe. *Storia del diritto italiano,* 8th ed. rev. Turin, 1921.

Sánchez Agesta, Luis. *El pensamiento político del despotismo ilustrado*. Madrid, 1953.

Sánchez de Aguilar, Pedro. *Informe contra idolorum cultures del obispado de Yucatán . . . impreso por primera vez en 1639*, 3rd ed. Mérida, 1937.

Sánchez Gallego, Laureano. "Luis de Molina, internacionalista." *Anuario de la Asociación "Francisco de Vitoria,"* 5 (1932–1933): 41–69.

Sanders, William T. "The Population of the Central Mexican Symbiotic Region, the Basin of Mexico, and the Teotihuacán Valley in the Sixteenth Century." In William M. Denevan, ed., *The Native Population of the Americas in 1492* (Madison, Wisc., 1976), pp. 85–150.

Sarabia Viejo, María Justina. *Don Luis de Velasco, virrey de Nueva España, 1550–1564*. Sevilla, 1978.

Sarrablo Aguareles, Eugenio. *El conde de Fuenclara*. 2 vols. Sevilla, 1955–1966.

Sarrailh, Jean. *L'Espagne éclairée de la seconde moitié du XVIIIe siècle*. Paris, 1964.

Sauer, Carl Ortwin. *The Early Spanish Main*. Berkeley and Los Angeles, 1966.

Schäfer, Ernst. *El consejo real y supremo de Indias. Su historia, organización y labor administrativa hasta la terminación de la casa de Austria*. 2 vols. Sevilla, 1935–1947.

Scholes, France V., and Eleanor B. Adams, eds. *Documentos para la historia del México colonial*. 7 vols. Mexico City, 1955–1961.

Semo, Enrique, coord. *Siete ensayos sobre la hacienda mexicana, 1780–1880*. Mexico City, 1977.

Serrano y Sanz, Manuel. *Orígenes de la dominación española en América. Estudios históricos. Tomo primero*. Madrid, 1918.

[Sierra O'Reilly, Justo.] "Consideraciones sobre el origen, causes y tendencias de la sublevación de los indígenas, sus probables resultados y su posible remedio." *El Fénix*, Campeche, July 25, 1849.

Las Siete Partidas. See Spain: Laws, Statutes, etc.

Simmons, Marc. *Spanish Government in New Mexico*. Albuquerque, 1968.

Simpson, Lesley Byrd. *The Encomienda in New Spain: The Beginnings of Spanish Mexico*. Berkeley and Los Angeles, 1950.

———. *The Encomienda in New Spain: Forced Native Labor in the Spanish Colonies, 1492–1550*. Berkeley, 1929.

———. *Exploitation of Land in Central Mexico in the Sixteenth Century*. Ibero-Americana, vol. 36. Berkeley and Los Angeles, 1952.

———. *Studies in the Administration of the Indians in New Spain: I. The Laws of Burgos of 1512; II. The Civil Congregation; III. The Repartimiento System of Native Labor in New Spain and Guatemala; IV. The Emancipation of the Indian Slaves and the Resettlement of the Freedmen, 1548–1553*. 3 vols.; Ibero-

Americana, vols. 7, 13, and 16. Berkeley and Los Angeles, 1934–1940.

———, ed. and trans. *The Laws of Burgos of 1512–1513: Royal Ordinances for the Good Government and Treatment of the Indians.* San Francisco, 1960.

Soberanes Fernández, José Luis. "La administración superior de justicia en Nueva España." *Boletín mexicano de derecho comparado,* 13, no. 37 (January–April 1980): 143–200.

———. *Los tribunales de la Nueva España.* Mexico City, 1980.

Solórzano Pereira, Juan de. *Política indiana,* new ed. 5 vols. Madrid and Buenos Aires, 1930.

Spain: Laws, Statutes, etc. *Cedulario indiano recopilado por Diego de Encinas.* 4 vols. Madrid, 1596; facsimile ed., Madrid, 1945.

———. *Los códigos españoles concordados y anotados,* 2nd ed. 12 vols. Madrid, 1872–1873.

———. *Colección de los decretos y órdenes que han expedido las cortes generales y extraordinarias.* 10 vols. Madrid, 1820–1823.

———. *Disposiciones complementarias a las leyes de Indias* (DCLI). 3 vols. Madrid, 1930.

———. *Novísima recopilación de las leyes de España; dividida en xii libros, en que se reforma la recopilación publicada por el señor don Felipe II en el año 1567 . . . y se incorporan las pragmáticas, cédulas, decretos, órdenes y resoluciones reales, y otras providencias no recopiladas, y expedidas hasta el de 1804.* 6 vols. Madrid, 1805–1807.

———. *Recopilación de leyes de los reynos de las Indias* (RLI). 3 vols. 4th ed., Madrid, 1791; facsimile ed., Madrid, 1943.

———. *Las Siete Partidas del sabio rey d. Alonso el IX, con las variantes de mas interés, y con la glosa del Lic. Gregorio López del Consejo Real de Indias de S.M.* 4 vols. Barcelona, 1843–1844.

———: Valladolid. *Recopilación de las ordenanças de la Real Audiencia y Chancillería de su magestad, que reside en la villa de Valladolid.* Valladolid, 1566.

Spain: Ministerio de Fomento. *Cartas de Indias.* Madrid, 1877.

Spell, Jefferson Rea. *Rousseau in the Spanish World before 1833: A Study in Franco-Spanish Literary Relations.* Austin, Texas, 1938.

Spores, Ronald E. *The Mixtec Kings and Their People.* Norman, Okla., 1967.

Stein, Stanley J. "Bureaucracy and Business in the Spanish Empire, 1750–1804: Failure of a Bourbon Reform in Mexico and Peru." *Hispanic American Historical Review,* 61 (1981): 2–28.

Suárez, Federico. "Sobre las raíces de las reformas de las Cortes de Cádiz." *Revista de estudios políticos,* no. 126 (November–December 1962): 31–64.

Swadesh, Mauricio, María Cristina Álvarez, and Juan R. Bastarrechea. *Diccionario de elementos del maya yucateco colonial.* Mexico City, 1970.

Taylor, William B. "Cacicazgos coloniales en el valle de Oaxaca." *Historia mexicana*, 20 (1970–1971): 1–41.

———. *Drinking, Homicide, and Rebellion in Colonial Mexican Villages*. Stanford, Calif., 1979.

———. *Landlord and Peasant in Colonial Oaxaca*. Stanford, Calif., 1973.

Teicher, J. L. "Laws of Reason and Laws of Religion: A Conflict in Toledo Jewry in the Fourteenth Century." In *Essays and Studies Presented to Stanley Arthur Cook . . . in Celebration of His Seventy-Fifth Birthday* (London, 1950), pp. 83–94.

Tena Ramírez, Felipe, comp. *Leyes fundamentales de México, 1808–1964*, 2nd ed. rev. Mexico City, 1964.

Tierney, Brian. *Medieval Poor Law: A Sketch of Canonical Theory and Its Application in England*. Berkeley and Los Angeles, 1959.

Tomás y Valiente, Francisco. *El derecho penal de la monarquía absoluta, siglos XVI–XVII–XVIII*. Madrid, 1969.

———. *La venta de oficios en Indias, 1492–1606*. Madrid, 1972.

Torquemada, Fray Juan de. *Monarquía indiana*. 3 vols. Facsimile of Madrid, 1723, ed., with Introduction by Miguel Leon Portilla. Mexico City, 1969.

Torre Revello, José de. "Relación de los méritos y ejercicios literarios del doctor don Eusebio Ventura Beleña, 1772." *Revista de historia de América*, no. 15 (1942): 315–323.

Torres Campos, Rafael. *Carácter de la conquista y colonización de las islas Canarias*. Madrid, 1901.

Torres Ramírez, Bibiano. *Alejandro O'Reilly en las Indias*. Sevilla, 1969.

Torriani, Leonardo. *Die kanarischen Inseln und ihre Urbewohner*, ed. Dominik Josef Wölfel. Leipzig, 1940.

Tutino, John. "Life and Labor on North Mexican Haciendas: The Querétaro-San Luis Potosí Region, 1775–1810." In Elsa Cecilia Frost, Michael C. Meyer, and Josefina Zoraida Vázquez, eds., *El trabajo y los trabajadores en la historia de México* (Mexico City and Tucson, 1979), pp. 339–378.

Van Kleffens, E. N. *Hispanic Law until the End of the Middle Ages*. Edinburgh, 1968.

Vargas Urgarte, Rubén. *Historia del Perú*. 5 vols. Lima, 1949–1958.

Vázquez de Espinosa, Antonio. *Compendio y descripción de las Indias Occidentales*. Washington, D.C., 1948.

Vera Cruz, Fray Alonso de la. *The Writings of . . . : The Original Texts with English Translation*, ed. Ernest J. Burrus, S.J. 5 vols. Rome, 1968–1972.

Viera y Clavijo, José de. *Noticias de la historia general de las islas Canarias*, ed. Elías Serra Rafols. 3 vols. Santa Cruz de Tenerife, 1950–1952.

Villapalos Salas, Gustavo. *Los recursos contra los actos de gobierno en la baja edad media: Su evolución histórica en el reino caste-llano, 1252–1504.* Madrid, 1976.

———. "Los recursos en materia administrativa en Indias en los siglos XVI y XVII: Notas para su estudio." *Anuario de historia del derecho español*, 46 (1976): 5–76.

Villarroel, Hipólito. *Enfermedades políticas que padece la capital de esta Nueva España en casi todos los cuerpos de que se compone y remedios que se la deben aplicar para su curación si se quiere que sea útil al rey y al público*, with Introduction by Genaro Estrada. Mexico City, 1937; facsimile ed., Mexico City, 1979.

Viñas Mey, Carmelo. *Estatuto del obrero indígena en la colonización española.* Madrid, 1929.

Vitoria, Fray Francisco de. *Relecciones del estado de los indios, y del derecho de la guerra*, with Introduction by Antonio Gómez Robledo. Mexico City, 1974.

———. *Relectio de Indis o libertad de los indios; edición crítica bilingüe*, ed. L. Pereña, J. M. Pérez Prendes, V. Beltrán de Heredia, et al. Madrid, 1967.

Vives, Juan Luis. *Opera omnia.* 8 vols. Valencia, 1782–1790; facsimile ed., London, 1964.

Vryonis, Speros, Jr. *The Decline of Medieval Hellenism in Asia Minor and the Process of Islamization from the Eleventh Through the Fifteenth Century.* Berkeley and Los Angeles, 1971.

Walsh, John K., ed. *El libro de los doce sabios o tractado de la nobleza y lealtad, ca. 1237.* Madrid, 1975.

Warren, J. Benedict. *Hans F. Kraus Collection of Hispanic-American Manuscripts: A Guide.* Washington, D.C., 1974.

Wittram, Reinhard. *Baltische Geschichte: Die Ostseeland, Livland, Estland, Kurland, 1180–1918.* Munich, 1954.

Zavala, Silvio. *Los esclavos indios en Nueva España.* Mexico City, 1968.

———. *Estudios indianos.* Mexico City, 1948.

———. *La "Utopía" de Tomás Moro en la Nueva España, y otros estudios.* Mexico City, 1937.

———, comp. *Ordenanzas del trabajo, siglos XVI y XVII.* Mexico City, 1947.

——— and María Castelo, comps. *Fuentes para la historia del trabajo en Nueva España.* 8 vols. Mexico City, 1939–1946.

Zorita, Alonso de. *Breve y sumaria relación de los señores de la Nueva España*, ed. Joaquín Ramírez Cabañas. Mexico City, 1942.

———. *Historia de la Nueva España . . . Tomo primero.* Madrid, 1909.

Index